Nihil Obstat

Ex Libris

Nihil Obstat

Religion, Politics, and Social Change in

East-Central Europe and Russia

Sabrina P. Ramet

Duke University Press Durham & London

1998

To Valerie Millholland

Contents

Imprimatur ix

I Cross-Regional Overview in Comparative Perspective 1

1. Introduction: The Communist Legacy and the New Religious Landscape 3
2. Phases in Communist Religious Policy 10

II The Northern Tier
East Germany, Poland, Czechoslovakia, and Hungary 51

3. Varieties of Christianity in East Germany 53
4. Catholicism and National Culture in Poland, Hungary, and Czechoslovakia 90
5. The Catholic Church Among the Czechs and Slovaks 121

III The Balkans 145

6. Nation and Religion in Yugoslavia 147
7. Holy Intolerance: Romania's Orthodox Church 181
8. Albania's Triple Heritage 202

IV The Former Soviet Union 227

9. The Russian Orthodox Church in Transition 229
10. A House Divided: Ukraine's Fractious Churches 246

V Postcommunist Trends and Conclusion 263

11. In Hoc Signo Vinces: The New Evangelism in Postcommunist Europe 265
12. Mores Ecclesiae et Potestas Fidei: A Contrast of the Bulgarian Orthodox Church and the Polish Catholic Church 275
13. Nihil Obstat: The Rise of Nontraditional Religions 308
14. Ego Te Absolvo: The Nature of Religio-Political Interaction 335

Notes 341
Index 409

Imprimatur

In January 1997, after presenting a public lecture based on sections of this book, I was very much taken aback when a prominent East Europeanist, seated in the audience, asked rather pointedly if I did not agree that Central and Eastern Europe were characterized by an all-engulfing "spiritual vacuum" as of the end of the communist era. When I responded that I did not agree and that the traditional Churches were still much in evidence, my questioner, far from retreating, began to insist that a vacuum existed and endeavored to insinuate that I must be blind not to admit it. The advocates of the "spiritual vacuum" view generally have in mind either of two theses: (1) that communism had largely wiped out all religion, leaving the people of the area dazed, confused, and hungry for the Christian gospel; or (2) that Catholicism, Orthodoxy, Islam, and Judaism, together with traditional Protestantism, cannot qualify as legitimate spirituality, so that their presence does not disqualify one from speaking of a "spiritual vacuum." Both of these theses are false and pernicious, but nonetheless they have become prevalent in some quarters. I cannot tell why, since the leaderships of new evangelical Churches do not themselves underestimate their competition. All the same, illusions persist.

One encounters other common illusions when one talks of religion in the area, such as the notion that all priests and pastors were "heroes" in the struggle against communism, or that communism was uniformly injurious to all religion, or that variously the political establishment and/or the religious associations might be viewed as monoliths. These and other illusions have led some casual observers far astray. It is my hope that this book can make a small contribution toward correcting some of them.

I have benefited in the preparation of these pages from the assistance of a number of individuals. My gratitude goes to my research assistants Dasha Koenig and Linda Tapp for translating the cited Czech (or Slovak) and Russian materials, respectively, and to Marija Jankówska and Henry Szymonik who translated the Polish materials cited. Ms. Jankówska's assistance is reflected in chapter 4; Polish materials cited elsewhere in the book were translated by Mr. Szymonik. I am also grateful to Professor Richard Johnson, Chair of the University of Washington History Department, for authorizing a salary to be paid to Mr. Szymonik. I would like to thank Joan McCarter, who printed out the copy sent to Duke University Press. I am also deeply indebted to Gjon Sinishsta for generously sharing Italian-language materials about the Albanian Orthodox Church with me, Roman Solchanyk for sending me many materials concerning the Ukrainian religious scene and for helping to clarify certain points concerning Ukraine, to Adele Barker for sending information about the Vissarion Brotherhood, and to Ivan Grdešić for providing extensive materials about sects and cults in contemporary Croatia. I am greatly indebted to Peter Sugar, James Felak, and the two anonymous readers contracted by Duke Press for taking time from their busy schedules to share the benefit of their wisdom and experience. I also wish to thank Jack Dull and James Townsend for comments on an earlier draft of chapter 2, John Haley and Glennys Young for their feedback on an earlier version of chapter 13, and Nathaniel Davis for helpful comments and corrections on an earlier draft of chapter 9.

Some chapters have been published in earlier drafts. A version of chapter 2 was published as "Adaptation and Transformation of Religious Policy in Communist and Post-Communist Systems," in Sabrina Petra Ramet (ed.), *Adaptation and Transformation in Communist and Post-Communist Systems* (Boulder, Colo.: Westview Press, 1992), and a version of chapter 3 as "Protestantism in East Germany, 1949–1989: A Summing Up," in *Religion in Communist Lands* 19, nos. 3–4 (Winter 1991) and also in Sabrina Petra Ramet (ed.), *Protestantism and Politics in Eastern Europe and Russia: The Communist and Postcommunist Eras* (Durham, N.C.: Duke University Press, 1992). Chapter 4 was published in a version with the same title given here, in Pedro Ramet, *Cross and Commissar: The Politics of Religion in Eastern Europe and the USSR* (Bloomington: Indiana University Press, 1987). Chapter 5 was first published as "The Catholic Church in Czechoslovakia, 1948–1991," *Studies in Comparative Communism* 24, no. 4 (December 1991): 377–93; this article is reprinted from *Studies in Comparative Communism* with permission of the editor and of Elsevier Science, Ltd., The Boulevard, Langford Lane, Kidlington OX5 1GB, United Kingdom. Chapter 6 appeared as "Religion and Nationalism in Yugoslavia," in Pedro Ramet (ed.), *Religion and Nationalism in Soviet and East European Politics,* Rev. and expanded ed. (Durham, N.C.: Duke University Press, 1989). An earlier version of chapter 8 bore the title, "The Albanian Orthodox Church," in Pedro Ramet (ed.), *Eastern Christianity and Politics in the Twentieth Century* (Durham, N.C.: Duke University Press, 1988). I am grateful to the publishers of these books for permitting me to use this material here, to the editor of *Religion in Communist Lands* (since renamed *Religion, State and Society: The Keston Journal*) for permission to use the material in chapter 3, and to the editor and publisher of *Studies in Comparative Communism* for allowing use of the material in chapter 5.

Chapters 1, 7, and 9–14 were written specifically for this book and are not derived from any published articles or chapters. However, chapter 13 grew from a paper that I originally presented at the 1994 convention of the American Association for the Advancement of Slavic Studies (Philadelphia, November 1994) and that I presented, in much revised form, in a public lecture at the University of Washington in November 1995. During the autumn of 1996 some materials in the book were presented as public lectures at Florida State University, the University of Arizona, and Linfield College in McMinnville, Oregon. These occasions to present my ideas to the public afforded the opportunity to receive useful feedback.

Finally, it is a great pleasure for me to acknowledge two rather special debts: To Valerie Millholland, my editor at Duke University Press, without whose encouragement this book might never have come about and to whom it is dedicated; and to my spouse, Chris Hassenstab, who has listened to me as I have read her earlier drafts of these chapters and who has given me the benefit of her wisdom and common sense.

Sabrina P. Ramet

I

Cross-Regional Overview in

Comparative Perspective

Chapter 1

Introduction: The Communist Legacy and the New Religious Landscape

Nihil obstat—nothing stands in the way. These words, signed by the Catholic diocesan censor, once were inscribed on the reverse of a book's title page, thereby signifying, to the faithful, that the volume in question contained no doctrinal or moral errors. This inscription was followed by the word, *imprimatur*—let it be printed—which was signed by the archbishop or bishop.

In affixing *nihil obstat* as the title of this book, I do not imply any guarantee that its contents are "doctrinally without error." Rather, the words are employed to suggest that, with the collapse of the communist power monopoly throughout what used to be called the Soviet-East European region, literally *nothing stands in the way* of new religious movements, groups, and associations, including many previously illegal.

In the 1960s, 1970s, and 1980s the religious landscape throughout the region gave the striking impression that traditional religions, generally organized on a hierarchical basis, clearly predominated. Here, one found the Roman Catholic Church of Poland, headed by the primate and supported by archbishops and bishops, the Romanian Orthodox Church, headed by a patriarch and supported by metropolitans and archimandrites, the Lutheran Church of Hungary headed by its bishop, and so forth. The processes of secularization and religious innovation which had spread throughout North America and Western Europe seemed unable to penetrate the communist domain, while traditional religions seemed to flourish. Communism in its own brutal way ultimately protected the religions of which it approved, crushing rival religious associations that failed to obtain its sanction.

A comparison with the precommunist era is revealing. In Russia, for example, the communists should be credited for eradicating the Flagellants (the *Khlysty*) as well as the so-called Sect of the Castrated (the *Skoptsy*), which split off from the Flagellants in the late eighteenth century in the province of Oryol.[1] The Sect of the Flagellants, centered in the city of Kostroma, was created in the mid-seventeenth century by Danilo Filippovich, a Russian peasant who claimed to be an incarnation of God. At first, the sect displayed marked tendencies toward political protest, but these evaporated in the course of the nineteenth century.[2] The Castrates, also known as the "White Doves," broke away from the Flagellants in the 1770s. They were largely inspired by Andrei Ivanov Blokhin, a runaway serf, and Kondratii Ivanovich Selivanov, a peasant from the village of Stolbov—Selivanov claiming to be the reincarnation of both Jesus Christ and the murdered Tsar Peter III of Russia.[3] The Bolsheviks did not object to the sect's practice of self-mutilation, but they abominated its members' antiestablishment attitudes; after 1929 the Sect of the Castrated was subjected to stiff repression.[4] In its abomination of radical, antihierarchical sectarian movements, the Bolshevik regime displayed attitudes that paralleled and underpinned those of the Russian Orthodox Church.[5] The Bolsheviks were especially suspicious of mystical and occult groups, and as early as February 1918 they issued an order to local Theosophists, Anthroposophists, and other unorthodox societies to terminate their activities by year's end.[6] Although the Bolshevik government disbanded Moscow's Free Academy of Spiritual Culture, closed presses that had been publishing occult and mystical materials, confiscated occult books from libraries, and exiled almost all of the leading intellectual figures associated with these currents, accompanying these actions with a barrage of volleys in the party press, occult societies continued their work in Russia until 1929, when a dramatic escalation of antireligious campaigns (including the arrests of members) wiped out almost all traces of them.[7] The Bolsheviks also were responsible for the suppression of the Old Believers, the True Orthodox Church, the Belorussian Orthodox Church, and the Ukrainian Orthodox Church, and they erected formidable barriers to the continued work of various Protestant groups, not to mention the Sufi (Islamic) orders, while some believers, such as the Mennonites, fled Russia at that time.[8] Some pockets of sectarianism remained (e.g., small groups of *priguni* (jumpers), *nostoiannie* (insisters), and *maksimisti* (maximalists) in Armenia in the late 1970s), but most Soviet-era writers on religion expressed confidence that the general trend was toward the eventual extinction of these groups.[9]

In Romania, Baptists, Pentecostals, and other evangelical Christian groups enjoyed relative freedom from 1928 until 1937 before being repressed under Marshal Antonescu.[10] But after the communists seized power, these groups were seen as "posing very serious internal security problems, and great vacillation and perplexity always have existed among state authorities regarding the wisest ways to deal with them."[11]

Or again, in Czechoslovakia the Jehovah's Witnesses, who began their activity in the Czech lands in 1907, were a registered religious community from 1934 until 1939. Banned by the Nazis in 1939, they resumed their activity in 1945, only to be outlawed for a second time by the communists in 1949.[12]

The most celebrated case of suppression involved the Greek-Rite Catholics, banned in Ukraine, Romania, and Czechoslovakia after World War II. But in one or more communist countries other groups also were denied legal registration—among them, Christian Science, the Christ Believer Nazarene Congregation, the Church of Jesus Christ of Latter-Day Saints (Mormon), and the Jehovah's Witnesses. Newer religious associations, such as the Unification Church of the Rev. Sun Myung Moon and the Krishna Society, likewise were denied legal registration—in most cases until 1988 or 1989.

But communism sometimes worked in the opposite direction, offering certain groups degrees of latitude and equality to which they had been unaccustomed. In Poland, for example, the Mariavites, a mystical sect founded by the Franciscan nun Maria Felicja Kozkowska in 1806, which allowed women as well as men to serve as priests and bishops,[13] was able to function freely only *after* the communist takeover. The same applies to the Methodist Church, the Reformed Church, the Seventh-Day Adventists, and the Baptists in Poland,[14] the Church of John in the German Democratic Republic, etc.[15]

In general, communist authorities distinguished among three categories of religious associations: (1) legally recognized, co-opted associations; (2) legally recognized associations treated with distrust, kept at a distance, but "tolerated"; and (3) proscribed associations. To obtain "co-opted" status, religious associations often had to make adjustments. In the GDR the Evangelical Church was forced to sever its organizational ties with Evangelical dioceses in West Germany and to create an Evangelical Church Federation that coincided with state boundaries. In Bulgaria the Congregational Church was pressured to subordinate local parishes to a central authority, contrary to Congregational teachings, in order to simplify communist control. Muslims in Central Asia were required to set up a governing board that would simultaneously decide policies for Islamic communities and coordinate those policies with Soviet authorities. And in Romania a "board of electors" was established on

communist instructions to assume responsibility for electing bishops—
the board to include both party officials and Church representatives.[16]
More examples could be cited, but the point is clear: the communists
wanted to control religious life and therefore "adjusted" religious organizations, where possible, to suit their needs. Religious associations such
as the Karaites[17] and the Bah'ai,[18] which dispensed with clergy, or the
Doukhobors (a pacifist sect of Russian Christians), who disdained any
form of ecclesiastical organization or hierarchical institution-building,[19]
were unlikely to obtain the approval of communist authorities.

This overall form of control, however, was only one aspect of the communist program vis-à-vis religion. To complete the picture, it should
be noted that the communists also aspired to control specific aspects of
Church organization and to censor and repress religious life. The communists further controlled religion by reserving the right to approve
or reject candidates for ecclesiastical office, seminary entrants, seminary curricula, the content of Church newspapers, church construction,
and even in some countries the content of parish bulletins. They censored religion by determining which organizations would be allowed to
function, and they often succeeded in reshaping the ideologies of the
Churches (as in the case of Hungary, where both the Reformed and
Lutheran churches subscribed to the so-called Theology of Diakonia, or
Service to the State).[20] Last, they repressed religion—selectively where
more "moderate" communists were concerned or entirely (in due course)
where hard-liners held sway—because religion always remained a rival
worldview.

Communist guarantees were often two-edged swords. For example,
the assurance that religion was "the private affair of the individual"
meant primarily that religious associations had no right to play any role
in public life or to speak out on public issues. Or again, communist guarantees of the right of worship also pointedly excluded other activities
(this exclusion varied considerably from country to country).

Communism, supposedly dedicated to the eradication of religion
("unutterable vileness" in Lenin's phrase), produced some interesting
anomalies. In the GDR the Socialist Unity Party (s e d) as late as 1956 enforced the legal obligation of citizens to pay a Church tax, and it allowed
theological faculties to function within the state universities right up
until the end. In Poland the state allowed a Catholic university to function in Lublin, and (after 1980) it increasingly treated the Church as a
partner in policy. In Czechoslovakia and Bulgaria the communist state

paid salaries to clergy. In Yugoslavia the communist party financed the reconstruction of a number of churches after the destruction of World War II. And in Czechoslovakia in the 1950s the communist party even organized pilgrimages to religious sites, compelling its cadres and others to take part (for reasons explained in chapter 5).

These activities were complemented by activities of a different nature —the bugging of Catholic confessionals and the apartments of Protestant ministers,[21] the enlisting of priests and pastors in the service of the secret police, and, at the height of Stalinism, the trials and imprisonment of bishops and metropolitans on various pretexts, in some cases including treason.

Communism defined democracy in terms of strict adherence to approved content; liberalism defines democracy in terms of strict adherence to approved procedures.[22] Although the systems that have replaced communism in the Russian-East European region have had a mixed record in moving toward liberal democracy, most of them have adopted at least some elements of liberal proceduralism. In the process, the rights and possibilities of religious associations have expanded enormously— not merely among religious denominations that have been functioning in the region, but among new entrants to the local religious competition.

The postcommunist transition has not been smooth in strictly political areas—or as it applies to religious associations. In several countries, including Hungary, the Czech Republic, and Romania, serious disputes have occurred over restitution of Church properties confiscated by the communists. In Bulgaria and Ukraine, communism had such a subversive effect on local Orthodox churches that rival patriarchs have appeared, mobilizing rival congregations that have not refrained from force in their quest for aggrandizement and facilities. Albania's Orthodox community has faced a rather unusual difficulty with the ecumenical patriarch insisting on the presence of a *Greek* patriarch to head the *Albanian* Church. In Poland, theocratic impulses have polarized the country and caused many citizens to worry about excessive clerical influence. And in Belarus, Slovakia, Croatia, and Serbia, authoritarian systems remain in place, with the result that local Churches (at least in all but Belarus) have found themselves replaying the oppositionist roles to which they became accustomed under communism.

This book is concerned primarily, but not exclusively, with the politics of religion in the twentieth century. Certain chapters delve more deeply into the past, while some focus exclusively on the postcommunist period.

Chapter 2 sets forth a theory about policy change in communist systems, taking the Soviet Union, China, Yugoslavia, Cuba, and Poland as case studies. It outlines a kind of ideal type of revolutionary political development and argues that communist systems tended to progress through stages of one or another variation of this ideal type, with parallel processes affecting all policy spheres, including the religious.

Chapter 3 surveys the wide spectrum of Christian experience in the German Democratic Republic (1949-90), focusing particularly on the activities of the Evangelical Church. Chapters 4, 6, and 8 take a long view, tracing the development of patterns of religio-political interaction over centuries in Poland, Czechoslovakia, Hungary, Yugoslavia, and Albania. Chapter 5 takes up the convoluted history of the Catholic Church's relations with the communist and postcommunist governments of Czechoslovakia (1948-92) and with the governments of the Czech and Slovak successor states. The emphasis in chapter 5 is on the concept of communist culture as an artifact of systematic policy construction and programmatic design. Chapter 7 examines the ways in which the Romanian Orthodox Church has become infected with intolerance, taking up the story in 1878.

Chapters 9 and 10 deal with post-Soviet religious affairs, examining the Russian Orthodox Church and the Ukrainian religious scene. Chapter 9 includes a retrospective survey of the years 1927-89 and then pursues the story in more detail. In chapter 10 the plight of three rival Orthodox Churches and of the Greek-Rite Catholic Church is discussed.

The book's final section examines the new evangelism sweeping the region (chapter 11) and the contrast between the Bulgarian Orthodox and Polish Catholic Churches (chapter 12). New cults and sects making their appearance in the area are discussed in chapter 13. Chapters 11 and 13 reveal a proliferation of new religious organizations and movements, including fringe groups ranging from the Church of Witchcraft to Satanism to UFO cults, while chapter 12 examines how the contrasting histories of the Bulgarian and Polish Churches have led to virtually opposite results. In the conclusion some points about the politics of religion are summarized.

"Under communism," Jakub Karpiński has noted, "it was easier for the Church to determine what was moral and immoral. Everything linked to communism was immoral. Now it is not so clear."[23] Where once there was one big demon and one big champion, now there are a multitude of little demons and little champions; what is more, far more actors are situated within a gray zone of moral ambiguity or ambivalence. A big demon can appear without a big champion, but a big champion must have a big demon. This is one reason why, as Karpiński has observed, "Communism was paradoxically a time of tremendous influence for the Church."[24]

Chapter 2

Phases in Communist Religious Policy

Two questions among others arise when one deals with developments inside certain regions: can one identify patterns across societies within a region which reveal similar preoccupations, challenges, tasks, and complications; and can any such identifiable patterns be derived from cultural or other locally specific factors (and hence be unique to the region under scrutiny) or, instead, could they stem from more generalized political syndromes not bound by factors limited to a single region?

This chapter investigates these two issues, proposing that changes in religious policy in revolutionary systems follow an identifiable and partially predictable script that is independent of prerevolutionary cultural patterns. Of the five cases analyzed, three are taken from the East European/Russian area, while two (China, Cuba) are drawn from outside. Unlike chapters 3–13, which are largely historical, and chapter 14, which has a more philosophical orientation, this chapter is the province of political science model-building, although it does employ historical material to support the theory outlined below. Readers uncomfortable with or uninterested in such model-building may safely skip this chapter and pick up the narrative with chapter 3.

Conventionally, studies of Church-state relations are concerned with outlining the basic contours and parameters of the relationship within a given span of time. Even when the analysis is self-consciously diachronic, the analyst is usually more concerned with comparing and contrasting two or more definable periods in an evolving Church-state relationship than in investigating the processes of transition between these phases. A study of adaptation is necessarily different. Although, in the following pages, my concern is with ascertaining the differences in religious policy across developmental phases, my interest also lies with the processes of system change that effect change in religious policy over time.

Adaptation is necessarily the adjustment of one thing to something else. It is in a sense reactive, suggesting that a change of policy is dictated by signs of stress or inadequacy in a policy's earlier history. Such change may or may not be anticipated, but in general whenever such modification takes place the analyst should be alert for the presence of both advocates and antagonists of policy modification.

As a preliminary caution, it should be emphasized that not all forms of adaptation are necessarily the result of decisions by the central authorities. Some forms of de facto policy adaptation are adopted by local authorities either within the scope of the delegation of jurisdiction (as, for instance, in the decentralized context of Yugoslav politics between 1963 and 1991) or on their own initiative, which is to say, in defiance of the central authorities. Local policy adaptation thus may assume the form of corruption. The Soviet Union provides examples of corruption in relations between local Orthodox hierarchs and local religious affairs commissioners.[1] Or again, there is the case of Central Asia, where local Soviet authorities repeatedly turned a blind eye to officially illegal practices, such as the unlicensed construction of mosques and the illegal teaching of Islam to children. One such instance came to light in October 1986 when *Pravda vostoka* criticized A. Meliev, the commissioner of the council of religious affairs for Samarkand oblast, for "passivity" in his attitude toward growing mosque attendance and the activities of unlicensed mullahs.[2] Local policy adaptations are unlikely to adumbrate change at the highest level unless the architect(s) of those local adaptations should achieve high rank at the center.

This distinction also shows that policy adaptation may be planned or unplanned. Planned policy adaptation in which the ruling authorities are involved is clear enough. Unplanned adaptation is probably best understood as policy modification, which could not be foreseen and for which there may have been little time to prepare. For example, the sundry meetings organized in late 1980 and early 1981 in Lithuania in response to a new confidence displayed by that republic's Catholics—itself the result of both the activity of Pope John Paul II and the entire Polish syndrome, including the role of the Roman Catholic Church in Poland at that time—were hastily organized on short notice[3] and represent policy adaptation at a lower level of generality.

In the present chapter I propose to assess the extent to which policy adaptations in the religious sector have reflected broader systemic changes and to trace the adaptation of religious policy across four broad developmental phases. In so doing, I hope to demonstrate that modulations in religious policy have coincided closely with modulations in other policy spheres. The experiences of three cases germane to the area

Table 2.1 Phases in the Revolutionary Development of Communist States

Soviet Union	System destruction	1917–23
	System building	1923–38
	Consolidation	1923–28
	Mobilization	1928–38
	System stabilization	1938–82
	System decay	1982–91
China	System destruction	1949–53/55
	System building	1953/55–76
	Consolidation	1953/55–57
	Mobilization (1)	1958–66
	Mobilization (2)	1966–76
	Interregnum	1976–78
	System stabilization	1978–present
Yugoslavia	System destruction	1943–53
	System building	1953–63
	System reform	1963–80
	Polarization	1963–66
	Liberalization	1966–71
	Construction of a Titoist center	1971–80
	System decay	1980–89/91
Cuba	System destruction	1959–61
	System building	1961–86
	Consolidation and revolutionary messianism	1961–67
	Mobilization (1)	1967–70/75
	Mobilization (2)	1970/75–86
	System decay	1986–present
Poland	System destruction	1944–48
	System building	1948–70
	System stabilization	1970–80
	System decay	1980–89

(the USSR, Yugoslavia, and Poland) will be contrasted to those of two other communist states (China and Cuba) to offer a broadly comparative framework.

It has become commonplace at this point to analyze the evolution of communist systems in terms of distinct phases, distinguished by differing systemic tasks and strategies. As Kenneth Jowitt put it in a now-classic statement of this approach,

in the history of Leninist regimes, one can identify at least three elite-designated core tasks and stages of development. The first is transformation of the old society; the second is consolidation of the revolutionary regime; the third . . . is inclusion [and is characterized by] attempts by the party elite to expand the internal boundaries of the regime's political, productive, and decision-making systems, to integrate itself with the nonofficial (non-*apparatchik*) sectors of society rather than insulate itself from them.[4]

These phases will be identified here as system destruction, system-building, and system stabilization. In addition to these three, a subsequent phase may take the form either of system reform or system decay in which the growing tension between vested interests, both corrupt and authorized, and the rising demands for reform is resolved one way or the other. System decay ends with the complete transformation of the system (albeit not without some inherited legacy from the past).

Within these broad phases certain "left" adjustments and "right" adjustments may occur.[5] Some of these adjustments may be dramatic enough to warrant the term "subphase," but as long as the core systemic tasks stay unchanged, the basic principles governing Church-state relations will likewise remain stable. Hence, as society progresses and the pattern of tasks with which it is confronted evolves, policy in the programmatic spheres (economy, media, nationalities, gender relations, religion, etc.) must be adapted to the changing tasks.

The First Phase: System Destruction

The system destruction phase is necessarily short.[6] The revolutionary party, not yet secure, must defend its position against internal and external foes, and it seeks to uproot traditional culture and traditional elites as a preliminary to constructing a new society. Mao Zedong in an early essay called for the destruction of all "feudal" culture "whose exponents include all those who advocate the worship of Confucius, the study of the Confucian canon, the old ethical code and the old ideas in opposition to the new culture and the new ideas. . . . This kind of reactionary culture serves the imperialists and the feudal class and must be swept away. Unless it is swept away, no new culture of any kind can be built up."[7] In this phase a degree of inner-party democracy is apt to be present, even as the spectrum of permissible political activity outside the party steadily shrinks.

In the Soviet Union this phase lasted from 1917 to roughly 1923, the year in which the Mensheviks and Social Revolutionaries were finally snuffed out, a new constitution was passed, and the ruble stabilized. It was in 1923, after the second failure to export revolution to Germany, that the Comintern was demoted and revolutionary millenarianism put on the back burner.

This phase was characterized by radical egalitarianism in class, inter-ethnic, and gender relations. "Bourgeois marriage" was mocked, and sexual promiscuity was encouraged.[8] In the army, military ranks were temporarily abolished and decisions were made on the basis of discus-sions and votes. Commissars entrusted with the supervision of music, wanting to create a new proletarian culture that would break totally with prerevolutionary culture, organized studio workshops in hundreds of Russia's towns and villages. In the spirit of musical collectivism a con-ductorless orchestra ('PERSIFANS') was established in Moscow in 1922, which achieved consensus on interpretation among the players through exhaustive discussions and consultations.[9]

In the religious sphere the chief tasks were the undermining of the Old Order, of which the Russian Orthodox Church was an organic part, and the whittling down of the church. To accomplish these twin goals, the Bolsheviks were prepared to harness the energies of selective religious liberalization, and they authorized the publication of various Protestant religious books and pamphlets. With Bolshevik encourage-ment, the Old Believers and other breakaway sects came into the open; the Ukrainian Autocephalous Orthodox Church declared its secession from the Moscow Patriarchate in 1921, and a Belorussian Autocephalous Orthodox Church was proclaimed in July 1922.[10] This policy of religious fragmentation echoed the policy of ethnic *razmezhevanie* through which the Bolsheviks encouraged larger nationality groups to split into smaller ones. Meanwhile, Russian Orthodox clergy members were attacked and sometimes murdered or sent to labor camps, and Orthodox churches and monasteries were looted. The combination of pressure on the largest reli-gious institution and encouragement of smaller, previously repressed in-stitutions had predictable results. By 1923 the party abandoned the policy of religious *razmezhevanie*, and the smaller sects began to experience dif-ficulties in publishing and functioning.

In the People's Republic of China the phase of system destruction began toward the end of World War II and lasted until 1953 to 1955. As in the Soviet case, China's communists came to power through civil war, and early policy decisions were taken with an eye to destroying the chief sources of resistance. The result was a series of mass campaigns from 1950 through 1952, aimed at prosperous landowners (kulaks), private merchants, and provincial party officials accused of corruption. Altogether, the "suppression of the counterrevolutionaries" between the 1949 takeover and 1955 claimed considerably more than 800,000 lives.[11] One of the more dramatic pieces of legislation during this period was the marriage law of 1950, which abolished bigamy and child-bride marriages and proclaimed equal rights for women and men in both marriage and divorce. But even here the party felt the need to organize mass propaganda meetings around the country as angry husbands, who refused to be divorced by their spouses, killed off tens of thousands of their wives.[12]

Contradictory trends were visible in the religious sphere. On the one hand, in the non-Chinese "border" provinces of Sinkiang, Tsinghai, and Kansu, Muslim ulema and Lamaist[13] priests were placed on platforms and forced to listen to ritual accusations, while crowds howled at them. And beginning in 1951, traditional drama was subjected to extensive rewriting to eliminate all references to the supernatural.[14] Catholic missionaries and priests as well as Protestant pastors were imprisoned or beaten, and churches were required to display portraits of Mao and Stalin at all times. Taoists, whose blend of folk religious practices and traditions of antigovernment opposition in secret societies made them particularly unpalatable to the new regime, were subjected to particularly harsh treatment. Shortly after the communist takeover, many Taoist temples were seized outright and revamped for other uses, such as headquarters for peasants' associations, cooperative stores, jails, or barracks. Some five thousand people, including members of a Taoist secret society known as *Hui Dao Men*, were executed on 24 March 1951.[15]

On the other hand, if some signs pointed to a policy of uprooting religion, other signs suggested incipient efforts to bring religious organizations under state control. One such effort was the establishment in the early 1950s of a series of national associations for the respective "sects" and, more particularly, the founding of the monthly periodical *Modern Buddhism* in 1950, which was entrusted with transmitting government policy to the Buddhists and promoting the reform of Buddhist doctrine, specifically its adaptation to communist social norms.

In Yugoslavia the phase of system destruction began during World

War II when Tito's partisans shot priests and uprooted traditional social structures in areas that fell under their control. The system received a sharp jolt in June 1948 when the Soviet Union expelled communist Yugoslavia from the Cominform. By 1950 the Yugoslav leaders realized that the rift could not be healed, and in a series of policy decisions over the next three years they introduced a system of workers' self-management (designed to challenge the USSR ideologically), dismantled the Stalinist constitution of 1946, called a halt to the campaign of harassing and assaulting clergy, and signed a mutual defense pact with Greece and Turkey, both of which were members of NATO. The end of this phase may be conveniently marked as 1953, the year in which legislation to revise the constitution was passed.

During much of this phase the communist party of Yugoslavia (which renamed itself the League of Communists of Yugoslavia in 1952) was confronted with the self-appointed task of eliminating the nine non-communist parties which appeared on the political scene at war's end. These included reincarnations of some interwar parties (the Croatian Republican Peasant Party, the Agrarian Party, the Socialist Party, and the Social Democratic Party). Soon these parties experienced difficulties publishing their papers, articulating their views, and organizing outside Serbia and Croatia. Communist agitators organized mobs to intimidate noncommunist politicians, while noncommunist deputies in the Federal Chamber of the assembly were hooted down and prevented from speaking. By 1949, political pluralism in Yugoslavia was dead.[16]

For three years beginning in 1948 the communist government of Yugoslavia was threatened with external intervention by fellow communist states (the USSR and its East European satellites) and "Cominformist" discontents in exile.[17] By 1951, however, the danger had largely passed.

In the religious sphere the Yugoslav communists wanted to strip away land and other properties held by the Churches, to stigmatize the Orthodox and Roman Catholic Churches for "collaboration" (the Orthodox with the Chetniks, the Catholics with the Ustaše), and to bring religious organizations under control. These objectives, of course, were at odds with each other. Thus, in putting Zagreb's Archbishop Alojzije Stepinac on trial in 1946 for alleged collaboration, the regime inflicted a still unhealed wound and created a long-term impediment to good relations with the Catholic Church.[18]

The chief instrument for promoting state influence—albeit an ambiguous one—was the system of priests' associations that sprang up after the war with the regime's encouragement. When the Serbian priests' association was established in December 1947, the Orthodox synod declared it uncanonical. But the various associations offered the priests social insurance, pensions, a say in Church affairs,[19] and, accordingly, the range of these groups spread. By July 1952, 80 percent of Orthodox priests were members of the principal association. During these years the priests' associations served as the main vehicle through which the communist regime conducted business with the Serbian Orthodox Church. This situation changed abruptly in 1954, however, when the regime found it increasingly feasible to deal directly with the hierarchy. Thereafter, the influence of the priests' association eroded.

In the early years of its power, the government not only confiscated church buildings, but fined Orthodox clergy on various pretexts; autocephalist currents among both Macedonian and Montenegrin clergy appeared to be encouraged. In October 1953, however, Patriarch Vikentije, accompanied by members of the Holy Synod, called on President Tito to express support for Tito's position in the international dispute over Trieste.[20] After 1954, the patriarch began to attend official gatherings such as Tito's birthday reception in 1955. And in August 1956 Tito decorated the churchman on his sixty-seventh birthday.

For the Catholic Church, more particularly, the initial postwar years saw great hardship. Property was confiscated, publications curtailed, clergy jailed or harassed, and ecclesiastical prerogatives in education rolled back. For the Catholics, as for the Orthodox, the situation began to change around 1953. In January of that year the government amnestied forty-three Catholic priests, and shortly thereafter, in a speech at Ruma, Tito called for an end to physical assaults on the clergy. On 27 April 1953 Yugoslavia passed a new law on the legal status of religious communities, which guaranteed freedom of conscience and of religious belief.[21]

In Cuba the phase of system destruction was unusually brief, being telescoped into a mere two years: 1959–61. During that time the revolutionary regime of Fidel Castro snuffed out economic free enterprise, nationalized industry, and expropriated all foreign-owned lands (as well as Cuban holdings in excess of 995 acres); it also began collectivizing agriculture and launched a six-month literacy campaign that recorded dramatically positive results.[22] In November 1959, as the regime veered leftward, the anticommunist moderates (Felipe Pazos, Faustino Perez, and Manuel Rey) tendered their resignations. The regime continued to face resistance from organized "counterrevolutionary" guerrillas in the

Escambray Mountains until mid-1961, and it successfully faced down the Bay of Pigs invasion in April of that year.

Some difficulties occurred in relations with the Catholic Church in these years because the Spanish-born prelates who dominated the Cuban hierarchy identified with the upper classes and were hostile to prospects of radical socioeconomic change.[23] The Church was divided over the agrarian reform law of May 1959, but clearly it was most concerned with the sanctity of private property. Religious processions began to take on the character of antigovernment rallies, as Catholic suspicion grew of the new regime's Marxist tendencies. For a while, the Catholic Church seemed headed for a role as the bulwark of the opposition, perhaps akin to the experience of the Polish Church. As evidence of this tendency, the annual National Catholic Congress of 1959 drew more than 1 million participants, although previously only about 10,000 had attended the event.[24]

In the course of 1961 the Cuban regime nationalized all private schools, including Catholic schools, and after someone was killed during a riotous religious procession, the government banned such ceremonies in the streets. Several clergy were expelled before the end of 1961, although later some of them were permitted to return. Recalling this period almost twenty-five years later, Fidel Castro told Fr. Frei Betto:

No churches in Cuba were ever closed down — none of them. There was a time when the political confrontation became really fierce, and because of the militant political attitude taken by some priests — especially the Spanish ones — we requested that they be withdrawn from our country, and we revoked their authorization to remain here. That happened, and that was the measure that was taken. However, we authorized other priests to come to Cuba and replace the ones who were asked to leave. That was the only measure that was taken — and it, only once. After that, relations were normalized.[25]

And indeed, after the early 1960s, Church-state relations in Cuba, according to most observers, became remarkably trouble-free.

Finally, in Poland, the phase of system destruction lasted from 1944 (declaration of the provisional government) to 1948 (the fall of Władysław Gomułka and the absorption of the socialist party by the communist party to form the new Polish United Workers' Party [PUWP]). During this phase Polish communists were preoccupied with the suppression of the anticommunist guerrilla resistance (accomplished by 1947)[26] and with the neutralization of the Peasant Party, the Socialist Party, and the rest of the noncommunist opposition. Party Secretary Gomułka tried to advocate a gradualist approach, reminiscent of Nikolai Bukharin in the USSR in the 1920s at what proved to be the height of Stalinism: Gomułka's assertion of the importance of sensitivity to Polish specificities, above all, cost him his position.

Where the Church was concerned, the authorities moved relatively slowly, especially when compared to the treatment accorded to elites in other East European countries at the time. On 12 September 1945 the council of ministers declared the concordat of 1925 null and void, and the regime successfully dissuaded the Church from reestablishing the Catholic Workers' Party. By 1948 Catholic printing presses were under state control, and Catholic publications were banned from public libraries.[27] Earlier, in 1945 the pro-regime priests' association PAX was created by Bolesław Piasecki at the instigation of the communist party, and in May 1949 PAX was allowed to establish a publishing house.[28]

Reviewing the five cases of system destruction, one finds that this phase varied from two years in the Cuban case to nine years in the Yugoslav (the added years there being a factor of the prolonged crisis in Soviet-Yugoslav relations). In every case surveyed, the fledgling communist regime had to deal with both internal and external foes, and in every case the leadership of some religious organization was hostile to the new secular authorities. Except in Poland[29], the communist authorities nationalized Church schools, and in some cases they confiscated Church lands; in every country, except for Cuba, limits were imposed on Church publications, and the Church press was subjected to censorship. Since even in Cuba most believers were antagonistic toward communism, the new political elites sometimes adopted a policy of divide and rule (as with the Chinese Buddhist Association and associations for other religions in China, the Yugoslav priests' associations, and the Polish association PAX). In the Soviet, Chinese, and Yugoslav cases, repeated, systematic incidents of harassment, deportation, jailing, and even murder of clergy occurred, while in Cuba about 8 percent of Catholic clergy members were expelled.

During the phase of system destruction, Church and state confronted each other as independent actors with divergent preferences. Given the uncertainty that surrounds the establishment of a new political order, conflict was almost foreordained.

The Second Phase: System-Building

Once it has successfully repulsed external threats and tranquilized the internal order, the revolutionary party is able to set about its programs of political and economic modernization and socialization to communist-collectivist mores. The development of a leadership cult, entailing the subordination of the party to the will of the leader, typically takes place during this phase. The process of system-building (or "socialist construction" in Marxist jargon) is complex; hence, this phase typically breaks down into two or three composite subphases, which vary from case to case.

While the five systems shared a great deal in common in the first developmental stage, some tangible second-phase differences emerged in the way in which the respective regimes tackled common tasks. In the first phase, the Marxist-Leninists in these countries tended to believe that they could bridle national culture and national tradition and that they could introduce ideologically motivated changes with little regard for anything besides the class structure and the question of ownership of the means of production. In the second phase, revolutionary elites are forced to take national culture and traditions, and local conditions in general, more seriously. The past comes back to haunt the present, with the result that the systems start to show important developmental differences, even if many of the institutional and policy instruments appear to be similar or the same from one country to the next. Later, as a result of differences at this stage, as well as differences in national context and experience, international conditions, leadership, generational changes, and no doubt others, differences become even greater at the third stage, as we shall see.

Differences among these systems in the second developmental phase are highlighted in table 2.2. Consolidation is a central preoccupation of all the elites during this phase, and mobilization figures as an ingredient in all but the Yugoslav case. (Although even in Yugoslavia there have been aspects of mobilization—for example, in the annual youth day celebrations, which were given an austere cast during Tito's primacy.) In four cases, the party faced the necessity of calling a retreat during this phase: tactical retreats in the Soviet Union and China, strategic retreat in Yugoslavia, and temporary tactical retreat *cum* strategic adjustment in Poland. In no case were the tasks of this phase completed, although the Soviets and Chinese came closer than the East Europeans or the Cubans. Also, diverse problems that prevented the tasks from being

Table 2.2 Subphases in System-Building in Communist States

Country	Subphases	Years
Soviet Union	consolidation: tactical retreat, strategic debate	1923–28
	mobilization	1928–38
China	consolidation: tactical retreat	1955–57
	mobilization: collective leadership	1958–66
	mobilization: cult of the leader	1966–76
Yugoslavia	consolidation: strategic readjustment	1953–61
	liberalization: strategic retreat	1961–63
Cuba	consolidation: strategic debate	1961–67
	mobilization, noninstitutionalized	1967–70/75
	mobilization, institutionalized	1970/75–86
Poland	consolidation and mobilization	1948–56
	retrenchment: temporary tactical retreat, strategic adjustment	1956–70

completed "on time"[30] likewise contributed to permutations at the third stage.

In the Soviet case, the system-building phase (1923–38) consisted of two subphases: *consolidation* (1923–28) and *mobilization* (1928–38). The general relaxation which characterized the consolidation subphase in all spheres—from economics to cultural life to party politics to nationalities policy and religious policy—was unmistakably a retreat. But whether it would be treated as a tactical retreat (as the party's left wing wanted) or as a strategic retreat (as the party's right wing preferred) itself depended on the combined power struggle and strategic debate that divided the party in the 1920s. Non-Russian cultures flourished with party approval and active support in the years up to 1928, while in gender relations, cadres advocated more conventional forms of liberation, promoting female employment, women's right to divorce, and, in Central Asia, mass unveilings, while they reversed their earlier encouragement of promiscuity.[31] In literature, the so-called Serapion Brothers advocated nonconformism in literary art, winning a guarantee of their views from the Central Committee of the Communist Party in 1925, while in the music the broader strategic debate was reflected in the uneasy and mutually antagonistic coexistence of the leftist Russian Association of Proletarian Musicians and the musically modernist, politically moderate Association for Contemporary Music.[32] The spirit of the time was one of laissez faire, typified in the New Economic Policy (NEP). By putting its transformational programs on hold, the party gained time to consolidate and institutionalize its power and to develop its administrative apparatus.

The mobilization subphase corresponds to the first two Five-Year Plans and thus to the programs of agricultural collectivization,[33] forced industrialization, partial Russification of the non-Russian peoples,[34] and mass recruitment of women into the labor force. (Abortion, legalized in 1920, was recriminalized in 1936 as a component of the Stalinist policy of encouraging the growth of the future labor force.)[35] The reliance on both charisma and terror increased exponentially during this phase, culminating in the savagery of the Great Terror, 1934-38. In literature, music, and art, the party imposed the doctrine of "socialist realism" in 1932, which prescribed a programmatic approach in which socialist leaders were to be portrayed in heroic proportions and capitalists and counterrevolutionaries as nefarious enemies of the people. Andrei Zhdanov (1896–1948), central committee secretary for ideological questions from 1944, told a conference of the Writers' Union of the USSR in 1934 that the doctrine required them "to portray reality in its revolutionary development" and "to combine the truthfulness and historical concreteness of this portrayal with the ideological reforming and education of the workers in the spirit of socialism."[36] This doctrine was legitimated through the cult of Stalin. As the publication *Tvorchestvo* put it in 1939, "Comrade Stalin's words of genius about Soviet art as an art of socialist realism represent the peak of all the progressive strivings of the aesthetic thought of mankind."[37] But nothing better symbolized the spirit demanded by the communist party at the height of Stalinism than the so-called Stakhanovite movement, a mass campaign of supposedly self-inspired workaholics seeking to emulate the example of coal miner Aleksei Stakhanov (1906–77), who claimed to have mined 102 tons of coal in a single six-hour shift in 1935.[38]

In the religious sphere the party hoped to enhance its political supremacy by backing a schismatic "Renovationist Church" (created 1922–23). Reformist and theologically modernizing, the Renovationist Church was loyal to the Bolshevik regime, and, indeed, its strategy and tactics were planned by a department of the GPU, the secret police.[39] This Renovationist Church was able to compete with the patriarchal church for only a few years, and once Patriarch Sergii issued his well-known declaration of loyalty in June 1927, the regime no longer needed the Renovationists, who therefore were included among the targets of the general offensives against religion of 1929–30, 1932–34, and 1936–38.

But while there was a general atmosphere of laissez faire in most policy spheres in this subphase, the parallel relaxation in the religious sphere owed more to deficiencies in infrastructure and control and (in the case of the Ukrainian Orthodox, Belorussian Orthodox, and Renovationist Churches) to continuing tactics of *razmezhevanie* than to any Bolshevik decision to ease up on religion. A limited "exception" of sorts occurred in Central Asia, where serious antireligious measures had to be delayed because of the still smouldering *Basmachi* revolt. Orthodox clergymen and scholars were given death sentences, and many believers were imprisoned throughout the Russian republic. In 1924, the state publishing house for antireligious literature was established and the weekly newspaper, *Bezbozhnik* [The Godless], was launched. The following year the authorities established the League of Militant Atheists under Emelyan Yaroslavsky (1878–1943). Yet despite all of these efforts, the authorities clearly were still in the process of setting up the apparatus for control of the religious organizations, and religious policy, like policy in other spheres, remained in a premobilization stage. Several bits of evidence support this interpretation. First, the central apparatus had not yet established its control over education in the provinces, and religious education continued to be offered in many communities, despite Moscow's instructions to terminate the practice.[40] Second, public religious lectures of an expository nature, which attracted young people on a regular basis, continued to be offered until 1928.[41] And third, there was a general rise in religious behavior in this period, with membership increases of 9 to 19 percent during 1925 alone for the Orthodox, Old Believer, Islamic, Jewish, and Evangelical Christian communities.[42]

Antireligious activity on the part of the Komsomol also was moderated in this period. Whereas the Komosomol had been giving priority to the development of new *secular* holidays beginning in 1920, launching the first "Komsomol Christmas" in 1922, and sponsoring Bolshevized "Easter" celebrations in 1923, punctuated with antireligious lectures, the Komsomol leadership called for a temporary cessation of all antireligious campaigns in September 1924. The new "moderation" was confirmed at the Fourteenth Party Conference (1925), which heard complaints about counterproductive excesses in antireligious work and called on the Komsomol to expel self-willed activists from its ranks. In the wake of this conference, Komsomol activists were advised not to close down churches by force but to rely on persuasion, for example, by advocating that the village church be converted into a library.[43]

In 1928, as the first Five-Year Plan was being set in motion, religious policy was put on a mobilization footing. A new religious law (1929) invalidated the earlier guarantee of the freedom of "religious propaganda" and left only the freedom of "antireligious propaganda." Under the new legislation, religious organizations were banned from any social, charitable, or educational activities, or from organizing special activities for women or young people.[44] Beginning in 1929, "godless shock brigades" were dispatched to factories and collective farms with the assignment of lecturing against religion while taking part in work. At the same time, the League of Militant Atheists launched an antireligious campaign, closing down the vast majority of houses of worship. New industrial cities such as Magnitogorsk were built without churches, creating purely secular environments for the growing working class.[45] Of the 50,000 Russian Orthodox churches functioning as of early 1917, only 200–300 remained by 1939.[46] Over the same years, some "80,000 Orthodox clerics, monks, and nuns had lost their lives at the hands of the Bolsheviks. This figure represents about half the total number of clerics, monks, and nuns serving before the 1917 revolution."[47] In 1928, coinciding with the launching of the first Five-Year Plan, anticlerical propagandists started to incorporate political elements in their arguments, accusing Muslim learned men (*ulema*), for example, of encouraging popular observance of traditional religious customs in order to sustain relations of exploitation.[48] That same year Soviet authorities began imprisoning Muslim ulema, confiscating Islamic community property, and destroying many mosques. By 1930 the process, by and large, was complete, and those mosques that remained open were without independent means of support. Arabic script was banned at this time, while traditional Muslim (*shariat*) courts had been abolished in 1927. Muslim schools (both the *mektep*, or primary schools, and the *madrassahs*, or secondary schools) were suppressed by 1928. The onslaught against Islam lasted from 1928 to 1938 and dramatically reduced the number of mosques. There had been some 26,000 mosques in Central Asia in 1917; by 1942, only 1,312 "working" mosques remained.[49]

During the mobilization subphase, the Ukrainian and Belorussian Orthodox Churches were suppressed, and the Russian Orthodox Church was gradually weakened. Popular priests were imprisoned in order to leave parishes in the hands of mediocre clergy.[50] The intensification of the antireligious campaign between 1936 and 1938—at the height of the Terror—resulted in nearly complete enervation of religious life in the country.[51] "Hundreds of churches and temples were simply torn down," Roy Medvedev writes, "dozens of monasteries were dissolved, and the OGPU [secret police] even rounded up hermits and put them in camps. In many cities precious monuments of church architecture were destroyed—the Church of Christ the Savior and the Spasskii Monastery in Moscow, for example."[52]

The basic tasks of the system-building phase in the religious sphere as elsewhere were essentially accomplished by 1938; the rehabilitation of Russian nationalism in that year and the winding down of the Terror were expressions of Stalin's recognition of that fact. Some observers may prefer to date the end of this phase from 1956, with Khrushchev's de-Stalinization speech, but the limits of de-Stalinization were clearly shown in the antireligious campaign of 1959-64. More particularly, I would argue that a disjunction may exist between leadership styles and systemic tasks, and that leaders may not always be able to adapt to changes in system tasks.

In China, things moved at a faster pace. In the "consolidation" subphase, there were already clear signs of mass mobilization—as in the collectivization campaign of 1955-57, the abortive Great Leap Forward of 1958-60, and the Socialist Education Movement of 1962-66. Several factors distinguish the consolidation subphase from the mobilization subphase. First, the earlier campaigns were directed toward changing forms of economic and social organization, while the Great Proletarian Cultural Revolution of 1966-76[53] placed a great emphasis on changing the culture and political thought of the people. Second, the earlier campaigns were still directed by the party, whereas the Cultural Revolution was launched by Mao and carried out by the Red Guards (communist youth brigades), serving the purpose of establishing Mao's unquestioned supremacy *over* the party.[54] Third, the Cultural Revolution was more intense in terms of general turbulence (in the early phase), the degree to which people were affected and involved, and the impact on party cadres. In these last two respects the differences parallel the Soviet case.

In other areas the Chinese case was remarkably different from the Soviet. For example, China's communists were faster in taking NEP-like steps to restore economic stability than their Bolshevik counterparts had been. As early as March 1949 Mao told the second plenum of the Seventh Central Committee that the immediate priority was to prevent the collapse of the economy. The remedies adopted included generous credit policies that revived the private business sector.[55] But unlike the Soviets, the Chinese experienced only a short "NEP," and as early as December 1955, 75 million peasants (63.3 percent of the total peasant population) had been drawn into agricultural collectives. At the same time, socialization of the business sector was essentially complete by the end of 1956.[56]

Soviet leader Khrushchev's anti-Stalin secret speech of February 1956 had its effect on elite circles in China, and moderates tried to put the brakes on what they called "economic adventurism."

In this context the Hundred Flowers Campaign of 1956–57 figured as a tactical retreat. The campaign was initiated in May 1956, when Lu Dingyi, head of party propaganda, delivered a speech entitled "Let a Hundred Flowers Blossom and a Hundred Schools of Thought Contend." Lu claimed that he had borrowed the slogan from Mao himself.[57] Whatever the truth of that claim, Mao Zedong gave a speech to the Eighth Party Congress on 27 February 1957, urging his listeners, "Can criticism of Marxism be allowed? Of course Marxism may be criticized. Marxism is not afraid of criticism."[58] In late April 1957 the party even issued an official "instruction" encouraging people to criticize any and all mistakes committed by the authorities. Within the context of this short-lived campaign, some ephemeral changes took place in religious policy. For example, several Catholic bishops, priests, and laypersons were released from prison, and priests once more were allowed to wear their religious attire and to visit their parishes. Among Protestant clergy and Muslims alike, a number of them took advantage of the sudden liberalization to speak out, criticizing the regime for discriminatory practices. A Rev. Marcus Cheng cautiously mentioned on one occasion that Marx had criticized the Bible, adding, "Even we fundamentalist Christians are glad to accept his criticism."[59] Less than a year later, this remark would draw stiff criticism on the argument that Cheng was needlessly suggesting some possible conflict between believers and nonbelievers. A more lasting concession of the "Hundred Flowers" period was the opening of a Buddhist academy in Beijing in September 1956 with 110 students enrolled (in 1957) in either two-year or four-year programs.

The antireligious campaign which followed that of the Hundred Flowers resulted in criticism of those who had dropped their guard, but there were both positive and negative developments from the standpoint of believers in the years before the Cultural Revolution. Among the positive developments could be numbered the addition of a research department to the Buddhist academy in 1961, and a department of Tibetan Buddhism the following year. On the other hand, the publication of *Modern Buddhism* was suspended briefly in 1960 and resumed with an altered format—more news about Buddhism abroad, less about Buddhists at home—only to be suppressed altogether in 1964. Where Protestants were concerned, the large-scale forced "consolidation" of churches in 1958 reduced the number of functioning churches and strengthened state control. In Beijing, sixty-five churches were "consolidated" to four; in Shanghai, two hundred churches were "consolidated" to twenty-three. And in the process of "consolidation," many Protestant pastors lost their jobs and were assigned to work teams in other sectors.[60]

The anti-rightist campaign of the mid-1950s resulted in the persecution or harassment of more than half a million intellectuals, while the disastrous economic policies of the Great Leap Forward (1958–60) resulted in the deaths of 25–30 million people, mainly in rural areas.[61] The lurches and hesitations in China's policies—the result of intra-elite factional struggles—must be set against the firmly established radicalism of Mao and his closest associates. Eight years before the launching of the Great Proletarian Cultural Revolution, Mao would tell the Supreme State Conference (January 1958): "I advocate continuous revolution. Do not mistake mine for Trotsky's permanent revolution. A revolution has to be struck while the iron is hot, one revolution has to be followed by another, a revolution has to move forward incessantly."[62]

China was given a foretaste of things to come on National Day, 1 October 1964, when "a monumental show, *The East Is Red*, was staged by the army. The press described it as a 'hymn to the Thoughts of Mao Zedong.' Monster choirs and ballet girls in military uniform fired rifles and danced *jete passe* steps. . . . The show ended with apotheosis; an immense gold flag adorned with a huge figure of Mao fluttered on the heights and the chorus sang: 'Chairman Mao, the sun is in our hearts.' "[63]

When the Cultural Revolution itself was proclaimed in 1966, the entire country was pushed into disarray. Lin Biao, fifth vice chairman of the party and minister of defense, addressed a "great meeting" of Red Guards on 18 August 1966, calling on them to "smash the old way of thinking, the old culture, old custom, and old habits."[64] Revolutionary zeal became more important than originality or creativity or productivity or previous success in one's work. One symptom of this fanaticism came in the form of a sudden fad for painting the walls of private residences red. So many people did so that a widespread shortage of red paint developed. The Red Guards disrupted offices, destroyed traditional shrines, destroyed priceless works of art from the precommunist era, and adorned city streets with revolutionary slogans. Red Guards even stopped citizens on the streets and gave them haircuts if they felt that their comrades' hair was too long. Mao told the Red Guards, "Do not be afraid to make trouble. The more trouble you make and the longer you make it, the better. Confusion and trouble are always noteworthy. It can clear things up. . . . Wherever there are abscesses or infections, we must blow them up."[65] Some of the country's leading economists, writers, and scientific experts were sent to collective farms to work in the fields and—it was thought—"learn from the masses." Schools were shut down for several months at the end of 1966 as a result of Red Guard rampages, and when they reopened in February 1967 the old textbooks were gone, replaced by Mao's works, and class time was devoted to the study of wall posters, the acquisition of industrial and agricultural skills, military training, and above all, the study of the thoughts of Chairman Mao.[66] Mao even saw fit to regulate private life, declaring that it was petit bourgeois to keep animals as pets.

The Cultural Revolution was scaled down in 1968, but its legacy—the replacement of bureaucratic dictatorship with charismatic despotism—lasted until Mao's death in 1976. Apart from its debilitating effects on government administration, the economy, and the educational system,[67] the Cultural Revolution also had an impact on the arts. Indeed, at the movement's height, only eight "model works" of music could be performed in China, and concert and opera audiences had to suffer through years of musical repetition. Five of these "model works" were operas (whose plots, on instruction from cultural commissar Jiang Qing, invariably placed a heroic woman in the commanding position). All traditional operas and even most revolutionary operas were banned.[68] Sexual references in fiction, poetry, or drama were strictly taboo, and when the famous play, *The White-Haired Girl,* was revived in its "purified" version as a "model revolutionary ballet," it no longer made any mention of the rape of the girl by the landlord's son.[69]

The decade-long Cultural Revolution (1966–76) changed conditions for believers in a number of ways. The Chinese Buddhist Association, the Islamic Association, the Patriotic Association of Chinese Catholics, and similar groups were dormant during this period.[70] Given the groups' totally docile and subservient nature,[71] it is clear that it was not a question of suppressing critical voices, but that these groups of sycophants no longer had a useful role to fill given the new tasks of the mobilization subphase.

The central task of the Cultural Revolution in the religious sphere was to destroy the institutional and spiritual bases for religion. The Red Guards figured prominently in the early years of this campaign, forming a "Revolutionary Struggle Group for the Abolition of Islam" and raiding Protestant churches to haul their Bibles, books, and other religious materials to the street to be burned. Churches, temples, and mosques of all religions were closed although the Islamic community was able to maintain a few functioning mosques in order to reduce the offense to the Muslim states with whom China maintained relations.[72] Seminaries for all faiths were closed.[73] Religious periodicals were terminated, and religious literature became unobtainable. Religion and religious life disappeared from the dispatches of the China News Agency and from the press. In the Chinese case, as in the Soviet, trends in religious policy clearly coincided with more general trends throughout the system.

In Yugoslavia the years 1953–63 could be described as a decade of *strategic adjustment*. This period most closely approximates the *system-building* phase. During that time the Yugoslav authorities attempted, not to implement the model with which they had started, but to adjust the old model to changed conditions. Symptomatic of this approach was the fact that the Basic Law of 1953 did not replace the 1946 constitution but merely amended it—albeit very extensively. One important aspect of this process of "adjustment" was a reform of the legal system set in motion in 1951, designed to remove unqualified judges from judicial posts, and to rehabilitate those who had been unjustly convicted of criminal charges (estimated at 40 percent of all convicted people in Serbia and 47 percent in Montenegro).[74] But only in 1961–62, toward the end of this phase, did the party enter into a lengthy debate about the political and economic formulae that ought to be applied. This debate ended only in 1991 when the country broke up, but decisive steps were taken in 1961 in the economic sphere and in 1963 in the political sphere. Until 1961 the economy was still regulated by a system of "planning by global balances."[75] In that year the first of a series of economic reforms was passed, and in 1963 a decentralizing "third" postwar constitution was instituted, which opened the door to gradual liberalization.

The distinctive features of Yugoslavia's political path were reflected in the religious sphere. The period from 1953 to 1964 (roughly coinciding with the duration of this phase) can be characterized as years of mutual search for a modus vivendi in the state's relations with the Catholic Church,[76] and the years from 1953 to 1966 can be described as a time of tense coexistence in the state's relations with the Serbian Orthodox Church.[77] Indeed, government authorities agreed to a program of "restoring Orthodox monasteries from 1956 onwards, partly for touristic purposes, and partly because a slightly more cosy relationship had now been established between senior Orthodox clergy and the state."[78] Where the Muslims are concerned, the possibilities for Islamic religious life improved in tandem with Tito's quest for allies in the Arab world— although in terms of group recognition, that period figures as one of cultural denial and ethnic subordination to the "Yugoslav" idea. Unlike the Soviet and Chinese experiences, the system-building phase in Yugoslavia brought not systematic repression, therefore, but liberalization and the extension of legal guarantees. In essence, this phase abandoned much baggage of mobilization and undertook the task of *inclusion* at an earlier stage than occurred in either the USSR or China. ("Inclusion" as a systemic task will be discussed in the next section of this chapter.)

In Cuba, system-building can be dated from 1961, when Castro signaled his intention to pursue an (independent) socialist course. From 1961 until 1963, socialist institutions of a Soviet type were introduced in Cuba, albeit without a formal, institutionalized communist party in control. A style of mobilization was adopted to pursue specific campaigns in education (the Schools of Revolutionary Instruction, 1960–67), and agriculture (the second phase of the collectivization campaign, 1963–68, and the well-known sugar harvest campaign of 1968–70). The late 1960s saw a strategic debate being waged, with the radical "Sino-Guevarist" approach[79] temporarily ascendant over the more moderate/liberal approach championed by economist Carlos Rafael Rodriguez and others. The death of Ernesto "Che" Guevara in 1967 and the failure of the sugar harvest campaign made adjustment inevitable. In the autumn of 1970 Castro declared that Cuba was entering a "new phase," which he characterized as a step forward in democratization. In practice, the years 1970–73 saw greater regimentation in Cuban life, including education and the arts,[80] and increased centralization of political power. Finally, in mid-December 1975 the Cuban Communist Party (which had been established in October 1965) held its first national congress, installing a new central committee, a new politburo, and a new secretariat. By then, the regime had established some thirty-seven party schools, with a total enrollment of 6,000 students, and it had created a system of local organs of "people's power," which strongly resembled local soviets in the USSR.[81]

From 1969 through 1975, party membership nearly quadrupled, reaching 200,000 in 1975. As William LeoGrande notes,

the institutionalization of Cuban politics since 1970 has had a profound effect on the Cuban Communist party: the size of the party has been greatly expanded, internal coordination and control have been systematized, institutional functions have been specified, and individual roles have been codified. Moreover, the functional boundaries *between* the party and other institutions are, for the first time, clearly delineated and enforced, and the subordination of the P C C to Fidel Castro's charismatic authority has been reduced.[82]

After the failure of the tactics of confrontation and resistance, the Catholic and Protestant Churches adopted a quiescent posture from about 1963 to 1968, corresponding roughly to the first subphase of Cuban system-building.[83] In the early 1960s the Castro regime encouraged people to burn their Bibles, and in 1965 Castro declared the "abolition" of Christmas.[84] Some clergy in the mid-1960s were drafted into so-called military units to aid production, a labor force that mobilized "tramps, pimps, homosexuals, common criminals, and others regarded as deviants" to perform manual labor.[85] Despite notions of creating a "new Cuban man and woman," however, the regime did not view atheization as a central component of its program and therefore was receptive to a rapprochement with ecclesiastical authorities. By the 1970s, as political institutions were stabilized and government offices came under the supervision of the party, Church-state relations also stabilized, and Christian Marxist dialogue became increasingly satisfying to both parties. Marxists rethought their classic antireligious postulates, and Christians reconsidered their traditional assumptions about Marxists.[86] The process of institutionalization also affected the religious sphere, for which a religious affairs office was "belatedly" established in January 1985.

Castro wanted to limit religious activity, but not to extirpate religion itself. Hence, while Cuban Church people might complain about occasional religious discrimination, about their lack of access to the media, and about their inability to engage in mass evangelism,[87] Havana played host to an international Catholic Ecclesiastical Congress in February 1986, attended by 181 delegates including guests from the Vatican, Spain, the United States, and various Latin American countries.[88]

In Poland, the system-building phase lasted a record thirty-two years, dissolving finally amid the political chaos and uncertainty of 1980. From 1948 until 1956, the years during which Bolesław Bierut and Edward

Ochab held power, the party strove to accomplish the goals of consolidation and mobilization in tandem, telescoping the revolutionary process in line with Stalin's postwar program of *Gleichschaltung*. Assisted by Soviet advisers, the Polish apparatus drew up a "Six-Year Plan of Economic Development and Construction of Socialist Foundations" in 1950, and it simultaneously pushed for extensive industrialization and agricultural collectivization, hoping to bring as much as 25 percent of arable farmland into the socialist sector by 1995.[89] In conformity with the system-building phase, the PUWP extended its control over all educational institutions—except for the Catholic University of Lublin—even down to establishing ideologically acceptable curricula, and strict guidelines were established in music, literature, and art. Igor Stravinsky's *The Rite of Spring*, for example, was not allowed to be played.[90] Although there were no show trials or executions, such as those that took place elsewhere in Eastern Europe at the time, the party purged nearly 350,000 of its members between 1949 and 1951 and in other ways tried "to create a loyal and disciplined political cadre that would be ideologically cohesive and effectively socialized in their obedience to commands."[91] The consolidation/mobilization subphase came to a crashing end in October 1956 when it became clear to everyone that the simultaneous and accelerated achievement of the twin tasks of consolidation and mobilization exceeded the capacity of the PUWP; a retreat of some sort, whether tactical or strategic, was inescapable. The result was Władysław Gomułka's return to power.

The Stalinist years were those of greatest hardship for the Church. In January 1950 the authorities closed down the Catholic relief agency, Caritas; soon after, they confiscated all Church estates. By January 1949 some 350 priests, brothers, and nuns had been incarcerated, and by the spring of 1950 this number had risen to 500.[92] Cardinal Primate Stefan Wyszyński (1901–1981) himself spent the years from 1953 until 1956 in prison. At the same time, the PUWP briefly attempted to persuade Catholic clergy to break with the Vatican and establish a national Catholic Church.[93] A church-state accord of 1950 was stillborn, and in November 1952 the state began engaging in anti-Western polemics.[94] But just as the party failed in its self-appointed tasks of socialist transformation, agricultural collectivization, and orchestrated political mobilization, so it failed to capture control of the Church on, say, the Bulgarian model. By 1956 the time was ripe for a new direction in policy, both generally and more specifically in the religious sphere.

Gomułka entered office as the idol of the liberals, and he made a few concessions that seemed to fulfill these expectations: legitimating the grassroots workers' councils, allowing the decollectivization of agriculture, and signing (in December 1956) a new Church-state accord with the newly released primate, Wyszyński. But ultimately the second Gomułka era was a time of retrenchment in which the PUWP tried to complete the task of consolidating its power.[95] The third congress of the PUWP (10–18 March 1959) sounded the clarion call of the Gomułka regime when it resolved that "the consolidation of party influence over all aspects of life is the indispensable condition for socialist democratization as well as the fundamental element in the strengthening of the people's state."[96] As with any retrenchment, the emphasis was on stabilization. But, ironically, this very strategy of stabilization contributed to eroding Gomułka's authority within the party, provoking an increasing amount of criticism.

Cardinal Wyszyński met with Prime Minister Józef Cyrankiewicz on 14 January 1957, and the result was a kind of "truce" based on the mutual realization that neither side could win outright and, on the Church's part, a realization that destabilizing the communist regime would risk Soviet intervention.[97] Over the ensuing years the Polish Church staged a revival similar to that experienced by religious organizations in Yugoslavia during this phase. First, the right to publish the newspaper *Tygodnik Powszechny* was withdrawn from the collaborationist PAX and reverted to its original publishers. The suppressed Catholic periodical *Znak* was revived, and Catholic laity were given independent representation in the *Sejm* (the parliament). In March 1957 the Catholic Intelligentsia Clubs were organized and received permission to operate in Warsaw, Kraków, Toruń, Poznań, and Wrocław. The regime also returned the Catholic University at Lublin's faculties of law, economics, political science, and education to Church control.[98] These significant concessions notwithstanding, Church-state relations were rocky throughout the Gomułka era, with ostensible rapprochements followed by renewed disappointments and frictions. The fundamental reason for the difficulties was that while Church and state could agree that they were "indispensable allies,"[99] and while both genuinely wanted a stable modus vivendi, they could not agree on the terms of that arrangement. This contradiction explains the superficially inconsistent religious policy in which, for example, the state permitted Wyszyński to lead a delegation of Polish bishops in attending the Vatican Council at a time when the secular press was engaged in anti-Church polemics.

A review of the five cases in the second phase of revolutionary development reveals that only two regimes adopted full-fledged mobilization strategies, targeting the Churches for coerced extinction: the USSR and China. In Yugoslavia the decision in the 1960s to broadly liberalize the system resulted in lasting gains for the Churches. Cuba's relatively chaotic path to institutionalization made considerable allowance for religious activity. Polish policies ran aground for a combination of reasons, two of which stand out. The PUWP was encumbered by system overload: in the 1950s the regime had been goaded into pursuing the tasks of consolidation and mobilization simultaneously, while in the 1970s the Gierek regime was faced with twin crises of distribution and participation and was unwilling to come to grips with participation in a meaningful way. Because of the differences among these five systems in the second phase of revolutionary development, policy differences and system imperatives should be expected to widen in the third phase.

In looking at the process of policy change from one phase to the next, three conclusions emerge. First, policy adaptation is often incremental by religious denomination, with some religious groups experiencing change in the political climate before others. Second, while the general context of change is the same for all religious groups, different aspects of that context may be more important—or important in different ways—for some groups than for others (e.g., the impact of the fall of Ranković in Yugoslavia). And third, policy adaptation in the religious sphere regularly has been institutionalized through changes in legislation, the creation of new political bodies, and changes of personnel or procedure, so that processes of adaptation are often announced by the passage of signal legislation.

The Third Phase: System Stabilization

The first two phases of system evolution correspond to what communist theorists have called the *dictatorship of the proletariat* (with the chief task of "uprooting the vestiges of the capitalist order") and the *construction of socialism* (with consolidation, mobilization, and transformation as goals). The terms *socialism, developed socialism,* and *communism* refer to subsequent stages, with the construction of communism figuring as the central effort in the first two of these three later stages. Thus, the theory adapted here from the writings of Jowitt, Meyer, Tucker, and Kolankiewicz[100] is sensitive to the self-appointed tasks of communist elites. Following this course of phases, the terms *socialism* and *developed socialism* should correspond to *system stabilization*, and communism should relate to *total system transformation*.

As Jowitt notes, the turbulence created by processes of transformation and mobilization in the system-building phase impedes the regime's effort to command support and obedience at all levels of society and party. "Success with the task of transformation redefines the regime's internal and external environments by creating a less turbulent situation, thereby depriving local cadres and social groups of control over a major locus of uncertainty and power."[101] On the other hand, failure with the task of transformation (as in the Polish case) has been shown to lead to widespread social unrest and political destabilization, while avoidance of that task altogether (as in Yugoslavia) creates a confused situation in which the continuance of a one-party monopoly appears not merely illegitimate but anomalous.

The five systems show some variation in the third phase, as table 2.2 makes clear. Having passed beyond the system-building phase, the five systems divide into three groups: those in which the party continues, at this writing, to set the agenda for political debate and social development (China and Cuba); those that have fractured into a plurality of successor states (the USSR and Yugoslavia); and Poland, in which the party monopoly was broken in 1989 and in which multiparty pluralism has been reestablished.

As Jowitt notes, this phase is associated with an enhanced role for technocratic elites, expanded possibilities for their participation in decision-making, the expansion of consultative relations with technical experts, and the abandonment of social domination in favor of organizational manipulation.

In all of these cases, regardless of phase, religious policy was always differentiated according to religious group. In the USSR in the 1920s this meant encouraging anything that would whittle down the Russian Orthodox Church; hence, the Bolshevik encouragement of the Renovationist Church, the Ukrainian Orthodox Church, the Belorussian Orthodox Church, the Old Believers, and even Protestants. Later, in the system-building phase, priorities were reversed, as Stalin sought a rapprochement with the Russian Orthodox Church. The Soviet Union also explicitly differentiated policy, banning some groups outright (e.g., the Ukrainian Greek-Rite Catholics, the Jehovah's Witnesses, the Sufi brotherhoods, Pentecostals, and the Hare Krishna), while meting out particularly unfavorable treatment to Jews, even though Judaism was never actually banned in the USSR. Similar patterns of differentiation could be found in the other cases.

I have discussed the dynamics of Soviet religious policy in the *system stabilization* phase elsewhere.[102] Here, only the chief points relevant to the Soviet context will be mentioned. To begin with, the triple imperatives of deescalation from the Great Terror (1934–38), seeking new poles of legitimation in Russian nationalism (from 1938 on), and mobilizing the population to face the Nazi onslaught (1941) entailed changes in the religious sphere, just as they did elsewhere. The Nazi invasion was particularly important. Stalin could not afford to continue to bulldoze churches and shoot priests if he expected to rally the Russian people to defend the USSR against the aggressors. Thus, the League of Militant Atheists was closed down just three months after the German invasion; its antireligious journals were terminated. Stalin received Orthodox Metropolitan Sergii in September, and, in the wake of this meeting, Russian Orthodox churches were opened in a number of towns and villages. By 1947, because of this relaxation and the incorporation of new land into the USSR, the Russian Orthodox Church had jurisdiction over some 14,039 parish churches.[103]

The arrival of the system-stabilization phase did not mean an end to antireligious campaigns, however. As a result of Khrushchev's antireligious drive of 1958–61, the Russian Orthodox Church lost more than 40 percent of its remaining church facilities; among other groups, the hardest hit were the Armenian Apostolic Church (which lost 33 percent of facilities) and the Jewish community (32 percent).[104] Moreover, steady efforts under Brezhnev to strangle religion indicate both that certain essential tasks of the system-building phase remained unfinished and that the regime had not lost its will to press its program forward. As the 1980s wore on, however, realization grew in the USSR that the battle against religion was not being won, that closing up church buildings and controlling the number of young persons allowed to enter the seminary did not extinguish popular religious belief. As John Anderson put it in a 1994 study, it was becoming "increasingly evident to many within the [Brezhnev] leadership . . . that repression as a means of coping with nonconformity was both unacceptable and inefficient."[105] As early as 1983, Borys Lewytzkyj concluded that the number of believers in the USSR was actually increasing.[106]

Within the broader scheme of things, the system-stabilization phase

was marked—in the Soviet Union as elsewhere—by the alternation between efforts at reform (Khrushchev) and a longer period of retrenchment and the reaffirmation of "doctrine" (Brezhnev). This same pattern
asserts itself in the Chinese, Yugoslav, and Polish cases.

Mao's death in September 1976 triggered a power struggle involving three factions: a radical group led by Mao's widow, Jiang Qing; a
reformist group led by the twice-deposed one-time general secretary,
Deng Xiaoping; and an anomalous opportunist grouping consisting of
Hua Guofeng and other beneficiaries of the Cultural Revolution, who
wanted to find a way to deconstruct the Cultural Revolution without becoming political casualties in the process.[107] As early as August 1977, the
Eleventh Party Congress declared an official end to the Cultural Revolution. Even earlier, however, the radicals had been dealt a dramatic blow
on 6 October 1976 when the "Gang of Four" was arrested. The campaign
against the partisans of the radical line continued until the Third Plenum
in December 1978. Both for this reason and because of the continued
contest between Hua and Deng, it seems appropriate to designate the
months from September 1976 to December 1978 as an interregnum, and
to date China's system-stabilization phase only from December 1978.[108]

As in the Soviet context, system stabilization in China meant system reform: the four modernizations, the explosion of publishing, the
opening to the West, and the liberalization of religious policy were all
consequences of the change in the political winds.[109] As early as 1979-
83 a series of agricultural reforms tantamount to decollectivization were
introduced.[110] The Deng leadership also showed recognition of the need
to make a transition from charismatic to bureaucratic rule. As Deng
Xiaoping noted in a conversation with his speech writers on 2 December
1978, the pattern of governance needed to be "stabilized in legal form. It
must be institutionalized so that it is protected by the system."[111]

Beginning in 1978, the Deng leadership allowed thousands of
churches, temples, and mosques to reopen. Catholic and Protestant
seminaries were allowed to operate again in a number of larger cities on
the coast. Muslim seminaries also reopened. The Buddhist academy in
Beijing renewed its activities. Some believers drew more encouragement
from these developments than the party had intended, and in June 1981
the CCP Central Committee passed a resolution advising that "religious
believers . . . must not engage in propaganda against Marxism-Leninism
and Mao Zedong Thought. . . ."[112] Furthermore, the party's new tolerance of religion has been qualified in three important ways.

First, China's latest constitution (1982) guarantees *freedom* of religion, but it does not recognize a *right* of religious belief. On this basis, the constitution spells out the limits of that freedom, noting, inter alia, that no religion will be permitted which is subservient to any foreign center (the Vatican, in particular, is signified here).[113]

Second, liberalization was accompanied by resurrecting institutional mechanisms of control and reactivating supervisory organs. The bureau of religious affairs was reestablished in 1979 to coordinate the party's religious policy. The Three-Self Movement of the 1950s, the Christian Patriotic Association, and other institutions were likewise revived. Decrees and laws closely regulate the activities of religious organizations. For example, under the terms of a regulation issued by the bureau of religious affairs in 1994, Chinese printing enterprises are authorized to accept contracts to print Chinese editions of the Bible, but only under strictly monitored conditions, including the requirement that all Bibles, together with all originals, plates, and films, are returned to the originating contractor.[114]

Third, Deng's form of liberalization has been associated with a tightening of controls on religion. Having watched as Mao's repressive policies drove religion underground and, thus, beyond party supervision and control, Deng and his coterie were determined to reassert party control in this sphere. Thus, for example, the toleration of a reopening of officially sanctioned places of worship was accompanied by a new effort to suppress underground "house churches," of which there were said to be about 10,000 among various faiths in 1982.[115] Indeed, an internal party memorandum, dated 2 April 1982, expressly warned cadres to assure that clergy and believers restrict their services and prayers to legally established houses of worship.[116] Consistent with this policy, Catholic priests who refused to join the Patriotic Catholic Association or to break with the Vatican were arrested and imprisoned (e.g., Bishop Geng Pinwei and three priests, who were arrested in March 1983 and given prison terms of up to fifteen years for "colluding" with a foreign power).

In China the rehabilitation of religious practice under Deng resulted in a deepening of policy differentiation. Mao had shown some favor toward Buddhists earlier and had allowed a token number of Islamic mosques to function in the larger cities in order to impress visitors from Muslim countries. But under Deng, officialdom has been markedly more supportive of Islam than of Christianity, allegedly because of fears of infection by Islamic fundamentalism.[117] Buddhist and Taoist temples and monasteries have been restored with state money, partly because officials have realized that these sites have potential tourist value. On the other hand, institutionalized religious practices have repeatedly been attacked by the party, including—perhaps predictably—the assortment of witches, sorcerers, and fortune tellers who have cropped up since the early 1980s.

In 1983 and 1987 the government launched ideological campaigns which had negative effects on the Churches. But in 1987–89, as part of a groundswell of general popular pressure for democratization, Christians openly criticized the practice of the bureau of religious affairs and demanded reforms.[118]

The precondition of toleration in Deng's China has been regime supervision. When a religious body has violated this principle, consequences have inevitably ensued. In May 1986, for example, an unauthorized Catholic seminary in Hebei province was forcibly closed by armed police.[119] More particularly, a new wave of repression followed the crushing of the student democracy movement at Tiananmen Square on 3–4 June 1989. In November 1989 four Buddhist monks in Tibet were sentenced to three years of "labor reeducation" for demonstrating in support of Tibetan independence. In the summer of 1990 some twenty Protestant house churches were uncovered and suppressed in Fujan province; about the same time, twenty-three leaders of an unauthorized Buddhist sect in Guizhou province were arrested and thirteen of their temples were closed. The Catholic Church likewise came under pressure, first in 1990 when officials arrested and sentenced various leaders of the underground (pro-Vatican) Catholic Church in two waves (February and November), and later in February 1991 when three more bishops loyal to the Vatican were arrested.[120]

Zhao Ziyang, briefly general secretary of the Chinese Communist Party, was identified with a defense of economic and political liberalism. When he fell from office in May 1989, party conservatives benefited.[121] The fall of Zhao coincided with the protests at Tiananmen Square and preceded the collapse of communist rule in Eastern Europe by only a few months. These three developments, taken collectively, made a deep impression on China's communist leaders, who were accustomed to drawing lessons from political vicissitudes in Eastern Europe. In April 1989, for example, Deng warned: "Events in Poland prove that making concessions provides no solutions. The greater the concessions made by the government, the greater the opposition forces became."[122]

The CCP concluded that religious organizations, particularly the Catholic Church, had played a role in destabilizing the communist systems of Eastern Europe, and it was determined to take the necessary steps to prevent the same thing from happening in China. Where religion began to flourish in the relatively liberal atmosphere of the 1980s, the 1990s have seen reemphasized control of religious life. The new line was confirmed at a November 1993 meeting of the United Front Work Department of the CCP, which called for a toughening of legal restraints on religion.[123] This call was followed on 31 January 1994 by the issuing of two sets of religious regulations that provided "a legal basis or license for local cadres to crack down on a wide assortment of religious activities" and enhanced police powers of surveillance and intervention in religious affairs.[124] Later in the year the government adopted regulations limiting the rights of foreigners by requiring them to obtain official permission before participating in religious services in China.[125] Authorities have targeted unofficial churches for closure and have arrested members of illegal sects, such as the so-called Shouters, otherwise known as the Little Flock of Watchman Ni.[126]

It is questionable whether China's communist leaders will be able to stabilize the system—whether in political terms, economic terms, or terms of religious policy. The broad swings from encouraging democratization to suppressing it reflect uncertainties about the present and the future. Chinese politics in the mid-1990s remains the preserve of gerontocrats (as was the case in the Soviet Union in the late Brezhnev era). When the gerontocrats pass from the scene, political change will be expected.

In Yugoslavia this phase of system stabilization ran from 1963 to 1980, but, as is typical in the history of that country, it took a course which dramatically departed from anything undertaken elsewhere in the communist world. By the end of the Tito era many Western observers had asked themselves whether Tito had "gone bourgeois," whether Yugoslavia had become a confederation, whether, indeed, Yugoslavia could still be considered a "communist" country. The key events during this phase were the Eighth Party Congress in December 1964, the fall of Ranković in 1966, the experimentation with national-liberalism in 1967–71, the adoption of Yugoslavia's "fourth" postwar constitution in 1974, and Tito's death in May 1980.

Significantly, it was at the Eighth Party Congress, held in Belgrade, that the League of Communists of Yugoslavia overturned the assimilationist orientation that had underpinned the party's nationalities policy until then and adopted a resolution announcing that "the erroneous opinions that our nations have, in the course of our socialist social development, become obsolete and that it is necessary to create a unified Yugoslav nation [are] expression[s] of bureaucratic centralism and unitarism. Such opinions usually reflect ignorance of the political, social, economic, and other functions of the republics and autonomous provinces."[127] Aleksandar Ranković, vice president of Yugoslavia and chief of the secret police, was closely identified with the assimilationist policies previously pursued and was known to be a champion of centralism. With his removal from office in 1966,[128] Tito signaled a change of course, and the Yugoslav ship of state now veered in the direction of increased federalization, decentralization, development of a market economy, and (up to a point) laissez faire. Thus, while the years 1963–66 figured as a period of continued struggle between the assimilationist and reformist wings of the party (hence constituting the *polarization* subphase), the years 1966–71 constituted a *liberalization* subphase. But toward the end of 1971 Tito became convinced that the pendulum had swung too far in the opposite direction and decided to move against his erstwhile liberal allies. The purge which resulted swept through Croatia, Slovenia, Serbia, and Macedonia. In Croatia tens of thousands of persons were expelled from the communist party, while at higher echelons of power 741 people were removed from their posts and banished from the party.[129] Many newspaper and magazine editors were dismissed, too. In Serbia about six thousand people lost positions of responsibility in administration, economic management, the media, education, and culture.[130] In the wake of these purges Tito and his loyalists attempted to *construct a Titoist center* which would, in their view, guarantee the system's stability. Despite the purge of the liberals, however, many (though certainly not all) of the liberals' policies were retained.

The partially liberalizing character of this phase in Yugoslav political development was reflected in the religious sphere. To begin with, a series of changes from 1965 until 1968 dramatically changed the conditions in which all three major religious groups in the country were able to operate. First, in 1965 the earlier Law Concerning the Legal Status of Religious Communities was amended, removing certain harsh provisions.[131] Second, Ranković's slide from power in early 1966 and his final fall on 1 July coincided with changes in the regime's policy toward the leading Christian Churches. Just a few days before Ranković was forced to resign the vice presidency, Belgrade signed a protocol with the Vatican (25 June 1966), agreeing to exchange governmental representatives and to certain guarantees for the Catholic Church. For the Serbian Orthodox Church, Ranković's fall was a mixed blessing. True, he had bullied the Serbian Church into compliance with regime directives. But at the same time he had protected the Belgrade Patriarchate from the threat of Macedonian autocephalism. Within five months of his removal, the Macedonian clergy, now with regime support, demanded autocephaly and made preparations for unilateral action.

From 1966 until 1971 religious policy in Yugoslavia was adapted to the general strategic liberalization that penetrated all policy spheres. In February 1968 this flexibility also affected the Muslim community, which from that point was recognized as "a separate nation."[132]

During these years the Catholic Church launched several new periodicals, of which the most important were the newspaper *Glas koncila*, the family weekly *Kana*, and the youth magazine *Ognjišće*. The Church also was able to open youth centers and recreation clubs, and it started sponsoring sporting events and other activities for Slovenian and Croatian youngsters. Similarly, the Serbian Orthodox Church launched a biweekly newspaper *Pravoslavlje* in 1967, the youth magazine *Svetosavsko zvonce* in 1968, and the theological journal *Teološki pogledi* in 1968. Overall, between 1945 and 1970, the Serbian Orthodox Church built 181 churches and eight monasteries and repaired 841 churches and 48 monasteries, with the expense of repairing about 450 of these churches borne by republican or local authorities.[133] For the Islamic community, this period saw the construction of numerous mosques, minarets, and other buildings and the establishment of beneficial ties with Libya and other Arab countries.[134]

The tasks associated with *retrenchment* (insofar as the construction of a project such as the Titoist center may be understood in such terms) are arguably more complex than those of liberalization—at least judging from the Yugoslav case. The post-1971 retrenchment saw not only the passage of the 1974 constitution but the concomitant issuing of a series of draft laws on religion (in 1975). Religious policy was increasingly entrusted to the jurisdiction of the eight constituent federal units, which set up their own committees for social questions of religion under the umbrella of the local branch of the Socialist Alliance of Working People of Yugoslavia (SAWPY).[135]

In Cuba the third developmental phase in the communist era cannot properly be called one of stabilization, because what occurred after ten years of abortive charismatic politics was a belated decision to institutionalize the revolution, which entailed shifting gears in terms of mobilization. Economically and politically weakened by the failure of the sugar harvest campaign of 1970, Castro opted for Soviet-style orthodoxy. Political power was incrementally institutionalized and centralized, Cuban life was subjected to increased regimentation from 1970 through 1973, and finally, in mid-1975, the Cuban Communist Party held its *first* national congress. The leadership now set up various party bodies, and by 1975 it had established some thirty-seven party schools with a total enrollment of 6,000 cadre. The party's second congress was not held until 1980. Cuba was midstream in the third subphase of its system-building phase when Gorbachev came to power in the USSR, began the incremental dismantlement of Marxist orthodoxy, and revised the economic terms of the Soviet-Cuban relationship. These changes in the Kremlin directly affected the developmental course in Cuba, cutting short the system-building phase, and jolting the country headlong into a phase of *system decay*, thus bypassing the phase of system stabilization. From 1990 through 1993 Cuba recorded a series of catastrophic declines in GDP: -5.0 percent in 1990, -19.0 percent in 1991, -20.0 percent in 1992, and -15.0 percent in 1993. Only in 1994 did the economy begin to stabilize with a meager 0.7 percent growth in GDP.[136] These trends fueled growing public discontent and reinforced the country's small but vocal dissident movement which had been demanding democratization. Although Castro has held onto power, thanks mainly to his liberal use of state security forces, he has endeavored to ease Cuba toward a more market-oriented economy on the Chinese or Vietnamese model, and he has encouraged carefully screened foreign investment in Cuba, particularly in the tourist industry.[137]

By the early 1990s Castro felt constrained to revise his thinking about the place of believers in Cuban society. In 1991 his regime gave permission for believers to join the Communist Party, and in July 1992 the constitution was amended to prohibit discrimination on religious grounds. Although the dominant Catholic Church welcomed these changes, Cuba's Catholic bishops continued to criticize the government, and in mid-September 1993 they issued a pointed pastoral letter (read from church pulpits across the country); in this letter, the bishops called on the ruling Communist Party to give up its political monopoly and permit the introduction of a multiparty system.[138] This political challenge was paralleled by a new *religious* challenge offered by Protestant and other non-Catholic Christian groups. More than 150,000 Bibles were imported into Cuba from 1990 through 1992,[139] and religious communities such as the Pentecostals, the Baptists, and the Jehovah's Witnesses recorded membership gains. The Castro regime responded by harassing the Pentecostals, imprisoning Rev. Orson Vila Santoyo (a popular evangelist and head of the Assemblies of God in Cuba) in the summer of 1995; Jehovah's Witnesses and Seventh Day Adventists were prosecuted as "active religious enemies of the revolution" because of their refusal to accept obligatory military service or participate in state-run institutions.[140] But with the system sliding ever deeper into crisis, many Cubans have been turning their backs on Castro's strain of communism (even in its reformed variety) and have been embracing religion in increasing numbers. In 1995 a British newspaper referred to the religious tide sweeping Cuba as a "Spiritual Revolution."[141]

Perhaps partly as a result of this "Spiritual Revolution" but, most certainly, in part as a result of Castro's need to expand his base of support, Church-state relations began to ease further around 1995. By mid-1996 both sides were talking of a new era of dialogue.[142] The new temper culminated in a historic visit by Fidel Castro to Rome in November 1996 for an audience with the pope, amid rumors that the Church might shortly gain greater freedom for its social and charitable work in Cuba.[143]

Finally, in Poland the collapse of the Gomułka regime amid meat price riots in December 1970 left the incoming regime of Edvard Gierek with the task of reconstituting a seriously weakened central authority. The Gierek regime (1970-80) tried a new approach to the still unresolved challenges left from the system-building phase. Gierek, once the Silesian party boss, understood the need to build public confidence in the system. The "Gierek formula," devised to meet this need, combined unabashed populism with stable food prices, climbing wages, and ambitious economic investment projects funded by massive loans from the West. But Gierek was unwilling to grant the chief popular desideratum—meaningful political participation. Some Western analysts recognized the weaknesses in this formula.[144]

Under Gierek, religious policy was overtly adapted to the broader needs of the system. On the one hand, Gierek hoped to assuage the Church hierarchy and to win it over to a supportive relationship vis-à-vis the state. On the other hand, he wanted to erode the Church's ties with the people. This dual policy, he hoped, would underpin his more general policy of stabilization without democratization. Hence, as early as July 1971 the new Polish government transferred to the Polish Church property confiscated from the German Catholic Church at the end of World War II.[145] Some seven thousand church buildings, chapels, monasteries, and parish halls were involved. The regime also remitted all unpaid rents on the Church's part, and it established lower Church taxes for the future.[146] Under Gomułka, the state had obstructed the construction or renovation of church buildings; under Gierek, in contrast, authorization for such purposes became much more easily obtained. Yet, overall, Gierek pushed for an increase in the "socialist content" in elementary school curricula and, in particular, for recasting curricula on Polish history to minimize the Church's role.

But just as the more general "Gierek formula" failed, leaving basic system tasks unfulfilled, so did his religious policy run aground, leaving the premises of Church-state coexistence uncertain. The two most important political moves taken by Gierek, which contributed to friction with the Church, were his efforts in 1976 to amend the Polish constitution to describe Poland as a "socialist state" (rather than a "people's republic"), to include a reference to Poland's indissoluble ties with the USSR, and to place added stress on the duties of citizens to the state. These moves pushed the Church back into an oppositionist role, and the Church hierarchy established regular contacts with dissident intellectuals of the Committee for the Defense of the Workers (KOR). KOR began to coordinate with the hierarchy before issuing public statements about the regime, and the Church publicly supported KOR's work for human rights.[147] That the hierarchy had entered into a cooperative relationship with the nation's most visible dissident organization clearly showed the failure of Gierek's religious policy.

The Fourth Phase: System Decay

According to Marx and Engels, the phase following the construction of communism would, rather inevitably, be communism. In Hegelian terms such a phase might be called *system sublation*, meaning (as Hegel did by this term) that the previous phase was simultaneously both canceled and preserved in this new phase, raising the system to a new, qualitatively different level. And if fitted into the Hegelian teleology, such a phase would have to be equated with what Hegel termed Absolute Knowledge.

The difficulty is that in the phase of *system stabilization*, when the construction of "communism" was supposed to be under way, elites tended to be preoccupied with making such adjustments as would enable the system to continue functioning more or less as before. When these adjustments failed, the elites in the USSR, Cuba, Yugoslavia, and Poland undertook adjustments that would clearly effect changes so that the system, if it functioned at all, no longer would function as before. Thus, this crisis phase would be a phase either of *system reform* (if successful) or of *system decay* (if unsuccessful). The Chinese case is a hybrid and too complex, in my view, to allow for adequate elucidation within these pages. Certainly the Deng leadership undertook reforms which dramatically changed the functioning of the system, but at the same time the elite has confronted the tasks associated with system stabilization. This hybrid character gives the post-Deng leadership some prospects of success, but it also has led me to omit China from a discussion of this final phase.

Not surprisingly, as the system in general decays, religious policy undergoes a process of "decay"—which is apt to mean flexibility and liberalization stemming from governmental weakness and chaos, a degree of unpredictability in the Church-state relationship, and recurrent polemics in the press. In this sense, it becomes difficult even to speak of a process of adaptation of religious policy. The reason is that, although religious policy continues to reflect more general trends in the political system, as power and process undergo decay, the capacity for adaptation itself decays. Yugoslavia, with its federalized and highly decentralized system, in which religious policy came to be determined at the level of the federal unit, aptly illustrates this phenomenon.[148] Likewise in the Soviet Union, in a number of instances in the late 1980s the Soviet press admitted that local cadres had disregarded government guidelines and strictures.[149]

By the mid-1980s the communist system in the USSR, Yugoslavia, Cuba, and Poland was in decay. The sources of system decay included the declining capacity of the political structure to control participation in politics, economic deterioration and consequent mass economic discontent, and a complete breakdown of the attempt to create a legitimate basis for communist rule.[150] As the political structure began to weaken, other institutions stepped into the breach, including, prominently, the Churches. In Poland, the Catholic Church in the 1980s presented itself as the spokesperson for the nation, and indeed it was. In the USSR an embattled Mikhail Gorbachev strove for a new formula that might save both system and Soviet society itself from disintegration.[151] In the process, he rehabilitated religion and, in a rather transparent effort to find a new basis for legitimation, joined the Russian Orthodox Church leadership in June 1988 in celebrating the millennium of the Christianization of Russia and Ukraine. And in the Yugoslav republic of Serbia, local party boss Slobodan Milošević held ostentatious meetings with the Serbian Orthodox patriarch and reversed the Titoist proscription of Church involvement in nationalism. On the contrary, Milošević now insisted that Serbian Orthodoxy was the core of Serbian national identity and the pride of all Serbs.[152] Even Cuba, where Fidel Castro had stubbornly tried to resist Gorbachev's influence,[153] was faced with growing economic strains and pervasive crises of ideology, political institutions, and social morale.[154] In these conditions the Havana regime has had to make serious adjustments, one symptom of which is the fact that, like the USSR, Poland, and Yugoslavia, the Cuban regime felt itself compelled to pass new legislation governing religious bodies.

At first sight, these four countries—especially the first three—display many similarities. All of them adopted a form of glasnost; in the Yugoslav and Polish cases, this took the form of open official admission that the country was in crisis and that the ruling elite was groping for solutions. All of them began experimenting with ways in which to boost economic production; extensive economic reform was discussed, as were greatly liberalized policies in literature, music, and the arts. Boris Pasternak's *Doctor Zhivago* was now published in the USSR, as was Evgeni Zamiatin's *We*. In Poland, George Orwell's long-banned *1984* became available in Polish translation even before the communists were swept from power. Religious materials also became vastly easier to obtain in the USSR and Cuba, and, sporadically, they could be found in China somewhat more easily than before. (Such materials had been readily available in Poland and Yugoslavia for years.) All of these countries were confronted with the need for legal reformulation. In China this process involved constitutional revisions in 1978, the passage of an entirely new constitution in 1982, and the passage of new civil and criminal codes; in Yugoslavia it involved the extent to which the constitution could be amended; and reformulation in the Soviet Union had to deal with strong hints of new legislation governing religious communities.

Below the surface in each of these countries, however, naturally important differences had consequences for religious policy. These differences included the degree of federalization, the kinds of tasks left unfulfilled as a result of earlier developmental contrasts, the nature of the crises confronting the elites in this phase (e.g., largely economic and political in Poland, but also ethnic and charismatic in the Yugoslav case). Ultimately, these differences involved the very structure of Church-state relations.

Conclusion

Too often, political analyses of communist religious policy have discussed policy changes as if they took place in a vacuum, which is to say as if the religious sphere were an entirely autonomous part of human activity about which decisions could be made without referring to, or being influenced by, developments in any other areas. I have been arguing, instead, that religious policy is adapted and attuned to the general characteristics of system strategy; that as a system evolves, religious policy necessarily evolves with it; and that differences among regimes in coping with systemic tasks at any given phase contribute to a widening of differences in subsequent political development—differences that are likely to affect the religious sphere.

If religious policy is differentiated across phases and among different religious groups, it also is true (as has been shown) that the religious balance may likewise change, and the relative advantage or disadvantage accorded to any specific religious organization in one era later might be completely reversed. For example, the Russian Orthodox Church was singled out for persecution in the 1920s, but it was accorded prejudicially "favorable" treatment in the late Stalin era. Or again, the Serbian Orthodox Church, which underwent the most severe treatment of any of the major religious organizations in Yugoslavia in the 1970s and early 1980s, was rehabilitated by Slobodan Milošević after 1987, and within the borders of the Republic of Serbia, it was granted a special status.

But although there were differences in the treatment meted out to specific religious groups, there were also some broad consistencies in religious policy within a given country at a given time, reflecting an understanding on the part of the given elite as to what goals were desirable and feasible, and what policy instruments were appropriate to the realization of those goals.

Policy adaptation is a response to a change in perceptions. Perceptions change when a system changes, when the circumstances change, or when the perceiver changes. Even when circumstances have changed so drastically that the unchanged system produces new side effects, incumbents may be so incapable of creative thinking that they cannot perceive the changes clearly or respond to them. Hence, as the Soviet, Chinese, and Yugoslav cases demonstrate, often a change of political leadership must occur before the system is able to adapt.

The countries examined here have had some common problems, tasks, and perceptions, but local conditions, historical experiences, and aspects of intraparty factionalism differed considerably, not to mention their degrees of success in confronting systemic tasks. For this reason, even though the dynamics of policy adaptation may be comparable, the sequences and alternative policies which were developed vary greatly.

II

The Northern Tier:

East Germany,

Poland, Czechoslovakia,

and Hungary

Chapter 3

Varieties of Christianity in East Germany

Here [in the GDR] the clergymen sound like revolutionaries,
and the officials like clergymen. STEFAN HEYM (1982)

The reunification of Germany in October 1990 brought an end to an era. For the forty years of the German Democratic Republic's existence, Soviet military occupation was a fact of life. The state attempted to construct a communist system on the Soviet model. And—where religion was concerned—the Protestant churches played an ever greater role in harboring political opposition to the regime and its policies. With the dismantling of the GDR, however, the Churches, which had been invigorated by their politicization, lost their unique political role and have watched helplessly as their congregations steadily drifted away.

The GDR (1949-90) had the distinction of being the only communist system in which Protestantism was clearly the predominant religious force. Combined with the division of Germany, this fact made for an almost unparalleled intensity of interaction between the GDR Churches and Churches in the noncommunist world, particularly in West Germany and Austria. Clergy members enjoyed an exemption from the general proscription against travel to noncommunist countries, and they frequently visited the West for ecclesiastical and ecumenical meetings.

At first sight, Church life in the GDR in the late 1980s looked vigorous. In particular, the public forums organized by the Evangelical Church drew large and interested crowds. Services were regularly attended, vocations revived, and the Churches themselves operated an impressive number of hospitals, old age homes, and other facilities. Thanks in part to subsidies from sister churches in the West, they functioned in relative financial comfort.

Yet East German pastors were aware that secularization was eating away at their base. The Evangelical Church, which numbered 14.2 million adherents in 1946, had only 10.1 million in 1964, and as of 1986 it claimed just 6.4 million members. A publication of the Institute for Marxism-Leninism in 1984 suggested an even lower figure, estimating real membership at 5.0–5.5 million.[1] Statistics for the Evangelical Church in Anhalt province illustrate the trend. In 1955 the province counted 422,800 members and recorded 56,591 communions, 5,406 baptisms, and 6,311 confirmations. In 1975 the province tallied only 221,000 members, recording 31,684 communions, 628 baptisms, and 1,161 confirmations. Ten years later, the province numbered 130,000 church members, recording 32,531 communions, 588 baptisms, and 549 confirmations. Or again, in Berlin-Brandenburg the Church lost more than half of its members between 1962 and 1987. In villages, as much as 90 percent of the population might still be Christian, while informed sources estimate that only 10 percent of the inhabitants of big cities adhere to Christian Churches.

Pastors also were aware that while the Church's ability to attract non-believers to its events enhanced its prestige, in the long run the Church cannot prosper on the basis of nonconverts who attend specific events out of specific interests. To survive and prosper, a Church must, at a minimum, maintain its base if not actually expand.

The Religious Sector: An Overview

In every respect the Evangelical Church (Lutheran and Reformed) dwarfs all other denominations in what is now eastern Germany. Maintaining 7,347 parishes, it had 4,161 active clergy in 1988 and operated 44 hospitals (with a total of 6,244 beds), 105 homes for the mentally and physically disabled, 200 old age homes (with about 11,000 places), 19 orphanages, 310 communal service outlets, and 278 kindergartens and day nurseries.[2] In addition, in 1988 the Evangelicals maintained three ecclesiastical training missions (in Berlin, Naumburg, and Leipzig), two schools for preachers (in Berlin and Erfurt), and one pedagogical institute (in Potsdam). Six of the state universities included theological faculties whose salaries from 1949 through 1989 were paid out of the communist state budget (at the universities of Berlin, Halle, Leipzig, Jena, Greifswald, and Rostock). These faculties are specifically Protestant and are used almost exclusively by members of the Evangelical Lutheran and Reformed Churches. Finally, the Evangelical Church was able to publish five regional newspapers: *Die Kirche* (Berlin, circulation 42,500; also a Greifswald edition), *Der Sonntag* (Dresden, 40,000), *Mecklenburgische Kirchenzeitung* (Mecklenburg, 15,000), *Glaube und Heimat* (Jena, 35,000), and *Potsdamer Kirche* (Potsdam, 15,000).[3] All of these periodicals were printed on state presses, which made it easy for state authorities to check copy before publication. This leverage proved important in 1988 when the state repeatedly censored or banned specific issues. The monthly journal, *Standpunkt,* which for years was viewed as no more than a regime tool, was operated by pro-regime Protestants. In the last years of the GDR, however, *Standpunkt* published a number of probing articles, and, as a result, its credibility improved.

The only other denomination registered in the German Democratic Republic with more than 1 million members was the Roman Catholic Church, which claimed some 1.05 million in 1990, with 1,083 priests and 1,753 members of women's orders (as of 1987).[4] The Catholic Church's most important periodical was the *St. Hedwigsblatt,* published in Berlin, although, as in the case of the Protestants, a pro-regime monthly journal (*Bewegung*) also was published. Unlike the mainline Protestant Churches, the Roman Catholic Church refused to accommodate itself to socialism or to make any effort to suggest, imply, or initiate any form of cooperation. Bishop Otto Spulbeck of Meissen captured the essence of the Church's approach in 1956: "We live in a house, whose structure we have not built, whose basic foundations we even consider false. We gladly contribute, living worthy and Christian lives. But we cannot build a new story on this house, since we consider its foundation false. This house remains an alien house. We thus live in a diaspora not only in terms of our Church, but also in terms of our state."[5] But if the Catholic Church refused any form of accommodation, it also declined to assume any form of opposition, practicing a kind of "political abstinence," in Robert Goeckel's apt phrase.[6] As of 1987, the Catholic Church comprised 1,037 churches, 11 seminaries and retreat houses, 330 convents and monasteries, 34 Church hospitals, 11 nursing homes, 107 old age homes, 44 orphanages, one theological faculty, and other facilities.[7]

The Russian Orthodox Church also has maintained an incongruous presence, having its headquarters for the Central European Exarchate in Dresden. With the collapse of the USSR, between 70,000 and 100,000 Russians fled westward, settling in Berlin, infusing new energy into the cultural life of the Russian diaspora in Germany, and potentially providing new blood for the Russian Church.[8]

The remaining Christian denominations of the GDR can be divided into three broad groups. *Traditional Protestants* include the Evangelical Church (in both its Lutheran and Reformed districts), as well as Methodists (28,000 in 1988), members of the Baptist Federation (20,000),

Reformed (15,000), Old Lutherans (7,150), Evangelical-Lutheran Free (3,200), Moravians (Unity of Brethren, 2,600), Free Evangelicals (1,000), Mennonites (250), and Quakers (52). A second grouping comprised *Apostolic Communities:* the New Apostolic Church (80,000–100,000 members), the Apostolate of Jesus Christ (12,000–14,000), the Shepherd and Flock (7,000), the Community in Christ Jesus (Lorenzianer, 5,000), the Apostolate of Juda (3,000), Catholic-Apostolic (2,000), and Reformed Apostolic (2,000). Finally, a heterogeneous collection of *other Christian Churches* includes Jehovah's Witnesses (not legally registered in the GDR, but numbering 25,000–30,000 adherents), Seventh-Day Adventists (9,000), Christian Community (*Christengemeinschaft*, 5,000), Mormons (4,700), the Church of John (*Johannische Kirche*, 3,500), Old Catholics (1,000), Anderson Community of God (200), Reorganized Mormons ("a few"), and Darbyists (no figures reported).[9] In addition, a number of Christian Science members in eastern Germany were placed under ban by the SED in 1951 and remained illegal until November 1989 when they belatedly reacquired legal status.[10]

Some non-Christian religious groups, specifically the Muslims (2,000), the Jews (250 in 1988), and the Rastafarians (15 in 1988) are present. Evidence, albeit ambiguous, also suggests that a handful of Satanists may exist in Berlin and Leipzig, but this matter is hard to verify.

Traditional Protestants

Two Churches bore a special relationship to the numerically preponderant Evangelical Church of the GDR: (1) the Federation of Evangelical Reformed Communities in the GDR and (2) the Unity of Brethren. There was no Reformed Church in the GDR per se, but Reformed parishes were organized in one of two ways. Most parishes exist as parts of the Evangelical Church itself—a legacy of the Union Church created by King Friedrich Wilhelm III of Prussia in 1817. In some cases (for example, Berlin-Brandenburg) the separate origin of the Reformed parishes is recognized by according them the right to reject synodal decisions that contradict their teachings. Three parishes—Dresden, Leipzig, and Bützow—are autonomous units not integrated into district Churches. All Reformed parishes, whether separate or integrated, were represented in the Federation of Evangelical Reformed Communities in the GDR, established in 1970. These communities shared theological training institutes with the Evangelical Church in Berlin, Leipzig, and Naumburg, and they took advantage of the theological faculties attached to the state universities.

The Unity of Brethren (Moravian Church) was distinguished by having become an associate member of the Federation of Evangelical Churches in 1969. Associate membership left the Brethren Church theologically and financially independent but enabled it to take part in Evangelical Federation deliberations and to associate itself with the Evangelical Church's posture vis-à-vis the state. Church life centers on the village of Herrnhut (population, 2,000), where about one-fifth of the Church's 2,600 members (in eastern Germany) live. In 1970 the community experienced a brief crisis when Werner Morgenstern, a pastor, announced that he and his family had been rebaptized, and he started to build a small circle of born-again Christians. Unity of Brethren parishes in Herrnhut, Niesky, Kleinwelka, and Ebersdorf were affected by his preaching, and for a while the issue of rebaptism was hotly discussed. The debate ended with Morgenstern's expulsion from the Moravian Church.

The largest traditional Protestant Church in the GDR, after the Evangelical Church, was the Methodist. With some 120 active pastors and more than a thousand lay workers, the Methodists, although a minority denomination in the GDR, played a larger role in Saxony where many of the church's adherents are concentrated. (Saxony, in fact, is confessionally the most diverse province in eastern Germany, and a number of groups that have no other base operate there.) The Methodist Church was actively involved in ecumenical activities in the GDR, and the secretary of the Working Community of Christian Churches in the GDR (*Arbeitsgemeinschaft Christlicher Kirchen in der DDR*), the country's most important forum for ecumenical activity, in 1988 was a Methodist (Martin Lange). With pacifism strong among Methodists of the GDR, some 40 percent of young Church members volunteered for the construction brigade in preference to regular military service. The Methodist Church operates a theological seminary at Bad Klosterlausnitz and, in communist times, published a biweekly bulletin, *Friedensglocke*, with a print run of 10,000 copies.

With some 20,000 members, the Federation of Evangelical-Free Church Communities in the GDR united three distinct denominations: the Baptists, the Evangelical Brethren, and the Elim Community. The Baptists and the Elim Community combined in a joint Baptist Federation in 1938. The Brethren joined them three years later. All three groups are lay movements in which ordained ministers do not enjoy anything like the authority exercised by priests of the Catholic or Orthodox Churches, or even like pastors of the Evangelical Church.[11] For all three groups, emphasis is on parish life. But some differences in orientation occur. (The Baptists to some degree are more concerned than the others about developing parish life in accord with a strict interpretation of the New Testament, while the Elim Community places greater emphasis than the others on the role of the Holy Ghost.) Like many church organizations, the Evangelical-Free Church Federation has experienced a decline in membership, down from a postwar level of 30,000–35,000. Regular retreats for young people emphasize Bible study. The federation operates a four-year theological seminary at Buckow, a one-year Bible school for laypeople at Burgstadt, a nursing home for the mentally disturbed (140 beds in 1988), and three homes for the aged (Berlin-Hirschgarten, Crivitz, and Sonneberg). The federation also issued a monthly periodical, *Wort und Werk*, with some 12,000 readers in communist times, and it published eight to ten books a year.

Of the remaining traditional Protestant Churches, only the Old Lutheran Church has more than five thousand members in eastern Germany. Formed by Lutherans who refused to go along with the administratively decreed amalgamation of the Lutheran and Reformed Churches in 1817, the Old Lutheran Church became skeptical of ecumenism, fearing that in searching for a common ground, ecumenists were in danger of reducing Christian doctrine to just Christ and love. A representative of the Old Lutheran Church attended an ecumenical meeting in Dresden in early 1988 and found that he objected to some of the participants' conclusions; peace and justice, he felt, could not be the Church's *primary* tasks. That Church (affiliated with the Missouri synod) views itself as extremely conservative and criticizes the main Evangelical Church for allegedly having modified its doctrines. The Old Lutheran Church's twenty-seven parishes were organized into three dioceses in the 1980s, served by twenty-five pastors.[12] For a number of years it sought permission from the authorities to publish a newspaper—without success until the communist regime collapsed. State permission, however, was not required to print its informational bulletin "for internal use only."

The Free Evangelicals, with a thousand members, work closely with the Baptists, sending potential ministers to the Baptist seminary at Buckow for theological training. The Free Evangelicals are actively involved in social work, concentrating efforts on the psychologically disturbed, alcoholics, the aged, and the socially isolated (for example, those recently released from prison). Some 1,700 copies of a Church bulletin for internal use only, *Glaube und Dienst,* appeared seven times a year during communist times.

The Mennonites did not inhabit the territory of the former GDR until after World War II when their established communities were forced to leave East and West Prussia. Most of them settled in West Germany, but about a thousand moved to the GDR. In 1988 about 250 Mennonites were dispersed among two hundred towns and villages across the GDR. Normal parish life was impossible, but the Mennonite community adopted the practice of holding monthly religious services in Berlin and additional services two to three times a year in Halle, Erfurt, Schwerin, Rostock, Torgau, Potsdam, and Dresden.[13] The community published 240 copies of a monthly bulletin, *Gemeindebrief,* for "internal use."

Finally, the Society of Friends (Quakers) is able to survive with scarcely more than a dozen adherents in eastern Germany (1988) because of its independence of any hierarchy or structure. Considering their numbers, the Quakers were surprisingly active in discussing social issues, supporting the initiative to introduce the construction brigade in 1964, and backing the drive for a social service alternative to military conscription.

Apostolic Communities

The bulk of this chapter is concerned with those Churches listed as "traditional Protestants" and their experiences under communism and immediately thereafter. However, a few words should be said about Churches in the other two main groups.

The Apostolic Churches trace their inception to the early nineteenth century when sentiment among some European Christians that Churches had decayed spiritually gave rise to a hope that a new age was dawning. From 1832 until 1835 these impulses took institutional shape in England, where twelve men started to call themselves "Apostles." They built up a community, which soon spread to the Continent, and they taught that other Churches had become the tools of Satan and that therefore it was necessary to resurrect the "original" Church. The new community professed to be that Church. Members of the Apostolic community were also convinced that they would see the Second Coming within their lifetimes, specifically during the apostolate of the twelve. By 1861 six of the apostles had died, and the community experienced a sense of crisis in which some members favored electing new apostles to replace the deceased, while others considered this approach sacrilegious. The debate led to a schism, with those favoring election of new apostles forming what is now the New Apostolic Church. The original group, known today as the Catholic-Apostolic Community, continued its refusal to elect new apostles, even after the last of the original apostles died in 1901. Since the community is hierarchically organized, with apostles required to consecrate bishops, bishops required to ordain ministers, ministers to anoint upper deacons, and upper deacons to anoint lower deacons, it steadily atrophied until by 1988 its highest-ranking official in the GDR was a lower deacon (*Underdiakon*). In the 1960s the Catholic-Apostolic Community still numbered 8,000-10,000 adherents in the GDR, but by the late 1980s this number had shriveled to about 2,000. Other Apostolic communities resulted from splits within the New Apostolic Church. The first of these schisms gave birth in 1902 to the Apostolate of Juda, which split again in 1923, giving rise to the Apostolate of Jesus Christ.

All Apostolic Churches believe that the Second Coming is a historical fact and will occur soon. The lower deacon of the Catholic-Apostolic Community told me that his Church expected the Second Coming in the year 2000. All members of the Apostolic Churches are socially and politically conservative and view other Churches (even within the Apostolic movement) with condescension. The Apostolic Churches therefore, with the sole exception of the Apostolate of Jesus Christ, have displayed essentially no interest in ecumenical dialogue.

The Apostolic Churches had correct relations with the communist state, but they were not given to the kind of effusiveness that occasionally characterized, say, the Evangelical Church's post-1978 relationship (or, in the case of Bishop Mitzenheim and certain others, even the pre-1978 relationship). The Apostolics view earthly government as a reflection of the divine monarchy, and they organize their own Churches on a monarchical basis. This outlook seems to have colored the New Apostolic Church's orientation to the GDR in the early years, when the Church was openly critical of the proletarian and social democratic tendencies unleashed by the new regime.[14] But this criticism never assumed a political aspect because, like the other Apostolic communities, the New Apostolic Church has completely avoided politics. This, of course, has consequences for the regime's Christian Democratic Union. As a member of another Apostolic community told me in 1988: "A Christian cannot be in a party. A Christian party is, in our eyes, not possible. Christian teaching teaches one to love one's neighbor; and party life is narrowed to serve partial interests."

Other Christian Communities

If clergy members from diverse Churches are asked whether they consider other Churches to be Christian, one finds that various Churches which see themselves as Christian—particularly the Church of John, the Church of Jesus Christ of Latter-Day Saints (Mormons), and the Jehovah's Witnesses—often are not recognized as Christian by other clergy. Of the six "larger" Churches listed in this category, one (the Jehovah's Witnesses) never succeeded in obtaining legal registration from the GDR's communist authorities; the Witnesses were granted legal status only in March 1990 by the coalition government of Lothar de Maiziere.[15] Therefore, the Witnesses were unable to engage in ecumenical contacts (which they surely would have spurned). Two other Churches (the Old Catholic Church and the Mennonites) joined the Working Community of Christian Churches in the GDR, which was dominated by the Evangelical and Methodist Churches. In addition, the Seventh-Day Adventists enjoyed observer status in the Working Community (alongside the Roman Catholic Church, the Quakers, and the Apostolate of Jesus Christ). The small Christian Community (*Christengemeinschaft*) thinks of itself as ecumenically oriented, although it did not take part in the Working Community. Its clergy argued that ecumenism was better fostered at the parish level between individual pastors and laypersons than among the leadership.

These Churches vary considerably in their degree of social engagement. For example, in 1972, when a law legalizing abortion was being passed, the Seventh-Day Adventists mobilized their ranks and contacted the state secretary for church questions. The Adventists also have been interested in environmental questions, but chiefly in an ecumenical context, taking part in the assemblies devoted to "Peace, Justice, and the Integrity of Nature" and at one time sending medical supplies, automobiles, and other items to Angola, Mozambique, Ethiopia, and Tanzania. The Adventists reported productive contacts with the East German CDU—one of the few religious organizations to express this view. GDR authorities allowed the Adventists to publish a monthly newspaper, *Adventgemeinde*, in a print run of 6,000 copies.

The Church of John is treated as a kind of pariah by most other Churches in eastern Germany because it teaches that God the Father manifested himself through Moses, God the Son through Christ, and God the Holy Ghost through Joseph Weissenberg (1855–1941), the Church's founder.[16] As a result, the Church of John took no part in the Working Community and has no official ecclesiastical contacts with the Evangelical Church, although its clergy members have personal contacts with individual clergy of various Churches. On social issues, the Church of John considers military duty a matter of individual conscience, and it showed its ecological commitment in the second half of the 1980s by organizing volunteers to clean up the long-polluted Blankensee tributary.

In contrast, the Christian Community and the Mormons decline to become involved in environmental issues and other social questions, arguing that "this is the sphere for the state, not the Church." The Mormons also do not object to military service per se, although some members opted for alternative service in the GDR's construction brigade. The Mormons have kept their distance from other churches in eastern Germany, abstaining from the continually increasing ecumenical forums—unlike the Christian Community, which, incidentally, accepts the Church of John as a fellow Christian church.

The Structure and Hierarchy of the Evangelical Church to 1991

The Evangelical Church in the GDR was not a unified body but a federation of eight district Churches (*Landeskirchen*) which had somewhat different traditions. In five districts (Berlin-Brandenburg, Görlitz, Greifswald, Anhalt, Saxony-Magdeburg) it is heir to the Union Church, established by the Prussian government, which unified Evangelical and Reformed churches. These district Churches are influenced in part by the Reformed tradition, which translates into a greater tendency than with traditional churches to become involved in social and political affairs. The other three district Churches (Mecklenburg, Thuringia, and Saxony-Dresden) are purely in the Lutheran tradition and have inherited Martin Luther's view that Church and state have different tasks and that the Church should acknowledge the state as God's instrument in the secular realm (a sentiment contributing to the state's enthusiasm for Luther during the 1983 quincentenary celebrations).[17] In concrete terms, this attitude was illustrated in an intra-Church controversy in 1988. Bishop Gottfried Forck of Berlin, of the Union tradition, responded to pressures from East German citizens who sought emigration by opening his offices for consultations with them. Others in the church criticized him for supposedly overstepping the bounds of legitimate Church activity.

Some differences in style are apparent among the bishops of the district Churches, which at times can translate into differences in posture vis-à-vis the state or in orientation and effectiveness vis-à-vis local congregations. Bishops Werner Leich of Thuringia and Horst Gienke of Greifswald[18] were described as more conservative than others, while Bishops Forck, Christoph Stier of Mecklenburg, and Christoph Demke of Magdeburg were more liberal—which sometimes translated into their greater readiness to confront authorities over social issues. But Stier and Bishop Rogge of Görlitz, who was a trained historian with expertise on Luther, were described as oriented toward ecumenical thinking and open to dialogue.

The Federation of Evangelical Churches in the GDR was created in June 1969 and lasted until February 1991.[19] Its highest organ was the synod, consisting of eighty members: seventy-two from the eight district Churches, and eight from the Conference of Church Leaderships, which was responsible for the federation's administrative and business affairs. In 1970 the Unity of Brethren became affiliated with the federation, and, after that, it was represented in the conference. Much of the responsibility for coordinating operations fell to the secretariat, which oversaw eleven standing commissions. These commissions were responsible for theology, parish work, social questions, information, radio and television, ecumenism, work with children, preparation of candidates for confirmation, work with adolescents, training of pastors, administration, and finances. Beginning in 1971, the federation and its district churches belonged to the Ecumenical Council of Churches and took an active part in the council's work.[20]

The Evangelical Church in the Early Postwar Period

The Nazis destroyed the institutional structures of the Churches, which had to be rebuilt after World War II. But many clergy members emerged from the war with great prestige because of their resistance to the Nazis and to the government-styled German Christian movement; these anti-Nazi clergy came to be called the "Confessing Church" (*Bekennende Kirche*). New synods had to be elected, although the Confessing Church had maintained an illegal Council of the Brethren to hold synods and carry out administrative tasks paralleling those of the administration conducted by Nazi-controlled Church offices.

After World War II the traditional district Church structures re-emerged, and all of the Evangelical Churches in the Soviet zone of occupation reestablished episcopal offices (or, in the case of Anhalt, the office of Church president). Otto Dibelius, ousted as general superintendent of Kurmark by the Nazis in 1933, had been active in the Confessing Church throughout the Nazi period, and on 7 May 1945 (when Germany surrendered) he took the lead in establishing the Church's consistory in Berlin-Brandenburg.

Pastors and communists had been together in Nazi concentration camps, and strong personal ties had developed. These connections contributed to a honeymoon from 1945 to 1948. During this period a Conference on Culture, sponsored in January 1947 by the Socialist Unity Party (*Sozialistische Einheitspartei Deutschlands*, SED), declared:

the brave conduct of a part of the clergy in the struggle against the barbarism of Hitler has also earned the recognition and respect of socialist laborers. Faith and socialism are not the antagonists that some would arbitrarily make them. The position of the party toward religion is one of absolute tolerance. That which Christianity seeks from faith, socialism seeks from knowledge. In their efforts to achieve their eminently secular objectives, the socialists have no desire to misuse the Church in a propagandistic manner.[21]

The Church began eliminating Nazis from its ranks immediately after the war, a task that it was able to carry out without interference from any of the occupation authorities. In this denazification process the Church was particularly concerned with removing pastors who had been involved in the German Christian movement.

At times, pressure was exerted on local pastors to endorse the new communist authorities. In July 1946 the Evangelical Church of Saxony responded by issuing a circular letter to its pastors, asking them to refrain from open political activity lest their spiritual role as pastors be compromised.[22] The Church's position was "that Christian life would only be possible at all if the state were constructed on democratic principles of organization and if the Churches received constitutionally anchored guarantees that they could fulfill their Christian mission."[23]

By 1948 a change in atmosphere had occurred. Villagers and townspeople in many municipalities were ordered to report for work on farms and in factories on Sundays, thus preventing them from attending church. In addition, state authorities interfered with religious instruction in some communities. The Churches grew apprehensive. In a Pentecostal letter dated 1 June 1949 Bishop Dibelius wrote: "More than anything else, we are concerned with the fact that the pattern of the state which is arising here is already showing signs of the same things which we struggled against under Nazi rule: power which overrules law, inner deception and untruth, and enmity to the Christian Gospel."[24] Shortly after the GDR's establishment in October 1949, two "progressive" pastors, Mehnert and Kehnscherper, were foisted on the Church's weekly radio broadcasts. In response, the Church decided to withdraw from the program. Subsequently, the government issued orders forbidding schools to commemorate Christmas and requiring them to celebrate the birthday of Joseph Stalin on 21 December. Christmas vacation was renamed winter vacation, and the Christ child was called the "Solidarity child."[25] At one point, a history textbook was issued in which one passage denied that Christ had ever existed; in the face of strong remonstrations from Church officials, a revised edition was issued in 1950 with this passage deleted.

About this time, schoolteachers began requiring children to write essays expressing the materialist point of view. In response, Bishop Dibelius repeatedly protested to Prime Minister Otto Grotewohl, as did bishops in the district Churches. But such expressions of concern were unavailing, and in the summer of 1952 state authorities went further and banned almost all Bible study groups.[26] The authorities obstructed the Church's work with young people on the grounds that it involved an "illegal" youth organization; this illegal status was vigorously denied by the Church. And systematic discrimination against Christians took place at all levels of sociopolitical life.

On the other hand, no state interference occurred in religious services or diaconical work. No bishops underwent show trials, as happened in other communist countries. And relatively few believers had to suffer imprisonment for their faith, although more than seventy Evangelical pastors and lay workers were imprisoned beginning in January 1953, some after show trials, such as Erich Schumann and Manfred Klain—an ardent young Catholic—both of them without just cause.

The S E D was intent in the early 1950s on breaking the inter-German links of the Churches and on pressuring the Evangelical Church into docile cooperation. In particular, the SED wanted the Church to co-operate with its National Front and to give prominence to "progressive" pastors. In 1950 the SED press published a series of defamatory articles, alleging that Bishop Dibelius was a Western agent. Until then, the SED had faithfully honored the obligations assumed by the state in the nineteenth century to make regular payments to the Churches. But in 1952 payments to the Church of Brandenburg were reduced by 20 percent, and in early 1953 all subsidies to Churches were (temporarily, as it turned out) discontinued. Lest the Churches turn elsewhere to make up the difference, they were hindered from making street collections (for which a special permit was required) and barred from making house collections. In addition, several West German Church periodicals were banned, including the official Lutheran Church organ, *Evangelisch-Lutherische Kirchenzeitung;* up to then, such periodicals had freely entered the GDR in the mails.

In these years state authorities regularly interfered in Church events, harassed student congregations and student pastors at the universities, and at times published defamatory press articles. But on 10 June 1953 Grotewohl promised an end to reprisals against Christian students, the reinstatement of teachers fired for their support of expelled students, and a retraction of certain limitations on religious instruction. These assurances improved the atmosphere temporarily, but by July 1954 the situation was souring again, and pastors were subjected to police surveillance. Even as Church publications experienced difficulties in obtaining adequate paper supplies, a new religious monthly magazine printed on high-quality paper, *Glaube und Gewissen,* made its appearance; the magazine was produced by East Germany's "progressive pastors."

The SED was especially interested in weaning young people from religion. It introduced a requirement that schoolteachers had to be Marxists; then, under pressure in 1953, it dropped the requirement, only to reintroduce it later. In 1954 the SED inaugurated a youth dedication ceremony (*Jugendweihe*), at the culmination of which each adolescent was presented with a book, *Weltall, Erde, Mensch* (The Universe, the World, Humanity), which explained that religion was a tool for "holding down the masses and oppressing them."[27] The SED exerted strong pressure on young people to take part in the nominally voluntary dedication ceremony, widely interpreted as an atheist alternative to the sacrament of confirmation. By 1958 the *Jugendweihe* had established itself as a normal outlet for young people.

On 15 February 1956 the city council of East Berlin issued the so-called

Fechner Decree; it forbade the conduct of religious instruction *before* school, requiring at least a two-hour interval between regular school and any after-class religious instruction, and demanding that parents who wanted their children to obtain religious instruction secure written permission, renewable on a three-month basis. About the same time, Hilde Benjamin, the minister of justice, issued a decree making the payment of Church taxes voluntary. (Up to then, the GDR state machinery had enforced individual payments of this tax!)

In these years the state's relationship with the Churches was entrusted to Deputy Prime Minister Otto Nuschke, head of the CDU-East, who also was a member of the Evangelical Church. Nuschke presided over a special Office for Church Relations, established within the framework of the CDU. But in March 1957 this office was eliminated, and a new State Secretariat for Church Affairs was created, headed by Werner Eggerath, former GDR ambassador to Romania. This organizational change was accompanied by intensified pressure on East German clergy to sever their organizational connections with their West German counterparts. More specifically, the government announced that it no longer would consult with clergy members who were not GDR citizens. Dibelius, who as bishop of Berlin-Brandenburg had been living in West Berlin, was suddenly ostracized and barred from entering the GDR. The same approach applied to Heinrich Grueber, the EKD representative to the East German government, who was likewise a West Berlin resident. Dibelius was not merely ostracized but vilified; posters were put up, linking him with Hitler's henchman, Heinrich Himmler, and with a convicted sex criminal named Balluseck. But for the time being, the Evangelical Church refused to divide itself along state lines.

In his first letter to all bishops in the GDR Eggerath asked them to devote their Easter sermons to a rejection of the atomic bomb and to advocacy of the peaceful use of atomic energy; compliance would have signified subservience to the government. Bishop Moritz Mitzenheim of Thuringia, as the senior Evangelical bishop resident in the GDR, replied that the Church had long ago rejected the use of atomic weapons and that he construed Eggerath's request as an attempt to discredit the episcopacy and divide the church. But not only bishops were singled out. Police pressured pastors to report on parishioners' political attitudes, and at least one attempt was made to persuade a pastor visiting West Germany to observe and report on Western military installations and troop movements.[28]

On 5 April 1957 came the arrest of the popular Siegfried Schmutzler, a pastor at the University of Leipzig. After a show trial, he was imprisoned for five years for "agitation to boycott the republic."[29] He also was accused of having expressed sympathy for the Hungarian revolt in 1956 and for supporting the Evangelical Church's agreement with Bonn to establish a chaplaincy in the West German military.

Meanwhile, the *Jugendweihe* was creating a crisis within the Evangelical Church. Some members suggested that the Church simply abandon confirmation since it had no biblical basis; others suggested postponing confirmation until young churchgoers reached the more mature age of seventeen; still others suggested splitting confirmation into its component parts, forgoing the completion of instruction, vow-taking, and the granting of constitutional rights. A rift emerged within the hierarchy over its posture toward the *Jugendweihe*. Dibelius led the majority, who felt that Church confirmation and the *Jugendweihe* had to remain mutually exclusive, even if that meant fewer members. Mitzenheim was the principal voice of a minority who felt that refusing confirmation to those taking part in the *Jugendweihe* would needlessly contribute to Church shrinkage; he recommended tolerance of the atheist youth dedication ceremony.

This controversy adumbrated a deeper rift between Mitzenheim and most of the hierarchy. Mitzenheim believed the Church had to choose between a prophetic/critical role and an effective protective role, and he felt that only the protective choice could be justified. He thus tried to maintain cordial and supportive relations with the regime and to seek concessions from it through persuasion and consultation. Typical of his controversial style was his acceptance of an invitation in October 1959 to attend a CDU rally in Dresden, even though the local bishop had declined. The bishop of Dresden was angered and took "revenge" by refusing to allow Mitzenheim to speak in one of Leipzig's large Lutheran churches. Mitzenheim, who served as bishop of Thuringia from 1945 to 1970, would be rewarded by the regime in August 1961 when it decorated him with the Order of Service to the Fatherland in Gold.

However, Mitzenheim was terribly isolated and had few followers outside Thuringia. He spoke of a "Thuringian path" (*Thüringer Weg*), and his concessions were said to be calculated to preserve the strongly Christian character of village life. While he was bishop, a number of Church people from Thuringia joined the CDU, and Mitzenheim's son, the director of the *Landeskirche* office, became a member of the *Volkskammer* (People's Chamber). In 1964 Mitzenheim was elected an honorary member of the CDU-East.

By the late 1980s (let alone in post-GDR Germany) Mitzenheim was no longer so controversial, chiefly because the controversies of the 1950s and 1960s no longer were relevant. Once branded in some circles as the "red bishop," he was honored years later by the Thuringian *Landeskirche*. In fact, the street leading up to the *Landeskirche* office in Eisenach was named for him. Some clergy in Thuringia told me in 1988 that Mitzenheim was a precursor of the "Church in Socialism" concept developed in the 1970s. Outside Thuringia, this assertion was disputed. Some recall Günter Jakob and Johannes Hamel, who, in the 1950s and 1960s, spoke about the need for critical solidarity with the state—with a strong accent on *criticism,* and with no attempt to obtain special concessions for the church (on which Mitzenheim placed his emphasis). They represented, in fact, an opposition to Mitzenheim, who felt that the Church had no critical role to play. Some argued, thus, that the "Church in Socialism" concept more accurately could be traced to their ideas. Yet it was Mitzenheim who as early as 1964 said, "We don't want to be a Church against socialism, but a Church for the people who want to be Christians in a socialist order."[30] Mitzenheim was not alone in his approach. As early as April 1962 Manfred Stolpe, then legal consultant in the consistory of the Berlin-Brandenburg *Landeskirche,* was advocating that the Church and the SED could find a modus vivendi.[31]

Mitzenheim's efforts also brought about the Church-state accord of 21 July 1958, which produced a softening of party secretary Walter Ulbricht's Church policy. In the joint communiqué cosigned by Mitzenheim and Ulbricht it was asserted that "the Churches . . . are in fundamental agreement with the peace efforts of the GDR and its regime."[32] The communiqué was controversial within the Church. But it was a dramatic change to hear Ulbricht declare in its wake that "Christianity and the humanistic ideals of socialism are not in contradiction."[33] Again, it was Mitzenheim whose efforts led to the granting of permission in 1962 for pensioners to travel to the West. And on 18 August 1964 Ulbricht and Mitzenheim met in Wartburg Castle (in Eisenach) and signed a follow-up document on Church-state understanding. Ulbricht commented on that occasion: "We have no basis for differences. . . . In the basics, in the questions of securing the peace and building socialism, we are of one mind. . . . The common humanist responsibility unites us all."[34]

Splitting the Churches from the West

As long as the question of German reunification remained open, it was reasonable to argue that no point was gained in hurrying organizational changes to conform to what might prove to be transient political realities. But with the creation of the GDR in 1949 and the failure of the last Soviet initiative on German reunification in 1957,[35] it became clear that the division of Germany would last for some time. Perhaps the first Church to adapt to the new situation was the German Unity of Brethren, which in 1945 divided into one organization for the Soviet zone of occupation and one for the other three zones. The Federation of Evangelical-Free Church communities soon followed, severing its ties with congregations in West Germany shortly after the GDR was established and setting up a separate organization for the GDR in 1950. In 1954 the Old Lutheran Church in the GDR likewise initiated its own organizational structure.

The authorities, of course, were most interested in splitting the Evangelical Church. In 1967 they stepped up the pressure. At a conference of the CDU-East in Jena on 10 February, CDU Chairman Gerhard Götting spoke of an "independent" Evangelical Church in the GDR that could "not be mentioned in the same breath" with the Evangelical Church in West Germany.[36] This sounded like praise, perhaps, but Church leaders reacted with alarm. Church President D. M. Müller of the *Landeskirche* of Anhalt wrote a letter to Götting, dated 4 March 1967, in which he said that the supposed ecclesiastical division was only wishful thinking on Götting's part; he further argued that the GDR Churches' abstention from the West German chaplaincy agreement of 1958 could scarcely be interpreted (as Götting seemed to think) as evidence of ecclesiastical secession. Bishop Hans Joachim Frankel of Görlitz was of the same mind. He declared: "We would be repudiating God's call for Christian unity if we were to allow ourselves to be separated from our sister Churches in the Fatherland."[37] An Evangelical Church synod was convened 2–7 April in Fürstenwalde, and on 5 April it issued a statement rejecting pressures to split the German organization in two. In a key passage the Fürstenwalde synod stated: "We Evangelical Christians in the GDR have no reason to destroy the community of the EKD. We have good reasons to preserve it."[38]

The new GDR constitution of 1968 specified that the Churches had to conduct their activities in conformity with the GDR's legislative and administrative limitations. This provision seemed to narrow the Churches' options. In April 1968 the *Landeskirchen* of Saxony, Mecklenburg, and Thuringia dissolved organizational ties to the Churches of the United Evangelical Lutheran Church of Germany, and on 1 December they established a new association, the United Evangelical Lutheran Churches in the GDR. For a while, the five Churches of the Evangelical Church Union held back from conforming. But by mid-1969 the separation was complete, and a new organization, the Federation of Evangelical Churches in the GDR, was set up on 10 June. About this time the Quakers, the Reformed, and the Methodists likewise separated from their West German coreligionists.

Organizational adaptation led to adaptation in ideology. Meeting in Eisenach in July 1971, Evangelical Church leaders accepted the programmatic formula—associated with the Evangelical Federation's then chairman, Bishop Albrecht Schönherr—that the Church did not want to be a Church alongside socialism, or a Church against socialism, but a Church *in* socialism.[39] What this statement meant was to some extent left vague. It clearly signified a pledge of loyalty, while at the same time it implied that some reciprocation was expected. It did not entail "ideological coexistence," as the Church made clear.[40] Indeed, State Secretary Hans Seigewasser's immediate reaction was dismissive; he considered this formulation inadequate and demanded that the Church make an explicit affirmation of socialism.[41] Be that as it may, some clergy members and believers initially feared that the Church was somehow selling out, and that concept stirred brief controversy. The other Protestant churches divided over the idea. Some (the Unity of Brethren, the Baptist Federation, the Seventh-Day Adventists) applauded the formula. Others were skeptical. (The Catholic Church repudiated the concept altogether.)

Shortly before the Eisenach synod of July 1971, Bishop Schönherr met with Seigewasser, the state secretary for Church questions, who had succeeded Eggerath in 1960. Schönherr complained of continued discrimination against young Christians in university admissions and of the fact that people fulfilling their military service in the construction brigade were barred altogether from university education.[42] Discrimination against believers, both in these forms and in hiring and promotion, remained an issue as long as the SED was in charge. The Church might have been *in* socialism, but in a number of ways its believers were made to feel they were only *alongside* socialism.

The Social Engagement of the Church

After the massive destruction of World War II, pacifist sentiments were widespread, especially among young people. The Evangelical Church responded to these feelings, and as early as 1962 it became engaged in political debate by promoting the idea of a social service alternative to newly introduced military conscription.[43] Introducing the construction brigade in 1964 was the state's reply to this pressure. On the surface, things seemed calmer after that response. But voices were raised within the Church—such as that of Heino Falcke, Evangelical provost in Erfurt, at a Dresden meeting in 1972—urging involvement in society's concerns.[44] In fact, Falcke became deeply involved in promoting pacifist and ecological activism on the Church's part, and he addressed an assembly in Buckow (28–29 January 1978) on the subject of a "Theology of Nature," arguing that the Old Testament lies within the environmentalist tradition.[45]

Ironically, it was on the eve of the Church's dramatically escalated involvement in peace-related and ecological concerns that Bishop Schönherr was received by General Secretary Erich Honecker for a kind of summit meeting on 6 March 1978. The meeting came at the Church's suggestion and had been carefully prepared in negotiations between responsible parties for months in advance to assure that it would have some substance rather than being merely a formal ceremony.[46] The Church wanted access to television and radio, a pension for clergy over the age of sixty-five, the construction of facilities in so-called "socialist cities" (churchless cities built after the war). A more specific issue also was raised. Ownership of the Augustine monastery in Erfurt was divided 50-50 between Church and state, and the Evangelical Church wanted full ownership. All of these requests were granted. In addition, the meeting created an atmosphere of trust between Church and state and led directly to a series of routine contacts in which questions were resolved issue-by-issue. The State Secretariat for Church Questions increasingly viewed itself as a go-between for the state apparatus and the Church rather than merely as an instrument of the state. Secretariat officials were highly knowledgeable, understood the needs of the Churches, and liked to think that they were useful to the Churches. Other Churches benefited from the new atmosphere, and almost every clergyman with whom I talked in 1988 said that his Church, either directly or indirectly, was a beneficiary of this meeting.

What did the state gain? First, the March 1978 meeting represented the culmination of Honecker's efforts to set Church-state relations on a new footing. Honecker wanted to break with the confrontational policies of his predecessor, Walter Ulbricht, and to see Church-state relations become more tranquil. Second, the authorities were already planning to introduce obligatory "pre-military" training in the ninth and tenth grades in September 1978. They may have welcomed the chance to work out a modus vivendi with the Church before embarking on a course that was certain to inflame many church people. And third, the Honecker regime was already showing a new approach toward the German past, "rehabilitating" long-denigrated giants of German history. Martin Luther was central to this project. The state planned to celebrate the Luther quincentenary in 1983, and Honecker would chair the official Martin Luther Committee of the GDR, which was established on 13 June 1980. The arrangement achieved in March 1978 established the basis on which Church-state cooperation in celebrating Luther would become possible.

Meanwhile, the Evangelical Church reacted quickly to the announced introduction of pre-military training. At a national conference on 14 June 1978 the Evangelical Church Federation warned that the planned educational changes would encourage young people to think in terms of "enemies," thereby cultivating prejudice and hatred. In July the Conference of Church Leaderships adopted an "Education for Peace" action program, underlining the Church's duty to work for a broadly conceived definition of peace. In September 1978 a Church synod at Berlin-Weissensee urged the regime to scrap its pre-military training program and instead introduce a "peace education" program, which would emphasize independent thinking on moral questions.[47] The SED was not interested.

In 1980, on the initiative of young people in the Church, the first "Peace Decade" was organized under the auspices of the Evangelical Church. This ten-day event mobilized Christians and non-Christians each November for discussions and seminars on peace, environmentalism, the arms race, and other social issues. In the GDR's larger cities, small groups of pacifists began forming spontaneously in late 1981, and by 1983 they numbered 2,000–5,000 activists and 30,000–50,000 sympathizers and supporters. Perhaps as many as 95 percent of these groups were Church-linked (until late 1989) because, with the sole exception of Church-associated activities, the authorities (up to late 1989) required citizens to register in advance for any "large" get-togethers, which even

applied to regular meetings of a half-dozen people. Although they depended on the Churches for use of their premises, 30–50 percent of the
members of these groups were non-Christians—some activists, in fact,
generally antipathetic to the Church, and some groups having no particular Christian character. The Church, however, was receptive to independent initiatives. In 1987 a group of so-called punks came to Berlin's Church of the Samaritan and asked for use of a room to set up a
punk club. The Church turned down the request. But some members of
a peace group already making use of the premises were sympathetic and
allowed the punks to join their group.

In 1981 the Evangelical Church commissioned an East German
graphic artist to design an emblem with the scriptural words, "Swords
into Plowshares" (*Schwerter zu Pflugscharen*). The resulting emblem was
used on shoulder patches distributed by the Church at its second "Peace
Decade" in November 1981. Authorities initially seemed to approve the
emblem, but in April 1982 the patch was banned and police were ordered
to stop young people from wearing it.[48]

Other Churches, including the Methodist, the Reformed, the
Seventh-Day Adventists, and the Church of John, likewise became active in environmental concerns, and they organized volunteers to help
clean up polluted streams and to plant trees. The environment came to
be a central theme of ecumenical meetings in the GDR, thus involving
all Churches that took part in such meetings. Some Churches, such as
the Apostolic communities and the Mormons, have not been interested
in ecumenism or in the environment. The Evangelical Church, however,
made the environment a focus of its "Peace Decade" in the late 1980s.
The Evangelical Church branched out into other areas, one prominent
example being its support for the GDR's small gay and lesbian rights
movement, which began to make its presence known in the 1980s.[49]

As the peace work of the Evangelical Church developed, it became
clear that six bones of contention existed between Church and state.
First, the Church remained opposed to what it termed the militarization
of East German society and, in particular, to programs of pre-military
training in the schools. Yet the regime repeatedly extended and expanded
these programs, both in the schools and in the Pioneers (the organization for boys and girls ages six to fourteen).[50] Second, the Church
continued to plead for the introduction of a social service alternative to
military service, as it had protested past discrimination against young
people who fulfilled their military duty in the construction brigade. In

1984 a panel discussion in St. Sophia's Church in Berlin revealed that more than a hundred former members of construction units had been admitted to university study and concluded that discrimination against veterans of the construction brigade was no longer a problem.[51] Third, the Church continued to protest broader discrimination against Christians—whether in education, jobs, or other areas. Fourth, the Church continued to plead for the right of emigration, and a consultation service was established in Berlin for those seeking to leave.[52] Fifth, the Evangelical Church's protection of independent peace groups opened it to the charge of harboring political opposition and made it more complicated to hold onto what Bishop Werner Krusche once called "the narrow space between opposition and opportunism."[53] Sixth, the Church increasingly addressed environmental concerns and identified with those who believed that the SED's economic policy was leading to ecological disaster. Peter Genischen of Wittenberg played a special role here. (As the head of the Wittenberg Church Research Center, he edited an irregular series of information bulletins about environmental questions.)[54]

When Honecker received Bishop Johannes Hempel of Dresden, the chair of the Federation of Evangelical Churches, for a meeting in February 1985, the conversation centered on the Church's peace activism and the SED's policy on peace. Honecker pointedly reminded Hempel of the GDR's alliance with the Soviet Union and acknowledged the contribution of East German Christians to building GDR socialism.[55] The compliment implied a warning.

Criticism and opposition, however, were only part of the story of the Church's relationship to the state. The other is a tale of cooperation and collaboration. The SED was eager to put its Churches to use, much as Moscow, Sofia, and Bucharest had done with their Orthodox Churches. A striking example of this eagerness came in April 1977 when the State Secretary for Church Questions, Seigewasser, informed Bishop Schönherr of his plan to involve the Churches in the celebrations of the sixtieth anniversary of the Bolshevik Revolution later that year. The Church was receptive to the suggestion, with Manfred Stolpe offering to evaluate the concepts of peace, security, and détente "in the light of the great October Revolution."[56] On 2 June 1977 the Evangelical Church leadership decided at the end of an intense discussion to send a representation of all member Churches to take part in the state celebrations.[57] To use another example, representatives of the GDR's religious communities, including Evangelical Bishop Schönherr, Harmut Fuchs (chair of the presidium of the Berlin Conference of European Catholics), and Gerhard Bassak (vice president of the Christian Peace Conference), took part in August 1982 in a Moscow-hosted conference on averting nuclear catastrophe.[58]

Collaboration was not limited to ceremonial events, however; it extended to contacts with the state security service (Stasi), which included sharing information with Stasi officers. Among those Church representatives later shown to have had unwarranted contacts with Stasi were Bishop Wilhelm Krummacher (onetime bishop of Greifswald and, from 1960 to 1968 chair of the Conference of Church Leaderships in East German),[59] Bishop Hans-Joachim Frankel (bishop of Görlitz, 1964–1979),[60] Siegfried Wahrmann (president of the Synod of the Evangelical Church Federation of the GDR, 1977–1986, the second highest post in that apparatus),[61] and Manfred Stolpe (president of the Consistory of the Berlin-Brandenburg Church, 1982–1990), whose first contacts with Stasi occurred in 1962 and who was in regular communication with Stasi officers from 1969 to 1989.[62] In Saxony, at least fourteen Catholic priests worked with Stasi in an unofficial capacity,[63] while at least seventy-three members of the Evangelical *Landeskirche* of Berlin-Brandenburg collaborated with the state security agency.[64] Altogether, about 5 percent of clergy members and other Church functionaries worked with Stasi.[65] Patricia Smith has documented that Stasi penetration extended even to the pacifist and environmentalist groups that met on church premises, with some pastors involved with those groups sharing information with Stasi.[66] It is interesting to note that "there were frequently conflicts between the groups and Church authorities,"[67] although no evidence indicates that Stasi had anything to do with these conflicts. But the Stasi network ultimately proved unavailing. Stasi was able to monitor the work of these groups from the inside and to obtain inside information about the workings of the Church; what Stasi could not do was terminate the critical work of these groups or curtail the growing pressure on Church leaders from their congregations to speak out on social issues.[68] The upshot was that collaboration with Stasi did not undermine the Church's opposition activity; on the contrary, it may even have made that opposition possible.

The Luther and Müntzer Celebrations

In the early postwar years the S E D drew a sharp contrast between Martin Luther and his contemporary, Thomas Müntzer. Luther was criticized for having served the interests of princes and nobility, while Müntzer, a chiliastic zealot who stirred up a peasant revolt in Germany in 1525, was hailed as "the true representative of the revolutionary forces" in Reformation times.[69] In a 1947 publication Luther was cast as the spiritual ancestor of Hitler,[70] while another East German historian, writing in 1946, charged Luther with being "counterrevolutionary".[71] By the mid-1960s, however, Luther was credited with contributing to the early "bourgeois" revolution against "feudal" Roman supremacy, which thus conceded that, relative to his time and context, he had been progressive. As Luther's star rose in East German historiography, Müntzer's declined. In 1967, as the GDR prepared to commemorate the 450th anniversary of the Reformation, consensus was reached in elite circles:

it is neither scientifically nor politically justified to content ourselves with this "Babylonian captivity" of the progressive Luther heritage. Marxist historical research has, on the contrary, through the exposition of the legitimate (*gesetz-mässig*) interrelationship of the Reformation and Peasant War as phases of the bourgeious revolution, uncovered the progressive meaning of the Lutheran Reformation and with it has created the scientific basis for the national jubilee marking the passing of 450 years since the Reformation, which appreciated Martin Luther as belonging to the good traditions of our republic.[72]

The decision to celebrate the Luther quincentenary in 1983 entailed his further rehabilitation, even though the SED continued to insist that he had been unable to perceive the full social ramifications of the revolutionary upheaval that he helped to inspire. The state's new interest in Luther provided a basis for a deepening of Church-state rapprochement, although some Church officials were critical of the SED's transparent attempt to adopt him as a forerunner of socialism.[73] Indeed, Luther was now described as "one of the greatest sons of the German people."[74]

For the SED, celebrating Luther reinforced its wider effort to reclaim its German past and to establish historical precedents and roots for the socialist system. In this way the SED hoped to convert German nationalism, which long had been a source of contempt for the East German state, into a source of support. Moreover, Luther's theology explicitly traced temporal authority to divine ordinance, leading him to preach obedience to secular authorities under most circumstances. (He preached passive resistance to authorities whose actions were contrary to Christian teaching.) Thus, Luther could be reinterpreted as a forerunner of "progressive" thinking, even of socialism, and also as an advocate of rendering unto Caesar that which is Caesar's.

Church representatives took part in the official Martin Luther committee's work, and the state provided funds for restoring a number of churches and sites of historical importance. The state even provided logistical support for Church-sponsored events connected with the celebrations. In the wake of the festivities a new trust had developed in relations between the state and the Evangelical and other traditional Protestant Churches. (Since the Catholic, Apostolic, and other Christian Churches placed no particular importance on Luther—or at least no positive valuation—the quincentenary had no effect on their relations with the state.)

Thomas Müntzer was a different matter. A utopian and political radical who entertained dreams of realizing far-reaching equality in an earthly republic, Müntzer has far less importance for the Church than Luther. Indeed, both Church and SED tended to see him as a "theologian of revolution"[75]—which explains the SED's interest and the slighter interest of the Church in commemorating his birth. In a three-page "Theses on Thomas Müntzer" the party organ *Neues Deutschland* declared that he had "aspired, on the basis of his revolutionary understanding of Christian teachings, to bring about a radical transformation of society in the interest of the exploited and subjugated people. He developed a theology of revolution with the goal of overcoming every form of class rule. He perceived in simple people the agent and revolutionary instrument of this transformation."[76] Honecker was even more explicit, claiming that Müntzer's heritage lived on in GDR socialism and that this legacy was "especially valuable" for the SED.[77]

The Evangelical Church established a committee to organize its commemoration of Müntzer's quincentenary in 1989, and it appointed three "observers" to attend the state committee's sessions (nominally headed, as in the case of the Luther celebrations, by Honecker).[78] Following the model established in 1983, the state commissioned a number of biographies of Müntzer as well as musical and dramatic works celebrating him, prepared a series of conferences and ceremonial events to honor him, and changed the name of the town of Stolberg to Thomas-Müntzer-Stadt Stolberg. Yet the celebrations had no particular impact on Church-state relations because the Church, by and large, viewed Müntzer as a "*Schwärmer*" (a fanatic) on the fringes of its tradition.

Trends and Developments in the GDR's Final Years

The Evangelical Church's increased involvement in pacifist and ecological concerns after 1978 was associated with grass-roots mobilization. Indeed, the bishops often have taken stands because of pressures generated from below. In 1986 this mobilization reached the point that could be described as a rebellion at the base—a revolt aimed at the laicization of the Church. In October a group of pastors, Church workers, and laypersons issued a declaration setting forth the principles of a "Solidarity Church." The laity, according to the declaration's authors, could not allow themselves to become passive objects of the Church's pastoral care; instead, they should take an active role in formulating programmatic Church statements.[79]

In June 1987 the Evangelical Church convened a synod in Berlin on the theme of Christian-Marxist coexistence. Supporters of the "Solidarity Church" decided that they wanted to hold an opposition synod, which they called the "Church Congress from Below" (*Kirchentag von unten*). Charging that the Church hierarchy had become too quiescent vis-à-vis the state, advocates of the Church Congress from Below nonetheless ultimately depended on the Church's benevolence since Church premises were the only legal place they could meet. Bishop Forck decided to make church facilities available to them, and the "countersynod" was held at Berlin's Church of the Pentecost, attended by some 1,200, mostly young people.[80] In general, the Church Congress from Below was dominated by the notion that the concept of a "Church in Socialism" had become obsolete and should be replaced by a new "grassroots movement for a different socialism." That is, some movement adherents did not see Western parliamentary pluralism as attractive, but they hoped instead to refashion socialism in accordance with certain humanist ideals.[81] The Church from Below also aspired to restructure the Church—*from below*.

Church from Below groups appeared in other cities, although the strongest was the original group in East Berlin. In general, these groups saw themselves as presenting an alternative to the Evangelical hierarchy's traditional methods. But in Erfurt, the local Church from Below group enjoyed good relations with the local hierarchy, and the two sides cooperated in putting on a critical exhibit about downtown Erfurt's reconstruction after World War II.

In Berlin the Church of Zion became deeply involved in environmental concerns, putting together a library on the subject that published the samizdat journal *Umweltblätter*. The Church also organized the country's first unofficial peace march in September 1987. On 25 November 1987 East German security police raided the library, confiscating copying machines and various publications and materials that criticized GDR authorities. Twenty-one people were arrested. Similar actions were carried out in Rostock, Dresden, Jena, Weimar, Wismar, and Halle. The raid on the Church of Zion marked the first time since the 1950s that church premises in the GDR were searched. Protests took place throughout East Germany, including some from Bishop Werner Leich, chair of the Federation of Evangelical Churches.[82]

Two months later, an official parade in honor of Rosa Luxemburg and Karl Liebknecht, founders of the German communist party, sparked new tensions between Church and state. Some 200,000 participants were joined in the parade by unofficial protesters who unfurled a banner bearing a quotation from Luxemburg: "Freedom is always only the freedom to think differently." These activists were quickly rounded up and imprisoned, and the Church loudly complained. Evidently, the party had had enough, and Bishop Leich was invited to a private meeting with Werner Jarowinsky, a member of the politburo. In that meeting Jarowinsky allegedly told the bishop:

Recently, the number of occurrences and events in the sphere of [the] Evangelical Churches has increased, which cannot be left unchallenged and in some cases exceed the limit of what can be tolerated. These events must be taken very seriously. They are in direct contrast with the form and understanding of togetherness which has proved its worth for a long time, respect for what is due the state, the parties, and the social organizations, and respect for the Church's constitutional tasks and duties. It must be clear that in the Church, too, there cannot be any zones exempt from [the] law. We must take very seriously such occurrences as the provocations on the fringes of the Rosa Luxemburg demonstration, and the obstructionist and virulent campaigns against the GDR, that are connected with the Church of Zion and the subsequent series of events in some Berlin churches. . . .

Churches are organizing purely political agitprop events, and anti-state slogans and calls for riots and confrontation are being tolerated there. . . . The limit of what can be tolerated has been surpassed, the opposition groups have gone too far.

We cannot allow things to continue like this. In a number of cases, events are organized without the knowledge of the allegedly competent municipal Church councilors, under pressure from the outside and from above, over which the "well-meaning" initiators no longer have control in the end. These are indeed signs of a disintegration of Church structures, which, according to the wishes of people acting in the background, should apparently be replaced by different structures. If even Church representatives openly admit that real substructures are forming, that there is discernible logistic control from outside and corresponding cooperation, this must be an occasion for reflection, for a reversal, for a necessary clarification, and for a change on the part of the responsible bodies. Attempts are being made to turn the churches into tribunals, lawyers' officers, or prosecutors' offices. At official [church] offices, people answer the phone saying "contact office," "Solidarity office," or "coordination center."[83]

New tensions in the relationship between the Evangelical Church and the state began to develop in September 1986 when clergy attending the Erfurt synod sharply criticized the regime's policies in education and, once again, demanded a social service alternative to military duty. Klaus Gysi, state secretary for Church questions from October 1979 to July 1988, finally agreed to take up these issues with appropriate Church representatives. But he was overruled by higher authorities, and no meeting took place. In 1987 a state official attending one of the Church congresses was asked about the prospects for Gorbachev-style democratization in the GDR. When the official ruled it out, he was loudly booed.

The example set by President Mikhail Gorbachev in the Soviet Union was probably responsible in great part for encouraging Church leaders in their outspoken course. In early 1988, for example, the Rev. Manfred Becker, head of the Berlin-Brandenburg synod, told a crowd of young people who had gathered in front of East Berlin's Galilee Church, "Much hope in our country is linked with the name Gorbachev. . . . Glasnost and perestroika belong on the agenda in our country too."[84] A few months later, in June, in a document circulated at the Church congress in Görlitz, activist cells of the Church from Below said that "current events in the Soviet Union have prompted us to consider certain fundamental questions concerning a social and political renewal."[85] The six-page letter called for initiating action to bring about democratization from below. Later that same month another regional Church congress held in Halle heard explicit calls for the introduction of Gorbachev's programs of glasnost and perestroika in the GDR.[86] Participants in the congress also raised the key question of what the Churches might do to "alleviate the glaring injustice of the division of our fatherland."[87] Subsequently, at a synodal meeting in Dessau (16–20 September 1988) Bishop Leich criticized what he called a two-class system developing in the GDR that consisted of people allowed to travel to the West and people denied that prerogative, and he called for a society with a "human face"[88]—a phrase strikingly reminiscent of Czechoslovak reformer Alexander Dubček's calls in 1968 for "socialism with a human face." Other congresses in 1988 took up other sensitive issues.

The authorities responded by barring West German television crews from taping or filming the proceedings in Dessau and by censoring issues of Church newspapers that sought to report on the various ecclesial assemblies. This clampdown marked the first time since the early 1980s that Church publications had been censored. All five regional Church newspapers, as well as the Evangelical Church news service, were affected. On one occasion the Berlin newspaper *Die Kirche* was banned because it attempted to reprint a German translation of an article on religious policy in the Soviet Union, which had been published originally in *Moscow News*.[89]

On 24 June, Bishop Leich met with representatives of the State Secretariat for Church Questions to discuss these interventions. But the meeting failed to resolve anything. Subsequently, Bishop Leich made a formal protest to East German Prime Minister Willi Stoph. Meanwhile, independently, a peace group and a working circle of the "Solidarity Church" sent a letter of protest to state authorities. As the censors' intrusions continued, Berlin pastor Wolfram Huelsemann led a silent march of some two hundred people on 10 October; the procession was forcibly broken up by security police on the grounds that it was an unregistered and hence illegal assembly.[90] During 1988 alone, the authorities censored *Die Kirche* fifteen times, and other Evangelical Church papers also were affected.[91]

As tensions grew, the GDR authorities banned an international Church congress scheduled for East Berlin on 12 November. Sixty-five representatives of Evangelical Churches from ten European countries had planned to discuss peace issues and Moscow's reform policy. Authorities said the meeting would put "pressure" on the Church-state relationship in the GDR.[92]

The Church and the Revolution

By 1988 the formula Church in Socialism was coming under fire within the Evangelical Church itself. Writing in the West Berlin periodical

Kirche im Sozialismus, East German theologian Richard Schröder criticized the formula for suggesting that the Church was somehow incorporating socialism into its self-image. He suggested that "Church in the GDR" might be more appropriate and politically less loaded.[93] But the suggested name would have been politically less useful to both Church and state. Moreover, although developed within Evangelical Church circles, the formula Church in Socialism was widely accepted among other Protestant Churches as well as by the Church of John, although not by the Apostolic Churches, the Mormons, or, of course, the Roman Catholic Church. By March 1989 Schröder was no longer a "voice in the wilderness," as Thuringian Bishop Werner Leich, chair of the Evangelical Church Federation, called the concept Church in Socialism "rather worn out." Leich had come to agree that the term suggested that the Church was *for* socialism.[94] On the contrary, the Church was becoming — Stasi informers and all — a leading force in the growing opposition to the sed regime. The Church began to distance itself from the concept,[95] but the entire idea of the Church in Socialism would soon be overtaken by events.

On 7 May 1989, elections were held in the GDR. Opposition groups sheltered by the Evangelical Church closely monitored the vote, and when the GDR announced the results, the opposition charged the regime with fraudulent underreporting of negative ballots. In East Berlin's Prezlau Hill district alone, the opposition said that some 2,659 negative votes had been confirmed; yet the regime had reported only 1,998 such ballots in all of East Berlin.[96] About two hundred young people demonstrated against the elections in front of St. Sophia Church; GDR security forces roughed them up, arresting 120. Under Church pressure, the jailed demonstrators were released.

In the summer of 1989 Hungary opened its borders with Austria and announced it would no longer honor its earlier agreement to return to the GDR those East German citizens seeking foreign asylum. Within weeks, hundreds of thousands of East Germans fled to West Germany — most of them via Hungary and Austria, but some by scaling the walls of West German embassies in Warsaw and Prague. An Evangelical Church synod held in Eisenach in September declared that fundamental political and social reforms were "urgent"; in particular, it demanded the introduction of a multiparty system in the GDR.[97] The regime refused. Church officials then sent a letter to the Honecker leadership requesting bilateral talks on political and social reforms. The authorities "took note" of this request but — until events forced their hands — shelved it.[98]

The GDR's fortieth anniversary celebrations on 7 October 1989 proved to be the East German experiment's final curtain. The Evangelical Church organized peace prayers and vigils in support of reform in Berlin, Leipzig, and Dresden, to which hundreds of thousands of people came. The vigils ultimately brought the regime down. Honecker, secretary of the SED since 1971, was forced to resign (fleeing to the USSR and eventually to Chile); Egon Krenz, former head of the East German youth organization and Honecker's handpicked successor, briefly took the reins. His first day on the job, Krenz met privately with Bishop Leich—a clear sign of the Church's political power at that juncture. In December, when roundtable talks on East Germany's future were convened in Berlin, Bishop Forck of Brandenburg-Berlin was chosen to chair the discussions.

New elections were held in East Germany in March 1990, bringing into office a coalition government headed by Christian Democrat Lothar de Maiziere and committed to German reunification. De Maiziere viewed himself as a caretaker for the brief transition before eventual reunification on 3 October 1990. His cabinet included four Protestant pastors, among them Rainer Eppelmann, minister of defense and disarmament, and Markus Meckel, minister of foreign affairs. Fourteen of the four hundred members of the transitional parliament were pastors.[99]

Some observers have exaggerated the ecclesiastical contribution to the East German revolution, painting the event as a "Protestant revolution,"[100] or casting all the clergy monochromatically as revolutionary "heroes."[101] The truth is far more complex, and it is important to keep in mind that only a small portion of the clergy played significant roles in opposition activities and that people from other walks of life made contributions.[102] As an unidentified Church pastor from the GDR admitted in early 1990, "Many of our fellow pastors, who today loudly trumpet the word 'Revolution' and who play up their supposed role in it, actually took a rather different position before and during the transformation. If people in the GDR today look to us Church leaders with trust, then we have to hang our heads in shame, because many of us have really not earned this trust; we were able to work quite well within the old system."[103]

Be that as it may, the Christian Churches benefited immediately from the collapse of communism. Maiziere's transition government restored several Church holy days (including Christmas and Easter) as state holidays, removed governmental pressure on the Church, and released internal documents revealing Stasi strategies for undermining and subverting the Churches.[104] The reunification of Germany also made the reuniting of the divided Evangelical Church possible, and this process, started in September 1990, was accomplished by and large by February 1991.[105] Thus ended the independent existence of the "East German Church."

Robert Goeckel, a seasoned American observer of the East German religious scene, noted, however:

despite its ideological conflict with the SED regime, the Church is ironically more likely than other institutions to retain elements of its past experience of socialism. Little appears likely to remain of "real existing socialism" in much of GDR society. . . The *Wende,* or transformation, has left no segment of society unaffected, even "non-political" areas like sports and the music scene. Yet because the Church was less affected by the Leninist system, its rejection of the GDR legacy is less sweeping than in these other institutions. There have been few purges in the Church leadership and the Church's call for social justice stand in stark relief to the popular embrace [as of mid-1990] of West German-style capitalism. . . . Nor is the resurgence of religion after the collapse of the Nazi regime likely to be repeated in the post-communist regime. . . . Yet, more than other institutions in the GDR, the Church is likely to embody elements of the past in the new Germany.[106]

Since Reunification

As elsewhere in the region, the collapse of communism removed institutional and cultural obstacles to proselytization by Christian groups based in the United States or elsewhere, by neo-Oriental sects, and by sundry other religious organizations and movements. By 1995, cults and sects of various kinds claimed about 2 million members across Germany.[107] Nontraditional Christian communities began springing up, not only in the former GDR but throughout western Germany. Between 1988 and 1993 alone, about three hundred new communities of a charismatic or Evangelical-charismatic or fundamentalist[108] bent were established across Germany.[109] Judaism shared in this sudden boom, chiefly as a result of the immigration of some 84,135 Jews from Russia and Ukraine between 1990 and March 1995. In May 1995 a new Jewish center was opened in Berlin, where the largest synagogue in Germany had once stood. And pressure mounted for the return of former Jewish properties in eastern Germany confiscated by the Nazis.[110]

But even as the confessional landscape was becoming more heterogeneous, the larger Churches—the Evangelical and Catholic—expressed concern about the large numbers of people who chose to leave them. (In the Federal Republic of Germany the government levies a Church tax on all citizens unless they formally renounce the Church and declare that they do not wish to be affiliated with any religious group. This tax has impelled people not attached to any Church to declare this fact explicitly—in turn, making an exact accounting possible.) In 1992 the Evangelical Church lost 360,000 members, and in 1993 another 280,000; for the Catholic Church, the loss tallied 193,000 in 1992 and 154,000 in 1993.[111] This flight has had worrisome financial consequences for the Churches; indeed, looking at the exodus historically, the Evangelical Church recorded a total loss of about 3.9 million members between 1970 and 1993.[112] The torrent of revelations regarding the extent of clerical collaboration with Stasi, among which the case of Manfred Stolpe, elevated since 1990 to the post of minister-president of Berlin-Brandenburg, was raised to the status of a cause célèbre,[113] scarcely helped the Churches. The Evangelical and Catholic Churches have attempted to deal with this hemorrhaging, and the Catholics even hired an advertising agency to promote Church membership.[114] Clergy in both Churches warned that "without reform, the Church will collapse, just as communism did."[115]

Meanwhile, German unification had other repercussions for the Church-state relationship. In the GDR abortion had been available on demand since 1972, while in the Federal Republic abortion had been available on a highly restricted basis, with women required to meet fixed social, medical, and/or psychological criteria, and with the ultimate decision being left to an attending physician. The Bundestag passed a law on abortion in June 1992 that was intended to resolve the controversy. The law sought to create a unified system throughout the country and authorized abortion only during the first twelve weeks of pregnancy, with counseling required three days before the actual abortion was to be performed.[116] Conservatives appealed the law to the Constitutional Court, the highest judicial forum in Germany, and in May 1993 the court ruled 6 to 2 that the law was unconstitutional, that the "right to life" begins at conception, and that state-supported hospitals were to perform no abortions at all. Regine Hildebrandt, minister for social affairs in Brandenburg province, denounced the ruling as "a return to the Middle Ages." She added, as she and other angry women politicians left the courtroom: "This is a catastrophe. This is just impossible at the end of the twentieth century."[117]

Probably no one would have anticipated that *any* court anywhere would find it within its jurisdiction to rule when the "right to life" begins—as if legal and judicial training equipped one with special expertise in resolving this tangled biological, philosophical, and moral question. But by November the FDP was talking in terms of preparing new legislation to provide for regulated access to abortion,[118] while, reportedly for the first time ever, German women began organizing a nationwide strike. This strike, scheduled for 8 March 1994, was seen as a protest against the dismantlement of women's rights in eastern Germany generally (including access to abortion), rising female unemployment throughout the nation, the curtailment of social services both East and West, and widespread poverty in old age.[119]

But if in the state of political fluidity induced by the unification of unlike systems women's rights could be questioned and debated, then the Churches' prerogatives also could be reassessed. A rather startling illustration of this proposition came on 1 January 1994, when, reacting to Church objections to eliminating state observance of two religious holidays, Federal Minister of Labor Norbert Blüm suggested that the Church tax could be discontinued.[120] Blüm's statement inflamed passionate reactions, and, two days later, government spokesperson Dieter Vogel reassured Church circles that the government had no intention of altering the Church tax system.[121]

One of the bigger surprises in the postcommunist transition has been the growing popularity of the *Jugendweihe* ceremony. Originally devised by the SED as an alternative to Church confirmation, and more concretely as an occasion for young people to pledge themselves to work for socialism, the *Jugendweihe* has demonstrated real resilience. In 1992 some 50,000 eastern German adolescents voluntarily chose to take part in the ceremony; in 1993 this figure rose to about 70,000, and in 1995 the number of young persons interested in the ritual continued to grow, with some 86,000 adolescents signing up.[122] Participants in the *Jugendweihe* are no longer given copies of *The Universe, the World, Humanity*, as in the Ulbricht era, or of *Socialism—Your World* as under Honecker. Instead, they receive copies of *Germany—So Beautiful Is Our Land* (published in the nation's western part).

By the summer of 1996 a new controversy flared up over a religion course scheduled to be introduced in state schools in Brandenburg during the 1996–97 school year. The Evangelical Church had been accustomed to having religion taught in West German schools from an engaged point of view, but the new course has been designed to be taught from a nondenominational, detached perspective. In this respect, Brandenburg betrayed the influence of four decades of SED rule. Moreover, in the other four states created out of the GDR—Saxony, Saxony-Anhalt, Thuringia, and Mecklenburg-western Pomerania—students have been given a choice between a traditional religion course and a nonreligious ethics course. Charging that the new course promoted "de-Christianization," its critics took the Brandenburg school system to the Constitutional Court for judgment.[123]

Conclusion

During the era of communist rule, 1949–89, the Evangelical Church by virtue of its preponderant size set the general tone for Church-state relations to some extent. But there were important exceptions to this rule. In the early postwar period, while the Evangelical Church's relations with the state were thorny, other Churches banned or forced to suffer severe limitations under the Nazis felt relief at being able to organize anew. Moreover, whereas earlier German governments had favored the Evangelical Church, the SED treated all registered religious organizations more or less equally. The result was that the smaller Churches often took a more positive view of SED policy (a perspective encouraged by an awareness of their own weakness and a consequent circumspection).

The Schönherr-Honecker meeting of March 1978, on the other hand, produced positive effects for all Churches. Religious life became more normal, communities generally found it easier to build churches, and the entire Church-state climate improved. By contrast, the falling out after 1986 was specific to the Evangelical Church's relationship with the state and did not affect other Churches. Only the Evangelical Church's publications were censored. And officials of other Churches insisted that no particular tension arose in their relations with the state during the GDR's last few years. In fact, as tensions were growing between the Evangelical Church and the state in 1988, the Church of John sent an open letter to Honecker, warmly commemorating the March 1978 meeting and noting "the positive effect of the separation between state and Church and of equal respect to all Churches and religious communities in our state." The letter gratefully acknowledged the "expansion of the publication of Church materials" and underlined acceptance of the principle that the Church is "neither a political nor a social organization."[124]

The Churches discussed in this chapter are highly diverse; their theologies, ecclesiologies, and perspectives on politics all have differed considerably. Even within the Evangelical Church there have been debates —some traceable to differences between the Lutheran and Reformed traditions, some associated with differences of personality or differences in the experiences of the given *Landeskirchen*. But the regime itself generally succeeded in presenting a united front.

Reunification has presented the Churches of the former East Germany with a powerful challenge. Unlike Churches in the western portion of the country, their ranks have been dramatically depleted by regime-sponsored secularization. Until reunification, their political role assured them of continuing as society's advocate against a monopolistic state. Now, shorn of that task, Churches in the former East Germany are having to accommodate themselves rapidly to the political balance and social realities with which Churches in West Germany have lived for the past fifty years.

Chapter 4

Catholicism and National Culture in Poland, Hungary, and Czechoslovakia

Poland, the Czech Republic, Slovakia, and Hungary are all predominantly Catholic countries, although strong Protestant Churches are active in both the Czech Republic and Hungary. All three countries experienced being parts of traditional feudal empires (specifically, of tsarist Russia and Habsburg Austria). All three emerged as new states after World War I (although in Hungary the transition from virtual independence under the *Ausgleich* system was not nearly as dramatic as the transition experienced by the Poles, Czechs, and Slovaks). All three countries in the interwar period were concerned with questions of ethnic heterogeneity (although revisionism in Hungary had a much stronger claim on the popular mind). In fact, in the 1930s the Catholic portion of each country's population was nearly identical. And all three countries came under the sway of Moscow-controlled communist parties in the late 1940s and were ruled by communist parties for more than forty years.

Yet despite these salient commonalities, for a long time Church-state relations in each country have diverged. In Poland the Roman Catholic Church has obvious grassroots strength, and in the communist era Poland was able to maintain a defiant posture toward a regime that had shown its hostility to the Church by unleashing at the outset of the 1980s a systematic campaign of harassment and intimidation. Religiosity in Poland remains intense, and candidates for the priesthood are still numerous.

By contrast, in Czechoslovakia the Catholic Church has waned in the Czech lands and held its own only in more agrarian Slovakia. The Husák regime placed the Church under pressure in both parts of the country. Whereas Polish communists from the beginning ruled out as unrealistic any notion of drawing the Catholic Church away from communion with the Vatican,[1] Czechoslovak communists, including the Slovak party's onetime first secretary, Vasil Bilák, suggested at one point that a break between the local Church and the Vatican might be a precondition for a "normalization" of Church-state relations. Religiosity among Czechs is generally characterized as weak, while the training of priests was controlled and obstructed by the party. In Kádár's Hungary (1956–88) the Catholic Church enjoyed the protection of the state, was able to operate eight high schools, and did not have to worry about harassment or obstruction by the authorities. The price paid for this relationship was a generally supportive attitude toward what was, in any event, a relatively liberal communist regime.

Given the many factors common to the three societies, how is one to account for these strikingly different patterns of Church-state interaction in the communist era? This chapter argues that religio-national symbiosis has played a key role as an intervening variable between remote events and more recent ones. To put it another way, the aspect of religio-national symbiosis in the communist era and after reflects the distillation of historical patterns and, in turn, sets limits to the possibilities in present Church-state relations.

Factors Affecting Religio-National Symbiosis

The presence or absence and the particular configuration of religio-national symbiosis cannot be presumed. In some regions religion may be the most important formative agent of national identity, while in others and among other peoples it may be secondary. Pašić, for instance, lists religion as the fourth most important factor in the formation of nations in the Balkans, behind political states, ethnic and linguistic variables, and cultural factors.[2] Nations may view their Churches as bastions of defense of the national culture, as in the case of the Poles, Croats, Serbs, and Bulgarians or, like the Czechs, they may view their Churches as somehow antinational. Or sentiment may fall somewhere between these extremes, as in the case of the Slovaks, Hungarians, Romanians, and Germans (albeit for different reasons).

Among the factors affecting religio-national symbiosis in Central and Eastern Europe (including the Baltics, Belarus, and Ukraine) are these:

Ethnic mix. Is the country ethnically homogeneous or not? If not, do the component national groups have common external foes and allies?

Confessional mix. Are there two or more rival Churches, each claiming to be the authentic voice of a given group (as in the case of the Slovaks, Hungarians, Romanians, and Ukrainians), or does a single Church have a monopoly on protectorship of the national culture (as in the Polish, Croatian, Serbian, Bulgarian, and Lithuanian cases)? Is the dominant religion of the largest national group also the dominant religion of other national groups? Are other confessional groups indifferent to national mythology?

Previous history of Church co-optation or opposition. If nationalism is identified with the governing class or party, a co-optive relationship with the Church may foster religio-national symbiosis. Alternatively, foreign rule may confront the Church with a choice between governmental hostility and popular rejection.

Traditional class roots of the Church. Is a given religion perceived as being the legacy of the upper class (as may be the case in Bohemia), or is it also viewed as the traditional religion of the lower class (as is clearly the case in Poland)?

The specific content of the given faith. What is the dominant confession's attitude toward history, culture, authority, and conscience? How much emphasis does the dominant confession place on the good of the collective, and how much on the integrity of the individual? Croatian theologian Šagi-Bunić describes Catholicism as a "point of departure" for nationalism insofar as it engenders values caring for the community.[3] Protestantism, by contrast, is generally understood to place less emphasis than Catholicism (especially Catholicism's conservative wing) on authority and received tradition (what the Catholic Church calls the magisterium), and more emphasis on individual judgment and conscience.

The Polish, Czechoslovak, and Hungarian cases will be used to examine the test of these hypotheses:

1. Trauma concentrated in one sphere of society necessarily affects other spheres. Insofar as trauma necessitates policy reappraisal, its effects will penetrate issues in several areas.

2. The closer the religio-national symbiosis, the more difficult it is for the state to maintain a purely confrontational attitude toward religion.

3. The experience of the Counter-Reformation created a tradition of anticlericalism that makes the Catholic Church more vulnerable in those areas where it was associated with the suppression of the indigenous nobility and local autonomy.

4. Confessional strength is positively correlated with national symbiosis and resistance to foreign oppression; it is negatively correlated with antinational demeanor and co-optation by or alliance with foreign rulers.

5. If nationalism is oppositionist in orientation, Church posture also must be oppositionist if religion and nationalism are to be symbiotic.

The Church in Poland: Oppositionist Nationalism

The Polish Catholic clergy is fond of speaking of the historical association of Christianity with Polish culture[4]—by which it means Catholicism and Polish culture. Yet Protestantism was an important social force in Poland for some 130 years (from about 1520 to about 1650); in Silesia the population was overwhelmingly Protestant as recently as the later 1600s.[5] Lutheran, Calvinist, Socinian, Anabaptist, and other groups spread into Poland from Germany, France, Bohemia, and Italy. Polish Calvinism had its center in Little Poland (Malopolska) after its introduction there in 1546.[6] By the end of the sixteenth century these diverse Protestant denominations had developed a dynamic presence in many Polish towns. The failure of Polish Protestantism to leave any important mark may be traced to at least three causes. First is the lack of organization among the Protestant Churches and the consequent difficulties experienced by them in trying to cooperate.[7] Second, whatever its strength in the towns, Protestantism failed to take root among the peasantry.[8] Third, in contrast to the situation elsewhere, Polish Protestantism failed to produce intellectual advocates of the caliber of the Catholic intellectuals Jan Laskii, Andrzej Frycz Modrzewski, and Stanisław Hozjusz.[9]

The central fact in the development of modern Polish nationalism is the century of partition from 25 November 1795 to the end of World War I. The partition not only colored Poland's attitude toward the outside world, but it cemented its bond with Roman Catholicism, even though the Holy See—concerned above all with protecting its own interests, whether in annexed territories or in a sovereign Poland—assured the partitioning powers (Austria, Prussia, and tsarist Russia) that it "accepted" the partition as "inevitable."[10] A series of autonomous or nominally autonomous national reincarnations (the Duchy of Warsaw, 1807–46; the Kongresówska, 1815–17; the Republic of Kraków, 1815–46; the Grand Duchy of Posen, 1815–49; and the "Kingdom of Poland" set up in November 1916 under German auspices) helped keep alive the Polish idea. But they were no substitute for self-determination, and, in consequence, Polish nationalism took on the character of resistance and sometimes insurrection. To be a Polish patriot meant to be in opposition.

Ironically, the Roman Catholic hierarchy in the eighteenth and nineteenth centuries was unsympathetic to Polish nationalism, and the Polish-Catholic equation was more important in border areas than in homogeneously Catholic areas. Even so, Catholicism has been a major component of Polish identity. Indeed, the loss of statehood encouraged

Polish national consciousness to focus above all on religion and language as the mainstays of national being. Moreover, of the three partitioning entities, only Austria, the sole Catholic power, pursued a tolerant policy toward the Poles; that tolerance prevented the Austrian Catholic ecclesiastical hierarchy from being seen as inimical to the survival of Polish culture. Protestant Prussia and Orthodox Russia posed more fundamental threats. It is also worth noting that although the Austrian occupation of Bohemia and Moravia accompanied the Counter-Reformation and was, indeed, part and parcel of it, the Austrian occupation of Galicia and Lodomeria followed the Counter-Reformation by more than 150 years and therefore was not seen as evidence that the Catholic Church was a "foreign" or "foreign-imposed" institution.

In the Russian pale (sometimes called Vistulaland) the Church fared the worst. The Russian court viewed Catholicism as a tool of Polish nationalism within Russia, and, as early as 1772, immediately after the first of the three partitions that removed Poland from the map, Catherine II forbade the Catholic clergy to communicate directly with the Holy See.[11] Some Poles tried a conciliatory tactic, aspiring to play the role of Greeks to the new Rome.[12] Fr. Stanisław Staszic (1775-1826), for instance, hoping to use Russian political leadership and power to buttress Polish cultural hegemony, claimed for Poland a special "civilizing" mission. Similarly, August Cieszkówski (1814-94), a Hegelian trained at the University of Berlin, believed that the Catholic Church and the Polish nation alike had a divine mission and looked forward to a Catholic utopia that he called the Era of the Holy Spirit.

Ultimately, however, persistent efforts at Russification, together with unremitting pressure on the Catholic faith, undermined the conciliatory line and reinforced the insurrectionary spirit.

In "Vistulaland," Catholic clergy were subject to control, and obstacles were erected to the promotion of Catholics in the army and the bureaucracy; the Catholic clergy lost its estates, and its dioceses were reorganized. The Greek-Rite (Uniate) Catholic Church suffered especially harsh treatment. During three periods (the 1770s-90s, the 1830s, and the 1860s) the Russian army was summoned to compel mass conversions to Orthodoxy.[13] Norman Davies stated in his history of Poland:

Papal bulls could not be published in Russia without the assent of St. Petersburg, and were often ignored or countermanded. . . . Books were burned; churches destroyed; priests murdered; services conducted according to the Orthodox rite under the shadow of bayonets. In 1839, all contact between the Uniate Church in Russia and the Vatican was severed. In 1875, the Union of Brest [signed in 1596] was itself officially annulled. By 1905, when a decree of religious toleration was finally exacted, no more than 200,000 Uniates were left to practise their faith openly. In all these religious policies, there is no doubt that the prime motivation was political.[14]

Roman Catholicism was a religion of the West, subject to a foreign prelate (the pope) and thus suspect. Russian Orthodoxy, by contrast, was under the tsarist thumb and was viewed as a pillar of imperial stability.

Indeed, St. Petersburg remained suspicious of the Polish provinces per se and therefore excluded them from even the limited grants of self-government that were extended (e.g., to the cities in 1775, to the *zemstva* [rural assemblies] after 1864). When the Poles revolted, the tsars struck back at the "Polish Church." Hence, after the Polish insurrection of 1831, which also spread to Lithuania, the tsar took reprisals against the Catholic Church, which he viewed as a den of "Latin propaganda," and shut down the University of Wilno. That university's theological faculty members were transferred to St. Petersburg where authorities could keep a close watch on them. And after the insurrection of 1863 the tsar began shutting down monasteries and closing schools (usually monastic) in which Polish was the language of instruction. According to Davies,

As a result of the November [1830] Rising, almost half of the Latin convents of Russian Poland were closed, while payment of the stipends of the clergy was turned over to the state. Unauthorized correspondence with Rome was punishable with summary deportation. All sermons, pronouncements, and religious publications were to be approved by the Tsarist censorship. All seminaries were to be inspected by the Tsarist police. As a result of the January [1863] Rising, the great majority of Catholic orders were disbanded. The entire landed property of the Church was confiscated together with the estates of lay patrons of Catholic benefices. The conduct of the Sacred College was placed under the Ministry of the Interior, and all business between the College and the diocesan curias was handed over to lay police-approved delegates.[15]

In November 1864 Russian troops took possession of more than a hundred monasteries, convents, and religious houses and imprisoned their former occupants. Adam Krasiński, the bishop of Wilno, was banished, together with about four hundred Catholic priests.[16] The dioceses of Kamieniec (1865), Podlasie (1867), and Minski (1869) were abolished by state decree. St. Petersburg even made some efforts to establish a Polish National Church under state jurisdiction.[17]

Around midcentury, Russian intellectuals and authorities began extolling the "superiority" of the Russian language over all other European languages; the speaking of a foreign language was equated with political disloyalty. Russification began in earnest. A Russianized Catholic Church, with the rituals in Russian, was supposed to serve as a vehicle of Russification. Accordingly, a Russian-language liturgical book was issued to replace the Polish one.[18] In addition, after 1864 Polish teachers were obliged to use Russian as the medium of instruction for all subjects, including religion, and even for teaching Polish to Polish children.[19] Field Marshal Iosif Hurko (1828–1911), governor-general in Warsaw from 1883 to 1894, was a leading advocate of the Russification of the Poles. Under his governorship the Cyrillic alphabet was actively promoted in public places, and street signs appeared in both Russian and Polish. The legacy of Russian occupation, then, was to reinforce an earlier tendency to view Orthodoxy as a foreign religion, Roman Catholicism as the Polish religion, and tsardom as hostile to the Polish soul.

The Prussian partition initially fared better, enjoying some autonomy in the "Grand Duchy of Posen" between 1815 and 1848 and benefiting from the generally more tolerant policy toward religion.[20] Prussian policy as it affected Polish culture began to change under Chancellor Otto von Bismarck. Indeed, shortly after German unification, Bismarck launched his Kulturkampf (1873). As a result, the use of Polish in state schools was banned, except for religious instruction, and teachers were barred from joining either Polish or Catholic societies. The Prussian government transferred priests whose politics were considered dangerous to remote parishes, and, beginning in 1885, it expelled Poles who could not prove Prussian citizenship.[21] Earlier, in 1872, the Reichstag had forbidden the Jesuit order to establish new offices in Germany, and it had authorized the expulsion of Jesuits already working in the country.[22] That same year, under regime pressure, the primate of Prussian Poland, Archbishop Mieczysław Ledochówski of Gnesen (1822–1902), had agreed that *Boże cos Polske* would no longer be sung at mass. The following year, after Ledochowski had displayed continued resistance to government interference in religious instruction and the operation of theological seminaries, he was imprisoned, along with ninety other Polish priests. As Davies notes, the anti-Catholic edge of the Kulturkampf served to identify Polishness and Catholicity, and in Silesia the Polish national movement was now captured by such radical priests as Fr. Józef Szafranek (1807–74).[23]

Ironically, until the Kulturkampf and its attendant aggressive German assimilatory efforts, Germanization had steadily proceeded. The sharpening of policy backfired and engendered resistance. Protestant Germany, like Orthodox Russia, showed itself inimical to Polish culture and nationality. The German attitude is well summed up by Max Weber's remark, "Only we Germans could have made human beings out of these Poles."[24]

By contrast, Austrian rule seemed benign almost to the point of altruism.[25] In 1869, for instance, the Polish language was put on an equal footing with German in Galicia and came to be used in all official business. In 1870 the Jagiellonian University was allowed to reinstate Polish as the principal language of instruction; two years later, the Academy of Fine Arts (Akademia Umiejetnosci) was established in Kraków. A Polish literary, cultural, and scholarly renaissance, centered in the universities of Kraków and Lemberg (Lwów), developed under Habsburg rule. In Lemberg, theaters presented plays in Polish and operas in Polish and Italian (solos generally in Italian, choruses in Polish). Earlier, in 1827, Józef Maksimilian Ossoliński had created the Ossolineum in Lemberg for the dissemination of Polish arts and sciences. After 1871 the University of Lemberg (founded in 1784) and the Polytechnicum (founded in 1844) were allowed to offer instruction in Polish, and in 1879 the National Polish Museum was opened in Kraków. The Habsburgs also permitted the founding of the Polish Historical Society in Lemberg and, in 1884, the Polish historical journal *Kwartalnik Historyczny*. Among the cultural figures of Kraków was Count Alexander Fredro (1793-1876), who wrote comedies in the style of Molière and staged them in Kraków and Lemberg.[26]

In political terms the *Ausgleich* Law of 21 December 1867 created an elective legislature and a provincial executive body for Galicia, which was tantamount to semiautonomy. In 1871 a ministry of Galician affairs was established in Vienna to defend Galicia's interests. In Habsburg theory the Poles were considered a "historical people," alongside Germans and Hungarians, and thus they were entitled to greater consideration and privileges than such "unhistorical" peoples as the Slovaks and Romanians.

The Catholic Habsburg regime viewed Polish Catholicism with favor. The only difference was that instead of praying to "the Virgin Mary, Queen of Poland," Austria's subjects in Galicia were urged to pray to "the Virgin Mary, Queen of Galicia and Lodomeria."[27] And while

Habsburg rule meant a policy of subordinating Church to state and re-sulted at one point in the closing of hundreds of monastic orders, the Holy See displayed complete equanimity in regard to Galicia—and, for that matter, in regard to the Prussian and Russian occupations. During the period of the partitions, the Holy See did not in fact show any particular interest in the Polish question per se, advising Poles to let the established authorities administer the affairs "of this world." Pope Leo XIII (1810-1903; pope, 1878-1903) even issued an encyclical urging Polish bishops to adopt a posture of loyalty toward their respective governments. Still, the Holy See was not indifferent to its own interests, as shown in an encyclical dated 24 April 1864, issued by Pope Pius IX (1792-1878; pope, 1846-78). In this encyclical Pius IX chastised "the [Russian] potentate who oppresses his Catholic subjects."[28]

At least two factors prevented anticlericalism (which would have sun-dered the religio-national linkage) from becoming a dominant trend in Galicia: First, by contrast with Germany and Russia, Catholic Austria was permitting, even encouraging, a Polish cultural renaissance and Galician prosperity; and second, by contrast with the Holy See, the lower clergy—in Galicia as well as in "Vistulaland" and eastern Germany—was closely bound with the lives of the parishioners and took an active role in the political movements of the day.[29]

The restoration of independence did not erase the Church's opposi-tionist legacy. The constitutions of 1921 and 1935 assured the Roman Catholic Church of preeminence among the religious denominations of Poland, with the government paying Catholic priests' salaries and en-forcing religious instruction at state schools; under the terms of the concordat of 1925 the Church was guaranteed complete freedom in its internal affairs. In spite of these important advantages many clergy were dissatisfied. Jesuit Jan Pawelski criticized the rather limited constitu-tional concession to the principle of separation of Church and state, calling it an "echo of confused liberalism and secularism."[30] In some ways, indeed, the Catholic Church "was pushed to the fringes of politi-cal life."[31]

The attitude of at least part of the Polish citizenry was captured by *Głos Prawdy* in a 22 February 1927 article. Immediately below the satiric head-line "The Roman Catholic Republic of Poland" came a subhead, "The people have had enough of fattening the bellies of priests."[32] And while the Church found some supporters in the *Endecja*, a political party led by Roman Dmowski (1864-1939), this support became increasingly irrele-vant after Marshal Józef Piłsudski's (1867-1935) seizure of power in 1926.

Piłsudski's government immediately called for a revision of the concordat, arguing that the agreement had granted the Church too many concessions; the government also blocked the Catholic Church's efforts to take control of formerly Catholic churches that had been Orthodox since the nineteenth century.[33] But in spite of these firm stances, the Piłsudski government ultimately gave in to most of the Church's demands, which included the granting of clerical immunity (as per a decree of 23 February 1927). These concessions did not prevent the Church from fretting about the apparent secularization of society. The establishment of Catholic Action in Poland in 1930, like the convening of the plenary synod at Częstochowa in 1936 (for the first time in three hundred years) and the International Congress of Christ the King in Poznan the following year, was a symptom of the Church's anxiety about the spread of atheism.[34]

It was the political right—rejecting notions of toleration of non-Polish culture—that was most enthusiastic about the role of the Catholic Church as protector of the Polish nation. This liaison proved abortive. As the Catholic monthly *Znak* noted in 1945 or 1946:

The problem of nationalism had especial meaning for the history of Polish Catholicism in the two decades (of the interwar period). For a large part of Polish school youth found itself under the political influence of national democracy and its student organization, Mlodziez Wszechpolska (All-Polish Union), as well as of the radical-nationalist organizations that arose in the last years before the second war. These influences led the youth to positions of radical nationalism, often of a chauvinism that called into question the rights of national minorities, linked with anti-Semitism and racism, with distinct sympathies for fascism. Moreover, those nationalist tendencies were quite usually joined with a rather strange religious formation; that was a superficial, traditional, sentimental Catholicism—a religion that did not form a world view and had a rather limited influence on mores. Odrodzenie [the Catholic academic organization], although it was an apolitical organization and jealously guarded its apolitical character, stood in sharp conflict with the circles of the "national youth," combating the latter's nationalism and anti-Semitism. For Odrodzenie, nationalism could not be conjoined with Catholicism properly understood, because nationalism was at the same time antipersonal (insofar as it subordinates the human person to the welfare of the nation) and antiuniversal (insofar as each nation is posed against other nations and insofar as [nationalism] posits the principle of struggle rather than cooperation).[35]

The Catholic Church has always been suspended between the principle of universalism and the claims of local national culture. Had the interwar republic lasted, the Church in time might have become divorced from nationalism. It was the advent of Soviet-style communism that ensured the perdurance of oppositionist nationalism on the part of the Church.

State seizure of control of the Caritas charitable organization and of much of the Church's holdings in land and livestock from January through March 1950[36] ensured that the Church would not be seen as somehow part of "the establishment." The arrest and imprisonment of Stefan Cardinal Wyszyński (1901–81), Bishop Czesław Kaczmarek, and other Catholic prelates revived the image of the suffering church and stimulated religious loyalty among the Poles. (Wyszyński remained in prison from September 1953 until October 1956.)[37] Hence, when protesting workers marched on provincial party headquarters in Poznań in June 1956, they shouted, "We want God and bread."[38] Even the suppression of all religious instruction in the schools in 1961 produced the opposite effect from that intended by the authorities; not only did the resultant network of catechistic cells thrive on Polish determination to defend their Catholic culture, but it indirectly contributed to identifying that culture with the Polish heritage.

The communist party drew the Church into nationalist concerns more directly by its efforts to rewrite Polish history through the lenses of Marxist dialectical materialism. These efforts, which downplayed the role of individuals and attempted to blot out the memory of the Church's close identification with Polish culture over the centuries, stirred the Church to action. In a series of pastoral letters, sermons, and official remonstrations presented to the government, Cardinal Wyszyński defended the Church against historical falsification.[39]

Wyszyński's "Great Novena" of 1957–66, a mass demonstration of folk piety and the bonds of Catholicism, figured in this struggle over history and, as such, was a direct challenge to the communist regime. As George Weigel has noted, Wyszyński anticipated that the regime would try to use the occasion of the Polish millennium in 1966 to engage in systematic historical revisionism; but by mounting a ten-year-long program of prayer, pilgrimage, poetry, literature, drama, and historical writing, the Catholic Church could fight to keep alive its own understanding of that history.[40] At the center of the Church's sundry activities was a "pilgrimage" of the Black Madonna herself. This icon, credited with the Polish victory over the attacking Swedish forces in 1655, was carried around the country for nine years from parish to parish, village to village. By itself, the impact of the traveling icon was tremendous.[41]

After 1970 the Church became bolder. The episcopate subsumed its concern for social justice and civil rights under Polish nationalism, linking "true democracy" with Polish traditions "since the times of the kings" and underlining the nation's "right to existence and independence."[42] In a series of sermons in 1974, Wyszyński criticized the regime for obstructing the construction of new churches, opposed the amalgamation of all youth organizations into a single Polish socialist youth organization, and underlined the Church's concern for freedom of association, press, opinion, and scientific research. To the regime's claim that Polish interests were identical to Soviet interests, Wyszyński countered that Polish interests had a life of their own, distinct from those of other countries. In Wyszyński's words:

Next to God, our first love is Poland. After God one must above all remain faithful to our Homeland, to the Polish national culture. We will love all the people in the world, but only in such an order of priority.

And if we see everywhere slogans advocating love for all the peoples and all the nations, we do not oppose them; yet above all we demand the right to live in accordance with the spirit, history, culture, and language of our own Polish land—the same which have been used by our ancestors for centuries.[43]

Hence, when at the end of 1975 the regime published its proposed changes to the Polish constitution, one of which would have based Poland's foreign policy on its "unshakable fraternal bond with the Soviet Union," the Church joined numerous intellectuals in voicing concern. Ultimately, the regime toned down the wording to read that Poland "strengthens its friendship and cooperation with the USSR and other socialist countries." In response, the episcopal conference issued a statement in March 1976 regarding these final proposals, arguing on the subject of foreign policy that nothing should be introduced into the constitution to limit the nation's sovereignty. Curiously, the Church had allied itself with the opposition to champion Polish freedom and sovereignty *against* its own government's position.

During the late 1970s the Polish Church became the chief focus of opposition, defending the underground "flying university," maintaining contacts with the workers' defense committee KOR that had been set up by a small group of intellectuals, and launching a series of "Days of Christian Culture," which provided an annual occasion for probing historical and cultural issues through lectures, concerts, poetry readings, films, art exhibits, and informal discussion groups.[44] In December 1979 the episcopate convened the 171st Plenary Session of the Conference of Polish Bishops. The bishops criticized the regime for having allowed the economic and social condition of the nation to deteriorate and issued a communiqué at the end of the conference, stating the case for internal reform. The Church had clearly and unmistakably allied itself with the moderate wing of the opposition.[45] The establishment of the independent trade union Solidarity in August 1980 permanently changed the political landscape in Poland, and from that time on, the Church ceased to be the focal point of opposition.

Not that Solidarity weakened the religio-national symbiosis in Poland. On the contrary, what the religiously inflected workers' protest in Gdańsk (July–August 1980) showed was that "after thirty-five years of socialism in Poland religious symbolism had become the only language capable of expressing the ideals of social emancipation."[46] Solidarity also was clearly a nationalist movement in that it strove to maximize the people's control over their own fate, and it stimulated a wave of expressions of anti-Russian sentiment. During 1980 and 1981 Poles reopened both the question of the Soviet massacre of thousands of Polish officers at Katyn during World War II and discussion of the Polish resistance during the war and the subsequent occupation. Solidarity set up a working group to revise the history textbooks used in Polish schools, and it invited exiled Polish writer Czesław Miłosz to come to Poland to address Polish workers.[47]

The Solidarity episode reinforced the Church's identification with nationalism in yet another way: by drawing attention to the dependence of the opposition on Church support. Thus, while some members of Solidarity clearly saw religion as inseparable from national life, others, like Adam Michnik, a member of KOR and an adviser to Solidarity, first espoused anticlerical views but then came to see the Church as an essential ally in the struggle for human and national rights. In his book, *The Church and the Left*, Michnik warned, nonetheless, that "Church attacks on 'liberals and Masons' are part of a bad tradition. They are associated with attacks on values that secular leftists hold dearest: freedom, tolerance, and human rights. It is the sound of the past one hears here, full of anger and fury."[48] The Church, for its part, cautiously welcomed Solidarity's appearance as an ally. A token of the Church-Solidarity alliance was seen at Solidarity's first national congress in Gdańsk in September 1981. It was opened with a mass concelebrated by Archbishop Józef Glemp and Bishop Kazimierz Kus of Gdańsk. Indeed, various delegates referred to the role of the Church and religion in Polish society, and the official report of Solidarity's national coordinating commission stressed the support given to Solidarity on numerous occasions by the Church.

By contrast with the pro-governmental stance taken by the Holy See in the nineteenth century, Pope John Paul II repeatedly underlined the Church's commitment to national self-determination and human rights. In a particularly striking move on 15 September 1981, John Paul II issued his encyclical *Laborem Exercens,* in which he defended the right of workers to organize unions.

After the military coup of 13 December 1981 and the suppression of Solidarity, the Catholic Church repeatedly spoke out on behalf of Polish workers. In late January 1982, for instance, the episcopal conference issued a pastoral letter demanding

a return to the normal functioning of the State, the release of all those interned, cessation of all duress on ideological grounds and of dismissals from work for political views or trade-union membership. We make it clear that the right of working people to organize themselves into independent self-governing trade unions and of the youth to form their own associations must be restored in the name of freedom.[49]

On 21 January 1982 Archbishop Glemp set up the Primate's Committee for Help to the Internees to deliver food and clothing to imprisoned members of Solidarity, dispense legal advice, provide for their religious needs, collect information on those imprisoned, and draft petitions to the authorities. Later that year, in July, the Church tried again to persuade the regime to permit Solidarity to resume legal activity. Subsequently, in a homily delivered at Jasna Gora, Archbishop Glemp identified the Church with jailed Solidarity activists and drew a pointed analogy between the workers' uprising in 1980 and the January 1863 Polish uprising against Russian tsarist rule, with which the lower clergy had displayed a similar level of sympathy. Glemp specifically demanded freedom for the interned Solidarity leader Lech Wałęsa, restoration of free trade unions, release of imprisoned Solidarity activists, and agreement on a date for a second papal visit to Poland.[50]

But it would be misleading to leave the impression that the hierarchy adopted a purely oppositionist stance. On the contrary, the posture assumed by the Church was complex and riddled with contradictions, and for every statement by one of Poland's bishops defending Solidarity and advocating Polish self-determination, another statement can be found by another bishop (or, often, by the same bishop) advising caution on the part of Poles generally, advising Poles not to resort to violence, and calling for compromise and coexistence. Nor can one ignore Glemp's willingness to transfer priests deemed "troublesome" by the regime to small and obscure parishes.[51] Glemp himself came, in time, to be called "Comrade Glemp" by his detractors.

But it is important to recognize that the increasingly political role played by the Polish Catholic Church over the years and extending into the postcommunist period (discussed in chapter 13) was a result not merely of the Church's conviction of its duty to promulgate its values throughout society, nor even of its institutional and popular strength, but of the illegitimacy of state power. It was the illegitimacy of the occupation by the partitioning powers that first brought the Polish Church into opposition politics, and the illegitimacy of communist rule revived that oppositionist role. If in the postcommunist era the Polish Church seems to become only more vocal and more ambitious, at least part of the explanation lies in institutionalized attitudes developed over decades of repression.

The Church in Hungary: Co-optive Nationalism

The Reformation was brought into Poland by immigrants, achieved a measure of toleration in the mid-sixteenth century and was by and large expunged by the mid-seventeenth century. With this development, Protestantism ceased to be an important factor in Polish national life. In Hungary and Czechoslovakia, by contrast, the manner in which Protestantism was combated in each case had long-lasting effects.

In seventeenth-century Hungary the emphasis in the early stages of the Counter-Reformation was placed on persuasion, as reflected above all in the cultural activities of Cardinal-Primate Péter Pázmány (1570–1637), founder of the University at Trnava. As Robert Kann notes, "The complete victory of the Catholic cause in the hereditary and Bohemian lands in general and the ideological fallout of the Magyar nobles' revolt under the leadership of Count [Ferenc] Wesselényi and counts Miklós and Péter Zrinyi between 1666 and 1669 helped to change all this."[52] The result was a shifting of gears as Count Leopold Kollonitsch (1631–1707), the bishop of Neutra (Nitra) and later cardinal-primate of Hungary, began to pursue policies inspired by intolerance and force. The campaign that followed was one of forced conversions, confiscation of the property of "heretics," and the jailing of Protestant ministers. In 1672 Jesuits, accompanied by soldiers, "traveled through the country forcibly converting the [religious] dissidents. Catholic magnates confiscated Protestant churches and schools on their estates, expelling ministers and teachers."[53] But unlike the Bohemian situation, where the Hussites had been identified with spiritual and national glory and in which the Battle of White Mountain provided a symbolic reference point for the simultaneous defeat of Czech national aspirations and Czech "Protestantism," the Hungarian situation involved no military confrontation of comparable magnitude or psychological resonance and hence no symbolic military defeat. Not only that, but Hungarian Protestants had been assured of religious freedom by the Habsburg authorities in 1645—an assurance that was reconfirmed in 1681, 1691, 1712, and 1781. Indeed, all told, the lands of the Hungarian crown were, among Habsburg possessions, the least affected by the Counter-Reformation. This fact is reflected in that, as of 1880, practising Catholics made up only 56.14 percent of Hungary's population; most of the remainder were Protestants.[54]

The Counter-Reformation had its effect on Church-state relations all the same. In the Counter-Reformation's aftermath the Church found that the state had already established commissions under Ferdinand I (1503–64) to check clerical misconduct and inspect monasteries and churches, and it had proscribed the sale of monastic property without government approval. Maximilian II (1527–76) had established a monastic council to supervise the administration of monasteries and convents. Conflicts concerning ecclesiastical property were now to be settled by secular courts. Later, Leopold I (1640–1705) introduced the practice of submitting other decisions by ecclesiastical courts to judicial review by secular courts.[55]

The Habsburgs expected the Catholic Church to preach obedience to secular authority, and the Church by and large did so. For this service the primate of the Hungarian Church was granted the dignity of princely rank. But the Habsburgs also wanted a tame Church, and between 1740 and 1792 (the reigns of Maria Theresa, Joseph II, and Leopold II) the chief issues in Church-state relations were state control and centralism. Maria Theresa (1717–80) barred apostolic delegates from visiting the dioceses, and she frowned on inspections of monasteries by foreign generals of orders. Her son and successor, Joseph II (1741–90), generally subjected the Church to close control, abolishing monastic schools, cutting monastic ties abroad, requiring royal approval for the promulgation of papal encyclicals and the issue of excommunications, and even prescribing the number of candles to be used in specific church services.[56] In the early 1750s, moreover, after the tax reform of 1748 abolished tax exemptions of both Church and nobility, the government assumed control of, but not administrative responsibility for, the Church's property; henceforth, the Church needed governmental approval to purchase or acquire additional land. But the Catholic Church's privileges remained extensive:

> the episcopacy was among the richest of the country's landlords. To a considerable extent, the Church regulated the spiritual life of Hungary. It controlled all schools from the elementary to the university level, and by strictly enforcing the regulations of censorship, it controlled the publication of books and thus everything the public was able to read.[57]

The Josephinian concept of the Church held that Church activity had to serve government interests and follow government regulations; it effectively treated the Church as a branch of the civil service. This concept was continued by Franz II (1768–1835) and influenced the thinking of Kaiser Franz Josef (1830–1916). The Church-state symbiosis worked in both directions. In the age of Metternich, Austrian censors devoted part of their attention to assuring the adequate protection of the Catholic faith. Catholic publications were treated with a certain favor. Protestant publications, on the other hand, "were severely censored for religious errors, although Jewish ones were the most strictly censored of all."[58] But this protection came at a price, and Catholic ecclesiastical hierarchs were noted for their docility.

The revolution of 1848–49 overthrew the old Church-state balance. In Vienna the revolutionary Reichstag even declared the disestablishment of the Roman Catholic Church.[59] After the crushing of the revolution and of Hungarian separatism, Vienna looked for a new strategy, and, in the course of the 1850s, it was decided to try to enlist the hierarchy as an "ally" of the crown. Accordingly, in 1850 new legislation expanded the powers of the bishops over the lower clergy and even freed the seminaries of state control. In line with this new approach, Vienna signed a concordat with the Holy See in 1855, granting wide-ranging concessions to the Church.[60]

This concordat ceased to apply in Hungary after the *Ausgleich* of 1867. With its autonomy now guaranteed, the Hungarian government in

Budapest abrogated the concordat and restored the religious bill drafted in 1848 during the Hungarian Revolution. It is worth recalling here that Joseph II's Edict of Toleration of 1781 had allowed individuals to convert from Catholicism to Protestantism. But the Hungarian religious bill of 1848/1867—which remained in force until 1948—went much further: it guaranteed the full equality of all religions and disestablished the Catholic Church, which had been the state religion until then.[61] Thus, from 1867 to 1918 Catholicism was the state religion in the Austrian half of the empire (including Galicia and the Czech lands of Bohemia and Moravia) but it enjoyed a more qualified status in the Hungarian half of the empire (which included Transylvania, Slovakia, and Croatia).

For a few decades after the *Ausgleich* the Budapest government clearly favored the Protestant Churches over the Catholic Church, paying subsidies to the Protestants but not to Catholics. Only in 1909 did the government agree to make a contribution to paying the salaries of the poorer members of the Catholic clergy. Education had long been the preserve of the Churches, but, beginning in the early part of the twentieth century the state had begun paying subventions for teacher salaries in ecclesiastical schools; with the subventions came state interference and the dependence of Church schools on the state. Yet the Catholic Church was still—in a backhanded sense—a "quasi-established" Church, insofar as all its responsible appointments, including archbishops, bishops, abbots, provosts, and canons, had to be approved by the government.[62] That was the legacy of Josephinism in Hungary.

The late nineteenth century was the high-water mark of Hungarian Protestant nationalism. Pushed to the geographic periphery at the time of the Habsburg Counter-Reformation, Hungarian Protestants bounced back under the *Ausgleich* and "became the rallying point of all anti-Habsburg nationalist sentiments."[63] The years from 1890 until 1895 saw a Hungarian Kulturkampf, a Protestant-backed legal campaign that introduced civil marriage, a civil register of births and deaths, and new regulations regarding children from mixed marriages; legalized divorce and a religious status; and allowed Christians to convert to Judaism. Needless to say, the Catholic Church was opposed to all of these changes. What should be underscored is that the legacy of the Hungarian Kulturkampf, which was in part anti-Catholic in inspiration, was a strong Catholic revival and the birth of a new political party, led by Count Nándor Zichy (1829-1911). Essentially a Catholic organization, Zichy's People's Party initially swore complete loyalty to the terms of the *Ausgleich* and pressed for reversal of the Kulturkampf, revision of the laws governing Church-state relations, and passage of a moderate social program to benefit the lower classes.[64]

The Roman Catholic Church in some ways became a victim of Hungarian nationalities policy, however. Specifically, in 1907 the Hungarian parliament passed a school law drafted by Albert Apponyi, minister of cults. The law mandated the closing of all confessional schools offering instruction in Romanian, Slovak, and Serbian and their replacement by state schools with instruction in Hungarian only.[65] The Catholic Church in Hungary viewed any injury to the autonomy of the Churches of the nationalities as a dangerous precedent, and the dissolution of confessional schools sharply clashed with the policy of firm support of broader religious schooling and church interests that the regime had been pursuing.[66] The law excited widespread protest and outrage in Transylvania, where mass demonstrations took place (in Bonyhad, for example, organized by Romanian priests); in Belenyes, protests against the law ended in bloody confrontations.[67]

While the *Ausgleich* era had been characterized by liberal predominance and a liberal aspiration to narrow the public role of the Churches (especially the Catholic Church), the era of Admiral Miklós Horthy (1868–1957) between the two world wars was more conservative. The Horthy government regarded the Churches as important pillars of morality and gave them extensive support. Indeed, the interwar regime discouraged irreligiosity and anticlericalism, and religion was a compulsory subject in state schools.[68]

While the Holy See sought concordats in many European countries at this time, it desisted in the case of Hungary, fearing for good reason that it could alienate non-Catholics and possibly revive the Kulturkampf. Yet the Catholic Church, perhaps more than other Churches, was clearly part of the Horthy-era establishment. Hence, in the initial upper house of the interwar Hungarian parliament, thirty-three of the 244 members enjoyed seats by reason of ecclesiastical office (nineteen Catholics, six Calvinists, four Lutherans, one Unitarian, one Greek-Orthodox, and two Jews).[69]

In interwar Hungary, which had been stripped of two-thirds of its territory and population by the punitive Treaty of Trianon (4 June 1920), revisionist irredentism was the dominant political force. All of the Churches were "nationalist" in the sense of supporting demands for the restoration of the irredenta.[70] Children were taught a Hungarian credo that summoned God's authority on behalf of irredentism: "I believe in one God. I believe in one Fatherland. I believe in eternal, divine justice. I believe in the resurrection of Hungary."[71] Moreover, Catholic and Lutheran clergy members proved enthusiastic apostles of Magyarization in the schools, steadfastly blocking the aspirations of Catholic ethnic minorities to establish schools in their own languages.[72]

When the communists took power in Hungary after World War II, they found religion stronger than in Czechoslovakia but less homogeneous and arguably less independent than in Poland. Unlike Poland, Hungary saw no hesitation by the new regime in launching policies aimed at whittling down and taming the Churches. The less organized and less centralized Protestant Churches quickly succumbed to communist pressure and made peace. The Catholic Church put up tougher resistance.

A reform in 1945 nationalized 34.6 percent of the Catholic Church's landholdings. A decree of 9 July 1945 banned most Church social organizations, including the youth organization. In September 1947 the independent Catholic press was suppressed. Between 1946 and 1948 the Church lost 3,163 of its 3,344 educational facilities, along with 600,000 of its students. And beginning with the 1949–50 school year, religious instruction ceased to be compulsory.[73] Church and state were officially separated on 18 August 1949, and on 30 June 1950 the Catholic theological faculties in Budapest and Pécs and the Evangelical theological faculty in Debrecen were separated from their respective universities. Between 6 June and 12 July 1950 security forces assaulted the country's monasteries and convents, deporting some 3,820 monks and nuns, many of whom were imprisoned and, according to Steven Polgar, tortured.[74]

Hungarian Primate József Cardinal Mindszenty (1892–1975) refused to compromise with the authorities and was arrested on 23 December 1948, remaining in prison until the revolution of October–November 1956. "József Grósz, the Archbishop of Kalocsa, followed him into prison soon afterwards, as did other Catholic and Protestant clergymen."[75] But other Catholic clergy decided to cooperate with the Stalinist regime on the regime's terms. A "peace priest" movement that came into being in the summer of 1947, was followed in August 1950 by the establishment of the Peace Committee of Hungarian Catholic Clergy under the chairmanship of Miklós Beresztóczy. The following year saw the creation of the state office for Church affairs, entrusted with the task of bringing the Churches under the regime's authority and supervision. The bishops were compelled to entrust responsible posts to "peace priests," and less cooperative prelates gradually were forced out of office. As a result, a new pattern of neo-Josephinism was inaugurated; with time it began to take on some characteristics of a co-optive relationship. In September 1966, under pressure from the Church affairs office, the episcopate established a Committee for Foreign Affairs of the Hungarian Episcopate, which provided the mechanism for state control and supervision of the foreign contacts of the Catholic Church.[76]

In 1964—by which time the Hungarian Catholic Church was only a shadow of its former self[77]—the Hungarian government of János Kádár (1912–89) signed a major agreement with the Vatican. The agreement provided that episcopal appointments were to be acceptable to both sides (an earlier stipulation of both the Habsburg and Horthy governments), that the clergy were to be bound by an oath of allegiance to the Hungarian constitution, and that the Hungarian Papal Institute in Rome was to be administered by priests acceptable to Budapest.[78]

Church-state relations became distinctly more cooperative in the 1970s. Two factors that contributed to this amelioration were the departure of Cardinal Mindszenty from Hungary in September 1971[79] and the accession of László Lékai to the posts of archbishop of Esztergom in 1974 and primate of Hungary in 1976 after Mindszenty's death in 1975. Lékai (who died in July 1986) embraced a policy of survival rather than confrontation—a choice that inevitably sparked controversy. The government welcomed this shift and decorated Lékai with the Order of the Banner of Rubies of the Hungarian People's Republic. The award was said to recognize his "exceptional efforts to promote good relations between the Hungarian State and the Catholic Church."[80] Indeed, governmental decorations of Hungarian bishops and priests became commonplace, with a veritable proliferation of honorary titles, medals, sashes, orders, and decorations for cooperative clergy.[81] A more tangible token of Church co-optation was the election of three Catholic "peace priests" (Imre Bíró of Esztergom, János Kis of the bishops' office at Székesfehérvár, and István Pregun of Hajdúdorog) to the Hungarian parliament in June 1985. Although contrary to canon law, their candidacy had been expressly approved by Cardinal Lékai.[82]

Yet change was not entirely superficial. On 17 July 1970, for instance, the Catholic news agency KNA reported that the peace committee was "no longer very successful" and would shift its focus from political problems to philosophical and educational issues. On 15 January 1975 a new regulation on religious instruction went into force, culminating long negotiations between the bishops' conference and the office for Church affairs. The regulation allowed religious instruction to be conducted twice a week on church premises on a voluntary basis.[83] In 1976 Budapest lifted its proscription on the grass-roots basic communities, which had been meeting illegally for some time, and granted them legal recognition[84] despite the fact that they had not proven amenable to supervision by either the government or the ecclesiastical hierarchy. Early in the 1970s the Bible was printed in a Hungarian-language edition of 200,000 copies, and in 1980 it was announced that secondary schools would be allowed to study the Bible as literature. In 1984 talk was heard of establishing a new Catholic religious order for women.[85] And according to figures provided by State Secretary for Church Affairs Imre Miklós, there were 497 theological students in Hungary in the 1983–84 academic year—a marked increase from the roughly three hundred in 1963–64. All the same, officially sanctioned secularism had its effects, seen most clearly in the Church's increasing difficulties in attracting young men to the priesthood. By 1988, the average age of the active clergy was close to sixty, and fewer young men entered the priesthood each year than the number of priests who had died.[86]

The 1980s saw a reawakening of national self-consciousness among Hungarians, as exemplified in the revival of interest in King Stephen (970?–1038; ruled 997–1038), who brought Christianity to Hungary, and the production of a rock opera based on his life. The Catholic Church played its part in his rediscovery, celebrating the one thousandth anniversary of his birth in 1970 and drawing attention to his "religious fervor."[87] The Hungarian Church's nationalism, unlike the Polish Church's, was consistently supportive of the Kádár regime. In an interview with the Budapest periodical *Kritika* in September 1983, for example, Bishop József Cserháti, secretary of the Hungarian conference of bishops, drew attention to "training in patriotism as a separate task [for both the state and the Church] . . . . I [have] always believed that the question of patriotism is primarily an ethical question. It is the statement of the purified, noble man toward his own kind, own brothers, own history and contemporaries."[88] The bishop continued by praising Church-state dialogue in Hungary and by slyly suggesting Church-state collaboration in the communist project of creating the New Communist Man and Woman—naturally, on the basis of Church teachings and the inspiration of the lives of the saints. In Cserháti's words:

We still suffer from the negligence or lack of Hungarian unity, the sought-after national unity. Thus, the task of the present is to form a new type of man; on the basis of the gospel, contemporary man must be told to "love your neighbor as yourself" and to "do unto others as you wish them to do unto you." In this regard, the possibilities remain unchanged: the churches are open, we are not prevented from describing an ethical humanistic vision of man from the pulpit and from inspiring people to work together to create a new Hungarian homeland. The Church can also illuminate the values from the past very effectively with their discovery, and with the introduction of Hungarian saints and outstanding personalities, we could certainly influence the present generation positively, especially the youth.[89]

Then, on the basis of this argument for the utility of the Church in buttressing nationalism and patriotism and in building socialism, Cserhati appealed for the Church to have greater access to youth and to offer more constructive criticism of social policies.

It is only when its eyes were turned outward that the Catholic Church's Hungarian nationalism assumed a critical edge in communist times. Both the Catholic and Protestant press amply discussed the difficulties of the Hungarian diaspora in Slovakia and Transylvania, and, according to Leslie László, "they were the first to open their columns to contributions from Magyar writers and scholars in the successor states."[90] Yet even here the Church conformed to policy objectives of the regime. The Hungarian Church under communism had reverted to a Josephinian cast.

The communist political monopoly in Hungary disappeared in 1989. This dramatic change was reflected in the passage of a new law concerning religion on 24 January 1990, which ended state interference in Church affairs. As the communist chapter of its history ended, however, the Catholic Church joined the Lutheran, Reformed, and Evangelical Churches in reexamining their recent past and admitting their complicity in supporting the communist dictatorship.[91]

The Church in Czechoslovakia: A Mixed National Heritage

Although most citizens of Czechoslovakia were nominally Catholic as of 1985—with 36 percent of the residents of the Czech lands and more than half of Slovaks counted as believers[92]—the Catholic Church in Czechoslovakia is neither national nor, where the Czechs are concerned, nation-

alist. It was not national in the sense in which the Church is national in
Poland and Hungary because no Czechoslovak nation ever existed; the
split of the country during 1992 into independent Czech and Slovak republics only confirmed that its halves had autonomous national histories
and identities. And in the Czech lands of Bohemia and Moravia, where
most Czechs lived, the Catholic Church, far from being nationalist, was
widely viewed as divorced from or outside the authentic national tradition. Hence, its institutional weakness.

Two developments ensured the disassociation of Catholicism and
Czech national feeling. The first was the religious reform movement in
the fourteenth and fifteenth centuries, which resulted in the emergence
of the Hussites, whose radical faction grew into the Unity of Czech
Brethren. This movement, though strictly illegal for some 150 years,
nonetheless became the most widely diffused congregation among the
Czechs (before the 1620s).[93] Jan Hus (martyred in 1415) was the movement's central figure. He polished the Czech vernacular and inspired an
armed rebellion that was finally subdued only in the 1430s. The movement bequeathed to the Czechs the idea of a Czech national Church, a
"Hussite" Church.

The second development that ensured the disassociation of Catholicism and Czech national sentiment came two hundred years later with
the defeat of the Czech Protestants by Catholic Austria at the Battle of
White Mountain (8 November 1620). Ironically, as late as 1609 Kaiser
Rudolf II (1552–1612) issued a letter of toleration, legalizing both the
Lutheran "Utraquists" (Evangelicals) and the Unity of Czech Brethren
and granting them the right to build churches and schools. At that time,
more than 90 percent of Czechs may have been Protestant, though most
of the Czech nobility had returned to Catholicism.[94]

Actually, the Catholic establishment had begun its Counter-Reformation in Bohemia in the 1560s, and it was showing some results within
a decade. The years leading up to 1618 saw growing uncertainty in the
rivalry between the armed camps of Protestants and Catholics in Bohemia, leading to a Protestant revolt in the war of 1618–20, which in turn
ignited the Thirty Years War. Ferdinand II (1578–1637), who had become emperor in 1619, was only too glad to have done with Protestantism—which he equated with disloyalty.[95] The war resulted in the total
defeat of Protestant arms and the flight of Protestant King Friedrich V
von der Pfalz (1596–1632) from Bohemia. After White Mountain, Protestantism was banned; Protestants were persecuted; Protestant nobility

were driven abroad and their estates turned over to "reliable" Catholics (including Germans, Walloons, Frenchmen, Spaniards, Irish, and Italians); the Jesuits were put in control of all higher education in Bohemia; and uncounted books and manuscripts were confiscated and burned.[96] Ferdinand II's attitude was summed up in his comment, "A desert is better than a country with heretics."[97] Protestantism was declared to be a crime punishable by death. Accordingly, the population of Bohemia and Moravia fell from about 3 million to some 900,000 people as Ferdinand's forces applied pressure to bring about the re-Catholicization of the Czechs.[98] The resultant "Ferdinandian Church" was quintessentially antinational.

The Czechs lost the right of self-rule; much of the Czech cultural heritage was destroyed by the Jesuits; and German settlers were brought in to fill the sudden demographic vacuum. German quickly became the dominant language of government and business. Hence, the glories of the baroque period were associated in the public mind with Habsburg rule, that is, with foreign overlordship. Indeed, the unity of purpose of Habsburg political power and Catholic religious power was unmistakable in Czech eyes. Not only was the Roman Catholic faith enshrined as the official religion of state, but under a law passed in 1874 the government was authorized to regulate internal Church affairs. This, in turn, meant that the Church had no *legal* basis for objecting to state policies, since it was legally subordinate to the state.[99]

During the nineteenth century, when nations created nationalism by looking to their pasts, the Czechs reclaimed Hussite Protestantism as the national ideology. This reawakening was reflected in the conversion of sundry Czech intellectuals (including Tomáš Masaryk) to Protestantism and culminated at the end of 1918 in the creation of a revived Hussite church after the establishment of the Czechoslovak Republic.[100]

The Czechs could not overlook the preponderance of German aristocrats among the leading Catholic Church dignitaries in Habsburg Bohemia or the Church's distance from the Czech national renaissance of the nineteenth and early twentieth centuries. During World War I, as sentiment for independence grew among Czechs, the Catholic Church again remained aloof. The end of the war saw an upsurge of anti-Catholic and anticlerical feeling among the Czechs, who saw the establishment of the Czechoslovak Republic as the reversal of White Mountain, which in turn was blamed on the Counter-Reformation. Strikingly, in November 1918, in one of the first gestures of independence:

Exultant Czechs tore down and demolished the statue of the Virgin Mary, "Our Lady of Victory" in the Old City Square of Prague. The statue was seen as a reminder of White Mountain, and at this historic moment—the birth of a new state—Czech nationalism expressed itself in a symbolic act of vengeance against the Catholic Church. Nor did it stop there. In the first year after the war, hundreds of statues of the Madonna, of St. John Nepomucene, and of St. Wenceslaus were destroyed, and about three hundred churches were expropriated by the authorities. Significantly, . . . these acts of vengeance were confined to the Czech parts of the country; the Slovaks did not succumb to the anti-Catholic temper of their Czech compatriots.[101]

The new Czechoslovak government supported Hussite churches and festivities and viewed the creation of a schismatic Czech National (Hussite) Church with favor. This national Church, set up by a group of alienated Catholic clergymen, was antipapal and pro-nationalist, using the vernacular in the liturgy and introducing a variety of changes, including lay representation on parish governing bodies and the abolition of priestly celibacy. Czechoslovak President Tomáš Masaryk (1850-1937), a freethinker, obtained a separation law on the French model and introduced a series of statutes inspired by Czech anticlericalism and French precedent.[102] Czech anti-Catholicism lost much of its steam by the 1930s, however, and Czech Catholics were able to assume their places in Czech politics and social life.[103] At least part of the credit for this development goes to Fr. Jan Šrámek, founder of the Czechoslovak People's Party and government minister from 1921 until 1938.[104]

Slovakia had been an integral part of Hungary since 1000 and naturally remained under Budapest's jurisdiction after the signing of the 1867 *Ausgleich;* the Church in Slovakia was therefore shaped by the religious and nationalities policies fashioned in Budapest. Above all, the ecclesiastical hierarchy's support of Magyarization, while wedding it to Hungarian nationalism, alienated nationally conscious Slovaks. After World War I, de-Magyarization was often associated with anticlerical sentiment.[105] At the same time, however, the Slovaks found an advocate in Fr. Andrej Hlinka (1864-1938), a charismatic orator who denounced *Ausgleich* Hungary's policy toward Slovaks and rebelled against the hierarchy for its support of that policy. Hlinka went on to found the Slovak People's Party, which worked for Slovak autonomy.

Already in 1919, as he was en route to the peace talks in Paris, Hlinka drew the connection between Catholic loyalism and autonomism:

When Catholicism is persecuted, monasteries are taken away and monks chased out, the Hussites and the Protestants keep their properties. . . . Nothing will help us against it but autonomy. . . . They insult our religion, they take away our faith, and that is the reason, and nothing else, for which I set out on the journey! . . . Today we don't need so much the national or economic principle as we need the religious principle.[106]

Hlinka never retreated from his interpretation, struggling persistently for a Slovak autonomism that he interpreted as regional confessional autonomism. Shortly before his death in 1938, Hlinka received a visit from Karl Frank, a parliamentary deputy of the Sudeten German Party, at Hlinka's home in Ružomberok. Hlinka indicated to Frank that he was in favor of cooperation with Konrad Henlein's (Nazi) Sudeten German Party, and he professed to see in Henlein an advocate of "the great role of Catholicism in the fight against Bolshevism which threatens Christian culture."[107] But, as James Felak has pointed out, in spite of friendly public professions on both sides, Hlinka was perturbed by certain anti-Catholic policies being carried out in Nazi Germany, and he was concerned, too, about German support for the pro-Hungarian Slovak émigré, František Jehlička.[108] Ultimately, Hlinka's successor, Msgr. Jozef Tiso (1887–1947), found himself charged with administration of the nominally independent Nazi puppet state of Slovakia. Because of this development, and in particular because of the activity of the Slovak People's Party and the experience of the wartime Slovak Republic, Catholicism has not become similarly divorced from Slovak national consciousness.

Although most Slovak Catholic clergy supported Tiso's quisling regime, a few joined the opposition, along with most Slovak Lutheran ministers. Protestants resented the regime's close identification with Catholicism and flocked to the resistance. As a result, the regime muzzled the Protestant press and put Protestant ministers in prison.[109]

As the war drew to a close, the provisional government promised complete religious freedom. But even before the communist coup, the Slovak National Council—which consisted entirely of communist and Protestant members—ordered the nationalization of all Church schools in Slovakia on 16 May 1945. In the first weeks of the provisional government, important publishing houses of the Catholic Church were nationalized, several Church newspapers were suspended, and others were throttled by the cutoff of paper supplies.[110] Even at this stage some leading Catholic figures were being arrested, including Bishop M. Buzálka of Trnava and Bishop Jan Vojtaššák of Spiš. It is clear that, independent of the communist takeover in 1948, Czechoslovakia was susceptible to anticlerical programs.

Once it had carried out its coup, the communist party ordered crosses to be taken out of the schools, removed teachers and professors who belonged to religious orders, eliminated religious instruction in the middle schools (the equivalent of American high schools), abolished the Central Catholic Agency (the executive organ of the bishops of Czechoslovakia), and banned the League of Catholic Women. In February 1949 the bishops tried to reach an accommodation with the regime, which demanded a declaration of loyalty and the reinstatement of certain "progressive" priests. Shortly thereafter, Czech priest Josef Plojhar drew up a manifesto calling for a new Catholic movement that would be free of "foreign" (i.e., Vatican) control. That revived sentiments of the "*Los von Rom*" tendency that had gained currency in the late nineteenth century and was understandably viewed by the bishops as a schismatic movement. In 1949 Plojhar organized the association of "patriotic priests."[111] At the same time, the Greek-Rite Catholic Church was banned, Uniate parishes were forcibly placed under Orthodox jurisdiction, and the term *Greek Catholic* soon disappeared from Slovak dictionaries.

As of 1945, the Roman Catholic Church had a theological faculty in Bratislava (separated from the University of Bratislava that year) and theological seminaries in Nitra, Spišska Kapitula, Banská Bystrica, Košice, Žilina, and Sv. Križ; the Greek Catholic Church had a seminary in Prešov; the Protestant Church of the Augsburg Confession had a seminary in Modra near Bratislava. In August 1950 the regime closed all existing seminaries and in their place set up the Cyril and Methodius Faculty for Catholics in Bratislava and a theological faculty for Evangelicals. The regime also ordered all theologians to enroll in a political awareness class during the summer of 1950; the course included instruction in Marxism. Of some four hundred Catholic theologians, only twenty-four enrolled.[112] Not until 1968 did the bishops reestablish their control over the seminary.

In 1950 police seized the monasteries and convents, locked up the 3,000 monks and 10,000 nuns in "concentration monasteries" or placed them in work camps, and launched a press campaign accusing them of participating in bacchanalian sex orgies and plotting "counterrevolution." The population had already been tranquilized by a series of strategic arrests. But in many Slovak villages police were unable to arrest pastors, whom the villagers guarded day and night.[113]

The religious climate remained oppressive until the Prague Spring of

1968. Then, during Alexander Dubček's brief rule, Plojhar's organization of "patriotic priests" was closed, the Catholic Church was allowed
to set up its own clerical organization, and the Uniate Church was legalized again.[114] Those priests still languishing in prison were released in
May 1968.[115] The Dubček era, however fleeting, had its lasting effects.
In an internal memorandum in 1970 Slovak government administrators, after bemoaning the fact that religious consciousness was allegedly
spreading, explained that the Dubček episode had restored Christians'
self-confidence.[116] Another official document, smuggled out of Czechoslovakia in 1974, said that the number of atheists in Slovakia was stag-
nant, that workers were anti-atheist, and that too many youths were
enrolled in religious instruction; it also urged the necessity of preventing
Christian girls from becoming medical nurses.[117]

A quarterly journal devoted to atheism was launched in 1973, and
the Husák regime extended its "normalization" program to the religious
sphere. Under regulations issued by the state in March 1975, seminarians
were forbidden to have (1) contact with any lay persons except family,
(2) free movement outside the seminary other than in groups and with
permission of the authorities, and (3) any radio equipment or foreign
literature on hand. Churches were barred from any activity with youth
other than limited religious instruction, and as regime pressure began to
produce results, 1976 saw a rapid drop in the number of children attending religious instruction. The seminary was controlled by the ministry of
culture, the Church was supervised by the state office for Church affairs,
and even the clergy in many cases, depended on the state for salary subsidies and pensions. In fact, the communist state used its salary stipends
to reward priests who gave up religious instruction, avoided contact with
young people, and preached less frequently. As a result, Slovakia had
impoverished priests living alongside rich ones. In this atmosphere of
planned stultification, clergy tended to prefer evasion to confrontation,
accommodation to martyrdom, shrewdness to defiance. As Teinhold
Lehmann put it in 1983, "There is no high regard in this country for the
hero who is prepared to act in desperation. The goal is survival."[118]

In 1980, in the face of the outbreak of labor protests in Poland, the
Czechoslovak regime intensified its containment strategy and stepped
up raids on Church members and arrests of clergy. (This campaign, as
well as later developments, are described in chapter 5.)

A few words should be said about the contrast between Czech and Slovak religiosity. According to official government statistics released in the

mid-1980s, 71.6 percent of all children born in Slovakia in 1984 were baptized, compared with 31.2 percent in Bohemia and Moravia; 53 percent of all weddings in Slovakia that year were church weddings, compared with only 15.8 percent in the Czech lands; and 80.5 percent of Slovak funerals were held in church, compared with 50.6 percent of Czech.[119]

The difference in religiosity between Czechs and Slovaks was more graphically displayed at the commemorative ceremonies on the occasion of the 1,100th anniversary of the death of St. Methodius, bishop of Moravia, held in the Moravian village of Velehrad on 7 July 1985. Though Methodius lived and worked in the traditional Czech lands, the ceremonies attracted 100,000 to 200,000 Slovaks, many singing religious hymns, but only "a sprinkling" of Czechs.[120]

The contrasts between Czech and Slovak religiosity result from differences in national heritage, history, availability and selection of intellectual leaders in the nineteenth century (mainly secular intellectuals in the Czech lands; mainly Lutheran pastors, as well as some Catholic priests, in Slovakia), and even levels of urbanization. Taken collectively, these differences have translated into those in the Church-state relationship and in the vulnerability of the Catholic Church to pressure in the Czech lands as opposed to the Slovak lands. Thus, the rehabilitation of Fr. Hlinka and Msgr. Tiso after 1989 might appear, in Slovakia, to signify a nation's reclaiming of legitimate heroes.[121] In the Czech lands these rehabilitations were inevitably perceived in another light.

Conclusion

This concise comparative history has emphasized the evolution of patterns of institutional behavior, the legacy of the Counter-Reformation and of variegated Habsburg religious policy, and the genesis of popular attitudes toward religion, tying them to considerations of nationalism. The argument, in brief, has been that a state's religious policy has a direct impact on religio-national symbiosis, which in turn shapes the environment in which Church-state relations subsequently evolve. Central to this analysis has been the assumption that popular attitudes, routine policy proclivities, and even institutional resources are affected by trends spanning decades and even centuries.

The overall conclusions can be summarized as follows. First, national traumas (e.g., the partition of Poland or the Battle of White Mountain and ensuing Counter-Reformation), insofar as they have direct religious consequences, are apt to become part of a religio-national mythology linking religion and nationalism. Second, the closer the linkage of religion and nationalism, the less able an anticlerical government will be to assault religious institutions. The clear correlation between religio-national symbiosis and relative policy liberality under communism across these three countries provides supporting evidence. Third, while the Counter-Reformation restored the numerical preponderance of Catholicism, it also created and reinforced a tradition of anticlericalism, at least in the Czech lands. Fourth, in Poland, Czechoslovakia, and Hungary, the role of the Catholic Church in resisting foreign domination has been directly correlated with national symbiosis and overall confessional strength. The Church is strongest in Poland, where, since 1795, it most often has been in opposition. The "Josephinian Church" syndrome exemplified in Hungary preserves the nationalist character of the Church but not its opposition role, and the legacy in the communist era was a pattern of accommodation—arguably, out of necessity. The "Ferdinandian Church" syndrome, as exemplified by the Catholic Church among the Czechs, combines an antinational demeanor with co-optation by an antinational, foreign power (the Habsburg empire). Its legacy includes estrangement from the people, powerful currents of anticlericalism, and confessional weakness. And fifth, among the peoples whose nationalism has been predominantly oppositionist (defensive) in character—Poles, Czechs, Slovaks—the Churches which supported that opposition have retained their strength and their nationalist base.

Chapter 5

The Catholic Church Among
the Czechs and Slovaks

When communist countries and their policies are compared, their common roots must be acknowledged. Their shared ontogenesis had historical, political, and cultural dimensions. Hence, even as diverse forms of communism evolved in specific national contexts and under the influence of local cultural conditions, these forms developed specific strains that preserved earlier currents and modes of thinking, depending on a host of factors, including generational experiences and local conditions.

In the religious sphere this diversity was manifested in a wide range of policy differences, even within East Central Europe. In the German Democratic Republic and in Titoist Yugoslavia, Church and state achieved a kind of mutual understanding and modus vivendi. In these two systems, religious rights were by and large respected and dramatic examples of Church-state cooperation occurred (such as the Luther celebrations in the GDR in 1983 and the resumption of construction of St. Sava's Cathedral in Belgrade beginning in 1986). In Czechoslovakia and Romania, by contrast, entire denominations remained illegal throughout the communist era (the Jehovah's Witnesses and Nazarenes in Czechoslovakia, the Greek-Rite Catholics in Romania), and conditions even for legal Churches were harsh and often unpredictable. If the fifteenth-century religious reformer Jan Hus had been a German from the region that became the GDR, he would have been the object of major state-sponsored celebrations; as he was a Czech from Bohemia, the Czechoslovak Communist Party (CzCP) only saw him as positive insofar as he was critical of the pope and the established Church.

Advocates of Church-state dialogue, including those in East Central Europe, sometimes would say that Marxism would be fine if only atheism were taken out of it (to which could be replied, Christianity would be fine if only God were taken out of it). Even certain Marxist theorists (e.g., Ivan Cvitković in Yugoslavia in the mid-1980s) suggested that a de-atheization of official Marxism was not an excluded possibility.

For communists, however, atheism figured in two important ways. First, it was seen as a *political* prerequisite to the establishment of a complete institutional monopoly. Atheism was politically necessary as long as a communist regime aspired to break the allegiance of people to the Churches and as long as a regime feared that the Churches might serve as institutional foci for rival loyalties. The fear of the Churches as institutional rivals was explicitly voiced by the journal *Questions of Peace and Socialism* in 1986, for example.[1] And while it is true that the aspiration to achieve and maintain institutional monopoly had been attenuated in various communist countries by the mid-1980s (Yugoslavia, Poland, and Gorbachev's USSR come to mind), change was much slower in Czechoslovakia, where bureaucratic forces resisted any small concessions until the entire system finally collapsed.

Second, for communists, atheism was *culturally* necessary. In its early utopian (Stalinist) phase communism aspired to create a universal culture — this, without realizing that, formally at least, a universal culture is a contradiction in terms. Etymologically and ontogenetically, culture is a value system of the cult, just as a party is the political mouthpiece of a part of the body politic, not of the whole. While culture has produced diverse variegations that often move far beyond any religious or "cult" boundary, the prominence of religion in promoting past and present culture is betrayed in everything from Bach cantatas to the cathedral at Chartres, to the frescoes in the Sistine Chapel, to the rhythmic Missa Luba that gained widespread Western recognition in the 1960s, to the Alan Hovhaness *Magnificat*. The essence of Stalinism, thus, was the aspiration to end politics and to redefine the meaning of culture, replacing politics, as Marx had suggested, with the "administration of things," and transforming culture in accordance with procedures of central planning. The aspiration to create a universal culture has been dead for some time. But for many years, communists in Czechoslovakia and elsewhere continued to think in terms of creating an atheist culture, defined as one whose artifacts derive from so-called class concepts defined by the party, and hence not derived from ecclesiastical sources. So we are back to politics. Culture, it seems, is the ideational bedrock of politics. If the regime can mold culture, it can mold the sources of political ideas, political meanings, and political language. Political control will be secured at its source. Indeed, in a 1985 essay, Leszek Kolakówski described communism itself as a "cultural formation."[2]

The concept of atheist culture was attacked in 1986 by the poet Yevgeni

Yevtushenko (b. 1933) in the Soviet newspaper *Komsomol'skaia pravda*, sparking a debate in intellectual circles about the relationship between religion and culture.[3] For Yevtushenko, there is no culture aside from what is religiously derived. This is surely an overstatement; what may be said is that the major premises underlying much of contemporary culture may be traced to certain aspects of specific religious heritages. In and of itself, the possibility of culture that is atheist should not be excluded. But it is clear that communist culture was not merely atheist; it was party-molded. In fact, it is more nearly accurate and much more useful to speak of communism as party-molded culture rather than as atheist culture, since the concept of atheist culture could refer to spontaneous and uncontrolled development.

The Political Apparatus and the Structure of Control

The supervision and control of religious life in communist Czechoslovakia was entrusted to the state office for religious affairs, which was established by law no. 217 in October 1949. This body, which was subordinated to the ministry of culture, supervised all activity of the Churches: approving and censoring all pastoral letters and other intraecclesiastical communications; monitoring the activities of all clergy; and, through state-appointed commissars ("Church secretaries"), controlling the day-to-day administration of the dioceses.

The communist state paid the salary of clergy (an obligation incurred by the state in the eighteenth century, in compensation for Josef II's nationalization of Church lands), but it did so in a discriminatory fashion to reward clergy it favored and to punish those it did not.[4] The state also reserved the right to disapprove all church construction or repairs, issued sacerdotal licenses authorizing priests to say Mass or otherwise carry out the priestly office, and severely restricted the foreign travel of its clergy. In 1987, for example, when Pope John Paul II convoked an episcopal synod in Rome, the only delegates who failed to obtain permission from their governments to attend were the two delegates from Czechoslovakia and the one from Laos.[5]

Moreover, the admissions, hiring, and curricula at the country's six theological faculties (two of them—at Bratislava and Prague—Catholic) were controlled by the state. These, like the two Catholic seminaries (in Litoměřice and Bratislava), were in effect state-run institutions.

For example, the dean of the theological faculty in Bratislava for years was an official who regularly countermanded the wishes of the bishops.[6] Exploiting its control of admissions, the state systematically choked off enrollments. In 1984, ninety-four people from Bohemia and Moravia applied for admission to the seminary at Litoměřice; the regime approved admission for only thirty-eight.[7] As a result of these constrictive policies, the number of active priests steadily fell. Through most of the 1980s in Slovakia fifty priests were dying each year, while only thirty new priests were being ordained. And whereas Bratislava had 160 Catholic priests for 150,000 inhabitants in 1948, it had only twenty for 400,000 in 1987.[8]

The seminaries themselves were under the control of the ministry of culture, which took precautions to cut the seminarians off from contact with the population. Seminarians were forbidden to have foreign religious literature in their possession or to listen to foreign broadcasts; special permission was required before they could leave the confines of the seminary for any purpose.[9] Partly to enforce these measures, the state security service habitually recruited informers from among young seminarians and theology students.[10] In addition, members of the secret police were trained as priests at the Litoměřice seminary, according to some seminarians there.[11]

One of the most important institutional instruments of regime control was the priests' association, Pacem in Terris, which was established in late August 1971 after the Prague Spring had swept away the earlier pro-regime Peace Committee of Catholic Clergy. Condemned by both the Vatican and Prague's František Cardinal Tomášek (1899–1992), who had become apostolic administrator of Prague in 1965, Pacem in Terris propounded the regime line and kept its members docile and cooperative. An official in the office for religious affairs described Pacem in Terris as "a part of our social structure."[12] It was clearly not part of the Church. The association never helped to ease conditions for religious instruction. It turned a blind eye to regime harassment of priests and to its insistence that a state license be required for saying Mass. And it ignored security police recruitment of young seminarians. In any dispute between the Church leadership and the state, the leadership of Pacem in Terris simply agreed mechanically with whatever was said by the minister for religious affairs.[13] As a West German publication put it in 1983, "the priests' association 'serves and helps' neither the believers and priests nor the Church, but rather the construction of social society."[14] Only 5 percent of the priests in Bohemia and Slovakia and 10 percent in Moravia were members of Pacem in Terris as of 1988.

Finally, in contrast to East Germany, for example, where the Churches made their episcopal appointments independently and merely informed the state, in Czechoslovakia the communist state enjoyed the prerogative of approving—in effect, controlling—all episcopal and hierarchical appointments. This prerogative was inherited ultimately from the Habsburg empire and passed down to the communists by the First and Second Czechoslovak Republics. The regime used this power to try to ensure that, as bishops' sees became vacant, they were entrusted to collaborationist clergy, specifically to members of Pacem in Terris. But the Vatican balked at this, with the result that by mid-1972, only one of Czechoslovakia's thirteen dioceses had a resident bishop. The following year, however, the Vatican decided to accept the regime's terms, and the two sides agreed on the appointment of four new bishops: Jozef Feranec, Ján Pasztor, Julius Gabris, and Jozef Vrana. All four were members of Pacem in Terris, while Vrana, in addition, had been serving as the association's president.[15] The Vatican hoped to fill the remaining eight vacancies with nonmembers of Pacem in Terris, but throughout most of the 1980s it failed to come to any agreement with Prague.[16] This situation changed only in 1988 with the appointment of three new bishops, none of them members of Pacem in Terris: Ján Lebeda (seventy-five) and Antonin Liška (sixty-three) were appointed auxiliary bishops to the ailing František Cardinal Tomášek in Prague, while 54-year-old Ján Sokol was appointed bishop and apostolic administrator of Trnava following the death of Archbishop Gabris. At the same time, once having secured it, the regime was evidently intent on keeping a firm grasp on the diocese of Olomouc; following the death of the incumbent Bishop of Olomouc Fr. František Vymetal, Jozef Vrana's successor as president of Pacem in Terris, was advanced by Vrana to assume responsibility for Olomouc. Finally, in April 1988 Tibor Spišak was appointed temporary apostolic administrator of Rožnava, following the death of the 74-year-old vicar capitular, Zoltán Belak.[17]

Aside from these sundry mechanisms, mention should be made of the professional atheists whose job it was to undercut popular trust in the Churches. The Institute for Scientific Atheism in Bratislava, established in 1971 as a principal center for professional atheism, published a bimonthly journal, *Atheism*. There was an Institute of Scientific Atheism attached to the Czechoslovak Academy of Science. In addition, a faculty of atheism had been attached to every university in Slovakia by the early 1970s.[18]

The Central Features of Regime Strategy

Five features were central to the communist strategy toward the Catholic Church in Czechoslovakia:

(1) Smash its infrastructure;

(2) seize control of its surviving institutions;

(3) launch a concerted atheization campaign in the schools and public life;

(4) divide the Catholic Church from other Churches;

(5) divide the hierarchy from the lower clergy.

First, the communists smashed the infrastructure of the Church. Many of the Church's elementary schools, high schools, and vocational schools had been nationalized in 1945, and, shortly after the communist coup in February 1948, the state nationalized the remaining private and ecclesiastical schools, including kindergartens. Catholic Action was dissolved by state decree on 22 November 1948 and replaced with a state-controlled agency taking the same name. A month later, the Catholic Union of Slovak Women was dissolved and its branches were ordered to integrate into the structure of the communist women's organization. The Church's youth and other social organizations also were suppressed. The communists moved quickly against the Church's publishing activity. In January 1949 twenty-five religious magazines (five weeklies, two biweeklies, fifteen monthlies, one bimonthly, and two quarterlies) were shut down, along with parish periodicals.[19] The publishing house of the Salesians was closed, and five other Catholic book publishing houses were assigned special commissars to supervise their work. Bishop Jan Vojtaššák of Spiš and Bishop M. Buzálka of Trnava protested these actions and as a result were imprisoned for several months.[20] Tomášek himself, at that time bishop of Olomouc, was taken into custody in July 1951 and interned in Zeliv until May 1954.[21] Most of the Church's seminaries and theological teaching institutions were closed down.

In 1950 monastic life was forcibly terminated. Male and female orders were forced to disband and forbidden to accept new members. Many monks and nuns were arrested and incarcerated in so-called "concentration monasteries." Altogether, some five hundred monasteries and convents were confiscated. A few were used as prisons; most were converted to other uses, without compensation to the Church. Many priests were drafted into the army, where they were typically assigned to heavy labor on meager rations.[22] Others were sent to forced labor camps. As of October 1950, some two thousand Catholic clergy were in prisons or work camps.[23] Despite the ban, at least some of the orders, including the Franciscans, were kept alive and continued to recruit new members underground.[24]

Taken in sum, these draconian measures were designed to destroy the Church's ability to conduct its institutional life in a normal way. Leaving aside Albania, where religious life was completely banned from 1967 to 1990, the only parallels in Eastern Europe were Bulgaria and Romania.

Second, having smashed much of the Church's infrastructure, the communists sought to seize control of what they had allowed to remain (e.g., the charitable organization Caritas, the seminaries, theological faculties, and the diocesan offices themselves), and at the same time they created a series of bogus Catholic institutions ranging from the pseudo-Catholic Action to the Peace Committee of Catholic Clergy (headed by the defrocked and excommunicated Jozef Plojhar) to the regime's newspaper, *Katolické noviny,* to an advisory body known as the "Church Six," which included Plojhar and was subordinated to the presidium of the communist party's central committee.[25]

Religious policy was centralized and conducted through various organs. Initially, the state security service was entrusted with responsibility for supervising the Churches. Later, in 1949, a Senate for Church penalties was established within the framework of the judiciary with the task of assessing penalties for ecclesiastical "infractions" of the law. In October 1949 the state office for religious affairs was established; its jurisdiction extended to monitoring and supervising the Church's financial activities. Alexej Čepička was named the office's first chairman. Finally, in June 1950 a special coordination commission was established, which consisted of representatives from the state office for Churches, from the state security service, from the ministry of justice, and from the general procuracy; a branch office was established in Bratislava to coordinate policy in Slovakia.[26]

In all dioceses, the episcopal ordinariat was subordinated to a local commissar who supervised all Church activity, even including the bishops' pastoral letters. The Church's newsletter for the clergy was replaced by a state newsletter, the *Gazette of the Roman Catholic Clergy;* the bishops, of course, had no control over the newsletter's contents.

Archbishop Josef Beran managed to circumvent state controls and arrange for the clandestine distribution of two pastoral letters, dated 28 May and 15 June 1949. In these, he condemned the *Gazette,* along with several other journals aimed at Catholics, and he banned clerical participation in pseudo-Catholic Action on pain of excommunication. After Beran's arrest on 19 June, the remaining archbishops and bishops managed to hold a final independent meeting, at which they issued a joint pastoral letter, providing details of state harassment and repression. The government responded by requiring that all meetings of the clergy be preapproved by the state and by making the subscription to and retention of the *Gazette of the Roman Catholic Clergy* mandatory for all Church functionaries.[27]

The communist party pursued this tactic of trying to establish its control over religious life with such consistency that it even started sponsoring pilgrimages. In doing so, the party hoped that it could arrange for "progressive" speeches to be given at the shrines, which would win the believers over to communism. However, priests and believers stayed away from these events, ironically forcing the party to order its members and trade unionists to attend so that the party would not lose face.

Seizing control of the Church's institutions necessarily meant establishing a measure of control over the bishops themselves. Aside from the assignment of "church secretaries" to the bishops, the party tried to promote the advancement of compliant bishops. For example, in January 1950 Bishop Skrabik of Banská Bystrica died, and the metropolitan chapter elected Msgr. Daniel Briedom to the office of vicar capitular; the state office for religious affairs refused to recognize his election, however, and instead appointed Decan Jan Dechet, a "patriotic priest" excommunicated by the pope, as administrator of the diocese. The state also unilaterally named priests from pseudo-Catholic Action to serve as canons in the metropolitan chapters. On 3 March 1951 four new canons (all "patriotic priests") were installed at the metropolitan chapter in Prague, among them Antonin Stehlik, a parish priest from Holesovice; five days later, upon the forced resignation of the incumbent vicar general, Stehlik was named vicar capitular of the archdiocese of Prague. In fact, between November 1950 and March 1951 ten of the thirteen dioceses of the Catholic Church received new vicars capitular. Finally, on 14 March 1951 Bishops Picha of Hrádec Králové, Čarský of Košice, Trochta of Litoméřice, and Lazik of Trnava took the state's oath of loyalty in the hope of preventing the transfer of all dioceses into the hands of "patriotic priests." Some five years later, in October 1956, Bishop Robert Pobozny, who had been removed from his duties in Rožnava for refusing to take the oath of loyalty, finally agreed to take the oath and was then allowed to resume his episcopal office.

From the party's point of view, Bishop Vrana of Olomouc was a model bishop. Vrana, who died in 1987, kept strict silence about the difficulties facing the Church and refused any form of contact with discontents. In December 1977, for instance, a group of Catholics in the Moravian town of Kroměříž drew up a document detailing the conditions in which the Catholic Church functioned and outlining some proposals for realizing religious freedom in Czechoslovakia; they submitted it as a petition to Cardinal Tomášek and to Bishop Vrana, in the hope that it would be discussed at the episcopal level. Vrana returned it unanswered, while Tomášek gave the petition his public endorsement.[28] Later, in the wake of *Quidam episcopi,* the papal encyclical proscribing membership in politically oriented priests' associations, Cardinal Oddi, prefect of the Congregation of the Clergy (in Rome), issued a pastoral letter making it explicit that the injunction in *Quidam episcopi* applied to Pacem in Terris; Tomášek sent a copy of Oddi's letter to Bishop Vrana (a member of Pacem in Terris) but received no reply.

Atheism in the Schools

Third, the communist party launched a coordinated drive in the schools and media to undercut popular support for the clergy and the Church by sowing doubts about Church doctrines. The party was emphatically clear about the incompatibility of religion and communism. *Rudé pravo* asserted in 1953 that "every religion, with its faith in eternal life, with its preaching of humility, resignation to fate, love even to the enemy, with its rejection of the active fight of the workers for true happiness on earth is in absolute and sharp contradiction to the communist world view."[29] In December 1957 the Central Section of Scientific Atheism of the Czechoslovak Society for the Dissemination of Political and Scientific Knowledge organized a four-day conference in Prague on how best to carry out antireligious work in schools and public life. In July 1959 the national assembly passed a law on educational activities to carry out a "cultural revolution in the period of completion of the socialist construction in our country."[30] During 1959 state filmmakers started to produce anti-Catholic movies, often drawing on Hussite themes: for example, "Jan Hus," "Jan Žižka," "Against All," and "Fates of the Fearless."[31] And from 1948 onward, it became impossible to publish any books that portrayed religion positively, whether in the fields of philosophy, ecclesiology, or history or the lives of the saints.[32]

The schools, of course, received special attention. The Czechoslovak constitution of 1960 specified that all education would be conducted "in the spirit of the scientific world view of Marxism-Leninism."[33] In accord with that principle, teachers were required to swear an oath that they would teach in harmony with Marxism; teaching positions therefore were closed to Christians.[34] Almost any subject of instruction could become the vehicle for implicit or explicit atheist points of view, and where this was not considered sufficient, after-hours lectures were organized. In addition, a mandatory course on atheism was introduced at the universities in 1958 and 1959. The Prague Spring evidently produced a retreat in this area, as the party had to reintroduce the course in 1975.[35]

At the same time, rather than forcing religious instruction underground, the party decided to allow it to be conducted openly in the schools where it could be monitored and controlled. Under this system, which continued until the end of communist rule, religious instruction was available in all elementary schools for grades 2–8 within the regular school schedule, once or twice a week, usually in the afternoon.[36] Religious instruction was carried out by clergymen or by laymen. Until the summer of 1968, parents wishing to enroll a child in religious instruction were required each year to submit a written request to state school officials. They would then be required to meet with the regular schoolteacher, who received a monetary bonus for every withdrawal from religious instruction. (The 1988 change is discussed below.)

The pressure exerted during these meetings and in other ways paid off, and the proportion of children enrolling in religious instruction declined in the 1970s.[37] Despite the official co-optation of religious instruction, the party clearly viewed these classes with disfavor. In 1975, for instance, the Prague periodical, *Tribuna*, lamented: "Unfortunately, in some instances we meet also hidden attempts designed to disorient the educational influence and activities of school organs and of social organizations especially on young people during hours of religious instruction . . . , i.e., on age groups of young people who are only slowly beginning to form a world view."[38] It would appear that religious instruction was not supposed to impart religious belief and religious values.

During Alexander Dubček's brief rule, 1968–1969, the ministry of education issued an "Action Program" which authorized the schools to go beyond Marxism and to devote time "to other philosophic explanations of natural and social laws."[39] During the months of liberalization, the number of children attending "nonobligatory" classes in religious instruction noticeably increased.[40] This was reversed in the 1970s. On the other hand, despite the threat of disciplinary action, some party members continued to send their children to receive religious instruction—especially in Slovakia.[41]

Sowing Division

Fourth, the regime hoped to increase distrust between Catholics and non-Catholics. To achieve this goal, the central action committee of the communist party issued secret instructions to party officials to discriminately favor the Czechoslovak (Hussite) Church, the Evangelical Church, and the Czechoslovak Orthodox Church.[42] Among Protestant clergymen, Josef Hromádka became a particularly strong supporter of the regime.[43] The regime also tried to use the trial of Msgr. Josef Tiso, the wartime president of Slovakia, to aggravate relations between Catholics and Protestants, although it turned out to have little effect.

And fifth, the communist regime aspired to sow division within the ranks of the Catholic clergy itself—in particular to foment discord between the hierarchy and the lower clergy. Czechoslovak President Klement Gottwald noted as early as April 1949, "Our task is to provoke a political crisis among the clergy, and thus create hostility and conflict among them."[44] In considerable part, Pseudo-Catholic Action and the Peace Committee of Catholic Clergy were both designed to achieve this goal. And when Archbishop Beran condemned these agencies, the government promised impunity for their members, specifically assuring them that even if they were suspended and excommunicated by the church, the state would guarantee their continued ability to carry out the priestly office.

The regime wanted to draw the lower clergy away from both the bishops and the Vatican. The state's *Gazette of the Roman Catholic Clergy* called the bishops "isolated individuals within the Church"[45]—a description that reflected communist wishes rather than reality. As for the Vatican, the office for religious affairs saw no immediate possibility of undermining the clergy's loyalty toward the pope or the Vatican, but it decided to adopt a strategy of emphasizing "the necessity of preserving the national spirit and identity of our Catholic Church."[46] The press also adopted the tactic of reporting papal pronouncements in highly selective and tendentious ways.

An internal report (issued around 1951) of the office for religious affairs divided the Catholic clergy into four categories. Fifty clergymen were described as "patriotic" and politically reliable. These priests could safely be entrusted with positions of administrative authority. Another 500 clergymen were said to have a favorable attitude toward many concrete measures adopted by the regime. A third group of about 1,750 clergy was quiescent, passive, intimidated. And a fourth group, numbering about 700, was said to be openly hostile to the communist regime.[47] Judging from various reports and writings, the proportions were probably about the same in 1988 and 1989.

At the same time, the communist regime itself was internally divided. In the early years, for example, certain functionaries of the state security service, the ministry of justice, and the party itself favored more "radical" solutions than the party was willing to embrace; within the state security service some influential voices advocated the simple liquidation of all leaders of the Catholic hierarchy.[48] Subsequently, Vasil Bilák seems to have been the leading figure in a group that at one point talked in terms of forcing the Catholic Church to break its ties with the Vatican and subordinate itself to the Patriarchate of Moscow.[49]

Tomášek and Charter 77

With the appearance of the dissident Charter 77 at the end of the 1970s, a new complication was added to the Church-state balance. The regime applied pressure on the Church to distance itself from this new grouping, but a number of Catholic priests—including Frs. Josef Zvěřina, Václav Malý, František Lizna, and Josef Kordik—not to mention certain Evangelical pastors, were lending it strong support.[50] During the papacy of Paul VI (1897-1978; reigned 1963-78) the Holy See sought to obtain concessions from communist regimes through quiet diplomacy and a level of cooperation that bordered on docility. Archbishop František Tomášek (who had been elevated to the College of Cardinals in 1977) "was an obedient son of the Church"[51] and adopted a quiescent demeanor that alienated many Czech and Slovak Catholics. At one time he even criticized Catholic participation in Charter 77—a criticism that may have been shaped not only by the exigencies of papal Ostpolitik but by his own recollection of the earlier behavior of some of the ex-communists who were now advocating human rights under the rubric of Charter 77.[52]

There were purely internal concerns as well. For example, Vicar General František Vanek and others warned the cardinal of the danger that the government might arrest the clerical signators of Charter 77 if he, as primate of the Church in Czechoslovakia, were to issue a statement in its support.[53] At one point Tomášek even issued a formal denunciation of Charter 77.

Tomášek's behavior abruptly changed a short time after the election of Karol Wojtyła as Pope John Paul II.[54] The Polish pontiff was utterly clear about the importance he attached to a firm defense of human rights. Perhaps coincidentally, it was also about this time that Cardinal Tomášek came under the influence of Marie Rut Križkova, a signatory of Charter 77, who met with the cardinal two to three times each year. Tomášek gathered around himself a group of priestly advisers who were committed to an active policy in defense of human rights: Fr. Zvěrina, Fr. Oto Mádr, Fr. Tomáš Halík, and others.[55] By 1984 Tomášek was regularly receiving and blessing spokespersons of Charter 77.[56] Tomášek also became more outspoken generally, and he came to be seen as a champion of human rights in Czechoslovakia. Nonetheless, many people could not forget his "indecent compromises" and "concessions to the [communist] nobility" from 1965 until 1978, years that closely coincided with the reign of Pope Paul VI.[57]

The Religious Situation in the 1980s

The consistency with which the five-pronged integrated strategy was pursued in communist Czechoslovakia partly explains the weaker position of the Catholic Church there when compared to other East European countries, although historical factors are involved, too. The 1980s saw a clear sharpening of the regime's effort to undermine religion, especially from 1980 until 1983, reflecting the party's nervousness about a possible spillover from Poland, where the Church had stepped into a new role as a result of Solidarity's rise. It was during this period—specifically, on 27 March 1983—that the state security service carried out large-scale operations against illegal religious orders, resulting in the arrest of some 250 members of the Franciscan order.[58]

Under Dubček, nuns had been able to resume some of their earlier activities, including catechistic work and the acceptance of novices. In October 1969 a decree from the office of religious affairs limited the activity of nuns in Slovakia to the following spheres: work in social institutions for the severely handicapped or mentally impaired, in charitable institutions for elderly nuns and priests, and in health-care facilities with the specific approval of the ministry of health. Nuns and monks were specifically forbidden to work in homes for the retired, to engage in social activity in families and villages, to teach catechism, to assist in parish administration, or to accept novices.[59]

The Husák regime added to the Church's problems in 1976 by issuing an ordinance forbidding priests to administer the sacraments in hospitals or in homes for the aged. Later, in 1986, the regime would even withdraw permission for nuns to work in homes for the mentally impaired.[60] But the principal hardship for the Catholic Church, which became the subject of repeated discussions between the Vatican and Prague, was Czechoslovakia's unwillingness to accept the Vatican's candidates for vacant episcopal sees. In consequence, as of November 1988, ten of the country's thirteen episcopal sees remained vacant.[61]

Throughout the 1970s and 1980s, Catholic clergy and lay activists had been subjected to harassment, intimidation, arrests, the confiscation of religious materials, and even murder.[62] In one instance of official murder, a popular 47-year-old priest, Fr. Štefan Polák, pastor of Borovce in West Slovakia, was brutally assassinated by secret police on 7 October 1987.[63] As of the early 1980s, about a hundred priests were languishing in Czechoslovak prisons.[64]

Gradually, however, instead of caving in, Catholic believers became more resolute and perhaps even more confident—especially in Slovakia. This may be attributed in part to the galvanizing effect that repression sometimes has on its victims. But the election of fellow Slav Karol Wojtyła as pope in 1978, the succession of Mikhail Gorbachev as general secretary of the Communist Party of the Soviet Union, and the more subtle but far-reaching changes in culture and social expectations that had built up since the 1960s, all played a part. The joyful and spirited celebration of the 1,100th anniversary of the death of St. Methodius, bishop of Moravia, by some 150,000–250,000 believers, mostly Slovaks, at Velehrad in July 1985 was already a symptom of a changed atmosphere.[65] The Church's annual pilgrimages to Levoča, Šaštín, and Gaboltov became tests of will. The authorities were determined to dissuade young people from taking part. Yet young people were drawn to these pilgrimages in large numbers; the 5 July 1987 pilgrimage to the shrine of Levoča drew about 230,000 participants, for example, 70 percent of them young.[66]

As noted, Cardinal Tomášek by this time was adopting a more outspoken stance. He began, in particular, to draft protest letters and to encourage others to show their opposition. In April 1986, for example, Tomášek submitted a memorandum to the Czech Minister of Culture, Milan Klusak, calling for a radical revision of the laws governing religious matters and demanding what the Czechoslovak constitution seemed to guarantee, namely, the complete separation of Church and state. The officials rejected Tomášek's appeal, noting that no one should think of reducing or impeding the state's supervision of religious life.[67] But just over a year later, on the eve of the convocation of an episcopal synod in Rome, Pope John Paul II released an address devoted specifically to appraising the severe restrictions on Church life in Czechoslovakia. The pope described religious conditions in Czechoslovakia as a "sad situation with no analogy in countries of Christian tradition."[68]

Subsequently, in November or December 1987 a group of Moravian Catholics drew up a 31-point petition, calling for religious freedom. By early January 1988 some 5,000 people had signed. On 4 January 1988 Cardinal Tomášek put his name to the petition and urged Czech and Slovak Catholics to do likewise. By early May some 500,000 people had signed, most of them Catholics, although some Protestants, Jews, and nonbelievers also endorsed the document.[69] The West German Episcopal conference in Bonn lent its support to the petition, which received widespread sympathetic coverage in the Western media.[70] Eventually, some 600,000 people signed it. Specifically, the petition demanded:

(1) That the state not interfere in Church activities;

(2) that the state not impede the appointment of new bishops by the Vatican;

(3) that state organs not interfere in the naming of parish priests;

(4) that theological faculties be able to admit students independently, without state interference or quotas;

(5) that the theological faculty at Olomouc be reopened;

(6) that a permanent deaconate be allowed to be established;

(7) that all religious orders be allowed to function openly and to admit new members;

(8) that believers be permitted to establish independent lay organizations;

(9) that religious instruction be permitted in the churches or on church premises, rather than taking place in the state schools;

(10) that priests be allowed to visit prisons and hospitals, on request;

(11) that spiritual retreats be permitted;

(12) that every parish be allowed to establish a parish council, consisting of laypersons;

(13) that Czechoslovak Catholics enjoy the possibility of free contact with Christian organizations throughout the world;

(14) that all believers be allowed to participate in pilgrimages abroad;

(15) that believers have complete access to religious publications and that it be possible to set up religious publishing houses under Church guidance;

(16) that the production and dissemination of religious texts not be considered an illegal activity;

(17) that the import of religious literature from abroad be permitted;

(18) that the broadcast of religious programs on radio and television be permitted;

(19) that the jamming of Czech and Slovak broadcasts of Radio Vatican and of the Sunday Mass on Radio Free Europe be stopped;

(20) that the advocacy of Christian ideas enjoy equal legal status with the promotion of atheist ideas;

(21) that all confiscated church buildings, constructed with the believers' own resources, be returned to the Church;

(22) that the construction of new churches be permitted;

(23) that the arbitrary removal of crosses, statues, chapels, and other religious and cultural monuments be ended;

(24) that the power of state-appointed church secretaries to interfere in the appointment and transfer of priests be abolished;

(25) that unlawfully sentenced priests, members of religious orders, and laypersons be rehabilitated;

(26) that the discrimination against Christians be ended;

(27) that Christians be able to express their views on diverse problems within the context of the right of petition;

(28) that those laws which criminalize normal priestly activities be rescinded;

(29) that articles 16, 20, 24, 28, and 32 of the constitution be amended in the light of the foregoing;

(30) that all laws in force which deal directly or indirectly with religions be brought into conformity with international accords on human rights;

(31) that a mixed commission be appointed to take up such issues, that commission consisting of representatives of state organs and the Catholic Church, including laypersons to be named by Cardinal Tomášek.[71]

The authorities seemed disinclined to listen. František Jelinek, head of the office for religious affairs of the Czech Republic, delivered a speech to representatives of Pacem in Terris attacking the petition, and on 20 February 1988 the Prague party daily, *Rudé pravo*, criticized Cardinal Tomášek for his support of the petition. Later, when Tomášek sent a letter to the authorities proposing Church-state "dialogue" on all unresolved questions, the head of the religious affairs office, Vladimír Janků, dismissed the proposal with the claim that the cardinal "simply wants to provide the Western press with new motives for 'attacking the ČSSR.'"[72]

Two events in March 1988 demonstrated the growing confidence and sense of expectancy among Catholic believers in Czechoslovakia. On 6 March some eight thousand Catholics attended a Mass in honor of Blessed Agnes of Bohemia. After the Mass, several thousand of them walked from the cathedral to the cardinal's residence, where they shouted, "Long live the cardinal!" and "We demand religious freedom!" and "We want bishops!"[73] Less than three weeks later, on 25 March, some two thousand Catholics assembled at Hviezdoslav Square in downtown Bratislava in defiance of a police ban. They lit candles, prayed, and sang Slovak and Czech anthems in symbolic protest against religious repression in their country. Eventually, the police moved in with clubs, dogs, water cannon, and tear gas, beating the believers and arresting more than a hundred. The loud denunciations from abroad, however, signaled to the authorities that their brutality would not go unnoticed.[74] A short time later, signs of change became evident in the religious climate.

An early sign was the publication in the Bratislava party daily, *Pravda*, in mid-June 1988 of a lengthy article conceding that religions had often played a "moral and progressive" role in history and that religion would not be overcome even in the twenty-first century.[75] Reminiscent of Yevtushenko's article for *Komsomol'skaia pravda*, the piece created a sensation.

Within a matter of months the Prague authorities authorized some five hundred Catholic nuns to resume their activities caring for the old and the sick, authorized the expansion of Catholic Charity's publishing activities to assure the ready availability of Bibles, catechisms, prayer books, and biographies of saints; authorized the importation of Czech-language Bibles from West Germany and of illustrated children's Bibles from Yugoslavia; and granted permission for the appointment and training of deacons to help with pastoral work in the parishes (something hitherto forbidden by law). In a significant revision of the procedures regulating religious instruction, the authorities also ruled that parents need not turn in requests for such instruction to the schools; parents would now be able to register their children for religious instruction with the parish priest, who was authorized to submit the necessary paperwork to the authorities.[76]

In a speech delivered in Prague on 31 May 1988, J. Andrs, central secretary of the Czechoslovak People's Party, linked changes in Czechoslovak religious policy to changes signaled in the Soviet party organ *Kommunist,* suggesting that, with Miloš Jakeš now heading the Prague regime, Czechoslovakia would be susceptible to Gorbachev-style glasnost and perestroika.[77] Shortly after this speech, Janku, the head of the office for religious affairs, signaled an ostensible willingness on the state's part to resolve outstanding problems in Church-state relations and to improve relations with the Vatican.[78]

Revolution and Transformation

The years 1988 and 1989 were characterized by inconsistencies in the communist regime's religious policy. On the one hand, the communists agreed to talks with the Vatican concerning episcopal appointments. On the other, even while questioning the value of those talks in the pages of *Rudé pravo,*[79] the authorities confined the internationally renowned Catholic civil rights activist Augustin Navratil to a psychiatric hospital and sentenced Slovak Catholic activist Ivan Polansky to four years in prison.[80] As of January 1988, ten of Czechoslovakia's thirteen dioceses were vacant, but in May 1988 the Czechoslovak government reached an agreement with the Holy See, and on 18 May the appointments of a resident bishop and two auxiliary bishops were announced; four more episcopal appointments went into effect on 26 July 1989.[81]

By that point, however, the political fabric of Czechoslovakia was unraveling, and tensions were rising between rulers and ruled. Cardinal Tomášek issued a public warning about these tensions in early August, and he offered to serve as mediator for roundtable talks, on the Polish model, between the regime and the opposition. Later, in November, after the "velvet revolution" had begun and such talks were actually under way, Tomášek issued an open letter, addressed to Czechoslovakia's citizens. In it, he said, inter alia,

We need a democratic government because otherwise we will be unable to halt ecological disaster and other ills. . . . It is time now when we are called to assume responsibility for our present and future and that of our children. We are with you, friends, who call for justice for all. I speak with thanks and respect above all to the victims of brutal violence. . . . In this hour of fate in our history, nobody can remain uninvolved. Raise your voice again, this time united with other citizens, Czechs and Slovaks and members of other ethnic minorities—believers as well as non-believers. The right of faith cannot be detached from other democratic rights. Freedom is indivisible.[82]

Changes in the Catholic Church's legal status followed immediately after the revolution. These changes included the dissolution of Pacem in Terris in December 1989, the restoration of Czechoslovak-Vatican diplomatic ties, an invitation to the pope to visit Czechoslovakia (which he did in April 1990), the filling of all the vacant episcopal seats by candidates selected by Rome, the establishment of Czechoslovakia's first standing Bishops' Conference (originally urged by Pope Paul VI at the conclusion of the Second Vatican Council in 1965), the restoration of confiscated property to the Church (sixty-four buildings and other properties by 1 February 1991),[83] and passage of a law in May 1990 permitting private and religious schools. The Church has also been able to open new seminaries (in Olomouc, Spiš, and Prešov), alongside the previously existing seminaries in Litoměřice and Bratislava, and female and male religious orders (banned for forty years) have been resurrected. *Teologičke texty*, the distinguished underground journal, was allowed to publish openly and officially. And inevitably, work began on a new law governing religious organizations. In March 1991, after having served more than twenty years as archbishop of Prague, Cardinal Tomášek retired. His successor, Miloslav Vlk (b. 1932), had served earlier as bishop of České Budějovice.

The collapse of communism was accompanied by a flare in Czech-Slovak frictions, which culminated in the precipitous dismantlement of the Czechoslovak federation at the end of 1992.[84]

In a number of respects, however, forty years of communism had their effects on Church life. At the most obvious level, much of society (especially in the Czech Republic) had been secularized, and even among those who remained believers, there were few laypersons as of 1989 who were truly knowledgeable about their faith. The shortage of priests had contributed to a weakening of religious life; as of January 1990, almost half of the 1,500 parishes in Bohemia and Moravia were vacant, while about 200 of Slovakia's 1,500 parishes also lacked priests.[85] Under communism, the underground church, desperate for deacons, had ordained a number of women to serve as deacons[86] — a practice otherwise not condoned at that time in the Catholic Church. About thirty priests, and even one or two bishops had married[87] — again a breach of Church discipline, though arguably unavoidable in the tough conditions of the Gottwald, Novotný, and Husák eras. The regime policy of strangling the institutional Church also produced a situation in which the 800 nuns working in Czechoslovakia as of January 1990 had an average age between sixty and seventy.[88] Even the long-standing communist practice of paying the clergy's salaries (a device used to encourage dependence and docility) would be continued in postcommunist Czechoslovakia, on the argument that as a result of communist confiscations and other policies, the Church was no longer able to survive financially on the basis of believers' donations and its own resources.[89]

After the Split

At the end of 1992, Czechoslovakia split in two. The states which resulted immediately gravitated in sharply different directions.[90] One of the most controversial issues affecting Church-state relations in both republics has been the question of the restitution of property confiscated from the Churches after World War II. Here the Slovak government has been quicker to accommodate the Churches' wishes. As early as 27 October 1993 the Slovak parliament passed a bill returning both movable and immovable property to the Church, including forests, meadowland, and church buildings. The law covered property held by the state or by local municipal governments, but specifically excluded were properties on which state hospitals, social service providers, and schools had been constructed and properties operated by cooperative farms and trading companies.[91] After the law was passed, Ján Cardinal Korec, the bishop of Nitra, commended the parliament for having "shown a sense of justice" and for having "achieved a leading [moral] position in Central and Eastern Europe."[92]

In the Czech Republic, by contrast, property restitution has moved far more slowly. Before the Czech-Slovak split, about 250 buildings and land plots in Bohemia and Moravia were returned to Catholic religious orders and congregations, but the Church laid claim to an additional 3,300 buildings and 600,000 acres of wooded and nonwooded land, of which 200,000 acres had been attached to the archbishopric of Olomouc alone.[93] But although the Church has had her parliamentary advocates, such as the Christian Democratic Union,[94] several parties, including the Social Democratic and Communist, categorically opposed any restitution of Church property. As progress on legislation slowed to a standstill, however, tensions grew between the Catholic hierarchy and Czech Prime Minister Václav Klaus.[95] By way of a compromise, Cardinal Vlk suggested that the hierarchy would be content with the return of just 800 of the 3,300 buildings in dispute.[96] But between 1993 and 1996, discussions of Church restitution had been tabled on eight separate occasions,[97] and as of the spring of 1997, no breakthrough is in sight. The Christian Democratic Union, a new addition to Klaus's ruling coalition in 1996, promptly let it be known that it gave top priority to a final resolution of this question.[98] But according to a 1993 publication, the Church, which has been dependent on the state for subsidies, might not become economically self-sufficient, even if granted the maximum extent of property restitution.[99] Moreover, the larger dioceses (facing more considerable expenses) actually obtain smaller sums in the Sunday collection plate than smaller dioceses.[100] Representatives of the Catholic Church have therefore insisted in discussions with government officials on the need for the continuance of state subsidies.[101]

In other respects, too, the issues affecting the Church in the two successor states are strikingly different. In the Czech Republic, for example, while some conversions to Catholicism have occurred, non-Catholics are said to have become increasingly hostile to the Church.[102] Resentments focus on fears that the Church wants to assert its hegemony and that other Churches would not share in a fully proportional way in Church restitution. These fears and hostilities were only aggravated when Pope John Paul II visited the Czech Republic in May 1995 and used the occasion to announce the canonization of Jan Sarkander (1576–1620). Sarkander, a priest tortured by Protestant nobility and ultimately put to death, is seen by Czech Protestants as a symbol of the Catholic Counter-Reformation.[103] Cognizant of this problem, the pope tried to turn the occasion to his advantage and, addressing a large throng at a rain-soaked open-air Mass in Olomouc, pleaded for reconciliation, even asking forgiveness "for the wrongs inflicted on non-Catholics" by the Church.[104]

Moreover, given the more complex confessional structure of the Czech Republic (by comparison with Slovakia), the Catholic Church has been unable to obtain the introduction of religious instruction per se into the public school system. Instead, a class on "civic education" has been introduced, designed to inform schoolchildren about morals and ethics and to provide some basic information about religious life in the country. There have been problems, however, ranging from lack of attention on the part of "civics" teachers to the importance of tolerance (religious, sexual, ethnic, racial) to the virtual silence about Jewish life, even though Jews have lived in the Czech lands for more than a thousand years, with about two hundred synagogues still functioning.[105] But even this compromise has seemed to some to violate the principle of Church-state separation. Critics such as A. Ambrůz have insisted that the state (and hence the state school system) should play no role in moral education and that the Churches should accomplish this task outside publicly financed institutions.[106]

In Slovakia, by contrast, even though its property was returned and religious instruction introduced as an elective course in public schools in the autumn of 1990,[107] the Catholic Church has again found itself thrust into the role of opposition, remonstrating against a controversial language bill passed in 1995[108] and protesting the passage of an amendment to the penal code in March 1996 that provided for three years' imprisonment for anyone spreading false information damaging to Slovakia's reputation.[109] In late 1995 Slovak security police searched the house of Bishop Rudolf Baláž, chairman of the Slovak Bishops' Conference, as well as the episcopal offices at Banská Bystrica, provoking Church protests.[110] Yet in spite of such acts, April 1996 would find Slovak Prime Minister Vladimír Mečiar complaining, in a pose of feigned innocence, "I don't have the support of the bishops at home."[111]

There have been some shared trajectories, of course. For example, in both republics the Catholic Church has been concerned (as it has been in Poland, among other places) about plans to introduce sex education in public schools. In the Czech Republic the Christian Democratic Party has insisted that any eventual curriculum of sex education must be based on "Christian principles"—a proposal that suggests the enforcement of strict ideological guidelines in sex education.[112]

Conclusion

Catholicism in the Czech and Slovak lands surprised many observers. Nineteenth-century efforts to associate Protestantism with Czech nationalism and Catholicism with antinationalism certainly had some impact, and throughout the nineteenth and twentieth centuries the Catholic Church in Czechoslovakia, more than in other countries of East Central Europe, was markedly more vulnerable to self-doubt, internal division, anticlericalism (including from Protestants), and repressive policies by the communist regime. But the displays of spiritual resilience among Czechoslovak Catholics in the late 1980s suggest that the picture is not a simple one. Indeed, even the religio-national interaction is not simple, as shown in the fact that certain cultural conservatives in Bohemia were pointing (in the late 1980s) to negative features of the Hussite movement, recalling the Counter-Reformation as a golden age (the "Bohemian Baroque"), and praising the Habsburg monarchy for its positive impact.[113] For them, the Catholic Church has nothing for which to apologize and can face the future with boldness and a clear conscience.

Perhaps even more surprising is the fact that despite the consistency and resolution with which the communist regime pursued its five-pronged strategy vis-à-vis the Churches—the Dubček era of course being an exception—this strategy encountered unexpected difficulties and resistance. The communist regime smashed much of the Church's infrastructure, but later it had to allow the Church to rebuild certain portions. The regime seized control of various ecclesiastical institutions, such as Pacem in Terris, only to find that a difference exists between controlling certain institutions and controlling religious life; the emergence of underground channels of cooperation and communication— the so-called "secret Church"—spelled failure for this tactic. The regime organized an atheization campaign in the schools, but it found that the demand for religious instruction remained high; meanwhile, the regime dared not strike religious instruction from the school curriculum because that would only drive it underground. The regime tried to divide the Catholic Church from the other churches, but as the multiconfessional support for the 31-point petition showed, there was tangible solidarity among believers. Finally, the communist regime tried to divide the hierarchy from the lower clergy, hoping to isolate the hierarchy and to intimidate, buy out, and control everyday religious; the regime achieved partial success here, at least among the 5–10 percent (or more) of the clergy who were members of Pacem in Terris, but ultimately it failed to cow the Church. To what extent the Church's resilience was dependent on and derivative from the late Cardinal Tomášek's principled constancy and John Paul II's leadership is unclear.

Now, in the postcommunist, post-Czechoslovak era, the Catholic

Church faces new challenges, which are different in the two republics. These challenges include correcting the widespread ignorance about religion that resulted from forty years of communist control of education,[114] coexistence with Orthodox and Protestants under new conditions, maintenance of an effective presence in a semisecularized society (more of an issue in the Czech Republic), adjustment to the postcommunist depoliticization of religion, and, in the case of Slovakia, coping with the Mečiar government's erosion of democratic rights.

III

The Balkans

Chapter 6
Nation and Religion in Yugoslavia

For several reasons, religion is a constitutive element in the group identity and nationalism of most nationality groups. First, it is the historical core of the culture that shaped the evolution of primitive tribes into politically conscious nations. Second, it is a badge (though not the only one) of group identity, distinguishing "us" from "them," establishing a basis for identification or distance. Third, religious groups always have been in the forefront of the development of national languages, national literature, and the dissemination of literature in the national tongue through the printing press. Fourth, being more highly educated, more respected, and more politically conscious, the clergy naturally stepped into leadership roles and does so even today. Finally, encounters with other nationality groups with different religious practices encourage the group to think of its religion as particularly its own, even as essential to its national survival.

In multiethnic Yugoslavia, religious organizations could be divided roughly into three groups in terms of their relation to national identity and nationalism. The first group consists of the historical Churches that have acted as the cultural guardians of their respective peoples for more than a millennium. There are only two Churches in this group: the Roman Catholic Church, closely identified with the Slovenes and Croats, and the Serbian Orthodox Church, closely identified with the Serbs and the Montenegrins. The second group consists of the ethnic Churches and comprises ecclesiastical organizations linked with particular groups but lacking the claim to historical guardianship. Claiming only a small minority of the nationality group to which they cater, they can be viewed as "national" in form, but they do not have any chance of playing the role of national guardians. In this group I would include the Czech Brethren, the Slovak Evangelical Church (long established in Vojvodina), the Hungarian Evangelical Church (with local headquarters in Subotica), and the Old Catholic Church (in Croatia). The third group consists of non-national Churches, usually of recent vintage, which tend to be uninterested in national culture as such. Among this group are Seventh-Day Adventists, Baptists, and Jehovah's Witnesses.

This categorization, however, excludes two extremely important religious organizations, which, I believe, are more accurately viewed as special cases: the Macedonian Orthodox Church and the Islamic community. The Macedonian Church, which came into being only in 1967 as a product of a schism still repudiated by the Serbian Orthodox Church, is indeed national but it is not historic, since official affirmation of Macedonian ethnicity is of recent vintage (a post-World War II phenomenon) and since Orthodoxy has variously treated Macedonians either as Serbs or as Bulgarians (depending on whether the clergyman was Serbian Orthodox or Bulgarian Orthodox). The Islamic community, on the other hand, is distinct both because its institutional organization is looser and less politically conscious, and because the enveloping Islamic culture (which, since 1968, has been taken as constitutive of a distinct Muslim or, since 1992–93, Bosnian nationality) is perhaps entirely a product of the synthesis of the peculiarly religious element (i.e., Islam as a way of life) and of Ottoman culture (i.e., the culture of a conqueror whose very conquest was inspired in large part by the drive to spread Islam). While Yugoslav Marxists painstakingly emphasized that some ethnic Muslims in Yugoslavia were not religiously Muslim, and that some of those who were Muslim by religion were of Turkish, Albanian, or even Macedonian ethnicity, the identification remains a close one.

I shall argue in this chapter that Yugoslav policy toward the various religious groups from 1945 until 1991 was, to a significant extent, affected by the relationship that the religious groups bore toward nationalism and that, at the same time, the policy adopted by the League of Communists of Yugoslavia (LCY) toward each nationality group determined in large part the policy that was adopted vis-à-vis the "local" religion. I shall also review the behavior of the major religious groups since 1991, and I shall argue that in spite of the replacement of Titoist communist leaders with new leaders inspired by nationalism, the nationalism of the religious organizations has remained an important force in creating frictions between each respective religious faith and the political leadership of the state with which that faith is most identified.

In the years before 1987 the LCY sought to banish the Churches to the liturgical and strictly ritual sphere as their exclusive domain, a banishment termed the "privatization" of religion. Under such "privatization," the party recognized religion as "the private affair of the individual," but it denied religion any legitimate place in public life.[1] Obviously, however, while religious belief is certainly in some sense a "private affair,"

Churches have always been public organizations involved in the community's public life. To deny the Churches any place in the public sphere is not merely to assail the linkage of religion and nationalism at a pivotal point but to undercut the basis of Church life altogether.

Yugoslav nationalities policy, while described by its apologists Kardelj, Purivatra, and others[2] as cohesive and unified whole, was a logical whole only in theory. In practice, until 1987 the party both denied the existence of a Yugoslav nationality and applauded the denationalization of those who declared themselves "Yugoslavs" at census time. The party both encouraged the ethnic self-consciousness of some groups (Macedonians and Muslims, and to an extent Montenegrins) and condemned the ethnic consciousness of other groups (Croats, Albanians, and sometimes Serbs). It both preached "brotherhood and unity" (*bratstvo i jedinstvo*) and stirred up, without respite, the memories of the civil war of 1941–45, the vivid recollection of which was the surest guarantee that brotherhood and unity would always remain fragile.[3] Even the chief insight of Yugoslav nationalities policy, namely, that a multiethnic community can be harmonious only when far-reaching powers are devolved to federal units coterminous with constituent ethnic groups, was undercut by the party's refusal to consider the extension of federalization to its own apparatus. Moreover, as Yugoslavs were to learn to their own horror, the creation of federal units defined by ethnic criteria deepened the fault lines of the society and contributed directly to satisfying an important precondition for the outbreak of ethnic war, namely, the existence of competing political elites, with distinct power bases, each appealing to rival ethnic constituencies.

Religious and nationalities policy interacted in party favoritism toward the religious organizations of favored nationality groups (especially where the Macedonian Orthodox Church was concerned) and in the escalation of Church-state frictions in cases where the Church retained the role of defender of its nationality group (e.g., the Catholic Church in Croatia and the Serbian Orthodox Church in Serbia).[4]

Historical Origins

Orthodoxy and Serbian Nationalism

The period of the Great Migrations, from the fourth through the tenth centuries, coincided with the institutional entrenchment of Christianity in the Balkans and elsewhere in Europe. By the ninth century, Christianity had acquired a dominant influence in both Croatia and Serbia,[5] though Christians and polytheists in both lands continued to live side by side for some time.[6] It is understandable, then, that the formation of ethnic-national identity (ethnogenesis) was associated with Christianization. Moreover, since the Church gave definition to the content of human culture and social mores, diluted tribal identities were readily supplanted by "national" identities founded on the conjunction of Church and state. Orthodoxy became the badge of Serbdom, just as Catholicism was the mark of a Croat. The ethnogenesis of the Bosnian Muslims is a tangled web, however, whose various threads historians have failed to untangle. Croatian nationalists (such as Ivo Pilar) usually have described the Muslims as Islamicized Croats, who through conversion acquired a new locus of cultural identification that entailed the loss of Croatian national consciousness. Similarly, for Pilar, as incoming Vlahs and local Croats converted to Serbian Orthodoxy, they became part of a community whose heartland was Peć and Mileševo, and they came to regard themselves as Serbs.[7] A study published by Noel Malcolm in 1994 confirms that Vlah immigration into Bosnia made an essential contribution to the Orthodox presence there and that the Ottoman authorities deliberately encouraged Orthodox immigration.[8]

Far from being an accidental byproduct of the expansion of political power, confessional homogenization was consciously sought by the Balkan princes. Prince Bodin (1082–1101) sought to strengthen Church organization in Serbia and, still looking to the West at that time, obtained papal recognition of the elevation of the bishopric of Bar to the status of metropolite. Later, in 1219, Sava, youngest son of Serbian Prince Stefan Nemanja, who had united Serbia, obtained recognition of the Serbian Church as an autocephalous member of Orthodoxy. Nemanja himself vigorously suppressed the heretical Bogomil sect, which he viewed as a threat to civil order, and the Bogomils fled from Serbia. In Croatia, too, King Tomislav (910–c. 928) aspired to make the Church liturgically more monolithic and organizationally more unified. Therefore, Tomislav allied with the pope and with the bishop of Split in the early tenth century to assert the primacy of the bishop of Split throughout Croatia and to ban continued use of the Old Slavic Glagolitic liturgy, replacing it with the Latin.[9] In the principality of Bosnia, where an autonomous Christian Church functioned which was neither Roman nor Orthodox, both Bogomils and Dalmatian Catholic priests who refused to give up the Glagolitic liturgy found safe haven in Bosnia's relatively tolerant atmosphere.[10] In a certain way, the Bosnian Church figured as a national religion, synthesizing disparate elements from Catholicism, Orthodoxy, Bogomilism, Islam, and even paganism. But the Bosnian Church was never strong institutionally, and thus the Bosnian regional identity that began to develop lacked a confessional anchor.[11] By the second quarter of the fifteenth century, energetic proselytization by the Franciscan order had seriously eroded the adherence of the peasantry to the Bosnian Church. By 1460, according to John Fine, "most of the nobility seems to have been won over to Catholicism [and] . . . the Bosnian Church stood alone without mass popular support and without the backing of [the] nobility. . . . Even within the Church itself loyalty and interest were lacking."[12] This same institutional weakness facilitated the penetration of elements of Islamic culture and faith after the Ottoman conquest (1463). But that conquest also led Bosnian Catholics and Orthodox to identify with the neighboring states of Croatia and Serbia, respectively.

During the Ottoman occupation the Serbian Orthodox Church assumed the role of guardian of the Serbian people's national culture and traditions. The Church fostered education and cultivated resentment of the Islamic conquerer. At the same time, however, it directly benefited from the Ottoman occupation of Bosnia. Before Ottoman dominance of Bosnia-Herzegovina, the Orthodox Church had little presence in Bosnia proper, and it was important only in parts of Herzegovina. But the Ottoman authorities consciously favored the Orthodox Church and brought in large numbers of (Orthodox) Vlachs as early as the 1470s and 1480s, settling them in parts of eastern Herzegovina. In general, Ottoman authorities preferred the Orthodox Church, because its seat was in the Ottoman capital, to the Catholic Church, which was seen as the Church of the Turks' great enemy, Austria.[13] In 1593, as Austria and Turkey went to war, the Serbs staged a major rebellion in Banat. Patriarch Jovan II of Peć (whose patriarchate had been reestablished in 1557) "directly stimulated" the uprising and blessed the banners of the insurgents. In retaliation—and perhaps in the conviction that if power is demonstrated by destroying the religious shrines of a people, the power of that people to resist is also destroyed—the Turks opened the grave of St. Sava at Mileševo, removed the corpse, and on 27 April 1594, burned it in Vračar, near Belgrade.[14] When the Austrians made peace with the Turks in 1606, the Serbian revolt caved in. Yet in 1689, during a later Austro-Turkish war, when the Serbs once more rose against the Turks and collaborated with the Austrians, the patriarch of Pec, Arsenije III Čarnojević, urged the rebels on, invited the Venetians to send troops in support of the rebellion, and, after the collapse of the Austrian campaign, led a large migration of Serbs from the area of present-day Kosovo through Belgrade into what is today Vojvodina.

The Turks tried to dampen the nationalist temper of the Serbian Orthodox Church, abolishing in 1766 the Serbian patriarchate at Peć; in the years that followed, they banned everything Slavic or national in Serbian liturgy and Church life. The Turks subjected the Church to thorough Hellenization, but this policy only ensured that the Serbian clergy would give their strongest backing to the Serbian liberation movement that began in 1804. Archpriest Matija Nenadović procured ammunition and served in the cavalry during the First Serbian Insurrection (1804–13), and Serbian monasteries were regularly used as meeting places and safe havens for anti-Ottoman Serbian rebels, as headquarters for Serbian commanders, and even as weapons storehouses. In fact, the rebellious Serbs several times set up command posts in Serbian monasteries. In 1830 the sultan reluctantly conceded Serbs the right to internal self-government, and the following year the Serbs freed their Church from Greek supervision.

Both in Ottoman Bosnia and in Habsburg Vojvodina, the Serbian Orthodox Church and the Roman Catholic Church competed for the loyalty of the populace; in both cases, confessional loyalty was equated with ethnic loyalty. As a result of the 1848 revolution, Patriarch Josip Rajačić of the Serbian Orthodox Church was named "patriarch of the Serbian nation" by the Viennese court that same year. Rajačić tried to live up to the title by demanding in 1860, for example, that the Austrian ministry of war change the name of the Romanian-Banat border regiment to the Serbian-Banat border regiment.[15]

Subsequently, as the Serbian state consolidated its independence, Serbian nationalists continued to emphasize the importance of Orthodoxy for the state and the nation. The symbiotic strength of the linkage of religion and nationalism was so alluring that no less a figure than Vuk Karadžić, the linguistic reformer and Serbian nationalist, declared that not only were the Serbs "the greatest people on the planet," but in fact Jesus and his apostles were themselves all Serbs.[16] Church leaders themselves became spokespersons for national expansionism. Already in 1794, a Serbian monk named Jovan Rajić had laid claim to Bosnia-Herzegovina as ethnically Serbian. Drawing back with horror at the concept of an ancient "Illyrian" people inhabiting the eastern shore of the Adriatic, a concept being propagated by some Croatian Catholic writers, the Serbian Orthodox Church insisted that Serbs would not give up their name and their identity for some artificial Illyrian idea. Teodor Pavlović, a particularly vociferous opponent of Illyrism, asked in 1837, why "Serbs of the Roman law do not call themselves Serbs." By his count, there were 5 million Serbs, but only four thousand "true" Croats.[17] Others promoted Serbian identity more directly. For example, Teofil Petranović, a teacher at an Orthodox school in Sarajevo in the 1860s, "formed a group of people to go out into the village and tell the Orthodox peasants that they must stop calling themselves 'hrišćani' (the local term for 'Orthodox') and start calling themselves Serbs."[18]

Ironically, the Serbian Orthodox Church was probably better off in the interwar Kingdom of Serbs, Croats, and Slovenes (1918–41, renamed the Kingdom of Yugoslavia in 1929) than it had been in the Kingdom of Serbia. In Serbia after 1881, the state packed the Holy Synod with its own lay appointees and effectively controlled the Church, reducing it to little more than a state agency. Orthodoxy, of course, was the official state religion of the Serbian kingdom, and Orthodox religious instruction was everywhere mandatory. But the Church enjoyed considerable munificence after 1918. Besides, following the establishment of the unified kingdom in 1918, the Serbian patriarch sat on the royal council, while a number of Orthodox clergymen had seats in the national assembly.[19]

During these years the Serbian Orthodox Church established a metropolitanate in Zagreb and erected three Serbian churches in Catholic Slovenia. But the Serbian Orthodox Church's greatest victory in the interwar kingdom was to block the Catholic Church's quest for a concordat with Belgrade, thereby preventing the Vatican from obtaining guarantees of complete freedom of access to Catholic clergy and laity, among other things.[20]

The spread of World War II to Yugoslavia in April 1941 divided the Serbian Orthodox Church. Some senior clergy in the Serbian church cooperated with the quisling regime of Milan Nedić.[21] Others gave their support to the Chetnik movement, which offered a restorationist program.

The Croats and Catholicism

The active involvement of the Catholic clergy on behalf of Croatian nationalism came somewhat later, although some parish priests openly supported a Croatian peasant rebellion against Emperor Maximilian in 1573.[22] Vinko Pribojević (Vincentius Priboevius), a Dominican priest, was one of the first clergymen to write on national themes; in a work published in 1525, he hypothesized the existence of an Illyrian people, understood by him to be Slavic in language and culture.[23] Another Dominican priest, Juraj Križanić (1618–83), developed Illyrian ideology further by identifying Serbs, Croats, and Bulgarians as three stems of the "Illyrian branch" of a still broader "Slavic nation" that also included Russians, Poles, and Czechs. Influenced by Levaković, Križanić tinkered with patching together elements of the speech patterns of these different peoples to produce a synthetic South Slav language—what Reinhard Lauer calls "a kind of Slavic Esperanto." Križanić, as did most of his ecclesiastical contemporaries, viewed Croatia as merely a geographic part of Illyria.[24] Many other Catholic clergy became vehicles of Illyrian ideology, especially the Franciscans, who spread the political credo throughout Bosnia-Herzegovina. Many clergymen viewed the Illyrian mythology as an effective tool in propagating Catholicism, and the efforts by Jesuit priests F. K. Pejačević and K. Pejkić to introduce Illyrism in Bulgaria in the mid-eighteenth century can be best understood as serving the purpose of propagating Catholicism.

Josip Juraj Strossmayer (1815–1905), appointed bishop of Djakovo in 1849, has come to personify the Illyrian movement because of his active endeavors to create a political union of Croatia and Serbia. Strossmayer shares this distinction with Ljudevit Gaj (1809–72), a publicist, journalist, and linguistic reformer who published a series of political and literary periodicals.[25] For his part, Strossmayer negotiated with the Serbian government, orchestrated an uprising in Bosnia, and championed a revival of the autochthonous Glagolitic liturgy (which had reemerged as an issue in 1848 during the revolutionary upheaval when it was taken up as a cause by Illyrian nationalists). Strossmayer's close friend, Friar Franjo Rački (1828–94), spelled out the essence of Illyrism when he declared that Croats and Serbs had no basis for claiming to be ethnically distinct and that only the Vatican was hindering the rapprochement of Catholic and Orthodox "Illyrians."[26]

Strossmayer has come to symbolize the integrative, embracing strand in Croatian national ideology, in which the common language is stressed and the religious divide is overcome by drawing the Catholic and Orthodox Churches together into a "national Church." Not surprisingly, Yugoslav communists repeatedly held up Strossmayer as a true Yugoslav; probably no major Yugoslav town in communist times lacked a "Strossmayer Street" or "Strossmayer Square."[27]

A second strand of Croatian national ideology evolved in the course of the nineteenth century, however, and ultimately became more closely identified with the Catholic Church than had the Illyrian strand. The alternative to a broader South Slav state was seen by most Croats to lie in a restoration of Croatian independence. The Croatian Party of Right, created by ex-seminarist Ante Starčević (1823-1896), was in essence a Catholic movement working for the political independence of a Catholic Croatia.[28] Thus, from the mid-nineteenth century until the 1920s the Church in Croatia was riven into two factions: the progressives, who favored the incorporation of Croatia into a liberal Slavic state and envisioned union with Serbia on lines drawn by Strossmayer; and the conservatives, who preferred the ecclesiastical security of union with Austria-Hungary if outright independence could not be secured and who were loath to bind Catholic Croatia to Orthodox Serbia. By 1900 the exclusivist orientation seemed to have gained the upper hand in Catholic circles, and the First Croatian Catholic Congress, held in Zagreb that year, was implicitly anti-Orthodox and anti-Serb.[29] So consonant were the aims of the Church's Croatian Social Party and Starčević's Croatian Party of Right that the two organizations were merged in 1910.

After the Habsburgs annexed Bosnia-Herzegovina in 1878, some efforts were made to encourage the development of a Bosnian national consciousness and a distinctive Bosnian language in order to cut the Bosnian Croats off from their ethnic kin to the north. The Croatian Franciscans in Herzegovina played a decisive role in resisting both this policy and the endeavors of Serbian nationalists, mainly through their weekly newspaper, *Glas Hercegovca* (1885–95). Croatian Franciscans played an active role in the literary life of Herzegovina, Dalmatia, and Croatia proper, working on *Narodni list, Katolička Dalmacija,* and other periodicals.[30] Catholic clergy were tangibly involved in the foundation of *Matica hrvatska* (the Croatian Cultural Society, originally named *Matica ilirska*), the Croatian National Museum, and even the first Croatian savings bank. Bishop Juraj Dobrila also contributed to the growth of national consciousness by founding the newspaper *Naša sloga;* and two other Catholic clergymen, Ivan Antunović and Boža Šarčević, established the *Bunjevačke i šokačke novine.* Antun Mahnić (1850-1920), bishop of Krk, was the leading figure in the Croatian Catholic Movement (*Hrvatski Katolički Pokret*), which figured as part of a broader European Catholic campaign against liberalism and secularization. In 1903 Bishop Mahnić founded the monthly magazine *Hrvatska Straža* (Croatian Guard), which continued publication until 1945.[31] The Roman Curia disdainfully viewed the prospects of union of Catholic Slovenes and Croats with Orthodox Serbs; instead, full appreciation of Austria-Hungary, the Vatican's most reliable ally, could not survive the creation of a united Yugoslav state.[32] But by 1917–18 the Vatican had come to regard the creation of a Yugoslav state as affording an opening for possible proselytization eastward, and "although the Catholic bishops in the South Slav lands of the Austro-Hungarian monarchy were not decided in regard to the creation of a Yugoslav state outside the Habsburg monarchy, the priesthood played its own role in the movement for national unification," strongly endorsing and supporting the unification of South Slavs.[33]

Religious faiths were not equal in the interwar Kingdom of Serbs, Croats, and Slovenes (renamed, Kingdom of Yugoslavia in 1929). While the Serbian Orthodox Church signed an agreement with the ministry of faiths in 1926 and began to benefit enormously from generous state subventions, the Roman Catholic Church was unable to obtain a similar arrangement. A concordat between the Holy See and the Belgrade government was actually signed on 25 July 1935, but thanks to the energetic and strenuous opposition of the Serbian Orthodox Church, parliament never ratified the concordat.[34]

In part because of this unequal treatment in the interwar kingdom, the Catholic Church remained broadly sympathetic to Croatian separatism. Fred Singleton reports that Archbishop Ivan Šarić (1871–1960), Stadler's successor as archbishop of Sarajevo (1919–45), joined the secessionist *Ustaše* organization in 1934, and Bishop Josip Garić of Banja Luka also may have been a member.[35] Opinions differ as to whether Šarić was "inherently" nationalist or not; be that as it may, it is clear that he calculated that Croatian independence might be more propitious for the Catholic Church's operations. *Katolički list,* the leading Catholic newspaper of Croatia at the time, repeatedly condemned Naziism, calling it "the worst heresy" and "a falling away from Christianity."[36] In 1938, on the eve of World War II, *Katolički list,* in an editorial, condemned Nazi anti-Semitism in the strongest terms, adding, "Healthy nationalism warms and enlivens a nation and, especially with a small nation, keeps it from disappearing, but exaggerated nationalism is chauvinism, hatred joined to envy and malice. It leads to war as the culmination of all the evils of our time."[37] But the dangers of Naziism did not make the inconveniences associated with Belgrade's twin policies of subtle cultural Serbianization and discrimination against non-Serbs any the more bearable.[38] Hence, upon the proclamation of the Independent State of Croatia (*Nezavisna Država Hrvatska*, or NDH) by the *Ustaše* in 1941, Zagreb's Archbishop Alojzije Stepinac (1898–1960), though not affiliated with the *Ustaše*, initially welcomed the establishment of the new state, having become convinced of the dangers posed by Greater Serbian hegemonism and communism alike for the Catholic Church in Croatia.[39] Even *Katolički list* set aside its earlier caution and described the NDH as "the fulfillment of [the Croats'] legitimate aspirations."[40] But *Katolički list* soon lost its independence as NDH authorities instructed its editors on what to write and censored news articles before publication.[41] The Catholic hierarchy's ambivalence concerning the *Ustaše* policy of the forced conversion of Serbs to Catholicism[42] would later become a source of considerable embarrassment to the postwar Croatian Church. On the other hand, Stepinac's repeated criticism of *Ustaše* excesses (e.g., on 23 February 1942) and his repeated efforts to circumvent NDH policy, saving some 6,717 children from the *Ustaše*, among them about 6,000 children of Serbs or of Partisans, as well as a number of Gypsies, confute the postwar communist claim that he collborated with the *Ustaše*.[43]

In the early postwar years Tito tinkered with the idea of encouraging the establishment of a schismatic national Catholic Church that might be more amenable to regime manipulation and pressure. When Croatia's leading prelates showed resistance to the idea, however, the communists attempted to brand the Catholic Church as fascist and thus to sever it from the wellsprings of Croatian nationalist feeling. Stepinac's trial was central to this endeavor. But the attempt failed, and the assaults on the good name of the archbishop produced a backlash, transforming a sincere and reputable churchman into a Croatian national hero, a symbol of Croatian national aspirations. Worse yet, from the regime's point of view, the crushing of the so-called Croatian Spring in December 1971 and the concomitant suppression of all institutions (such as *Matica hrvatska* and the newspapers *Hrvatski tjednik* and *Tlo*) that had served as forums for Croatia's exclusivist nationalists had as a byproduct the effect of strengthening the Church's role as guardian of Croatian national interests.

The Slovenes and Catholicism

Slovenian national identity owes an enormous debt to Protestant leader Primož Trubar (1508–86), who printed his *Abecedarium* with a small catechism in Tübingen in 1551 and who wrote some twenty books in all, including a translation of the New Testament into Slovenian (completed between 1557 and 1577). When Trubar started his work, Slovenian had very limited uses, chiefly of an utterly mundane nature. There was no literature in Slovenian, and Latin and German were viewed as the appropriate mediums for serious dialogue on any subject. But thanks to Trubar, to Jurij Dalmatin's translation of the Bible into Slovenian (published in 1584), and to the literary activity of other Protestants, Slovenian began to spread and to express class solidarity.[44] Slovenian Protestant reformers also established a string of primary and secondary schools teaching in the vernacular.

With the launching of the Counter-Reformation in the early seventeenth century, Slovenian elementary schools were largely eliminated. Slovenian-language elementary education survived only in the countryside, and graduates of these schools were ineligible for enrollment in secondary schools.[45] As Catholic friars slowly responded to the continuing demand for books in Slovenian, the output focused on sermons, prayer books, and homilies. Capuchin friar Janez Svetokriški, for example, published five volumes of sermons in Slovenian under the Latin title, *Sacrum promptuarium* (The Sacred Handbook, published 1691–1707). Another Capuchin friar, Michael Kramer—known as Rogerius—also published sermons (1731–43); his efforts adopted a baroque style that reflected the literary fashions of the age. In 1768, the Augustinian monk Marko Pohlin (1735–1801) published his Slovene grammar, marking the revival of the Slovenian literary language.[46] Slovenian secular poetry was pioneered by another friar, Franciscan Valentine Vodnik (1758–1819), whose earliest collection of verse appeared in 1806. Didactic in tone, the poems were based in part on the rhythm of folk songs. When Slovenian territories came under French occupation from 1809 until 1813 and were reorganized as part of the so-called Illyrian Provinces, the French authorities introduced the Slovenian language throughout the elementary school system as well as in the secondary schools, giving Vodnik one of the leading posts in education. But after the defeat of Napoleon, the Habsburg authorities restored the educational system's status quo ante.[47] An attempt to restore Slovenian-language education was made in 1848, but with the restoration of absolutism the issue of Slovenian instruction was temporarily removed from the agenda, and the Church's control over the schools became stronger than ever. Only after Austria's military defeat by Prussia and Italy in 1866 were the hands of the liberals strengthened and new legislation passed. These new laws attenuated the prerogatives granted to the Church in education under the concordat of 1855 and took control of elementary and secondary schools away from the Church, turning it over to the state. Only religious instruction remained under Church supervision.[48]

In the mid-1880s the conservative forces dominating the Slovenian Catholic Church launched a new offensive against liberalism, talking of the need to effect a "Christianization" of Slovenian society. Catholic organizations demanded that education, science, art, the media, and social and political work all take into account Catholic doctrines and values and set their compass by Catholic teaching. Much as the Catholic Church wanted to assert a cultural monopoly in Slovenia, it could not do so at that time. In the years before World War I, for example, six secondary schools were run by Protestants.[49]

The Slovenian Catholic Church played to a regional audience in the interwar kingdom, but, all the same, some interesting changes occurred. In 1922, for instance, a conference of archdeacons and deans of the archdiocese of Ljubljana granted that art and "humanist sciences" had some claim to a degree of autonomy from Church control.[50]

Slovenian Catholic priests made significant contributions to Slovenian literature and culture in the nineteenth and twentieth centuries. Here, one might mention in particular the activities of Archbishop Anton Martin Slomšek of Maribor (1800–1862);[51] Fr. Franc Saleški Finzgar (1871–1962), who edited the popular monthly periodical, *Mladika* (1924–32);[52] and Fr. Franc Ksaver Meško (1874–??), whose writings highlighted the importance of Christian values in contemporary life.[53]

The Muslim Community

At the time of the Austrian occupation of Bosnia-Herzegovina in 1878 the Muslims were the least nationally conscious of the three principal confessional groups under survey. Their position within the Ottoman empire had been a privileged one, and it was only with the imposition of rule by Catholic Austria that collective identity was stimulated by cultural threat. The Austrians harbored no intention of suppressing Islam or of discriminating against Muslims, but, as Joint Minister of Finance József Szlávy observed in a report to Emperor Franz Josef in 1881, Bosnian Muslims were dissatisfied—at least in his opinion—because after enjoying a privileged position under the Turks, they objected to being treated as equals with Christians by the Austrians.[54]

In fact, neither the Muslims nor the Serbs of Bosnia accepted Austrian occupation, and both groups began to campaign, soon thereafter, alternatively for religious-cultural and political autonomy; in any event, eventual political goals were never far from sight.[55] The Austrians' hope was to reinforce tendencies toward regional identity, to cut the local population off from ethnic kin abroad, and, above all, to block any spread of Serbian nationalism among the Muslims, even while impeding the development of a national consciousness among the Bosnian Muslims: they should think of themselves as Bosnians, as Austrian subjects, but not as ethnic Muslims. The Austrian authorities were, in particular, eager to instill in the population a feeling of "Bosnianness," which would weaken the ties of Orthodox and Muslims to Serbia and the Ottoman empire, respectively. They therefore welcomed the founding in 1891, by Mehmed-beg Kapetanović and several other pro-Austrian Sarajevo Muslims, of a weekly newspaper, *Bošnjak,* whose underlying principle was that all Bosnians, regardless of faith, had a common nationality. The paper was written in Serbo-Croatian, which the editors in harmony with local custom identified as the "Bosnian" language.[56]

The Austrians also endeavored to insulate Bosnian Islam from the Ottoman caliphate, and in October 1882 they created the new office of Reis-ul-ulema, as head of Bosnian Islam, with a state salary of 8,000 gulden per year. But a series of conversion incidents in 1893, 1897, and 1899, in which Muslims converted to Catholicism, mobilized the Muslim community and catalyzed its autonomy movement. In December 1900 a group of prominent Muslims drew up a proposed autonomy statute and presented it to Benjámin von Kállay, joint minister of finance and ipso facto chief administrator of Bosnia-Herzegovina (1882–1903). The petition enumerated Muslim complaints, including the conversion of a number of mosques into Christian churches, the neglect of Muslim cemeteries, and alleged aggressive Catholic proselytization among Muslims, said to have been inspired by Archbishop Stadler of Sarajevo. Finally, the Muslims complained that the Austrian-created institution of the Reis-ul-ulema and Austrian control of appointments to the Medzlissi-ulema and the Vakuf commission had usurped control of religious affairs from its rightful charge, the "Islamic nation." The Muslims demanded religious autonomy and self-regulation.[57] This petition marked the beginning of the Muslim National Organization that was formally established six years later. The groundwork had been laid for the emergence of Muslim ethnic consciousness.

Islamic religious identity, of course, had been heightened by the Austrian occupation and the conversion incidents, but it was still possible for Muslims to declare themselves Serbs or Croats when it suited them, and "some Muslims changed from one camp to the other on several occasions," calculating their tactics on the basis of shifts in the political wind.[58] But most of these affirmations and alliances were largely tactical, and *Glas slobode*, the organ of the Social Democratic Party in Bosnia-Herzegovina, could report on 24 May 1911 that "the endeavors of Serbs and Croats to see the Muslims adopt their [respective] names have been, to date, completely unsuccessful. Only a few individuals call themselves Serbs or Croats. The rest are simply Muslims."[59]

With the establishment of the interwar kingdom, the Muslims were relegated, both by the regime and by the socialist opposition, to the position of one branch of the "Yugoslav nation" or even, in the eyes of some Serbs, of confessionally deviant Serbs. Jovo Jakšić, an apologist for the theory of the "tri-named people" ("Serb," "Croat," and "Slovene" being, in this view, alternative names for a single "Yugoslav" people), denied that any differences other than religion differentiated the people of Bosnia-Herzegovina—as if that were not potent enough—and suggested that Muslims be viewed as a fourth "tribe" of the Serbo-Croato-Slovenian nation.[60] In spite of this assertion, when the first Yugoslav parliament was opened, twenty-two of the twenty-four Muslim deputies from Bosnia declared themselves Croats, and the Yugoslav Muslim Organization, the strongest Muslim party, was tangibly closer to Croats than to Serbs. Later, at the first national conference of the Communist Party of Yugoslavia (November 1940), Moše Pijade told delegates that Bosnian Muslim consciousness was largely religious and not ethnic. This judgment would later receive some corroboration in the wartime split among the Muslims, with many actively supporting the Croatian *Ustaše*, even identifying themselves as "Croats of Muslim faith," and many joining the communist partisans.

Religious Organizations and Cultural Homogenization

In the case of both "historical" Churches and Bosnian Islam, religion proved a defining factor in ethnic differentiation, perhaps even the single most important factor. By the end of the nineteenth century, if not long before, it seemed almost inconceivable that a Croat could be anything but Catholic, a Serb anything but Orthodox, and rival claims made upon

Muslims could not conceal the fact that Islam likewise had come to define an ethnocultural collectivity.

Religious organizations reinforce the tendency to identify religion and nation, of course, by endeavoring to have the state suppress or discriminate against adherents of other faiths. In Serbia, for instance, proselytism among Orthodox believers was first forbidden in 1349,[61] while in the case of the Catholic Church, the reforms of Austrian Emperor Josef II, extending religious freedom to Protestants and Greek Orthodox in 1781 and requiring monarchical consent before any papal bull could be made public in his lands, so agitated Pope Pius VI that he hurried to Vienna in 1782 to admonish the emperor to reconsider his reforms.[62]

Religious organizations also have been forces for cultural homogenization—and thus nation-building—in other ways, for example, by dictating dress codes and social mores and molding the national language. The Serbian Orthodox Church backed promulgation of the Serbian language in its antiquated church variant, and both the Orthodox and Catholic Churches ardently advocated discrete alphabets. But where the Orthodox clergy was united in its promotion of Cyrillic, the Catholic Church was divided between Glagolitic and Latinic supporters. The appearance of an Old Croatian Catholic sect in 1923 may be taken as a culmination of this long-simmering rift between papal loyalists and those inclined to resist papal regulation. But where the restoration of an independent Serbia placed the Serbian Orthodox Church in a politically dominant position, the fact that Croats were repeatedly thrust into the position of being a minority (whether in Hungary, in Austria-Hungary, or in Yugoslavia) tended to place the Church in Croatia, insofar as it defended the interests of Croats, in the role of opposition. In an early instance of this opposition, Church leaders and lower clergy fought Magyarization in Croatia and lent support to the nascent Croatian national movement in the mid-nineteenth century. The consequences of this evolution were that religion took on a nationalist coloration, that religious tensions could easily spill over into ethnic tensions and vice versa, and that the Yugoslav communists, hostile to religion of all kinds, found that they could not launch an assault on religion without inflaming nationalist temper.

Orthodoxy Under the Communists

Of all the religious organizations in communist Yugoslavia, the Serbian Orthodox Church was the first to reach a modus vivendi with the ruling CPY. Its relations with the party were repeatedly described by regime spokespersons as "satisfactory," even "good"—characterizations with which the Serbian Church occasionally disagreed, for example, when it came to difficulties in obtaining approval to build new churches. The problem, however, lay in that murky frontier zone where religious affirmation spilled over into national sentiment and where an unmistakably *Serbian* Church spoke out for Serbian interests while a *Yugoslav* regime endeavored to balance the interests of the country's sundry peoples, always safeguarding the interests of the ruling party itself. Thus, almost the only criticism that the Tito regime ever lodged against Serbian Orthodoxy was that it was nationalist[63]—and indeed, it was, and is, unabashedly so. The Serbian Orthodox Church had become involved in nationalist causes on all of its frontiers: in Macedonia and Montenegro, where the Church continued to view the local populations as Serbs; in Croatia, where the Croatian nationalist euphoria of 1971 stimulated anti-Croatian sentiments among the Serbian minority within Croatia, provoking a strong reaction on the part of the Serbian Orthodox Church; and in Kosovo, where the Church took a strong stand in defense of church monuments and the rights of Serbs allegedly threatened by Albanian nationalist riots and violence in 1981.

The long-standing controversy between the Serbian Orthodox Church and the Macedonian Orthodox Church was the most dangerous issue affecting the Serbian patriarchate's relations with the Belgrade regime. The crux of the matter is that the Tito regime welcomed the creation of the Macedonian Orthodox Church as a validation of its claim —contested by Bulgaria—that the Macedonian people should be considered ethnically distinct from Bulgarians, while the Serbian Church, already having suffered one schism in the secession of overseas dioceses, was loath to endure yet another upheaval in what it considered its heartland.

After the abolition of the 800-year-old archbishopric of Ohrid in 1767, the first demand for a revived independent Macedonian Church was made by Metropolitan Teodor of Skopje in 1891, when the Macedonian eparchy of Veles was administratively part of the Bulgarian exarchate. With the creation of Yugoslavia after World War I, jurisdiction for Orthodox Church affairs in Macedonia was transferred to the Serbian patriarchate. The demand for an independent Macedonian Church was revived only twenty-five years later when, in March 1945, a council of local clergy and laity met in partisan-held Skopje and adopted a resolution proclaiming the right of the Macedonian nation to a national

Church. Although this demand was brushed aside, the government of the new Yugoslav republic of Macedonia backed continued efforts to establish an independent Macedonian Church. In 1958 a council of Macedonian clergy took a first step toward autocephaly by reestablishing the archbishopric of Ohrid, declaring the Macedonian Church autonomous, though in canonical unity with the Serbian Orthodox Church, and electing Bishop Dositej Stojković, a native of Smederevo, archbishop of Ohrid and metropolitan of Macedonia. The Macedonian government publicly supported these moves.

Finally, in the autumn of 1966, the Macedonians made a formal request for autocephaly, warning the Serbian patriarch in a memorandum of 3 December 1966 that they would act unilaterally if he should deny his concurrence.[64] When the patriarch nonetheless turned them down, the Macedonians summoned an ecclesiastical *sobor* in Ohrid in mid-July 1967 on the bicentennial anniversary of the abolition of the archbishopric of Ohrid and proclaimed the autocephaly of the Macedonian Orthodox Church, seceding from the Serbian Church.[65] The government attended the *sobor* in force, sending two members of the Macedonian government, the heads of the federal and Macedonian commissions for religious affairs, and the mayor of Ohrid. Once the proclamation of autocephaly had been read, moreover, the president of the federal commission for religious affairs announced that President Tito had awarded the cordon of the Order of the Yugoslav Flag to Metropolitan Dositej. Macedonian party chief Krste Crvenkovski telegraphed his congratulations, and the Macedonian party daily, *Nova Makedonija,* wrote that the proclamation would strengthen the brotherhood and unity of Yugoslav peoples.[66] Another Yugoslav writer, expressing the official line, described the declaration as an important step in "the full establishment of the independence of the Macedonian people and nation."[67]

The Serbian Holy Synod denounced the secession and condemned the schismatic clergy. In a series of articles in *Pravoslavlje* and *Glasnik,* the Serbian Orthodox patriarchate cast doubt on the existence of a separate Macedonian people altogether.[68] The Serbian Church refused to accept the autocephaly of the Macedonian Church, and the communist regime refused to withdraw its support for the Macedonian clergy. The situation remained deadlocked.

But if the Serbian Orthodox Church's stance in the Macedonian Church dispute had a defensive character, its activity in other spheres was simultaneously more active and more celebratory. Such activity ranged from doting commemorations of turning points in the development of the Serbian literary language,[69] to celebrating Vuk Karadžić and other heroes of Serbian history,[70] to reinterring the remains of Tsar Dušan the Mighty (1308–55) in an ornate sarcophagus weighing 1.5 tons in St. Mark's Cathedral in Belgrade (1968) as tens of thousands watched.[71]

In May 1982, just over a year after violent Albanian riots shook the province of Kosovo, *Pravoslavlje* published an "Appeal for the Protection of the Serbian Inhabitants and Their Holy Places in Kosovo," signed by twenty-one priests. Accusing the Albanians of destroying an entire wing of the ancient patriarchal church in Peć, the appeal assailed the regime for its weak and indecisive policy and called Kosovo "the Serbian Jerusalem."[72] After this initial act, the Serbian Orthodox Church adopted Kosovo as its own theme, returning to this issue time and again.

To some extent, the post-Tito regime even may have been happy to put the nationalism of the Serbian Orthodox Church to work in Kosovo, going so far as to ask the other religious organizations (in early 1987) to get involved in discussions about Albanian irredentism.[73] But the regime was playing with fire, and the longer the discussion of Kosovo continued to be conducted from a nationalist point of view, the more the Serbs cast themselves as innocent victims and adopted a posture of wounded self-righteousness. A few years earlier, the regime had been more sensitive to the dangers of exclusivist nationalism. For example, Serbian Orthodox Bishop Nikolaj Velimirović (who had died in the United States in 1956) was attacked in a series of articles in *Oslobodjenje* in September 1981, which charged him with nationalist chauvinism.[74] But after 1982, such harsh actions became much rarer, and by 1984 a decisive shift in the wind occurred where the Serbian Church was concerned.

In that year, Serbian Republic authorities granted permission to the Orthodox Church to resume construction of the colossal Church of St. Sava (begun in 1935 and suspended in 1941). After Slobodan Milošević's seizure of power in Serbia in late 1987, the Church's fortunes began to improve all the more rapidly. The new atmosphere was effectively symbolized by an audience that Milošević granted to a group of high-ranking Serbian Orthodox bishops in July 1990.[75] Specific concessions since 1987 included permission for the Church newspaper *Pravoslavlje* to be sold on newsstands (granted in December 1989), permission for Christmas to be celebrated publicly (granted in January 1990), the removal of Marxism from the school curriculum (achieved in June 1990), and the Church's full rehabilitation by actually praising its nationalism![76] Encouraged by the new policy line, the Church sent a letter to the ministry of education of Serbia and demanded that Orthodox religious instruction be introduced in all elementary and secondary schools as a required subject, beginning in the 1991–92 academic year.[77] The proposal came before parliament, where deputies loyal to the Church attempted to obtain the bill's passage, but Milošević used his influence to block the measure, causing it to fail. Meanwhile, the Church indulged once again in the cult of the dead, exhuming the bones of Tsar Lazar and bearing them aloft in a solemn religious procession through parts of Serbia, burying them ultimately in Kosovo. As Renata Salečl has pointed out, for the Serbian celebrants of this macabre ritual "Lazar's return to Kosovo constitute[d] symbolic confirmation of the 'fact' that Kosovo has always been the cradle of 'that which is Serbian.'"[78]

Catholicism and Nationalism

Throughout the nineteenth century, Catholic clergy championed the interests of Croats and Slovenes. In Croatia, the Catholic Church actively backed the struggle for national autonomy (threatened by Magyarization), and in Slovenia, the Church fought to protect the Slovenian language in the face of cultural Germanization by defending its use in Church liturgy. The Church continued to act as the guardian of the secular interests of its Croatian and Slovenian flock. In practice, the linkage of Catholicism and "nationalism" has been manifest in the Church's protection of (1) the interests of Croats in Croatia, (2) the interests of Slovenes in Slovenia, (3) the interests of Croats in Bosnia, Vojvodina (where it remonstrated, at one point, against "the danger of Hungarianization threatening Croats in Bačka"),[79] and elsewhere in Yugoslavia, (4) the interests of Croats abroad, and (5) its own interests (in which it found important symbols of ecclesiastical achievements denigrated by the LCY).

The missionary expansionism that fueled the Church's earlier equation of Croatian or Slovenian national identity with adherence to the Catholic faith is a thing of the past. Most important Church leaders in postwar Yugoslavia, including Franjo Cardinal Kuharić of Zagreb, Archbishop Frane Franić of Split, Franciscan theologian Tomislav Šagi-Bunić, and Fr. Živko Kustić, long-time editor of the weekly Catholic newspaper *Glas koncila*, at one time or another publicly repudiated the equation of national identity with Catholicism.[80] This repudiation, however, did not prevent communist spokespersons from portraying the Church's protection of its flock as a species of "clerical nationalism."[81]

The LCY's hostility to the Catholic Church originally derived from its resentment of any independent institution representing the interests of a part of the population. The LCY ascribed to itself exclusive legitimacy as the advocate of the interests of Yugoslav society—Kardelj's theorizing in the late 1970s notwithstanding. The Church's concern for human rights in Slovenia and Croatia and for national rights in Croatia was a challenge to the LCY monopoly. To buttress its position, the LCY frequently reiterated its ritual incantation that "every nationalism is dangerous." But the Catholic Church has always refused to accept this proposition. In his papal encyclical, *Populorum progressio,* Pope Paul VI condemned "exaggerated nationalism," i.e., racism, but emphasized that some nationalism is constructive. In the same vein, Croatian theologian Šagi-Bunić distinguished between "healthy nationalism"—which he allowed might also be termed "patriotism"—and "unhealthy nationalism," and he argued that Christianity "must be national, must be patriotic; Christians must be patriots."[82] The Church, moreover, now views itself as the legitimate representative of Catholic peoples in general—regardless of whether the government is communist or not—and thus of Croats and Slovenes.

The Croatian Catholic Church's defense of Croatian interests enmeshed it in the politics of the Croatian Spring, 1967–71. Some clergymen, perhaps most, welcomed *Matica hrvatska*'s more active profile and encouraged Croats to join the nationalist organization. The Church entered into negotiations with the Croatian government of Savka Dabčević-Kučar and Miko Tripalo and was confident that Catholics soon would be granted greater equality with atheists and afforded wider opportunities in Croatia.[83] Franciscans in Bosnia-Herzegovina became more active in defending equal employment for Croats. But the removal of Dabčević-Kučar and Tripalo from power in December 1971 and the subsequent suppression of many periodicals and institutions in Croatia delivered a setback, not only to Croats who had hoped to improve Croatia's position within the federation, but also to advocates of Catholic-Marxist dialogue.[84]

Not only the Church's desire to address contemporary issues on the home front annoyed the LCY, however. Almost as unpopular with the regime was the Croatian Church's resolve to maintain contact with Croats abroad—in Germany, Austria, or elsewhere. When Archbishop

Josip Pavlišić of Rijeka and Senj made a private visit to South America and North America in December 1974, he was upbraided for being a guest of "notorious *Ustaše* exiles," a charge later denied by the Episcopal Conference of Yugoslavia. Again, in late 1986, *Borba* tried to portray a routine pastoral visit by Cardinal Kuharić to the Croatian community in Peru as an *Ustaša* event. In this instance, the Croatian daily *Vjesnik* sprang to Kuharić's defense and cited Yugoslav diplomats in Peru to the effect that *Borba*'s claims were "without foundation."[85] The Catholic Church was, and is, in some sense nationalist—but *not in that sense*. Kuharić and others in the Croatian Church could be characterized as nationalists in that they have wanted to nurture and protect the spiritual values and historical memory (embedded in culture) of the Croatian people. But even this form of nationalism is vulnerable to criticism by the regime. Hence, publication by the Croatian Church of the book *Katolička crkva i Hrvati izvan domovine* [The Catholic Church and Croats Outside the Homeland] in 1980 drew criticism from *Vjesnik* for its emphasis on ties of language, culture, and tradition, rather than on the political system.[86]

Finally, the Croatian Church became entangled in nationalist issues through its defense of its own institutional interests. Specifically, since some of its leading clerics of the nineteenth and twentieth centuries, attacked by the party for genocide and other sins, had also acquired the status of Croatian heroes (Archbishop Stepinac being the most important example, but Catholic Action activist Ivan Merz and wartime Bishop Kvirin Klement Bonefačić of Split-Makarska also figuring in LCY criticisms in the 1980s), the defense of its own prelates became, ipso facto, a "nationalist" position.

The situation was closely similar in Slovenia, where Catholic Bishop Gregorij Rožman, who had fled the country in May 1945, was repeatedly characterized as a fascist and a traitor to Slovenia. An attempt even was made on the life of auxiliary bishop of Ljubljana Anton Vovk in early 1952.[87] But as in the Croatian case, Church-state relations in Slovenia improved markedly after the signing of a protocol between the Yugoslav government and the Vatican on 25 June 1966 and, more particularly, after the reestablishment of diplomatic relations between Yugoslavia and the Holy See on 14 August 1970.

Still, from time to time there were reminders of the limitations imposed by the state. In December 1984, for instance, Živko Kustić, the editor of *Glas koncila*, was summoned "by the appropriate state bodies" for an investigative interview in connection with charges that his newspaper had disseminated misinformation embarrassing to the state. The following month, Kustić was sentenced to two months' imprisonment.[88] Ironically, the sentence came just three months after Kustić's ambivalent comment, "The truth is that the only people who have real religious freedom in this country are we priests."[89] It appeared as if the authorities wished to correct Kustić's illusions about a clerical exception. Examples could be multiplied, but the conclusion is clear enough. As Cardinal Kuharić pointed out in an interview with the Slovenian daily newspaper *Delo* in 1989, it was the communist state's insistence on setting the parameters for the institutional life of the religious associations and on controlling the ideological agenda of public life that accounted for Church-state relations remaining so much more problematic in countries ruled by self-described communist parties (or "leagues") than elsewhere.[90]

Muslim Nationalism

Muslim nationalism differs from the preceding cases in at least three ways: (1) the absence of an institutionalized hierarchical Church infrastructure; (2) the difficulty in denying the link between Islam and Muslim ethnicity (although such difficulty has not prevented the LCY from doing just that, albeit obliquely); and (3) the LCY's interests in reinforcing Muslim national consciousness as a foil against the Serbs and Croats of Bosnia.

Although a separate Bosnian republic was created precisely to prevent either Croatia or Serbia from dominating the postwar federation, Belgrade was slow to accord to Muslims their status as a nationality group. The 1948 census allowed the Muslims to list themselves as "Serbian Muslims" (161,036 did so), "Croatian Muslims" (29,071 did so), or "Macedonian Muslims" (37,096). The only other option was "Muslims with undecided nationality"—pointedly unflattering terminology. Only in the 1961 census were Muslims permitted to declare themselves "Muslims in an ethnic sense" (as 842,247 did).[91] Muslims (and Croats) continued to be treated as second-class citizens in Bosnia, however, until the reversal of policy signaled by the removal of police chief Aleksandar Ranković in July 1966. Finally, in February 1968 the central committee of the League of Communists of Bosnia-Herzegovina elevated Muslims from the status of "ethnic group" to that of "separate nation."

In the wake of the 1971 census, Muslim nationalists in Bosnia had become inflamed with the desire to have Bosnia redesignated a "Muslim Republic" in the same way that Serbia was recognized as the Republic of the Serbs and Macedonia as the Republic of the Macedonians.[92] The Muslim learned men (*ulema*) became outspoken advocates of change, and time and again they applied for permission to establish Muslim cultural institutions such as they had enjoyed in Habsburg times.[93] But despite LCY eagerness to have Muslim national identity entrench itself and thus cut off the Muslims from Catholic Croats and Orthodox Serbs, the party consistently refused to allow the establishment of a *Matica muslimanska,* even though a *Matica srpska* continued to function. The reason for this refusal is simple: the regime wanted a "Muslim national identity," but it did not want that identity tied too closely to Islam or to the *ulema,* and a cultural society would inevitably reinforce those taboo linkages.

Relations between the *ulema* and the communist regime remained uneasy. Illustrative of that tension was an article (published in 1981) reporting that Muslim children in Bujanovac were "being overburdened with religious instruction" and claiming that religious instruction was being used as a vehicle for the dissemination of Muslim nationalism.[94]

In 1983 a lengthy Pan-Islamic declaration came to light. Written by a 58-year-old Bosnian lawyer, Alija Izetbegović, the declaration not only rejected socialism, but spurned both coexistence between Muslims and non-Muslims and any secular or non-Islamic system for Muslims. According to Izetbegović's statement, "there is no peace or coexistence between the 'Islamic faith' and other non-Islamic social and political systems. . . . Islam clearly denies the right and opportunity of activity in its own domain to any alien ideology." He went on to reject as alien any nationalism based on folklore and language, linked authentic Muslim self-identity exclusively with Islam, and concluded that "in the Muslim world there is no patriotism without Islam."[95] Izetbegović and twelve other Muslim intellectuals, including an imam and a teacher at a Muslim religious school, were subsequently arrested for having conspired to execute the principles set forth in the "Islamic Declaration" and ultimately sentenced on 20 August 1983 to prison terms averaging eight years.[96]

A new trial of alleged Muslim nationalists was conducted in the spring of 1987. The accused—Fadil Fadilpašić, Munib Zahiragić, and Ibrahim Avdić—were tried for conspiring to overthrow the Yugoslav political system and to establish an "ethnically pure Islamic republic" in Bosnia-Herzegovina, if necessary by means of a jihad. They also were said to have made contact with "hostile émigrés" in Turkey and to have obtained from those émigrés a copy of the "Islamic Declaration." Given the gravity of the charges, it came as some surprise that they were sentenced to prison terms ranging from only two to five years.[97]

The Outbreak of War

Tito's League of Communists of Yugoslavia, which expired under centrifugal pressures in early 1990, long pursued a doubly self-contradictory policy. The first contradiction consisted, on the one hand, in the LCY speaking of creating a cultural basis for "brotherhood and unity" among the peoples of Yugoslavia and extending respect and tolerance to religious believers in the spirit of reconciliation, while on the other hand, the LCY never tired of stoking old hatreds and prejudices associated with Croatian Archbishop Stepinac (hated by Serbs) and Serbian Archbishop Velimirović (whose pro-Chetnik sympathies made him unsympathetic to Croats), although such measures could have the effect only of sowing and preserving interethnic rancor. Moreover, despite all its talk of "unity," the LCY on a number of occasions obstructed ecumenical contacts among the three principal faiths of Yugoslavia.

The second contradiction was between the Titoist system's "modernism" in the sense of aspiring to depoliticize and weaken ties to family, village, religion, and ethno-national groups and the policy of according protection to those ties within the framework of ethnically based federal republics.[98]

Ideally, the Titoists wanted the Churches "denationalized" so that the Catholic Church's link with Croatian nationalism and the Serbian Orthodox Church's link with Serbian nationalism would be severely attenuated, if not sundered altogether. But not only did the Churches themselves resist this policy, but the very strategies and tactics adopted by the communists served to consolidate the symbiotic relationship of religion and nationalism, thus achieving the exact opposite of what many LCY officials genuinely hoped for.

Only in 1989–90, as the political system was disintegrating, did ecumenical contacts become reasonably vigorous, and then only between Catholic and Islamic theologians.[99] During this time, however, the Serbian Orthodox Church's relations with both of these communities actually soured, chiefly if not exclusively as a result of the rising tide of Serbian chauvinist nationalism. By early 1990 Serbs were writing anti-Muslim graffiti such as "Death to Muslims!" on Islamic buildings.[100] Similar graffiti also have been scrawled on Catholic Church buildings in Belgrade. As nationalist and religious hatreds exacerbated and found increasing expression, Catholic Archbishop Franjo Cardinal Kuharić of Zagreb appealed for dialogue with the Serbian Orthodox leadership, only to be rebuffed. By then, anti-Catholic propaganda had reached a fever pitch in Serbia with the publication of Vladimir Dedijer's slanderous book about the Catholic Church[101] and the proliferation of loose talk, both in the media and among the public, of a Vatican "conspiracy" against the Serbs. Although Serbian Orthodox clergy could be said to have eagerly jumped onto the nationalist bandwagon as early as 1982 (in the wake of the Albanian riots in Kosovo in April 1981), the Milošević regime clearly encouraged the Serbian Church's adoption of a siege mentality, both by approving the publication of Dedijer's book and others like it[102] and by increasingly giving Serbian bishops access to *Politika* and other public forums for the expression of nationalist sentiments. A clear relationship can be detected between the conspiratorial mood that seized the Serbian Church as it worried about a worldwide Vatican-Islamic plot against Serbdom and the Milošević regime's claims that a Vatican-German-Croatian-Muslim conspiracy existed against the Serbian nation—a line which predated the ethnic war's outbreak in June 1991 but which received added emphasis later.

On 7 May 1991 the newly installed Serbian patriarch, Pavle, who in some key ways appeared to be more moderate than his predecessor, received Cardinal Kuharić for friendly talks.[103] At the discussion's conclusion the two prelates issued a joint statement, warning of the imminent danger threatening their peoples. Referring to the "almost hopeless difficulties in our Homeland," the bishops spoke "of the need to maintain civilized and brotherly relations in this grave and difficult time," stressing that the failure to do so would result in "the destruction of property, the desecration of sacred places, and the threat to the lives of people."[104] But this last-minute dialogue had no meaningful impact on Serb-Croat relations, and at best its impact was at the inter-episcopal level. After the Yugoslav war broke out on 27 June 1991 between the federal army and Slovenia, subsequently evolving into a Serb-Croat confrontation, the Serbian Orthodox Church seemed less interested in ecumenism and once again showed its nationalist colors. A reading of the Serbian patriarchal organ *Pravoslavlje* illustrates this attitude all too well. *Pravoslavlje* in 1990 started publishing voluminous chauvinistic, anti-Croatian articles, often dredging up distorted and one-sided information about World War II; in July 1991, as Serbian troops were laying siege to Osijek, the newspaper devoted a full page to an overtly political expostulation on "the contribution of the Serbian Orthodox Church to the development of the culture of the city of Osijek."[105] It was only after the war had spread to Bosnia and as it became apparent that Serbian hostility was not limited to Catholic Croats that the Serbian Orthodox hierarchs adopted a more moderate position, even articulating pacifist views on occasion.[106]

Jure Kristo, a seasoned observer of the Croatian ecclesiastical scene, has strenuously denied that the Yugoslav war might, in any sense, be construed as "religious."[107] Yet it is clear enough that the war soon developed salient religious dimensions. To begin with, all three sides deliberately targeted each other's religious objects for destruction — not only in the heat of battle, but even within areas already under their control. The Bosnian Serbs, led by former psychiatrist Radovan Karadžić, were the most systematic in this regard. They razed the last remaining Islamic mosques in Banja Luka in the summer of 1994, even though no challenge to their control of the city had arisen since they had seized it two years earlier; the Bosnian Serbs also dynamited six Catholic churches in Banja Luka within a matter of weeks in the spring of 1995.[108] To take another example, Serbian forces attacked the historic Catholic cathedral at Ilok on the Danube on three occasions in 1993, succeeding during one attack in blasting away the cathedral's doors.[109] In areas "ethnically cleansed" (i.e., subjected to systematic genocide) and swept of earlier historic mosques and Catholic churches, the conquering Bosnian Serbs took to rewriting the past, telling Western journalists, whom the Serbs took for fools, that no mosques or Catholic churches had ever existed in the area — only Orthodox churches.

Those Catholics living in Serbia were harassed, with the result that the number of Catholics in the Belgrade archdiocese, for example, plummeted from 34,000 in 1987 to 8,000–9,000 in 1993.[110] Meanwhile, in Croatia the tension became so intense that many of the country's remaining 100,000–150,000 Serbs agreed to have their children or themselves baptized as Catholics, in order to prove their *confessional and, hence, political* loyalty to Croatia.[111] Metropolitan Jovan, the head of all Serbian Orthodox believers residing in Croatia, protested against these baptisms, claiming that they were "forced."

In March 1992 the Serbian Orthodox patriarchate declared that "in this new independent state of Croatia, as in the earlier one, there is no life for Orthodox Serbs."[112] And in repeated public pronouncements and published articles the Serbian patriarchate and bishops laid stress on the *past* sufferings of the Serbian people in World War II, ignored the fact that people other than Serbs had suffered in that war, portrayed the Serbs as guiltless, blameless, innocent victims (even comparing the Serbian nation in one article to the biblical victim Job), and adopted the pose of guardians of the nation. On 28 May 1992, however, after the expansion of the war into Bosnia-Herzegovina, the synod of bishops of the Serbian Orthodox Church issued a strong statement calling on Milošević to step down and accusing the authorities in Serbia and Montenegro of refusing to attempt a policy of "national reconciliation." But even with that statement, the synod stuck to its "victim" interpretation of Serbian history, declaring: "This is not the first time for the Serbian people in their history to have experienced crucifixion."[113] Two weeks later, on 14 June, Patriarch Pavle led a procession of several thousand Serbs through the streets of Belgrade. The crowd demanded that Milošević immediately resign.[114]

In the months that followed, Patriarch Pavle reestablished contacts with Franjo Cardinal Kuharić, the Catholic archbishop of Zagreb, and collaborated with him in issuing a series of statements calling for peace.[115] In one joint statement, issued in Geneva on 23 September 1992, Pavle and Kuharić urged the immediate cessation of all hostilities, the freeing of war prisoners and hostages, an end to "ethnic cleansing," the facilitated return of all refugees to their homes, etc.[116] By the beginning of November 1992 these two Church leaders had issued three such statements. Then, on 25 November they were joined by Reis ul-ulema Jakub Selimoški, the head of the Bosnian Islamic community, in a wider appeal for peace in Bosnia-Herzegovina.[117]

Yet, despite Patriarch Pavle's occasional pacifism, he took Karadžić's side when a rift appeared between Milošević and Karadžić in the summer of 1994.[118] Milošević wanted the Bosnian Serbs to sign the latest peace plan, while Karadžić insisted on rejecting the plan and continuing to advance Serbian aims on the field of battle. In an interview with *Svetigora*, the official monthly magazine of the Orthodox metropolitanate in Cetinje, Karadžić even claimed that God personally endorsed the Bosnian Serbs and that their conquests were "God's work."[119] Meanwhile, imams and Christian clergy increasingly appeared alongside their respective troops, blessing them before battle. By the autumn of 1994, in truncated Bosnia, imams were telling people that confessionally mixed marriages should be the exception, while Bosnian Muslim women increasingly covered their heads with scarves in deference to Islamic leaders and to an unnamed Arab organization that reportedly was paying them DM 50 each to cover their heads. For some Western observers, these were small straws in the wind, indicating a turn toward a stricter observance of Islam. Indeed, within Bosnian President Alija Izetbegović's party, a struggle between moderates and fundamentalists was said to be waxing.[120]

The Serbian leadership and the Serbian Church hierarchy have each promoted the notion that Serbdom means Orthodoxy, albeit for distinctly different reasons. For the leaders, this manipulation serves to create a point of cultural unity, to build a bridge to nationalism as an alternate source of legitimacy (replacing the defunct communist ideology), and to resurrect traditional values such as the primacy of the nation and male dominance. And lest anyone doubt that male dominance is politically relevant in this context, George Mosse reminded observers of the historic linkage between nationalist policies and the suppression of women by means of supposedly "traditional" values.[121]

For the Serbian Church hierarchy, this manipulation served the obvious objective of placing the Serbian Church at the ideological center and of creating an artificial (i.e., nonspiritual) attraction to the Church. But the shift in aims accomplishes something even more significant, namely, the rehabilitation of the Serbian Church as a political entity, a restoration of its ability to address public issues, and a renewed assertion of its self-proclaimed "right" to speak on behalf of "Serbs everywhere."

Defining the nation as specifically Orthodox in religion (or Catholic or Muslim, for that matter) is one way to draw the boundaries of a nation. Violence directed against members of the out-group (or out-groups) likewise serves to define the boundaries of the in-group by throwing them into sharp relief and by underlining the importance of clear criteria for determining group membership. Here, I agree with the argument offered by the collaborators in the Project on Religion and Human Rights to the effect: "one may understand violence as one way that groups of people seek to establish boundaries between themselves and others, boundaries intended to protect a communal way of life, . . . or in general to secure a place in the universe. With this understanding in mind, one is justified in thinking that the potential for religion to be a root of conflict is always present in human societies."[122]

War, Intolerance, Seeds of Despair

The Serbian Insurrectionary War of 1991–95—the name I use because
the conflict began with insurrection by Croatian and Bosnian Serbs— [123]
had features characteristic of both civil war and international war, fueling
endless and ultimately irreconciliable controversies about terminology.
Some observers suggested calling the war "an ethnic war" because the
Serbian forces in Croatia and Bosnia, and to a lesser extent Croatian
forces in those same republics, relied on the systematic inculcation of
hatred of designated "others," but also because both Serbian and Croatian media were soon awash with emotionally charged diatribes against
entire national groups.[124] Still others denied that this approach was
valid, often claiming that the Bosnian side was largely immune to ethnic
hatred. Be that as it may, the war proved to have tremendous power to
foster and/or reinforce ethnic and religious intolerance and to engender
organizational dismemberment, manifested, inter alia, in the dismantlement of the Catholic bishops' conference of Yugoslavia (in 1992),[125] the
establishment of an autocephalous Montenegrin Orthodox Church over
the protests of Serbian bishops (in 1993),[126] the creation of a separate
Islamic council of elders in the Sandžak in the face of denunciations by
officials of the FRY ministry of religion (in 1994),[127] the rupture by the
Montenegrin Islamic community of organizational-administrative unity
with the Islamic Community of Serbia in the face of insinuations that
the move was part of a plan to "Albanianize" the Slavic Islamic population of Montenegro (in 1995),[128] and the reorganization of the Croatian Islamic community as an administratively independent body (also
in 1995).[129]

Although the fighting cannot usefully be characterized as a "religious
war," the religious aspects of the conflict all the same were unmistakable. Serbs destroyed Catholic churches and Islamic mosques,[130] Croats
destroyed Serbian Orthodox churches and Islamic mosques,[131] and both
Croats and Bosnians were accused of attempting to convert people of
other faiths against their will.[132] Pressures on non-Muslims to convert
to Islam took the form of introducing Koran instruction into the program of the Bosnian army's 7th Corps,[133] and the prohibition (in 1994) of
marriage between Muslims and non-Muslims on the part of the Islamic
Community of Bosnia-Herzegovina.[134] So estranged from each other did
the peoples of Bosnia become that they lost the ability even to understand the pope's exhortation during a visit to Zagreb in September 1994

asking for fraternal and sororal harmony. The pope, in urging that "we are all brothers and we must remain brothers" and that "no one can avoid the course of unity and peace,"[135] was thinking of the sisterhood and brotherhood of all humankind and of what he might call "unity in Christ" and not referring to any special ethnic or linguistic similarities between Croats and Serbs, let alone to their shared history. But a Serbian journalist, attempting an exegesis of the papal speech, fastened on the words "brothers" and "unity" and gave the pope's words an entirely different interpretation, imagining that "the general impression is that the writers of the pope's Zagreb 'encyclics' . . . made ample use of the 50-volume *Collected Works of J. B. Tito.*"[136] Pope John Paul II, who proposed to speak as the Vicar of Christ and an Apostle of Peace, was portrayed instead as the vicar of Tito and the apostle of the Titoist formula of "brotherhood and unity."

But because this war was fueled by hatred, it became impossible to restrict its destructiveness to the battlefield. While the Croatian army's excesses during military operations in the so-called Krajina are well known, it is only the Bosnian Serb forces loyal to Radovan Karadžić who made it a policy to *systematically erase all traces of the heritage of other religious traditions in areas far removed from the front lines or from military operations.* Of the various cities held by the Bosnian Serbs, perhaps none suffered so much as Banja Luka where, in the course of three years of "peace," Bosnian Serb forces destroyed all 212 mosques and destroyed or seriously damaged seventy out of seventy-five Catholic churches of the city.[137] Indeed, as of May 1995, thirty attacks on Catholic nuns had occurred in Banja Luka, and seven Catholic priests were being held in Bosnian Serb prison camps.[138]

Interestingly enough, even Serbia, nominally at least a nonbelligerent, has seen some religious violence. At least two cases are relevant here. On the night of 31 May 1994, unknown persons planted explosives in the Catholic church in Subotica.[139] And, more vexingly, the seventeenth-century Bajrakli mosque in downtown Belgrade—the city's only mosque—withstood seven bombing attacks between 1990 and April 1996 (at least two of them in 1996) in a transparent attempt on the part of unknown perpetrators to bring confessional "cleansing" home to Serbia.[140]

But an even more striking case of the repercussions of war-related hatreds on the home front involves the Jews. In the old Kingdom of Yugoslavia there were about 80,000 Jews. As of 1995, however, only about 3,000 Jews lived in the Federal Republic of Yugoslavia (Serbia and Montenegro), an equal number resided in Croatia, and only 525 in Sarajevo.[141] But in spite of these small numbers or, rather, *because* the numbers have been so small, anti-Semitism has reared its head in both Serbia and Croatia. In Serbia in 1994 an article, "Jewish Vampire Balle," appeared in a newspaper published by the Serbian National Renewal in *Bijelo polje*. The article was roundly condemned not only by members of the Jewish community, but by many ordinary Serbs as well as by government spokespersons in Belgrade.[142]

In Croatia, by contrast, anti-Semitism has revived as a byproduct of the Tudjman government's policy of rehabilitating the wartime N D H, including some of its leading figures such as Ante Pavelić and Mile Budak. Strong reactions from the world public compelled Tudjman to retrace some of his steps, but in July 1994 the coordination committee of the Jewish communities of Croatia still considered it necessary to send an open letter to the government in Zagreb. I quote the full text of the H T V broadcast about the letter:

The Coordination Committee of the Jewish Communities of the Republic of Croatia states with regret that there has been no response to its letter sent to the highest-ranking state officials [on 29 November 1993].

In the letter, demands were made for the return of monuments on the site of the former concentration camp in Jadovno and on other sites of mass *Ustaša* crimes against members of the Jewish and other peoples. The Committee also protested against increasingly frequent instances of the distortion of historical facts through the rehabilitation of the criminal Independent State of Croatia [N D H] and warned of unfavorable reactions to and consequences of the name kuna given to the new Croatian currency.

We note with pleasure, the letter goes on, expressions of sympathy with the Jewish people and commiseration with the victims of fascism and other antifascist statements which have come from President Tudjman in recent months. We also welcome a move to rename Mile Budak School in Zagreb. Unfortunately, at the same time, there are a growing number of events in Croatian public life which cause our concern and indignation, the letter says, adding that various newspapers have fomented national intolerance and hatred, directly offending Jewish and other peoples.

For instance, the Croatian [newspaper] *Vjesnik* of 10 April 1994 and various rightwing parties and groups are organizing public celebrations to mark the anniversary of the N D H and of Ante Pavelić, while the state television carries extensive reports of these events without any critical remarks or reservations.

We find these phenomena offensive to the Jews and to the entire democratic public, and worrying for Croatia. Because of all this, the Coordination Committee of the Jewish Communities of the Republic of Croatia demands that, on the basis of Article 39 of the Constitution of the Republic of Croatia, the public prosecutor take legal action against Croatia's *Vjesnik* for fomenting national intolerance and hatred and institute proceedings on a regular basis whenever and wherever similar articles appear. We also propose that the Croatian Parliament pass special legislation which, on the basis of the above-mentioned article of the Constitution, will prohibit and stipulate penalties for the spreading of national and religious intolerance and hatred, as has already been done in most countries of the developed democratic world, we read in the public letter signed on behalf of the Coordination Committee of the Jewish Communities of the Republic of Croatia by its president, Ognjen Kraus.[143]

In this context, it will come as no surprise that some members of the Croatian political opposition urged the Catholic Church in 1996 to condemn alleged strains of fascism within Franjo Tudjman's ruling party.[144]

Intolerance has been provoked not merely by hate-mongering and intercommunal warfare, but also by two specific and interconnected processes of politicization of religion and sacralization of politics. As Srdjan Vrcan has noted, these processes entailed, among other things, "the ontologizing of existing social, political and cultural differences, projecting them onto a metaphysical backdrop" and the promotion of "an interpretation of national history in terms of a sacred martyrology of Calvary made glorious by the quality and quantity of the suffering of the victims" and an associated belief that that suffering "has to be recompensed or revenged in terms of a privileged quasi-salvational historical mission within the eternal plans of Providence."[145] The translation of national causes into religious causes and ethnic hatreds into confessional antagonisms not only politicizes religion, but it transforms religion, subtly changing the meaning of its terms of reference and substituting a national ontology for divine ontology as the centerpiece of religious life.

Conclusion

Yugoslav religious policy was affected by ethnic and nationality considerations in at least three ways. First, the linkage of religion and nationalism strengthens the religious organization, reinforcing its legitimacy as a political actor and compelling the regime to calculate the effects of religious repression on individual nationality groups. Second, the LCY's desire to reinforce Macedonian and Muslim ethnic identities led the communist regime to adopt a very cooperative attitude vis-à-vis the Macedonian Orthodox Church and to tread softly where Muslims were concerned (e.g., far fewer Muslim learned men were imprisoned—if any —than either Catholic or Orthodox clergy, and Muslim *ulema* from the past were never calumniated in the press). Regime endorsement of the religio-nationalist linkage in Macedonia is corroborated by the fact that while other universities were named for Yugoslav socialists and communists (e.g., the Edvard Kardelj University of Ljubljana, the Veljko Vlahović University of Titograd, the Djemal Bijedić University of Mostar, and the Svetozar Marković University Library of the University of Belgrade), the University of Skopje was named for the medieval monks, Cyril and Methodius.[146] Third, insofar as the LCY may have feared that ethnic tensions in one republic might spread to other republics (as was said to be the case after the massive Albanian riots in Kosovo in April 1981), the linkage of religion and nationalism may have served to stimulate antireligious attitudes.

This chapter has reviewed the position and activities as they have impinged on nationalism of the principal religious bodies in the lands of the South Slavs. I have dwelled at length on the Serbian Orthodox Church, the Croatian Catholic Church, and the Islamic community in Bosnia, devoting some attention, as well, to the Catholic Church in Slovenia and to the Macedonian Orthodox Church. With the breakup of Yugoslavia in June 1991, some of these Churches have come to dominate their respective republics (the Catholic Church in Slovenia and Croatia, the Serbian Orthodox Church in Serbia); elsewhere, religious divisions deprive any single religious body from playing a superordinate role (as in Macedonia and divided Bosnia-Herzegovina). But in all of these cases the breakup of the country and the accession of new political leaderships have meant a transformation of Church-state relations and a change in the religio-nationalist connection.

Chapter 7
Holy Intolerance: Romania's Orthodox Church

Every society experiences problems of intolerance, and almost all—if not all—religions encourage and sanction specific forms of it. Indeed, often religions *require* intolerance in order to pursue their objectives. Intolerance rooted in religion is perhaps the strongest strain of intolerance, because its lack of charity and its willful injury to others are given what is presumed by believers to be "divine" sanction. Romania is a case in point. Indeed, in the years since 1878, which this chapter covers, Romania has displayed persistent strains of both anti-Catholic and anti-Semitic intolerance.

Intolerance may be understood as the endeavor on the part of those subscribing to a simpler, preexisting paradigm to press complex reality into it without making any meaningful adjustments. In sociological terms, simpler paradigms have tended to be associated with the countryside, where inhabitants operate within narrower horizons, tend to have a smaller circle of friends (usually from the same ethnic group or religion, or both), experience fewer opportunities for social mobility, and in general are exposed to a largely homogeneous social and cultural environment. Even today, most villages in Central Europe and the Balkans are ethnically homogeneous and generally have, at most, two religious faiths represented within the village. In *the Balkans* confessionally homogeneous villages have tended to be the norm (especially in Bosnia, Romania, and Bulgaria). The entire cast of the village is such as to foster distrust of "outsiders" and to define the notion of "outsider" broadly, with multiple levels of distance and distrust.[1]

The city is inevitably different. With increased opportunity to encounter people of different faiths, ethnicities, sexual orientations, attire, culture, languages, etc., the inhabitants of an urban environment are habituated to take a more openly embracing view of who is "one of us," if not, indeed, to begin to move away from outsider/us thinking altogether. Cosmopolitanism is specifically the ambience of the city and the culture in which tolerance may thrive.

In societies where urbanization keeps pace with exposure to new cul-

Table 7.1 Illiteracy in Romania (1930)

Region	Percent illiterate
The Regat	44.1
Bessarabia	61.4
The Banat	27.5
Transylvania	33.6
Bukovina	34.2

Source: Armin Heinen, Die Legion 'Erzengel Michael' in Rumänien: Soziale Bewegung und politische Organisation (Munich: R. Oldenbourg, 1986), p. 558.

tures, adjustment may be hard enough (as the example of the United States in the late nineteenth and early twentieth centuries amply illustrates).[2] But when urbanization fails to keep pace—as, for example, when a nation suddenly annexes large swathes of territory that had been operating for centuries under different social and legal systems—the appearance of certain problems of cultural adjustment is to be expected.

Romania in 1918 was essentially a textbook case of a society ripe for intolerance. To begin with, the society was overwhelmingly rural and agrarian, and many residents of larger cities were at best one generation out of the village. As late as 1938, 78 percent of the population of Romania was employed in the agricultural sector.[3] Educational levels and literacy levels were low (see table 7.1). Nicolae Iorga commented on the situation of the peasantry in interwar Romania in these terms: "There is no doubt that our peasantry is the most backward of all in Europe; in no other country, not even in Turkey, has the peasantry been left so far behind as the peasantry in the Romanian kingdom."[4]

Second, the peasantry lived in grinding poverty, which was only compounded by a 54 percent growth in population between 1859 and 1899 alone.[5] Rural overpopulation reinforced low productivity, which in turn resulted in poor nutrition and health; these factors, in turn, combined with landlord absenteeism to stimulate social friction in the countryside[6] —a friction which could, with some manipulation, be deployed against designated "enemies."

Third, thanks to a combination of ruthless military action and clever diplomacy during World War I, Romania more than doubled its size and population after 1918, acquiring land from Austria (Bukovina), Hungary

(Transylvania), Russia (Bessarabia), and Bulgaria (southern Dobruja). Fourth, Romania was flushed with ethnic nationalism, as a concomitant of this rapid expansion, although 28 percent of Romania's population in 1919 consisted of ethnic non-Romanians.[7]

And fifth, this society, which many nationalist politicians viewed as "the village writ large," was confessionally diverse. In addition to the large Orthodox and Greek-Rite Catholic Churches, interwar Romania also counted 710,706 members of the (Hungarian) Reformed Church, 650,000 Jews, 645,544 Roman Catholics, 69,257 (Hungarian) Unitarians, 70,000 (mostly Swabian) Lutherans, 30,000 members of the newly formed Hungarian Evangelical Church, 30,000 Baptists, and additional numbers of Muslims and members of other faiths.[8]

The challenges posed by this combination of elements were enormous, and the results predictable. But to set the Romanian Orthodox Church in perspective, three other themes that have played significant roles in the life of that Church—government domination, nationalism, and competition with other faiths—need to be highlighted.

A Brief Retrospective (1878–1918)

The theme of government domination of religion in Romania leaves the strongest impression from the start. Indeed, during Romania's first half-century of independence (1878–1928), political parties with diverse philosophies and programs constantly interfered in the life of the Romanian Orthodox Church, often by passing laws in which the Church enjoyed little input, at other times by appointing hierarchs who would be useful to the state (though not necessarily to the Church).[9] A law passed in 1872, on the eve of independence, for example, specified the procedures to be observed in the selection of metropolitans and diocesan bishops as well as the composition and responsibilities of the synod. An 1893 law regulated theological education, while a 1904 law established a governmental agency to maintain and improve Church properties. These laws were followed in 1908 by passage of a statute establishing the so-called Supreme Church Consistory as a quasiecclesiastical parliament to give laity, regular clergy, and monastics a voice in the Church's affairs.[10] The ministry of religion and public instruction played a key role in regulating and channeling Church-state relations, so much so that as Baptist and Adventist missionaries established bridgeheads in Romania, the Orthodox hierarchy looked to the government to protect it and to uphold its legally sanctioned privileged position. The state, however, declined to involve itself in the interconfessional conflict.

Orthodox clergy members resorted to less than delicate tactics in pursuing their competition. The Adventist and Baptist missionaries commonly expressed contempt for Orthodox clergy and insulted the Church.[11] The clergy, in turn, accused the missionaries of making "foreign propaganda," depicting them as agents of foreign powers. Nationalism was thus exploited in the context of interconfessional rivalry.

The Jews faced much different obstacles in that article VII of the constitution of 1866 provided that "only foreigners belonging to a Christian confession can obtain naturalization."[12] This meant that the formal assurance of the equality of all religions required by the Great Powers as part of the 1878 Treaty of Berlin remained a dead letter until such time as Bucharest might adopt a new constitution.

The Jewish presence owed something to the encouragement given them to immigrate to Moldavia between 1834 and 1849.[13] By 1859, some 118,000 Jews resided in Moldavia, though only 9,200 lived in Wallachia. Intermittently, the Romanian authorities imposed restrictions on Jewish immigration, but these were not properly enforced and the wave of new arrivals continued. By 1899, 201,000 Jews lived in Moldavia, 68,000 in Wallachia. The Jewish community constituted, thus, 4.5 percent of the population of the kingdom of Romania.[14]

Religious intolerance mixed with jealousy of the Jewish community's economic talents to induce Christian Romanians to lend unanimous endorsement to the withholding of civil equality from the Jews. From time to time, attacks were carried out on Jewish synagogues, which were viewed by local Christians as the physical and symbolic embodiment of Jewish "foreignness." In Paris the Alliance Israelite agitated in favor of the Jews, even offering to raise a low-term loan of Fr 25,000,000 in exchange for incorporation into the constitution of a clause affirming that "religion constitutes no obstacle to naturalization."[15] This initiative failed to achieve its objective; indeed, the Romanian authorities now hardened their stand against the Jews.

Rather than cave in to foreign pressure, the commission appointed by the Romanian legislature adopted an openly obstreperous manifesto (on 5 July 1879), which held that "there are no Roumanian Jews and never were...."[16] But Romanians could not hold out over the long term against consistent pressure by the Great Powers, and on 18 October 1879 the legislature voted, 133 to 9, to amend article VII to read that "difference of religious creed does not constitute an obstacle to the acquisition or exercise of civil and political rights."[17] This resolution was largely superficial, and various restrictions and evasions continued to consign Jews to second-class status. But the Great Powers were eager to put the issue of Romanian anti-Semitism aside, and they accepted the compromise as sufficient.

Meanwhile, the Orthodox clergy were swept up in the rising tide of peasant discontent. In the peasant revolt of 1888, many village priests revealed strong sympathies with the impoverished peasants. Subsequently, in 1907 when the peasants rose again in revolt against the boyars and landlords, many Orthodox parish priests joined them, even in some cases accompanying bands of armed peasants. After the government finally suppressed the uprising, dozens of priests were rounded up and imprisoned on charges of having incited the peasants. Three priests were even shot by authorities.[18]

Interwar Romania

Romania's rapid expansion after World War I dramatically changed the country's confessional composition. Before 1918 the chief poles of religious rivalry were between the Orthodox Church on the one hand, and Roman Catholic, Adventist, and Baptist congregants on the other. In any event, the ethnic association was largely marginal. Aside from these inter-Christian rivalries, the only other interconfessional issue to attain the level of a national controversy was the so-called "Jewish question" (as noted).[19] After 1918 the large Greek-Rite Catholic Church was added to the mix, figuring simultaneously as ethnic ally and ideological rival of the Orthodox Church;[20] the Hungarian and Swabian congregations in Transylvania also assured that interconfessional competition would assume a clear ethnic coloration.

The social and cultural climate of interwar Romania might be characterized by situating the country within the general European reaction against rationalism and logical positivism. As Keith Hitchins notes,

Rumanian intellectuals rejected the rationalism represented by Kant and his successors, who struck them as hopelessly out of touch with the real world. They turned for guidance to others: to Nietzsche, whose anti-rationalism fascinated them; to Dilthey and Einstein, whose relativism converted them from Darwin's determinism; to Spengler, whose theories about the inevitable decline of civilizations, especially of the West, provided them with new analytical tools. . . . A veritable wave of irrationalist and mystical ideas seemed to break across Rumanian intellectual life.[21]

The repudiation of Kantian rationalism went hand in hand with the rejection of moral universalism; in its place, intellectuals embracing irrationalism and antirationalism placed moral relativism and moral nihilism, constructing upon this twin foundation the ideological turrets of intolerant nationalism.[22]

The religious climate in interwar Romania was shaped in part by two highly influential writers, Nichifor Crainic (1889–1972) and Onisifor Ghibu (1883–1972). Crainic, whose ideas influenced the fascistic Iron Guard and whose influence continued into the Ceauşescu era, idealized the Romanian village and Orthodox spirituality, which he linked. Crainic argued "that the Romanian village had assisted nation-building by its ability to screen out foreign influences and keep alive a fundamental spirituality deriving from Byzantine orthodoxy. To survive, Romania had to remain faithful to its traditions and avoid becoming contaminated by western values." In Crainic's view, as Gallagher has pointed out, "democracy was unsuitable for Romania because of its association with western bourgeois civilization."[23]

Crainic lent his explicit endorsement to the anti-Semitism rampant in his country. According to Crainic,

The point of view of Judaism in our country is the uprooting of our people (*neamului*) from their own country. In this respect a clear distinction is necessary between Christian minorities and the Jews. In our ethnic body, the minorities are localized islands, sometimes with centrifugal tendencies, but with very few tendencies of internal expansion. The Jews, however, represent the force of general infiltration, and a multiple assault toward our subjugation.[24]

Crainic was, in his own way, one of the ideologists of the age. Ghibu's role was different. His calling was not that of political bard but of polemicist and provocateur. Ghibu's ire was directed against the Hungarian Catholic Church and against the Vatican's quest for a concordat. His writings contributed tangibly to interconfessional resentment and hostility. A professor at the University of Cluj, Ghibu argued for the abrogation of the legal guarantees enjoyed by the (mostly Hungarian)

Roman Catholic Church in Transylvania since long before the region's annexation by Romania. He also was opposed to the prospect of the Holy See obtaining a concordat with the government in Bucharest.

In 1923 Ghibu began writing articles for *Patria*, a daily newspaper, demanding that some Roman Catholic churches be turned over to Romanians, whether Orthodox or Greek-Rite Catholic; he further characterized the "Status," the autonomous legal rights enjoyed by the Roman Catholic Church in Transylvania since the seventeenth century, as "a state within a state."[25] Fired up by Ghibu's charges, Ioan Bianu, an Orthodox senator, approached the minister of religious affairs on 24 February 1924 and demanded an investigation of the Status of the Catholic Church. Romanian authorities responded by harassing the Roman Catholic hierarchy and raising questions about the 250-year-old Status. In some localities the authorities confiscated Hungarian Catholic properties. The Romanian Orthodox Church also became involved in anti-Catholic politicking. After considerable delay, negotiations were initiated with the Holy See in 1932; Valer Pop (the government's chief negotiator) hoped to obtain a transformation of properties of the ancient Status (of *Roman*, hence Hungarian, Catholics) into "general Catholic properties," which also would benefit Greek-Rite (Romanian) Catholics.[26] A general agreement was reached on 30 May 1932, granting concessions to both sides. Ghibu attacked the "Roman Accord," as it was called, and launched a hysterical polemical campaign against it. Largely under the influence of Ghibu's attacks, the Romanian courts declined to recognize the Roman Accord, which therefore died on the table. In the meantime, individual Roman Catholic parishes were being compelled to surrender many treasures and properties to the Greek-Rite Catholics, including the Minorite Church and the Church of Monostir.[27]

It was only in 1938 that a committee appointed by Bucharest once again took a serious look at the Roman Accord. Negotiations with the Holy See were resumed, dragging on for months, and eventually the accord was signed and recognized as valid, its announcement duly recorded in *Monitorul Oficial* on 2 March 1941. Not only Hungarian Catholics were subjected to endless delays, however. Bucharest also held up recognition of the Hungarian Evangelical ecclesiastic organization for some twenty years (1920–40).[28] This prolonged delay suggests that anti-Hungarian prejudice may have played more than a small role in framing Bucharest's religious policies in that era. This conclusion is reinforced by a reading of section 22 of the Romanian constitution of 1938: "Since the

Orthodox Church is the religion of the great majority of Romanians, the Orthodox Church is the ruling Church in the Romanian state, whereas the Uniate Church is granted priority with regard to other denominations."[29] The designation of a given Church as the official, established Church of the country was customary in Europe at that time; but it was unusual to grant a second Church something on the order of runner-up status. Then there is the fact that both of these privileged Churches had ethnic Romanian congregations.

This reading is reinforced by the provisions of the Law on Religion (1928) which classified the Romanian Orthodox Church and the (Romanian) Greek-Rite Catholic Church as "Churches"; all other religious bodies were classified as "cults."[30] According to Sándor Bíró, this law also "prescribed what amounted to police control over every [activity] of the non-Romanian churches."[31] For example, the law hindered contributions from coreligionists abroad, set limits on donations by believers, and prescribed supervision by state authorities of some aspects of the internal life of non-Romanian Churches. Even where the law appeared to prescribe equal treatment of religious bodies, it was applied unequally, for example, in the confiscations of properties owned by the Hungarian Unitarian and Reformed Churches and their transfer to the Romanian Orthodox and Greek-Rite Catholic Churches.[32]

Bucharest also practiced discrimination in the disbursement of the *Congrua* (or salary subsidy) distributed to clergymen of all faiths. From 1898 to 1918 the *Congrua* had been distributed to clergy in Transylvania by the Hungarian government; Budapest had done so by treating all religious denominations and nationalities equally. Beginning in 1920, the Romanian state disbursed the *Congrua* in Transylvania (as elsewhere in Romania); for the first ten years, Bucharest adhered to the letter of the law, treating all clergy equally, dispensing equal salaries to equivalent ranks. But starting in 1932, the subsidy was variegated and was tied to the number of faithful; this method of calculation greatly favored Romanian Orthodox clergy, while condemning the clergy of smaller Churches to impoverished conditions. In some instances, the minister of religious affairs even deprived clergymen of their *Congrua*, often on charges of Hungarian irredentism, which were neither justified nor investigated.[33] Discrimination manifested itself in other ways as well. In some locales, for instance, Hungarian children were forced to attend Orthodox or Greek-Rite liturgy. Moreover, beginning in 1930 the Romanian government also pressed for the forced conversion of Szekelys to the Romanian national religions from 1934 onward.[34] After 1937, missionary work by "nontraditional" Churches became impossible.

On the other hand, the government signed the concordat with the Vatican in 1927, despite the criticism of Ghibu and arguments by (Orthodox) Metropolitan Nicolae Bălan of Alba Iulia to the effect that the document was unconstitutional and would give the Catholic Church a "privileged" position.[35] Ratified by the legislature in 1929, the concordat provided for the establishment of new dioceses in Maramures (Greek-Rite) and Oradea (Roman). Catholic orphanages, schools, and hospitals were assured of their right to operate under direct Church control without government interference. And Catholic bishops were assured of their right to communicate directly with the Holy See without the legal necessity of recourse to a governmental intermediary.

In considering the case of interwar Romania, the Legion of the Archangel Michael (or Iron Guard) must be mentioned. The Iron Guard counted about 270,000 members at the end of 1937, and in the December 1937 national elections it drew 478,000 votes.[36] Founded by Corneliu Zelea Codreanu (1899–1938) in June 1927, the fascistic legion was inspired by fanatical devotion to the Orthodox Church and catered to and exploited the rampant anti-Semitism of the time. Indeed, as Heinen notes, the anti-Semitic movement enjoyed the sympathy of many Romanian Orthodox clergy, and the patriarch himself delivered anti-Semitic sermons.[37] Hundreds of Orthodox priests actually joined the Iron Guard, and four of them occupied seats (as of 1993) in the so-called Legionnaire Senate.[38] *Gindirea*, an Orthodox Church periodical, had a markedly right-wing orientation and published submissions by well-known Guardists such as Nichifor Crainic. For that matter, the editor of *Gindirea*, Nae Ionescu, was himself a Guardist.[39] The legionnaires opened their meetings with prayers and hymns and viewed themselves as warriors defending the presumably endangered traditional institutions— monarchy, Church, family, and private property. In their view, the Jews were the foremost threat to these institutions. For the Orthodox Church, the "clerics saw in the young people of the Legion a welcome reservoir of religious revival."[40]

Authoritarianism and War

By the late 1930s many prominent Romanian intellectuals, including Nae Ionescu, Nichifor Crainic, and Nicolae Iorga, had declared themselves against democracy and modernism, against Jewish and Western influences alike, and in favor of the promotion of a cultural "traditionalism" based on Orthodoxy.[41] Thus, a tangible reservoir of support for authoritarianism existed which King Carol II (1893–1953; reigned 1930–40) could tap in 1938 upon establishing his royal dictatorship. Carol II implemented a new constitution, which made no mention of civil rights,[42] and he dissolved the historical political parties. Two years later, the Romanian government became openly fascist. As part of its turn to fascism, anti-Semitism became official policy when Horia Sima, Codreanu's successor as leader of the Iron Guard, was named undersecretary of state in the ministry for public education.[43] The construction of concentration camps in Romania further confirmed this trend.

Insofar as the wartime government's policy was anti-Semitic rather than, say, antireligious, the Romanian Orthodox Church found little reason to play an opposition role. On the contrary, prudence seemed to dictate continuing the same cautious combination of ambiguity and obscurantism that had characterized the metropolitan's comments about fascism as early as 1924.[44]

The Communist Era (1945–1989)

The difficulties for the Churches began as early as 1947 with the passage of a law granting the government a larger role in the election of Orthodox bishops and with government confiscation of Church-run schools; state approval was required for even pastoral letters and other major public communications. That same year the communists assimilated Church youth organizations into the communist youth infrastructure.[45] By 30 December 1947 communists had compelled King Michael to abdicate, and they had proclaimed a People's Republic. In 1948 authorities forbade Churches and monastic orders to operate schools of any kind, and they annulled the autonomy granted to Catholics of both rites under the interwar concordat. At the same time, the authorities forbade the Churches and their representatives to carry on any contact with their counterparts in other countries, except with the express permission of the ministry of cults.[46] Justinian Marina, who had displayed leftist leanings as a simple parish priest and who had hidden communist leader Gheorghe Gheorgiu-Dej (1901-65) when Gheorgiu-Dej escaped from Marshal Antonescu's prisons, was installed on communist instructions as patriarch of the Orthodox Church in 1948, just in time for him to engage in the canonically questionable act of signing an order abolishing the Greek-Rite Catholic Church. The liquidation of the Greek-Rite Church became effective on 1 December 1948 with its properties and clergy being assigned to the Romanian Orthodox Church. The following year Patriarch Justinian convoked a meeting of all the major faiths represented in Romania. The Roman Catholic Church (with 1 million adherents) was the only invitee to refuse to send a representative, wishing in this way to signal its protest of the Orthodox Church's collaboration in the suppression of a sister (Greek-Rite) Church.[47]

During 1949-50 Romanian communist authorities tried to launch a so-called Democratic Action Committee among Catholic clergy members, who were pressured to sign the Stockholm Peace Appeal. Monsignor Glaser, an assistant bishop, instructed Catholic clergy not to sign; but Glaser was arrested in May 1950 and, according to the official report, "died of heart failure" in prison.[48] In due course, "a 450-man labor brigade made up entirely of Catholic priests was detained to work on the Danube-Black Sea canal project; almost half of the brigade died at the work site."[49] During the same period Stalinist-style purges decimated the Orthodox hierarchy. Three Orthodox archbishops died unexpectedly, while thirteen other archbishops and bishops were imprisoned. The communist strategy was to remove recalcitrants and to secure the cooperation of those who proved more pliant.[50] By January 1953 some 300-500 Orthodox priests had been incarcerated in Romanian concentration camps.[51] That same year Patriarch Justinian was awarded the Star of the Republic, First Class.

Superficially, the Romanian state paid honor and respect to the Orthodox Church. Thus, although the constitution of 1948 (later amended in 1952) declared all recognized religious bodies to be equal before the law, it took note of the traditional "predominance" of the Romanian Orthodox Church in society.[52] And in October 1953 the Romanian state joined in celebrating the seventieth anniversary of the autocephaly of the Orthodox Church. On the other hand, the government made no secret that it expected complete obedience from Patriarch Justinian. In 1956 the government drew up a decree for Justinian to sign, mandating a reduction in the number of nuns and monks. Justinian hesitated, and the government put him in prison briefly, just long enough to persuade him of the disadvantages of disobedience.[53]

Shortly after becoming patriarch in June 1948, Justinian had undertaken a major reform of monastic life, aspiring to revive the spirit of service and the traditional regimen emphasizing prayer, study, and work. He promulgated new ordinances affecting the monasteries in 1950, and these soon stimulated a revival of spiritual and intellectual life among the monastic orders.[54] The government, however, watched this monastic revival with concern, and in the summer of 1958, a few months after the death of former Prime Minister Petru Groza (1884–1958), it undertook to close some monastic schools, limit the number of nuns and monks, and impose strict limits on the number of novices. By the end of the year, Gheorghiu-Dej had had more than four hundred Orthodox priests arrested.[55] From 1958 through 1962 "more than half of the Orthodox Church's remaining monasteries were closed, more than two thousand monks [were] forced to take secular jobs, and about fifteen hundred clergy and lay activists [were] arrested. Throughout this period, Patriarch Justinian was careful to say the right things and to avoid giving offense to the government."[56] In 1962, however, possibly as a byproduct of Romania's emerging independent course, Church-state relations suddenly thawed. Gheorghiu-Dej died in 1965, but the thaw continued into the Ceauşescu era, manifesting itself, for example, in a flourishing of theology and theological publications in post-1962 Romania. (As of 1975, the Romanian Orthodox Church was publishing eight theological journals of high quality.) The Romanian Orthodox Church benefited in particular from the Ceauşescu regime's embrace of Romanian nationalism and its desire to exploit mythologies of the past for present-day purposes. As Trond Gilberg has pointed out, Ceauşescu's love affair with Romanian history extended to "claims about the superiority of Romanian culture and its extensive contributions to world civilization."[57]

At the same time, this cult of history fed directly into Ceauşescu's leadership cult, as the Romanian leader encouraged comparisons of himself with bygone Romanian heroes such as Stephen the Great, Michael the Brave, and Vlad Tepeš (the Impaler). Ceauşescu (1918–89) feigned innocence when he informed a *Newsweek* correspondent that the cult was a spontaneous affair. He told the U.S. magazine that he was "lucky to be so popular."[58] But in reality, politicians, journalists, other writers, and clergymen alike were required to adhere to strictly ritualized formulae in making their mandatory obeisances to "the eternal star on the Romanian sky," aka "Romania's greatest son." Optimism and gratitude also were mandated in the Ceaușescu era. All of Romania was to be depicted as if it were a Hollywood musical revue of the 1930s, with everyone constantly singing, dancing, and smiling.

On 29 February 1968 Ceaușescu received the heads of the religious communities and made a short speech thanking them for their support in the building of socialism. Patriarch Justinian, in reply to Ceaușescu's speech, used the prescribed vocabulary, observing,

The understanding and cooperation established between the cults in this country, the religious freedom we enjoy, the good will and extensive material and moral support given to the religious cults by the State leadership, the religious faith in itself, as well as the atmosphere and feelings of lofty patriotism prevailing in all sons of our homeland, are inspiring us. . . .[59]

Nearly twenty years later, the same formulae were still being strictly observed by the Orthodox hierarchy. On the occasion of the installation of Teoctist Arapasu (b. 1915) as patriarch on 9 November 1986 (following the death of Justinian's successor, Justin Moisescu (1910–86)), *Agerpress* news agency reported:

the hierarchs, the clergy, and the believers, like all the sons of the homeland, are highly appreciative of President Nicolae Ceaușescu's creative capacity, activity [as] genuine builder of a new life in Romania, and daring thought put in the service of Romania's continuous progress, of the entire people's happiness. The [patriarch] also expressed thanks and deep gratitude for the conditions of full religious freedom in which the Romanian Orthodox Church, [and] the other denominations in Romania carry out their activity.[60]

Or again, in January 1988, during public celebrations of Nicolae Ceaușescu's seventieth birthday, Patriarch Teoctist assured the dictator that the Church was "thinking of you with great appreciation, deep gratitude, and unlimited love."[61]

At the same time, Orthodox prelates were expected to represent the communist regime's interests abroad. Hence, in August 1988, when the central committee of the World Council of Churches took up the subject of human rights violations in Romania, Romanian Orthodox Metropolitan Antonie of Transylvania threatened to walk out of the meeting unless the subject were dropped. (The threat achieved its purpose.)[62] If the prelates did not "cooperate," they had to reflect on the fact that the department of religious cults was operationally subsumed within the Securitate, an organizational detail not without import.[63]

Relying on such devices as the "rotation of cadres," nepotism,[64] and sheer terror, Ceauşescu asserted his absolute supremacy for nearly a quarter century. When, in 1976 he decided to build a large palace for himself, he pulled Romania out of a UNESCO agreement on the preservation of architectural heritage and proceeded with the wholesale demolition of much of downtown Bucharest, destroying some thirty churches and monasteries, while having additional ecclesiastical buildings literally *towed* to new locations.[65] Or again, in 1982, when Ceauşescu began to entertain fantastic fears about a small group of people in Bucharest who were practicing yoga and meditating, the Securitate, acting on Ceauşescu's orders, arrested more than thirty on charges of having indulged in Transcendental Meditation, among them, Andrei Plesu, who would serve as minister of culture after Ceauşescu's fall.[66] Legend even has it that during one of Ceauşescu's periodic inspections of the countryside, local authorities panicked because the grass had been allowed to yellow. They therefore ordered the grass painted green, lest the *Conducator*'s eyes be offended. It was enough to cause Lewis Carroll to flash a Cheshire grin from beyond the grave.

Foreign governments were somehow drawn into Ceauşescu's cult. The French government bestowed the Legion d'Honneur on him. The British government, acting on the recommendation of Foreign Secretary David Owen, decorated the Romanian president with the Grand Cross of the Order of the Bath. Even Disneyland proved eager to laud the *Conducator*, awarding him honorary citizenship in the world of Mickey Mouse.[67]

The Ceauşescu Legacy in Minority Affairs

The Ceauşescu regime and the Romanian Orthodox Church were, in a sense, natural allies in that they combined heterophobia in the religious and ethnic realms with homophobia in the sexual domain. Although ideological foes in the spiritual dimension, they cooperated in other spheres.

Ethnic Chauvinism

In Ceaușescu's view, "Romania belongs to the Romanians, and only the Romanians, because only Romanians live here, even though many of them speak different languages."[68] In this short sentence Ceaușescu betrayed a deep-seated intolerance of any other culture and provided a key to understanding Bucharest's policy of subverting and assailing the national consciousness and national culture of Romania's ethnic minorities. Numerous German and Hungarian cultural and educational institutions were closed down under Ceaușescu, including the famous (Hungarian) Bólyai University and a renowned (Hungarian) medical and pharmaceutical institute. In many municipalities, ancient gravestones of non-Romanians were confiscated in order to erase vital traces of past diversity. In the schools, Hungarian and German children were taught that the great figures in their respective cultures were actually Romanians, and in sundry ways they were subjected to an educational system that translated "non-Romanian" as *inferior*.[69] Toward the end of his rule Ceaușescu set about bulldozing thousands of Hungarian and German villages in order to destroy the infrastructure that sustained their cultures. Throughout all of this onslaught, the Romanian Orthodox Church hierarchy never raised its voice in protest, never suggested that Ceaușescu's policies were anything but "brilliant" and "lofty."

Indeed, in some ways the Romanian Orthodox Church actually profited from the communists' ethnic policies, as, for example, when the churches and other ecclesiastical facilities belonging to the small ethnic Greek minority were confiscated by the authorities and reassigned to the Romanian Orthodox patriarchate.[70] To the extent that the Romanian Orthodox Church has thought of "national reconciliation," its audience has been fellow Orthodox believers of neighboring Moldova. Thus, in March 1992 the Romanian patriarch blessed the "cross of the reunion" being borne by advocates of Moldovan-Romanian reunification who had marched from Chisinau to Bucharest.[71] And it was with this audience in mind that, on 21 June 1992, Patriarch Teoctist canonized Stephen the Great (Prince of Moldova, 1457–1504) in a solemn pageant, attended by 5,000 people, at St. Spiridon's Cathedral in Bucharest. Among those attending the ceremony was Prime Minister Theodor Stolojan.[72] Prince Stephen had to share honors with twelve other new saints that day, but on 2 July, Patriarch Teoctist presided over a ceremony honoring only Prince Stephen. More than 15,000 people attended this ceremony, which was held at the Putna monastery in northeastern Romania where Saint Stephen is buried. Among those attending this second service were Romanian President Ion Iliescu, then-Foreign Minister Adrian Nastase, and Minister of Defense Nicolae Spiroiu. "God has brought us together under the same skies," Patriarch Teoctist told the assembled crowd, "just as Stephen rallied us under the same flag in the past."[73]

This happy view of things has not, of course, been shared by everyone. Among the more outspoken critics of "the ideology of the Orthodox Romanian national state" is László Tökés, a Reformed bishop and honorary chair of the Democratic Union of Hungarians in Romania. In early January 1992 he sent an open letter to the authorities, declaring:

I protest against the tendency of the upcoming national census to discriminate against national and religious minorities. This census, prepared in the spirit of the ideology of the Orthodox Romanian national state and of the division of national minorities, wants to implement the homogeneous, assimilative, and nationalist principles of Article 1 of the new Romanian Constitution.[74]

Three years later, the Hungarian Churches of Romania joined with the Democratic Union of Hungarians in Romania (UDMR) to protect the newly adopted Romanian education law, which, it was claimed, "threatened the existence" of the Hungarian ethnic-cultural community.[75]

Religious Chauvinism

Where "confessional heterophobia" is concerned, the patriarchate's complicity in the suppression of the Greek-Rite Catholics has been noted. But having lost some 1,800–2,000 places of worship in 1948, the Greek-Rite religionists have inevitably been concerned, now that their Church has been made legal again, that these facilities be promptly returned. Instead, however, the Romanian Orthodox Church has dragged its feet, advising the Greek-Rite Catholics to give up notions of ecclesiastical independence (on the spurious argument that the Holy See aspires, in the long run, to reunite with the Orthodox Church) and advertising itself as a "Church of love."[76] Church of love or not, Romanian Orthodoxy since 1989 has carried out a "smear campaign" against the Greek-Rite Church, even characterizing it as "unpatriotic" and "foreign."[77] Greek-Rite clergy and congregants initially expected the government to take responsibility for assuring the return of confiscated churches. But the government has ignored appeals and demands to this effect, contenting itself with passage of a law in 1990 obliging "the Orthodox Church, not the state, to restore Church property voluntarily, even though it had been seized by the latter."[78]

To the extent that the Romanian Orthodox Church has demonstrated a genuine concern for the adherents of other Churches, its concern has been limited to fellow Orthodox believers in sister Churches, in particular in Moldova[79] and Serbia.[80] Patriarch Teoctist mourned the suffering of Orthodox Serbs in the Serbian Insurrectionary War of 1991–95, but he made no mention of the suffering experienced there by Catholic Croats and Bosnian Muslims. When it comes to non-Orthodox Churches in Romania, solidarity fails. Although not speaking on behalf of the patriarchate, the so-called Reflection Group for the Renewal of the (Orthodox) Church appeared to mirror patriarchal thinking in offering a damning prediction in 1991 that "national-chauvinist political activities will find a fertile ground in the [Roman] Catholic churches in Transylvania."[81]

Sexual Phobias

Within sexual minorities in Romania, two major groups are found: gays and lesbians on the one hand, and transsexuals on the other. In this sphere as well, the communist regime and the Orthodox Church worked hand in glove. For the Church, "any departure from the [heterosexual] norm was looked on as a sin," while transsexualism was construed as a desire to tamper with "God's handiwork."[82] As for the communists, the 1947 penal code drawn up by the communist authorities included an article 200 that criminalized homosexual acts, mandating penalties ranging from one to five years in prison for anyone convicted of breaking this rule.[83] The Securitate, which kept a close eye on suspected gays, resorted to blackmail to press some gays into ancillary service, informing on persons about whom the secret police were interested.[84]

In the wake of Ceauşescu's fall, Romania applied for admission to the Council of Europe, which in turn identified eleven conditions that needed to be met before membership could be granted. Among these conditions was repeal of the law criminalizing homosexuality.[85] Romania also has signed and ratified the European Convention on Human Rights, which recognizes a right of choice in sexual orientation. The Romanian parliament in due course took up the subject, but it found the path strewn with obstacles thrown up by the Romanian Orthodox Church and conservative deputies, who argued that the Council of Europe was imposing "alien" notions on Romania. As the dispute in parliament dragged on, Patriarch Teoctist sent a letter to the speaker of the Chamber of Deputies, Adrian Nastase (the former foreign minister), demanding that homosexuality continue to be punishable by imprisonment.[86] The parliament eventually adopted a measure in September 1995 permitting homosexual contacts provided they did not disturb public order. Immediately after this vote, Patriarch Teoctist addressed the nation on the state television channel, criticizing the parliament and characterizing homosexuality as "a sin that has nothing to do with human rights."[87]

Admitted to the Council of Europe, Romania proved unable to leave the issue alone, and in early September 1996 the Chamber of Deputies, the lower house in Romania's bicameral National Assembly, took up the question once more, urging that even private, concealed same-sex relationships be punished by three years in prison, with three Christian Democratic deputies in the lower house suggesting the establishment of "control teams" authorized to inspect people's homes to verify that only certified heterosexuals enjoy freedom in Romania.[88] Horia Pascu, another Christian Democratic deputy "claimed [that] homosexual relations were unknown in the 'animal world,' with the exception of ducks, 'which are known to be the most stupid among birds.'"[89] Emil Popescu, yet another Christian Democratic deputy, shared with the assembled deputies his opinion "that 'incest is preferable to homosexuality,' because it 'gives breeding a chance.'"[90] Finally, after listening to these and similar opinions, the chamber voted to stiffen the penalties for same-sex relationships.

Transsexuals' uphill struggle has confronted similar attitudes and difficulties, but an important victory was scored in April 1995 when a Romanian court handed down a ruling authorizing a nineteen-year-old male-to-female transsexual to undergo Romania's first sex-change operation.[91] Rodica Cojocara, a Bucharest gynecologist, has championed transsexual rights and has made slow progress in the face of widespread ignorance and incomprehension.[92]

The Church's stance on homosexuality and transsexualism is rooted in its conservative worldview, a conservativism also reflected in its position on abortion. In Ceauşescu's time, abortion was, for all practical purposes, unavailable, and when the Ceauşescus fell, one of the new regime's first moves was to relegalize abortion. Between January 1990 and March 1994 some 3.3 million abortions were performed in Romania, according to official statistics.[93] But the Orthodox Church, which has never reconciled itself to abortion becoming legal again, persisted in a crusade to restore the ban. In February 1994, in an open letter to the president, the cabinet, and the parliament, Patriarch Teoctist made his point succinctly: "The adoption of a law against abortion . . . such as other Christian countries have, will cease the national infant genocide."[94]

Under Ceauşescu, abortion was strictly banned, and physicians warned women that oral contraceptives would lead to obesity and heart disease.[95] As a result, many women resorted to illegal, back-door abortions or do-it-yourself abortions. The *New York Times* reported that "some 10,000 women are believed to have died from complications [resulting] from illegal abortions, and many more were permanently maimed."[96]

The Church Since 1989

Outwardly, Ceauşescu seemed firmly ensconced as late as the first week of December 1989. But within two weeks a popular revolt broke out, ignited by the refusal of Reformed parishioners in Timişoara to allow Securitate troops to remove their parish priest, László Tökés. Ceauşescu's initial response to this resistance was to send in reinforcements. After the Securitate had massacred more than a hundred locals, Patriarch Teoctist sent a telegram to Ceauşescu, perversely congratulating him on having dealt with the "hooligans."[97] After the balance had shifted against the *Conducator*, however, Teoctist reconsidered his position and on 24 December, the day before the Ceauşescus were executed and with a new regime already in place, the patriarch belatedly denounced Nicolae Ceauşescu as "a new child-murdering 'Herod,' "[98] declaring further, "The Romanian Orthodox Church is by the side of the Romanian people also at these crucial times."[99] But the patriarch was unable to regain his credibility—at least for the time being—and on 19 January 1990 he stepped down as patriarch, delicately citing "ill health" and "old age" as the reasons for his decision. Fr. Casian Craciun, the official Church spokesperson, tried to exonerate the patriarch by offering a relativistic and universal exculpation. "Nobody is guilty and nobody is innocent," Craciun claimed.[100] But on 4 April the Holy Synod voted to restore Teoctist to the patriarchal throne, noting that his health had, in the meantime, been "restored." On the streets of Bucharest, protesters greeted the news by calling Teoctist "Antichrist."[101]

Circumstances have changed dramatically for Romania's Churches

Table 7.2 Public Approval of Public Institutions in Romania (1995)

Institution	Percentage approval
The army	91
Romanian Orthodox Church	82
Judiciary	43
The government	32
Parliament	25

Source: Survey conducted by the Urban and Regional Sociology Center, Bucharest, and reported in Christian Century, 5–12 July 1995, p. 674.

since 1989. A new 78-article law on religion restored considerable freedom to the Churches, while recognizing Orthodoxy as "the national Church." Interestingly enough, however, the new law requires that individuals changing their religious belief or affiliation notify state authorities.[102] Change has been comprehensive. Mandatory religion classes were introduced in state primary schools, with optional religion classes offered in state secondary and vocational schools.[103] The army chaplaincy was revived. A new Orthodox Church publishing house (Lumina) was established, which immediately set about publishing lives of the saints and other religious materials. The Orthodox Church set up a new National Church Assembly. And in 1993 the Orthodox Church joined the Reformed and Lutheran Churches in launching the Ecumenical Association of Churches of Romania.[104]

The Orthodox Church also has taken up the nationalist banner once again, deploring the fact that there were fewer Romanian national saints than Russian, Bulgarian, or Serbian. The Holy Synod accordingly canonized some nineteen new saints in June 1992, declaring the second Sunday after Pentecost "Romanian Saints' Day."[105] Some critics noted that the Church showed no particular interest in canonizing any of the 6,000 Orthodox clergymen imprisoned between 1946 and 1964 or any of the 500,000 or so political prisoners sent to prison in the 1950s or early 1960s; none of these victims of the communist era were declared "martyrs," let alone canonized, by the Romanian Orthodox Church.[106] Perhaps this selective nationalism may account for the Church's high approval rating (see table 7.2).

When it comes to present-day conditions, the Orthodox Church has complained of "unfair competition from other denominations, which are heavily financed from abroad,"[107] demanding that the state continue to pay salaries to Orthodox clergy, as was done under Ceauşescu, and to adopt other measures conducive to the Orthodox Church's material advantage.

Conclusion

The transition from communism to pluralism (understanding by pluralism *only* that there are some political alternatives presented to Romanians, and *by no means* suggesting that an intolerant society can ever sustain anything worthy of the name "democracy") has brought mixed results. From the standpoint of the Romanian Orthodox hierarchy, the post-Ceauşescu liberalization of abortion is particularly abhorrent, as are Western pressures to allow gays, lesbians, and transsexuals to enjoy civil rights on a par with other citizens. Some "members of the 'Orthodox nomenklatura' have started looking back at the communist era with nostalgia. As one professor of theology put it: '[Before 1989] we were forced to live within very strict limits; but inside that space we enjoyed complete freedom.'"[108]

Romania is changing, but as many commentators have noted, continuity as well as transformation marks its path. Up to now the Romanian Orthodox Church has displayed more continuity than transformation, but as social conditions, political circumstances, and hierarchical personnel change, the Romanian Church is likely to evolve. And as it evolves, it may shed aspects of its traditional holy intolerance.

Chapter 8

Albania's Triple Heritage

Albania's communists were fond of justifying their forcible extirpation of all religious organizations by describing them as foreign implants and denying them any link with Albanian national culture. In fact, however, Christianity spread among the Albanian people in the first century, albeit in the face of resistance from the adherents of local polytheist faiths, and by the time of the Emperor Justinian it had established its dominance.

Islam came to the area much later, when the Ottoman empire expanded into the region in the fourteenth and fifteenth centuries. Catholicism was largely found in the northern Gheg regions, while Orthodoxy's adherents were among the Tosks of the south. Islam won adherents among both Ghegs and Tosks. For a number of reasons it was the Roman Catholic Church in the Gheg regions that, among Albanians' three religions, was most strongly animated by the nationalist impetus.[1]

Albanian Christianity lay within the orbit of the bishop of Rome from the first century to the eighth. But in the eighth century Albanian Christians were transferred to the jurisdiction of the patriarch of Constantinople.[2] With the schism of 1054, however, Albania was divided between a Catholic north and an Orthodox south. At Bar at the end of the eleventh century Rome established an archbishopric that gradually was able to bring the bishoprics of Shkodër, Ulcinj, Drivast, and others under its jurisdiction. As a result, Catholicism spread in northern Albania, and in the second half of the twelfth century the Catholic Church even made inroads in southern Albania.[3] In spite of this advance, Roman Catholicism remained a minority religion among Albanians, and up until the beginning of the nineteenth century the Orthodox faith was clearly dominant among the Tosks of southern Albania.[4] Yet doctrinal differences between Rome and Constantinople were slow to evolve, and the sense of true separation between Catholic Albanians and Orthodox Albanians dates only from the mid-eighteenth century.[5]

After the arrival of Ottoman power in the fourteenth century, Islam gradually spread, and the number of Christian churches and monasteries declined. Mass conversions to Islam did not begin until the seventeenth century, but before the end of the nineteenth century less than half of the Albanian population was still Christian.[6] Albania thus became a confessionally mixed society in which no stable boundaries stood between the faiths. In fact, over the centuries Albanians often abandoned one faith for another for purely opportunistic reasons, such as the desire to obtain protection from a given power or the desire to escape the special tax levied on non-Muslims by the Sublime Porte. This would incline one to expect that Christian faiths would be weaker in Albania than elsewhere in the region. One may add that the Orthodox Church in particular was long the champion of Greek liturgy and Greek-language instruction, so that when the Albanian national movement appeared, nationalists of the Orthodox faith considered their first task to be the capture of the Orthodox Church and its adaptation to the national effort. This meant, in effect, that Albania's Orthodox Church had to be autocephalous. By contrast, the Catholic Church played a vanguard role in the provision of Albanian-language education and in the development of publishing activity in Albanian. The Franciscans opened a school in Pdhanë as early as 1638, and by 1644 this school issued the first Italian-Albanian dictionary.[7] The Jesuits, who established themselves in Albania in 1841, opened a seminary in Shkodër in 1859 (the Kolegja Papnore Shqiptare), the curriculum of which included the study of the Albanian language.[8] Shortly thereafter, in 1877, the Jesuits founded the College of St. Francis Xavier (Saverianum); Albanian language was among the subjects taught there. In the meantime, the Jesuit press had published a book concerning Christian doctrine (in 1876), which was the first volume ever printed in the Albanian language. The Jesuit press also launched a series of Albanian-language magazines, including *Lajmtarii Zemrës së Krishtit* (The Messenger of the Sacred Heart) and *Leka* (an abbreviation of *Lidhja*, Union).[9]

Albanian Orthodoxy Before the Communist Takeover

Albania's Christian population was largely unaware of the gathering rivalry between Rome and Constantinople until the early thirteenth century, when the East-West ecclesiastical schism came to be reflected in local politics. The Ottoman conquest between the end of the fourteenth century and the mid-fifteenth century introduced a third religion — Islam

—but the Turks did not at first use force in its expansion, and it was only in the 1600s that large-scale conversion to Islam began—chiefly, at first, among Albanian Catholics.[10]

The Orthodox community enjoyed broad toleration at the hands of the Sublime Porte until the late eighteenth century. Under the millet system the Orthodox Church regulated the social life of its adherents, and in the absence of an autocephalous Church, Albania's Orthodox population came under the jurisdiction of the patriarch of Constantinople. Orthodox learning and culture therefore were Greek, and the schools opened by the Orthodox Church in Ottoman times used Greek as the language of instruction. A Greek school operated in the monastery of St. Nahum on Lake Ohrid from the sixteenth century on. Additional Greek schools were opened in Zagorie and Himarë by the seventeenth century and in Vlorë by the mid-eighteenth century. After 1750 the number of Orthodox schools rose sharply, to a considerable extent as a result of the efforts of Kosmas Aitolos, who is said to have founded more than two hundred Greek schools in the country.

The towns of Voskopojë (Moskhopolis) and Janina emerged as important centers of Greek culture, and by 1744 Voskopojë boasted a "New Academy" that rivaled the best Greek high schools of that age. A large number of religious and ecclesiastical works were also published in Voskopojë for distribution among Orthodox Christians in Albania and elsewhere. The clergy was itself active in this endeavor, and Archpriest Theodore Kavalioti and Mast Dhanil from Voskopojë left two polyglot dictionaries, while Bishop Grigor Argjirokastriti of the island of Eubea supervised the translation of the Gospels into Albanian. This translation was published in Korfu in 1827.[11]

In the late eighteenth century Russian agents began stirring up the Orthodox subjects of the Ottoman empire against the Sublime Porte. In the Russo-Turkish wars of 1768-74 and 1787-91 Orthodox Albanians rose against the Turks. In the course of the second revolt the "New Academy" in Voskopojë was destroyed (1789), and at the end of the second Russo-Turkish war more than a thousand Orthodox fled to Russia on Russian warships.[12] As a result of these revolts, the Porte now applied force to Islamicize the Albanian Orthodox population, adding economic incentives to provide positive stimulus. In 1798 Ali Pasha of Janina led Ottoman forces against Christian believers assembled in their churches to celebrate Easter in the villages of Shen Vasil and Nivica e Bubarit. The bloodbath unleashed against these believers frightened Albanian

Christians in other districts and inspired a new wave of mass conversions to Islam.[13]

Throughout the period of Ottoman rule, the Ecumenical Patriarchate (at Constantinople) opposed the creation of Albanian-language schools for the Orthodox, fearing that language teaching would diminish Orthodoxy's cultural influence and possibly even lead to the emergence of an autocephalous Albanian Church. After disturbances in 1878–80, the Porte relaxed its prohibition on use of the Albanian language in schools and periodicals. Soon a number of Albanian-language schools sprang up in villages near Korçë and in the district of Kolonjë. Albanian-language books, newspapers, and periodicals also appeared. Up until then only Catholic schools had been conducted in Albanian; Muslim schools used Turkish as the language of instruction, while Orthodox schools taught in Greek and figured, thereby, as vehicles of Hellenization. In 1892 Philaretos, archbishop of Kastoria, anathematized all who associated themselves with the new Albanian-language Orthodox schools, declaring that the Albanian language "does not exist" and that the true aim of these schools was to spread "freemasonry and Protestantism" among Albanian Christians. Under pressure from the Ecumenical Patriarchate, the Porte again imposed the ban on Albanian publications and shut down the Orthodox schools teaching in the language.[14]

Not surprisingly, under these circumstances the Greek idea had considerable influence on the thinking of the Albanian Orthodox. Bilingual in Albanian and Greek, some educated Orthodox Albanians in the later years of the nineteenth century desired union with independent Greece, and two émigré Orthodox patriots in Egypt, Thimi Mitko and Spiro Dine, argued for the creation of a Greco-Albanian dual monarchy, based on the model of the Austro-Hungarian monarchy.

Meanwhile, Bulgarian nationalists sought to enlarge ethnic "Macedonia," which they viewed as "western Bulgaria," by establishing Bulgarian-language schools and seminaries in ethnic Albania. In 1894 a group of three hundred Albanians addressed a letter to the Ottoman sultan, objecting to the permission granted Bulgarian and Serbian Churches (the Serbian, by then, in Prizren) to extend their influence, and demanding authorization to open Albanian-language schools. The appeal complained that Bulgarian schools were being established in Dibër and Tetovo, "where not a word of Bulgarian is spoken," and it charged the Bulgarian Church with aiming to Bulgarianize the local Albanian population. Albanian nationalists began to promote the idea of an autocepha-

lous Albanian Orthodox Church as a necessary bulwark against denationalization. Opposition to the Hellenizing and Bulgarianizing thrust
of local Orthodox hierarchs also encouraged the conversion of a small
number of Orthodox Albanians to the Uniate Church; they hoped that
Habsburg protection would safeguard their Albanian heritage, but under
strong pressure from Russia the Uniate movement in Albania petered
out by 1907.[15] The Albanian Uniate movement continued among Albanians in Italy.

The nationalist cause was given impetus in 1905 when the Albanian
priest and poet, Popa Kristo Negovani, was killed by Greek chauvinists
after he had introduced the Albanian language into Orthodox liturgy
for the first time.[16] Yet the first Albanian Church was to be the creation
of émigrés. In the course of the nineteenth century, groups of Albanian
Orthodox believers had settled in Romania, Bulgaria, and the United
States. The Romanian and American communities played a role in the
establishment of an Albanian Orthodox Church, a central goal of Albanian nationalists of Orthodox faith from about 1880 onward. On 27 May
1900 the Albanian Orthodox in Romania promulgated a program demanding autocephaly and liturgy in the Albanian language; two vain
attempts to erect an Albanian church in Bucharest were subsequently
undertaken.

It was thus not until 1908 that the Albanian Orthodox Church was
born—its first incarnation being among Albanian émigrés in Boston.
Its founder and first bishop, the Harvard-educated Fan Noli, who later
translated Shakespeare, Ibsen, and other playwrights into Albanian, was
actually ordained a priest only on 8 March 1908. Although his formal
ordination as a bishop did not occur until 1919, he was unable to secure
recognition from the Ecumenical Patriarchate.[17]

Independent Albania came into being in 1912 on the eve of World
War I. The Great War turned neutral Albania into a battlefield as Greek,
Serbian, Italian, and even French armies took up positions on its ter-
ritory.[18] But by 1920 the last troops (the Italian) departed from Alba-
nia, which regained its independence and entered the nascent League of
Nations.

A central issue facing the new Albanian government was land reform, which divided the population to some extent along religious lines
in that most of the large landowners, especially in the south, were Muslims, whose estates generally were worked by Orthodox Christians. Predictably, the Muslim landowners favored preservation of the status quo,

while the Orthodox generally urged land reform. Rival political parties sprang up advocating these rival interests. The Progressive Party, opposed to land reform, was led by Shevket Verlazi, the largest landowner in the country; the Popular Party, which favored land reform, was led by Ahmed Zogu and Bishop Fan Noli. Fan Noli had in fact been elected to the National Assembly as a representative of the American Albanian community.[19]

Zogu and Noli cooperated with each other at first, but they split in 1922 over policy vis-à-vis Kosovo, which Zogu was willing to write off despite its large Albanian population. Meanwhile, Noli had campaigned for an independent ecclesiastical organization *within* Albania in 1921, and in September 1922 the Albanian government under Prime Minister Zogu convened a congress at Berat to address this issue. Predictably, the congress declared the Church autocephalous, proclaimed that the liturgy should be conducted in Albanian, and set up a council under Vassili Marco to appoint bishops to an Albanian Church synod and to oversee Church activity. At that time, some 200,000 Orthodox believers resided in Albania.

The Congress of Berat issued a Church constitution for the "Albanian Autocephalous Orthodox Church," and in its endorsing of ecclesiastical autocephaly the government entered the Church constitution into its official gazette on 26 October 1922. The ecumenical patriarch responded cautiously and sent two bishops of Albanian origin as his representatives: Ierotheos, bishop of Militopoli, and Kristofor Kissi, bishop of Synada. They recommended to the ecumenical patriarch that he accord the Church autonomy but not autocephaly. Subsequently, Bishops Ierotheos and Kristofor, by then elevated to the rank of metropolitans, consecrated Fan Noli a bishop in St. George's Cathedral in Korçë in what may well have been Noli's third episcopal consecration.

Noli was deeply involved in both ecclesiastical politics and national politics. In January 1924 a national synod of the Albanian Orthodox Church convened at Korçë. In attendance were Bishops Ierotheos, Kristofor Kissi, and Fan Noli.[20] That same month Zogu's parliamentary faction went down to defeat in national elections, and Noli's faction was able to put together a coalition government. Zogu fled to the Kingdom of Serbs, Croats, and Slovenes (Yugoslavia). But Noli's government lasted only five months, when Zogu returned from Yugoslavia with a force of two thousand troops and seized power. By 1928 Zogu had crowned himself King Zog, thus turning Albania into a monarchy.

Zog, like Noli, wanted ecclesiastical autocephaly. But in the absence of a local hierarchy, the decisions of the Congress of Berat had not been carried out even by the end of 1928. Hence, King Zog convened a meeting in his villa in February 1929 with Greek-educated Bishop Vissarion and Serbian Bishop Viktor, naming them to a five-man synod and persuading them to consecrate three uneducated priests for the remaining three seats. The Ecumenical Patriarchate excommunicated four of the five members of this synod, all but the Serb, hoping in vain that the patriarch of Belgrade would decide to chastise Bishop Viktor. In reply, the Albanian government expelled the first patriarchal representative, Ierotheos, and imprisoned the second, Kristofor Kissi, in a monastery. Understandably, under these circumstances the rank and file of Orthodox believers remained suspicious of the new synod.[21]

The Albanian Orthodox Church thus created an archbishop ("of Durrës, Tiranë, Elbasan, and all Albania") and three metropolitans. Its diocesan jurisdiction was divided among (1) the archbishopric of Tiranë-Durrës, headed by the archbishop and subdivided into districts of Tiranë, Durrës, Shkodër, Kavaga, and Elbasan; (2) the bishopric of Berat, subdivided into Berat, Vlorë, Fieri, and Lushnja; (3) the bishopric of Gjirokastër, subdivided into Gjirokastër, Pogoni, Delvina, Saranda, Himarë, and Permeti; and (4) the bishopric of Korçë, subdivided into Korçë, Kolonya, Leskoviku, and Pogradeci.[22] In many parishes the Albanian Church replaced Greek liturgy with liturgy in the Albanian language, allowing the use of Greek to continue where desired.

The Greek Orthodox Church, the Church of Cyprus, the Patriarchate of Alexandria, and the Moscow Patriarchate joined the Ecumenical Patriarchate in condemning Albanian autocephaly. On the other hand, other Orthodox Churches, such as the Serbian, Romanian, and Polish, and the Patriarchate of Antioch maintained a discreet silence, which, at least in the Serbian case, reflected acceptance.[23]

Searching for a way out of the impasse, the government finally proposed Kristofor Kissi as a candidate to head the Church. This move came in October 1933. The Ecumenical Patriarchate at first seemed to reject this olive branch, however, and it proposed Eulogio Kurila, a priest of Albanian origin. Either way, Primate Vissarion Xhuvani had become an obstacle to settlement, and by May 1936 the Albanian synod reached the decision that Bishop Vissarion had to be retired. Rumors now conveniently emerged that Bishop Vissarion was leading a loose and scandalous life, and eventually an agreement was reached whereby Kristofor

Kissi would be named primate of the Church, which in turn would be recognized by Constantinople.[24]

Early in 1937, therefore, King Zog relieved Vissarion of his post and appointed Kristofor Kissi to succeed him. The Holy Synod of Constantinople accordingly convened in an extraordinary session on 15 March 1937 to consider the proposed accord and approved it unanimously a month later, issuing an official "Tomos" ceding autocephaly to the Albanian ecclesiastical organization.[25]

Islam and Catholicism in Precommunist Albania

In pre-Ottoman Albania local lords and bishops switched back and forth between Catholicism and Orthodoxy, according to what best served their interests at the time.[26] The Ottomans first invaded Albania in 1385. A second Ottoman force was sent to Albania 1394–96, occupying the country. Given both the Ottoman disposition to tolerate religious diversity among loyal subjects and the generally bellicose traditions of the Albanians, Ottoman authorities adopted a conciliatory policy toward Albanian Christians in the early decades of occupation. Still, although conversion to Islam was not required, a Christian Albanian lord could count on winning favor if he converted.[27]

If the Ottomans did not believe that religious reasons could compel a Christian to convert to Islam, they nonetheless looked askance when a Muslim converted (or reconverted) to Christianity. This happened in 1443 when Gjergj Kastrioti (called Skenderbeg), who had been reared as a Muslim in the sultan's palace, abandoned the Islamic faith and publicly reverted to the creed of his forefathers. But this conversion was not merely a public gesture of defiance. It was the first act in a revolutionary drama. For, after changing his religious allegiance, Skenderbeg demanded that Muslim colonists and converts alike embrace Christianity on pain of death, declaring a kind of holy war against the sultan/caliph.[28] In 1444 at a convention of Albanian lords Skenderbeg was elected commander-in-chief of Albanian forces, which he led in wars against the Ottomans for twenty-four years, until his death in 1468. With the eventual suppression of his revolt, some Albanian Orthodox lords and subjects fled to southern Italy and Sicily, embracing Catholicism; today, most of their descendants are Greek-Rite Catholics.

Throughout the sixteenth century Catholicism held its own, especially in the villages and remote regions. The people of the cities and lowlands, on the other hand, were exposed to more visible social and economic pressures to convert to Islam.[29] Only in the course of the seventeenth century, therefore, did the number of Catholics in Albania begin to decline despite the activity of the Franciscans. Then, in 1644, war broke out between Venice and the Ottoman empire. At the urging of the clergy, many Albanian Catholics sided with Venice. The Ottomans responded with severe repressions, which in turn drove many Catholics to embrace Islam (although a few elected to join the Orthodox Church instead).[30] The year 1649 saw the outbreak of a fresh insurrection among the Albanians; the Ottomans crushed the revolt, and in its wake more conversions to Islam took place, alongside the flight of Christian missionaries. Within a span of just twenty-two years (1649–71) the number of Catholics in the diocese of Alessio fell by more than 50 percent, while in the diocese of Pulati (1634–71) the number of Catholics declined from more than 20,000 to just 4,045.[31] In general, Albanian insurrections during the Ottoman-Venetian wars of 1644–69 resulted in stiff Ottoman reprisals against Catholics in northern Albania and significantly accelerated Islamization.

In 1689 Austrian armies pushed deep into the Balkans, backing up the Venetians; Catholic Albanians once more rose in revolt and, under the Proveditore General Daniele Delfino, enjoyed temporary success against Ottoman armies. A year later, Austrian armies were in retreat, and the Pasha of Peć deported great numbers of Catholics from northern Albania; most of them settled in southern Serbia.[32] In general, a pattern emerged. When the Ottoman empire was attacked by Catholic powers, local Catholics were pressured to convert, and when the attack on the Ottoman empire came from Orthodox Russia, the pressure was on local Orthodox to change their faith. In some cases Islamization was only superficial, however, and in the nineteenth century many villages and some entire districts remained "crypto-Catholic" in spite of their adopting the externals of Islamic culture.[33]

Confessional heterogeneity proved to be no obstacle to collaboration in the interests of local culture and autonomy. In 1878, for example, both Muslims and Catholics participated in the work of the newly established League of Prizren, which sought to block Montenegrin and Serbian annexation of Albanian-inhabited areas (a move that enjoyed the support of the great Powers).[34] In October 1880, having already lost the purely Albanian city of Ulcinj to Montenegro, delegates from all of Albania assembled in Dibra to petition the Sublime Porte once again to grant autonomous status to Albania.[35] The league attempted a show of force to win autonomy, but in May 1881 league leaders in the south were arrested, effectively breaking the power of the league of Prizren. But Albanian discontent could not be so easily dispelled, and in 1896 local Albanians in Elbasan raised the autonomist banner. Albanian autonomists, however, remained a kind of loyal opposition, as was shown during the Greco-Ottoman War of 1897 when Albanians fought side by side with Ottomans against the Greeks.[36] In November 1898 Albanian representatives petitioned the sultan to introduce education in the Albanian language in all schools in the Albanian vilayets.[37]

Albanian Muslims and Christians alike resisted the nineteenth-century Tanzimat reforms, resenting the replacement of their own begs by centrally appointed officials from Istanbul. They likewise opposed army reforms, including the establishment of a recruitment system.[38] Understandably, then, Bektashi notables in Albania at first greeted the Young Turks with the hope of their greater sensitivity to local needs. When the Young Turks disappointed these tentative expectations, Albanian Bektashis began to talk of independence.[39] Several thousand Albanians now took up arms and congregated in Prizren, Djakovo, Priština, and Vucitrn. In early 1909 renewed disturbances occurred in the vilayet of Kosovo. In March 1910 Albanian discontent flared into a large-scale uprising in Kosovo, provoked by the authorities' attempt to impose new taxes on all wares being brought into Priština.[40]

On 23 June 1911 Albanian insurgents, including Ismail Kemal Bey and Luigj Gurakuqi, met in the Montenegrin village of Gerče and drew up a thirteen-point memorandum, which emphasized the long-standing loyalty of the Albanians to the Porte but demanded respect for the religious and traditional needs of the Albanians, the introduction of instruction in the Albanian language in public schools, reorganization of the vilayet, free elections of Albanian assembly deputies, use of the Albanian language alongside Ottoman Turkish in local administration and courts, military service within the vilayet, the return of confiscated weapons, etc.[41] Although Ottoman authorities agreed to these conditions, both Ottomans and Albanians were quickly overtaken by events when in the autumn of 1911 war broke out between Italy and the Ottoman empire. The Italo-Ottoman War of 1911 prepared the ground for the Balkan Wars of 1912–13, which, in turn, set the stage for the continental war that broke out in 1914.

King Zog, who, except for a few months in 1924, ruled Albania from 1922 until 1939 — albeit as king only from 1928 on — created an authoritarian system in which he wanted to bring, as far as possible, all three major religious associations under his control. The key to success in this regard was to persuade the respective religious associations to sunder their subordination to foreign centers. Zog achieved immediate results within the Islamic community, which separated itself from external authority in 1923.[42] With the Orthodox Church, though, it was only in 1937 that he was able to realize his goal of obtaining full ecclesiastical autocephaly. In contrast, where the Catholics were concerned, resistance to pressure for separation from the Vatican was boldly intransigent. Accepting the impossibility of extending this scheme to the Roman Catholic Church, Zog nonetheless hoped that the institution of civil marriage and divorce and the development of an extensive network of state schools (at the elementary and secondary levels) would attenuate Catholic influence among the population.[43] As this state school system developed and despite the signing of a concordat with the Holy See (1927), Zog in 1933 ordered — over the protests of Albania's Catholic bishops — that all Catholic and other private schools be closed. These schools were reopened in 1936, after the Italian dictator, Benito Mussolini, who favored Catholic education, briefly suspended loans to Tiranë.[44] In spite of these difficulties the Catholic Church continued to build up its infrastructure. In 1922 the Jesuits opened the Sacred Heart Orphanage in Shkodër, launching an apostolic preparatory school in the same city in 1932. This act was followed by the founding of the Jesuit alumni association called "Don Bosco" in Shkodër in 1933 and the consecration of the Sacred Heart Cathedral in Tiranë in 1941.[45]

Although commanding the allegiance of fewer adherents than either the Islamic community or the Orthodox Church, the Catholic Church, in excess of its numerical strength among the population, exerted significant cultural, social, and pedagogical influence on Albanian society. Some of this influence came from the well-developed state of that Church's institutional infrastructure. Some was the result of the direct contribution of Catholic priests to the development of Albanian literature, poetry, historiography, musical life, and philosophy. Among the Catholic clerics who made noteworthy contributions during the interwar era were Fathers Vinçenc Prendushi, Anton Harapi, Bernardin Palaj, Martin Gjoka, Pal Dodaj, Justin Rrota, Luigj Marlekaj, Gjon Shllaku, and Paulin Margjokaj.[46]

In 1942 a wartime census recorded the presence within Albania of 763,723 Muslims (representing 68.9 percent of the population), 299,080 Orthodox (20.7 percent), and 113,897 Catholics (10.4 percent). Of the total Muslim population, 599,524 were Sunnis and 164,199 were Bektashi.[47] There was also a small Jewish community, dating to the late twelfth century.[48]

On the eve of the communist takeover, Sunni Muslims operated 1,127 mosques and 17 medresas and had 1,306 clergy at their disposal; the Bektashi had 260 Tekke cloisters, 65 Baba abbeys, and 468 celibate dervishes. The Orthodox Church counted 844 churches; and the Catholic Church operated 147 churches, 70 of them attached to monasteries.[49]

The Communist Era (1944–1990)

Many Orthodox clergymen had supported Enver Hoxha's (communist) partisans during World War II, as had a number of Bektashi "monks."[50] They therefore hoped to be allowed to continue their religious activity unobstructed in Hoxha's communist republic. Indeed, the regime at first seemed to favor the Bektashi, co-opting two of their leaders, Baba Faja and Baba Fejzo, into the People's Assembly in 1945.[51] Moreover, the constitution of 1946 guaranteed freedom of religion and conscience to all citizens.

Yet as early as May 1945 the communist regime took repressive measures designed to whittle down the strength of the religious associations. In that month Hoxha ordered the expulsion of Archbishop Leone G. B. Nigris, the apostolic delegate to Albania. He then summoned Metropolitan-Archbishop Gasper Thaçi of Shkodër, primate of the Church, and Archbishop Vinçenc Prendushi of Durrës, to his office, where he demanded that they cooperate in separating the Catholic Church in Albania from Rome and establish a new "national" Catholic Church. They refused. Both prelates were subsequently harassed, their physical movements restricted. Thaçi died in 1946 while under house arrest; Prendushi was sentenced to twenty years at hard labor and died in prison in 1949.[52]

On 21 June 1945 the authorities arrested two Jesuit teachers, Frs. Jak (Giacomo) Gardin and Gjergj Vata, along with twenty-four other priests and Catholic laypersons; at the end of a show trial, all of them were sentenced to hard labor. Later that same year the authorities arrested the Jesuit vice provincial, Fr. Gjon Fausti, and the pontifical seminary rector, Fr. Daniel Dajani.[53] Both Fausti and Dajani were executed on 4 March 1946 at the end of a two-week political trial. The following month the regime closed down all Jesuit institutions in Albania and outlawed the order. After suppressing the Jesuits, the communists turned on the Franciscan community and the remaining episcopal presence. Bishop Fran Gjini, abbot of Shen Llezhri i Oroshit, was shot in Shkodër in 1948.[54] Priests brought to trial were labeled "enemies of the people" and upon their conviction were isolated from other prisoners and kept under close guard.[55] Some priests were sent to labor camps; one such labor brigade, which included priests, was assigned to reclaim the Maliq marsh. Another labor brigade, to which Fr. Gardin was assigned, was involved in building the Vlorë Prison.[56] By the end of 1946 almost half of all Catholic clergy members were behind bars.

The *muftis* of Tiranë, Durrës, and Shkodër were either imprisoned or shot on allegations of wartime collaboration with occupation authorities.[57] Among Bektashi leaders, Baba Murteza of Kruje was tortured and defenestrated from a prison window in 1946; Baba Kamil Glava of Tepelen was executed in Gjirokastër that same year; in 1947 both Baba Ali Tomori in Gjirokastër and Baba Sheftet Koshtani of Tepelen were executed.[58]

During these repressions the communist regime had passed a land reform law nationalizing Church lands in August 1945, and in December of that year it set up a Union of Orthodox Priests to divide the lower clergy from their bishops.[59] The years 1945 to 1950 saw an assault on the position of all three religious organizations. Church revenues were curtailed. Religious instruction was forbidden. All religious publications and communications, including sermons, pastoral letters, and even public memoranda, had to be approved by the government before dissemination. The Churches were banned from operating charitable institutions. And the state asserted control and veto power over the election and appointment of candidates to ecclesiastical posts. In the first five years of communist rule most Orthodox hierarchs were either killed, imprisoned, or sent to labor camps, including Archbishop Vissarion Xhuvani of Elbasan, Bishop Irine of Appolonia, Bishop Agathangjel Cance of Berat, Bishop Irine (the deputy metropolitan of Korçë and Gjirokastër), and Papas Josif Papmihaili, an advocate of Uniatism.

At that time Albania's regime wanted to place the Albanian Orthodox Church under the care and authority of the Moscow Patriarchate, but this proposed action met with resistance from the clergy. Finally, in January 1948 a small group of Albanian clergy visited Moscow, Kiev, and Leningrad and consulted with Russian Orthodox hierarchs. At the end of this visit, a statement was issued:

Whereas all the other Churches, and especially the Vatican, wanted to put an end to the existence of the Albanian Church, the Russian Orthodox Church is its great defender.

The Russian Orthodox Church is national and patriotic. The emancipated Albanian nation is moving rapidly along the path of progress and wishes its Orthodox Church to be likewise national and patriotic. In this connection the experience of the Russian Church provides a valuable lesson.

In the common struggle against Fascism, the Albanian nation has come [to feel] close to the Russian people and wishes to be in close relationship with its Church.[60]

Later that year a Russian bishop visited Tiranë, and Moscow played host to the 1948 Orthodox Church conference. Archbishop Kristofor Kissi's absence from these meetings was a sign that he was opposed to the direction in which the Church was being forced. His refusal to cooperate led to his early removal. Deposed on 28 August 1949 for "plotting to detach the Church from the Eastern Orthodox faith and surrender it to the Vatican,"[61] Kissi was imprisoned and replaced by Archbishop Paisi Vodica, who was distinctly sympathetic to the communists.

On 26 January 1949 the Albanian regime issued a general decree (no. 743) on religious organizations and required that Sunni Muslim, Bektashi Muslim, Orthodox, and Roman Catholic organizations each draw up statutes within three months to present to the council of ministers. None of them complied,[62] so the state issued statutes on their behalf. The Orthodox statute (decree no. 1065) was issued on 4 May 1950. In a key clause it declared: "The Autocephalous Orthodox Church of Albania will report connections or cooperation with the Orthodox sister-Churches who practise the high principles of the Gospel with regard to peace and true brotherhood among the nations of the whole world."[63] Although vague, this clause evidently codified the Church's responsibility to report its activities to the state and subordinated it to the Moscow Patriarchate, especially insofar as it could easily be argued that Orthodox Churches in countries other than Stalin's "socialist camp" were not "sister-Churches who practise the high principles of the Gospel with regard to peace."

The Islamic community, like the Orthodox Church, accepted the government-dictated charter in a docile fashion. But the Catholic hierarchy insisted on modifying the charter's terms. Further arrests of Catholic clergy failed to deflect the hierarchy from its position, and at that point Tuk Jakova, the minister of the interior, initiated negotiations with the Catholic hierarchy. For this breach of party discipline, Jakova was dismissed from office amid accusations that he was linked with the Church.[64] The regime eventually agreed to a compromise allowing the Catholic Church to retain its ties with the Holy See, but when the communist press reported on the agreement, it falsified its contents and announced that all ties between the Albanian Catholic Church and the Holy See had been severed.[65] In July 1951 the government issued a decree unilaterally nullifying the Catholic Church's link with Rome.

At first, the Islamic community seemed to enjoy somewhat better treatment than the Christian churches. At least part of the explanation for this difference lay in the regime's desire to demonstrate to visitors from Muslim countries the "harmonious compatibility" of Islamic faith and communism.[66] At first, therefore, instruction in Islamic faith and attendance at mosques were merely discouraged, but by the early 1950s this policy began to change as the authorities imposed direct and indirect restrictions on Islamic religious activity.

The party introduced antireligious propaganda in the schools at an early date, and in April 1955 a party plenum resolved that religious beliefs were obstructing "the spread of . . . socialist culture among the masses."[67] As early as 1965 Albanian students were organizing meetings with the encouragement of the party to persuade citizens that religion was outdated and that places of worship should be closed down. Some places of worship were, as a result, shuttered; of those that remained open, many were vandalized by gangs of adolescents.[68] Yet it was only in 1967 that the Albanian Communist Party made its decisive move to eliminate all forms of religion in Albania—Orthodoxy included.

In a speech to the party's central committee on 6 February 1967 Hoxha announced the inception of a new policy toward religion as part of the party's Cultural Revolution. Hoxha returned to this theme in his address to the Fifth Party Congress in June 1967:

To be a revolutionary means not only to have no religious faith but also to struggle continuously against religious beliefs, which are an expression of feudal and bourgeois reactionary ideology; it means not only to condemn with words and on principle the backward habit of despising and enslaving woman or other backward habits which stem from the remnants of feudal and bourgeois relationships in life and in the family, but it also means to struggle concretely and courageously for the liquidation of these reactionary habits and for the creation of new, socialist and communist, habits.[69]

Teams of young agitators were dispatched throughout the country with the assignment of persuading or forcing people to abandon their religious practices and, ultimately, their religious beliefs.

On 13 November 1967 the Albanian People's Assembly approved a decree annulling the religious statutes governing the Islamic, Orthodox, and Catholic communities and rescinded the guarantee of freedom of worship. By the end of 1967 all 2,169 churches, mosques, and monasteries of the three faiths had been closed and confiscated. For the Orthodox Church this meant the loss of 608 churches and monasteries (including those at Ardenica, Narta, Vlorë, and Voskopojë) and its only seminary.[70] The Catholic Church lost 327 churches. The Jews lost their synagogue in Tiranë. The other affected places of worship were Muslim.

Archbishop Damian, who had inherited the primacy of the Orthodox Church in 1966, died in prison in November 1973; within two years the entire surviving hierarchy of the Albanian Orthodox Church, as well as most of its priests, were held in prison.[71] As for the Catholics, with the death of Bishop Ernest Coba, apostolic administrator of Shkodër in 1979, the only remaining Catholic bishop in Albania was Nikolle Troshani, titular bishop of Cisamo and apostolic administrator of Lezha and Durrës. He was confined in the labor camp at Tepelana, near the port of Vlorë.

Illegal since 1967, religious organizations also became unconstitutional under the new document adopted in 1976. Article 55 of the new constitution declared: "The formation of any organization of a fascist, anti-democratic, religious or anti-socialist nature is forbidden. Fascist, religious, warmongerish, anti-socialist activity and propaganda are forbidden, as is the incitement to hatred between peoples and races."[72] In June 1977 a new penal code was issued, which prescribed penalties for engaging in religious activities.

In the mythology of the Albanian Party of Labor the suppression of religion—which was carried out with speed and vigor—was portrayed as having enjoyed broad popular support. An account in *Studime Historike*, which clearly reflected the communist regime's outlook, held that "the struggle against religious dogmas, rites, and beliefs was carried out in conformity with the line of the masses. It was the people themselves who rose up and condemned the religious ideology. This job was done through discourse and reasoned polemics. Persuasion, the elevation and activation of public opinion—these were the decisive factors that assured success in this struggle."[73]

In its desire to expunge all traces of religious heritage the regime began advising parents on the appropriateness of names for their children. Official lists of "Illyrian" names were published, but people ignored them until, finally, on 23 September 1975 the government issued a decree (no. 5339) requiring everyone to assume a nonreligious name.[74]

The antireligious campaign was portrayed as a reflection of authentic Albanian nationalism, and all three religions were described as foreign penetrations.[75] Repeated appeals from the two Albanian Orthodox ecclesiastical organizations in the United States had no impact on Tiranë's tough policy. Still, repeated complaints about party activities in this area were sufficient to indicate that religion was far from dead in the self-proclaimed "first atheist state." In 1975 a Yugoslav observer noted that Orthodox believers in the south, some of them Greeks, *always* observed religious holidays and refused to work at Easter.[76] In the summer of 1980 an Albanian sociologist revealed that during the previous ten years only 3 percent of rural marriages and only 5 percent of urban marriages involved people of different religious backgrounds—itself a measure of the tenacity of religious consciousness. As if supporting that point, a Tiranë publication conceded the following year that religious marriages and rituals continued to be practiced.[77]

The Albanian communist regime tried to popularize the notion that the Albanian people had never been religious and that Catholicism, Orthodoxy, and Islam alike were *foreign* religions, opposed to the natural atheism of the people. This claim was disputed in the West, but it does appear that the religious *institutions* were too weak to put up an effective resistance to Hoxha's repression.

The death of Enver Hoxha resulted in no immediate changes in the fortunes of Albania's religious associations. Ramiz Alia, Hoxha's successor, continued the antireligious policies of his predecessor. At the Ninth Congress of the Albanian Labor Party in November 1986 Hulusi Hako lamented the fact that, despite the party's "powerful revolutionary movement against religion and backward customs," there was still evidence of "certain manifestations and remnants of religious preconceptions and practices and related superstitions."[78] Hako reiterated the Stalinist line without modification, asserting, "We must fight not only against these remnants and the harm they cause, but also to ensure the total triumph of the line of the Party."[79] In pursuing this line the party continued to make use of Cultural Youth Brigades which traveled around the country investigating and countering manifestations of religious loyalty.[80] Perhaps the only measure adopted during Alia's first year in office which reassured the religious associations was the release from prison of Bishop Troshani on 13 January 1986 after twenty-two years of incarceration.[81] Subsequently, in 1988 Tiranë began to permit émigré Albanian religious leaders to visit the country; Mother Teresa, an ethnic Albanian from Skopje, paid a three-day visit in August 1989. Finally, on 8 May 1990 Tiranë repealed the law banning religious propaganda. Six months later, religious associations were granted permission to reopen their churches and mosques. This move was followed by the official reopening of the Bektashi main office in Tiranë in March 1991.

Religious Communities After the Fall of Communism

Nowhere in Eastern Europe was the communist legacy harsher for religious associations than in Albania. Most places of worship were destroyed under the communists, and those that were spared were converted into warehouses, movie theaters, and sports arenas. Most clergy of all faiths died in prison camps. And because of the blackout on religious instruction, Albanians were left knowing little of their faiths, even when they might identify themselves as members of a specific creed.

Now, in the wake of religious activity becoming legal again, religious life is making an energetic return, albeit in ways that may signify religious transformation rather than a return to the precommunist status quo. From 1991 until 1995 the Islamic Community built more than five hundred new mosques, the Orthodox reopened about ninety churches, and several hundred Catholic churches opened their doors (many of them prefabricated buildings). Sacred texts have enjoyed a boom. In 1994 alone, more than a million copies of the Bible and the Koran were introduced into Albania, some of them bypassing legal channels. Missionary work has been frantic as well. As of the summer of 1995 about 450 evangelical missionaries reportedly were active in Albania (representing at least seventy evangelical Churches, most of them American), alongside at least 200 Catholic nuns and eighty Catholic priests involved in missionary work, several hundred mullahs from Persian Gulf states, and twelve Orthodox priests.[82]

The Americans and Arabs represent different traditions, and their work in Albania may change the character of Albanian religion. Some Albanians worry that the country's traditions of religious tolerance and interconfessional harmony may be eroded by American evangelicals and Islamic fundamentalists who preach that there is only one road to God. Up to now, Albanians of all faiths have tended to venerate the religious shrines of *all* faiths—a token of unique tolerance.[83]

The Islamic Community

Of Albania's current population of 3.3 million, nominally 2.24 million are Muslims. Of the 1,127 mosques in Albania before the communist take-over, only fifty survived that era, most of them dilapidated. As of 1991, only two mosques in Tiranë were fit for use by worshipers.[84]

The rebuilding of Islamic religious life in Albania inevitably has been premised on outside assistance. Here the governments of Saudi Arabia, Kuwait, and United Arab Emirates have played an important role, funding the construction of new religious buildings, albeit buildings often designed in unfamiliar styles.[85] From 1991 until 1995 more than ten Islamic schools were built with the help, big and small, of Arab countries; this work was crowned with the reopening in October 1995 of the Abu Bakr mosque, Albania's largest. Built in 1760, the mosque can hold 1,200 worshipers and is the only one of Shkodër's more than thirty mosques to have survived communist-era demolition campaigns.[86] The historic Rhodes mosque on the shore of the Adriatic, built in the fifteenth century but converted into a theater under Hoxha's rule, also has been repaired by the International Islamic Relief Organization.[87]

Ignorance of the content of the Islamic faith has been widespread. Abdullah Al-Mudaidab, director of the East European Committee of the World Assembly of Muslim Youth (WAMY), admitted in 1994, "If you ask someone [in Albania] about his religion, he will say Islam, but when you ask him who is your prophet, he will tell you he doesn't know."[88] To correct this deficit, WAMY produced some 14,000 cassettes for distribution among Muslim young people and handed out more than 6,000 veils to Muslim women in Albania. WAMY has financed the teaching of Arabic and the Shari'at in Albanian cities, and it conducted a two-week Dawah campaign aimed at propagating Islam in early 1994.[89] Some Albanians have been offered scholarships to study Islamic theology in Tripoli, Teheran, Jeddah, and elsewhere.

Not everyone welcomes these developments. Gramoz Pashko, a former deputy prime minister and leader of the centrist Democratic Alliance opposition party, is convinced that much of the imported Islamic presence is "militant" and "aggressive."[90] The teachings of Ayatollah Khomeini have been published in Albanian since 1994, if not earlier, conveying a mixture of religious intolerance and hostility toward the West.[91] Albanians partial to fundamentalist Islamic ideas even formed an Ayatollah Khomeini Association in Shkodër in June 1996, reportedly the first of its kind in the country.[92]

Controversy flared in September 1996 when Muslim squatters occupied the premises of two Orthodox monasteries (near the towns of Saranda and Gjirokastër). The squatters were reported to have illegally built some forty huts on monastery grounds in Saranda and to have defiled twenty-three rare frescoes, scrawling "Allah is great!" across images of medieval saints. The government took no immediate action to eject the squatters, however. About the same time, Teodor Laco, the minister of culture, announced that the Albanian Orthodox Church would not obtain full restitution of facilities confiscated by the communists.[93] Lest these developments be interpreted to signify that the Albanian government was acting in league with the Islamic community, the ministry of culture soon indicated its decision to close several Islamic theological schools. The official reason for the closing was the schools' alleged inability to assure the technical and material conditions for their operation.[94]

In October 1996 there were reports of Islamic fundamentalist activity in Albania,[95] some of it alleged to be the work of outsiders. Others denied that Islamic fundamentalism represents a phenomenon in Albania, and they cited Albania's long history of religious tolerance. For example, Ali Hoxha, an otherwise unidentified Albanian Muslim, told the Czech magazine *Pozor,* "There is no danger of Islamic fundamentalism here. Many Muslims think that all this talk of fundamentalism comes from people who are hostile to the Koran. Albanian tolerance could be an example to other Islamic countries."[96]

The Orthodox Church

About 700,000 inhabitants of Albania are Orthodox in religion. Tiranë claims that 640,000 of these are ethnic Albanians, conceding that the remaining 60,000 are Greek. Athens claims, on the other hand, that between 250,000 and 300,000 Orthodox Greeks reside in Albania.[97]

The reconstruction of Orthodox religious life has involved work on many levels. The restaffing of the Church has been pursued with the reopening of a seminary, which in 1995 graduated twenty-eight students, twenty-one of them immediately being ordained into the priesthood.[98] The return of surviving church buildings also has been high on the Church's agenda, but the government of Sali Berisha was slow to move on this matter.[99] Moreover, as of December 1995 the government was still holding onto various icons, other religious objects, and archives belonging to the Orthodox Church on the grounds that the Church was not yet equipped to adequately protect them.[100]

But the ethnic element has constituted the greatest challenge to the normalization of Orthodox religious life in post-1990 Albania. Part of the difficulty lies in the Greek government's ambiguous attitude toward southern Albania, a region that many Greeks call Northern Epirus, and the government's desire to act as guardian of Albania's Greek minority. In 1993, for example, Albania expelled a Greek Orthodox clergyman (Chrysostomos Maidonis) on charges that he had been inciting ethnic Greeks in southern Albania to campaign for unification with Greece; the Greek government repudiated the charge and expelled some 20,000 Albanians in response.[101] Irredentism cropped up again the following year, when Albanian authorities arrested five ethnic Greek Albanians, members of an association called Omonia, on charges of having airdropped antigovernment leaflets.[102]

It is against this background, as well as against the background of the historic role of the Greek Orthodox Church in efforts to Hellenize the Albanian population, that the nomination of an ethnic Greek in 1992 to serve as head of the Albanian Orthodox Church must be assessed. Archbishop Anastasios Iannoulatos, a professor at Athens University, was charged by the ecumenical patriarch in 1991 to undertake the reorganization of the Albanian Autocephalous Orthodox Church. In June 1992, over the protests of local Albanians, he was appointed head of the Albanian Church. Even his installation ceremony was marred by noisy protests. Albanian President Berisha had misgivings about this nomination but approved it on the condition that no more Greek bishops be appointed for Albanian assignments.[103] In the course of 1994 the government drew up and passed a new constitution, article 7 of which affirmed: "The heads of the religious communities must be Albanian citizens, born in Albania with permanent residence in Albania during the past 20 years."[104] This article immediately drew fire. The General Church Council of the Albanian Autocephalous Orthodox Church charged that it was incompatible with the lay character of the state and was aimed *exclusively* at the Orthodox Church.[105] The Greek government also voiced an opinion, declaring that the article constituted unwarranted interference in the internal affairs of the Church. An Albanian-based Union for Human Rights, headed by Vasil Mele, went further and objected to the government's backing for the autocephalous status of the Albanian Orthodox Church, calling even this act "an intrusion into religious affairs."[106] Since the Orthodox Church's ethnic Albanian members favor ecclesiastical autocephaly, Mele's objections, if successful, would risk splitting the relatively small Albanian Orthodox community in two.

On the other side of the barricades, a number of political organizations (the National Association of Former Political Prisoners and the Politically Persecuted; the Party of Balli Kombëtar; the Albanian People's League Party; the Albanian Union Democratic Movement; the Ecology Party; and others) declared that even the presence of Archbishop Anastasias as head of the Church was unacceptable[107] and that the constitutional article was the minimum necessary to safeguard the autocephaly and national character of the Albanian Church. Finally, the Albanian government rebutted the Greek government's remonstrations, characterizing them as "unacceptable interference in the internal affairs of the Albanian state."[108] Moreover, some political figures were eager to interpret the constitution's passage as entailing the departure of Archbishop Anastasios.[109]

But Anastasios remained in office, albeit in a situation resembling siege. Then, in 1996 the Ecumenical Patriarchate in Istanbul, ignoring the protests of Albanian believers and disregarding the letter of the Albanian constitution, appointed three ethnic Greek bishops to senior posts as metropolitans of Gjirokastër, Vlorë, and Korçë. Archbishop Anastasios, more sensitive to the political climate in Albanian religious circles, objected, refusing to perform the rite of induction.[110] On 4 August the archbishop called on the World Orthodox Center in Istanbul to review its appointment of the three bishops and to consider other possibilities.[111] The National Committee for the Defense of the Autocephaly of the Albanian Orthodox Church, based in Tiranë, registered a strong protest to the Ecumenical Patriarchate, as did the Albanian government.[112] Archbishop Anastasios himself conceded, "Fear and concern have now been intensified in Albania that the Greeks [intend] to penetrate and realize their ethnic plans through the Albanian Orthodox Autocephalous Church."[113]

The Roman Catholic Church

Perhaps as many as 450,000 Roman Catholics reside in Albania today.[114] A total of twenty-seven priests and one bishop (not in office) survived the communist era, having an average age of sixty-seven in 1991.[115] By 1993 the number of priests had inched upward to thirty-one, as compared with eighty-two secular priests and 123 religious clergy in 1936.[116] Only about a hundred Catholic church buildings survived, and all of these had been adapted for other purposes and needed to be renovated for liturgical use.

Albania and the Vatican resumed diplomatic ties in July 1991, and in October of that year the Holy See appointed Ivan Dias to serve as papal nuncio in Tiranë.[117] The Jesuit order also was granted permission to return to Albania, and it announced the reopening of the pontifical seminary in Shkodër in September 1991.[118] Early in 1993 the printing house Dispenca in Tiranë became the property of the Catholic Church, while an agreement signed between the ministry of health and environmental protection and the Albanian Catholic Church on 29 September provided for construction of a 250-bed hospital in Tiranë, to be operated by the Church; in this connection, the government made some 12.5 acres available for rent.[119] The Catholic Church also has informed the government of its plans to construct religious educational institutions.[120]

Also in 1993, Pope John Paul II consecrated four new bishops for the Albanian Church, and in December 1994 he elevated Albanian Archbishop Mikel Koliqi to the College of Cardinals.[121]

The Jews

As of 1990 about 350 families of Jewish origin still lived in Albania.[122] That year efforts were initiated by the Israeli Foreign Ministry, the Jewish Agency, and an American Jewish welfare organization to arrange for the transfer of Albania's small Jewish population to Israel and other countries.[123] In a series of top-secret flights the entire Jewish population was flown out of Albania, the process being completed by 11 April 1991. Almost all concerned opted to be transferred to Israel, with about thirty families indicating a preference to be resettled in the United States.[124] Most Albanian Jews were said to be well-educated and with professional careers. But a year after being airlifted to Israel, some immigrants were said to be experiencing "acute social isolation" and difficulties in being absorbed into Israeli society.[125] By 1993 some of them even were expressing a desire to return to Albania.[126]

Evangelical Christians and Other American-based Christian Groups

No published statistics indicate the number of converts to American-based religious organizations, which, in addition to Jehovah's Witnesses and other evangelical Christians, include Lutherans, Mormons, Baptists, and Seventh-Day Adventists. These groups created an umbrella organization known as the Albanian Evangelical Alliance, which has complained of administrative obstacles to the building of churches and access to the media.[127]

The evangelicals insist on a clear religious choice and show disdain for the Albanian tradition of honoring all religious shrines. "Most people [in Albania] think that Jesus and Mohamed are just two different roads to the [one] God," said Bill Babione, an American missionary with the fundamentalist student organization, Campus Crusade for Christ. "But two roads that diverge cannot lead to the same place."[128] Babione's organization, which offers Bible study classes in dormitories of the University of Tiranë, attracts about two hundred students per week. Babione and some of his colleagues toured the countryside in the summer of 1994, showing *The Jesus Film* in about 250 villages.[129] As they drove from village to village, the message was the same everywhere. "We believe that unless someone has a personal relationship with Jesus Christ, he or she is on the way to Hell," said Dave Fyock, administrator of the Albanian Encouragement Project, an evangelical coordinating body.[130] Not surprisingly, Islamic leaders have expressed concern about the activities of the missionaries. Nasuf Dizdari, managing editor of an Albanian Islamic newspaper, put it this way in 1994: "We are a very small country with a lot of religions. We don't want to be an experimental country for sects coming in from abroad. The different sects coming here are neither Christians nor Muslims. They only damage the equilibrium of Albania."[131]

Conclusion

Albanian President Berisha noted the obvious in 1992 when he pointed to the religious "boom" being experienced by all religious associations in Albania.[132] But while religious sentiment experiences a revival, remnants of Albanian Marxism have made a few feeble efforts to show that their faith is not entirely dead. Latter-day Marxists showed their colors as recently as 1994, unfurling a national flag shorn of the Albanian eagle; they also tacked photos of Enver Hoxha onto obelisks in Korçë. One ambitious activist even affixed a large portrait of Lenin on the marquee of the Morava cinema.[133]

There was a time when it meant something to declare that the religion of Albanians was Albanianism. It meant something during the Ottoman period, when the competing faiths seemed to represent foreign interests. It meant something in interwar Albania when King Zog was intent on consolidating an independent Albanian religious life under his control and influence. And it meant something in the days of Enver Hoxha, when the equation of religiosity with foreignness and nationalism with atheism reinforced and underpinned the regime's idiosyncratic, autarkic line. But in the postcommunist era, as evangelicals engage Albanians in a new discourse and as Albania's more traditional faiths draw on foreign resources in an effort to fight back and compete for "souls," the discourse about Albanianism has lost its meaning. Not only can one no longer speak of "Albanianism" as a religion, but one can no longer even use the phrase "the religion of Albania" coherently.

IV

The Former Soviet Union

Chapter 9

The Russian Orthodox Church in Transition

For more than sixty years (1927–88) the Russian Orthodox Church was subordinated to and controlled by the Soviet state. Its chief newspaper was proofed by the KGB before publication. Its clergy were promoted, demoted, and assigned according to the preferences of state authorities. The curriculum and admissions at its seminaries were subject to the veto of authorities, and all repair work on churches had to be cleared with the appropriate officials. Some clergymen and bishops turned KGB informers. As for the patriarch, he was obliged to make "positive propaganda" for the Soviet Union abroad, most especially at the World Council of Churches. The Russian Orthodox Church, which from 1721 to 1917 had been the handmaid of the tsars, had proven capable of adapting to the service of atheist, even atheizing, masters.

The collapse of the Soviet state, therefore, could only have huge consequences for the Russian Orthodox Church—consequences in some ways greater than for many other religious bodies in the lands that made up the Union of Soviet Socialist Republics.

Communist Years (1927–1953)

At first, of course, the Russian Church—or a part of it, at least—resisted Bolshevization. Patriarch Tikhon pronounced an anathema on the new government and called on the faithful to resist state policies and defend the Church. But some clergy saw the Bolshevik Revolution as a great opportunity, and they tried to create a (schismatic) Church organization along "modernist" and "democratic" lines. The resulting Renovationist (or Living) Church at its peak controlled most of the Orthodox parishes,[1] maintaining "close organizational identification with the security organs of the state."[2] Meanwhile, persecution whittled away the strength of the patriarchal Church.

In April 1925 Patriarch Tikhon died, having dictated a statement some two years before his death that he was "henceforth not an enemy of the

Soviet government."[3] Soviet authorities imprisoned Tikhon's designated successor, Metropolitan Petr, who was serving locum tenens. Church leadership was then conferred on Metropolitan Sergii (Stragorodsky), who for a time had been associated with the Renovationist Church. The Bolshevik government ordered Sergii, as the new locum tenens, to excommunicate clerical and lay members of the Synodal Church, but when he refused, the Soviets imprisoned him in February 1927.[4] Sergii was released the following month, and in July 1925 he issued a declaration of loyalty to the Soviet state and his motherland, "whose joys and successes are our successes, and whose setbacks are our setbacks."[5]

By then, the League of Militant Atheists was already two years old. Designed as the organizational arm of the communists' propaganda onslaught against religion, the league recruited former clergy into its ranks—among them, Mikhail Gorev, one-time curator of the Spaso-Preobrazhenskaia Church in St. Petersburg, and Ivan Brikhnichev, former parish priest at the Tbilisi Railway Station Church.[6] By 1932 membership in the league had risen to more than 5 million.[7]

As of 1928 Joseph Stalin had consolidated his supremacy within the communist regime. This new dominance coincided with a dramatic shift across policy spheres. The religious sphere was among those affected. Significantly, a new Decree on Religious Associations was issued on 8 April 1929, which confirmed the earlier rights of religious profession (changed in 1936 to a right of religious *worship*) and of *antireligious* propaganda, but dropped any mention of any right of *religious* propaganda. The revision signaled the antireligious drive of the first five-year plan. Indeed, aside from attendance at religious services in registered buildings, almost every other kind of confessionally associated activity was now illegal. The following month the Council of People's Commissars added financial pressure, placing clergy in the same tax category as private peasants and shopkeepers (other occupations destined for extinction under the Soviet plan).

The years 1929–33 witnessed a massive wave of church closures. The regime also began to choke off religious life in other ways. *Izvestiia* boasted in February 1930 that the USSR had "already really built [a] State without God, and a government without any of God's laws."[8] But Metropolitan Sergii was impressed with the importance of "cooperation," and at a tightly controlled press conference orchestrated for Western journalists he "denied priests and the pious laity were persecuted, declaring there was no illegality in the way they were treated. He said he had not heard that all the churches in the Odessa region had been closed by the local Soviet despite the fact this appeared in all the official Moscow papers."[9] Sergii was cooperative in other ways, too. For example, later in 1930 he signed an order dismissing Metropolitan Evlogi as head of the Russian Church in Western Europe. Evlogi had been accused of having engaged in anti-Soviet propaganda and of having played a key role in organizing meetings in Paris and elsewhere to protest religious persecution and the demolition of churches in the USSR.[10]

But the Soviet authorities did not restrict themselves to church closures and interference in episcopal appointments. In the spring of 1932, for instance, a decree banned the display of colored Easter eggs, the baking of the tall sweet cake called *kulich*, or the preparation of paskha (a traditional sweetened cheese dessert).[11] The Young Pioneers suggested that stores instead display toy automobiles and toy tractors to celebrate socialist progress.

The omni-intrusiveness of the Stalin regime also had a brutal side. Although the regime tried to throw a cloak of secrecy around its misdeeds, some incidents came to public view even at the time. In one instance, Romanian newspapers published stories on 9 May 1932 of Bolshevik massacres of believers participating in a religious procession on the banks of the Dniester while they sang hymns to celebrate Easter.[12]

Meanwhile, the demolition of churches continued. On the eve of the Bolshevik Revolution in 1917, the Russian Orthodox Church owned some 50,000 church buildings; the number rose to 80,000 if one counted chapels, convent churches, institutional prayer houses, etc. By 1939, according to Nathaniel Davis, only 200-300 (Orthodox) churches were still functioning in the entire country.[13] Of the 1,242 Orthodox monasteries reported to have been operating in 1917, none remained open as of the early 1930s. Many of these monasteries were simply demolished, while others were converted to new uses (such as military schools, prisons, theaters, administrative offices, even a swimming pool).[14] (The numbers of clergy who lost their lives during this period are documented in chapter 2.)

Part of the hierarchy and clergy had fled the country by 1921 and established a separate Church organization outside Russia that came to be known as either "the Russian Orthodox Church Abroad" or "the Synodal Church."[15] Inside Russia the Church split again when a movement calling itself the True Orthodox emerged. Itself bifurcated, the movement reached the height of its activity from 1943 to 1947, during World War II and its immediate aftermath. But with the revival of harsh antireligious measures in 1948, the movement found itself targeted for special attention, and by the early 1950s it was defunct.[16]

Meanwhile, so thoroughly debilitated was the (patriarchal) Russian Orthodox Church by 1939 that, for the most part, it could think only of supplicating itself before the regime that was causing it to rapidly expire. Ironically, World War II proved to be a godsend for the Church. Stalin could not afford to further alienate the Church during the period of the Nazi invasion and occupation, which began on 22 June 1941. Antireligious propaganda ceased, the League of Militant Atheists was shut down barely three months after the Nazi invasion, and in late 1941 a small number of churches were reopened (around Ulyanovsk). A few seminaries also were reopened during the war, as were two religious academies. Permission was granted for resumed publication of the journal *Patriarkhiia*.[17] The Russian Orthodox Church, which since 1927 had been administered by a metropolitan, was allowed in 1943 to elevate Sergii to the post of patriarch, and the episcopate was granted permission to establish administrative structures and resume printing religious literature. Other religious denominations were granted similar prerogatives. In 1943, moreover, Soviet authorities set up the Council for the Affairs of the Russian Orthodox Church, which was followed in 1944 by the founding of the Council for the Affairs of Religious Cults.[18] The establishment of these two bodies implied a pledge (not honored in practice) on the part of the authorities (at least for the interim) to respect the legal norms of the Soviet state in dealings with the Churches.

As a result of this partial "liberalization," as well as the USSR's acquisition of new territories not yet subjected to Stalinist terror, the Russian Orthodox Church tallied some 10,504 registered parish churches as of January 1946. Then came the delegalization of the Greek-Rite Catholic Church in Ukraine in March 1946[19] and the transfer of its parishes to the jurisdiction of the Russian patriarchate. This move brought the total number of Russian Orthodox churches to 14,039 as of 1 January 1947. Moreover, as a result of the continued "liberalized" policy in Moscow, this figure rose to 14,421 two years later.[20]

This total proved to be the high-water mark for the Russian Orthodox Church for many years to come. The number of churches began to decline in 1950, and by 1953, the last year of Stalin's reign, the number of Russian Orthodox churches had slipped to 13,508.[21]

Communist Years (1953–1991)

After a brief interregnum, Nikita Khrushchev became First Secretary of the CPSU, adding the title of Prime Minister (literally, Chairman of the Council of Ministers) in 1958. Although less brutal than Stalin, Khrushchev was no less ideologically driven, and in his mind it was the duty of the state to expunge religious superstitions and prejudices from the minds of Soviet citizens. As early as 7 July 1954 the Central Committee of the CPSU adopted a resolution concluding:

many party organizations are providing inadequate leadership of scientific atheist propaganda among the population, as a result of which this important aspect of ideological work is in a neglected condition. At the same time, the Churches and various religious sects have revitalized their activities, strengthened their cadres and adapted flexibly to modern conditions, thus reinforcing their influence on some sections of the population.[22]

In spite of this summons the first four years of Khrushchev's reign were largely benign as far as the Churches were concerned. Indeed, between 1954 and 1958 periodic reports appeared in the *Journal of the Moscow Patriarchate* about the construction of churches. "A few were newly built," as Pospielovsky notes, "but most were churches that [had been] damaged or partly ruined during the war."[23] Bishop Arsenii of Kostroma even felt emboldened to conduct unsanctioned prayer services outdoors and to violate "cult" legislation in other ways during 1955–56. His activities provoked a great deal of concern on the part of the authorities, however.[24]

Renewed pressure on the Churches began at the end of 1958 when the Council of Ministers abolished certain tax exemptions on monastic properties, which had been introduced in 1945 (at a time when about a hundred Orthodox monasteries were reopened) and called for measures to curb monastic activity. In 1959 sixty-four monasteries still functioned. The vigor of the antimonastic measures reduced their number to eighteen by 1965.[25] *Pravda* carried an editorial on 21 August 1959, explaining the new line: "Our party's premise," it wrote, "in defining its attitude towards religion is that religion is inimicable to the interests of the working masses, that it is the most conservative form of social consciousness, and that it hinders the active struggle of the people for the transformation of society."[26] The *Pravda* editorial reiterated the party's commitment to the "complete eradication of religious prejudices"[27] and made it clear that the new spirit of antireligion would not be limited to closing monasteries.

On the contrary, believers were subjected to new forms of harassment, while more decisive moves were taken to undermine the institutional strength of the Russian Church. These included closing the Cathedral in Perm in February 1960 (on the grounds that the crowds gathered outside on Sundays created a traffic hazard) and shutting down the theological seminary in Kiev as well as churches across Ukraine, Belorussia, and Moldavia.[28] The Orthodox Church was constrained to change its statutes in 1961, giving up priestly control of parish councils and reducing the parish priest to a kind of "employee" of the lay council.[29] In 1962 Soviet authorities revised legislation to make it more difficult to open a new parish and to essentially abrogate the right of believers to appeal a decision on the part of local authorities to close a given church.[30] The authorities likewise declared it illegal for parents to teach catechism to their children. By 1963, according to Nathaniel Davis, "children and teenagers under the age of eighteen were being prevented, even more systematically than previously, from entering and attending church services."[31] By 1964, only 7,600 Russian Orthodox churches remained open throughout the USSR, or just over half as many as in 1947.[32]

Authorities also employed the KGB in attempts to infiltrate religious institutions, and they routinely endeavored to entice or intimidate seminarians and priests into collaboration.[33] The Znanie ("Knowledge") Society was also put to work, organizing lectures on antireligious subjects. In 1959 the society held some 400,000 antireligious lectures, which rose to 660,000 in 1963 (as compared to 120,000 such lectures organized by the Znanie Society in 1954).[34] At the same time, Soviet officials more vigorously designed new "socialist rituals," which, it was hoped, would displace Christian rites of baptism, marriage, and interment.

Khrushchev's fall from power in October 1964 resulted in yet another respite for the churches. The closing of church facilities fell off, arrests of religious activists all but ended, and some believers even were released from prison. In a striking departure that antedated Khrushchev's removal by a few months the Council for the Affairs of Religious Cults organized a conference (in June 1964) to discuss violations of the rights of believers.[35] This is not to suggest that religion now rebounded. On the contrary, the number of functioning Russian Orthodox churches would reach a new low (in 1988) of 6,740, with the inertia of the Brezhnev, Andropov, and Chernenko eras carrying into the third year of Gorbachev's rule (1985–91).[36] Still, priests no longer were subject to indiscriminate persecution, church closings became less frequent, and in January 1981 the rate of taxation of clergy was even slightly reduced.[37]

By 1980, moreover, an important new element had been introduced in the Russian Orthodox Church's declared intention to celebrate the millennium of the Christianization of Kievan Rus in 1988. The symbolic and catalytic importance of this event will become evident. But at the time of Gorbachev's accession to the post of General Secretary of the Communist Party in March 1985, few clues betrayed any shift in the wind. On the contrary, Gorbachev used the occasion of a stopover in Tashkent in November 1986 to endorse a continuation of the party's policy of "determined and pitiless combat against religious manifestations."[38] But gradually, in the wake of an article published by Yevgeni Yevtushenko (b. 1933) in *Komsomol'skaia pravda* in December 1986—in which the world-renowned Soviet poet declared that official atheism was incompatible with the principle of separation of Church and state—the first steps were taken to rehabilitate religion in both rhetoric and policy. The reexamination of the premises of state religious policy was played out in the pages of the official press[39] and gradually prepared the ground for the Church's restoration to public life. Work began as early as 1986 on the formulation of a new law on religious organizations; after four years of discussions and debate the eventual draft was passed into law in the early autumn of 1990. At this point the central authorities were more liberal than local officials, and from 1985 until 1988 the Council for Religious Affairs "reversed eighty-three refusals by local authorities to register religious societies."[40] During these years conditions improved for religious communities in other ways as well. For example, authorities gradually but steadily relaxed their controls over the production or importation of religious literature, and censorship was eased. From 1985 until 1989 some 2 million copies of the Bible or the New Testament had been imported into the USSR.[41]

In June 1988 came the millennial celebrations, the product of Church-state collaboration, in which Orthodoxy was celebrated as an important component of Russian (and Ukrainian) culture and history. The authorities also lifted the ban on Church involvement in charitable activities and volunteer work in hospitals, and at the same time they allowed Sunday schools and catechism classes to be held openly. Religious broadcasts, religious phone-ins, and faith healings became ever more common by the winter of 1990–91, and in April 1991 the first Orthodox radio station, *Radonezh*, began broadcasting.[42]

What should be emphasized, however, is that religious organizations in general, and the Russian Orthodox Church in particular, regained lost ground precisely at a time when the Soviet state was rapidly decaying, and more, they regained it *as a function of that political decay*. This breakdown of the state, in turn, set the stage for radical changes in the challenges and opportunities confronting the Russian Orthodox Church after 1991.

System Collapse, Civil Strife, and Religious Revival

When authoritarian systems[43] collapse, they are apt to do so under certain identifiable conditions and generally according to regular patterns. Growing civil strife is commonly associated with system collapse, and it also is often, though not inevitably, associated with foreign intervention (as in the Spanish Civil War of 1936–39 and the Serbian Insurrectionary War of 1991–95). System collapse usually follows an extended period of political decay and economic deterioration, as in Russia, and spotlights the entire question of system legitimation.

Indeed, the fundamental problem of politics is the creation and maintenance of a legitimate political order, and this dilemma is thrown into sharp relief in revolutionary systems, which are especially ill-equipped to resolve it. Legitimacy may be seen as consisting in consonance between the values embodied in the prevailing system and the dominant political values of a society. Revolution (treating this concept, for the moment, as synonymous with the notion of radical revolution) starts at a disadvantage, because it is defined by its attempt to remake political order in accord with values held by a minority party. (Radical) revolution thus operates in disjunction with a society's dominant values. Counter-revolution, by contrast, may be defined as the effort to undo revolution in order to bring political order into consonance with society's values. If we accept these definitions as heuristic devices, this analysis offers an explanation as to why revolutionary regimes remain vulnerable to counter-revolution and why it is much harder to launch a revolution than it is, ultimately, to overthrow it. That said, it is apparent that the question of political cohesion and national unity depends very much on the existence or achievement of some degree of consensus on values.

In ideal conditions a consensus on values is developed around the political system itself (or in some examples, especially before 1550, around the religio-political system).[44] With one exception, it is much harder to build a broad social consensus on values around any other institution than the state—that single exception being the Church. But that exception applies only in confessionally homogeneous societies such as Poland; Russia is already confessionally more diverse, and although Russian Orthodoxy is clearly the "traditional" religion, it is by no means the religion of all Russians. Now, when a political order fails to build a consensus on values that support its continuance, it decays. But there is no guarantee that political decay entails the emergence of some alternative consensus on values. And it is precisely this problem that provokes the greatest concern where the post-Soviet commonwealth is concerned.

Some analysts claim that a form of legitimation takes place through performance, that is, that a system may be considered legitimate insofar as its population is prosperous, well-fed, and freed of concerns about safety and survival (so-called "*eudaemonic* legitimation"). While conceding that Thomas Hobbes identifies the maintenance of public order as the minimal, most essential function of the state, I would argue that performance is not associated with legitimacy, and that, on the contrary, a population may consent to illegitimate government as long as it is kept "fat and happy." At the same time, it can be put forward that legitimate governments are less vulnerable to economic deterioration than are illegitimate ones; indeed, illegitimate governments may depend on performance factors as a substitute for legitimation.

The Russian pattern since 1991 has conformed closely to the pattern in other postcommunist societies. As Lilia Shevtsova has written,

Without exception, post-communist societies have shared the following characteristics: a poorly developed system of party formation; fragile coalitions among the ruling elite, which break down and are then recreated with frequency; continuous confrontation between the executive and legislature; periodic clashes between the president and the government; the pursuit of unregulated emergency powers by the executive, relying on a plebiscitary appeal and based on personal charisma; and an ideological vacuum caused by the wholesale repudiation of Marxism-Leninism. In no [postcommunist] country has a successful model of political development been carried out. In all countries political clashes have occurred between half-baked new ideologies—"Westernism" versus nationalism; democratization versus an iron hand.[45]

Whether this syndrome adequately describes, say, the Czech Republic and Slovenia is not the point. What matters is that a *typical* syndrome exists in the societies where the communist system has collapsed; that syndrome has *typical* features, and Russia exemplifies it rather well.

But there is something else, too, which is essential: the deepened uncertainty that characterizes periods of "transition" (*pace* Verdery).[46] As John Löwenhardt has wisely emphasized, "the main characteristic of the transition process is that during it, the rules of the political 'game' are not defined. Unlike the periods before and after transition, at least some of the main rules will be hotly contested, and many participants in transition may be in a state of uncertainty concerning these rules."[47] These two features—the legitimacy vacuum and the general state of uncertainty—contribute directly and indirectly to the intensified politicization of religion. The absence of operative principles of legitimacy is a great lure for Churches, which are (without exception in the modern world) committed to systems of values that they ideally would like to become dominant in society. Religious organizations, therefore, are naturally political, and a crisis of legitimacy inevitably plays to religion's greatest interest. At the same time, this general condition provides ample scope for Church involvement in politics, for when everything is uncertain, nothing is clearly forbidden. These two characteristics help explain why decommunization in Russia, far from leading to the depoliticization of religion, has, on the contrary, contributed to Russia's Churches being able to widen the scope of their political activity.

Religious Organizations and Social Change

Samuel P. Huntington, among other commentators, has remarked on the way in which growing social and political chaos seems to suck religious organizations into the political fray.[48] And when it comes to chaos, Russia has most certainly had its share since 1991. To begin with, all fourteen other Soviet republics withdrew from association with Russia in 1991–92. This severing of ties was followed by the outbreak of armed conflict in Nagorno-Karabakh,[49] Chechnya, Tajikistan, Abkhazia, South Ossetia, North Ossetia and Ingushetia, and Transdniester, with Russian troops being deployed in all of these conflicts. Between 70,000 and 80,000 people died in Chechnya by September 1996,[50] while the war in Tajikistan claimed more than 20,000 lives by May 1994.[51] As Russians streamed out of Central Asia by the thousands,[52] Moscow pledged to use military force if necessary to protect their native compatriots who lived in former Soviet republics.[53] Meanwhile, rumors from time to time were heard that Lithuania,[54] or Belarus,[55] or Russia itself[56] would shortly dissolve into civil war. For that matter, in the wake of military complications in Chechnya, Russian Defense Minister Pavel Grachev called for improving the Russian military's ability to fight in cities.[57] Even if no additional conflicts were to break out, the existing ones have seriously drained the Russian treasury, as renowned commentator Vasiliy Selyunin warned in the summer of 1993.[58] Russia appeared to be on the brink of civil war in the autumn of 1993 when President Boris Yeltsin ordered Russian army tanks to shell the Russian parliament.[59] In addition, one should take into account struggles over autonomy in the Crimea and in the Gagauz region of Moldova; the proclamation of the so-called Talysh-Mugan Republic in border districts of Azerbaijan bordering on Iran;[60] the mushrooming of organized crime and petty crime in Russia, with as many as five thousand distinct "mobs" active and with some of them having access to nuclear know-how;[61] and continued economic decline in Russia, Ukraine, and other former Soviet republics,[62] with some 75 million Russians said to be undernourished as of July 1995;[63] with all of these problems, it is no wonder that some Western analysts have begun to discuss whether Russia can avoid internal political collapse.[64] Nor is it any surprise that Stalin is enjoying renewed popularity in certain circles,[65] or that paranoia and conspiracy theories obtain ready audiences (e.g., Agrarian Party leader Mikhail Lapshin was said to believe that a "deliberate policy to destroy Russia's agricultural sector"[66] existed while KGB General Georgi Georgievich Rogozin was said to dabble in black magic and the occult to obtain insight into suitable policies to recommend to Yeltsin).[67] In the new Russia, sex symbol Yelena Kondulainen, a veteran of more than two dozen films, could create a so-called Party of Love, brandishing slogans "back to basics" and "Lovers of the world, unite!,"[68] while civil engineers set to work erecting a scaled-down version of Mount Rushmore in Moscow's Gorky Park (complete with gigantic stone likenesses of U.S. Presidents Jefferson, Washington, Lincoln, and Theodore Roosevelt).[69] In such conditions, with this degree of system overload, can Russia build capitalism at all? Russian President Yeltsin gave his answer in April 1996: "Russia is not building capitalism . . ., it is building a market economy with its own specific flavor."[70]

The politicization of religious organizations has been a general phenomenon throughout the CIS area—because political and social chaos have had their counterpart in religious chaos (as amply illustrated in Ukraine; see chapter 10); because in times of institutional weakness, people inevitably exploit nonpolitical institutions for political purposes;

and because religion, concerned with the values of society, is intrinsically political anyway. In Russia, Orthodox priests have served as deputies in the parliament, while the Church hierarchy itself played a small (and ultimately nugatory) role in mediating the conflict between Yeltsin and the parliament in October 1993[71] and openly endorsed Yeltsin for president in 1996;[72] in Belarus, Churches appealed to voters to support the Belarusian Popular Front;[73] in Lithuania, Catholic priests became involved in ethnic conflicts, and one priest even served briefly in parliament;[74] in Azerbaijan, leaders of the Islamic Party engaged in legally dubious activities from 1992 until 1995, with the goal of revamping the republic as an Islamic state "living in accordance with the laws of the Shari'ah and governed by religious leaders";[75] and in Tashkent, Islam Karimov has encouraged the development of a new Islam-based ideology to underpin the consolidation of a more united sense of Uzbek nationhood.[76]

The Russian Orthodox Church, which had been "gradually transformed into something resembling a classic Soviet institution" and which had become accustomed to maintaining "a stony silence about the tragic realities" of the USSR,[77] was thrust into a maelstrom in August 1991 when communist hard-liners arrested Gorbachev and attempted to take over the machinery of state. Unaccustomed to criticizing those wielding power, the patriarchate kept silent for twenty-four hours before issuing a timid statement on 20 August. In this curiously worded statement, Patriarch Aleksii II (elected in June 1990 after Pimen's death) declared that "the circumstances of [Gorbachev's] withdrawal [from power] remain unclear," adding, in what was at best a naive spirit, "we must listen to the voice of President Gorbachev and discover his attitude to the events now going on."[78] President Yeltsin had appealed to the patriarch on 19 August to make a public statement; this cautious declaration can only have been a disappointment to Yeltsin and others resisting the coup. During the night of 21 August, however, the patriarch issued a second statement, observing that "the Church does not and cannot give its blessing to illegality, violence and acts of bloodshed."[79] While more helpful than the patriarch's first statement, it still did not compare favorably with the decisive declaration issued the previous day by the superintendent and general consistory of the United Evangelical Lutheran Church of Russia:

Dear fellow countrymen! We appeal to you, regardless of religious denomination or ethnic origin, to remain loyal to the lawful, constitutionally elected authori-

ties of the USSR and the RSFSR. Only the peaceful restoration of M. S. Gorbachev's authority as President of the USSR and the preservation of the lawful
authorities of the republics will allow us to save the country from catastrophe.

We hope that our common prayer to God may give hope that arbitrary violence will not triumph again in our country.

We call on you to support President B. N. Yeltsin and the Russian Parliament.
In the current crisis they are the only power which can stop the plotters of the
Committee, who are trying to take us back to the bloody nightmare of the com-
munist past. May the Lord God preserve us to live a worthy life![80]

With the failure of the coup, the USSR hastened toward its demise
just four months later. In the wake of the Soviet Union's collapse, a parliamentary commission submitted a report to the Moscow Patriarchate
on 6 March 1992, giving details of KGB hiring of bishops and other rank-
ing Church personnel as agents. As Dimitry Pospielovsky has pointed
out, cognoscenti could easily decipher the identities concealed behind
the KGB code names; the documents showed that Metropolitans Pitirim,
Iuvenalii, and Filaret of Kiev, together with the late Metropolitan Nikodim of Leningrad, and even Patriarch Aleksii II, at the time when he
was a metropolitan, had all performed service for the KGB.[81] These documents thus confirmed the truth of Fr. Sergei Popov's charge in January
1990 that "the Russian Orthodox Church has become thoroughly entangled in the evil policies of the state, and has consciously associated
itself with them."[82]

The Russian Orthodox Church Since 1991

Predictably, inevitably, and obviously, the Russian Orthodox Church has
benefited in many ways from the final disappearance of communism. It
has enjoyed new freedoms and prerogatives,[83] including the chance to di-
versify its publishing activities, to expand its educational activities, and
to build (or rebuild) important places of worship (such as the Christ the
Saviour Church in Moscow, destroyed by Stalin in 1931).[84] But especially striking has been the Church's desire to retain the old communist
formula—although in reverse. From the standpoint of the Church, it
seems, there is nothing wrong with Church-state symbiosis as long as
the Church is in the driver's seat. In an early intimation of this theocratic spirit the Russian Orthodox Church egged the parliament to pass

a bill in mid-July 1993 that severely restricted the activities of foreign-based religious organizations.[85] Or again, in April 1995 as Russia's military entanglements in conflicts around its periphery became a subject of internal debate, the patriarch met with Col.-Gen. Andrei Nikolayev, director of the Russian border troops, to sign a joint statement of cooperation, providing, inter alia, for the religious education of border troops, regular pastoral visits to border garrisons, and the placement of Russian Orthodox literature, videos, and audio materials in the libraries of their units. Col.-Gen. Nikolayev declared, "Faith and homeland are synonyms; without faith there cannot be a homeland, and without a homeland, there cannot be faith."[86] In July 1995 the Moscow Patriarchate even established a department for cooperation with the armed forces and police organs.[87]

In fact, since 1991 the Russian Orthodox Church has increasingly comported itself as the leading exponent of the "Russian national idea." But in support of its new boldness, the Church can point to a dramatic reversal in the self-identification of Russians, at least according to some polls. Whereas in communism's final years, some 70 percent of Russians said that they were nonbelievers, today 49 percent say they believe in God, while 51 percent consider themselves Orthodox.[88] German researcher Georg Seide has suggested that the Russian Orthodox Church may be aspiring to become the official state Church (despite the denials of Aleksii II).[89]

Be that as it may, with the collapse of the old communist power monopoly, the Orthodox Church has become dramatically more independent in its politics. In May 1994, for example, the Church joined Human Life International (a U.S.-based antiabortion organization) in cosponsoring Russia's first major antiabortion conference. Coordinated with the Russian antiabortion group, Right to Life, the conference provided a forum to agitate for abortion's criminalization.[90] Then again, the Holy Synod of the Russian Orthodox Church decided to air a proposal to canonize the murdered Tsar Nicholas II and his wife and five children as Orthodox martyrs.[91]

But the most controversial aspect of the Church's politics has been the flirtation of some of its hierarchs with monarchist and fascist ideologies. In October 1992, for example, Metropolitan Vitalii (head of the émigré Synodal Church) gave an interview to *Den'*, a fascist-national-Bolshevik weekly published in Moscow. In the interview Vitalii "gave full support to *Den'*'s contention that a world Zionist-Masonic plot was gathering forces to destroy Russia and the Orthodox Church," and he "declared that all religions except the Orthodox Church were satanic cults, wherefore any form of ecumenism was treason."[92]

One may dismiss Vitalii's case on the grounds that his affiliation with the émigré Church renders his interview irrelevant to an assessment of the *patriarchal* Church. However, it is more difficult to dismiss evidence of the wide support enjoyed by the All-Russia Monarchist Center (established in 1992) and the monarchist Union of Christian Rebirth among both priests and lay activists of the patriarchal Russian Church.[93] In the case of Metropolitan Ioann of St. Petersburg and Ladoga, he became a favorite of the nationalist right through his repeated broodings about alleged Jewish conspiracies to destroy Russia.[94] Church hierarchs have not been oblivious to the problem, however, as indicated in a pastoral letter from the Church's episcopal council read to a Moscow audience in the spring of 1992. "Both the Church and society," the bishops warned, "have to liberate themselves from the legacy of totalitarianism."[95]

This may be a hard assignment. Different parts of the Soviet and Russian past appeal to different parts of the population, and in the newly pluralist Russian political landscape, new organizations are creating new combinations out of the conflicting elements of Russia's heterogeneous past. Even the notion of marrying elements of Bolshevism to theocracy has found a home in the Russian All-People's Movement, which champions economic planning and the unification of Church and state.[96]

Conclusion

In addition to the social and political challenges enumerated above, the Russian Orthodox Church faces several internal challenges. These have included the lure of overcoming the seven-decade-old schism with the Synodal Church, the participation of certain priests in the work of the Russian parliament (in defiance of long-established Church guidelines),[97] the secession of some Russian Orthodox dioceses in Ukraine, Moldova, and Estonia,[98] and—looking beyond the boundaries of the Church itself—competition from newly active religious organizations, many based in other countries. (For more on these groups, described by Patriarch Aleksii II as "pseudo-religious movements" preaching "pernicious" and "false teachings,"[99] see chapter 13.)

The history of Russian Orthodoxy in the twentieth century has been turbulent. In the years up to 1917 Russian Orthodoxy was the privileged handmaiden of dynastic tsardom, associated as much with authority as with spirituality. This period was followed by a decade in the proverbial wilderness—1917-27—when the Church was riven by splits and schisms and engaged in a contest of mutual anathematization with the new Bolshevik regime. The years 1927 to 1943 constitute a third phase in the Church's twentieth-century life. This phase was characterized by energetic efforts on the regime's part to uproot and destroy the Church and all traces of religion. The later Stalin era (1943–53) must be considered a phase in its own right, although it did not differ in its fundamentals from the fifth phase, running from the death of Stalin in 1953 to the bursting of the dam in 1988. Since 1988 the entire religious landscape is fundamentally different, as the preceding pages have endeavored to show.

When communism first collapsed, many optimists in both Russia and the West enthusiastically embraced the notion that Russia was now on the path to democracy. In a 1992 article for *Voprosy filosofii*, D. E. Furman, a researcher at the Russian Academy of Sciences, attempted to disabuse would-be optimists of their illusions about the meaning of the combined religious and political changes taking place. "The 'religious swing of the pendulum,'" Furman argued, "is considerably weaker than the preceding 'atheistic' swing and . . . , in addition to the pendulum-like movement, which is superimposed on and interacts with the turn toward religion, there is another movement as well, leading to fundamentally different consequences."[100] Part of the difficulty, according to Furman, is that the Russian Orthodox Church does not nurture democratic ideals, subscribing instead to "reactionary-romantic authoritarian" notions. Hence, Furman concluded,

the current "pendulum" movement is a movement not toward democracy but rather through democracy, bypassing it, toward authoritarianism with an opposite sign. It is these psychological and general cultural features of similarity between the two totalitarianisms (or authoritarianisms) that are the sources of the relative "softness" of Orthodox believers toward the actual institutional foundations of the communist regime (in contrast to its general ideological foundations), toward what it was in real terms, not in ideal terms—toward Stalin, the CPSU, and the vision of the leaders of the August 1991 attempt to restore a strong authoritarian regime. The political equivalent (in the mass consciousness) of the movement away from atheism and toward "integral" Orthodoxy is a movement from communist totalitarianism to "reactionary-romantic authoritarianism."[101]

It was, Furman argued, misguided associations of Orthodoxy with democracy that accounted for at least part of a crest of declared "conversions" to Orthodoxy in 1990–91, but it was a subsequent realization that the Orthodox Church was not democratically oriented at all—or, at the least, had no tradition of democratic thinking to which to look—that produced an abandonment of Orthodoxy by a certain proportion of its new "converts" beginning in 1991.[102]

There is no need to end on a note of ideological or cultural determinism, however. It is one thing to acknowledge that Russian Orthodoxy has developed and displayed certain identifiable political proclivities. It is another matter to foreclose all possibilities of change. On the contrary, changes in certain cultural factors will often change the meaning or functioning of still other factors, gradually inducing larger historical shifts. As William Fletcher has argued in an essay devoted to Russian Orthodoxy, even attitudes which historically have been associated with exploitative or discriminatory behaviors may be transformed into concepts of honor conducive to "the emergence of a transformed ethical sense."[103] This is, of course, still a far cry from entertaining notions that the Russian Orthodox Church is evolving into a democratically oriented champion of modernism. It is only to suggest that within the ideological corpus of Russian Orthodoxy may be found not merely "reactionary-romantic authoritarianism," but other proclivities, potentialities, and possibilities.

Chapter 10

A House Divided: Ukraine's Fractious Churches

During the years 1946 through 1989, Ukraine enjoyed the distinction of being the Soviet republic with the largest proportion of its inhabitants denied access to the religious denomination of their choices. The Ukrainian Autocephalous Orthodox Church had been suppressed since 1930, the Ukrainian Greek-Rite Catholic Church was suppressed in 1946, the *Pokutnyky* (Penitents) movement (which arose in 1954) was never legal;[1] even counting only the Greek-Rite Catholics and the *Pokutnyky*, at least 4–6 million Ukrainians were deprived of associating with the religious community of their choice.

Ukraine enjoyed another distinction in being divided into three identifiable demographic zones: the more urbanized and industrialized east, where Russian immigration had been heavy and where most Ukrainians spoke Russian as their primary, native language; central Ukraine, where Russian immigration had been moderate and where Ukrainians, although usually bilingual, typically counted Ukrainian as their primary language; and west Ukraine, where Russian immigration was virtually nonexistent and where Ukrainian was clearly the dominant language (and whose older generation was more likely to speak Polish than Russian). In religious terms east and central Ukraine were, in communist times, primarily Orthodox (at least nominally), while west Ukraine was (as it is today) overwhelmingly Roman Catholic.

The story of the experiences of Ukraine's religious communities under communism is fascinating and instructive, but it has been eloquently recounted before.[2] The account here will provide only a cursory overview of Ukraine's religious history before 1988, focusing primarily on events since the fallout of the millennium and the galloping liberalization of 1988–89. In particular, the story will be traced of how a republic that, for nearly sixty years, had only one legal Orthodox Church could suddenly face a situation in which four Orthodox Churches could compete for influence, with three of them in relationships of rivalry.

Confessional Politics (1596–1988)

In recounting the religious history of Ukraine it seems appropriate to begin with the Union of Brest of 1596. This union, which resulted from an initiative on the part of the Orthodox bishops of Ukraine and Belarus but which received encouragement from Antonio Possevino, the papal legate to the court of Ivan the Terrible,[3] allowed defecting Orthodox dioceses to retain their autonomy, their liturgy and vestments, and their local custom in exchange for doctrinal and juridical subordination to the Vatican. As Mikhail Dmitriev points out, the Union of Brest served to protect the Ukrainian and Belorussian dioceses both from the centralizing power of the newly established Patriarchate of Moscow and from cultural assimilation at the hands of Poland's Roman Catholic Church.[4] But in doing these things, the union made the Ukrainian religious scene more complex.

Another layer of complication was added about sixty years later, when Cossack leader Hetman Bohdan Khmel'nyts'kyi signed an agreement with the Russian tsar (1654) that recognized the tsar's sovereignty in exchange for a guarantee of autonomy plus military assistance against Poland. Thanks to this agreement, the Orthodox Church in Ukraine and Belorussia, which had staged an impressive recovery at the time of Khmel'nyts'kyi's uprising against Polish rule (1648), looked forward to some assurance of local ecclesiastical autonomy. But "the Kievan metropolitan had great difficulty in maintaining the unity of the Orthodox Church" in Ukraine,[5] or in retaining control of dioceses it claimed. Metropolitan Dionysii Balaban (reigned 1657–63) was unable to assert his authority, even over the city of Kiev, while his successor, Metropolitan Iosyf Tukals'kyi (reigned 1663–75), faced rivalry from a certain Antonii Vynnyts'kyi (claimed to reign 1663–79).

In fact, the Ukrainian-Belorussian Orthodox Church was rapidly disintegrating. In 1686 the patriarch of Moscow claimed to exercise full authority over the metropolitanate of Kiev, and by the 1720s, the metropolitan of Kiev exercised no authority whatsoever outside Kiev's territorial limits.[6] In 1722 the primate of the Ukrainian Orthodox Church for the first time was appointed, not elected; appointing him was the Holy Synod of the Russian Orthodox Church, a newly created body. There was another change: beginning in 1722 the Ukrainian Orthodox primate was no longer a metropolitan but only an archbishop. In the 1760s, during the reign of Empress Catherine II (1729–96, reigned 1762–96), state control of the Church increased steadily, while the prerogatives of the Ukrainian Church faded. By the end of Catherine's reign, all remnants of the autonomy of the Ukrainian Orthodox Church had been extirpated. During the last century and a half of tsarist rule the Russification of Ukraine continued, with the Russian Orthodox Church playing a major role.

The Bolshevik Revolution of 1917 seemed at first to reverse the tide of history. For instance, in July 1918 the Russian Church under Patriarch Tikhon recognized an exarchate of Ukraine under its own metropolitan, and in May 1920 an All-Ukrainian Orthodox Church Council proclaimed the reestablishment of an autocephalous Ukrainian Orthodox Church.[7] The new Soviet authorities gave the new Church their blessing. As of 1924 the Ukrainian Autocephalous Orthodox Church claimed to have some 3 million to 6 million members, who were organized in more than 3,000 parishes and served by thirty bishops and 1,500 priests and deacons. Ukrainian Greek-Rite Catholics at that time were largely under Polish rule, but the Ukrainian religious scene was divided all the same between the Russian Orthodox Church, the UAOC, and the Renovationist Church.[8]

Soviet authorities hoped that the UAOC would merge with the Renovationists. The Ukrainian prelates, whom the Soviets had been accusing of waxing nationalist tendencies, refused. Accordingly, in the summer of 1926 Soviet police arrested the UAOC primate, Metropolitan Vasyl' Lypkivs'kyi (1864-1938), and suppressed the All-Ukrainian Church Council. Soviet authorities demanded that the Church adopt more "acceptable" behavior. The UAOC hierarchy buckled, purging Lypkivs'kyi and other bishops considered "unacceptable" by Soviet authorities, and it elected at its second *sobor* (1927) Mykolai Borets'kyi as metropolitan.[9] The Soviets extended concessions but began to withdraw them the following year. In the summer of 1929 OGPU (the Soviet secret police) began arresting UAOC bishops and clergy. In November 1929 OGPU claimed to have discovered a "counterrevolutionary" League for the Liberation of Ukraine. The UAOC hierarchy was implicated in the work of this alleged secessionist organization. Finally, in January 1930 the remaining bishops and clergy of the UAOC were brought together for an Extraordinary *sobor* in Kiev, where they were forced for the second time to declare the dissolution of their Church.[10]

The Soviet occupation of eastern Poland in September 1939 placed some 10 million Catholics under Soviet rule. Between 3.2 million and 3.9 million of these were Ukrainian Greek-Rite Catholics. As soon as their forces assumed control of this area, Soviet authorities began to confiscate Church properties and imposed burdensome taxes. Authorities also closed Catholic schools, monasteries, and printing presses. Ironically, "full-scale repression" was set in motion only in June 1941, on the very eve of the Nazi invasion.[11]

The Nazis occupied Ukraine for three years (1941-44). Since they did not care one way or the other about Ukrainian religious life, the Nazis turned a blind eye as the Churches began to rebuild. It was during the short-lived Nazi occupation that the Greek-Rite Catholic Church, traditionally based in Galicia, first established a hierarchical structure in central and eastern Ukraine.[12]

In view of subsequent Soviet claims that the Greek-Rite Catholic Church behaved as a "stooge" of the Nazis, it is worth pointing out that Metropolitan Andrei Sheptyts'kyi repeatedly vented his outrage over Nazi persecutions and exterminations of the Jews. In a letter sent to Gestapo Chief Heinrich Himmler in 1942, Sheptyts'kyi remonstrated against the Nazi treatment of the Jews and protested the use of Ukrainian auxiliary police in their shooting.[13] Indeed, in his letter to Himmler, Sheptyts'kyi described the Nazis as "even more evil and diabolic" than the Bolsheviks.[14] By 1944 the Gestapo had had its fill of Sheptyts'kyi, and, shortly before being driven out of Ukraine by the advancing Soviet forces, Sheptyts'kyi's arrest was authorized. As an eyewitness describes it, armed Gestapo police beat their way into the metropolitan's study only to find themselves overwhelmed by his charisma. The officer in charge called off the mission with the words, "Nein, das ist Gott."[15]

Soviet forces reentered Ukraine in the summer of 1944. The Soviets seemed, at first, solicitous of Ukrainian religious sensitivities. Thus, when in November 1944 Metropolitan Sheptyts'kyi, primate of the Ukrainian Greek-Rite Catholic Church, passed away, Nikita Khrushchev, then First Secretary of the Communist Party of Ukraine, attended the funeral. Nor did the Soviets utter a word of protest or criticism when Metropolitan Iosyf Slipyi (1892-1984) was enthroned as the new primate of the Greek-Rite Church in Ukraine. It was only in April 1945 when five of that Church's prelates, including Slipyi himself, were arrested on trumped-up charges of collaboration with the Nazis, that the first signs of a shift in policy appeared. Then, in March 1946 a fraudulent Church *sobor* was convened, under heavy protection by the NKVD (the acronym at that time for the Soviet secret police), proclaiming the annulment of the Union of Brest and the "return" of the faithful to the arms of the Russian Orthodox Church. This pronouncement was followed by the systematic destruction and suppression of the Greek-Rite Catholic Church.[16] In one incident, Pavel Sudoplatov, a Soviet intelligence officer, acting on direct orders from Stalin, tried to kill Archbishop Teodor Romzha in a staged car "accident" (27 October 1947). Romzha was critically injured, but not killed; he was rushed to a hospital for surgery. An intelligence agent, masquerading as a nurse, then infiltrated Romzha's hospital room and administered a lethal injection of curare (a South American poison) on 1 November 1947.[17] From 1946 until 1989 neither the Ukrainian Greek-Rite Catholic Church nor the Ukrainian Autocephalous Orthodox Church could function normally. The Greek-Rite Catholics, for their part, routinely said Mass in "padlocked churches"—that is, in churches shut and bolted by the authorities.

From time to time, attacks were made on the Greek-Rite Catholics (also known as Uniates). One attack, an article by Klym Dymtruk for *Radyans'ka Ukrayina* in March 1981, excoriated Greek-Rite Catholic faithful as "yellow-and-blue traitors, remnants of the SS, fascist police, UNA bandits and other fascist scum,"[18] praising those Greek-Rite Catholics who had reconciled themselves to union with the Moscow patriarchate. Dymtruk continued,

Contrary to the ridiculous stories being disseminated in the West about an alleged "restriction" of freedom of conscience and religion, religious believers in our country, including those in the western oblasts of this republic, are satisfying all their religious needs and, together with the entire Soviet people, are taking active part in this country's sociopolitical affairs, are dedicating their efforts to the cause of preserving peace on our planet. Incidentally, the existence of full freedom of religion in the USSR has been confirmed time and again both by churchmen in our country and by numerous organizations of foreign Church organizations.

All of this is also well known at the Vatican, where the provocational "synod" of the UKTs [Ukrainian Catholic Church] was held. And the organizers of this anti-Soviet plot evidently have other purposes in mind. Ideological saboteurs, including those garbed in robes and soutanes, carrying the social commands of the sponsors of anticommunism, are doing everything in their power to conceal the great truth about the Soviet Union. . . .[19]

A second attack was conveyed in an article by S. Voznyak, head of the department of scientific atheism at the USSR Academy of Sciences. Likewise published in *Radyans'ka Ukrayina,* Voznyak's article began with the suggestion, "Remnants of Uniatism, which have found refuge in the countries of the bourgeois West, should be swept by the Ukrainian people onto the ash heap of [history]."[20] Characterizing the Greek-Rite Catholic Church as having served, historically, as "a spiritual instrument of [the] enslavement of the masses," Voznyak offered his own assessment as to "what kind of 'liberty' for the Ukrainian people the hierarchs of Uniatism are dreaming [of]: freedom to enslave the Ukrainian people."[21]

Until late in the 1980s, few, if any, reasons existed to hope for a relegalization of Ukraine's suppressed Churches.[22] Then, largely between 1988 and 1990, Soviet authorities rushed with hurtling speed toward the liberalization of conditions for the country's religious associations, including Ukraine's long-banned Churches.[23] But, as will be seen, liberalization not only has revived interconfessional jurisdictional battles, but, perhaps predictably, it has broadened the scope of interdenominational rivalry.

The Religious Scene

As of February–March 1996 some seventy religious denominations were registered in Ukraine.[24] The largest bodies, in order, are the Ukrainian Orthodox Church of the Moscow Patriarchate, the Ukrainian Greek-Rite Catholic Church, and the Ukrainian Orthodox Church of the Kievan Patriarchate. These three, together with the smaller Ukrainian Autocephalous Orthodox Church, make up the "traditional" Churches connected through a long history in Ukraine.

A second group comprises historical religions lacking roots in Ukraine or any basis on which to claim to be *the* (or *a*) "Ukrainian national faith." In many cases religious associations in this category appeared in Ukraine only during the twentieth century, but before 1985. They include the (Polish) Roman Catholic Church, the Armenian Orthodox Church, Judaism, the Lutheran Church, the Jehovah's Witnesses, and (primarily in Crimea) the Islamic faith.[25]

A third group consists of those religious organizations that have registered in Ukraine only since 1985. This category consists of several smaller Orthodox communities (two Old Believer Churches, a Ruthenian Orthodox Church, and the Russian Free Orthodox Church), new Christian missionary imports from the West, a neopagan group combining ancient Slavic religious beliefs with intense Ukrainian nationalism (the Native Ukrainian National Faith), and several Eastern religions and miscellaneous new religions (including Buddhism, Transcendental Meditation, Krishna Consciousness, and the Agni Yoga "Living Ethic" inspired by Russian mystic Nikolai Roerich).[26]

The strongest religious body institutionally is the Ukrainian Orthodox Church of the Moscow Patriarchate (UOC-Moscow Patriarchate). Granted autonomy in 1991, this body comprised 5,998 parishes in January 1994, with 4,854 priests, 48 monasteries, and eight theological schools (with 1,870 students enrolled). By February 1996 the number of parishes had increased to 6,564.[27]

The second-largest religious body in Ukraine is the Greek-Rite Catholic Church, which regained its legal registration in December 1989. In January 1994 this Church counted 2,932 parishes, 1,691 priests, 39 monasteries, and six theological schools (with 1,670 students). As of February 1996 the number of Greek-Rite Catholic parishes had risen to 3,079.[28]

The third largest Church in Ukraine is the Ukrainian Orthodox Church of the Kiev Patriarchate (Kiev Patriarchate). Fashioned by Metropolitan Filaret (Denisenko) in the summer of 1992, it claimed the allegiance of 1,932 parishes in January 1994, supported by 1,080 priests, 14 monasteries, and seven theological schools (with 774 students enrolled). In February 1996 the Kiev Patriarchate recorded only 1,332 parishes—a one-third decline in two years.[29]

The Baptists were Ukraine's fourth-largest religious body in 1994 and may have overtaken the Kiev Patriarchate since then. With 1,364 parishes (in 1994), the Baptists had 1,970 ministers, and 11 religious schools (with 440 registered students).[30]

Ukraine's fifth-largest religious body, the Ukrainian Autocephalous Orthodox Church (Autocephalous Church) was founded in 1921, suppressed in 1930, and re-created in 1991. The Autocephalous Church showed only 289 parishes in 1994, but by February 1996 this number had risen dramatically to 1,209 as parishes switched their allegiance from Filaret's Kiev Patriarchate.

None of the Orthodox Churches consider the splintering of Orthodoxy "normal," and repeated efforts have been made to either undermine each other or to orchestrate unifications. Thus, when the Autocephalous Church convened for an ecclesiastical congress in November 1995, unification with the UOC-Moscow Patriarchate ranked high on the agenda.[31]

Diversity and Conflict (1989–1993)

In 1988 there was only one legally registered Christian Church of the Eastern rite operating in Ukraine—the Russian Orthodox Church. Today there are more than a half-dozen.

In the course of 1989, Greek-Rite Catholics, whose Church had been suppressed in 1946, came into the open, staging a historic mass rally in Lvov (Lviv) on 17 September 1989 with more than 150,000 persons participating. As summer wore into autumn, village parishes across western Ukraine declared their identification with the Greek-Rite Catholics.[32] The renewed legalization of the Greek-Rite Catholic Church, which had been under serious public discussion since June, became an accomplished fact on 1 December 1989, when Gorbachev assured the pope that full legal status for Greek Catholics would soon be provided. "By the end of the year over 300 parishes were already functioning as Greek Catholic, 650 had applied for registration, and over 200 formerly Russian Orthodox priests had joined the Greek Catholic Church."[33]

At the same time, autocephalists undertook efforts to reestablish the Autocephalous Church in Lviv and among Ukrainians who resided in Lithuania. The Russian Orthodox bishop of Zhytomyr, Ioann Bodnarchuk (1929–94), abandoned his own Church and assumed the leadership of the Autocephalous movement in Ukraine, playing a key role in reviving that Church. A few months later, in June 1990, the Autocephalists staged a council in Kiev, electing 92-year-old Mstyslav Skrypnyk (1898–1992) of South Bound Brook, New Jersey, as patriarch.[34] Particularly striking at this time was the cooperation between Autocephalists demanding Church independence and the Popular Movement for the Reconstruction of Ukraine (*Rukh*) demanding national independence.

The UOC-Moscow Patriarchate realized that the situation could get completely out of its control unless a major strategic adjustment was made. That came on 9 February 1990 with the reconstitution of the Ukrainian Autonomous Orthodox Church "in canonical union" with the UOC-Moscow Patriarchate. A five-member episcopal synod was established to govern the newly autonomous body, with veto power controlled by the Moscow patriarch.[35]

In the meantime, interconfessional conflicts over churches were becoming ever more frequent and more nettling. An example of this trend came as early as 29 October 1989, when the Lviv parish of the Transfiguration withdrew from the Russian Orthodox Church and declared itself Greek-Rite Catholic. The Orthodox Church claimed that the Catholics had resorted to violence to seize control of the church, although a Canadian television crew on site broadcast the events of that day and recorded no instances of physical conflict.[36] Catholic-Orthodox quadrilateral negotiations got under way shortly thereafter, in the hope of achieving consensus on the distribution of church facilities.[37]

In March 1990, amid protests from Ukrainian Orthodox that "extremist Eastern-rite Catholics are illegally seizing Orthodox churches,"[38] Greek-Rite Catholics began to press local civil authorities to endorse their demand for the return of all properties seized from the Greek-Rite Catholic Church in 1946. The parishes that had been transferred in 1946 constituted a significant portion of all Russian Orthodox facilities, and, partly for this reason, the Moscow Patriarchate remained a reluctant partner in the continuing negotiations.

On 6 April 1990 the Lviv city council of people's deputies authorized the transfer of the St. George Cathedral to the Greek-Rite Catholic Church. The Holy Synod of the UOC–Moscow Patriarchate released a statement the following week, rejecting the decision: "By this decision," the statement read, "the Lvov City Council deprived Ukrainian Orthodox believers in Lvov of their last temple, without offering any replacement."[39] On the same day that this statement was released, the Orthodox side broke off talks with Catholics; those discussions had been aimed at settling Orthodox-Catholic differences peacefully.[40]

But even as Catholic-Orthodox tensions continued, intra-Orthodox differences surfaced. A key figure in this development is Metropolitan Filaret (Denisenko), a bright, energetic, and ambitious cleric who was consecrated bishop at age thirty-two and who, at age thirty-seven, was appointed to head the Ukrainian Exarchate of the Russian Orthodox Church. In 1990, after the death of Russian Orthodox Patriarch Pimen, the Holy Synod elected Filaret to serve as locum tenens, that is, interim head of the Church. Customarily, the locum tenens may expect to be elected patriarch. But Filaret, no customary candidate, inflamed controversy. For one thing, he had just been named head of the (autonomous) Ukrainian Orthodox Church; for another, he was widely blamed for having mishandled relations with the Greek-Rite Catholics. When the Church council made its decision in June 1990, its nod went not to Filaret, but to Metropolitan Aleksii (Ridiger) of Leningrad, a churchman viewed as "essentially 'apolitical' and a guarantor of a desirable 'quietness' and 'peace' within the Church."[41] These were precisely the qualities that Filaret was thought to lack.

The establishment of Ukrainian independence in 1991 stimulated aspirations for Ukrainian Orthodox autocephaly, and Ukrainian President Leonid Kravchuk (1991-94) threw his support behind the Autocephalist movement.[42] Kravchuk looked to the Autocephalists as natural allies in his bid for independence and a nationalist agenda, and he courted both Patriarch Mstyslav (Skrypnyk) and Metropolitan Filaret. Upon the proclamation of Ukrainian independence on 24 August 1991, Filaret "concluded that an independent state must have an independent Church . . . and, encouraged by Kravchuk, demanded complete autocephaly for the Ukrainian Church from Moscow."[43] In November 1991 an episcopal council of the Autonomous Church sent a formal petition to Moscow for a grant of full autocephaly. The Holy Synod of the Russian Orthodox Church rejected this request, which led to the Ukrainian Orthodox bishops convening again and deciding to submit a new petition. Three bishops of the Ukrainian Church resisted this second effort as well, and, as a consequence, Metropolitan Filaret dismissed them from their dioceses.[44]

As Filaret pushed forward, three interested parties took the trouble to cull the newly declassified KGB files in hopes of finding incriminating information. Their efforts were rewarded, and in January 1992 they published their findings, which, inter alia, showed that Metropolitan Filaret had collaborated with the KGB under the code name "Antonov."[45] Rumor has it that the files further revealed that Patriarch Aleksii also had been a KGB agent under the code name "Drozdov," but the investigators were not interested in undermining him and passed over his case in silence.[46] In the meantime, Filaret continued to clamp down on clerical critics of his drive for autocephaly. On 4 February 1992 Patriarch Aleksii II sent a telegram to Filaret, asking him to refrain from further sanctions against clergy who did not share his views, at least until a meeting of the Holy Synod scheduled for 18-19 February. On 19 February, the synod sent a note to Filaret, condemning his sanctions against clergy opposed to autocephaly. The synod also pressed Filaret to resign his post as head of the Church.

As Filaret hesitated, Patriarch Aleksii convened an extraordinary council of bishops in Moscow that in March 1992 stripped Filaret of his ecclesiastical office, citing "canonical violations." On 6 April the Holy Synod rescinded Filaret's transfers of the three bishops who had resisted his program.[47] On 6-7 May 1992 the Holy Synod of the Russian Orthodox Church met once more, demanding that Filaret, still unbowed, submit to its decisions; if he failed to do so by 15 May, the synod vowed, he would be brought before an ecclesiastical court. About the same time, the bishops of the UOC-Moscow Patriarchate convened in Kharkiv and elected Metropolitan Vladimir (Sabodan) to assume Filaret's duties and functions. On 11 June 1992 the Moscow Patriarchate charged Filaret with "cruel and arrogant" behavior toward the bishops under his jurisdiction and demoted him to the rank of a simple monk.[48]

Meanwhile, in May 1992 Filaret had initiated private discussions with Metropolitan Antoniy (Masendych) of the Autocephalous Church (headed by Metropolitan Mstyslav). Filaret, who is said never to have spoken Ukrainian in public until 1989,[49] now comported himself as an ardent Ukrainian nationalist and made a bid for co-optation into Mstyslav's Church. The bid was successful, and on 25 June 1992, with President Kravchuk's encouragement, representatives of Mstyslav's Autocephalous Church met with Ukrainian Orthodox clerics loyal to Filaret in a joint Church council. The following day this joint council proclaimed the unification of the two groups under the new name Ukrainian Orthodox Church-Kiev Patriarchate. Patriarch Mstyslav, by then ninety-four years old, was proclaimed head of this Church, with Metropolitan Filaret elected his deputy. A year later, Mstyslav was dead, and Metropolitan Volodymyr (Romanyuk) (1925-1995), a highly regarded advocate of human rights who had spent sixteen years in Siberian labor camps, was elected to succeed Mstyslav as patriarch;[50] Filaret was confirmed as deputy.

By this point, pitched battles were breaking out in city streets between Autocephalists and pro-Moscow activists.[51] In the meantime, the media published articles about Filaret's liaison with a certain Yevgeniia Rodionova and intimated that he had been guilty of various kinds of misconduct, both sexual and political.[52] *Moscow News* cited portrayals of Filaret as a "zombie," noting claims that he had "lost the capacity to react rationally and naturally."[53] These allegations assured that Filaret would remain controversial. In July 1993 a faction of clerics from the original Autocephalous Church, who had opposed the union with Filaret in the first place, withdrew from the union and established a rival Ukrainian Autocephalous Orthodox Patriarchate, electing Dmytriy Yarema (a Catholic priest until 1946) to serve as patriarch. Based in Lviv, Dmytriy's Autocephalous Church has its strength mainly in western Ukraine and predictably claims to be "the only true Ukrainian Orthodox Church and the legitimate successor to Mstyslav's patriarchate."[54] With the creation of this self-declared Autocephalous Church, the religious landscape in Ukraine assumed its present features.

Inter-Orthodox Struggles Since 1992

Kravchuk's support gave Metropolitan Filaret a certain advantage. As "deputy" patriarch of the Kiev Patriarchate, Filaret enjoyed effective control of both the Kiev cathedral and the Church's finances and publication activity. Metropolitan Vladimir (Sabodan) of the UOC–Moscow Patriarchate complained that Kravchuk was favoring Filaret; as Davis notes, he also maintained that there had been

a dozen instances of violence during the summer of 1992, when armed groups seized cathedrals, diocesan offices, and monasteries under Vladimir's jurisdiction, most of them in western Ukraine. Reportedly the Ukrainian National Self-Defense Guard (UNSO), a Ukrainian nationalist militia, forcibly occupied Ukrainian Orthodox churches and turned them over to Filaret's people.[55]

There appeared to be a waxing coalition between Filaret and the far-right UNA-UNSO, culminating in a bid, using UNA-UNSO paramilitary forces, to take control of the majestic Pecherska Lavra monastery (monastery of the caves) in Kiev.[56] But the presidential elections of July 1994 dramatically changed the political and ecclesiastical balance of power.

Without much oversimplification, the UOC–Moscow Patriarchate can be characterized as having its base in more Russified eastern Ukraine, with Filaret's Kiev Patriarchate centered in what I have called central Ukraine, and Dimitriy's Autocephalous Church the dominant Orthodox body in western Ukraine. Leonid Kravchuk, Filaret's champion, had his base of popularity in central and western Ukraine, while Leonid Kuchma, Kravchuk's rival, had made his career in the largely Russified (eastern) city of Dnipropetrovs'k. Kuchma carried the entire eastern half of Ukraine in July 1994, winning from 67 to 88 percent of the vote in the eastern districts. In central and western Ukraine the results were reversed, with Kravchuk garnering between 70 and 95 percent of the vote, depending on the district. Because of the population imbalance between east and west, Kuchma won by a narrow margin.[57]

Kuchma immediately sounded a different chord. Whereas Krawchuk had treated the Kiev Patriarchate as the semiofficial Church of Ukraine, Kuchma issued a statement on 29 July 1994 affirming the principle of Church-state separation and governmental noninvolvement in religious affairs.[58] In a token gesture to his commitment to Church-state separation, Kuchma ordered the creation of a new department in the cabinet of ministers: the ministry of nationalities issues, immigration, and cults.

He also ordered the dissolution of the Ukrainian Council for Religious Affairs.[59]

Filaret did not give up, however, and he periodically appealed to members of the other Orthodox Churches to "unite" with the Kiev Patriarchate. "It is necessary for Ukraine to create *one* Ukrainian national Church," he declared in August 1995. "Those who are struggling against the Kiev Patriarchate are fighting against Ukraine's independence."[60] Filaret also has pressed his Church's claims to houses of worship and other properties confiscated by the state during the Stalin and post-Stalin eras.[61] In September 1995 high-ranking clergymen of the Kiev Patriarchate appealed to President Kuchma and Prime Minister Yevhen Marchuk to authorize the transfer of several properties from the UOC–Moscow Patriarchate to the Kiev Patriarchate. Specifically mentioned were the Andriiv Church in the Podol region, the Vydubetskyy monastery, and the Pecherska Lavra monastery in Kiev, including the Refectory Church.[62]

Filaret, as noted, remained nominally second-in-command within the Kiev Patriarchate. But in July 1995 the incumbent patriarch, Volodymyr (Romanyuk), died under suspicious and as yet unclear circumstances. The 69-year-old patriarch had received a telephone call from an unknown person on 14 July and had agreed to meet with that person the following day. He was last seen alive when, in the company of a monk, he left for the meeting. He was later found dead by a passer-by. The monk was never seen again, and the caller has remained unidentified. Although Patriarch Volodymyr had four fractured ribs, the official bulletin attributed his death to a heart attack.[63]

As vexing as the circumstances of his death would seem to be, Volodymyr's burial proved even more distressing. To begin with, the Volodymyr Cathedral (controlled by the Kiev Patriarchate) simply had no suitable space to bury the patriarch, while the government refused to allow the Kiev Patriarchate to make use of the prestigious Baikovo Cemetery. The UOC–Moscow Patriarchate had facilities deemed appropriate by the Kiev Patriarchate, but it refused to make these available.[64] The Kiev Patriarchate then informed the government of its decision to bury Volodymyr in the eleventh-century St. Sophia Cathedral in downtown Kiev, which has been classified as a "national monument." However, the government gave notice that it would not permit the St. Sophia Cathedral to be used for such a purpose.

After all of these difficulties and despite the government's warning, the senior clerics of the Kiev Patriarchate (following Filaret's lead) decided to proceed with plans to bury Volodymyr on the grounds of St. Sophia's Cathedral on 18 July. The decision was ill-fated. Some thousand mourners, accompanied by uniformed members of UNA-UNSO, attended the funeral services outside the cathedral. But as the service got under way, Berkut (eagle) riot police poured into the square, firing tear gas canisters and beating mourners with truncheons. The UNA-UNSO militiamen offered resistance, and in the ensuing scuffle two people were killed and fifty-one hospitalized with injuries. Police arrested five UNA-UNSO militiamen. Meanwhile, about three hundred defiant mourners used pickaxes to dig a makeshift grave for Volodymyr next to St. Sophia's.[65] As of early 1997, the patriarch remains buried in this anomalous grave. In the wake of the tumult, the Kiev Patriarchate and the Kuchma government hurled recriminations at each other. "The authorities do not want Ukraine to have its own Church," said Metropolitan Filaret,[66] attributing the police action to political motivations. "Some people in the government and the president's administration," he added, "are supporting the privileged position of the Ukrainian Orthodox Church under the Moscow patriarchate."[67]

On 22 July, Metropolitan Filaret, acting as locum tenens, issued a formal statement on behalf of the Kiev Patriarchate, demanding an apology from the government and compensation for the Church's financial and moral losses, "an end to the persecution of the national Church, the Kiev Patriarchate," the transfer of various facilities, *including the St. Sophia Cathedral and the Pecherska Lavra monastery*, to the Kiev Patriarchate, and government support for the unification of Ukrainian Orthodoxy under the leadership of the Kiev Patriarchate.[68]

Four days later, the president's office released the full text of President Kuchma's statement about the events of 18 July. While conceding that the behavior of the riot police had been "unprofessional," Kuchma declined to yield on any substantive points. On the contrary, he insisted that "permission [for] a burial on the grounds of St. Sophia's Cathedral . . . would have provoked a needless conflict between the state and other religious communities and led to an increase in social tension in society." Kuchma repudiated any thought of concessions with "ultra-radical groups" and vowed "to neutralize extremist groups in their attempts to resolve society's problems by force."[69] It was hard to discern an olive branch in these comments.

A third noteworthy statement was drawn up by a cluster of political parties and organizations and made public on 22 July. This statement was signed by representatives of the Democratic Party of Ukraine, the Congress of Ukrainian Nationalists, *Rukh*, the Ukrainian Republican Party, the Ukrainian Conservative Republican Party, the Ukrainian National Assembly–Ukrainian National Self-Defense (UNA-UNSO), the Taras Shevchenko "Enlightenment" Society, the Ukrainian Officers' Union, the Ukrainian Cossacks, the Union of Ukrainian Women, the Women's Assembly International Organization, the Helsinki-90 Committee, the "Green World" Ukrainian Ecological Association, and the Ukrainian Democratic Alliance. Condemning the Kuchma government for an "unprecedented and brutal outrage," the statement warned that "a police regime is being established in Ukraine."[70]

Finally, former President Krawchuk sent an open letter to the mass media, declaring that 18 July "will go down in Ukrainian history as the beginning of an open onslaught launched by the state bodies on the Ukrainian Church."[71]

A government working group was now appointed to initiate negotiations with representatives of Ukraine's four "traditional" Churches with respect to the construction of an appropriate tomb or mausoleum for Ukraine's religious leaders.[72] At the same time, a government commission headed by Ukrainian Deputy Prime Minister Ivan Kuras held discussions with the Holy Synod of the Kiev Patriarchate in an effort to reach a compromise as to Volodymyr's final resting place. The government's idea of a compromise seemed to be that the deceased patriarch would be reburied in a location suggested by the Ukrainian cabinet.[73] Nor did Filaret appear to be disposed to compromise. "Either he will be buried in St. Sophia or he will remain where he is," Filaret asserted in an interview in early August.[74] Volodymyr therefore remained buried in the sidewalk near a trolley stop, amid flowers and antigovernment graffiti.

Compromise could be furthered by depoliticizing the issue. But the issue remained defined by politics, as shown a month later when more than 1,200 UNA-UNSO militiamen took part in ceremonies to honor the memory of the patriarch.[75] Finally, in June 1996 the Kiev Patriarchate reached an acceptable compromise with the government, thanks to the active engagement of the acting mayor of Kiev, Oleksander Omelchenko, who arranged for a memorial to be built on the sidewalk where Volodymyr is buried, authorizing the use of city funds (some $71,000 in all) to cover the costs of a marble monument.[76] Then, on 14 July 1996, on the first anniversary of the patriarch's death, a memorial service held at the grave was attended by close to a thousand people; Filaret and Acting Mayor Omelchenko delivered homilies.[77]

Metropolitan Filaret had long been the real power behind the Kiev Patriarchate, and on 20 October 1995 this reality was recognized with his election as patriarch. Metropolitan Andriy of Halychyna, the archbishop of Ivano-Frankivske, and three other bishops expressed their dissatisfaction with Filaret's election by disaffiliating from the Kiev Patriarchate at this point and joining Patriarch Dymytriy's Autocephalous Church. These defections were not the only ones, moreover, as priests and parishes in Zaporizhzhia, Dnipropetrovs'k, and Cherihiv left the patriarchate and joined Dymytriy's ranks.[78]

That same month brought revelations of a plan on the part of several parliamentary deputies to portray these defections as a kind of ecclesiastical "merger" and, on the pretext of that supposed "merger," to outlaw the Ukrainian Orthodox Church of the Kiev Patriarchate![79] These deputies had even formed an illicit Single Community Church Association for this purpose.[80] Oleksandr Moroz, chair of the Ukrainian supreme council, condemned these activities in late October and underlined the importance of maintaining church-state separation.[81]

In November 1995 hierarchs of the Autocephalous Church and the UOC–Moscow Patriarchate initiated discussions about a possible unification of their two organizations. As Oleh Gerus has noted, a union of these bodies "would represent the vast majority of the Orthodox faithful and thus qualify for canonical autocephaly, either from Constantinople or [from] Moscow."[82] As this initiative gathered momentum, President Kuchma felt constrained in March 1996 to reiterate his firm opposition to the establishment of a state church in Ukraine.[83]

Conclusion

When Krawchuk was president, Filaret's star was ascendant. Indeed, shortly before he was voted out of office, Krawchuk had even promised Filaret that he would transfer the symbolically important Cathedral of St. Sophia to the Kiev Patriarchate.[84] But Filaret's fortunes have risen and fallen with those of Krawchuk, and in the absence of governmental favoritism the Kiev Patriarchate has declined in strength. Much will depend on the outcome of discussions between the Autocephalous Church and the UOC–Moscow Patriarchate. As Filaret knows, if these two antagonists can overcome their differences and create a united Ukrainian Orthodox Church, that new body might exert an enormous pressure on both clergy and lay members of the Kiev Patriarchate, and the continued attrition of Filaret's organization might be all but assured. The fact that such a union would necessarily entail the effective loss by the patriarch of Moscow of any say over any part of Ukrainian Orthodoxy may, at first, seem to pose a not insignificant obstacle to that union. But, as all parties to the dispute realize, Moscow's jurisdiction within Ukrainian Orthodoxy is itself a relic of the tsarist and communist past, unlikely to endure long in independent Ukraine. Indeed, Oleh Gerus may be right in considering the emergence of a single large Ukrainian Orthodox Church (with only trivially small "rivals") to be inevitable.[85] If and when that result is obtained, the resulting Ukrainian Orthodox Church, with as many as 35 million faithful, would be the second-largest Orthodox Church in the world, trailing only the Russian Church, and would easily dwarf the Greek-Rite Catholic Church.

V

Postcommunist Trends

And Conclusion

Chapter 11

In Hoc Signo Vinces: The New Evangelism
in Postcommunist Europe

"Russia, turn to God and you will be great again in Jesus' name," television evangelist Paul Crouch of Tustin, California, shouted to a crowd of 16,000 Russians in Moscow's Olympic Stadium.[1] This modern-day version of God's alleged promise of triumph to Emperor Constantine in the fourth century—*In Hoc Signo Vinces*—is proving effective. Throughout the former communist lands, economic duress, social dislocation, and psychological stress have combined to make people ripe for conversion. They want desperately to believe in something transcendent, even if it assumes an unfamiliar (American) garb. Even so mundane a message as "I come here from America to tell you that Jesus loves you!"[2] could find receptive audiences in countries where atheism once reigned supreme.

This chapter briefly reviews the evangelical activities of Christian Churches not indigenous to the region, as well as the reactions of local governments and the Churches "traditional" to the region. Most Christian missionaries who have come to the region since 1989 are Americans, although some have come from parts of Western Europe. But the new Christian evangelism is only part of the story of religion in postcommunist Eastern Europe. That story has at least two other parts: the changed behavior of traditional Churches (see chapter 12) and the proliferation of non-Christian religious associations in the region, whether as a result of indigenous innovation or through importation from outside (see chapter 13).

The Christian missionaries benefited from a transitory fascination with everything connected with the United States, as well as from an openness to novelty, brought on by the sudden disappearance of the communist old order. A picture from Moscow's Red Square vividly captures the spirit of the times. Where a 40-foot poster of Lenin once hung, mounted on the front of the Museum of History, a huge religious placard was hoisted up for Easter 1992, depicting the unmistakable likeness of Jesus Christ. Next to it, where in earlier years one could find a giant

Table 11.1   Nonindigenous Protestant Missionaries in the European
Soviet Successor States (1994)

State	Missionaries	Population	Population per missionary
Armenia	10	3,290,000	329,000
Azerbaijan	N/A	7,130,000	N/A
Belarus	6	10,260,000	1,710,000
Estonia	45	1,600,000	35,556
Georgia	8	5,460,000	682,500
Latvia	29	2,610,000	90,000
Lithuania	4	3,720,000	930,000
Moldova	0	4,360,000	—
Russia	505	148,040,000	293,149
Ukraine	1,113	20,099,000	18,056

Source: East-West Church and Ministry Report 2, no. 1 (Winter 1994): 5.

Marx-Engels-Lenin display for May Day, visitors saw instead a large sign advertising a vacation trip to the Canary Islands.[3]

The Russian-East European region has been awash with Christian and non-Christian missionaries ever since the collapse of communism 1989–91. A study by Wheaton College's Institute of East-West Christian Studies identified more than seven hundred Western missionaries who had been sent to Russia and other former Soviet republics as of 1992; most of these were evangelical Christians.[4] By 1994 this figure had risen to more than 1,100 (see table 11.1). Relative to population density, the most intense missionary activity has been centered in Estonia and Latvia, followed—at some distance—by Russia, Armenia, and Georgia. But these figures do not tell the whole story because, as if to exact vengeance for more than seventy years of Moscow-directed official atheism, missionaries placed a special emphasis on converting Moscow and descended upon the city in droves. Some missionaries to Russia brought medicines, clothing, and food. Others launched English classes, using religious tracts in lieu of a textbook. Still others provided sermons during intermissions of wrestling bouts at the local sports arena. Lutherans in St. Petersburg took to distributing phonograph records such as those of the musical show *Jesus Christ, Superstar* to attract attention.[5] Between late 1991 and early 1993 alone, American evangelicals shipped at least 50 million bibles to Russia and Ukraine.[6]

Table 11.2 Nonindigenous Protestant Missionaries in Formerly Communist
Countries of Eastern Europe (1994)

State	Missionaries	Population	Population per missionary
Albania	182	3,300,000	18,132
Bosnia-Herzegovina	2	N/A	N/A
Bulgaria	77	8,470,000	110,000
Croatia	2	4,793,000	2,397,500
Czech Republic	87	10,310,000	118,506
Hungary	213	10,340,000	48,545
Poland	77*	38,000,000	493,506
Romania	165	23,210,000	140,667
Serbia/Mont.	53	10,643,000	200,811
Slovakia	10	5,300,000	530,000

*Does not include Mormons.
Source: East-West Church and Ministry Report 2, no. 1 (Winter 1994): 5.

Christian missionaries also have been active in the former communist countries of Eastern Europe (see table 11.2). As of 1994, at least
864 Protestant missionaries were proselytizing in the East European region. Of these, the greatest numbers were to be found in Hungary (213),
Albania (182), and Romania (165). The Bible has, as ever, served as the
bill of fare for itinerant evangelists. The shipment to Bulgaria of some
300,000 copies of a new Bulgarian edition of the Bible, for example, was
arranged as early as 1990.[7] In 1995 came the first Macedonian translation
of the Bible.

Broken down by denomination, the most energetic entrants into the
Russian-East European religious market have been Youth with a Mission, the Campus Crusade for Christ, the Church of Christ, the Navigators (a religious association that claims to be well represented on
American university sports teams), the Southern Baptist Convention,
and Church Resources Ministries (see table 11.3). Some denominations,
such as the Navigators, OMS International, and the Salvation Army have
emphasized work in the Soviet successor states. Others, such as the Assemblies of God, Biblical Education by Extension, the Calvary Chapel of
Costa Mesa, and Church Resources Ministries have concentrated their
efforts in East Central Europe.

The Church of Jesus Christ of Latter-Day Saints (Mormon) has

Table 11.3 Missionaries to the Former Soviet Union and East Central Europe:
The Twenty Most Active Religious Organizations (1995)

Organization	Former Soviet Union	Eastern Europe	Total
Assemblies of God	28	64	92
Biblical Education by Extension	12	51	63
Calvary Chapel of Costa Mesa	8	25	33
Campus Crusade for Christ	234	165	399
Child Evangelism Fellowship	25	64	89
Christian and Missionary Alliance	39	10	49
Church of Christ	104	128	232
Church Resources Ministries	17	129	146
Evangelical Free Church Mission	12	52	64
International Teams	20	47	67
InterVarsity Christian Fellowship	32	12	44
Lutheran Church—Missouri Synod	32	15	47
Church of the Nazarene	16	21	37
Navigators	193	27	220
OMS International	87	14	101
Operation Mobilization	40	43	83
Salvation Army	50	2	52
Seventh-Day Adventists	49	10	59
Southern Baptist Convention	80	76	156
Youth with a Mission	1,600	700	2,300
Totals	2,678	1,655	4,333

Source: East-West Church and Ministry Report 3, no. 2 (Spring 1995): p. 10.

established a foothold in Poland. By October 1994 some hundred Mormon missionaries were preaching in Poland, distributing copies of the Book of Mormon (in Polish translation) at a rate of seven hundred per month, and gradually winning converts.[8] In Hungary the charismatic Faith Church rented a large sports hall in the Buda hills and began holding five-hour meetings attended each time by up to three thousand born-again Christians, who came "for a potent American mixture of prayer, testimony of conversion, sermon, religious rock music, dancing, speaking in tongues, and laying on of hands."[9] In Hungary, as in Czechoslovakia and parts of Yugoslavia, the American television evangelist Morris Cerullo also was reported in 1991 to be building a mass following.[10] In Bulgaria, Orthodox clergy watched with apprehension as the Union of Evangelical Pentecostal Churches, the Union of Evangelical Congregational Churches, the Union of Evangelical Baptist Churches, the Bulgarian Evangelical Church of God, and other evangelical and charismatic religious organizations were granted juridical-legal status.[11] And in Ukraine, Baptists have been rapidly making inroads, baptizing 10,000 new members in 1994 alone, and opening eighty-three new churches and seventy prayer houses in that republic in 1994 alone. By October 1995 Ukraine was home to about 500,000 Baptists, organized in about 7,500 churches—the largest and fastest-growing Baptist community among the Soviet successor states.[12]

The Jehovah's Witnesses number some 4.5 million members in more than a hundred countries worldwide. Created in 1879 by Pennsylvania businessman Charles Russell, the association teaches that only Jehovah's Witnesses will survive Armageddon (variously set by the association to occur in 1914, 1925, and 1975) and that a mere 144,000 (a sacred number drawn from Revelation) will be taken into heaven to enjoy eternal bliss.[13] As of 1993 there were reported to be 107,876 Jehovah's Witnesses in Poland, 62,211 in the former USSR, about 50,000 in Romania, and slightly more than 60,000 in other Eastern European countries, from the Czech Republic to Macedonia.[14] Witnesses have been energetic in propagating their message, renting Moscow's Locomotive Stadium in the summer of 1993 (to baptize two thousand Russians in three portable swimming pools) and convoking three-day assemblies in Chorzow (Poland), Szczecin, Zagreb, Znojmo (southern Moravia), Bratislava, and elsewhere.[15]

"Traditional" churches have reacted with alarm and hostility to the appearance of these new rivals. Metropolitan Ioann of St. Petersburg and Ladoga spoke his mind in an open letter to the mayor of St. Petersburg dated 23 August 1992. "It is with alarm and regret," he admitted,

that I have lately observed a sharp increase in the onslaught of destructive forces that are hostile to Eastern Orthodoxy and are taking advantage of the economic and political collapse of the theomachistic Bolshevist state in order to spiritually disorient our people. The consequences of this spiritual aggression could be ruinous for Russia and could result in moral degeneration the likes of which the much-suffering Russian people have never known before. Taking advantage of the country's difficult situation, throngs of upstart preachers falsely calling themselves Christians have poured into our country, Holy Rus. These false teachers and false prophets . . . are trying to make the most of the ideological vacuum that formed in society after the collapse of official communist doctrine, filling it with . . . religious refuse. . . .[16]

Some people have read political functions into the activities of the new proselytizers, suggesting that they were specifically working to expunge the traditional communalism and solidarity from the Russian character and replacing them with individualism and self-seeking. In one interpretation, cited in *Pravda*, "Nothing will come of attempts to establish either a market economy or democracy in Russia until the casual Russian attitude toward wealth is replaced by the unquenchable Protestant thirst for getting rich."[17] Some Protestant missionaries have tried to allay these concerns. For example, Terry Townsend, head of the Russian-American Assemblies of God, has insisted that his organization wants "to strengthen the Russian Church, not to undermine it."[18] The Russian Orthodox Church remains unconvinced.

Elsewhere, there are parallel concerns. In Belarus, for example, President Alyaksandr Lukashenko criticized the "spiritual and ideological aggression" by Roman Catholics and Protestants in 1995, accusing them of having "embarked on a path close to political intrigue." In Lukashenko's view, the risk is that "the people of Belarus [will] lose their identity. . . ."[19] According to him, "It is not a political but a moral necessity to preserve and develop Orthodox Christianity in Belarus, Russia and Ukraine."[20] During a meeting with Patriarch Aleksii II on 22 July, Lukashenko told the Russian churchman, "If through our own unwise actions we lose Slav [i.e., Orthodox] culture as our foundation, we will thereby encourage spiritual and ideological aggression."[21] Belarusian authorities have endeavored to combat such "aggression" through a combination of bureaucratic obstructionism and outright prohibition of groups they find distasteful, refusing, for example, to register the Salvation Army or the Krishna Society as legitimate religious associations.[22]

In Moldova and Armenia the new postcommunist governments took a leaf from the communist cookbook and, as a device to freeze the religious status quo, simply passed laws prohibiting proselytization. In Armenia the law further specifies that legal registration may be denied organizations whose doctrines are not based on "historically recognized holy scriptures."[23] Adherents of new religious movements in Armenia have not escaped violence and coercion either. According to a report in

Moscow News, the religious leaders of local branches of the "50th Day" Church, the Jehovah's Witnesses, the Baptists, the Seventh-Day Adventists, the Bachaists, and the Hare Krishna were rounded up in 1995 and subjected to forms of harassment, while five young members of the so-called Warriors of Christ were forcibly drafted and, upon their refusal to bear arms, humiliated.[24] The *Moscow News* continued its report on developments in Armenia:

Two prayer houses of the "50th Day" followers in the town of Abovyan and in the Yekhegnadzorsky region were blown up. Some people threw a bomb at the window of the Seventh Day Adventists' church in Aragats. Several people burst into a prayer house of the Charismatic Church (a branch that separated itself from the Baptists). Vandals beat up the guard, broke computers and telephones and stole food intended for charity. In four Armenian regions, Charismatic Church missionaries who visited the villagers on their own request were attacked. Certain "unknown persons" [vandalized] the only Krishna temple in Yerevan. The headquarters of the charity mission [of the] Hare Krishna or "Food for the Soul" is also headquartered there. Thugs beat up the servicemen who happened to be there as well as guests . . . In accordance with the order of David Shakhnazarov, chairman of the department for national security, thousands of sacred Hindu books were burned in the furnaces of the Yerevan heating plant at the end of last year [1994]. Thousands of books burned recently in the village of Shatin in the Yekhegnadzorsky region added to the total. An explosion shook the village's church and seriously damaged the building. Even well-known athlete Ervand Zakaryan fell victim to the repressions against [the] Krishnaites. His apartment was attacked as the thugs kept repeating that there must be only one Church in Armenia, the Armenian Apostolic Church. In every case the victims applied for legal defense but no measures were taken.[25]

Other countries also have followed this restrictive model, such as Abkhazia, which in 1995 issued an edict banning the Jehovah's Witnesses,[26] and, up to a point, Lithuania, which in 1994 drew up a law distinguishing between "established" and "nonestablished" religions.[27]

In Romania, by contrast, the Romanian ministry of education in the summer of 1996 gave a green light to Jehovah's Witnesses to hold an evangelical event in Bucharest's soccer stadium (capacity: more than 40,000), while the Orthodox Church watched helplessly, fulminating against "an action meant to destroy the nation's moral unity."[28] Indeed, American and other Western evangelicals have become a common sight in Romania's municipalities.

In Bulgaria, similarly, as of 1992, the doors to evangelization were open, and Orthodox Bishop Natanail of Krupnik was complaining of the alleged "active participation of a government institution" in cooperating with evangelical Christian organizations at the expense of the Bulgarian Orthodox Church.[29] About the same time, Bishop Neofit, secretary of the Holy Synod of the Bulgarian Orthodox Church, lamented, "It is a shame that they should come to evangelize a nation which has been Christian for 11 centuries."[30] Be that as it may, the government refused entry to a planeload of Swedish evangelists in early 1993 when they landed at Sofia airport without visas. Following that incident, Bulgarian newspapers ran a series of articles painting extremely unflattering pictures of non-Orthodox religious organizations, and missionaries began to complain of harassment in sundry forms.[31]

Ecumenical Patriarch Bartolomeios spoke for Orthodox believers when in October 1995 he equated Christian fundamentalism with crime. In the patriarch's words: "too many crimes today are taking place in the name of faith. . . . Religious extremists and terrorists may be the most wicked false prophets of all, for not only do they commit horrible crimes—they do so in the name of a lie. . . . Fundamentalism is a danger. . . . The rise of fundamentalism has given greater urgency to the cause of East-West unity."[32]

Traditional Churches have viewed the ecclesiastical newcomers not as Churches but as sects or cults. Thus, the Church of Jesus Christ of Latter-Day Saints is considered a Church in the United States but is viewed as a sect in the Czech Republic.[33] In contemporary Central and Eastern Europe the Jehovah's Witnesses, the Children of God, the Mormons, Kip McKean's Church of Christ, and the so-called Jesus Freaks are all considered, and even officially classified by local authorities, as sects.[34] While it is possible to employ the terms "cult" and "sect" scientifically in accordance with strict definitions (see chapter 13), it is clear enough that these terms are used by Central and East European officials and laypersons alike in a disparaging way. Illustrating this usage were Russian General Aleksandr Lebed's public comments on 27 June 1996. "We have established, traditional religions—Russian Orthodoxy, Islam, and Buddhism," he observed, transparently signaling his approval for these traditional associations. "But," he continued, "as for all these other sects—Mormons, Aum Shinrikyo, [et al.]—all this is mold and scum that is artificially brought into this country with the aim of perverting, corrupting, and ultimately breaking up our state. Therefore, the state must rise to the defense of its citizens and outlaw all these foul sects."[35]

Inevitably, there have been ecclesiastical "counteroffensives." Perhaps the first such counteroffensive on the part of a mainline Church was signaled by the Holy See in late November and early December 1991 when it convened a European synod at Vatican City to launch a "new evangelization" of Eastern Europe.[36] Two years later, addressing a crowd of more than 100,000 people in Vilnius, Pope John Paul II returned to the theme of evangelical Protestant movements and nontraditional religious associations — "sects" in Vatican terminology. "People who hope to find happiness," the pope told his Lithuanian audience, "in sects which exploit their followers by holding out forms of esotericism and magic will fail in their search for happiness. They leave themselves open to great disillusionment."[37]

By 1993 the Russian Orthodox Church became sufficiently fearful of the nonindigenous Christian associations that it sought to obtain adoption of a law restricting the activity of any religious organizations based outside Russia. Although aimed at Jehovah's Witnesses, Mormons, the Assembly of God, the Faith Church, the Four-Square Gospel Church, Moonies, Baha'i, the Krishna community, and sundry evangelical groups, the draft law aroused profound concern on the part of Roman Catholic bishops lest their subordination to Rome be construed as sufficient grounds to brand them "nonindigenous."[38]

At first, the controversial legislation seemed to be stillborn,[39] but on 10 July 1996, the Russian Duma approved the first reading of a somewhat amended version of the original bill, by a vote of 376 to 3. The draft law establishes that only "Church-type" religious associations with doctrines, liturgy, and religious instruction may be registered as legal religious organizations. Religious associations not recognized as Churches still will be allowed to register, but they must register under other laws that will classify them differently and provide for a narrower range of prerogatives.[40] The new bill also provides that a person's religion will be listed on her or his passport (as is the case in Greece); at the same time, the bill scraps Article 5 of the previous law ("Guarantees of Religious Freedom").[41] Under the new bill, foreigners may serve as founders of religious associations operating in Russia *only* if they have earlier taken up permanent residence in Russia. "The chairman of the Duma Committee considering the law, Viktor I. Zorkaltsev, stated that the Committee 'receives thousands of letters in which citizens express fright at the seemingly uncontrollable activities of foreign missionaries. They request [that] the severest measures be undertaken.'"[42]

In June 1997 the Russian parliament passed restrictive legislation declaring the Russian Orthodox Church, Judaism, Buddhism, and Islam "traditional religions" of Russia and leaving all other religious organizations, including the Catholic Church and the Baptist movement, subject to withdrawal of legal registration, confiscation of property, and constriction of their right to proselytize. Under pressure from the United States, President Boris Yeltsin vetoed the law on 22 July, but on 26 September he in fact signed a slightly redrafted version of this law with the same four religions acknowledged.[43]

Evangelicals have visions of bounty. In Poland, Mormon missionaries have pointed to their Church's success in the Philippines where, after thirty years of proselytizing, there are now about 370,000 Mormons.[44] In Russia, American evangelicals projected in 1993 that their combined strength would be at least on a par with that of Russian Orthodoxy as early as 2003.[45] One does not need to take such claims at face value to appreciate the potential for shifts in the religious balance or the connection between such shifts and changes in the values of a given society. The traditional Churches have the example of Latin America to consider; there, in Brazil, about 20 percent of the population (or 30 million people) have converted to evangelical churches, with tangible rates of evangelical growth also in Chile, Guatemala, Peru, Bolivia, and Mexico as well.[46] This consideration gives a particular edge to the new evangelism in Eastern Europe.

That said, more recent reports suggest that missionary activity, at least in Russia, may have peaked around 1993 and that the high tide of evangelism in that country may have come and gone. At first, according to Lev Mitrokhin, Western religious groups attracted devotees because of the general popularity of anything connected with the United States. With the waning of Russians' love affair with Americana, as with the gradual exhaustion of the missionaries' resources, has come a waning in the fortunes of the evangelical Christian missionaries.[47] Waning or not, the religious configuration of Eastern Europe and Russia has changed permanently and will continue to change.

Chapter 12

Mores Ecclesiae et Potestas Fidei:
A Contrast of the Bulgarian Orthodox Church and
the Polish Catholic Church

The concept of Constantinism derives . . . from the name of the Emperor Constantine, under whose reign there first appeared the theory of dual power: spiritual and temporal. As a political model, Julianism is the opposite of Constantinism. In place of the cooperation of the spiritual and temporal powers, Julianism is marked by their conflict. The Church finds itself in opposition. Deprived of political power, it possesses only moral authority—and in this lies its strength . . . Its moral authority is inversely proportional to its participation in political power. . . . Moral authority is the fundamental feature of the Julianic Church, just as political authority is the mark of the Constantinian Church. . . . Yet Julianism is in a sense connected with Constantinism. . . . Julianism does not develop by itself; rather it is a contested form of Constantinism, arising where the state has departed from a previously accepted notion of collaboration with the Church. It would be wrong to say that the Julianic Church has nothing in common with political power: this is a Church that has been forcibly deprived of its participation in power. . . .

Constantinism means participation in state power. Julianism is marked by bitterness and resentment over losing that power, and not by voluntary acquiescence [in] the loss. This is why the Julianic Church, with all of its spiritual power, is never fully in solidarity with society, and never fully identifies with it. It does of course want society to identify itself with the Church, but this is not the same thing. Deprived of its political strength, it fights to preserve its spiritual leadership over the nation. It refuses to accept that there is any way other than the Church to bring about the spiritual or ideological integration of society, and it refuses to acknowledge the existence of any form of opposition other than those that it itself promotes and controls. If the existence of another form of opposition becomes quite obvious—one that offers society some kind of ideological alternative, allowing it to come together apart from the Church—then the Julianic Church condemns this opposition, or at least tries to disavow and devalue it in the eyes of public opinion. Never will the Julianic Church be anxious to engage in any form of collaboration against the state with any independent center of oppositionist thought. In its conflict with the secular rulers, the Julianic Church prefers to act alone, without partners, toward whom it feels no sense of solidarity. BOHDAN CYWIŃSKI, *Rodowody Niepokornyeh* (1971)[1]

Chapter 4 examined certain historically *remote* sources of religio-national interaction and Church-state relations, linking Church-state relations to both the nature of religio-national symbiosis or conflict and legal and institutional precedents inherited from the remote past. In particular, it was argued that patterns established in the eighteenth and nineteenth centuries had continuing importance today. In this chapter the focus shifts to history's more *proximate* sources of Church-state relations, and the argument is extended by showing that patterns of Church-state interaction in the nineteenth and twentieth centuries, and perhaps most especially the pattern of interaction during the communist era, have had an impact on the given Church's credibility and even legitimacy in the eyes of the people. A Church, after all, is judged not merely by the plausibility of its doctrines or the stability (or adaptability) of its rituals, but by its political behavior.

The Bulgarian Orthodox Church and the Roman Catholic Church in Poland provide a study in contrasts. The Bulgarian Orthodox Church, which assumed autocephalous form in 1870 in a region where Orthodoxy had found a modus vivendi with Ottoman authorities through the *millet* system,[2] was completely subordinated to the machinery of the state during the communist era. The Bulgarian Church, thus—even though it displayed *some* aspects of "Constantinianism," to use Cywiński's terminology—until the early 1950s never developed any habits of resistance to state authority, let alone any heroic tradition. The Polish Catholic Church, however, earned its nationalist credentials in the era of the partitions (1795–1918), when parish priests played highly visible roles in the rebellions of 1830 and 1863.[3] And although the Polish Church had its experience with Constantinist triumphalism in the Austrian zone of occupation (Galicia, 1795–1918) and more generally during the years 1918–26, its relations with state power became more problematic during the Piłsudski era (1926–35). The communists once more deprived the Church of political power, and once again it assumed the role of guardian of the national spirit and center of resistance. Unlike the Bulgarian Orthodox Church, moreover, the Polish Church produced two genuine heroes in the postwar era: Stefan Cardinal Wyszyński (1901–81) and Fr. Jerzy Popiełuszko (1947–84).[4] The Bulgarian Church's docility led to ecclesiastical atrophy and, in the wake of communism's fall, to internal division and vulnerability to competition from new Christian and non-Christian missionaries. The Polish Church's resistance, by contrast, gave that Church resilience and credibility, tempting it to succumb, in the wake of communism's fall, to theocratic ambitions.

If the Polish Church of 1918–26 (or, more loosely, 1918–39) can be described as *Constantinian,* and of 1947–89 as *Julianic,* the Bulgarian church of 1879–1945 possibly can be characterized as increasingly *Petrine* (meaning that it tended over time to increasingly assimilate to the model of state control of the Church established by Peter the Great of Russia in 1721).[5] The most useful term to describe the Bulgarian Church after 1950 is *Stalinist.* A Julianic Church is merely deprived of power in which it once shared; a Stalinist Church has lost all decision-making autonomy and has been reduced to a mere agency of the state.

Bulgarian Orthodoxy: A Controlled Church

An Orthodox Church centered in Ohrid had existed from 972 to 1767; there was also a patriarchate in Tŭrnovo between 1235 and 1393. But from 1767 until 1870 Bulgarian Christians were placed under the authority of the ecumenical patriarch in Constantinople, who allowed Hellenist influences to assert themselves throughout the Church. The Bulgarian national awakening in the nineteenth century coincided with a religious awakening, and in the 1840s a separate Bulgarian Church was set up in the Phanar district of Constantinople; the Porte's agreement had been obtained in 1848, and Bulgarian Christians were able to consecrate the St. Stefan church in October 1849.[6] Other denominations were quick to spot the opening created by the Bulgarian national awakening. The Roman Catholic Church, for example, stepped up its propaganda efforts among Bulgarians in the 1850s, while the newly created Eastern-Rite Catholic Church offered Bulgarians the use of their own language in the liturgy.[7] Protestants also smelled opportunity in Bulgaria. The Methodists and Congregationalists, followed by Baptists and Pentecostals, dispatched missionaries to work among Bulgarians. Protestant missionaries from the American Board of Commissioners for Foreign Missions hoped at first to divert the Bulgarian autocephalists from their appointed goal and to convince them of the satisfaction to be obtained by "merging" into the Protestant *millet*. But by the early 1860s it was becoming clear that whatever interest the autocephalists might have in such a move was purely tactical, seen by them as a step toward the ultimate goal of Bulgarian ecclesiastical autocephaly.[8] On the other hand, Protestant missionaries seem to have had a direct impact on Bulgarian Orthodox ecclesiology, according to Tatyana Nestorova, who cites the fact that several typical Protestant notions, such as lay participation in Church government and the removability of the exarch, were incorporated into the Orthodox Church at the time of its institutional rebirth in 1870.[9]

The first major concession to Bulgarian ecclesial sensitivities had come a decade earlier when in July 1860 the Ecumenical Patriarch Joachim offered to permit the use of Bulgarian in churches and schools and to appoint Bulgarians to take charge of a few bishoprics. The Bulgarian clerical spokespersons ungraciously rejected this concession with the observation that only complete autocephaly could be deemed adequate.[10] In 1867 there was a new offer, this time from Patriarch Gregory VI, Joachim's successor, who proposed to give his blessing to the establishment of an *autonomous* Bulgarian Church with jurisdiction in the lands between the Danube and the Balkan Mountains. The Bulgarians rejected this second offer because they aspired to jurisdiction over a more extensive territory.[11] The Greek-Bulgarian ecclesiastical dispute could not be ignored, however, and in early 1870 the Sultan issued a *firman* (an edict) establishing a Bulgarian exarchate with jurisdiction over seventeen dioceses.

The Bulgarian Orthodox exarchate had less than a decade of existence under Ottoman rule. In 1875, revolt broke out in the Balkans, and in 1878 the Congress of Berlin sanctioned the creation of an independent (albeit truncated) Bulgarian state. Liberation created immediate complications for the Church. The exarch had had his seat in Constantinople, and it seemed appropriate that he should move his seat to Bulgaria; but if he did so, a question would arise as to whether he should retain his authority over exarchist communities in Macedonia, Thrace, or for that matter, Eastern Rumelia.[12] Even more problematic was the fact that the Tŭrnovo constitution of 1879 described the Church-state relationship in terms that were open to interpretation, with the result that Church leaders read it as sanctioning Church authority over the state, while governmental leaders aspired to extend their controls over the Church, citing the same constitution in their support.[13] Indeed, Prime Minister Dragan Tsankov "insisted that the state had the right to legislate unilaterally with regard to the Church's secular activity."[14]

Relations between the Church hierarchy and Stefan Stambolov (1854–95), who served as prime minister from 1887 until 1894, were at least as problematic. Already in his first year in office, Stambolov adjusted the salary stipends paid to clergy. Later, when Bishop Kliment of Tŭrnovo refused to celebrate a *Te Deum* for Ferdinand, Bulgaria's new (Roman Catholic) monarch, Stambolov suspended financial subventions to the exarchate and even tried to engineer the removal of the exarch, albeit unsuccessfully. But in other ways Stambolov clearly helped the Church. In January 1888, for example, he persuaded the cabinet to agree to have new prayer books printed on state presses. And in 1894, in his last year in office, he obtained the transfer of two new bishoprics in Macedonia to the jurisdiction of the Bulgarian exarchate, in addition to the three Macedonian bishoprics transferred in 1890.[15] In what seems a wry hint of things to come, there was in Stambolov's day a joint ministry for foreign and religious affairs.[16]

Church and state seemed almost evenly matched until the reign of King Boris III (1894–1943; reigned 1918–43). Boris succeeded where his predecessors had failed. Early in his reign he transformed the Church into a de facto synodal institution, and he imposed the malleable Metropolitan Neofit of Vidin on the Church (as president of the Holy Synod) in 1934. Indeed, King Boris and his ministers "repeatedly tried to influence the elections of new metropolitans of Tŭrnovo, Vratsa, and Varna, but failed in their attempts to take direct control of the Church."[17]

There are several differences between the Petrine and Stalinist models for control of Churches. First, the Petrine model presumed that there was something valid in the Christian religion—an assumption not made by Stalin and his minions. Second, the Petrine model was founded on the concept of an official state religion, whereas Stalinism repudiated any formal establishmentarianism. Third, the Petrine model was a formula for *control;* the Stalinist model provided a formula for the *total control* of Churches and was, in consequence, far more intrusive.

Soon after their seizure of power, the communists imprisoned and tortured Metropolitan Kiril of Plovdiv (the future patriarch) and Metropolitan Paisi of Vratsa, and they murdered Archimandrites Paladi of Vidin, Iriney of Sofia, and Nahum of Ruse. At first, a vocal minority among the Orthodox clergy stood up to the communists, but these "recalcitrants" were assigned to labor brigades or sent to political reeducation camps. Out of 2,440 Orthodox priests, 316 were incarcerated in the brutal concentration camp on Belene Island alone.[18] This example inclined those still at liberty to view cooperation with the government as a basic necessity. "Gradually," as Spas Raikin recounts, "the Church was transformed into an obedient and useful tool in the hands of the government."[19]

In the early years the communist authorities ordered the demolition of many church buildings and allowed hundreds of others to fall into disrepair. Even as late as 1971 the St. Spas church, famous for its frescoes, was bulldozed to make room for a bank, over the protests of some 40,000 demonstrators. The authorities also confiscated Church lands and facilities. As early as 1946, for instance, the state confiscated about 5,900 acres of land and woods attached to the Rila monastery, including a timber plant, a distillery, and several dairy farms.[20] This is only one example. School prayer and religious instruction were discontinued. By 1947 the Orthodox Church had been deprived of its jurisdiction over issuing birth and death certificates, marriage, and divorce.

The communist party introduced a new constitution in December 1947. Article 78 declared, "It is forbidden to misuse the Church and religion for political ends."[21] Taking a cue from previous practice, the communists entrusted the supervision of the Churches to a branch of the foreign ministry.[22] The Bulgarian secret police were authorized to perpetrate certain provocations with an eye to subverting and undermining the Church.[23]

At this point the government essentially dictated new bylaws to the Church, granting the lower clergy a role in state government and a determinative role in the composition of the synod. By 1955 the government felt sufficiently confident of its control of the hierarchy that it could dispense with the Priests' Union, which it had hitherto wielded as a wedge, and ordered the union's dissolution.

The prescribed bylaws provided for an elaborate system of elections within the Church, with parish councils electing district delegates, who would in turn elect diocesan electoral colleges (consisting of clergymen and laymen), which in turn elected both diocesan metropolitans and, during patriarchal vacancies, the patriarchal electoral college. The entire system was designed to facilitate manipulation by state authorities. A hitherto secret document published in 1992 proves that from 1949 on, the minister of the interior had the final say as to who might be elected patriarch of the Church.[24]

With the elevation of Kiril of Plovdiv (d. 1971) to head the restored patriarchate in 1953, the Church-state relationship quickly took on the appearance of symbiosis. In fact, the hierarchy had, by then, consented to be at the state's beck and call, functioning as apparatchiks of the state. "As befits a bureau of state, the Church was required to add a course in Marxism to its curriculum at the Theological Faculty in Sofia."[25]

The Bulgarian Orthodox Church performed many services for the communist regime. It joined the Moscow-inspired Christian Peace Conference (based in Prague) and, in 1961, the World Council of Churches, supporting regime priorities in those bodies. It organized and hosted international peace conferences at which it upheld Moscow's line. It endorsed Warsaw Pact policies (e.g., through a patriarchal letter dated 3 May 1963). It channeled its publishing activity along lines pleasing to the regime. The Church weekly *Duhovna kultura* sounded the dominant theme of the Bulgarian Church's activity during the communist era in a 1984 article: "The Bulgarian Orthodox Church will continue to cultivate in its youth a love for our socialist motherland, [and] will make its contribution . . . towards the consolidation of the age-old fraternal friendship with the Russian people and with the other peoples of the Soviet Union."[26]

The Legacy of Stalinism

The Bulgarian Church's willingness to accommodate the regime cost it the trust and loyalty of many citizens. The communist state was clearly the enemy as far as most Bulgarians were concerned. And if the Orthodox Church served that state, then it followed that the Church, despite its protestations of nationalism and love of homeland, was the servant of the enemy. After 1989 there were repeated public attacks on the Church for its past behavior; these included publication of a book excoriating Patriarch Kiril.[27] There also were revelations and accusations in the press. In May 1991 *Demokratsiya* published allegations that the metropolitan of Vratsa had obtained his post as a result of unlawful interference on the part of local communist authorities and that he had repaid this favor by rendering loyal service to the secret police. The metropolitan was further accused of having collaborated in the repression of politically nonconformist clergy. Patriarch Maksim (b. 1915, elected Kiril's successor in 1971) also was implicated in collaborating with police authorities.[28] Public indignation reached such a pitch that in May 1991, during a visit of the ecumenical patriarch to Sofia, angry crowds shouted their demand for the resignation of Patriarch "Marx-im."[29]

This sentiment has made the Bulgarian Orthodox Church especially vulnerable to attrition, and a number of Protestant groups have stepped into the breach. Among the religious organizations (Christian and otherwise) which have carried out energetic missionary efforts in Bulgaria since 1989 are the Assembly of God, the Church of God, the Church of Jesus Christ of Latter-Day Saints, the Jehovah's Witnesses, the Krishna Society, the Union of Evangelical-Pentecostal Churches, the Evangelical Methodist Episcopal Church, and the Universal White Brotherhood.[30] The Roman Catholic Church also has seen opportunities for proselytization and expansion at the expense of Bulgaria's post-Stalinist Orthodox Church.[31]

But forty years of docile accommodationism also have had a direct impact on the Church's infrastructure, provoking a serious internal schism. The eventual rift was adumbrated in March 1989 when Fr. Hristofor Subev, a former physicist, set up a Committee for Religious Rights, Freedom of Conscience, and Spiritual Values. Proceeding without the approval of either Church hierarchy or party officials, Subev pledged to work to end state interference in religious life, to make religious instruction for the young legal again, and to spark spiritual renewal. The Church hierarchy issued a statement characterizing the "self-styled committee" as "counter to the canon of Orthodoxy," that is, illegal from an ecclesiastical point of view.[32] The Holy Synod contacted the state judiciary and asked that it decline to register Subev's committee.[33]

Subev not only campaigned for the institutional and spiritual regeneration of the Orthodox Church, but he worked actively "to promote understanding and tolerance among the different faiths of Bulgaria—Judaism and Islam included"[34]—offering support to Turks threatened with cultural assimilation. The communist authorities shared the hierarchy's displeasure with Subev and imprisoned him briefly during the summer of 1989. But by autumn Subev was out of jail—in time to play a vocal role in the political tumult of November that accompanied the last days of the Zhivkov dictatorship. Still committed to Church reform and spiritual renewal, Subev told a rally attended by 50,000 people in Sofia (on 18 November): "There should be a Bible in every home. God bless democracy!"[35] But while Subev was placing his stress on Bibles (though not without noting other issues), the Holy Synod prepared a statement for delivery to the National Assembly, emphasizing the synod's desire to obtain the return of churches, monasteries, and other facilities confiscated after 1945.[36]

The Holy Synod recognized that a problem existed with its authority and announced its intention to convoke a *Subor* (or Church assembly) sometime in 1990. The synod even—and rather surprisingly—named Subev to take part in the preparatory commission's work. Later, the synod reconsidered, dissolving the commission, and the *Subor* did not take place.[37]

But in 1990 Radko Poptodorov, a professor specializing in canon law, published an article in *Otechestvo*, noting, inter alia, that whereas canon law prescribed that the *Tsurkovno-naroden Subor* (the Council of Church and Nation) meet every four years to consider the most important issues affecting the church, no *Subor* had taken place since 1953. This signified that the election of Metropolitan Maksim of Lovech as patriarch in 1971, as well as all appointments of metropolitans since 1954, had been uncanonical and therefore invalid. Indeed, since Maksim had obtained his original appointment as metropolitan only in 1960, it followed that not only his election as patriarch but even his appointment as metropolitan had been invalid under canon law.[38] The article blew wind into the sails of Subev's movement for ecclesiastical reform.

"Our Church is sick and its disease comes right from the head," Subev said in a radio interview. "The diagnosis is dementia. The patriarch was appointed by the communists and has always served them faithfully. The Holy Synod must be renewed as soon as possible."[39] By then, Subev was head of the parliamentary committee for religion, which in February 1992 ruled that Maksim's election as patriarch had been illegal.[40] Subev also was in friendly contact with Metodi Spasov, head of the directorate of religious affairs. Poptodorov's arguments were instrumental in persuading Spasov to act, and on 9 March 1992 his directorate declared Maksim's election as patriarch null and void.[41] Shortly thereafter, Spasov gave Subev written authorization to proceed with moves to replace Maksim. Spasov would later be criticized for thereby involving state organs in internal Church affairs.

In the meantime, encouraged by the friendly attitude of the directorate, Church rebels led by Subev announced the creation of a Provisional Synod, declared Maksim's election invalid, and elected Metropolitan Pimen of Nevrokop to take his place as patriarch. The Provisional Synod, which enjoyed the support of four out of thirteen metropolitans, six out of sixteen bishops, and about forty priests, elevated Subev to the rank of archimandrite on the same day.[42] But, as Janice Broun has pointed out, the composition of the provisional Synod strained credibility. Its leaders were the three most compromised Metropolitans, all faithful lackeys of the Communist government. Pimen had, among other things, been responsible, in 1963, [for] expelling the best priests from the Bulgarian Orthodox parishes in the USA. Pankrati of Stara Zagora . . . as Chief of the Church Foreign Department had endorsed government policy and had been elected as Deputy in the new Assembly—for the Fatherland Union, a BSP [Bulgarian Socialist Party] front party. Kalinik of Vratsa was popularly known as the "Red Bishop." Furthermore, as members of Maksim's inner Standing Committee for years, they shared responsibility for his decisions.[43]

These compromised prelates were incongruous allies for the sincere Subev. But Subev probably appreciated the difficulty of locating hierarchs untainted by collaboration and/or uncanonical activity. Maksim himself is charged with having been a colonel in the communist secret police.[44]

On 25 May, less than a week after the establishment of the Provisional Synod, Spasov intervened a second time and declared Maksim and the old Holy Synod uncanonical. The Council of Ministers concurred with this intervention on 1 June. Meanwhile, on 26 May the Provisional Synod gave Subev his second promotion within a week, elevating him to bishop of Makariopol. The choice of Makariopol was not without problems in that it lies within the independent Republic of Macedonia and is already administered by the autocephalous Macedonian Orthodox Church.[45]

Bulgarian President Zhelyu Zhelev (b. 1935), expressing his belief that state organs should not interfere in Church affairs, asked the Constitutional Court to review the situation and, specifically, to hand down a ruling on the actions of the directorate of religious affairs.[46] On 11 June 1992 the Constitutional Court announced its decision, characterizing the directorate's actions as "inadmissible interference in the affairs of the Bulgarian Orthodox Church."[47] The Constitutional Court refused to rule on the question as to which synod was legitimate, however, and referred the matter to the Supreme Court. The high court ruled on 2 July that the original synod was invalid, but it reached this decision on the grounds of a technicality—the synod had been a day late in registering with the directorate. But this was not the end of the story, since the Holy Synod loyal to Maksim appealed this decision. On 5 November 1992 a five-member panel of the Supreme Court chaired by Blagovest Punev overturned the Constitutional Court's ruling, finding that the directorate "did not unduly interfere with the practices of the Bulgarian

Orthodox Church."[48] On the following day the Supreme Court ruled on the Holy Synod's appeal, declaring *both* synods invalid, the Holy Synod for reasons already cited, and the Provisional Synod on the grounds that only a synod duly elected by Church members was legally qualified to apply for registration.[49]

While these legal battles were being waged, physical battles were being fought between the supporters of the Provisional Synod and those of the Holy Synod. In late May, supporters of Metropolitan Pimen occupied the building of the Holy Synod and proceeded to fortify it. On 16 July, Patriarch Maksim led a procession bearing an alleged relic of the True Cross around Sofia's Aleksander Nevsky Cathedral and then marched, phalanx-like, against the occupied synodal building. Maksim's supporters used a park bench as a battering ram and hurled bottles and stones at the windows. From inside, the better-prepared supporters of Pimen and Subev responded by hurling tear gas cannisters out their windows and showering Maksim's loyalists with bottles.[50]

Hierarchs loyal to Maksim met with Prime Minister Filip Dimitrov on 24 August and tried to recruit his assistance. Dimitrov declined to get involved.[51] The following March, the Council of Ministers dismissed the controversial Spasov from his post in charge of the directorate[52] and pledged to do "everything within its power, *acting in compliance with the law and the canons of the Bulgarian Orthodox Church,* to help for the recovery and unification of the Bulgarian Church."[53] The lower clergy also became involved in efforts to restore Church unity, launching a campaign for this purpose in May 1994.[54] But as of 1996 the Bulgarian Church remained divided, with disputes extending even to ownership of a candle-making factory in Sofia.[55]

Weak, divided its very ranks depleted by decades of countersocialization, and shorn of virtually all credibility, the post-Stalinist Bulgarian Orthodox Church has been in no condition to evangelize effectively, having to concentrate its energies on solving its own internal disputes.

The Polish Church: From Constantinism to Julianism

The Polish Catholic Church provides a striking contrast in all respects. Far from having experienced the kind of Caesaro-papism that characterized the Bulgarian Orthodox Church in the interwar period, the Polish Catholic Church felt a distinct ambivalence about its relationship with the state. And far from having been weakened by communism, the Polish Church seems to have gained strength from it.

The politics of Polish Catholicism before 1945 were discussed in chapter 4, while the Polish Church's experiences under communism were summarized in chapters 2 and 4. This chapter will restrict itself to highlighting the principal points concerning the period up to 1989 and will focus primarily on the years since 1989.

In contrasting the Polish Catholic Church with the Bulgarian Orthodox Church, one is struck by the fact that whereas the Polish Church defined itself in the nineteenth century in competition with Protestantism (in German-occupied Poland) and Orthodoxy (in Russian-occupied Poland), the chief rivals confronting the Bulgarian Church (and especially in Macedonia) were the fellow Orthodox Churches of Greece and Serbia. Second, whereas Bulgarian ecclesiastical autocephaly preceded Bulgarian independence, in Poland state independence proved to be the prerequisite for the relief of religious pressure on Polish Catholicism. And third, whereas the Petrine model of interwar Bulgarian Orthodoxy was connected with issues of *control*, the Polish case must be discussed in terms of degrees and levels of alliance or competition between Church and state.

From the vantage point of the communist era, the interwar era certainly appeared Constantinian; in terms of generating a Julianic syndrome, it is the subjective recollection that matters. But at the time, matters looked more ambiguous. The constitution of March 1921 (article 114) simultaneously granted and denied the Catholic Church legal preeminence: "The Roman Catholic faith, being the religion of the overwhelming majority of the nation, occupies in the state a leading position among religions endowed with equal rights."[56] Nor was the Church entirely sure of its footing, especially at first. In 1920, for example, Aleksander Cardinal Kakowski (1862–1938), the archbishop of Warsaw, advised a foreign interviewer, "You must not . . . suppose that we have not also our difficulties. Infidelity and Freemasonry have spread their contagion among us, as elsewhere. Judaism constitutes with us a danger more serious than elsewhere. In a word, even in Poland, the Church is in a situation of combat, not in that of peaceful and undisturbed possession."[57]

The watershed in interwar Poland was May 1926, the month that Marshal Piłsudski seized power. Until his coup, the Church seemed to be making steady advances, though Neal Pease no doubt is correct in cautioning that "from the beginning the interwar Polish hierarchy understood that it could not get too cozy with [the] *Endecja* without trespassing on dubious ideological ground."[58] On the other hand, the Holy See was able to obtain a concordat on 10 February 1925 (ratified by the Polish *Sejm*, the lower house of parliament, in March of that year).[59] The concordat made some important concessions to the Church, guaranteeing that religious instruction would be part of the standard curriculum in all state schools, granting the Church the prerogative of appointing religion teachers, and committing the government to provide a partial salary for Catholic clergy.[60]

Piłsudski's ascent to power created immediate problems for the Church. Apart from the fact that many of his more radical followers displayed marked anticlerical proclivities, there was the fact that many bishops and priests had been sympathetic to the *Endecja* and hostile to Piłsudski.[61] Where the *Endecja* had given the Church favorable conditions in the concordat, Piłsudski's government believed that the Church had been given too much and endeavored to retract some concessions already granted, disputing the level of priests' salaries, among other things. And where earlier governments had seemed favorably disposed toward the Church's sundry property claims, the Piłsudski government blocked the return of certain formerly Catholic churches that had been turned over to the Orthodox Church during the nineteenth century.[62]

In reviewing the interwar period, thus, it is clear (1) that the Church faced the necessity of defending its interests against state encroachment and (2) that the Church enjoyed far more propitious conditions than would be granted to it after World War II.

The Vatican considered the communists completely impossible, and in July 1949 it announced the automatic excommunication of anyone cooperating with them. As Polish communist authorities took their first steps to whittle down Church power, Church and government signed an agreement on 14 April 1950. In exchange for Church pledges to respect collectivization, to oppose the channeling of religious feelings into antistate activity, and to condemn "the criminal activity of underground bands," the state agreed to desist from further restrictions of religious instruction, to desist from obstructing children's attendance at religious events, to refrain from creating difficulties for religious rituals of a public nature, and to allow convents, monasteries, and religious associations "complete freedom of activity" within their appropriate spheres.[63]

But in spite of this agreement, or rather because this agreement did not yield results pleasing to the communist authorities—say, something on the order of Bulgarian Church docility and obedience—the authorities had Bishop Czesław Kaczmarek arrested on 20 January 1951 and set a date for his trial.[64] On 28 January the government withdrew approval from five apostolic administrators, forcing the Church to replace them with (lower-ranked) vicars capitular. The government was actively trying to pit hierarchy and lower clergy against each other, and it even tried to set the bishops at odds. By 1952 relentless arrests of priests and other religious were being carried out. Then on 25 February the primate was informed that the censors would not permit *Tygodnik Powszechny* to publish the episcopate's memorandum on the constitution. When the mixed (Church-state) commission met on 20 March, the session became the scene for party accusations that the bishops were "sabotaging" the agreement of April 1950.[65] In January 1953 four priests and three lay workers of the Kraków archdiocese were tried on charges of having collaborated with the CIA.[66] In September 1953 Wyszyński himself was sent to prison—to regain his freedom only in October 1956. While the archbishop was locked up, the government closed down the theology faculty of Jagiellonian University in Kraków (in October 1954) and issued a decree arrogating to itself the authority to appoint bishops and pastors and to determine diocesan and parish boundaries.[67]

Bolesław Bierut (1892–1956), who served as General Secretary of the Polish United Workers' Party (PUWP) from September 1948 to March 1954 and as First Secretary of the PUWP from March 1954, died in March 1956 under mysterious circumstances; after a brief tenure by Edward Ochab (1906–89), Władysław Gomułka (1905–82) became the new First Secretary (in October 1956). Gomułka began his term by releasing Wyszyński and by negotiating a fresh agreement with the Church (on 8 December 1956), allowing religious instruction on an optional basis for children of parents who requested it in writing. At the same time, *Tygodnik Powszechny*, the Church's weekly newspaper which had been shut down in March 1953, was allowed to resume publication under the supervision, as before, of Jerzy Turowicz.[68] For the next four years optional religious instruction was conducted at state schools, despite the protests of certain communists. Then, during the summer of 1960 the authorities decided to remove religious instruction from the schools once and for all. The episcopate objected that this action violated the concordat, but to no avail. Adam Michnik has observed,

the Gomułka regime never thought seriously about a lasting coexistence with Catholicism. The declarations and compromises from the period of October 1956 were but tactical measures caused by a difficult political situation and the weakness of the new administration. Repression against the Church increased as the political situation stabilized and the episcopate, realizing the illusory nature of its post-October hopes for an honest compromise, began to formulate its views in more drastic language.[69]

The Gomułka era (1956–70) was characterized by gradual retreat from relative liberalism and by a degree of unevenness and unpredictability in state policy. That era overlapped the Church's decade-long celebration (1957–66) of the millennium of the Christianization of Poland. A key element in Wyszyński's vision of the celebrations was for the nation to renew the vows to the Virgin Mary taken by King Jan Kazimierz in 1656 (after the victory over the Swedes).[70] But during 1966, at the height of the commemoration, police interrupted Church celebrations in a number of locations and harassed participants. The authorities went so far as to lock up the icon of the Black Madonna of Częstochowa (credited with having granted the Poles victory over the Swedes in 1655) for six years, 1966–71.[71]

During this time the Polish Church's tendency to formulate its ideas independently of the Holy See became completely obvious to all concerned (offering a sharp contrast to the automatic obedience of Prague's Cardinal Tomášek). In 1965 Pope Paul VI (1897–1978; reigned 1963–78) mandated the creation of episcopal conferences at the national level, granting local Churches more discretion and autonomy on a national basis than they had enjoyed for some time.[72] But the Polish bishops had special needs and requested an audience with the pope. On 13 November 1965 the Roman pontiff received a delegation of thirty-eight Polish bishops, led by Cardinal Wyszyński. Addressing the pope in fluent Italian, Wyszyński made his case with force and eloquence:

We are aware that it will be very difficult, but not impossible, to put the decisions of the [Second Vatican] Council into effect in our situation. Therefore we ask the Holy Father for one favor: complete trust in the episcopate and the Church in our country. Our request may appear very presumptuous, but it is difficult to judge our situation from afar. *Everything that occurs in our Church must be assessed from the standpoint of our experience. . . .*[73]

Here was Wyszyński telling the pope that Vatican II did not apply to Poland and that he, Wyszyński, should be allowed a carte blanche within his own country. Hebblethwaite reports that the pontiff was "taken aback" at Wyszyński's chutzpah.[74] But Wyszyński found the results of the Second Vatican Council highly objectionable:

He was alarmed by its apparent lack of enthusiasm for popular devotions, for the mass processions and pilgrimages that were the staple of Polish piety. he was disconcerted by its understated mariology. He detested liturgical change, believing its effects would be unsettling. He thought the new-fangled "kiss of peace" would turn the Church into a salon. As for 'ecumenism,' it was irrelevant in Poland, there being no interlocutors. In Poland religious liberty was something the Church claimed [for itself], not something it conceded to others.[75]

Under Wyszyński, the Polish episcopate displayed the same sense of its own grandeur in its dealings with both the Holy See and the Polish communist regime.

The Church-state balance shifted perceptibly in the Gierek era (1970–80). Indeed, from Edward Gierek's accession as First Secretary until the end of the communist power monopoly in 1989, the party grew steadily weaker, while the Church grew steadily stronger. This mounting strength was graphically reflected in the numbers of pilgrimages to Częstochowa. These pilgrimages had declined in Poland's Stalinist era (1948–56), but they revived in the 1960s. By the 1970s, indeed, 1.5 million people were visiting Częstochowa annually. In 1977, of the 2 million who came to Częstochowa, 28,000 trekked on foot (50,000 in 1980).[76]

The Catholic Church's revived strength manifested itself in intensified resistance and opposition—displays that in turn reinforced the Church's waxing credibility and might. During the debate over proposed constitutional amendments in 1975–76, for instance, which would have added references to the "unshakeable and fraternal bonds with the Soviet Union" and to "the leading role of the Polish United Workers' Party," Wyszyński and Karol Cardinal Wojtyła of Kraków denounced the proposed amendments in their sermons.[77] Later, on 9 September 1976 the Polish episcopate issued a communiqué protesting against the prosecution of workers who had taken part in work stoppages the preceding June.[78] All too transparently, the Church was comporting itself as the champion of society against the state.

Communist authorities fought back in sundry ways. One mechanism the government used was censorship, which held the prospect of projecting substantial power. As part of a systematic effort to downplay the importance of the Catholic Church in Polish history, Poland's communist censors kept the names of many religious figures from Poland's past out of the press. Also prohibited was any mention of the Vatican; and limits were set as to what Catholics identified as Catholics could be reported to say about social problems such as alcoholism and hooliganism. "The censors were also instructed to see to it that Church publications did not discuss the role of the Church in community and educational work, even though it was perfectly legal. Detailed instructions prohibited coverage of various Catholic groups and movements in Poland."[79] The censors paid special attention to the Catholic print media. (The Church had no access to radio or television.) In fact, a specialized unit within the Polish censorship bureau devoted itself to scrutinizing religious periodicals and books. The other censors called the members of this unit "the Saints."[80]

But the Polish episcopate, unlike its equivalent in Bulgaria, refused to be cowed or silenced or erased from history. On 11 November 1978, in token of this refusal, the episcopate issued a pastoral letter in observance of the sixtieth anniversary of independence. Read from the pulpits, it declared:

The Polish nation never gave up this natural right of each nation to freedom, to self-determination within [its] own borders. . . . It is therefore imperative to keep reminding ourselves of this date, so important for our Nation—1918. Rightly then is the sixtieth anniversary of the regaining of our independence remembered. *The nation has the right to know the whole truth about its own history.*[81]

By the late 1970s the PUWP realized that it had no idea how it might effectively combat religion, as good Marxists were supposed to do, and that communist programs had failed to attenuate religious feeling. On the contrary, a survey of 4,969 citizens in 1978 found that 17.9 percent characterized themselves as "deep believers" with another 68.4 percent considering themselves "believers"—adding up to a total of 86.3 percent of Poles who subscribed to Church teachings. (The percentage of self-declared "Catholics" was tangibly higher than that of "believers" and "deep believers" combined.) Nonbelievers, on the other hand, made up a mere 6.5 percent of the sample.[82]

The PUWP began to beat a retreat. On 10 February 1976 the *Sejm* had amended the constitution of 22 July 1952. In its new incarnation, article 67 (formerly article 57) now stated: "The citizens of the Polish People's Republic have equal rights without regard to sex, birth, education, profession, nationality, race, creed, or social descent."[83] The communists viewed the Catholic Church "as a political force, whose operation interfered with the building of socialism or made it more difficult."[84] The sundry concessions by Gierek (see chapter 2) must be viewed in this light.

In the epigraph to this chapter Bohdan Cywiński observed in 1971 that the Julianic church "is never fully in solidarity with society, and never fully identifies with it," with the result that "it refuses to acknowledge the existence of any form of opposition other than those that it itself promotes and controls." If an independent opposition force should arise, Cywiński predicted, the Julianic Church will shy away from any form of collaboration with it against the state. As Cywiński concluded, "in its conflict with the secular rulers, the Julianic Church prefers to act alone, without partners, toward whom it feels no sense of solidarity."

Cywiński's analysis provides a useful guide to understanding the Church's dilemma with the emergence of the independent trade union Solidarity in the summer of 1980. Certainly the Church recognized that it shared certain ideals and programmatic goals with Solidarity. But it was not willing to be a mere "copilot," and it increasingly opted for the role of *mediator* between the communist state and Solidarity. But this assertion cannot be interpreted simplistically. After all, the Holy See passed funds to Solidarity and other opposition groups in Poland during 1980 and 1981, using Church offices and agencies as conduits. Some of the transferred funds came out of the budget of the Vatican's Institute for Religious Works.[85] But the Polish Church, now being steered by the uncharismatic Archbishop Józef Glemp (b. 1928), avoided an unambiguous embrace of the opposition and, at times, counseled docility. Glemp's statement immediately after the proclamation of martial law on 13 December 1981 shocked many. On that occasion he advised his listeners to trust General Wojciech Jaruzelski: "The authorities consider that the exceptional nature of martial law is dictated by higher necessity; it is the choice of a lesser rather than a greater evil. Assuming the correctness of such reasoning, the man in the street will subordinate himself to the new situation. . . ."[86] After that speech, Glemp started to be called "Comrade Glemp." In general, during the period of martial law (13 December 1981–22 July 1983) and after, the Church, headed now by Glemp, counseled against confrontation, participated ever more actively in negotiating forums with the state, and concentrated much of its energy on extracting concessions for itself.[87] This transformation in Church behavior did not escape public notice, as was found in a survey conducted in 1983. Asked whether the Church was more supportive of the government or of the opposition, some 24.2 percent of respondents said that the Church supported the government more often than it did the opposition, while only 6.5 percent felt that the Church was more supportive of the opposition. Almost a third of those questioned (29.6

percent) replied that the Church sometimes supported the government and sometimes the opposition—a response that presumed the same opportunism on the part of the Church as that entailed in the claim that the Church more often supported the government.[88]

The continuing strength of the Catholic Church in Poland has been explained in different ways by different scholars. Barbara Strassberg has chosen to emphasize the anthropocentric character of Polish religiosity, manifested in the cult of the Virgin Mary and the cult of the saints, as the key to understanding why "secularization" has led in the Polish context to the "deeper penetration of religion into the entire culture of the nation."[89] Vincent Chrypiński preferred a more traditional interpretation, ascribing "the success of Polish Catholicism in retaining the loyalty of the people to its religious authenticity and its union with national culture."[90] And I have suggested, in these pages, that the Church's independence of action, manifested at times in courageous resistance to state encroachment but likewise also in a shrinking from collaboration in opposition, has been a key factor in sustaining the Church's confidence, credibility, authority, and strength. But whatever differences of emphasis or interpretation there may be among scholars in their efforts to account for the Church's strength, none dispute that the Polish Church has been and remains a strong and politically effective institution.

The Legacy of Julianism

When a Julianic Church is given access to power, it is apt to become a *theocratic Church,* meaning that it will try to use state mechanisms to impose the rules and religious values of its own faith on everyone living in the territory of the given society, including those believers who subscribe to other faiths.

The election of Kraków's Cardinal Wojtyła to the papacy in 1978 and his subsequent pastoral visits to Poland also were influential in reinforcing the Church's social and political roles. (I have recounted this story elsewhere,[91] and another review of the details would serve no useful purpose, since the Catholic Church was already a Julianic Church *before* the era of the Polish pope.) What was clear to the Church by 1988 was that it was witnessing the dawn of an era of great opportunity, and it was determined to take full advantage of the new opportunities opened by the breakup of monopoly power.

The Church's first priority was to sweep the communists out of power.

Accordingly, in the spring 1989 elections, the Catholic hierarchy openly backed Solidarity candidates, providing office space, copy machines, and organizational advice, and using the pulpit to inform parishioners about election procedures. Some clergy members even showed up for Solidarity rallies and blessed Solidarity banners.[92] The Church realized immediate benefits. As early as 17 May 1989 new legislation governing religious matters granted the Roman Catholic Church full status as a legal person (a status withheld by the communists) and gave official sanction to the Church's various educational, cultural, and charitable activities, which hitherto had been pursued in the twilight zone of semi-illegality. The new legislation also assured the Church of its right to build facilities for its use, including hospitals, radio stations, and theaters, not to mention churches, and guaranteed the Church's legal right to operate private schools and seminaries.[93] As prime minister, Tadeusz Mazowiecki restored Catholic religious instruction in state schools, extended special tax breaks to the Church, and speeded up the return of properties confiscated from the Church ahead of the general schedule for other landowners. By August 1989 the restitution of confiscated Church properties had begun, and by the end of March 1994 the Church had obtained the return, inter alia, of some 45,000 acres of agricultural land.[94]

The Catholic Church now formulated a precise game plan, pushing for the restoration of Catholicism as the official state religion of Poland,[95] the introduction of Catholic religious instruction in public schools, the tightening of divorce laws, the proscription of abortion without exceptions of any kind, guarantees that "Christian values" (i.e., the values of the Roman Catholic Church) not be offended on the broadcast media, the redrafting of the constitution along lines pleasing to the Church, and the conclusion of a new concordat between the Holy See and the Polish government that would anchor some of these changes, along with other concessions, in a bilateral agreement. In early 1991 the Church succeeded in obtaining a tightening of divorce laws,[96] while de facto mandatory Catholic religious instruction was introduced in public schools in the fall of 1990 over the protests of non-Catholics and liberals alike. And while the Polish episcopate was constrained to withdraw its demand in May 1991 for the formal abrogation of the separation of Church and state,[97] it seemed to have achieved another of its chief goals in September 1993 when the lame-duck government of Prime Minister Hanna Suchocka approved and ratified a new concordat with the Vatican.[98] The Church even saw fit to attack sexual minorities. Homosexuality has been legal in Poland since the 1920s and had become a nonissue for the Polish public by the late communist era, if not before. The Church, however, has wanted to stigmatize homosexuality and has tried to make of it a public issue.[99] The Church also threw its weight against proposals to legalize gay and lesbian marriages.[100]

The Church's theocratic stridency has contributed to the polarization of Polish society. On the one hand, opinion polls show a decline in public confidence in the Church from 85 percent in 1990 to 41 percent in 1993, with 46 percent in 1993 expressing *disapproval* of the Church.[101] On the other hand, the Church has held onto its hardcore followers, radicalizing them. Wojciech Lamentówicz, a professor of law at Warsaw's Polish Academy of Sciences, spoke for many in warning that the Church was *reversing* the relationship between Church and state that had prevailed in the communist era. Accordingly, said Lamentówicz, "Now we have to protect democratic values . . . from a powerful authoritarian Church. The Church, which before had been the defender of the people, has become the new obstacle to self-expression."[102] "The logical consequence," Paul Hockenos explains, if the Catholic Church were to realize its agenda, would be "that all public space would come under the supervision of [a] strong, moral government, with the Church standing behind it as the final judge."[103]

One of the Church's earliest triumphs, as mentioned, was its success in getting Catholic religious instruction introduced into public school curricula. This success withstood an appeal to the Constitutional Tribunal submitted by ombudsman Tadeusz Zieliński; the court rejected the appeal.[104] At the same time, conservative Catholic prelates tried to have sex education removed from school curricula and, failing that, successfully blocked the adoption in 1994 of a comprehensive sex education syllabus developed by Zbigniew Lew-Starówicz, reported to be one of Poland's leading experts on sexology.[105]

From time to time, representatives of other faiths have complained of Catholic domination. For example, in April 1996 Orthodox Bishop Jeremiasz voiced objections before the Polish Ecumenical Council about Catholic priests allegedly forcing non-Catholics wishing to marry Catholics to convert to Catholicism and about difficulties in obtaining baptismal certificates for faiths other than Catholic.[106] Bogdan Tranda, a minister of the Evangelical Reformed Church in Warsaw, has claimed that,

many Protestants feel threatened by the increasing clericalization of everyday life. Everywhere—in political parties, in trade unions, in schools, in the army, in the hospital—they have to explain why they do not go to mass, do not receive Catholic communion; they have to explain that they are Protestants and that Protestants are [also] Christians. Many Protestants will tell that they honestly believe that nothing has in fact changed in the Roman Catholic Church and that the whole conciliar reform process is only a deceptive operation aimed at the Protestants.[107]

In these circumstances, many were surprised when Pope John Paul II in the course of his fifth papal visit to Poland (in May 1995) asserted that Polish Catholics were being "mocked and ridiculed," that they were victims of "an ever more powerful intolerance . . . spreading in public life and in the media," and that there was in Poland an "increasing tendency to marginalize [Catholics]."[108] Yet these sentiments were echoed less than two months later by a Fr. Czeslaw S. Bartnik, who alleged further that "the Church's spiritual existence is more endangered in our country than it was in the times of open Marxism."[109]

Without minimizing the strong emotions stirred up by disputes over same-sex relationships, divorce law, sex education, and mixed marriages —a set that has inspired parliamentary deputy Barbara Labuda of Wrocław to lament what she calls "the sex manias of Catholic clergy"[110]— or, for that matter, the controversy over religious instruction in public schools, the most inflammatory issues relating to the Church's agenda have been the controversies concerning (1) abortion, (2) the law on broadcasting, (3) the constitution, and (4) the draft concordat.

The Abortion Controversy: Act I

Abortion was legalized by the Polish communist regime in April 1956 for cases of medical necessity, economic hardship, or rape. In practice, abortion became readily available, and in the late 1980s and up to 1992 tens of thousands of legal abortions were performed annually.[111] The Church hierarchy never reconciled itself to this practice, and even during the communist era churchmen would periodically speak out against it. As early as the winter of 1988-89, while the Round Table discussions were still in progress, the Polish episcopate began to approach its supporters in the *Sejm* and in the opposition to press for an early abrogation of the 1956 law. In May 1989 Archbishop Glemp summoned Solidarity leader Wałęsa to his office to impress upon him the seriousness with which the Church regarded the high number of abortions in Poland. In the meantime, a *Sejm* committee had already taken up an abortion bill drafted by the episcopate. The Church promoted its case vigorously. "From May to June 1989 virtually every one of Poland's twenty most popular Catholic magazines devoted significant coverage to the evils of abortion and the virtues of natural family planning"[112] — "natural" meaning, of course, without recourse to contraceptives. But in December 1989 thirty-seven members of the new Senate asked that the debate be allowed to continue. While this debate was still in progress, the ministry of health announced in May 1990 that contraceptives no longer would be covered by national health insurance; overnight, this made contraceptives significantly more expensive. In the same announcement the ministry publicized new guidelines for abortion, restricting its availability.[113] Meanwhile, parish groups (of lay activists) pressured pharmacists to remove contraceptives from their shelves; those who refused to comply were criticized by name during church services.[114]

At the same time, the episcopate was exerting pressure on the Senate, and by September 1990 the Senate had adopted a restrictive bill on abortion. The measure now went before the *Sejm*. Pro-abortion activists were aware of the Church's considerable influence in the parliament and tried to arrange a national referendum on the measure. They collected more than 1 million signatures within less than three weeks, demanding a referendum.[115] Opinion polls taken at the time consistently showed that about 80 percent of Poles thought that abortion should be legally available, at least under certain circumstances.[116] But the episcopate wanted no compromise and urged the government to ignore calls for a referendum and to legislate the mandatory imposition of two-year prison terms on physicians performing abortions or on women performing abortions on themselves — with no exceptions. "[Our beliefs about] human life cannot be the subject of any kind of referendum," read a statement issued by the leadership of the pro-clerical Christian Democratic Party.[117] In November 1992 the *Sejm* settled on a draft bill that, among other things, excluded any and all prenatal tests.[118] This exclusion was later dropped. Against protests from the episcopate, the draft bill allowed that abortions could be performed in cases of rape or incest.[119]

Returning from Christmas vacation, the *Sejm* passed the antiabortion law on 7 January; the Senate ratified the *Sejm*'s version on 30 January by a vote of 35 to 34, with 20 abstentions.[120] President Wałęsa signed the measure into law on 15 February 1993.[121] Under this law, abortion would be allowed in only four situations:

when a panel of doctors certifies that the pregnancy endangers the mother's life or seriously threatens her health;

when a prosecutor certifies the pregnancy is the result of rape or incest;

when the fetus is determined by pre-natal tests to be seriously, irreparably damaged;

and during the course of emergency action if needed to save the mother's life.[122]

The Church had fought against all of these exceptions, viewing prenatal life as beyond compromise. But the exception considered most important by foes of prohibition, namely, in cases of financial difficulty, was not accepted by the legislature. Yet, as Senator Zofia Kuratówska noted, financial considerations were the main reason for about 90 percent of all abortions in Poland.[123]

In a society in which only 6–7 percent of Polish women use any kind of contraceptives,[124] the consequences of this legislation soon became clear. Women who could afford it contacted local travel bureaus and booked so-called "abortion vacations" to less restrictive countries. Less pecunious women either obtained illegal abortions, sometimes under less than sanitary conditions, or handled the matter themselves. While only 786 legal abortions were performed in 1994[125] and 559 in 1995,[126] the number of illegal abortions was several times as great. Where unwilling mothers were unable to obtain abortions, they sometimes threw their newborn babies into rivers or rubbish dumps (as 162 women did in 1994)[127] or abandoned their infants in hospitals (as 738 mothers did in 1995)[128] or sold them to foreigners.[129] As of 1995, 67 percent of children were being raised in families in which one of the parents was unable to find permanent work.[130] And while the government is legally obliged to extend economic assistance to pregnant women and women with infants, a report filed in mid-1995 found that "the number of pregnant women with difficult living conditions is increasing at a faster rate than the pool of money set aside for such assistance can handle."[131] Meanwhile, many state-run nurseries have been closed for budgetary reasons, leaving many women without acceptable alternatives. Not surprisingly, survey data collected in 1992–93 had found that most Poles wanted abortion to be available in cases of financial hardship;[132] a similar poll conducted in June 1994 found that 70 percent of Poles favored a relaxation of the abortion law.[133]

With the changes in the composition of parliament produced by the elections of September 1993, progressive deputies made an attempt to pass an amendment making allowances for financial difficulties. Defying insistent homilies from the pulpit, the *Sejm* approved a set of amendments to the bill in June 1994 by a vote of 241 to 107, with 32 abstentions.[134] In response, the Polish episcopate let fire a blistering cannonade: "Legalizing murder of the unborn," the bishops warned,

does not in any way alter the moral judgment of the act: evil remains evil, a sin remains a sin, and murder remains murder.

This [legislation] constitutes an open violation of natural law, of the first and most fundamental right to life inscribed in the conscience of humans and in the commandment: "Thou shalt not kill," and hence a great challenge to men of honesty and to the predominantly religious nation. In endorsing such legislation, the state is contradicting the very purpose of its existence, which is to protect and promote the natural rights of individuals and assist citizens in performing their duties.[135]

Yet in spite of this protest, the Polish Senate approved the amendments on 1 July by a vote of 40 to 36, with 4 abstentions.[136] Wałęsa vetoed the measure on 4 July, as expected; legislators now needed a two-thirds majority to override the veto. The *Sejm* met on 2 September and voted 232 to 157, with 22 abstentions, to override Wałęsa's veto, failing of its purpose by 42 votes.[137]

The Law on Broadcasting

Legislative action on a new law on radio and television broadcasting overlapped that relating to abortion, with the result that a new law was passed by the *Sejm* on 15 October 1992 and published on 29 January 1993. Controversy centered on the Catholic Church's insistence that the media had no right "to obscure and ridicule the values of Christianity and Polish national culture,"[138] and that the legislature should insert a clause into the bill that would require broadcast media to respect "Christian values."[139] The Church had its way, and the eventual law includes these passages:

Article 18

1. Broadcasts may not advocate activities conflicting with the laws, the Polish raison d'etre, or attitudes and views conflicting with morality and the common good.

2. Broadcasts should respect the religious feelings of audiences, and, in particular, they should respect the Christian system of values.

3. Broadcasts that may endanger the psychological, emotional, or physical

well-being of children and youth may not be disseminated between 0600 and 2300 hours.

4. The National Council, by issuing an executive order, may define specific guidelines for the dissemination of the broadcasts referred to in Paragraph 3.[140]

As for the "National Council" (or more properly, the National Radio and Television Council) which would have the authority to issue specific guidelines and prepare legal action for the courts, two of its eight members have close ties with the Church, while a third member served as a senator of the Polish Peasant Party, a party known for its strong sympathy with Church views.[141]

What kinds of issues have come up? One of the earliest complaints generated by this law came from the Catholic periodical *Slowo*, "which objected to the broadcasting of a program about Jehovah's Witnesses 'in a Catholic country' on Good Friday."[142] Sexual subjects, of course, have been a high priority of the Church, which lodged a formal complaint against the "PolSat" station because it objected to a talk show featuring transsexuals.[143] For that matter, several Church-linked groups initiated legal action against the Polish distributor of *The Priest* (1994), a British film about the moral dilemmas of a gay clergyman.[144] Catholic conservatives also have tried to use the law to enforce adherence to Church-approved vocabulary, raising a storm in July 1995 about the use of the expression "antiabortion law" on public television.[145]

The Constitution: Act I

The adoption of a constitution appropriate to Poland's new politics has been delayed, chiefly because of continued disputes between the Catholic Church hierarchy and its experts and supporters on the one side and progressive legislators and experts on the other. Among other things, the Church has wanted the constitution to begin with the invocation, "In the name of Almighty God," to include (in the preamble) a description of Poland as a Christian and Catholic country, and to guarantee the protection of human life "from the moment of conception until natural death."[146] In consequence, the bishops have objected to drafts in which there are references to the state being secular,[147] although if it is not to be a secular state, it can only be a religious one.[148]

At one point, the Church agreed to the inclusion of a clause affirming the separation of Church and state. For obvious reasons, Poland's other religious denominations have been eager to see such a constitutional clause. But in February 1995 the episcopate withdrew its consent to the formulation.[149] The government, led since September 1993 by a coalition of the Democratic Left Alliance (SLD) and the Polish Peasant Party (PSL), attempted to accommodate the Catholic Church, dropped the reference to the separation of Church and state, and proposed, as a compromise, to include a phrase alluding to the neutrality of the state's "worldview."[150] This also was deemed unacceptable by Church leaders.[151]

In May 1995 the text of a constitutional draft of 12 April 1995 was published. Article 16, which concerned religious affairs, guaranteed equal treatment for all religious associations, affirmed the Polish government's "impartial[ity] on matters concerning religious, personal, and philosophical beliefs," and asserted that Church-state relations should be founded on "the principles of respect for mutual autonomy and [the] independence of each within its own [sphere]."[152] The draft failed to include an invocation to God.

Poland's Catholic bishops met for a three-day plenary conference in June to consider the draft constitution. At the end of the conference, the episcopate released a statement: "A reference to God in the opening sentences of the constitution *guarantees* that human dignity is protected. Man is not the highest authority in laying down laws. Lawmaking, if it is to be binding for human conscience, must correspond to natural law."[153] Archbishop Józef Michalik, head of the episcopal team that had prepared a provisional report (to the conference) on the constitution, elaborated on this point for the Catholic Information Agency: "The vision of liberty [this draft constitution] contains," Michalik said, "is unacceptable. 'Everything that is not forbidden is allowed.' That is absurd. . . . The draft is unacceptable in its current form. It is nihilistic and underlying it is an appeal to fight all that is moral."[154] Only in June 1996 did the two sides soften their respective stances, at least on this issue, and move toward compromise (see below).

Religious War in Poland: The Concordat

Back in July 1993 the Catholic Church thought that the concordat was essentially wrapped up. But the parliamentary elections of September 1993 handed conservative parties a major setback, and the new, more progressive parliament immediately raised questions. To begin with, the draft concordat, as signed on 28 July 1993 by the Polish foreign minister and the papal nuncio, proved to be incompatible with sixteen existing Polish laws, two codices, and many decrees.[155] Then there was the problem that non-Catholic religious associations claimed that the draft concordat would grant the Catholic Church special privileges not accorded to other faiths.[156] There were some practical difficulties as well since under a 1989 law, where no municipal cemetery is available, the local Catholic parish cemetery is to be made available for the burial of deceased non-Catholics; the concordat, however, guarantees the "inviolability" of Church cemeteries. Or again, under the concordat, medical care facilities run by non-Catholic religious associations would be obliged to admit Catholic chaplains.[157]

As questions and concerns arose, one after the other, the pressure for postponement grew. Aleksander Malachówski, deputy speaker of the *Sejm*, put it simply. In his view, the Suchocka government's endorsement of the draft concordat in its given form was an "enormous" mistake, which could only provoke difficulties.[158] On 1 July 1994 the deputies of the *Sejm* voted 201 to 181 to postone ratification of the concordat, pending further study and renewed negotiations with the Holy See.[159]

Poland's primate, Cardinal Glemp, reacted with an expression of rage. "The Church wants peace, but the Church is not afraid of war," Glemp told *Gazeta Wyborcza*.[160] Bishop Tadeusz Pieronek, secretary of the Episcopal Conference of Poland, drew practical conclusions: "We now have an atmosphere which compels the Catholic Church to mobilize its forces and close ranks."[161] "It's the start of a religious war," said Ryszard Czarnecki of the Christian National Union.[162] The following month, the cardinal urged that Catholic Action quickly be set up in Poland.[163] SLD leader Aleksander Kwaśniewski responded to the cardinal's allusion to war. "I understand that there are issues on which the Church hierarchy and [the] current majority in Parliament may hold different viewpoints," Kwaśniewski said. "But this should not lead to a state of war, since this would imply that the Church is ready to accept democratic structures only so long as they act accordingly to its will."[164] This explanation did not impress some of the bishops, who described parliament as a "sick embryo," referring to its deputies as "mules."[165]

On whose behalf would the Church fight its war? According to an opinion poll conducted on the eve of the vote, only 17 percent of Poles favored ratification of the concordat in its draft form. Another 17 percent favored ratifying the concordat after appropriate amendments had been made (the *Sejm*'s position), while 22 percent opposed the concordat altogether.[166]

As Church prelates continued to criticize the *Sejm,* ascribing bad faith and ill will to the deputies, the *Sejm* closed ranks. "The bishops are suffering from megalomania," deputy Barbara Labuda charged.[167] "They tried to force us to approve the Concordat . . . on our knees, as it were," declared Ryszard Bugaj, leader of the Labor Union.[168] For all that, Kwaśniewski expressed confidence at one point that the concordat would be ratified by the end of 1994.

But the parliament failed to meet this deadline, and while parliamentary committees continued to sort through the sundry points of incompatibility between the concordat and Polish law, Polish bishops repeatedly used the word "arrogance" to characterize the parliament's attitude.[169] Archbishop Ignacy Tokarczuk claimed, at one point, that the government was working against the nation.[170] In October 1995 Bishop Pieronek chose to dramatize his latest criticism of the parliament by delivering his rebuke from the crypt of the Katowice Cathedral of Christ the King.[171]

As the parliament searched for a compromise formula, some speakers criticized SLD leaders for conceding too much to the Church.[172] But when the parliament finally offered its compromise formulations to the episcopate for review, the latter rejected them as incompatible with the spirit of the concordat.[173]

The presidential elections of November 1995 were conducted, thus, in an atmosphere of a declared religious war. The Church at first backed Hanna Gronkiewicz-Waltz, the president of the National Bank of Poland, candidate of the Saint Catherine Covenant, and firm advocate of the Church's interests. But Gronkiewicz-Waltz's support sank dramatically from 19 percent to 10 percent between September and October, while Wałęsa's support rose from 14 percent to 21 percent in the same period.[174] The Church therefore switched its support to Wałęsa. The bishops were unrestrained in their support of the former Solidarity leader, demonizing SLD candidate Kwaśniewski as "anti-religious," "anti-God," and "neo-pagan."[175] But for all that, Kwaśniewski won and the Church found itself facing the necessity of working with a president it had all but characterized as the Antichrist.[176]

In the wake of the 1995 presidential elections, President-elect Kwaśniewski held out an olive branch to the Church, but he called for further bilateral talks with the Holy See with regard to the concordat. However, Bishop Pieronek, speaking on behalf of the episcopate, ruled out further talks, "because, in his opinion, the Episcopate had already devoted too much time to the issue and had not been treated seriously."[177]

As of March 1996, Church and state remained at loggerheads. Bishop Pieronek had accurately stated (in September 1995) that "the war over the Concordat is a war of religion."[178]

The SLD-PSL coalition had, by then, fallen apart, almost entirely because of differences over the concordat and Church-related clauses in the constitutional draft. The SLD and its new coalition partner, the Social Democracy of the Polish Republic (sdRP), have remained in agreement that ratification of the concordat should follow, and not precede, the eventual adoption of the constitution.[179] Over the protests of the Church and, for that matter, of the Polish foreign minister, the parliament confirmed this schedule in July 1996 by a vote of 199 to 170.[180]

The Constitution: Act II

Soon after becoming president, Kwaśniewski began to back away from the tough anticlerical positions he had embraced during his campaign and sought to curry favor with the Church. In so doing, he earned the opprobrium of some of his erstwhile colleagues in the SLD.[181] Insisting all the same on the need for compromise, Kwaśniewski seemed to have secured a truce in the "religious war" as of June 1996 through direct talks with Cardinal Glemp. The compromise that seemed to be calming tempers involved allowing the Church to have its way with the preamble (thereby adding the words, "In the name of Almighty God") while retaining unaltered the draft of article 16 (as prepared in April 1995).[182]

The Abortion Controversy: Act II

If Church-state tensions seemed to be abating where the constitution was concerned, relations between the two institutions remained strained regarding abortion. After the presidential elections of November 1995, the parliament once more took up the abortion issue. Progressive-minded deputy Izabela Jaruga-Nowacka presented a draft bill on 1 March 1996 that would allow women to obtain an abortion until the twelfth week of pregnancy if financial difficulties or other personal problems were present.[183] In mid-March the measure withstood a minority motion to scrap it.[184]

By early June the *Sejm* subcommittee entrusted with the preparation of amendments to the abortion bill was nearing the end of its work. The committee proposed to make abortion available where financial hardship was an issue (during the first twelve weeks of pregnancy), to restore partial subsidization of contraceptives, to increase the maximum penalty for violation of this liberalized law to ten years' imprisonment, and to introduce sex education throughout the Polish public school system.[185] Archbishop Józef Michalik of Przemyśl said the draft amendments proved that the "libertarian-socialist parliamentarians" were "plotting against morality, the family, and the Church."[186] Sex education, he asserted, had no place in a school system, since it could only be "intended to . . . boost the sexual instincts of children and youth."[187] The Polish Federation of Pro-Life Movements, a Catholic front organization, echoed these sentiments, suggesting that instead of sex education, Polish schoolchildren should be given courses oriented to preparing them for family life, including such information as how to bring up their eventual children.[188] The *Sejm* ignored these and other protests and continued with its work, putting the bill into final form on 9 July.[189]

By this point, Glemp was delivering homilies on the subject, the Polish Catholic Lawyers' Association had issued a manifesto condemning the allegedly "anti-Catholic" policy of the government,[190] and progressives had defeated a last-ditch effort by a cluster of conservative parties on 28 August to scuttle the bill. Had the conservatives succeeded, they would have removed it from the agenda without submitting it to a vote.[191] Some two thousand antiabortion activists demonstrated outside the parliament building on 29 August, the day before the vote. The next day, the *Sejm* approved the bill by a vote of 208 to 61, with 15 abstentions and 120 deputies absent.[192] The Polish primate compared the measure to World War II, and he called it "an act of hostility towards those who honor Mary and follow Christ."[193] Speaking from his summer residence in Castelgandolfo, the pope, his voice quivering with emotion, lamented, "A nation which kills its own children is a nation without hope!"[194]

President Kwaśniewski also spoke after the vote, praising the measure as a step to counteract the hypocrisy of the earlier bill, which had immediately spawned a large "abortion underground." Kwaśniewski also suggested that legislation was a misguided way to combat abortion and urged, rather, that "treating women as individuals and as partners in marriage is the way to make the problem of abortion disappear. I will be happy if the problem of abortion ceases to exist, because that is the whole point."[195]

The Polish Episcopate mounted pressure to block final approval of the bill, organizing a demonstration in which more than 50,000 faithful took part.[196] On 4 October the Senate (the upper house of the bicameral legislature) reversed the *Sejm*'s verdict, rejecting the liberalization measure by a vote of 52 to 40.[197] Three weeks later, ignoring protest meetings involving several thousand antiabortion activists, the *Sejm* overturned the Senate's rejection with a vote of 228 to 195 with 16 abstentions.[198] Bishop Leszek Sławoj Głodz, the chief army chaplain, stirred up a storm in the wake of this vote by describing it as an "aggression against Polish independence," and by suggesting that the vote "called into question the state authorities' right to give orders to soldiers."[199] President Kwaśniewski duly signed the bill on 20 November, but even before he did so, Solidarity spokespersons promised to challenge the liberalized law before the Constitutional Tribunal.[200]

Et Abundantia in Turribus Tuis

The Roman Catholic Church of Poland is ideologically more diverse than this account has revealed, with clearly identifiable liberal and conservative camps.[201] But two points should be remembered. First, the so-called "liberals" of the Catholic Church are tangibly more conservative than the progressives of the SLD and agree with Church conservatives on several important points (including abortion). Second, conservative sentiment prevails at the Episcopate, and it is the Episcopate that has defined the dialogue—if one may call it that—between the Church and the state. The sheer predominance of conservative sentiment in the upper echelons of the Polish Church simultaneously reflects worldwide tendencies during the papacy of John Paul II and also may be, as Krzysztof Krzyzewski has suggested, "the product of totalitarian rule, an ideological current which surfaced as a reaction to the communist threat and which turned against democratic values once the totalitarian system was toppled."[202] If Krzyzewski's analysis is correct, liberal Catholicism's rather obvious present disadvantage may, thus, be partly attributable to the effects of communism.

Two rather different cases have been brought together in this chapter to suggest that historical trajectories may traverse distinct historical epochs and that patterns set under one system may carry over or exert influence into the next. The Bulgarian Orthodox Church, which worked within the frameworks set by the Sublime Porte, the monarchy, and the communists, found that its credibility and strength steadily

ebbed, leaving the Church divided, vulnerable, fearful of proselytization by foreign-based missionaries, and forced to the defensive. The
Polish Catholic Church, by contrast, which identified itself with anti-
tsarist and anti-Hohenzollern resistance from 1795 to 1918 and with
anticommunist defiance (1945–89), keeping its distance as well from the
Piłsudski regime of 1926–35, entered into the postcommunist era with
enormous credibility, an aura of legitimacy (partially squandered since
then), a united hierarchy, and an offensive posture. The contrast could
not be more striking.

Chapter 13

Nihil Obstat: The Rise of Nontraditional Religions

In all countries of the region, as long as the communists were in power, strict controls were maintained in the religious sphere. Religious organizations were required to meet regularly with state officials with supervisory responsibility for religion, to obtain building permits before undertaking any new construction, and to obtain "sacerdotal licenses" for clergy. In some cases, staff transfers and promotions, entries into the seminary, seminary curricula, and even parish bulletins were closely supervised and controlled. In Czechoslovakia the newspaper *Katolické noviny* was controlled by the state and regularly articulated views opposite those of the Catholic primate. In Hungary, Romania, and Bulgaria the larger Churches were expected to support state policies actively and vociferously, and every issue of *Romanian Church News,* for example, included a ritualized paean to the wisdom and magnificence of Nicolae Ceauşescu. Those religions which could not (or did not want to) obtain state approval had to contend with such developments as the bulldozing of unapproved church buildings, the harassment of believers, the beating of clergy, and even the occasional murder of priests and pastors. Approved religious organizations also were sometimes subjected to these measures, especially in the case of outspoken antiregime clergy. The case of Fr. Jerzy Popiełuszko, abducted and killed by Polish secret police in October 1984,[1] serves as an apt illustration of this possibility. For religious organizations such as the Nazarenes and the Jehovah's Witnesses, survival in communist Eastern Europe meant having to contend with the constant threat of imprisonment, their refusal to bear arms being perhaps the most important reason for the harshness of the penalties they faced.

To members of disadvantaged religions, and especially to nonindigenous religions which had experienced difficulty in establishing firm bases in the region, the collapse of communism signaled a dramatic new opportunity. Religion once again was no mere "private affair of the individual," as the communists always put it, but energetically pushed its way into the public arena. Whether one talks of the more established religious organizations such as the Catholic, Lutheran, and Orthodox

Churches or of more newly established organizations such as the Baptists and Methodists, or fresh entrants into the religious competition, such as the Baha'i and the Unification Church (the so-called "Moonies"), the collapse of communism has meant a significant expansion of the possibilities for proselytization and other religious activity.

The activity of Protestant missionaries from nonindigenous Churches and sects was discussed in chapter 11. But not only did "neo-Protestants" expand their activity in this area. Membership in nontraditional religious associations also has mushroomed in the region, and as of 1993 472,334 members of such associations resided in Eastern Europe (excluding eastern Germany) and the former Soviet Union. The highest concentrations of nontraditional membership were found in Poland (258,861 members), the former USSR (89,311), and Romania (50,801).[2] Data compiled by the *East-West Church and Ministry Report* of Wheaton College include Jehovah's Witnesses and Mormons in figures for nontraditional religious associations, referring to them as "cults" and "sects." The terms "cult" and "sect" have been avoided here because some people find them offensive. Also avoided is the common substitute "new religious movement," which reveals judgmental bias, both by including as "new" some associations older than some of those not counted as "new" and by referring to these groupings with the loaded word "movement." Using the Wheaton College figures (excluding those for the Jehovah's Witnesses and Mormons, which were included in the chapter 11 discussion) and breaking them down by religious association, there were 166,800 Hare Krishnas in the region as of 1993 (150,000 in Poland), 5,000 Scientologists (all in Hungary), 4,931 Baha'i (3,500 of these in the former USSR and 601 in Romania), 2,000 Children of God in Bulgaria and additional but unspecified numbers of "Children" in Russia and the Czech Republic, 900 members of the Unification Church of the Rev. Sun Myung Moon (all in the former USSR), and 800 Brahma Kumaris (all in the former USSR).[3]

In fact, these statistics are both incomplete and already outdated. For example, the statistics omit the Theosophist Society, which established a presence in Yugoslavia as early as 1924, while they predate plans by Scientologists for a big push into Albania in the spring of 1994.[4]

Inevitably, alternative religious organizations, each claiming to have a uniquely valid insight into morality and life, come into conflict. This is especially the case between traditional religious organizations and nontraditional associations, such as Scientology, which preach radically new concepts about gender relations and individual behavior.[5] But the very appearance and growth of nontraditional religious associations may be taken as symptoms of fundamental changes in values, assumptions, and needs, changes which are then channeled, satisfied, legitimated, and reinforced by the new religions.

One is struck by the sheer diversity that is emerging in the religious sector. After decades during which traditional Churches faced virtually no competition—thanks to the vigilance of the communist power monopoly—these established Churches are now confronted with a rich array of both exogenous and indigenous religious organizations, some offering to sharpen one's business skills (e.g., Scientology), some offering healing (e.g., the Faith Church), others offering salvation (e.g., the White Brotherhood), and still others offering "the wisdom of the East" (e.g., Oriental associations and mystic sects). Three factors account for this sudden frenzy of activity. To begin with, the communist control and surveillance mechanism artificially held back processes normal in modern society, resulting in a situation of a growing but unsatisfied demand for nontraditional religion. Second, the abrupt lifting of controls in the religious sphere has prodded exogenous religious organizations into a frenetic race to take advantage of the new opportunities, resulting in the religious equivalent of a bull market. And third, the psychological, social, political, and economic uncertainties created by the collapse of the old system and—in most countries of the region—by escalating class differences have stirred up levels of stress that appear to be best treated by magic, faith, miracles, and even the occult. Psychologist Adam Rozenblatt, an American based in Moscow, noted that people "are completely disoriented in the fast-changing Russian society."[6] Scarcity may also play a role. Rodney Stark and William Sims Bainbridge find the terms "cult" and "sect" to be more useful for their purposes. Differentiating between religious groups in low tension with society or no tension at all ("Churches") and religious groups in high tension ("sects" and "cults"), Stark and Bainbridge note that "low-tension religious groups are unable to provide as efficacious compensators for scarcity as high-tension groups readily offer."[7] Receptivity to extraordinary religious experiences also may be induced by sudden changes in reality that leave ordinary people confused and feeling adrift. As Paul Theroux, a noted novelist, has said, "People are vulnerable to messianic personalities and fad cures when there is a confusion between reality and virtual reality" or between a receding reality and an emerging reality.[8]

In the following pages, I shall examine some of the new religious phenomena of Eastern Europe and Russia under these headings: apocalyptic associations; faith healing and psychic healing; channeling; Satanism; occultism; Eastern faiths and associations; nontraditional Christian associations and other religious phenomena.

Apocalyptic Associations

Apocalyptic associations are distinguished from other religious phenomena by three central features: (1) their belief that the world is about to end (and usually, that the exact date of the day of judgment and resurrection can be precisely calculated); (2) a deemphasized liturgy and a corresponding emphasis on events related to the end of the world (whether awaiting it or provoking it); and, at least in some cases, (3) a belief that God is physically present in the world (usually entailing the claim that the leader or deputy of the cult is God Incarnate).

The three most important apocalyptic associations to surface in the Russian-East European region since 1989 are the White Brotherhood (centered in Ukraine, but, at its peak, counting followers in Poland, Moldova, Russia, Belarus, Kazakhstan, Canada, the United States, Israel, and perhaps other countries in Europe);[9] the Mother of God Center; and the Aum Shinrikyo sect (founded in Japan, but by 1995 having more adherents in Russia than in Japan). In addition, mention should be made of the Messengers of the Holy Grail, a nontraditional religious association with some Czech following.

The Mother of God Center

Very little is known about the Mother of God Center (*Bogorodechnyi*). The association traces its origins to 1985, when a former monk named Ioann Bereslavskii, a specialist on the ancient East and India, had a vision of the Mother of God in his apartment in Smolensk. Teaching that the era of "the Third Testament" is at hand and that two more "comings" will occur, Bereslavskii opened an office in Moscow, subsequently consecrating two bishops to assist him: Tikhon and Lazar.[10] Since 1990 the association has set up branches in many cities and towns across Russia, Ukraine, and Belarus. After moving its headquarters from Moscow to St. Petersburg, the center was renamed the Church of the Transfiguring Mother of God. Bereslavsky claims to receive six or seven revelations from the Virgin Mary each month, and he teaches that Mary appeared in the sky above the parliament building during the August 1991 coup attempt and "saved" Russia. The association places the Virgin Mary at the center of its worship and insists on women's enrollment, preaching hatred of women who decline to join the organization. Bereslavsky condemns marriage, childbearing, and family, and he portrays conception and birth as sins of lechery. While prophesying an early and rapidly approaching doomsday, the Church is said to encourage children to tear up photographs of their mothers. Membership figures are not available.[11]

The White Brotherhood of Maria Devi Khristos

The White Brotherhood — or, as it is sometimes called, the Great White Brotherhood — has been far more conspicuous. Led by former Komsomol official Mariya Krivonogova Tsvigun ("Jesus Christ Reincarnate," or sometimes, more simply, "The Living God") and milling-machine operator Yuri Krivonogov ("the second John the Baptist"), the association grew out of Krivonogov's sermons but took off only when Tsvigun joined up with this self-styled "John the Baptist." The turning point for Tsvigun came on 20 April 1990, about two weeks after her thirtieth birthday, when she submitted to the latest in a long string of abortions. To still her pain, nurses gave her an extra-powerful dose of anesthetic. The anesthetic was known to have hallucinogenic properties, and shortly after Tsvigun's abortion the hospital abandoned the procedure. As for Tsvigun, she suffered an overdose, actually died a clinical death in the hospital, but then revived, looking calm but strangely beautiful. When her friends tried to talk to her, she replied, "I am not Mariya. I am God."[12] The association now refers to 11 April as the "Day of the Great Explanation of the Planetary Logos of Jesus Christ into the body of the Mother of the World (Mother of God) Maria Devi Khristos."[13] She subsequently left her spouse, Mykola, and took Krivonogov as her second husband. The association took shape before the end of 1990 and was formally registered in March 1991. In addition to Tsvigun and Krivonogov, twenty-seven-year-old Vitaly Sidorov played a key role in the association, serving as its first "archbishop." He was replaced in this capacity by Vitaly Kovalchuk.

The White Brotherhood combined quasi-Orthodox symbology with mantra-chanting, and authorities at first viewed it as benign. By 1992 the association was already prophesying the end of the world, and at that point authorities decided to ban it.

But conditions in Ukraine were uniquely propitious for a doomsday cult. As of 1993, economic production was shrinking at a rate of 15-

20 per cent per month![14] "Economically and intellectually, the country looks as if a tornado has hit it," Juliusz Urbanówicz of the *Warsaw Voice* commented in 1993. "[And] so far, there's nothing to suggest that reconstruction is taking place."[15] Economic disorganization, combined with hyperinflation, shrinking income, political uncertainty, and widespread concern for the future, made doomsday appear a plausible—indeed, all too real—eventuality.

The association started recruiting heavily among children. In February 1992 Tsvigun, who by now styled herself Mariya Devi Khristos, and Krivonogov, who had taken to calling himself Ioann Swami, turned up in Yaroslavl. The children of Yaroslavl could relate to this message of doom and resurrection, and by June they were abandoning school and parents to follow these new prophets.[16] Predictably cast as the "Pied Pipers" of Ukraine,[17] the two leaders of the White Brethren were soon being sought by the criminal investigation department on charges of kidnapping. The brotherhood turned up in Donetsk in 1993 and was said to have recruited about twenty members in Lebork, a town in northern Poland.[18]

Tsvigun and Krivonogov announced that the end of the world would take place on 24 November 1993; then, a short time later, they came forward and "confessed" that they had made an error in their mathematical computations. The end of the world was advanced to 14 November. Tsvigun, who had been thirty years old at the time of her fateful abortion, became obsessed with the symbolism of her age (since, according to popular tradition, Jesus Christ had likewise begun to preach at age thirty), and she became increasingly convinced that she would be crucified by nonbelievers on the day of reckoning itself. As of November 1993 she would be thirty-three—the same age as Christ, according to tradition, when he was crucified. She forecast that she would lie in her tomb for three days, and on the third day she would rise to heaven together with 144,000 "saints." These saints were taken to be her followers.[19] The number 144,000 was the number of saved souls specified in the Book of Revelation, where it says,

And I heard the number of them which were sealed: and there were sealed an hundred and forty and four thousand of all the tribes of the children of Israel.[20]

Elsewhere in Revelation one finds:

And I looked, and lo, a Lamb stood on the mount Sion, and with him an hundred forty and four thousand, having his Father's name written in their foreheads. . . . And they sung as it were a new song before the throne, and before the four beasts, and the elders: and no man could learn that song but the hundred and forty and four thousand, which were redeemed from the earth.[21]

Meanwhile, estimates of the brotherhood's membership varied widely. TASS reported that, altogether, only about 3,200 members of the White Brotherhood resided in Ukraine as of November 1993; they were said to be organized into some thirty cells or branches.[22] The Ukrainian ministry of the interior, however, estimated the membership of the association at 150,000 for the very same month[23] — a figure based on a misreading of the association's opaque citations of Revelation[24] — while White Brethren themselves set the figure as high as 200,000 worldwide.[25]

As the preannounced doomsday approached, the Ukrainian interior ministry announced that it was bracing for a rash of illegal activity, including mass suicide and unspecified "provocations."[26] Metropolitan Filaret of the Ukrainian Orthodox Church denounced Tsvigun, alias Mariya Devi Khristos, as "the Antichrist."[27] For his part, Krivonogov claimed that the Russian and Ukrainian Orthodox Churches were operated by the KGB and controlled by Satan; in his view, Russian President Boris Yeltsin was the "Antichrist."[28]

In the weeks preceding 14 November, posters of Mariya Devi Khristos clothed in a white robe were put up by the White Brotherhood in cities across Ukraine, Russia, and Belarus. In St. Petersburg and Moscow, metro travelers found White Brotherhood posters plastered on station walls. Toward the end of October police began to round up association members, and by 3 November some 488 White Brethren were being held in protective custody.[29] By 14 November the number of association members in detention had risen to 570; 300 of them had begun a hunger strike to protest their incarceration.[30] But White Brethren continued to stream from Russia and Belarus into Kiev. At one point, Ukrainian government officials summoned Russia's ambassador to Kiev to complain that Moscow was doing nothing to prevent the influx of Russian members of the association across the Russo-Ukrainian border. The Ukrainian ministry of foreign affairs also alerted the Russian ambassador to the fact that the White Brotherhood's leaflets (in 500,000 copies) had been printed in Russia.[31]

On 1 November hundreds of devotees of the association gathered in Bogdan Khmelnitsky Square in downtown Kiev to begin a two-week prayer vigil that was supposed to culminate in the apocalypse. Police moved in "to keep order," and inevitably they attacked association members, while some three thousand bystanders watched.[32] Police and association members engaged in a second brawl on 10 November when members entered the cathedral, where they grabbed fire extinguishers and sprayed foam at the police, in the process damaging priceless icons. Police took another sixty association members into custody after the violence.[33]

One might well ask, Why would Christ want to be reincarnated specifically as a *Ukrainian*, and why would the association's members consider it important to assemble on Bogdan Khmelnitsky Square for the Day of Judgment? Both questions seemed to be answered by the association's claim that Kiev's St. Sophia Cathedral (located on Bogdan Khmelnitsky Square) is "the closest point to the cosmos"[34]—whatever that was supposed to mean.[35]

Police expected tens of thousands of association members to descend on St. Sofia Cathedral on 14 November and took appropriate security precautions, including obtaining authorization from Ukrainian President Kravchuk to expel from the capital all persons lacking a Kiev residence permit.[36] Police also seized about twenty tons of religious literature in the association's possession. In the event, however, only some three hundred people turned out for the day of judgment. Tsvigun and Krivonogov led about sixty of their followers into the cathedral, presumably to seize control of it. In the ensuing tumult, Tsvigun and Krivonogov were taken into custody and imprisoned.[37] Association members still at liberty now declared that the revised estimate had been based on a miscalculation and returned to the original date set for doomsday—24 November. This time only a few dozen people came to Bogdan Khmelnitsky Square, and most of them were police, journalists, and upset parents hoping to recover their children.[38]

Charges of inciting mass unrest, "infringing on personal and civic rights on the pretext of performing religious rituals," and "premeditated infliction of serious bodily injuries" were brought against the couple,[39] and after a lengthy delay, during which Tsvigun and Krivogonov were given extensive psychiatric examinations, trial began at Kiev's city court in March 1995. To no one's surprise, the defendants told the court that the trial was replicating Pontius Pilate's trial of Jesus Christ two thousand years earlier.[40] At one point in the proceedings Judge Lyudmila Borisovna asked Khristos-Tsvigun to name the person who had registered the association. The defendant replied, "God." The judge responded, in frustration, "I can't talk to God as an eyewitness"—to which came Kristos-Tsvigun's rejoinder, "You can talk to me. I am the Christ on Earth."[41]

In February 1996, as the year-long trial was coming to a close, public prosecutor Anna Mulyun urged Tsvigun to show repentance and throw herself at the mercy of the court, suggesting that the eventual sentence might be suspended. Tsvigun rejected this offer with disdain and continued to behave in court as Christ reincarnate.[42] She continues to forecast that, after the apocalypse, the sun and the moon will be dissolved, to be replaced by a new star: Jesus-Maria Devi Christ. In her vision of the future, the earth, cleansed of all its inhabitants, will then be repopulated by a "sixth race" consisting of "beautiful, strong, immensely tall prophets" able to communicate with each other telepathically.[43] By March 1996, *Moscow News* was reporting that this association, which some observers had written off three years earlier, was once again winning followers.[44]

The court eventually found the accused guilty of disorderly conduct, damaging citizens' health on the pretext of religious rituals, and incitement to public disorder. Krivonogov received the heaviest sentence—seven years' imprisonment. Vitalii Kovalchuk, another association leader, received a six-year sentence, while Tsvigun, the central figure in the association, received the lightest sentence—four years in prison.[45]

Aum Shinrikyo

Compared to the White Brotherhood, the Aum Shinrikyo (Sublime Truth) religious association impresses one as significantly more dangerous. Instead of merely waiting for the end of the world, Aum Shinrikyo proposed to hasten its arrival, manufacturing and stockpiling the deadly nerve gas sarin for that purpose.

Aum Shinrikyo was founded in 1987 by the weak-sighted Shoko Asahara. Starting with just ten followers, Asahara drew upon Tibetan Buddhism for his doctrines, but he downplayed the Tibetan Buddhist valuation of compassion. The movement he developed practiced total control over its members, including "limitation on the forms of participation with outsiders, refusal to take part in common societal activities, peculiar habits of eating and abstinence, and . . . even peculiarities of dress."[46] Although he lured adherents with promises to help them develop the ability to levitate, along with other supernatural powers, Asahara's writings reveal an unmistakable apocalyptic strain. Unlike the White Brotherhood, however, he viewed the apocalypse as the end result of human destructiveness, in essence as Armageddon. "As we move . . . toward the year 2000, there will be a series of events of inexpressible

ferocity and terror," Asahara promises in one of his religious association's pamphlets, without revealing that he intended to instigate these
events himself. "The lands of Japan will be transformed into a nuclear
wasteland."[47] As the price of membership in his doomsday cult, Asahara
exacted hefty donations from his followers. By 1995 Asahara counted
10,000 followers in Japan and 30,000 in Russia[48] as well as an undeter-
mined number in the Bulgarian coastal town of Varna.[49]

Along the way, Asahara built up a business empire worth tens of mil-
lions of dollars. Aum Shinrikyo used the offices of the Russian government itself to penetrate Russia. Back in 1992, Oleg Lobov, head of Russia's security council, met with Asahara in the course of a visit to Japan
and subsequently arranged for President Boris Yeltsin to approve the
founding of an Aum-sponsored Russian-Japanese University in Moscow.
Russian news media added that Aleksandr V. Rutskoi, then vice president of Russia, met with Asahara that same year, at Yeltsin's behest.[50]
Asahara subsequently set up several communes in Russia, including five
or six offices in Moscow alone. "The sect's grasp of modern media tech-
niques," *Inter Press Service* reported, was amply displayed at a promo-
tional rally held on 22 November 1993 in Moscow's Olympic stadium:

[For] what one observer called "an awe-inspiring and overwhelming experience"
thousands of Russians paid a hard-earned 1,000 rubles ($2) to be initiated in the
sect. They were given sweets, shown giant video images of Christ's crucifixion
with Asahara's face superimposed and taken through a series of mystical chants
and yoga poses accompanied by "Astral Cosmic Consciousness" music.[51]

The following year Aum Shinrikyo spent $300,000 to buy segments of
prime time on Russian television and radio, including a weekly half-hour
show called "Learning the Truth" on 2-times-2, an independent television network in Moscow.

Under Fumihiro Joyu, the spiritual leader of the Russian branch of the
association, Aum Shinrikyo opened five chapters in Moscow and one in
Vladikavkaz. The association also won adherents in Ukraine and Belarus, and in September 1993 it applied to Ukrainian authorities for legal
registration and permission to open a branch in Kiev.[52] In the meantime,
the association's members in Moscow were reported to be "increasingly
interested in mass destruction weapons, particularly war agents,"[53] and
authorities in Moscow revoked their license. At that point, authorities
in Kiev balked.

Meanwhile, Asahara used his skyrocketing income to stockpile dangerous chemicals. Police would later estimate that he had stockpiled enough toxic agents at the association's commune in Kamikuishiki (in central Japan) to create fifty tons of the nerve gas Sarin—enough to kill 4.2 million to 10 million people.[54] On 20 March, association members showed to what use they intended to put this stockpile by launching a nerve gas attack in the Tokyo subway. Eleven people were killed, and more than five thousand were sickened. Four days later, Russian authorities ordered the termination of the association's Russian-based radio broadcasts to Japan, confiscated sect property in Moscow, and froze the sect's bank accounts.[55]

On 15 March, five days before the nerve gas attack, Russian police had raided Aum headquarters in Moscow, confiscating an undisclosed quantity of drugs described as "possibly heroin."[56] Russian authorities ordered the immediate closure of all Aum facilities and banned the association from further broadcasting on Russian television and radio.[57] In the wake of the attack, Japanese police raided Aum sites around Japan, carting off hundreds of drums of chemicals, which weighed more than 150 tons.[58] Police also discovered materials that allegedly documented the association's intention to seize power in Japan before the year 2000 and to develop one of the most powerful armies in the world.[59] Further raids in July on the association's extensive weapons industry led authorities to conclude that the group was in the final phase of its war preparations; officials now suggested that the association intended to launch an offensive war of world conquest in 1997.[60]

In the meantime, Russian authorities canceled the registration of the Moscow branch of Aum Shinrikyo, while Belarusian officials turned down the group's application for registration on the grounds that it posed a threat to society's health and welfare.[61] Russian and Japanese law enforcement agencies also pooled their resources; in this connection, two officials of the Japanese national police agency arrived in Moscow in early April.[62]

Two months after the nerve gas attack in the subway, Japanese police, in quick succession, arrested Asahara and Yoshihiro Inoue, his righthand man, and prepared to put them on trial.[63] In March 1996, twenty-six-year-old Seiji Tashita, another of Asahara's collaborators, was sentenced to seven years' imprisonment for complicity in the nerve gas attack.[64] That seemed to bring the story to a close, but history has shown that a religious movement may survive the imprisonment (or even death) of the founder, and that it may even flourish. In Russia, some 30,000–35,000 association members and an additional 20,000–25,000 sympathizers remained at liberty, their potential activity open to question.

Messengers of the Holy Grail

One of the nontraditional religious associations to achieve cause célèbre status in the Czech press is a group founded and led by Jan Dvorsky (b. 1965). In 1994 Dvorsky's Messengers of the Holy Grail numbered about a hundred adherents, most of them in western Bohemia, but by 1996 this already small number had declined. Dvorsky achieved a certain notoriety in 1993 with the publication of *Son of Man,* a book which, among other things, warns of the threat allegedly posed by Czech President Václav Havel, Pope John Paul II, and Dvorsky's own mother-in-law. Dvorsky, alias Parsifal Imanuel, warned of the threat of apocalypse in the year 2000, but he offered adherents the assurance that they would be resurrected from the dead when a "new kingdom" would be created.[65]

Some former members of Dvorsky's cult have obtained treatment at the Psychiatric Clinic of Prague-Bohnice, under Dr. Prokop Remes. A few of them have attempted suicide.[66] One is reminded of American psychiatrist John Clark's claim, on the basis of extensive empirical research, that 58 percent of the people attracted to religious cults and sects suffer chronic psychiatric disorders while the remaining 42 percent for the most part experience difficulty in adjusting to society.[67]

Faith Healing and Psychic Healing

The association of religion with healing has a long history. Whether one thinks of the miraculous cures reported at Catholic Madonna sites, or the recourse to supernatural cures in medieval Chinese folk religion,[68] or the faith healing commonly found in Pentecostal and charismatic groups, or even the simple act of praying to God for relief from illness, the belief that the supernatural may be harnessed for medicinal purposes has been one of the most tenacious and widespread convictions of the human race.

Various kinds of healing without a physical curative agent are known. These include faith healing, paranormal healing, magnetic healing, New Thought healing, and psychic healing. In psychic healing, for instance, the curative process is said to involve "the transfer of the universal life force through touch or passes of the hand. The energy transfer often is accompanied by such sensations as heat, tingling, electrical shock, or impressions of colors."[69]

Although faith healing was known and hotly debated as early as the fourth century, it experienced a boom in the late nineteenth century and twentieth century, thanks in part to movements such as Christian Science and Pentecostalism and to evangelistic healers such as Oral Roberts and Kathryn Kuhlman.[70] Faith healing, along with all other forms of healing without known curative agents, was strictly forbidden in Soviet Russia; all such healing was seen by Soviet officials as a species of superstition and backwardness. But with the collapse of communism, healing has revived. In Russia alone there are today an estimated 300,000 folk healers, witches, wizards, or extrasensors. Yet only about three thousand people have registered with the Russian Association of Healers.[71] In early 1994 the Russian parliament passed a law requiring would-be witches and wizards (or warlocks) to submit to a test administered by the health ministry. If they pass the test, applicants are issued a certificate entitling them to go into practice—in effect, a witchcraft license.[72]

In Hungary, witchcraft has been given an explicitly religious—or quasi-religious—legitimation with the establishment of a Church of Witchcraft in Budapest. The high priest of this Church is József Meszaros who, for a price, will dispense love spells, cures, curse removal, and other magical spells.[73]

Healers, whether in Russia, Poland,[74] or elsewhere, have different styles. Take Bob Wilcox, an American charismatic preacher who appeared at the October Theater in Moscow's New Arbat Street in 1993. As people in the audience stretched out their hands, Wilcox drew himself up and cried: "I speak to back pain! In the name of Jesus, I command you to go!"[75] Other healers currently practicing in Russia include cat worshipers, shamans, sorcerers with potions, and wizards who make use of astral charts.

Tamara Nikolayeva blends Chinese acupuncture, Tibetan herbalism, pre-Christian Russian chants, and her natural extrasensory gifts and opens her private sessions with an incantation:

> Queen of the Sky, fountain, healer
> Heal the servant of God,
> Victoria, from this feebling infirmity
> As water flows from the mountains

So, by your grace,
Bring Victoria fruitfulness. . . .[76]

The best-known healer in Russia today is Anatoly Kashpirovsky, an associate of neofascist Vladimir Zhirinovsky, who performed highly controversial healing shows on television during 1989, claiming to effect cures through mass hypnosis.[77] He was later accused of having used mass hypnosis to influence Russians' voting behavior. Other well-known faith healers in Russia are worthy of mention. Dzhuna Davitashvili, director of a Moscow clinic who claims to use psychic powers to heal the afflicted, is reported to be close to Boris Yeltsin.[78] Then there is a renowned master wizard, Sergei Gordeev, who shocked the Russian public in 1990 with a television spot showing him in a wizard's robe conjuring an unclaimed corpse at a Moscow morgue; the TV audience watched as the corpse seemed to respond to Gordeev's supposedly psychic energy by raising his arms and rising jerkily off the slab. Gordeev's acclaim was unaffected by subsequent revelations that his revival of the dead had been a hoax.[79] Nor should one forget Russian faith healer Alan Chumak, who announced in September 1989 that he had transmitted his "bioenergy" to the next ten issues of the daily newspaper *Vechernyaya Moskva*. The paper subsequently received letters from thousands of satisfied readers who assured the editor that the "energized" issues did in fact make them feel good.[80]

Bulgaria in recent years also has experienced a boom in faith healers, clairvoyants, and others professing to exercise psychic and/or spiritual powers. One of the most renowned healers throughout much of the postwar period was a blind woman (1911–96) living just outside the town of Petrich, known only by her first name, Vanga, who claimed to foresee the future and who provided cures and advice for the equivalent of a day's salary.[81] She was consulted at one time or another by Leonid Brezhnev, Mikhail Gorbachev, Vladimir Zhirinovsky, and a number of Bulgarian leaders. When she died in August 1996, Bulgarian President Zhelyu Zhelev and Prime Minister Zhan Videnov traveled a hundred miles from Sofia to Rupite to pay their respects at her funeral.[82]

Faith in folk medicine runs deep. A 1995 poll among Muscovites found that while 72 percent of respondents believed in God, fully 85 percent believed in folk medicine.[83] The reverse is a pervasive, irrational fear of negative magic. A 1992 poll among residents of the Russian city of Vologda asked respondents what they most feared in life. Topping the list were "energy vampires" who threatened to suck the "life energy" from innocent people.[84] Witches and black magic came in second. Third place went to "silly superiors and their stupid orders."[85] Although Vologda has no history of earth tremors, three of the forty respondents polled confessed that they worried about earthquakes, floods, or the sudden appearance in town of visitors from outer space.[86] This last item, which reflects local concern about reports in 1989 of a mysterious flying craft landing in the vicinity of the town,[87] leads to the next category of nontraditional religious associations.

Channeling

Channeling is defined in *Harper's Encyclopedia of Mystical and Paranormal Experience* as "a form of mediumship in which information is communicated from a source perceived to be different from the conscious self. Sources are identified variously as nonphysical beings, angels, nature spirits, totem or guardian spirits, deities, demons, extraterrestrials, spirits of the dead, and the Higher Self."[88] Channeling occurs when the medium is in an altered state of consciousness. Spiritualism (which has a long history in Bohemia) and shamanism (with an even longer history in parts of Russia and Siberia) are perhaps the best-known examples of channeling. The Noah's Ark Society, which can be found in today's Croatia,[89] practices spiritualism and mediumship. In East Central Europe, however, the most dynamic manifestations of channeling are two new entrants: (1) the cult of Ramtha and (2) extraterrestrial visitations.

The story of Ramtha began in 1978, if one is a skeptic, or 35,000 years ago, if one is a believer. In 1978 Judy Knight, a twenty-nine-year-old waitress living in Washington state, started to feel the presence of an ancient Egyptian warrior stirring within her. Ramtha, as this warrior is known, would take over her body from time to time and speak in a low, gruff voice. It did not take long before Knight quit her waitress job and went into "partnership" with Ramtha. Speaking through Knight, Ramtha dispenses advice to the rich and ambitious, at a fee pocketed by Knight. By 1995 their "joint" income was estimated at $4 million per year.[90]

By 1994 Ramtha's fame had spread to Central Europe, and Ramtha considerably began dispensing advice and insights through a local—fifty-two-year-old German psychic, Julie Ravel. Ravel, who runs a parapsychological society called Light Oasis and who holds court in a castle in Austria, ended up with a copyright battle on her hands. Although her attorney argued forcefully that a spirit was not the property of any medium but a free agent who might choose to communicate through one medium on one day and through another on another day,[91] the court ultimately agreed with Knight's claim, "Ramtha feeds his thoughts and energies through me alone. I am his keeper."[92] The ruling is unlikely, however, to dampen the enthusiasm of Ramtha's German and Austrian devotees.

Whatever Ramtha's charms, it is when we turn to reports of UFOs that we see more clearly a correlation with the collapse of communism. The watershed year 1989, during which the Soviet Union lost its East European empire, also marked the spectacular visitation by vernaceous space aliens, eight feet to thirteen feet tall, to the east Russian city of Voronezh.[93] Pavel Mukhortov, a journalist for *Komsomol'skaia pravda*, could smell a good story and, according to reports, pleaded with the aliens to take him on an excursion to their planet, Red Star, in the constellation Libra.[94] The aliens declined to accept his request, leaving *Krasnaia zvezda* (Red Star), the army's daily newspaper, to wonder about the planet's name.

In Hungary a dramatic surge in UFO sighting began in November 1989, the month in which the political firmament in Eastern Europe shifted.[95] The conclusion seems inescapable that a connection exists between the emotional ferment stirred up by political and social changes and the growing number of sightings of UFOs, or—put more simply—that many sightings are stress-induced. Of interest in this connection is an estimate by the Munich daily newspaper, *Süddeutsche Zeitung*, that more than half of all Russians had reported seeing flying saucers by 1992.[96] For that matter, a 1966 Gallup poll reported that about 5 million Americans believed that they had seen a UFO.[97]

To some extent, people see what they want to see, or what they expect to see. *The UFO Encyclopedia* admits, albeit obliquely, that "there is some form of statistical link between sightings of UFOs and visions of the Blessed Virgin Mary."[98] Stated differently, the lights and sundry inexplicable phenomena that have occurred at Medjugorje since 1981 seem to locals to be manifestations of recurrent apparitions of the Blessed Virgin Mary, but they might well be given a UFO explanation if they took place in Arizona or Wyoming.[99]

Since 1989, UFOs have been sighted in the Czech and Slovak republics, Hungary, Croatia, Serbia, Romania, Albania, and, of course, Russia.[100]

György Keleti, Hungarian defense minister since July 1994, has gone on record as a UFO believer; he even contributed a story to *Ufomagazin* in 1992 under the headline, "We don't stand a chance in a UFO invasion."[101] A few months before being swept from office, Soviet President Mikhail Gorbachev himself endorsed the UFO phenomenon, cautioning, "The phenomenon does exist and must be treated seriously."[102]

Interest in UFOs extends to the populations at large. In Hungary there were fifteen UFO clubs and associations by 1992, and as of 1994 every large Hungarian town had at least one UFO society. In September 1994 Debrecen (in eastern Hungary) played host to an international UFO congress with participants from eleven countries.[103]

Although, in some ways, interest in UFOs may function as a surrogate for religion, it encroaches directly on religious terrain once channeling comes into play. Take, for example, Antrovis, an alleged extraterrestrial who advertises him- or herself as "the mysterious Center for the Revival of Life and Humans." Antrovis became the focal point for a small religious movement in Poland, whose members drew satisfaction from Antrovis's assurance that Poles were a "chosen people."[104] Antrovis offered some predictions in 1993, prophesying that Pope John Paul II would be killed in 1994 by some of his close associates, that many people would contract terrifying skin diseases from space radiation also in 1994, and that "in 1999 a group of people who attain universal space value will be evacuated by extraterrestrials."[105] The prophecy of Antrovis seemed to imply that Poles would be among those to be evacuated from this doomed planet. In further revelations, Antrovis promised that precisely 144,000 Slavs (mainly Poles) together with 600,000 persons of other races would be the lucky evacuees. The Poles would be picked up on Mount Sleza near Wrocław and flown in spaceships to the distant planet of Mirinda.[106]

The man behind the Cult of Antrovis is Edward Mielnik of Wrocław, who claims to have had a vision of the Blessed Virgin Mary in 1980, when he was thirty-five. Soon after this vision he began experiencing "contact" with Antrovis and set up the cult, which spread to Warsaw, Kraków, and Szczecin. The cult was registered as a religious association by the provincial court of Wrocław in mid-1990. Court documents show that its declared aims included "disseminating knowledge about man's physical and mental health, protecting the health of animals by natural means and propagating knowledge about regenerating the natural environment."[107] As of 1994, the Cult of Antrovis numbered twenty-seven "founding members" and fifteen "ordinary members." During its brief existence, the cult offered courses attended by some six hundred people. In 1994, however, the "founding members" decided to shut down the association.[108]

Nearby Bulgaria has put its space aliens to work, casting two willing alien personalities as local equivalents of Ann Landers and Dear Abby. It started in Plovdiv, when a space alien named Kiki was said to be contacting a chosen few at regular intervals, passing on advice and predictions. Kiki flattered Bulgarian sensibilities by revealing that Bulgarian is *the* intergalactic language of choice. Kiki's fame spread, but not everyone agreed with Kiki's dispensations, and soon a second space alien, named Rocky, established contact with receptive minds in Sofia and took to spending much of his time contradicting Kiki.[109] By 1990 Kubrat Tomov, a former engineer, launched the Bulgarian Society of Psychotronics, which soon claimed more than a thousand members. Tomov assured society members that they would "soon be able to see into the future and that contacts with extraterrestrials will be commonplace."[110]

UFO cultists also may be found in the Czech Republic, sharing in the conviction, typical of such groups, that extraterrestrials intend to save a select few human beings from impending doom.[111] Still other groups, such as Iso Zen (which has some adherents in Germany), worship UFOs,[112] while the Los Angeles-based Aetherius Society (founded in England in 1954), which has shown some interest in Eastern Europe, places UFOs at the center of its rather simplified belief system, teaching that Jesus came from Venus and that Earth is visited from time to time by a spaceship known as Satellite 3, which beams down positive energy.[113] Whatever one may make of UFOs, it is clear that belief in them and in space aliens has the power to excite the religious imagination.

Satanism

The more seriously people take their gods, the more fervently they are apt to believe in, and fear, their devils. Religious fundamentalism, in particular, prepares the soil for belief in Satan. Hence, it comes as no surprise that Satanism has been most tenacious in fervently religious Poland, throwing up a full-fledged Church of Satan in the 1920s and 1930s and resurfacing by means of the rock music scene in the mid-1980s. Nor should it be a surprise that, as evangelical missionaries intensify their work throughout the region, warning people of "the work of the Devil," some should react by embracing this devil. The innovative fieldwork of Dutch anthropologist Mart Bax confirms this observation. He has found that the intense religiosity of the Bosnian pilgrimage center at Medjugorje has stimulated a countervailing response in which "many local women [have felt] terrorized by a rapidly increasing number of devils, which make them feel uneasy, sick, and unable to properly care for the daily needs of their lodgers, the pilgrims."[114]

Actually, a wide variety of phenomena are subsumed under the rubric of Satanism, including worship of Satan, the seeking of pacts with the devil, the cult of violence and evil, and superficial fashion statements better understood as "pop Satanism."

Although Satanism has reared its head in several countries of Eastern Europe—Poland, the Czech Republic, Slovakia, Hungary, and Croatia —what is striking is that almost all reports of Satanist activity come from Catholic nations, not from traditionally Orthodox countries. This correlation is significant and reflects the greater importance of the devil in Catholic (and Protestant) theology. Moreover, just as communism kept the lid on fringe religions, so did it succeed in confining Satanism. It was only around 1986, as Polish communism was starting to crumble and as the clericalization of Polish society picked up momentum, that recurrent reports appeared concerning groups of young people calling themselves Satanists. Polish sociologists identified four strains of Satanism in their society in the late 1980s: Satanists who worshipped the devil without belittling the importance of God and who used either red wine or animal blood in their rituals; followers of Robert Szwed, who viewed God as nominally supreme but weak, and who advocated a gentle disposition, respecting nature and using red wine in rituals; Luciferians, who claim that Satan is the Supreme Deity and that God is a usurper and requiring the use of fresh blood in their rituals; and the Church of Satan, having a magic-occultist character and at best a blurred connection with true Satanism.[115] By 1991 about 20,000 Satanists were reported in Poland, although the divisions mentioned above had in large part broken down.[116]

Today, formal Satanist Churches function in at least three countries of the region. The Polish Province of the Church of Satan is affiliated with the San Francisco-based Church of Satan, founded by Anton Sandor La Vey, the so-called Black Pope. The highest-ranking clergyman in the Polish Satanic Church has the rank of cardinal; he reportedly has about twenty "priests" assisting him.[117] In the Czech Republic the so-called

First Church of Satan operates under the guidance of Grand Master Jiří Valter. In public forums, Valter says that his Church advocates living life to the fullest, pleads individualism, and asserts that "stupidity and agreeing with everything is the first sin."[118] In Russia, followers of the Macumba Satanic cult are said to practice human sacrifice and, accordingly, remain underground.[119]

Satanists are regularly said to perpetrate murder. In Yugoslavia in the late 1980s a Satanic movement called Dark seemed to promote suicide as a route to "mystic death" and "rebirth."[120] In the Czech Republic, Hungary, and Romania, local Satanists have been held responsible for the murder of various victims, both animal and human, usually within the context of a black mass.[121] In 1994, conflicting reports came out of an otherwise unidentified Satanist organization with its main bases in Hungary and Austria that was allegedly behind explosions set off in Subotica (in Serb-controlled Vojvodina), Szeged (in southern Hungary), and Budapest.[122] Satanist thinking seemed to be well reflected in comments by a self-declared anarchist with Satanist sympathies: "These hypocrite Christian pigs," this anarchist (who identified himself only by his cult name, "Grass") told the *Warsaw Voice*. "We need more freedom, more violence in this world."[123]

There is no evidence that pacts with the devil are common, but violence against ecclesiastical property is most definitely in vogue with Satanists. The usual targets are cemeteries—perhaps in part because they are less likely to be guarded than churches—but at least one Satanist attack was reported on a Catholic church. The most serious vandalism to date occurred in Niedow in southwest Poland in June 1994, when the sacristy was demolished and religious objects were destroyed. Satanic cult symbols had been painted on the church walls, and police speculated that a Satanist mass had been held.[124]

Finally, mention should be made of "pop Satanists." Although it would be misleading to portray Satanist fashions as somehow a religious phenomenon, the vogue sometimes entails actions with religious significance (such as vandalizing graves and throwing drinking parties in mausoleums), and it tends to presume and reinforce a critical distance from the Church. Pop Satanists are closely associated with the rock scene, whether in Poland, Hungary, or elsewhere. These are the so-called "tomb dwellers," the *Grufti*, who wear Satanist pins, listen to rock groups such as Budapest's War Pigs, and favor skateboards for short-distance travel. They also tend to know some Russian. One young woman in Hungary explained, "The ones who have a future studied English [in school]. The skinheads, tomb dwellers, and thieves studied Russian."[125]

Occultism

To some extent, occultism has been subsumed under the rubrics of Faith Healing and Psychic Healing and Satanism. But additional dimensions of occultism render a further consideration practical. Ordinarily when the occult is mentioned, what is meant are incantations, magic, contacts with the supernatural and the souls of the departed, spells, curses, etc. The definition of "occultism" in *The Encyclopedia of Psychic Science,* first published in 1934, is worth noting: "a philosophical system of theories and practices on, and for the attainment of, the higher powers of mind and spirit. Its practical side connects with psychical phenomena."[126] The best example of a religious movement inspired by occult thinking is Theosophy, a mystical society founded in 1875 by H. P. Blavatsky, but spiritualism (involving the holding of seances and seeking communication with the dead) also has religious, or at least quasi-religious, aspects. As recently as the 1980s some spiritualist activity was reported in Bohemia, Hungary, Serbia, and Croatia,[127] while in recent years Theosophists and their close cousins, Anthroposophists, have come to public attention in Poland and Russia.[128] Although Theosophy has not commanded much following or attention in recent decades, never really recovering from the death of Annie Besant (more or less Blavatsky's successor) in 1933,[129] Theosophists in 1991 were said to be printing about 50,000 copies of their scripture, *The Secret Doctrine,* in various East European languages, including Russian, in hopes of winning converts. By 1991, copies of *The Secret Doctrine* were on sale at metro stations in Moscow.[130] By 1995, Theosophy and Anthroposophy had reestablished a foothold in Croatia,[131] alongside New Acropolis, a neo-Theosophist current claiming about a hundred adherents in Rijeka.[132]

Other occult religious societies recently established (or reestablished) in Russia include the Psychological Culture Club (in St. Petersburg), the Lotus, Luminary, and Torch of Roerich Associations (Krasnodar), the Cosmos Club (in Moscow), the Citadel Club (in Moscow), and an occult religious association in Voronezh (the site of the UFO landing in 1989). Astrology was mentioned favorably by TASS in 1994, albeit in the context of reporting the recent work of researchers at the University of

California.[133] And in Yeltsin's government, Georgi Georgiyevich Rogozin has been said to consult horoscopes and communicate "with the cosmos" before giving Yeltsin advice on financial and economic matters; he also supposedly rotates tables and saucers to create a "favorable power field" around the Russian president. *Moscow News,* the source for some of these reports, also claimed that Rogozin had aligned Yeltsin's bed along a north-south axis to assure a favorable magnetic force.[134] These and other stories about Rogozin are, however, probably pure invention, designed to discredit Yeltsin.

Yet the occult *is* making a comeback in the region, sometimes in the most public way. This has taken the form, inter alia, of the staging of a paranormal festival in Nowa Huta, sponsored by the Polish monthly magazine *Out of This World;*[135] the convening of the first World Dracula Congress at a castle on Transylvania's Lake Snagov in 1995;[136] and the popularization of a ghoulish Devil Museum on Kredytowa Street in Warsaw.[137]

Mainline Churches have been anything but sanguine about occult phenomena. A pamphlet released by the Russian Orthodox Church in late 1993 warned, "Our ancestors realized what a danger such people were" and cautioned against "obsession" with the demonic.[138] In most places the scale of occultism has not reached the point where legislative action has been deemed necessary, but it is interesting to note that in Irkutsk, a commission of the Council for the Cultural, Spiritual, and Moral Perfection of Society recommended in 1992 that black magic, sorcerers, and thaumaturges be banned within the territory of Irkutsk.[139]

Eastern Faiths and Associations

This category subsumes both groups derived from authentic Asian traditions, such as Buddhism and Hinduism, and splinter groups which have their main followings outside Asia, such as the Baha'i and the Hare Krishna. All of these groups have at least some presence in the area. Buddhism can trace its first appearance in Poland back to the early years after World War I, but Polish Buddhism did not survive the combined effects of the destruction of World War II and the onslaught of Stalinism. Buddhism returned to Poland in 1972, however, and gained converts, particularly after the proclamation of martial law in 1981; for many Poles, martial law was taken to signify the failure of the Catholic Church.[140] In Sankt-Petersburg four Buddhist "congregations" were registered by the end of 1992.[141] Buddhism also won adherents in Bulgaria, Czechoslovakia, and Estonia. Secret Oriental devotional societies were set up in Bulgaria and Yugoslavia in the 1980s.[142]

The Hare Krishnas are perhaps the most energetic proselytizers among this set. The Krishna Society claims to have as many as 500,000 adherents in Russia alone[143] and has won adherents in every country of Eastern Europe, including Albania, as well as in Latvia, Georgia, Abkhazia, and even in Kazakstan.[144] The Baha'i have established informational centers in Moscow, Kiev, Minsk, and other cities, and they claim to have made tangible progress in Albania with the conversion of some 12,000 Albanians by late 1996.[145] Other Eastern-oriented religious associations found in the region today include the Baha'i, the Bhagwan Rajneesh movement, Soto Zen, Kwan Um, Nichiren Shoshu–Soka Gakkai (an association that originated in thirteenth-century Japan), and the cult of Sathya Sai Baba.[146]

Finally, the controversial Ananda Marga society, which advocates male dominance and the use of violence to achieve one's ends, has won a small following in parts of Eastern Europe.[147]

Nontraditional Christian Associations and Other Religious Phenomena

Even so delicate a label as "nontraditional" risks censure in this age of "correct thinking" and pervasive paranoia on grounds of normative bias. In applying this term to certain religious associations, however, no judgment is being made about the content of their doctrines or their behavior, but a distinction is being drawn based on duration and on the perceptions of mainstream society. Other writers have used far bolder terminology, such as a certain Benton Johnson, writing in 1963. According to Johnson, "A Church is a religious group that accepts the social environment. A sect is a religious group that rejects the social environment."[148] Johnson's definitions would signify that the distinction between Church and sect is relative to the given society and to the nature of the religious mainstream in that society.

The Vissarion Brotherhood (also known as the Church of the Last Precept), like Ukraine's White Brotherhood, would probably be viewed as nontraditional by most observers. Created by millionaire Sergei Torop, a former policeman, this Russian-based sect teaches its adherents to venerate Torop as Vissarion-Christ. Customarily attired in a red tunic, with a Jesus-style beard, Torop claims to have been sent to earth by God the Father to bring about the unification of all religions.[149]

Government officials estimated that the Vissarion Brotherhood had about five thousand adherents in early 1996, about a thousand of them residing in the villages of the Altai taiga.[150] Inspired by Vissarion's so-called "58th Testament," Vissarionites are vegetarians and practice urinotherapy, extrasensory perception, childbirth in water, and the accumulation of cosmic energy.[151] The association rejects urban life and contemporary mass culture and is reported to be building, in the Siberian forest, a "City of the Sun" (possibly inspired by the Utopian vision of the philosopher Tommaso Campanella [1568–1639]).[152] Devotees of the Russian Orthodox Church seem to have been particularly inflamed against this association, whose teachings they have called "Masonic" and whose leader they have described as a "seducer" (a term also applied by Orthodox Christians to Satan).[153]

The Church of Scientology, the Unification Church of the Reverend Sun Myung Moon, and Maharishi Mahesh Yogi's Transcendental Meditation are also active in the region, as are Tantra (in Russia), the Sri Radmish Mystical Cult (in Latvia), the sexually abstinent Holic Group (founded by Gottfried Holic, based in the former East Germany and active throughout Eastern Europe), and the tea-drinking Santo-Daime cult (active in Germany, blending Brazilian Indian, Christian, and spiritualist traditions).[154] None of these religious associations may claim to have been active in the region over many years. Of some interest is a report published in *Moskovsky Komsomolets* in October 1992, which promised that "at 10:00 p.m. on 22 October the vast area in front of Lenin's mausoleum will be filled with more than 7 million "astral ghostwarriors" . . . [who will] do battle with evil spirits which have held sway there for years."[155] The outcome of the battle was not reported.

The Church of Scientology has been especially active in building bases in Russia and Germany. In Russia the Scientologists donated a reading room to Moscow State University in 1992, together with hundreds of books, among them the writings of founder L. Ron Hubbard. The university showed its appreciation by announcing that it would observe a "Ron Hubbard Day."[156] A year later, the Church opened a Dianetics center in Moscow with a staff of eleven persons; by August 1994 the center had grown to eighty staffers, while Scientology officials boasted that their publications had obtained a greater resonance in Russia than anywhere else.[157] In Germany, federal and *Land* authorities have grown increasingly concerned about the Church of Scientology, tending to view it as a criminal organization with ambitious political goals, and they accuse the organization of activities contrary to the German constitution.[158] By 1996 Bavaria had decided to exclude Scientology members from public service, while similar exclusionary measures were being proposed at other echelons.[159] In late October, leaders of Germany's sixteen provinces announced that they were considering a proposal to place Scientology activists under government surveillance.[160]

Other religious (or religious-associated) associations that are new to the Central and East European region include the Templars, an outgrowth of Gnostic traditions,[161] self-described "pagans,"[162] and New Age centers, which have sprouted by the hundreds throughout the region that once comprised the Soviet Union.[163]

Conclusion

The region's "traditional" religions have greeted the arrival of nontraditional religious associations with particularly intense hostility and fear. Typical is the reaction of Archbishop Aleksandr of Kostroma and Galich, head of the Russian Orthodox Church's youth movement, who characterized such groups as the Unification Church, the Church of Scientology, and Aum Shinrikyo as "harmful and even dangerous."[164] The traditional Churches have organized conferences on "how to combat fanatical religious sects." One conference, hosted by the Greek Orthodox archbishop of Athens at a monastery outside Athens in November 1993, was attended by more than 120 participants from sixteen countries; the meeting's premise was the supposition that "these fundamentalist activities threaten the personality of the individual, European civilisation, and democratic institutions."[165] In some countries local citizens have set up their own organizations to fight against the new nontraditional religious associations. In Moscow, for example, there is the Committee for the Salvation of Youth from Totalitarian Sects.[166]

The contemporary explosion of cult and sect activity in the newly decommunized societies of Eurasia suggests certain general conclusions. First, the natural tendency for religious associations, as for all associations dependent on ideological, theological, or philosophical agreement,

is to fragment, split, and proliferate, unless checked by political obstruction. Second, this tendency is accelerated in periods of social stress, such
as the one that has characterized the region since 1989.[167] Third, the tendencies found in peripheral sectors (i.e., nontraditional religious associations) mirror and reflect those found in mainline religions (for example,
in the fragmentation of Orthodoxy in Ukraine). And fourth, some of
the evangelizing groups may derive advantages from certain characteris-
tically "American" features such as optimism (in regard to recruitment
and perhaps also in doctrine), pragmatism in organizational goals, and a
diminished "sense of the sacred," manifested, for example, in the notion
that a mere human being might have a "personal relationship" with the
Creator of the Universe.[168] A fifth observation may be added, namely,
that these phenomena mirror processes in the West of increasing interest in psychic phenomena, ghosts, angels, U F Os, and the like.

Religious organizations would have their target audiences believe that
they are merely "revealing" and "propagating" some received truth or
Truth, that they are but the vehicles for divine commands and divine
dogma. But, as this chapter makes clear, religious organizations may also
resort to varieties of conscious and unconscious manipulation. Much as
the Serbian Orthodox Church manipulated nationalism as a means to
restore its prominence and power, or as the Catholic Church in Poland
has manipulated the abortion issue in a kind of phalanx strategy that was
supposed to redefine sexual mores and remake Poland in the image of
the Catholic Church, so too have new cults systematically manipulated
agendas and information in an effort to control the minds of their followers.

For their congregations, submitting to manipulation offers a fulfillment of the deep-seated desire of most people to "escape from freedom,"
to use Erich Fromm's phrase, to the security of the womb, whether in
the form of a Mother Church or in the form of a radical right organization. And here one may add the need that many people have for
dogmas, for having their lives, or parts of their lives, reduced to black
and white, to clear rules, to simple slogans. Kip McKean, founder of the
Church of Christ, put it this way: "As Christians we have the answer to
all [our] problems—and that is Jesus Christ." [169] The persistent tendency
of Christian religions since the twelfth century to anathematize homosexuals is one example of the creation of dogma for the sake of effecting
a control that many people actually crave.[170] It is thus no accident that
the profile of one type of religious personality (specifically, the typical

adherent of fundamentalist religious associations, whether Christian or not) conforms closely in some key ways to the profile of the authoritarian personality as spelled out more than forty years ago by T. W. Adorno and his associates.[171]

The desire to proselytize—to convince others of the eternal truth of one's own suppositions and speculations—is common to most, if not all, Christian religions. It has, thus, not been surprising that alongside the sundry American fundamentalist churches and sects which have, like Scientology, taken advantage of the new "liberalism" in Eastern Europe, more "traditional" Churches such as the Roman Catholic and Orthodox Churches have likewise drawn up ambitious plans for expansion. Soon after the collapse of communism, Pope John Paul II convened a synod that sketched out plans for nothing less than a "re-evangelization" of Eastern Europe.[172] But, by the same virtue, Orthodox Churches have taken advantage of the disappearance of the "Iron Curtain" to attempt to expand their presence in *Western* Europe.[173] Nihil obstat. Praedicetur.

Responding to a question about the left's defensive measures against the Church in Poland undertaken in 1992, Jan Lopuszański, chair of the Christian-National Union Supreme Council, noted: "It is undoubtedly another stage in the battle to control people's hearts and minds. It is the battle that determines the course of history."[174] It is, indeed, for the ability to set the values of the community and the public agenda already brings any group a long way toward controlling the political system itself. In the sixteenth century the byword was *"cuius regio, eius religio"*—whoever rules the region may dictate the religion. This may easily be reversed, however: *"cuius religio, eius regio"*—whoever dictates the religion, rules the region.

Chapter 14

Ego Te Absolvo:

The Nature of Religio-Political Interaction

The quest for absolution of one's sins, for forgiveness, is a powerful driving force behind religion. There can be no greater relief of the scourge of guilt than to have someone in authority, sanctified by God, declare, "Your sins are forgiven!" That is not religion's only attraction, and it is not universal to all religions, but among those that offer the remission of sin, it is an important and powerful instrument.

Absolution may apply not merely to individuals but to regimes, political parties, and armies as well. Here the absolution is sometimes given in advance, as, for example, when Serbian Orthodox priests blessed the banners of Bosnian Serb troops (1992–95) on the eve before battle. Religious authority may, in this way, be politically useful. The story of Abraham and Isaac is revealing. The Book of Genesis tells us:

And he said, Take now thy son, thine only son Isaac, whom thou lovest, and get thee into the land of Moriah; and offer him there for a burnt offering upon one of the mountains which I will tell thee of.

And Abraham rose up early in the morning, and saddled his ass, and took two of his young men with him, and Isaac his son. . . .

And they came to the place which God had told him of; and Abraham built an altar there, and laid the wood in order, and bound Isaac his son, and laid him on the altar upon the wood.[1]

No matter that God sent an angel at the last minute to stay Abraham's hand. The point had been made: here was a God who did not recognize a morality higher than his own will, who demanded total obedience from his followers, extending even to the repudiation of the stirrings of conscience.

As Mark Juergensmeyer wrote in 1993, one does not need religion to know that killing is wrong; religion serves, rather, to identify where one may find legitimate exceptions to this moral dictum.[2]

However important absolution may be, it is only one form of religio-political interaction. Other forms, which may operate in either direction, include legitimation, ideological adaptation, organizational influence (i.e., on the structures of institutions), legislation, control of resources, and the interpenetration and interaction of religious values and regime values. To this list one may add the Churches' ability to generate mythologies of righteous national struggle and to bind people in collective loyalty.[3] Of these sundry levels of interaction, that of values is perhaps central. As I have observed elsewhere,

Political traditions presume value orientations and interpretations of the meaning of collective association. Insofar as these elements are also prescribed in *religious* traditions, it becomes clear that the religio-political system is a unified web and that the elements in the religious sphere and those in the political sphere tend to be mutually reinforcing. When there is compatibility between the two spheres, stability is promoted. When there is tension between the two spheres, the political system has difficulties with legitimation, and the result is social anomie, destabilization, and the potential for social chaos. . . . To say this is to suggest that politics is suffused with religion, as religion is with politics. . . .[4]

There are those who imagine that religion can be depoliticized bloodlessly, as it were, that the state can declare itself a secular state and that the Churches will learn "good manners" and retreat from public debate to their "natural sphere." But politics *is* the natural sphere of religion because, as Hegel realized, one way to comprehend religion is to view it as the spiritualization of politics. Take, for example, the statement released by the Polish episcopate in June 1995 (cited in chapter 12): "Man is not the highest authority in laying down laws. Lawmaking, if it is to be binding for human conscience, must correspond to natural law." The notion that positive law (civil law) must correspond with Natural Law to be valid is scarcely new; indeed, this assumption was common in medieval Central Europe, lying at the heart of Aquinas's ethical discourse,[5] and, for that matter, underpinned Cicero's thinking as well. Writing nearly two thousand years ago, Cicero observed,

For there is a true law: right reason. It is in conformity with nature, is diffused among all men, and is immutable and eternal; its orders summon to duty; its prohibitions turn away from offense. . . . To replace it with a contrary law is a sacrilege; failure to apply even one of its provisions is forbidden; no one can abrogate it entirely.[6]

But it is one thing to agree that positive law should be in accord with Natural Law (or, as I prefer to call it, Universal Reason). It is another matter to put this demand into operation. Clearly, someone has to make a judgment as to how close this correspondence is. But should this be the legislature (as in nomocracy) or the Church (theocracy) or through the discourse and binding decision of historians and jurists not subject to citizens' recall (a scheme that might be inspired by a reading of Plato or Ortega y Gasset)? And if the Church, then why? Because it is the body that advocates the ritual worship of a supposedly all-powerful being? The connection between power and morality, or again, between ritual and morality, is not clear. Moreover, the ancient Greeks did not see any particular association between religion and morality, except incidentally and more or less by coincidence.[7] And while Aquinas developed a sacerdotal system of Natural Law, which endured until the seventeenth century, Enlightenment figures beginning with Hobbes and continuing with Locke and Kant developed a secular theory of Natural Law, or Universal Reason, which set morality upon the foundation of right reason.[8]

The justification for the transference of religiously derived commands into secular law which is usually offered is that the connection is rooted in divine command. This is, for various reasons, unsatisfactory. The story of Abraham and Isaac hints at the problem. Either the good has value in and of itself, in which case God's command adds nothing to its validity or authority but constitutes merely a form of divine assent, or the good is subordinate to God's command, in which case the good does not have absolute value at all. If the good is dependent on and derivative from God's command, then it is God's will that has absolute validity, not morality. But whereas the motivation for obedience to absolute morality (Universal Reason) should be clear enough,[9] the demand for obedience to absolute power would appear to be based either on necessity or on fear of damnation, and not, in fact, on love of the good. (I would go even further and assert that a purported love of God, if not having the character of a love of the good and of Reason, cannot be said to constitute a position of harmony with moral law.)

Returning to the question of religious claims with regard to positive law, it appears that such claims would be registered not on behalf of Universal Reason but on behalf of obedience to divine authority. This, in turn, suggests that the demands of any religious association to bring laws into harmony with its specific values can be seen only as tending toward theocracy. Thus when, for example, the Romanian Orthodox Church demands strict laws against same-sex relationships and the use of the penal system to punish gays and lesbians, the Church is making a demand based on theocracy, not democracy. Democracy, as Joseph Raz has demonstrated, requires tolerance of difference;[10] theocracy does not, and it may even require *intolerance* of difference.

For a secular state to rise above theocratic pressures, without recourse to Bolshevik-style measures, it would be necessary to anchor morality firmly in Universal Reason, as an independent system. To be reasonably effective, thereby promoting a softening of Churches' ability to "demand" that the laws fit their own preferences, it would be necessary to abandon all illusions about morality being only relative. What, after all, does it mean to speak of genocide being only "relatively" reprehensible, or to claim that stabbing an innocent bystander without provocation is neither good nor evil but "depends on your point of view." Moral relativism, all too common today, in fact provides the seedbed upon which theocratic moralism can be built, by (1) suggesting that moral consciousness might be impossible outside a religious framework and (2) preparing the individual for the moral relativism of subordinating morality to divine command (like Abraham, who interpreted moral law as relative to the arbitrary commands of his God). But if morality is "absolute," does that mean that every last moral question has a definite answer? The answer is straightforward: no. In fact, there are apt to be a number of gray areas in human reason, where reasonable persons may hold different points of view, even strongly, and insofar as morality manifests itself through Reason, it follows that there also may be gray areas in morality. Abortion would seem to be such a gray area. After all, societies have argued the pros and cons of abortion since at least Roman times; thus, it appears that human reason is unable to achieve consensus on this issue, regardless of social system or dominant values. But conceding the moral ambiguity of abortion does not prevent one from asserting, at the same time, the absoluteness of moral dicta, any more than a short depth of field in a snapshot should cause an onlooker to feign inability to recognize objects in clear focus, just because objects in the background may appear fuzzier.[11]

But if some moral issues that bring Churches into the political arena are of ancient vintage, that does not mean that religio-political interaction is changeless. On the contrary, as is well known, such interaction is changing all the time. But when it comes to evaluating processes of change in the Russian/East European region, two points should be emphasized. First, one ought not assume that change in that region is inexorably in the direction of assimilating it to patterns already found in the West. Even granting that many of these states have modeled their constitutions on some synthesis of Western examples, that some of the same issues arise from one society to the next (e.g., the abortion controversy in Poland and in the United States; homophobia in Romania and the United States), and that many Western religious associations have been proselytizing energetically throughout the region since before 1989, nonetheless one must note that the region will preserve its own character, both because its dilemmas are different from those of the West and because it will amalgamate Western accretions into its own cultural firmament.

The second point is that not only are societies changing, but the vectors and axes of change themselves are changing. Whereas religious change in the fifteenth and sixteenth centuries could be effected by waging religious wars, signing treaties, and arranging formal unions, such as the Union of Brest (1596), religious change in the twentieth century has necessarily taken more account of the role of mass media and socialization, of media spectacles, and of appeals to individuals to look out for their own private interests ("save your soul"—a message that reduces religiosity to the level of personal gain). As the modalities of change themselves change, earlier wisdom, dicta, assumptions, texts are not forgotten, but come to be understood in new ways that may reflect a departure from the original understanding.

If (most?) religious associations seek power, it is because they want to ensure that their values and their moral agenda are reflected and protected in society; or, to put it in religious terminology, just as Man is said to have been created in God's image, so too human law (positive law) should be fashioned in the image of divine law. One does not need to be religious to apprehend the centrality of moral concerns in politics. As Kant once put it, "A true system of politics cannot . . . take a single step without paying tribute to morality."[12]

Rather obviously, religious associations are not the only organizations to promote moral agendas. Among such other organizations with moral agendas one might mention political parties (e.g., communist parties), labor unions, feminist organizations, Nazi front organizations, and groups such as the NAACP, the Boy Scouts of America, the Humane Society, Planned Parenthood, and Hands off Washington (an agency set up to combat homophobia). But religious associations bring other agendas and resources to bear, which are not available to secular associations, above all the linkage of moral dicta with divine command.

The more a Church absolutizes its values, the more it is apt to insist, where it thinks it has sufficient power to be successful, on those values being translated into law. In this regard, sdRP head Jozef Oleksy missed the point when he told a Polish journalist in 1996, "The Church forgets that infallibility in matters of faith does not mean infallibility in assessing the state's functioning."[13] On the contrary, that is precisely what it means. Once the former is granted, then the Church's claim to assert a veto over government policies and laws is already sanctioned.

Notes

1. Introduction

1. This is not to say that the phenomenon of religious sectarianism emphasizing castration as a rite of passage was new. On the contrary, *among Christian-influenced sects,* the phenomenon can be traced at least as far back as the sixth century. See Pavel Ivanovich Melnikov, *Polnoe sobranie sochinenii,* vol. 14 (St. Peterburg: Izdanie tovarishchestva m.o. Vol'f, 1898), p. 206.

2. Ibid., pp. 208-209; and A. I. Klibanov, *History of Religious Sectarianism in Russia (1860s-1917),* trans. from Russian by Ethel Dunn, ed. Stephen P. Dunn (New York: Pergamon Press, 1982), p. 72.

3. Melnikov, *Polnoe sobranie sochinenii,* vol. 14, p. 248; and N. M. Nikol'skii, *Istoriia russkoi tserkvi* (Moscow: Moskovskii rabochii, 1931), p. 355. See also Klibanov, *History of Religious Sectarianism,* p. 53; *Scotsman,* 24 July 1995, p. 7.

4. *Scotsman,* 24 July 1995, p. 7.

5. Regarding the Church, see, for example, a discussion of its abomination of the *Shtundists,* who organized Bible study circles among peasants in the second half of the nineteenth century, in Klibanov, *History of Religious Sectarianism,* pp. 229-231.

6. Maria Carlson, *"No Religion Higher than Truth": A History of the Theosophical Movement in Russia, 1875-1922* (Princeton, N.J.: Princeton University Press, 1993), p. 173. The Bolsheviks also decreed that henceforth only organization members were allowed to attend meetings organized by the Theosophical Society. See A. S. Rogozhin (compiler), *Put' teosofii* (Petrozavodsk: Sviatoi Ostrov, 1992), p. 27.

7. Carlson, *"No Religion Higher,"* pp. 176-178; and Rogozhin, *Put' teosofii,* pp. 34-41.

8. A. V. Belov, *Sekty, sektantstvo, sektanty* (Moscow: Nauka, 1978), p. 57.

9. Ibid., pp. 72-73.

10. Paul Mojzes, *Religious Liberty in Eastern Europe and the USSR: Before and After the Great Transformation* (Boulder, Colo.: East European Monographs, 1992), pp. 313-314.

11. Earl A. Pope, "Protestantism in Romania," in Sabrina Petra Ramet (ed.), *Protestantism and Politics in Eastern Europe and Russia: The Communist and Post-communist Eras* (Durham, N.C.: Duke University Press, 1992), p. 175.

12. *Lidové noviny* (Prague), 6 April 1996, p. iv; CTK, 16 August 1992, and 3 April 1994, both on *Nexis.*

13. For more details about this sect, see Barbara Strassberg, "Polish Catholicism in Transition," in Thomas M. Gannon, S.J. (ed.), *World Catholicism in Transition* (New York: Macmillan, 1988), p. 185.

14. Grażyna Sikorska, "Poland," in Janice Broun, *Conscience and Captivity: Religion in Eastern Europe* (Washington, D.C.: Ethics and Public Policy Center, 1988), p. 167.

15. On the Church of John, see Helmut Obst, *Apostel und Propheten der Neuzeit: Gründer christlicher Religionsgemeinschaften des 19. und 20. Jahrhunderts,* 2nd ed. (East Berlin: Union, 1981), pp. 326-344.

16. The Romanian example is derived from Owen Chadwick, *The Christian Church in the Cold War* (Harmondsworth, Middlesex: Penguin Books, 1993), pp. 32–33.

17. See *Independent* (London), 22 September 1991, p. 6.

18. See *New York Times,* 13 November 1994, on *Nexis.*

19. The Doukhobors also rejected the teachings of the Orthodox Church, the Bible, the divinity of Christ, and private property. See Belov, *Sekty, sektantstvo,* p. 67; George Woodcock and Ivan Avakumović, *The Doukhobors* (New York: Oxford University Press, 1968), esp. pp. 17, 19–20, 356.

20. See Joseph Pungur, "Theologies of Collaboration: The Rise and Fall of Theologies of Service and Diaconia," in Joseph Pungur (ed.), *An East European Liberation Theology* (Calgary: Angelus Publishers, N.D. [1994]).

21. AFP (Paris), 7 February 1989, in FBIS, *Daily Report* (Eastern Europe), 9 February 1989, p. 15.

22. On this point, see Valerie Bunce, "Rising Above the Past: The Struggle for Liberal Democracy in Eastern Europe," in Sabrina Petra Ramet (ed.), *Adaptation and Transformation in Communist and Post-Communist Systems* (Boulder, Colo.: Westview Press, 1992), pp. 243, 245–247.

23. Quoted in *Christian Science Monitor,* 5 July 1995, p. 7.

24. Quoted in ibid.

2. Phases in Communist Religious Policy

An earlier version of this chapter was published as "Adaptation and Transformation of Religious Policy in Communist and Post-Communist Systems," in Sabrina Petra Ramet (ed.), *Adaptation and Transformation in Communist and Post-Communist Systems* (Boulder, Colo.: Westview Press, 1992). Reprinted, with revisions, by permission of Westview Press.

1. See Dimitry Pospielovsky, *The Russian Church Under the Soviet Regime, 1917–1982* (Crestwood, N.Y.: St. Vladimir's Seminary Press, 1984), esp. vol. 2; Jane Ellis, *The Russian Orthodox Church: A Contemporary History* (Bloomington: Indiana University Press, 1986).

2. *Pravda vostoka* (25 October 1986), cited in *Keston News Service,* no. 265 (11 December 1986): 8.

3. For details, see Pedro Ramet, *Cross and Commissar: The Politics of Religion in Eastern Europe and the Soviet Union* (Bloomington: Indiana University Press, 1987), pp. 148–150.

4. Kenneth Jowitt, "Inclusion and Mobilization in European Leninist Systems," in Jan F. Triska and Paul M. Cocks (eds.), *Political Development in Eastern Europe* (New York: Praeger, 1977), p. 93.

5. Jan S. Prybula, "China's Economic Experiment: From Mao to Market," *Problems of Communism* 35 (January–February 1986): 21–22.

6. The Soviet case material in this section and the following one draws in part on my *Cross and Commissar,* chap. 3.

7. Mao Zedong, "On New Democracy" (1940), quoted in Richard C. Bush, Jr., *Religion in Communist China* (Nashville, Tenn.: Abingdon Press, 1970), p. 351.

8. Mikhail Stern and August Stern, *Sex in the USSR,* trans. Mark Howson and Cary Ryan (New York: Times Books, 1980), pp. 23–24.

9. Boris Schwarz, *Music and Musical Life in Soviet Russia, 1917–1981*, enlarged ed. (Bloomington: Indiana University Press, 1983), pp. 20, 46. See also Brandon Taylor, *Art and Literature under the Bolsheviks*, vol. 1: *The Crisis of Renewal 1917–1924* (London: Pluto Press, 1991).

10. On these two bodies, see Walter Kolarz, *Religion in the Soviet Union* (New York: St. Martin's Press, 1961), pp. 106–117, 124–127; also Bohdan R. Bociurkiw, "The Ukrainian Autocephalous Orthodox Church," in Pedro Ramet (ed.), *Eastern Christianity and Politics in the Twentieth Century* (Durham, N.C.: Duke University Press, 1988).

11. Arthur A. Cohen, "Maoism," in Milorad M. Drachkovitch (ed.), *Marxism in the Modern World* (Stanford, Calif.: Stanford University Press, 1965), p. 177.

12. See Ono Kazuko, *Chinese Women in a Century of Revolution, 1850–1950* (Stanford, Calif.: Stanford University Press, 1989), chap. 8.

13. Lamaism is the liberal, theistic form of Buddhism practiced in Tibet and Mongolia.

14. C. K. Yang, *Religion in Chinese Society* (Berkeley: University of California Press, 1961), pp. 388–389, 392.

15. Bush, *Religion in Communist China*, pp. 113, 172, 186; László Ladany, *The Communist Party of China and Marxism, 1921–1985: A Self-Portrait* (Stanford, Calif.: Hoover Institution Press, 1988), p. 180.

16. Vojislav Koštunica and Kosta Čavoški, *Party Pluralism or Monism: Social Movements and the Political System in Yugoslavia, 1944–1949* (Boulder, Colo.: East European Monographs, 1985), pp. 30–31, 63, 71–72, 87, 114.

17. Ivo Banac, "Yugoslav Cominformist Organizations and Insurgent Activity: 1948–1954," and Béla K. Király, "The Aborted Soviet Military Plans Against Yugoslavia," both in Wayne S. Vucinich (ed.), *At the Brink of War and Peace: The Tito-Stalin Split in a Historic Perspective* (New York: Brooklyn College Press, 1982); Ivo Banac, *With Stalin Against Tito: Cominformist Splits in Yugoslav Communism* (Ithaca, N.Y.: Cornell University Press, 1988).

18. See O. Aleksa Benigar, *Alojzije Stepinac, Hrvatski kardinal* (Rome: Ziral, 1974).

19. See Stella Alexander, *Church and State in Yugoslavia Since 1945* (Cambridge: Cambridge University Press, 1979), pp. 188–190, 200.

20. Ibid., pp. 169, 249–250.

21. For further discussion of this period, see Pedro Ramet, "Catholicism and Politics in Socialist Yugoslavia," *Religion in Communist Lands* 10 (Winter 1982): 257–260.

22. Carmelo Mesa-Lago, *Cuba in the 1970s*, rev. ed. (Albuquerque: University of New Mexico Press, 1978), pp. 1–5; Edward Gonzalez, *Cuba Under Castro: The Limits of Charisma* (Boston: Houghton Mifflin, 1974), pp. 125–133; Richard R. Fagen, *The Transformation of Political Culture in Cuba* (Stanford, Calif.: Stanford University Press, 1969), p. 50.

23. David Kowalewski, "The Catholic Church and the Cuban Regime," *Religion in Communist Lands* 11 (Spring 1983): 67–68.

24. Margaret E. Crahan, "Catholicism in Cuba," unpublished paper, Occidental College, 1987.

25. *Fidel and Religion: Castro Talks on Revolution and Religion with Frei Betto*, trans. from Spanish by the Cuban Center (New York: Simon and Schuster, 1987), p. 195.

26. Harry Rositzke, *The CIA's Secret Operations* (New York: Reader's Digest Press, 1977), pp. 169–171.

27. Bogdan Szajkowski, *Next to God . . . Poland: Politics and Religion in Contemporary Poland* (New York: St. Martin's Press, 1983), pp. 11–12.

28. See Andrzej Micewski, *Katholische Gruppierungen in Polen: Pax und Znak, 1945–1976*, trans. from Polish by Wolfgang Grycz (Munich and Mainz: Kaiser and Grunewald, 1978).

29. Church property had been exempted from the agrarian reform of 1945.

30. Leonard Binder, "Crises of Political Development," in Leonard Binder et al., *Crises and Sequences in Political Development* (Princeton, N.J.: Princeton University Press, 1971).

31. See Gail Warshofsky Lapidus, *Women in Soviet Society: Equality, Development, and Social Change* (Berkeley: University of California Press, 1978). See also Michelle V. Fuqua, *The Politics of the Domestic Sphere: The* Zhenotdely, *Women's Liberation, and the Search for a* Novyi Byt *in Early Soviet Russia,* Donald W. Treadgold Papers, no. 10 (Seattle: University of Washington—HMJ School of International Studies, 1996).

32. See Schwarz, *Music and Musical Life,* pp. 49–64.

33. As Robert Conquest notes, "By the end of 1934 nine-tenths of the sown acreage of the USSR was concentrated in 240,000 collective farms which had replaced the twenty million odd family farms existing in 1929." Conquest, *The Harvest of Sorrow: Soviet Collectivization and the Terror-Famine* (London: Hutchinson, 1986), p. 182.

34. Regarding the case of Ukraine, see Robert S. Sullivant, *Soviet Politics and the Ukraine, 1917–1957* (New York: Columbia University Press, 1962).

35. Regarding abortion and abortion policy in Stalin's Russia, see Wendy Z. Goldman, *Women, the State, and Revolution: Soviet Family Policy and Social Life, 1917–1936* (Cambridge: Cambridge University Press, 1993), chap. 7.

36. Frank J. Miller, *Folklore for Stalin: Russian Folklore and Pseudofolklore of the Stalin Era* (Armonk, N.Y.: M. E. Sharpe, 1990), p. 9. See also Peter Kenez, *Cinema and Soviet Society, 1917–1953* (Cambridge: Cambridge University Press, 1992).

37. Matthew Cullerne Bown, *Art Under Stalin* (New York: Holmes and Meier, 1991), p. 89.

38. Aleksei Stakhanov, "The Stakhanov Movement Explained" (1936), reprinted in James von Geldern and Richard Stites (eds.), *Mass Culture in Soviet Russia: Tales, Poems, Songs, Movies, Plays, and Folklore, 1917–1953* (Bloomington: Indiana University Press, 1995), pp. 239, 241.

39. Pospielovsky, *The Russian Church,* vol. 1, p. 52.

40. Larry E. Holmes, "Soviet Schools: Policy Pursues Practice, 1921–1928," *Slavic Review* 48 (Summer 1989); Larry E. Holmes, "Fear No Evil: Schools and Religion in Soviet Russia, 1917–1941," in Sabrina Petra Ramet (ed.), *Religious Policy in the Soviet Union* (Cambridge: Cambridge University Press, 1993), pp. 131–136.

41. Pospielovsky, *The Russian Church,* vol. 1, p. 100.

42. Exact figures given in ibid.

43. Isabel A. Tirado, "The Revolution, Young Peasants, and the *Komsomol's* Antireligious Campaigns (1920–1928)," *Canadian-American Slavic Studies* 26, nos. 1–4 (1992): 105, 109, 114. As Glennys Young has documented, in the early 1920s many members of Komsomol continued themselves to observe religious holidays and participate in religious rituals. See Glennys Young, *Power and the Sacred in*

Revolutionary Russia: Religious Activists in the Village (University Park, Pa.: Pennsylvania State University Press, 1997), pp. 88–91.

44. See Giovanni Codevilla, *Stato e Chiesa nell'Unione Sovietica* (Milan: Jaca Book, 1972).

45. Nathaniel Davis, *A Long Walk to Church: A Contemporary History of Russian Orthodoxy* (Boulder, Colo.: Westview Press, 1995), p. 7. For further details about the antireligious campaign, see Ramet, *Cross and Commissar*, p. 49.

46. Davis, *Long Walk*, pp. 12–13.

47. Ibid., p. 11.

48. Fanny E. Bryan, "Anti-Religious Propaganda in the Soviet Union: Attacks Against Islam During the 1920s and 1930s," *Modern Greek Studies Yearbook* 9 (1993): 197.

49. Alexandre Bennigsen and Marie Broxup, *The Islamic Threat to the Soviet State* (New York: St. Martin's Press, 1983), pp. 41, 48.

50. Pospielovsky, *The Russian Church*, vol. 1, p. 170.

51. Ibid., pp. 169, 173.

52. Roy A. Medvedev, *Let History Judge: The Origins and Consequences of Stalinism* (New York: Alfred A. Knopf, 1972), p. 238.

53. As it is now conventionally dated. See, for instance, Thomas B. Bernstein, "How Stalinist Was Mao's China?" *Problems of Communism* 34 (March–April 1985).

54. See Parris H. Chang, *Power and Policy in China* (University Park: Pennsylvania State University Press, 1975), pp. 164–173.

55. Lowell Dittmer, *China's Continuous Revolution: The Post-Liberation Epoch, 1949–1981* (Berkeley: University of California Press, 1987), p. 14.

56. Ibid., pp. 16–17.

57. Ladany, *The Communist Party of China and Marxism*, p. 210.

58. Quoted in ibid., p. 224.

59. Quoted in Bush, *Religion in Communist China*, p. 227.

60. Ibid., p. 231.

61. Merle Goldman, "China's Sprouts of Democracy," *Ethics and International Affairs* 4 (1990): 82.

62. Quoted in Dittmer, *China's Continuous Revolution*, p. 33.

63. Ladany, *Communist Party of China*, pp. 272–273.

64. Quoted in Yen Chia-chi and Kao Kao, *The Ten-Year History of the Chinese Culture Revolution* (Taiwan: Institute of Current China Studies, 1988), p. 55.

65. Quoted in Dittmer, *China's Continuous Revolution*, p. 87.

66. Julia Kwong, *Cultural Revolution in China's Schools, May 1966–April 1969* (Stanford, Calif.: Hoover Institution Press, 1988), pp. 113–116.

67. Regarding the impact on the educational system, see Maurice Meisner, *Mao's China: A History of the People's Republic* (New York: Free Press, 1977), p. 349.

68. Arnold Perris, *Music as Propaganda: Art to Persuade, Art to Control* (Westport, Conn.: Greenwood Press, 1985), pp. 110–111.

69. Harriet Evans, "Defining Difference: The 'Scientific' Construction of Sexuality and Gender in the People's Republic of China," *Signs* 20 (Winter 1995): 364.

70. Holmes Welch, *Buddhism Under Mao* (Cambridge, Mass.: Harvard University Press, 1972), pp. 19–25; Peter Humphrey, "Islam in China Today," *Religion in Communist Lands* 10 (Autumn 1982): 170; Angelo S. Lazzarotto, *La Chiesa cattolica in Cina—La politica di libertà religiosa dopo Mao* (Milan: Jaca Books, 1982), p. 56.

71. For example, at its second conference (Peking, 5–19 January 1962) the Patri-

otic Association of Chinese Catholics adopted a resolution swearing to "whole-heartedly accept the leadership of the Chinese Communist Party, follow the socialist Road, energetically serve socialist construction, hold aloft the anti-imperialist banner, take an active part in the anti-imperialist occupation of our territory of Taiwan and [in defeating] its plot of creating 'two Chinas,' support the national liberation movements, continue to be vigilant and expose the plot of U.S. imperialism and the Vatican to harm the new China by utilizing Catholics, resolutely shake off the control of the Vatican, and attain thoroughly the goal of independence and self-government for Chinese Catholics in the administration of the Church." Quoted in Bush, *Religion in Communist China*, p. 156.

72. Ibid., p. 296.

73. Lazzarotto, *La Chiesa cattolica*, p. 33.

74. Richard West, *Tito and the Rise and Fall of Yugoslavia* (New York: Carroll and Graf, 1994), p. 245.

75. World Bank, *Yugoslavia: Self-Management and the Challenges of Development*, 6 vols., Report No. 1615a-YU (21 March 1978), vol. 2, p. 71.

76. See elaboration in Ramet, "Catholicism and Politics," pp. 257–260.

77. See Sabrina Petra Ramet, *Balkan Babel: The Disintegration of Yugoslavia from the Death of Tito to Ethnic War*, 2nd ed. (Boulder, Colo.: Westview Press, 1996), chap. 8.

78. Noel Malcolm, *Bosnia: A Short History* (New York: New York University Press, 1944), p. 196.

79. Mesa-Lago's term. See *Cuba in the 1970s*, p. ix.

80. See Peter Winn, "The Cuban State and the Arts," in Irving Louis Horowitz (ed.), *Cuban Communism*, 4th ed. (New Brunswick, N.J.: Transaction Books, 1981), pp. 356–357; Carmelo Mesa-Lago, "Castro's Domestic Course," *Problems of Communism* 22 (September–October 1973): 36.

81. See Edward Gonzalez, "Castro and Cuba's New Orthodoxy," *Problems of Communism* 25 (January–February 1976).

82. William M. LeoGrande, "Party Development in Revolutionary Cuba," *Journal of Interamerican Studies and World Affairs* 21 (November 1979): 473–474.

83. Margaret E. Crahan, "Salvation Through Christ or Marx: Religion in Revolutionary Cuba," *Journal of Interamerican Studies and World Affairs* 21 (February 1979): 156.

84. On Bible burning, see *Independent* (London), 5 July 1995, p. 14; on the abolition of Christmas in 1965, see *The Times* (London), 28 May 1992, on *Nexis*.

85. Crahan, "Salvation Through Christ," p. 174.

86. Thomas Quigley, "The Catholic Church in Cuba," in Pedro Ramet (ed.), *Catholicism and Politics in Communist Societies* (Durham, N.C.: Duke University Press, 1990), pp. 307–309.

87. Crahan, "Catholicism in Cuba."

88. *Neue Zürcher Zeitung*, 8 March 1986, p. 3.

89. Jan B. de Weydenthal, *The Communists of Poland: An Historical Outline*, rev. ed. (Stanford, Calif.: Hoover Institution Press, 1986), p. 61.

90. See Andrzej Panufnik, "Composers and Commissars," *Encounter*, March 1955.

91. De Weydenthal, *The Communists of Poland*, p. 65.

92. Giovanni Barberini, *Stato socialista e Chiesa cattolica in Polonia* (Bologna: Centro Studi Europa Orientale, 1983), p. 55; Suzanne Hruby, "The Church in

Poland and Its Political Influence," *Journal of International Affairs* 36 (Fall/Winter 1982/83): 320.

93. On this tactic, see Ramet, *Cross and Commissar*, p. 29.

94. Barberini, *Stato socialista*, pp. 67 68, 77.

95. De Weydenthal, *The Communists of Poland*, p. 99.

96. Quoted in ibid.

97. Szajkowski, *Next to God . . . Poland*, p. 19.

98. Ronald C. Monticone, *The Catholic Church in Communist Poland, 1945–1985* (Boulder, Colo.: East European Monographs, 1986), pp. 28–30.

99. Szajkowski, *Next to God . . . Poland*, p. 19.

100. Jowitt, "Inclusion and Mobilization"; Alfred G. Meyer, *Communism*, 4th ed. (New York: Random House, 1984); Robert C. Tucker, *The Soviet Political Mind: Studies in Stalinism and Post-Stalin Change* (New York: Praeger, 1963); George Kolankiewicz, "Poland and the Politics of Permissible Pluralism," *Eastern European Politics and Societies* 2 (Winter 1988).

101. Jowitt, "Inclusion and Mobilization," p. 94.

102. Ramet, *Cross and Commissar*, pp. 46–48, 50–51.

103. Davis, *Long Walk*, pp. 20, 27.

104. John Anderson, *Religion, State and Politics in the Soviet Union and Successor States* (Cambridge: Cambridge University Press, 1994), p. 56.

105. Ibid., p. 136.

106. Borys Lewytzkyj, *Sovetskij narod, Das Sowjetvolk: Nationalitätenpolitik als Instrument des Sowjetimperialismus* (Hamburg: Hoffmann and Campe, 1983), p. 90.

107. On these groupings, see Immanuel C. Y. Hsü, *China Without Mao: The Search for a New Order* (Oxford: Oxford University Press, 1982), chaps. 1–2; Harry Harding, *China's Second Revolution: Reform After Mao* (Washington, D.C.: Brookings Institution Press, 1987), chap. 3.

108. Harding (*China's Second Revolution*, pp. 53–57) likewise refers to this period as an "interregnum."

109. For discussion of the politics of this period, see Stuart R. Schram, "China After the 13th Congress," *China Quarterly*, no. 114 (June 1988); John P. Burns, "China's Governance: Political Reform in a Turbulent Environment," *China Quarterly*, no. 119 (September 1989).

110. Lowell Dittmer, *China Under Reform* (Boulder, Colo.: Westview Press, 1994), p. 38.

111. Quoted in Ruan Ming, *Deng Xiaoping: Chronicle of an Empire* (Boulder, Colo.: Westview Press, 1994), p. 63.

112. Quoted in Foster Stockwell, *Religion in China Today* (Beijing: New World Press, 1993), p. 39.

113. Edward J. Malatesta, S.J., "Draw the bow, but do not shoot: The Religious Policy of the People's Republic of China," paper presented at the University of Washington, Seattle, 11 March 1991.

114. Human Rights Watch, *China: Religious Persecution Persists* (New York: Human Rights Watch, December 1995), appendix 6, pp. 43–44.

115. According to Christian groups in Hong Kong cited in Merle Goldman, "Religion in Post-Mao China," *Annals of the American Academy of Political and Social Sciences*, no. 483 (January 1986): 153.

116. Cited in Goldman, "Religion in Post-Mao China," p. 153.

117. Ibid., p. 152.

118. Anthony P. B. Lambert, "The Church in China—Pre and Post Tiananmen Square," *Religion in Communist Lands* 18 (Autumn 1990): 237–238.

119. *Keston News Service,* no. 263 (13 November 1986): 11.

120. *Christian Science Monitor,* 30 November 1989, p. 12, and 2 February 1990, p. 6; *Keston News Service,* no. 358 (13 September 1990): 9; *Neue Zürcher Zeitung,* 22 November 1990, p. 2; *Süddeutsche Zeitung* (Munich), 2–3 February 1991, p. 8.

121. On the fall of Zhao Ziyang, see Richard Baum, *Burying Mao: Chinese Politics in the Age of Deng Xiaoping,* updated ed. (Princeton, N.J.: Princeton University Press, 1995), chap. 11 (The Beijing Spring: April–May 1989).

122. Quoted in ibid., p. 250.

123. Human Rights Watch, *China: Religious Persecution Persists,* pp. 3, 6.

124. Ibid., p. 7.

125. Ibid., p. 10.

126. Details in Human Rights Watch, *China: Persecution of a Protestant Sect* (New York: Human Rights Watch, June 1994).

127. *Osmi kongres Saveza Komunista Jugoslavije* (Belgrade: Komunist, 1964), excerpted in *Nacionalno pitanje u djelima klasika marksizma i u dokumentima i praksi kpj/skj* (Zagreb: Centar Društvenih Djelatnosti ssoh, 1978), p. 360, as quoted in Sabrina P. Ramet, *Nationalism and Federalism in Yugoslavia, 1962–1991,* 2nd ed. (Bloomington: Indiana University Press, 1992), p. 51.

128. See Dušan Bilandžić, *Historija Socijalističke Federativne Republike Jugoslavije: Glavni procesi* (Zagreb: Školska knjiga, 1978), chap. 5.

129. *New York Times,* 23 May 1974, p. 5; Savez Komunista Hrvatske, Centralni komitet, *Izvještaj o stanju u Savezu komunista Hrvatske u odnosu na prodor nacionalizma u njegove redove* (Zagreb: Informativna služba ck skh, May 1972), pp. 127–128, as given in Ramet, *Nationalism and Federalism,* p. 131.

130. Aleksa Djilas, "Identities, Ideologies, and the Yugoslav War," *Balkan Forum* (Skopje) 2 (September 1994): 25.

131. Stella Alexander, "Yugoslavia: New Legislation on the Legal Status of Religious Communities," *Religion in Communist Lands* 8 (Summer 1980): 119. The text of the 1953 law is reproduced in Rastko Vidić, *The Position of the Church in Yugoslavia* (Belgrade: Jugoslavija, 1962), pp. 128–133.

132. Hamdija Pozderac, *Nacionalni odnosi i socijalističko zajedništvo* (Sarajevo: Svjetlost, 1978), p. 44.

133. Radomir Rakić, "Izdavačka delatnost crkve od 1945, do 1970, godine," in *Srpska Pravoslavna Crkva 1920–1970: Spomenica o 50-godišnjici vaspostavljanja Srpske Patrijaršije* (Belgrade: Kosmos, 1971); Alexander, *Church and State in Yugoslavia,* p. 274.

134. See *Politika* (Belgrade), 14 January 1964, trans. in *Religion in Communist Dominated Areas* 3 (31 March 1964): 48; *Politika,* 23 October 1970, p. 6; *Borba* (Belgrade), 9 October 1980, p. 4; Ahmed Smajlović, "Muslims in Yugoslavia," *Journal— Institute of Muslim Minority Affairs* 1, no. 2, and 2, no. 1 (Winter 1979/Summer 1980): 139–140, 142–143.

135. For details, see Alexander, "New Legislation," and Ivan Lazić, "Donošenje novih republičkih i pokrajinskih zakona o pravnom položaju vjerskih zajednica u SFRJ," *Naša zakonitost* (Zagreb) 30, nos. 11–12 (1976).

136. IBC USA Licensing, *Political Risk Services,* 1 May 1995, on *Nexis.*

137. *Washington Post,* 5 August 1992, *Agence France Presse,* 16 December 1993, and IBC USA Licensing, *Political Risk Services,* 1 August 1994, all on *Nexis;* and interview with Castro, in *Focus* (Munich), 6 November 1995, pp. 330–333.

138. *Reuter News Service,* 14 July 1992, and 2 October 1993, both on *Nexis;* U. S. Department of State, *Cuba: Human Rights Practices, 1994,* on *Nexis* (March 1995).

139. *Chicago Tribune,* 19 June 1992, p. 9.

140. *Independent* (London), 5 July 1995, p. 14; *Cuba: Human Rights Practices, 1994; Federal News Service,* 14 June 1995, on *Nexis.*

141. *Independent* (London), 5 July 1995, p. 14.

142. *National Catholic Reporter,* 28 June 1996, p. 16.

143. *New York Times,* 31 October 1996, p. A4, and 20 November 1996, p. A3.

144. See, for example, Adam Bromke, "A New Juncture in Poland," *Problems of Communism* 25 (September–October 1976); Ernst Kux, "Growing Tensions in Eastern Europe," *Problems of Communism* 29 (March–April 1980); Pedro Ramet, "Poland's Economic Dilemma," *New Leader,* 5 May 1980.

145. Dieter Bingen, "The Catholic Church as a Political Actor," in Jack Bielasiak and Maurice D. Simon (eds.), *Polish Politics: Edge of the Abyss* (New York: Praeger, 1984), p. 214.

146. Monticone, *The Catholic Church in Communist Poland,* p. 57.

147. Ibid., p. 69.

148. See discussion in Pedro Ramet, "The Dynamics of Yugoslav Religious Policy: Some Insights from Organization Theory," in Ramet (ed.), *Yugoslavia in the 1980s;* Ramet, *Cross and Commissar,* chap. 7.

149. See, for example, *Moscow News* (1987), no. 4, as cited in Vera Tolz, "Church-State Relations Under Gorbachev," *Radio Liberty Research,* 11 September 1987, p. 5.

150. These and other sources of destabilization are discussed in Sabrina Petra Ramet, *Social Currents in Eastern Europe: The Sources and Consequences of the Great Transformation,* 2nd ed. (Durham, N.C.: Duke University Press, 1995), chap. 2.

151. One of the best accounts of the Gorbachev era is Dusko Doder and Louise Branson, *Gorbachev: Heretic in the Kremlin* (New York: Viking Press, 1990).

152. *Politika* (Belgrade), 2 September 1990, p. 18.

153. Rhoda Rabkin, "Implications of the Gorbachev Era for Cuban Socialism," *Studies in Comparative Communism* 23 (Spring 1990).

154. Howard J. Wiarda, "Is Cuba Next? Crises of the Castro Regime," *Problems of Communism* 40 (January–April 1991).

3. Varieties of Christianity in East Germany

This is a significantly revised, updated, and expanded version of a chapter that appeared originally in Sabrina Petra Ramet, ed., *Protestantism and Politics in Eastern Europe and Russia: The Communist and Postcommunist Eras* (Durham, N.C.: Duke University Press, 1992); and in *Religion in Communist Lands* 19, nos. 3–4 (Winter 1991). Reprinted by permission.

1. Wolfgang Kaul, *Kirchen und Religionsgemeinschaften in der DDR—Eine Dokumentation* (Rostock-Warnemünde: Institute for Marxism-Leninism, 1984), pp. 5–6; *Zahlenspiegel Bundesrepublik Deutschland/Deutsche Demokratische Republik: Ein Vergleich,* 3rd ed. (Bonn: Federal Ministry for Inter-German Relations, 1988), p. 97.

2. *Zahlenspiegel,* p. 97.

3. *Frankfurter Allgemeine,* 23 April 1988, p. 12, trans. in JPRS, *East Europe Report,* no. EER-88-040 (23 May 1988): 2.

4. *Keston News Service,* no. 279 (9 July 1987): 19.

5. Quoted in Robert F. Goeckel, "The Catholic Church in East Germany," in

Pedro Ramet (ed.), *Catholicism and Politics in Communist Societies* (Durham, N.C.: Duke University Press, 1990), p. 103.

6. Ibid., p. 107.

7. Ibid., p. 115.

8. *Der Spiegel* (Hamburg), 28 August 1995, pp. 60–65.

9. Most of the figures given here come from interviews with responsible Church representatives or with state officials in East Germany, June–July 1988, or from Kaul, *Kirchen und Religionsgemeinschaften*. Some statistics were taken from Hubert Kirchner (ed.), *Freikirchen und Konfessionelle Minderheitskirchen* (East Berlin: Evangelische Verlagsanstalt, 1987); and Helmut Obst, *Apostel und Propheten der Neuzeit: Gründer christlicher Religionsgemeinschaften des 19. 20. Jahrhunderts*, 2nd ed. (East Berlin: Union, 1981).

10. *Christian Science Monitor*, 6 November 1989, p. 3.

11. Ulrich Materne, "Der Bund Evangelische-Freikirchlicher Gemeinden in der DDR," in Kirchner (ed.), *Freikirchen*, p. 51.

12. Werner Klan and Johannes Zellmer, "Die Evangelisch-lutherische (altlutherische) Kirche," in Kirchner (ed.), *Freikirchen*, p. 134.

13. Knuth Hansen and Hubert Kirchner, "Die Mennoniten-Gemeinde," in Kirchner (ed.), *Freikirchen*, p. 32.

14. Christian Pietsche, "Im Benehmen mit dem Staate: Die Neuapostolische Kirche in der DDR," *Kirche im Sozialismus* 12 (June 1986): 123–124.

15. DPA (Hamburg), 19 March 1990, trans. in FBIS, *Daily Report* (Eastern Europe), 20 March 1990, p. 33.

16. For an account of Weissenberg's life and the early experiences of his community, see Obst, *Apostel und Propheten*, pp. 326–344.

17. See Dan Beck, "The Luther Revival: Aspects of National *Abgrenzung* and Confessional *Gemeinschaft* in the German Democratic Republic," in Pedro Ramet (ed.), *Religion and Nationalism in Soviet and East European Politics*, rev. and expanded ed. (Durham, N.C.: Duke University Press, 1989).

18. Bishop Gienke aggravated members of his Church in 1989 by joining Honecker in reaffirming the continued validity of the "Church in Socialism" concept at a time when Church members were increasingly critical of the idea. As a result, the district synod tallied a vote of no confidence in November — 32 to 30 against him. The vote impelled the bishop to resign his office that same month. See ADN International Service (East Berlin), 14 November 1989, trans. in FBIS, *Daily Report* (Eastern Europe), 14 November 1989, p. 27.

19. See *Neue Zürcher Zeitung*, 28 September 1990, p. 3, 24–25 February 1991, p. 4, and 27 February 1991, p. 4; *Süddeutsche Zeitung* (Munich), 23–24 February 1991, p. 5.

20. For details, see Hans-Martin Moderow and Matthias Sense (eds.), *Orientierung Ökumene: Ein Handbuch*, 2nd ed. (East Berlin: Evangelische Verlagsanstalt, 1987), esp. chap. 7.

21. Quoted in Richard W. Solberg, *God and Caesar in East Germany: The Conflict of Church and State in East Germany Since 1945* (New York: Macmillan, 1961), p. 30.

22. Ibid., p. 57.

23. Horst Dähn, *Konfrontation oder Kooperation? Das Verhältnis von Staat und Kirche in der SBZ/DDR 1945–1980* (Opladen: Westdeutscher, 1982), p. 28.

24. Quoted in Solberg, *God and Caesar*, p. 74.

25. Ibid., p. 90.

26. Dähn, *Konfrontation oder Kooperation*, p. 44.

27. Quoted in Solberg, *God and Caesar,* p. 196.

28. Ibid., p. 234.

29. Ibid., p. 235.

30. Quoted in Florian Ehlert, " 'Suchet der Stadt Bestes!': Bischof Mitzenheims Bemühungen um Einvernehmen mit dem Staat," *Kirche im Sozialismus* 14 (June 1988): 97.

31. Ralf Georg Reuth, *IM "Sekretär": Die "Gauck-Recherche" und die Dokumente zum "Fall Stolpe,"* 2nd ed. (Frankfurt/Berlin: Ullstein Buch, 1992), p. 55.

32. Quoted in Ehlert, " 'Suchet der Stadt Bestes!,' " p. 98.

33. Quoted in ibid., p. 99.

34. Quoted in ibid.

35. Stephen R. Bowers, "East German National Consciousness: Domestic and Foreign Policy Considerations," *East European Quarterly* 13 (Summer 1979): 148.

36. Quoted in Peter Fischer, *Kirche und Christen in der DDR* (East Berlin: Gebr. Holzapfel, 1978), p. 28.

37. Quoted in ibid., p. 87.

38. Quoted in ibid., p. 89.

39. See *Kirche als Lerngemeinschaft: Dokumente aus der Arbeit des Bundes der Evangelischen Kirchen in der DDR* (East Berlin: Evangelische Verlagsanstalt, 1981), pp. 161–162.

40. Ibid., pp. 202, 206. See also the discussion in Günter Krusche, "The Church Between Accommodation and Refusal: The Significance of the Lutheran Doctrine of the 'Two Kingdoms' for the Churches of the German Democratic Republic," *Religion, State and Society* 22, no. 3 (1994): 323–332.

41. Robert F. Goeckel, *The Lutheran Church and the East German State: Political Conflict and Change Under Ulbricht and Honecker* (Ithaca, N.Y.: Cornell University Press, 1990), p. 176.

42. *Kirche als Lerngemeinschaft,* p. 169.

43. Theo Mechtenberg, "Die Friedensverantwortung der Evangelischen Kirchen in der DDR," *Deutsche Studien* 19 (June 1981): 176.

44. *Kirche als Lerngemeinschaft,* p. 208.

45. Ibid., p. 255.

46. See Albrecht Schönherr, "Nach zehn Jahren: Zum Staat-Kirche-Gespräch am 6. Marz 1978," *Kirche im Sozialismus* 14 (February 1988): 5.

47. *Frankfurter Allgemeine,* 27 September 1978, p. 1.

48. For further discussion, see Pedro Ramet, "Church and Peace in the GDR," *Problems of Communism* 33 (July–August 1984): 51–53; reprinted as chap. 5 in Pedro Ramet, *Cross and Commissar: The Politics of Religion in Eastern Europe and the USSR* (Bloomington: Indiana University Press, 1987).

49. Raelynn J. Hillhouse, "Out of the Closet Behind the Wall: Sexual Politics and Social Change in the GDR," *Slavic Review* 49 (Winter 1990): 592–593.

50. *De Tijd* (Amsterdam), 16 December 1983, trans. in JPRS, *East Europe Report,* no. EPS-84-015 (30 January 1984): 20; and Ulrike Enders, "Erziehung zum Hass: Zum staatlichen Erziehungsprogramm für Kindergarten," *Kirche im Sozialismus* 13 (April 1987).

51. *Frankfurter Allgemeine,* 5 September 1984, p. 3.

52. Ibid., 9 February 1988, p. 2.

53. Quoted in Gisela Helwig, "Zwischen Opposition und Opportunismus: Zur Lage der Kirche in der DDR," *Deutschland Archiv* 9 (June 1976): 578.

54. Wolfgang Büscher and Peter Wensierski, *Null Bock auf DDR: Aussteiger-jugend im anderen Deutschland* (Hamburg: Spiegel, 1984), p. 42; also *Glaube und Heimat* (Jena), 18 May 1986, p. 4, trans. in JPRS, *East Europe Report*, no. EER-86-103 (17 July 1986): 98–99.

55. *Neues Deutschland*, 12 February 1985, p. 1.

56. Gerhard Besier, *Der SED-Staat und die Kirche 1969–1990* (Frankfurt-am-Main: Propylaen, 1995), pp. 213–214.

57. Ibid., p. 214.

58. East German News Agency, 18 August 1982, in *BBC Summary of World Broadcasts*, 20 August 1982.

59. *Der Spiegel* (Hamburg), 26 July 1993, p. 58.

60. *Welt am Sonntag* (Hamburg), 22 October 1995, p. 5. On Frankel, see also Robert F. Goeckel, "The Churches and Collaboration with the Secret Police: The Case of East Germany," paper presented at the annual convention of the American Association for the Advancement of Slavic Studies, Boston, November 1996, p. 10.

61. *Die Welt* (Bonn), 2 March 1995, p. 2.

62. Reuth, *IM "Sekretär,"* p. 45; and *Welt am Sonntag*, 2 April 1995, p. 5. See also *Der Spiegel*, 13 March 1995, pp. 22–24; and *Welt am Sonntag*, 19 February 1995, p. 34.

63. *Süddeutsche Zeitung* (Munich), 17/18 April 1993, p. 5.

64. *Welt am Sonntag*, 23 April 1995, p. 5.

65. *Süddeutsche Zeitung*, 16/17 January 1993, p. 6.

66. Patricia J. Smith, "Democratizing East Germany: Emerging Political Groups and the Dynamics of Change," unpublished Ph.D. dissertation, University of Washington, 1995, chap. 6, p. 27.

67. Markus Meckel and Martin Gutzeit (compilers), *Opposition in der DDR: Zehn Jahre Kirchliche Friedensarbeit—Kommentierte Quellentexte* (Cologne: Bund, 1994), p. 53.

68. John S. Conway, "The 'Stasi' and the Churches: Between Coercion and Compromise in East Germany Protestantism, 1949–89," *Journal of Church and State* 36 (Autumn 1994): 733.

69. *Mittelalter, Beginn der Neuzeit* (Berlin: Volk und Wissen Volkseigener, 1958), a history textbook for senior schools in the GDR, as quoted in Arvan Gordon, "The Luther Quincentenary in the GDR," *Religion in Communist Lands* 12 (Spring 1984): p. 78.

70. Wolfram von Hanstein, *Von Luther bis Hitler* (Dresden, 1950), pp. 22–23, as cited in Stephen P. Hoffmann, "The GDR, Luther and the German Question," *Review of Politics* 48 (Spring 1986): 250.

71. Alexander Abusch, *Der Irrweg einer Nation* (Berlin, 1950), as cited in Hoffmann, "The GDR." First published in 1946.

72. Gerhard Brendler, "Reformation und Fortschritt," in Leo Stern and Max Steinmetz (eds.), *450 Jahre Reformation* (Berlin: VEB Deutscher Verlag der Wissenschaften, 1967), p. 67, as quoted in Hoffmann, "The GDR," p. 256.

73. Robert F. Goeckel, "The Luther Anniversary in East Germany," *World Politics* 37 (October 1984): 119.

74. Quoted in ibid., p. 121.

75. Friedrich Winterhager, "Thomas Müntzer und die Gegenwart in Beiden Deutschen Staaten," *Deutsche Studien* 24 (December 1986): 386; and Arbeitsgruppe *Thomas-Müntzer-Gedenken 1989* des Kirchenbundes, "Orientierungshilfe zum Ge-

denken des 500. Geburtstag von Thomas Müntzer im Jahre 1989," *EPD Dokumentation,* no. 52 (1987): 44.

76. "Thesen uber Thomas Müntzer," *Neues Deutschland,* 30-31 January 1988, p. 9.

77. Ibid.

78. Roland Hahn, "Müntzer ein Sozialrevolutionär? Die SED und die Kirche vor dem 500. Geburtstag Thomas Müntzer," *Kirche im Sozialismus* 14 (August 1988): 141; also *Thomas Müntzer Ehrung der DDR 1989* (East Berlin: Dietz, 1988).

79. Rita Hermanns, "Auf der Suche nach Freiraumen: über die Initiative 'Kirchentag von unten,' " *Kirche im Sozialismus* 13 (August 1987): 145.

80. *Frankfurter Allgemeine,* 24 June 1987, p. 5, and 29 June 1987, p. 5.

81. "Grössere Freiräume für Basisgruppen" (Rudiger Rosenthal, interviewed by Matthias Hartmann), *Kirche im Sozialismus* 13 (October 1987): 189, 191.

82. *Welt am Sonntag,* 29 November 1989, pp. 1-2, and *Frankfurter Allgemeine,* 31 December 1987, p. 2.

83. *Frankfurter Allgemeine,* 14 November 1988, p. 7, trans. in FBIS, *Daily Report* (Eastern Europe), 17 November 1988, pp. 19, 21. The statement was allegedly read to Leich and distributed in written form to only the first secretaries of SED *Bezirk* and *Kreis* leaderships.

84. Quoted in Vladimir Tismaneanu, "Against Socialist Militarism: The Independent Peace Movement in the German Democratic Republic," in Vladimir Tismaneanu (ed.), *In Search of Civil Society: Independent Peace Movements in the Soviet Bloc* (New York: Routledge, 1990), p. 167.

85. Quoted in Barbara Donovan, "Church Groups Call for Democratic Reforms," *Radio Free Europe Research,* 10 June 1988, p. 1.

86. *Frankfurter Rundschau,* 27 June 1988, p. 1.

87. Quoted in *Die Welt,* 7 June 1988, p. 10, trans. in FBIS, *Daily Report* (Eastern Europe), 8 June 1988, p. 36.

88. *Frankfurter Allgemeine,* 20 September 1988, p. 3; and Matthias Hartmann, " 'Hier ändert sich nichts' — Zur Synodaltagung des Kirchenbundes," *Deutschland Archiv* 21 (October 1988): 1025.

89. On this case, see *Frankfurter Allgemeine,* 20 June 1988, p. 1.

90. *Süddeutsche Zeitung,* 5 July 1988, p. 2; *Die Welt,* 5 July 1988, p. 1, trans. in FBIS, *Daily Report* (Eastern Europe), 6 July 1988, p. 29; *Frankfurter Allgemeine,* 23 July 1988, p. 4, and 9 August 1988, p. 3; and *Süddeutsche Zeitung,* 18 October 1988, p. 2, trans. in FBIS, *Daily Report* (Eastern Europe), 19 October 1988, p. 18.

91. Vienna Domestic Service, 30 December 1988, trans. in FBIS, *Daily Report* (Eastern Europe), 30 December 1988, p. 25; and Michael Burg, "Es geht nicht um die Kirchenpresse," *Kirche im Sozialismus* 14 (December 1988): 218.

92. *Die Welt,* 14 November 1988, p. 1; and DPA (Hamburg), 14 November 1988, both trans. in FBIS, *Daily Report* (Eastern Europe), 15 November 1988, p. 27.

93. Richard Schröder, "Was kann 'Kirche im Sozialismus' sinnvoll heissen?," *Kirche im Sozialismus* 14 (August 1988): 137.

94. *Frankfurter Allgemeine,* 13 March 1989, p. 4, trans. in FBIS, *Daily Report* (Eastern Europe), 17 March 1989, p. 22.

95. Heino Falcke, "Stellvertretendes Handeln: 'Kirche im Sozialismus' am Beispiel der DDR," *Kirche im Sozialismus* 15 (December 1989): 232-237.

96. *Frankfurter Rundschau,* 13 May 1989, p. 2.

97. *Frankfurter Allgemeine,* 21 September 1989, p. 2; also *Neue Zürcher Zeitung,* 24/25 September 1989, p. 3.

98. *Die Welt,* 16/17 September 1989, p. 4, trans. in FBIS, *Daily Report* (Eastern Europe), 19 September 1989, p. 28.

99. *New York Times,* 18 May 1990, p. A5.

100. See, for example, Gerhard Rein, *Die protestantische Revolution: 1987–1990 — Ein Deutsches Lesebuch* (Berlin: Wichern, 1990); and Ehrhard Neubert, *Eine protestantische Revolution* (Osnabruck: KONTEXT, 1990).

101. For documentation sufficient to refute this position, see Gerhard Besier and Stephan Wolf (eds.), *Pfarrer, Christen und Katholiken,* 2nd expanded ed. (Hamburg-Neukirchener, 1992); and Smith, *Democratizing East Germany.*

102. See the full-page article "Es gab nicht nur Helden und Heilige," *Süddeutsche Zeitung,* 8/9 February 1992, p. 10.

103. Quoted in Gerd Stricker, "Afterword," in Sabrina Petra Ramet (ed.), *Protestantism and Politics in Eastern Europe and Russia: The Communist and Postcommunist Eras* (Durham, N.C.: Duke University Press, 1993), p. 349. Regarding the post-1990 revelations of Stasi collaboration on the part of the clergy and the resultant accelerating exodus from the mainline Churches throughout reunified Germany, see Sabrina P. Ramet, "Religion and Politics in Germany since 1945: The Evangelical and Catholic Churches and New Religious Associations," in Brigitte Schulz (ed.), *Unified Germany: Domestic Problems and Global Challenges* (forthcoming).

104. See *Frankfurter Allgemeine,* 3 September 1990, p. 12, and 24 September 1990, p. 14.

105. *Neue Zürcher Zeitung,* 27 February 1991, p. 4.

106. Robert Goeckel, "The Evangelical-Lutheran Church and the East German Revolution," *Occasional Papers on Religion in Eastern Europe* 10 (November 1990): 43. See also Edelbert Richter, *Christentum und Demokratie in Deutschland* (Leipzig: Gustav Kiepenheuer, 1991).

107. "Beten auf Teufel komm raus — Sekten in Deutschland," *Stern,* 4 May 1995, pp. 32-42. See also chap. 14.

108. In the sense of taking the Bible literally, word for word, as an exact history and precise guide to action.

109. *Welt am Sonntag,* 26 March 1995, p. 26.

110. On immigration, see *Die Welt* (Bonn), 28 March 1995, p. 3. On the center, see *Neue Zürcher Zeitung,* 8 May 1995, p. 4. On the return of property, see *Süddeutsche Zeitung,* 8/9 April 1995, p. 6.

111. *Welt am Sonntag,* 9 April 1995, p. 31. See also *Süddeutsche Zeitung,* 12/13 August 1995, p. 5, and *Der Spiegel,* 8 March 1993, pp. 78-80.

112. *Welt am Sonntag,* 5 November 1995, p. 26.

113. Stolpe has published his own account, based on some of his speeches, essays, and interviews over twelve years. See Manfred Stolpe, *Den Menschen Hoffnung geben: Reden, Aufsätze, Interviews aus zwölf Jahren* (Berlin: Wichern, 1991). See also *Neue Zürcher Zeitung,* 25 March 1992, p. 5.

114. *The Times* (London), 22 October 1993, p. 16. See also *Der Spiegel,* 4 October 1993, pp. 108-117, and *Süddeutsche Zeitung,* 13/14 November 1993, p. 5.

115. This was the title of an article that appeared in *Stern* (Hamburg), 30 March 1994, pp. 146-153.

116. *Japan Times,* 30 May 1993, p. 5.

117. Quoted in *International Herald Tribune* (Tokyo ed.), 29/30 May 1993, p. 4.

118. *Süddeutsche Zeitung,* 16/17 November 1993, p. 2.

119. Ibid., 13/14 November 1993, p. 5. This protest notwithstanding, conservative Church circles could only feel encouraged by Chancellor Kohl's selection of 28-year-old Claudia Nolte, a strict Catholic from Rostock, in November 1994 to serve as minister for family, youth, and pensioners. A committed antiabortion activist who has maintained membership in three separate antiabortion organizations, Nolte has talked of wanting to compel women who terminate pregnancies to spend a year doing volunteer work in a hospital as a kind of "penance." *The European* (London), 25 November–1 December 1994, p. 9.

120. *Süddeutsche Zeitung,* 2 January 1994, p. 5.

121. Ibid., 4 January 1994, p. 5.

122. The figures for 1992 and 1993 come from *Der Spiegel,* 17 May 1993, p. 125; the figure for 1995 comes from *Die Welt,* 27 March 1995, p. 3.

123. *Christian Science Monitor,* 7 August 1996, p. 5.

124. *Neues Deutschland,* 31 May 1988, p. 2.

4. Catholicism and National Culture in Poland, Czechoslovakia, and Hungary

This is a revised and expanded version of a chapter which appeared originally in Pedro Ramet, *Cross and Commissar: The Politics of Religion in Eastern Europe and the USSR* (Bloomington, Ind.: Indiana University Press, 1987); reprinted by permission.

1. Andrzej Micewski, *Katholische Gruppierungen in Polen: Pax und Znak, 1945–1976,* trans. Wolfgang Grycz (Munich and Mainz: Kaiser and Grunewald, 1978), p. 69.

2. Najdan Pašić, "Faktori formiranja nacija na Balkanu i kod Južnih Slovena," *Pregled* (1971), no. 5, as cited in Tomislav J. Šagi-Bunić, *Katolička crkva i hrvatski narod* (Zagreb: Kršćanska sadašnjost, 1983), pp. 23–25.

3. Šagi-Bunić, *Katolička crkva,* p. 11.

4. See "Brief des Episcopats über die Pflichten der Katholiken in Polen gegenüber der Nationalen und Religiösen Kultur," *Dokumentation Ostmitteleuropa* 4 (28) (December 1978): 335–338.

5. Wiesław Müller et al., *Kościół w Polsce,* vol. 2: *Wieki XVI–XVIII* (Kraków: Znak, 1969), p. 16.

6. Ibid., p. 21.

7. Ibid., pp. 26–27.

8. Ibid., pp. 28–29.

9. Ibid., p. 28.

10. Lawrence Wolff, "Poland and the Vatican in the Age of Partitions: European Enlightenment, Roman Catholicism, and the Development of Polish Nationalism," Ph.D. diss., Stanford University, 1984, pp. 45–47, 89. But see also p. 4.

11. V. Stanley Vardys, *The Catholic Church, Dissent and Nationality in Soviet Lithuania* (Boulder, Colo.: East European Monographs, 1978), pp. 4–5.

12. Norman Davies, *God's Playground: A History of Poland,* vol. 2: *1795 to the Present* (New York: Columbia University Press, 1982), p. 62.

13. A period of relative toleration of both Latin and Uniate rites of the Catholic Church also began with the reign of Tsar Paul I (1796–1801) and continued to some

extent, during the reign of Alexander I (1801–1825). See ibid., p. 86; and Dennis J. Dunn, *The Catholic Church and the Soviet Government, 1939–1949* (Boulder, Colo.: East European Monographs, 1977), pp. 8–10.

14. Davies, *God's Playground*, vol. 2, pp. 86–87.

15. Ibid., p. 210.

16. Walter J. Kapica, "Major Socio-Political Movements and Catholicism in Partitioned Poland," Ph.D. diss., Catholic University of America, 1968, p. 67.

17. Ibid.

18. Vardys, *Catholic Church*, pp. 12–13.

19. Davies, *God's Playground*, vol. 2, p. 99.

20. See Sebastian Haffner, *The Rise and Fall of Prussia*, trans. Ewald Osers (London: Weidenfeld and Nicolson, 1980).

21. Lothar Gall, *Bismarck: The White Revolutionary*, vol. 2: *1871–1898*, trans. J. A. Underwood (London: Unwin Hyman, 1990), pp. 177–178.

22. William Carr, *A History of Germany, 1815–1990*, 4th ed. (London: Edward Arnold, 1991), p. 127.

23. Davies, *God's Playground*, vol. 2, pp. 126–127.

24. Quoted in ibid., p. 134.

25. Among the large number of excellent works dealing with Habsburg Austria, these deserve mention: Edward Crankshaw, *The Fall of the House of Habsburg* (New York: Viking, 1963); Péter Hanák (ed.), *Die nationale Frage in der Österreichisch-Ungarischen Monarchie 1900–1918* (Budapest: Akademiai Kiado, 1966); Oscar Jászi, *The Dissolution of the Habsburg Monarchy* (Chicago: University of Chicago Press, 1928); Robert A. Kann, *A History of the Habsburg Empire, 1526–1918* (Berkeley: University of California Press, 1974); Robert A. Kann, *Das Nationalitätenproblem der Habsburgermonarchie: Geschichte und Ideengehalt der nationalen Bestrebungen vom Vormärz bis zur Auflösung des Reiches im Jahre 1918* (Graz: H. Bohlaus, 1964); Robert A. Kann and Zdenek V. David, *The Peoples of the Eastern Habsburg Lands, 1526–1918* (Seattle: University of Washington Press, 1984); C. A. Macartney, *The Habsburg Empire, 1790–1918* (London: Weidenfeld and Nicolson, 1968); Arthur J. May, *The Hapsburg Monarchy, 1867–1914* (Cambridge, Mass.: Harvard University Press, 1960); Christoph Stolzl, *Die Ära Bach in Böhmen: Sozialgeschichtliche Studien zum Neoabsolutismus, 1849–1859* (Munich: R. Oldenbourg, 1971); and Adam Wandruszka, *The House of Habsburg*, trans. from German by Cathleen and Hans Epstein (Garden City, N.Y.: Doubleday, 1964). For useful biographies of Metternich and Kaiser Franz Josef, see Andrew Milne, *Metternich* (London: University of London Press, 1975), and Jean-Paul Bled, *Franz Joseph*, trans. from French by Teresa Bridgeman (Oxford: Basil Blackwell, 1992).

26. Kann, *A History of the Habsburg Empire*, pp. 390–391.

27. Davies, *God's Playground*, vol. 2, p. 142.

28. Ibid., pp. 212–213.

29. Ibid., pp. 216–217.

30. Ronald Modras, *The Catholic Church and Antisemitism: Poland, 1933–1939* (Chur, Switzerland: Harwood Academic, 1994), p. 37.

31. Davies, *God's Playground*, vol. 2, p. 404.

32. Quoted in Antony Polonsky, *Politics in Independent Poland 1921–1939: The Crisis of Constitutional Government* (Oxford: Clarendon Press, 1972), p. 208.

33. Ibid., pp. 210–211.

34. Davies, *God's Playground*, vol. 2, pp. 419–420.

35. Quoted in Micewski, *Katholische Gruppierungen*, p. 219.

36. Oscar Halecki (ed.), *Poland* (New York: Praeger, 1957), p. 208; and Jan Kubik, *The Power of Symbols Against the Symbols of Power: The Rise of Solidarity and the Fall of State Socialism in Poland* (University Park: Pennsylvania State University Press, 1994), p. 106.

37. *A Freedom Within: The Prison Notes of Stefan Cardinal Wyszyński*, trans. Barbara Krzywicki-Herburt and Rev. Walter J. Ziemba (San Diego: Harcourt Brace Jovanovich, 1982).

38. Cited in Bogdan Szajkowski, *Next to God . . . Poland: Politics and Religion in Contemporary Poland* (New York: St. Martin's Press, 1983), p. 17.

39. Vincent C. Chrypiński, "Church and Nationality in Postwar Poland," in Pedro Ramet (ed.), *Religion and Nationalism in Soviet and East European Politics*, Rev. and expanded ed. (Durham, N.C.: Duke University Press, 1989), p. 247.

40. George Weigel, *The Final Revolution: The Resistance Church and the Collapse of Communism* (Oxford: Oxford University Press, 1992), p. 114.

41. Ibid., p. 116.

42. Szajkowski, *Next to God*, pp. 31-32.

43. Quoted in Adam Bromke, "A New Juncture in Poland," *Problems of Communism* 25 (September–October 1976): 11-12.

44. Chrypiński, "Church and Nationality," pp. 250-251.

45. Ronald C. Monticone, *The Catholic Church in Communist Poland 1945-1985: Forty Years of Church-State Relations* (Boulder, Colo.: East European Monographs, 1986), p. 95.

46. Szajkowski, *Next to God*, p. 87.

47. Alain Touraine, François Dubet, Michel Wievorka, and Jan Strzelecki, *Solidarity: Poland, 1980-81*, trans. David Denby (Cambridge: Cambridge University Press, 1983), p. 45.

48. Adam Michnik, *The Church and the Left*, trans. from Polish by David Ost (Chicago: University of Chicago Press, 1993), p. 146.

49. Quoted in Szajkowski, *Next to God*, p. 168.

50. Archbishop Jozcf Glemp, "Homily Delivered on 26 August 1982 at Jasna Gora, Częstochowa," trans. in *Communist Affairs* 2 (April 1983): 252-253.

51. For details, see Sabrina Petra Ramet, *Social Currents in Eastern Europe: The Sources and Consequences of the Great Transformation*, 2nd ed. (Durham, N.C.: Duke University Press, 1995), pp. 187-188.

52. Kann, *A History of the Habsburg Empire, 1526-1918*, p. 115.

53. Kann and David, *Peoples of the Eastern Habsburg Lands*, p. 138.

54. Kann, *A History of the Habsburg Empire, 1526-1918*, pp. 115, 117; Jörg K. Hoensch, *A History of Modern Hungary 1867-1986*, trans. from German by Kim Traynor (London: Longman, 1988), p. 43; Peter F. Sugar, "The Principality of Transylvania," in Peter F. Sugar with Péter Hanák (eds.), *A History of Hungary* (Bloomington: Indiana University Press, 1990), pp. 132, 134; and Horst Haselsteiner, "Cooperation and Confrontation Between Rulers and the Noble Estates, 1711-1848," in Sugar with Hanak (eds.), *A History of Hungary*, pp. 138-141.

55. F. M. Mayer-Kaindl and Hans Pirchegger, *Geschichte und Kulturleben Österreichs, von 1493 bis 1792*, 5th ed. (Vienna: Wilhelm Braumüller, 1960), p. 150; and Kann, *A History of the Habsburg Empire, 1526-1918*, pp. 133-134.

56. Mayer-Kaindl and Pirchegger, *Geschichte*, pp. 315-324; Kann, *A History of the Habsburg Empire, 1526-1918*, p. 188; and Macartney, *The Habsburg Empire*, p. 120.

57. Haselsteiner, "Cooperation and Confrontation," p. 159.

58. Alan Sked, *The Decline and Fall of the Habsburg Empire 1815–1918* (New York: Longman Group, 1989), p. 47.

59. Ibid., p. 143.

60. For details, see Bled, *Franz Joseph,* pp. 80–82; and Macartney, *The Habsburg Empire,* p. 458.

61. Leslie László, "Church and State in Hungary, 1919–1945," Ph.D. diss., Columbia University, 1973, pp. 20–21.

62. Ibid., pp. 27–28, 30, 33–34.

63. Ibid., p. 39.

64. See Péter Hanák, "The Dual Monarchy (1867–1918)," in Ervin Pamlényi (ed.), *A History of Hungary* (London: Collet's, 1975), pp. 373–375.

65. Miron Constantinescu, Ladislaus Bányai, V. Curticapeanu, C. Göllner, and C. Nuţu, "Zur nationalen Frage in Österreich-Ungarn (1900–1918)," in Péter Hanák (ed.), *Die nationale Frage in der Österreichisch-Ungarischen Monarchie 1900–1918* (Budapest: Akademiai Kiado, 1966), pp. 76–77.

66. István Dolmányos, "Kritik der Lex Apponyi (Die Schulgesetze vom Jahre 1907)," in Hanák (ed.), *Die nationale Frage,* p. 238.

67. Ibid., p. 252.

68. László, *Church and State,* p. 458.

69. Ibid., pp. 214–215.

70. Leslie László, "Religion and Nationality in Hungary," in Ramet (ed.), *Religion and Nationalism,* p. 288.

71. Quoted in Mihály Bucsay, "Kirche und Gesellschaft in Ungarn 1848–1945 unter besonderer Berucksichtigung des Problems des Nationalismus," in *Kirche im Osten* 18 (1975): 106.

72. Joseph Rothschild, *East Central Europe Between the Two World Wars* (Seattle: University of Washington Press, 1974), p. 193; and Leslie László, "Nationality and Religion in Hungary, 1867–1918," *East European Quarterly* 17 (March 1983): 47.

73. Friedrich Hainbuch, *Kirche und Staat in Ungarn nach dem Zweiten Weltkrieg* (Munich: Dr. Rudolf Trofenik, 1982), pp. 9, 26–29.

74. Ibid., p. 37; and Steven Polgar, "A Summary of the Situation of the Hungarian Catholic Church," *Religion in Communist Lands* 12 (Spring 1984): 15.

75. Miklós Molnár, *From Béla Kun to János Kádár: Seventy Years of Hungarian Communism,* trans. Arnold J. Pomerans (Oxford: Berg, 1990), p. 142.

76. Hainbuch, *Kirche und Staat,* pp. 46, 71.

77. The Catholic Church had 6,900 priests in 1945, 4,500 in 1963; thirty seminaries in 1945, six in 1963; 3,163 elementary schools in 1945, none in 1963; forty-nine high schools in 1945, eight in 1963; nine hospitals in 1945, four in 1963; sixty-eight newspapers and journals in 1945, four in 1963; fifty publishing houses in 1945, two in 1963; about four thousand lay organizations and associations in 1945, one in 1963.

78. Polgar, "A Summary," p. 20.

79. Mindszenty, who had been imprisoned from 1949 until 1956, had enjoyed only a few days of liberty during the Hungarian Revolution of 1956. Subsequently, he had been living at the U.S. embassy in Budapest. His continued presence in Hungary exerted a strain on Church-state relations because Mindszenty was the symbol of uncompromising resistance to communist policies at a time when many in the Church were coming to favor compromise. His exit from Hungary was the result of long negotiations between the Holy See and the Hungarian government and hinged ultimately on Mindszenty's consent to go into exile.

80. Quoted in Trevor Beeson, *Discretion and Valour: Religious Conditions in Russia and Eastern Europe*, rev. ed. (Philadelphia: Fortress Press, 1982), p. 284.

81. E.g., Ferenc Magyar, ed. of the Hungarian Catholic weekly *Új Ember*, was awarded the Golden Medallion of the Order of Merit for Labor in 1986 by the chairman of the state office for Church affairs, Imre Miklós. See *Keston News Service*, no. 242 (23 January 1986): 11.

82. Ibid., no. 228 (27 June 1985), p. 9. Four Protestant church leaders were also elected.

83. Hainbuch, *Kirche und Staat*, pp. 4-6, 102-103.

84. Emmerich András, "Die Kirche in Ungarn," in Paul Lendvai (ed.), *Religionsfreiheit und Menschenrechte* (Graz: Styria, 1983), p. 158.

85. Alfred Reisch, "State Secretary for Church Affairs Goes on Television," *Radio Free Europe Research*, 1 June 1984, p. 25.

86. Leslie László, "The Catholic Church in Hungary," in Pedro Ramet (ed.), *Catholicism and Politics in Communist Societies* (Durham, N.C.: Duke University Press, 1990), p. 167.

87. László, "Religion and Nationality," pp. 294-295; and *Új Ember* (Budapest), 4 September 1983, trans. in Joint Publications Research Service (JPRS), *East Europe Report*, no. 84606 (25 October 1983): 16.

88. *Kritika* (Budapest), September 1983, trans. in JPRS, *East Europe Report*, no. 84830 (28 November 1983): 120.

89. Ibid., p. 119.

90. László, "Religion and Nationality," p. 296.

91. For further discussion, see Joseph Pungur, "Theologies of Collaboration: The Rise and the Fall of Theology of Service and Theology of Diakonia," in Joseph Pungur (ed.), *An Eastern European Liberation Theology* (Calgary: Angelus Publishers, N.D. [1994]), esp. pp. 140-145; and Joseph Pungur, "Protestantism in Hungary: The Communist Era," in Sabrina P. Ramet (ed.), *Protestantism and Politics in Eastern Europe and Russia: The Communist and Postcommunist Eras* (Durham, N.C.: Duke University Press, 1992), pp. 149-153.

92. According to official statistics of the Institute for Scientific Atheism, Brno, as cited in *Profil* (Vienna), 15 July 1985, p. 40.

93. Matthew Spinka, "The Religious Situation in Czechoslovakia," in Robert J. Kerner (ed.), *Czechoslovakia* (Berkeley: University of California Press, 1945), pp. 284-285.

94. Ibid., p. 285.

95. R. J. W. Evans, *The Making of the Habsburg Monarchy, 1550-1700* (Oxford: Clarendon Press, 1979), pp. 67-68.

96. Joseph F. Začek, "Nationalism in Czechoslovakia," in Peter F. Sugar and Ivo J. Lederer (eds.), *Nationalism in Eastern Europe* (Seattle: University of Washington Press, 1970), p. 174; and Kann, *A History of the Habsburg Empire, 1526-1918*, pp. 112-113.

97. Quoted in Jászi, *Dissolution*, p. 49.

98. Začek, "Nationalism in Czechoslovakia," p. 174.

99. Aleš Pejchal, "Takzvaný cirkevni majetek," *Listy* (Prague) 25, no. 3 (1995): 87-91.

100. Alexander Tomsky, "*Modus Moriendi* of the Catholic Church in Czechoslovakia," *Religion in Communist Lands* 10 (Spring 1982): 25. On the "Los von Rom" movement, see Ludvik Němec, *Church and State in Czechoslovakia* (New York: Vantage Press, 1955), pp. 117-131.

101. Pedro Ramet, "Christianity and National Heritage Among the Czechs and Slovaks," in Ramet (ed.), *Religion and Nationalism*, p. 273.

102. Anthony Rhodes, *The Vatican in the Age of the Dictators, 1922-1945* (London: Hodder and Stoughton, 1973), p. 89.

103. This sentence was closely paraphrased from Victor S. Mamatey, "The Development of Czechoslovak Democracy, 1920-1938," in Mamatey and Radomír Luža (eds.), *A History of the Czechoslovak Republic 1918-1948* (Princeton, N.J.: Princeton University Press, 1973), p. 141.

104. James Ramon Felak, "Priests in East Central European Politics: Ignaz Seipel, Jan Šrámek, and Andrej Hlinka," in Sabrina Petra Ramet and Donald W. Treadgold (eds.), *Render Unto Caesar: The Religious Sphere in World Politics* (Washington, D.C.: American University Press, 1995), pp. 273-275.

105. László, *Church and State*, p. 234.

106. Quoted in Alena Bartlová, *Andrej Hlinka* (Bratislava: Vydavatel'stvo obzor, 1991), p. 65.

107. Quoted in ibid., p. 104.

108. James R. Felak, *"At the Price of the Republic": Hlinka's Slovak People's Party, 1929-1938* (Pittsburgh: University of Pittsburgh Press, 1995), pp. 180-182.

109. Anna Josko, "The Slovak Resistance Movement," in Mamatey and Luža (eds.), *A History of the Czechoslovak Republic*, p. 369.

110. Anton Hlinka, "Zur Lage der Katholischen Kirche in der Slowakei—Pt. I: Geschichtliche Sicht," *Glaube in der 2. Welt* 6 (March 1978): 2.

111. Václav Vaško, *Neumlčena, kronika, Katolické cirkve v Československu po druhé světove válce II* (Prague: Zvon, 1990), p. 64.

112. Hlinka, "Zur Lage der Katholischen Kirche in der Slowakei—Pt. II: Hauptmomente der Auseinandersetzung zwischen Kirche und Staat," *Glaube in der 2. Welt* (April 1978): 16.

113. Ibid., p. 18; and *Rheinischer Merkur* (Bonn), 17 February 1978, p. 13.

114. See Michael Bourdeaux, "The Uniate Churches in Czechoslovakia," *Religion in Communist Lands* 2 (March-April 1974).

115. Ján Chryzostom Korec, *Od bárbarskej noci, na slobode* (Bratislava: Vydavatel'ske družstvo lúč, 1993), p. 18.

116. Hlinka, "Zur Lage der Katholischen Kirche in der Slowakei—Pt. III: Die Dekade 1968-1978," *Glaube in der 2. Welt* 6 (May 1978): 35.

117. Ibid., pp. 44-45.

118. *Rheinischer Merkur* (10 June 1983), trans. in JPRS, *East Europe Report*, no. 83906 (15 July 1983): 25.

119. Czechoslovakia/Situation Report, *Radio Free Europe Research*, 10 March 1986, p. 10.

120. J. P. Hensley, "Slovakia's Catholic Resurgence," *New Leader*, 1-15 July 1985, p. 10, and *Profil*, 15 July 1985, p. 40.

121. Regarding the rehabilitation of Hlinka, see Carol Skalnik Leff, "Czech and Slovak Nationalism in the Twentieth Century," in Peter F. Sugar (ed.), *Eastern European Nationalism in the Twentieth Century* (Washington, D.C.: American University Press, 1995), p. 115.

5. The Catholic Church Among the Czechs and Slovaks

This chapter is a revised and updated version of "The Catholic Church in Czechoslovakia, 1948-1991," originally published in *Studies in Comparative Communism* 24 (December 1991): 377-393. I am grateful to the editor of the journal (Andrzej Korboński) and to the publisher for permission to reprint this chapter here.

1. Cited in "Il Cardinale di Praga protesta," *Pro fratribus* (Rome), April 1986, p. 14.

2. Leszek Kolakówski, "Communism as a Cultural Formation," *Survey* 29 (Summer 1985).

3. See Sabrina Petra Ramet, "Religious Policy Under Gorbachev," in Ramet (ed.), *Religious Policy in the Soviet Union* (Cambridge: Cambridge University Press, 1993).

4. Anton Hlinka, "Zur Lage der Katholischen Kirche in der Slowakei," in 4 parts: pt. 2, "Hauptmomente der Auseinandersetzung zwischen Kirche und Staat," *Glaube in der 2. Welt* 6 (April 1978): 24.

5. "Slowakei: Die Kirche in Fesseln," Pro fratribus, *Stimme der Schweigenden* (Koblenz), no. 1 (March 1988): 3.

6. Josef Rabas, *Kirche in Fesseln,* Materialen zur Situation der Katholischen Kirche in der ČSSR, VI (Munich: Sozialwerk der Ackermann-Gemeinde, 1984), p. 45.

7. Interview with Cardinal Tomášek, *Il Sabato,* 14 June 1985, trans. into German in Pro fratribus, *Stimme der Schweigenden,* no. 3 (September 1985).

8. "Slowakei: Die Kirche in Fesseln," p. 7.

9. Anton Hlinka, "Zur Lage der Katholischen . . .": pt. 4, "Die Dekade 1968-1978," *Glaube in der 2. Welt* 6 (May 1978): 43-44.

10. Rabas, *Kirche in Fesseln,* pp. 48-49.

11. *Keston News Service,* no. 296 (17 March 1988): 4.

12. Matej Lúčan, on 12 November 1981, as quoted in *Priestervereinigung "Pacem in terris:: Eine kritische Analyse* (Munich: Sozialwerk der Ackermann-Gemeinde, 1983), p. 46.

13. Ibid., p. 64. See also *Pravda* (Bratislava), 23 October 1981, p. 2, trans. in Foreign Broadcast Information Service (FBIS), *Daily Report* (Eastern Europe), 2 November 1981, p. D10; *Neue Zürcher Zeitung* (27 January 1983), p. 4; *Süddeutsche Zeitung* (Munich), 14-15 November 1987, p. 12.

14. *Priestervereinigung,* p. 65.

15. Dennis J. Dunn, *Détente and Papal-Communist Relations, 1962-1978* (Boulder, Colo.: Westview Press, 1979), pp. 164-165.

16. *Aktuelnosti Krščanske Sadašnjosti* (AKSA), Zagreb, 30 December 1980, 21 May 1982, and 18 March 1983.

17. *Keston News Service,* no. 293 (4 February 1988): 4, no. 298 (14 April 1988): 9, no. 299 (28 April 1988): 19, no. 301 (26 May 1988): 2.

18. Alexander Tomsky, "Der Katholizismus in der Tschechoslowakei," in Paul Lendvai (ed.), *Religionsfreiheit und Menschenrechte* (Graz: Styria, 1983), p. 132.

19. Václav Vaško, *Neumlčena, kronika, katolické cirkve u Československu po druhé světove válce II* (Prague: Zvon, 1990), p. 58.

20. Rabas, *Kirche in Fesseln,* pp. 31-32.

21. Jan Hartman, Bohumil Svoboda, and Václav Vaško (eds.), *Kardinál Tomášek* (Prague: Zvon and České Katolické Nakladatelství, 1994), pp. 16, 19-21, 187.

22. V. Chalupa, *Situation of the Catholic Church in Czechoslovakia* (Chicago: Czechoslovak Foreign Institute in Exile, January 1959), pp. 24, 28–29.

23. Rabas, *Kirche in Fesseln*, p. 33.

24. "Intervista con Peter Rùčka, giovane Francescano della Slovachia," *Pro fratribus*, April 1987, pp. 3–14.

25. Karel Kaplan, "Church and State in Czechoslovakia from 1948 to 1956," trans. from Czech by Julia Joannou, pt. 3, *Religion in Communist Lands* 14 (Winter 1986): 274.

26. Rabas, *Kirche in Fesseln*, p. 35.

27. Ludvík Němec, *Church and State in Czechoslovakia* (New York: Vantage Press, 1955), pp. 270–271; Chalupa, *Situation of the Catholic Church*, pp. 12–15.

28. Josef Rabas (compiler), *Zeugnis und Zusage: Dokumente aus der Kirche der ČSSR*, Materialen zur Situation der Katholischen Kirche in der ČSSR, IV (Munich: Sozialwerk der Ackermann-Gemeinde, 1981), pp. 11–18.

29. Quoted in Chalupa, *Situation of the Catholic Church*, p. 34.

30. Quoted in ibid., p. 38.

31. For a discussion of the Hussite legacy in the religio-national symbiosis in Czech history, see Pedro Ramet, "Christianity and National Heritage Among the Czechs and Slovaks," in Ramet (ed.), *Religion and Nationalism in Soviet and East European Politics*, rev. and expanded ed. (Durham, N.C.: Duke University Press, 1989).

32. *Most* (Rome), nos. 1–2 (1987): 8, as cited in Czechoslovak Situation Report, *Radio Free Europe Research*, 3 June 1988, p. 25.

33. Article 16, as quoted in *Rudé pravo*, 23 February 1977, trans. into German as "Das Verhältnis zwischen Kirche und Staat in der Tschechslowakei," *Osteuropa* 28 (July 1978): A431.

34. Milena Kalinovska, "Czechoslovakia Ten Years After," *Religion in Communist Lands* 6 (Autumn 1978): 167.

35. *Vysoka škola*, no. 8 (April 1975), trans. into German as "Religion und atheistische Propaganda in der ČSSR," *Osteuropa* 25 (November 1975): A596.

36. "Eine Theologie des Dienstes," in Giovanni Barberini, Martin Stohr, and Erich Weingartner (eds.), *Kirchen im Sozialismus: Kirche und Staat in den osteuropäischen sozialistischen Republiken* (Frankfurt: Otto Lembeck, 1977), p. 169; confirmed in *Luxemburger Wort* (Luxemburg), 16 February 1984, p. 18, trans. in Joint Publications Research Service (JPRS), *East Europe Report*, no. EPS-84-040 (26 March 1984): 2–4.

37. For precise statistics, see Rabas, *Kirche in Fesseln*, p. 77.

38. *Tribuna*, 8 October 1975, p. 5, trans. in JPRS, *Translations on Eastern Europe*, 28 November 1975, p. 33.

39. Quoted in "Principles of Scientific Education in Schools," decree of the Ministry of Education of the Czech Socialist Republic, Act No. 10.824/72-200 of 4 April 1972, trans. in *Religion in Communist Dominated Areas* 17, nos. 4–6 (1978): 74.

40. *Nová Mysl* (Prague), no. 1 (January 1972), trans. in *Religion in Communist Dominated Areas* 12, nos. 7–9 (July–September 1973): 101.

41. On the 1950s, see Chalupa, *Situation of the Catholic Church*, pp. 42–43; on the 1980s, see Czechoslovak Situation Report, *Radio Free Europe Research*, 26 July 1983, pp. 5–7.

42. Němec, *Church and State*, pp. 253ff.

43. See Joseph L. Hromádka, *Theology Between Yesterday and Tomorrow* (Philadelphia: Westminster Press, 1957); Josef L. Hromádka, *Thoughts of a Czech Pastor,* trans. from Czech by Monika Page and Benjamin Page (London: SCM Press, 1970).

44. Quoted in Karel Kaplan, "Church and State . . . ," pt. 1, *Religion in Communist Lands* 14 (Spring 1986): 68.

45. Quoted in Chalupa, *Situation of the Catholic Church,* p. 13.

46. Quoted in Karel Kaplan, "Church and State . . . ," pt. 2, *Religion in Communist Lands* 14 (Summer 1986): 190.

47. Report cited in ibid., p. 188.

48. Kaplan, "Church and State," pt. 2, p. 191; Kaplan, "Church and State," pt. 3, pp. 277–278.

49. Czechoslovak Situation Report, *Radio Free Europe Research,* 7 September 1984, pp. 17–25.

50. Hartman, Svoboda, and Vaško (eds.), *Kardinal Tomášek,* pp. 64–65.

51. George Weigel, *The Final Revolution: The Resistance Church and the Collapse of Communism* (New York: Oxford University Press, 1992), p. 176.

52. Ibid., p. 176; and Hartman, Svoboda, and Vaško (eds.), *Kardinal Tomášek,* p. 66.

53. Hartman, Svoboda, and Vaško (eds.), *Kardinal Tomášek,* p. 67.

54. Weigel, *The Final Revolution,* p. 177.

55. Ibid.

56. Hartman, Svoboda, and Vaško (eds.), *Kardinal Tomášek,* p. 68.

57. Ibid., p. 92.

58. "Slowakei: die Franziskaner im Gefngnis," in Pro fratribus, *Stimme der Schweigenden,* no. 3 (September 1986).

59. "Slowakische Charta 1969," in Pro fratribus, *Stimme der Schweigenden,* no. 3 (September 1985).

60. *Frankfurter Allgemeine,* 5 April 1986, p. 6.

61. *New York Times,* 25 November 1988, p. A4; also Czechoslovak Situation Report, *Radio Free Europe Research,* 7 December 1988, p. 39.

62. For details and documentation, see A. Hlinka, "Katholiken in der Slowakei," *Kirche in Not* 23 (1975): 106–107; Pedro Ramet, "The Czechoslovak Church Under Pressure," *The World Today* 38 (September 1982): 358–359; "Slowakei: Die Kirche in Fesseln," pp. 3–4; "Arrestato sacerdotale: celebrava in casa," *Pro fratribus,* May 1987, p. 36; Milan J. Reban, "The Catholic Church in Czechoslovakia," in Pedro Ramet (ed.), *Catholicism and Politics in Communist Societies* (Durham, N.C.: Duke University Press, 1990).

63. For details, see "Der grausame Mord an Priester Štefan Polák," in Pro fratribus, *Stimme der Schweigenden,* no. 1 (March 1988): 2; *Frankfurter Allgemeine,* 16 March 1988, p. 3.

64. *Los Angeles Times,* 18 July 1983, p. 10.

65. J. P. Hensley, "Slovakia's Catholic Resurgence," *New Leader,* 1–15 July 1985, p. 10; *Profil* (Vienna), 15 July 1985, p. 40; *Informace o církví* (1985), no. 8, trans. into German as "Repressionen und Schickanen: Zur Lage der Katholischen Kirche in der Tschechoslowakei," *Osteuropa* 36 (July 1986): A393.

66. Czechoslovak Situation Report, *Radio Free Europe Research,* 14 October 1987, p. 15.

67. Ibid., 28 August 1987, pp. 5–6.

68. *New York Times*, 2 October 1987, p. 6.

69. *Keston News Service*, no. 293 (4 February 1988): 3; and *Frankfurter Allgemeine*, 5 May 1988, p. 1.

70. *Süddeutsche Zeitung* (Munich), 19/20 March 1988, p. 6.

71. "31 Punti di Libertà: Il Manifesto della Chiesa Ceco-Slovaca," *Pro fratribus*, March 1988, pp. 10-13.

72. *Frankfurter Allgemeine*, 7 June 1988, p. 1, trans. in FBIS, *Daily Report* (East Europe), 7 June 1988, p. 11. See also *Rudé pravo*, 25 May 1988, p. 2, trans. in FBIS, *Daily Report* (East Europe), 31 May 1988, pp. 5-7.

73. *Glas koncila* (Zagreb), 20 March 1988, p. 1.

74. *New York Times*, 27 March 1988, p. 6; *Frankfurter Allgemeine*, 30 March 1988, p. 6; *Die Zeit* (Hamburg), 8 April 1988, p. 6; *Glas koncila*, 10 April 1988, p. 4; Czechoslovak Situation Report, *Radio Free Europe Research*, 19 April 1988, pp. 19-24; and "Der Pressburger Karfreitag 1988," in Pro fratribus, *Stimme der Schweigenden*, no. 2 (June 1988), p. 5.

75. Cited in *Neue Zürcher Zeitung*, 9 July 1988, p. 5.

76. *Kurier* (Vienna), 6 July 1988, p. 3, trans. in FBIS, *Daily Report* (East Europe), 12 July 1988, p. 12; *Keston News Service*, no. 297 (31 March 1988): 16; Czechoslovak Situation Report, *Radio Free Europe Research*, 11 August 1988, pp. 21-22.

77. See *Lidova Demokracie* (Prague), 1 June 1988, p. 5.

78. *Rudé pravo*, 1 July 1988, p. 7.

79. Ibid., 19 September 1988, p. 3.

80. On Navratil, see *Die Presse* (Vienna), 17/18 September 1988, p. 2; on Polansky, see *Neue Zürcher Zeitung*, 10 September 1988, p. 3.

81. UPI, 19 April 1990, on *Nexis*.

82. *Lidova Demokracie*, 22 November 1989, pp. 1, 2.

83. ČTK (Prague), 1 February 1991, in FBIS, *Daily Report* (Eastern Europe), 5 February 1991, p. 17.

84. For a discussion of this period and of the frictions and tensions between Czechs and Slovaks, see Sabrina Petra Ramet, "The Reemergence of Slovakia," *Nationalities Papers* 22 (Spring 1994).

85. *Reuters*, 25 January 1990, on *Nexis*.

86. *Christian Century*, 6 December 1995, pp. 1171-1172.

87. ČTK, 2 April 1996, on *Nexis*.

88. On the age of nuns, see *Keston News Service*, no. 342 (25 January 1990): 19.

89. ČTK, 1 February 1991, in FBIS, *Daily Report* (Eastern Europe), 5 February 1991, p. 17.

90. For discussion, see Sabrina P. Ramet, *Whose Democracy? Nationalism, Religion, and the Doctrine of Collective Rights in Post-1989 Eastern Europe* (Lanham, Md.: Rowman and Littlefield, 1997), chap. 2 ("Eastern Europe's Painful Transition") and chap. 5 ("The Struggle for Collective Rights in Slovakia").

91. Sharon Fisher, "Church Restitution Law Passed in Slovakia," *RFE/RL Research Report*, 19 November 1993, pp. 51-53. See also *Süddeutsche Zeitung*, 8 October 1993, p. 10.

92. Quoted in Fisher, "Church Restitution," p. 54.

93. ČTK, 7 November 1995, and 22 February 1996, both on *Nexis*.

94. See, for example, *Lidové noviny* (Prague), 25 January 1994, p. 3.

95. *Frankfurter Allgemeine*, 10 January 1994, p. 10. See also "Kirchenbesitz und jüdisches Vermögen in der Tschechischen Republik," *Osteuropa* 44 (May 1994):

A259-A271; and *Respekt* (Prague), 25 September-1 October 1995, p. 2. On other sources of tension, see *Süddeutsche Zeitung*, 13 July 1993, p. 6, and 21 July 1993, p. 9.

96. ČTK, 1 February 1996, on *Nexis*.

97. Ibid., 26 January 1996.

98. *Süddeutsche Zeitung*, 20/21 July 1996, p. 6; *New Europe* (Athens), 25-31 August 1996, p. 19; and *Süddeutsche Zeitung*, 12/13 October 1996, p. 6.

99. *Církve a majetek* (Prague: Občanský Institut, May 1993), p. 9.

100. *Lidové noviny*, 26 September 1994, p. 3.

101. *Respekt* (Prague), 2-8 May 1995, p. 2.

102. *Prague Post*, 13 June 1995, p. 15.

103. *Balkan News and East European Report* (Athens), 21-27 May 1995, p. 46; *Die Welt* (Bonn), 22 May 1995, p. 1; *La Repubblica* (Rome), 22 May 1995, pp. 1, 11; *La Stampa* (Torino), 22 May 1995, pp. 1, 9; and *Slobodna Dalmacija* (Split), 23 May 1995, p. 10.

104. Quoted in *New York Times*, 22 May 1995, p. A3. See also *Balkan News and East European Report*, 28 May-3 June 1995, p. 17.

105. *Nedělní lidové noviny* (Prague), 9 December 1995, p. 7.

106. See A. Ambrůz, "Nemít, a tudíž nebýt," *Listy* (Prague) 45, no. 8 (1995): 40.

107. *Narodna obroda* (Bratislava), 26 July 1990, p. 1, trans. in FBIS, *Daily Report* (Eastern Europe), 30 July 1990, p. 18.

108. *Rozhlasova Stanica Slovensko Network* (Bratislava), 27 September 1995, trans. in FBIS, *Daily Report* (Eastern Europe), 28 September 1995, p. 13; *Pravda* (Bratislava), 11 November 1995, p. 1, trans. in FBIS, *Daily Report* (Eastern Europe), 15 November 1995, p. 23; *Smé* (Bratislava), 17 November 1995, p. 5, trans. in FBIS, *Daily Report* (Eastern Europe), 21 November 1995, pp. 13-14.

109. ČTK, 26 March 1996, on *Nexis; Independent* (London), 1 April 1996, p. 12.

110. *Pravda* (Bratislava), 7 October 1995, p. 2, trans. in FBIS, *Daily Report* (Eastern Europe), 20 October 1995, pp. 14-15.

111. Quoted in ČTK, 26 April 1996, on *Nexis*.

112. *Lidové noviny*, 11 January 1995, p. 5.

113. *Stredni Evropa*, no. 8 (July 1987), summarized in Czechoslovak Situation Report, *Radio Free Europe Research*, 3 November 1987, pp. 33-34.

114. On this point, see Václav Klaus, *Rok málo či mnoho v dějinách země* (Prague: Repro-Media, 1993), p. 73.

6. Nation and Religion in Yugoslavia

An earlier draft of this chapter was published under the title "Religion and Nationalism in Yugoslavia," in Pedro Ramet (ed.) *Religion and Nationalism in Soviet and East European Politics*, revised and expanded ed. (Durham, N.C.: Duke University Press, 1989).

1. Ivan Cvitković, "Stavovi suvremenih teologa o odnosu religije i religijskih zajednica prema politici u socijalizmu," *Politička misao* 15, no. 4 (1978): 653.

2. Edvard Kardelj, *Razvoj slovenačkog nacionalnog pitanja*, 2nd ed. (Belgrade: Kultura, 1957); Edvard Kardelj, "O naciji i medjunacionalnim odnosima," *Treći program*, no. 40 (Winter 1979); Atif Purivatra, "Stav komunističke partije Jugoslavije prema nacionalnom pitanju u Bosni i Hercegovini," in Milan Petrović and Kasim Suljević (eds.), *Nacionalni odnosi danas* (Sarajevo: Univerzal, 1971); Krste Crven-

kovski, *Medjunacionalni odnosi u samoupravnom društvu* (Belgrade: Sedma sila, 1967); Hamdija Pozderac, *Nacionalni odnosi i socijalističko zajedništvo* (Sarajevo: Svjetlost, 1978); and Jovan Raičević, "Savez komunista Jugoslavije i nacionalno pitanje," in *KPJ–SKJ: Razvoj teorije i prakse socijalizma, 1919–1979* (Belgrade: Savremana administracija, 1979). See also Walter Lukan, "Zur nationalen Frage eines kleinen Volkes: Edvard Kardeljs Darstellung zur Entwicklung der nationalen Frage bei den Slovenen," *Österreichische Osthefte* 15 (November 1973) and 16 (February 1974).

3. This was admitted by Božidar Gagro, president of the Socialist Alliance of Working People of Croatia, when he told *NIN* in early 1982 that memories of World War II constituted one of the most important obstacles to overcoming tensions and frictions, especially in relations between the state and the Catholic Church. Reported in *Aktualnosti Kršćanske Sadašnjosti,* informativni bilten (*AKSA*), 19 March 1982.

4. I was told by certain members of the Serbian Orthodox clergy in Belgrade in July 1982 that the rosy picture painted by the regime of harmonious and unruffled relations between the Serbian Orthodox Church and the LCY was, even aside from the Macedonian Orthodox Church and recurrent regime recriminations against Bishop Velimirović, fallacious and illusory. This claim was reaffirmed when I visited Belgrade in June and July 1987.

5. Branislav Djurdjiev, *Uloga crkve u starijoj istoriji Srpskog naroda* (Sarajevo: Svjetlost, 1964), p. 55.

6. On pre-Christian beliefs among Croats and Serbs, see Natko Nodilo, *Stara vjera Srba i Hrvata* (Split: Logos, 1981), and Ante Škobalj, *Vjera starih Hrvata* (Zagreb: Duće, 1986).

7. Ivo Pilar, *Die Südslawische Frage und der Weltkrieg* (Vienna: Manzsche K. u. K. Hofs-u. Universitäts-Buchhandlung, 1918), pp. 170, 185, 195, 213, 313–14. A more recent example of the argument that Bosnian Muslims are Croats is Mladen Dolić, "Narodna svijest i žrtve Bosansko-hercegovačkih muslimana," *Republika Hrvatska* (Buenos Aires), 36, no. 154 (September 1986). For an argument that Bosnian Muslims are Serbs, see Lazo M. Kostić, *Etnički odnosi Bosne i Hercegovine* (Munich: Iskra, 1967). For an elaborate analysis of competing theories about the ethnicity of Bosnia's Muslims, see Sabrina P. Ramet, "Primordial Ethnicity or Modern Nationalism: The Case of Yugoslavia's Muslims, Reconsidered," *South Slav Journal* 13 (Spring/Summer 1990).

8. Noel Malcolm, *Bosnia: A Short History* (New York: New York University Press, 1994), pp. 71–72.

9. Interestingly enough, the Croatian monasteries were excluded from the ban. See *Mali ključ povijesti crkve u Hrvata,* 3rd ed. (Zagreb: Nadbiskupski duhovni stol, 1981), p. 117.

10. Ibid., p. 136; John V. A. Fine, Jr., *The Bosnian Church: A New Interpretation* (Boulder, Colo.: East European Monographs, 1975), pp. 3–4, 15, 51–52; and Jaroslav Šidak, *Studije o 'crkvi bosanskoj' i bogumilstvu* (Zagreb: S. N. Liber, 1975), pp. 87, 89.

11. *Pregled* (Sarajevo), April 1970, trans. in Joint Publications Research Service (JPRS), *Translations on Eastern Europe,* 6 July 1970; and Fine, *Bosnian Church,* pp. 10–11, 14–15, 18–19.

12. Fine, *Bosnian Church,* p. 342.

13. Malcolm, *Bosnia: A Short History,* pp. 55, 71–72. For further discussion of the life of the Serbian Orthodox Church in Ottoman Bosnia, see Ivo Andrić, *The De-*

velopment of Spiritual Life in Bosnia Under the Influence of Turkish Rule, trans. from Croatian by Želimir B. Juričić and John F. Loud (Durham, N.C.: Duke University Press, 1990).

14. Harold W. V. Temperley, *History of Serbia* (New York: Howard Feitig, 1969), p. 125; and Djurdjiev, *Uloga crkve,* pp. 144–145.

15. Keith Hitchins, *Orthodoxy and Nationality: Andreiu Şaguna and the Rumanians of Transylvania, 1846–1873* (Cambridge, Mass.: Harvard University Press, 1977), pp. 185–86.

16. Oszkar Jaszi, *The Dissolution of the Habsburg Monarchy, 1867–1918* (Chicago: University of Chicago Press, 1929), p. 264.

17. Ivan Mužić, *Hrvatska politika i jugoslavenska ideja* (Split: n.p., 1969), pp. 9, 15.

18. Malcolm, *Bosnia: A Short History,* p. 126.

19. See Sabrina Petra Ramet, *Balkan Babel: The Disintegration of Yugoslavia from the Death of Tito to Ethnic War,* 2nd ed. (Boulder, Colo.: Westview Press, 1996), chap. 8.

20. For more details, together with documentation, see ibid.

21. Malcolm, *Bosnia: A Short History,* p. 195.

22. This section draws liberally from my essay, "From Strossmayer to Stepinac: Croatian National Ideology and Catholicism," *Canadian Review of Studies in Nationalism* 12 (Spring 1985).

23. Reinhard Lauer, "Genese und Funktion des ilyrischen Ideologems in den südslawischen Literaturen (16. bis Anfang des 19. Jahrhunderts)," in Klaus-Detlev Grothusen (ed.), *Ethnogenese und Staatsbildung in Südosteuropa* (Göttingen: Vandenhoeck und Ruprecht, 1974), p. 119.

24. See Ante Kadić, "Križanić and His Predecessors: The Slavic Idea Among the Croatian Baroque Writers," in Thomas Eekman and Ante Kadić (eds.), *Juraj Križanić (1618–1683): Russophile and Ecumenic Visionary* (The Hague: Mouton, 1976).

25. On Gaj, see Wolf Dietrich Behschnitt, *Nationalismus bei Serben und Kroaten 1830–1914: Analyse und Typologie der nationalen Ideologie* (Munich: R. Oldenbourg, 1980), pp. 60, 66, 133, 136, 140–147; and Ferdo Šišić, *Pregled povijesti Hrvatskoga naroda* (Zagreb: Nakladni Zavod MH, 1975), pp. 401–412.

26. For a detailed discussion of Strossmayer, see Charles Joseph Slovak III, "Josip Juraj Strossmayer, A Balkan Bishop: The Early Years, 1815–1854," unpublished Ph.D. diss.: University of Illinois at Urbana-Champaign, 1974.

27. In 1982 Stevan Nikšić and Milan Milošević defended Strossmayer against unnamed critics and repudiated Croatian nationalist claims that Strossmayer's "Yugoslavism" was actually a poorly disguised species of Croatian nationalism. See *NIN,* no. 1625 (21 February 1982): 12.

28. See Mario S. Spalatin, "The Croatian Nationalism of Ante Starčević, 1845–1871," *Journal of Croatian Studies* 16 (1975). Also see Mirjana Gross and Agneza Szabo, *Prema Hrvatskome gradjanskom društvu* (Zagreb: Globus, 1992).

29. Mužić, *Hrvatska politika,* p. 43.

30. Andrija Nikić, "Franjevci u Hercegovini od 1878. do 1892. godine," *Kačić* 10 (1978): 180, 219.

31. Stella Alexander, "Croatia: The Catholic Church and Clergy, 1919–1945," in Richard J. Wolff and Jorg K. Hoensch (eds.), *Catholics, the State, and the European Radical Right, 1919–1945* (Boulder, Colo.: Social Science Monographs, 1987), pp. 40–41. See also Bonifacije Perović, *Hrvatski Katolički Pokret: Moje uspomene* (Rome: Ziral, 1976), pp. 36–46.

32. Zlatko Matijević, "Katolička crkva u Hrvatskoj i stvaranje Jugoslavenske države 1918-1921. godine," in *Povijesni prilozi*, no. 5 (Zagreb: Institut za Historiju Radničkog Pokreta Hrvatske, 1986), pp. 7-8.

33. Ibid., p. 15. Also by Matijević, "Reformni pokret djela nižega Katoličkog svećenstva u Hrvatskoj (1919-1924. god.)," *Povijesni prilozi*, no. 8 (Zagreb: Institut za Historiju Radničkog Pokreta Hrvatske, 1989).

34. For details and documentation, see Ramet, *Balkan Babel*, chap. 8. For further in-depth discussion, see Ivan Mužić, *Katolička crkva u kraljevini Jugoslaviji* (Split: Crkva u svijetu, 1978).

35. Fred Singleton, *Twentieth Century Yugoslavia* (New York: Columbia University Press, 1976), p. 196.

36. *Katolički list*, 1 June 1934, quoted in Alexander, "Croatia: The Catholic Church," p. 43.

37. *Katolički list*, 18 August 1938, quoted in Alexander, "Croatia: The Catholic Church," pp. 43-44.

38. See Ivo Banac, *The National Question in Yugoslavia: Origins, History, Politics* (Ithaca, N.Y.: Cornell University Press, 1984), and Fikreta Jelić-Butić, *Hrvatska Seljačka Stranka* (Zagreb: Globus, 1983).

39. Ivan Mužić, *Pavelić i Stepinac* (Split: Logos, 1991), p. 69.

40. From a fuller extract, quoted in Fiktreta Jelić-Butić, *Ustaše i NDH* (Zagreb: S. N. Liber and Školska knjiga, 1977), p. 215.

41. Alexander, "Croatia: The Catholic Church," p. 52.

42. See ibid., pp. 53-55.

43. Mužić, *Pavelić i Stepinac*, pp. 71, 73. See also Ernest Bauer, *Aloisius Kardinal Stepinac: Ein Leben für Wahrheit, Recht, und Gerechtigkeit* (Recklinghausen: Georg Bitter, 1979); O. Aleksa Benigar, *Alojzije Stepinac, Hrvatski Kardinal* (Rome: Ziral, 1974); Anthony O'Brien, *Archbishop Stepinac: The Man and His Case* (Dublin: Standard House, 1947); Richard Pattee, *The Case of Cardinal Aloysius Stepinac* (Milwaukee: Bruce, 1953); Stella Alexander, *The Triple Myth: A Life of Archbishop Alojzije Stepinac* (Boulder, Colo.: East European Monographs, 1987); Ramet, *Balkan Babel*, chap. 7. Ivan Cvitković's *Ko je bio Alojzije Stepinac*, 2nd ed. (Sarajevo: Oslobodjenje, 1986), is a vicious anti-Stepinac diatribe which distorts the evidence and misrepresents the historical record.

44. Joze Pogačnik, "The Cultural Significance of the Protestant Reformation in the Genesis of the South Slavic Nations," in *Slovene Studies* 6, no. 1/2 (1984): 102-103; and "Slovene Literature," *New Catholic Encyclopedia* (New York: McGraw-Hill, 1967), vol. 13, p. 296.

45. Ervin Dolenc, "Culture, Politics, and Slovene Identity," in Jill Benderly and Evan Kraft (eds.), *Independent Slovenia: Origins, Movements, Prospects* (New York: St. Martin's Press, 1994), p. 70.

46. "Slovene Literature," p. 296.

47. Dolenc, "Culture, Politics," p. 71.

48. Ibid., p. 73.

49. Ibid., p. 77.

50. Ibid., p. 82.

51. "Slomšek, Anton Martin," *New Catholic Encyclopedia*, vol. 13, p. 292.

52. "Finzgar, Franc Saleški," ibid., vol. 5, p. 931.

53. "Meško, Franc Ksaver," ibid., vol. 9, p. 696.

54. Robert J. Donia, *Islam Under the Double Eagle: The Muslims of Bosnia and Hercegovina, 1878-1914* (Boulder, Colo.: East European Monographs, 1981), p. 98.

Under Ottoman law, the testimony of one Balkan Muslim carried the same weight as that of twenty Christians.

55. Juraj Kolarić, "Ekumenska djelatnost Nadbiskupa Stadlera," in Petar Babić and Mato Zovkić, *Katolička crkva u Bosni i Hercegovini u XIX i XX stoljeću* (Sarajevo: Vrhbosanska Visoka Teološka Škola, 1986), p. 138.

56. As a research scholar, Benjámin von Kállay concluded that Muslim Bosnians, Serbs, and Croats were all members of the same nationality. As joint minister of finance with administrative responsibility for Bosnia-Herzegovina, he banned his own book (in which he had argued the grounds for South Slav unity) and forbade its distribution in Bosnia-Herzegovina. See Herbert Adams Gibbons, *The New Map of Europe, 1911–1914* (New York: Century, 1916), p. 160n.

57. Donia, *Islam Under the Double Eagle*, pp. 140-141.

58. Ibid., p. 177; confirmed, with examples, in Muhamed Hadzijahić, *Od tradicije do identiteta: Geneza nacionalnog pitanja bosanskih muslimana* (Sarajevo: Svjetlost, 1974), pp. 39, 144, 164.

59. Quoted in Kasim Suljević, *Nacionalnost Muslimana* (Rijeka: Otokar Keršovani, 1981), p. 153.

60. Jovo Jakšić, *Ustavno pitanje u Jugoslaviji* (Belgrade, 1934), p. 14, as cited in Suljević, *Nacionalnost Muslimana*, p. 165.

61. Robin Okey, *Eastern Europe, 1740–1980* (London: Hutchinson, 1982), p. 106.

62. Jaszi, *Dissolution*, p. 69.

63. See, for instance, *Politika*, 10 May 1972, p. 8.

64. Stevan K. Pavlowitch, "The Orthodox Church in Yugoslavia: The Problem of the Macedonian Church," in *Eastern Churches Review* 1 (Winter 1967-68): 380-381. See also Suzanne Gwen Hruby, Leslie Laszlo, and Stevan K. Pavlowitch, "Minor Orthodox Churches of Eastern Europe," in Pedro Ramet (ed.), *Eastern Christianity and Politics in the Twentieth Century* (Durham, N.C.: Duke University Press, 1988).

65. See "Makedonska crkva samovoljno se otcepila od majke Srpske crkve," *Pravoslavlje* (Belgrade), 15 September 1967, pp. 1-2.

66. Pavlowitch, "Orthodox Church," p. 382; and "Die 'autokephale Mazedonische Kirche,'" *Wissenschaftlicher Dienst Südosteuropa* 16 (August 1967): 139.

67. Done Ilievski, "The Fifth Anniversary of the Macedonian Orthodox Church," *Macedonian Review* 2, no. 2 (1972): 213.

68. *NIN* (Belgrade), 5 March 1972, p. 25.

69. See *Vesnik: Organ Saveza udruženog Pravoslavnog sveštenstva Jugoslavije*, 1–15 January 1971, p. 10, and 1 February 1971, p. 7.

70. See, for example, *Vesnik*, 15 January 1967, p. 4; 1 February 1967, p. 2; 1 March 1967, p. 8; and 1-15 August 1971, p. 5. See also *Politika*, 12 December 1970, p. 6, *Pravoslavlje*, 15 May 1987, p. 2.

71. See Michael B. Petrovich, "Yugoslavia: Religion and the Tensions of a Multi-National State," *East European Quarterly* 6 (March 1972): 122.

72. *Pravoslavlje*, 15 May 1982, p. 1.

73. Reported in *AKSA*, 8 May 1987, trans. Stella Alexander, in *AKSA Bulletin*.

74. *Oslobodjenje*, 18-24 September 1981.

75. *Pravoslavlje*, 1 July 1990, p. 1.

76. *Süddeutsche Zeitung* (Munich), 23-24 June 1990, p. 8; Sabrina Petra Ramet, "The Serbian Church and the Serbian Nation," in Ramet and Donald W. Treadgold (eds.), *Render Unto Caesar: The Religious Sphere in World Politics* (Washington, D.C.: American University Press, 1995), p. 311.

77. *Pravoslavlje*, 15 December 1991, p. 7.

78. Renata Salecl, *The Spoils of Freedom: Psychoanalysis and Feminism After the Fall of Socialism* (New York: Routledge, 1994), p. 23.

79. Tanjug, 28 October 1972, trans. in JPRS, *East Europe Report*, no. 57563, 20 November 1972. See also *Borba*, 24 October 1970, p. 11.

80. *Guardian*, 17 April 1978, p. 7; *Nedjeljna Dalmacija*, 6 June 1971, pp. 5, 10, trans. in JPRS, *East Europe Report*, no. 53764 (5 August 1971); *Glas koncila*, 15 June 1969, p. 1; *Croatia Press* 32 (April-June 1979): 4; *Glas koncila*, 12 July 1981, p. 2, excerpted and trans. in JPRS, *East Europe Report*, no. 78682, 5 August 1981, p. 44. In July 1997, Josip Bozanić, the erstwhile Bishop of Krk was appointed to succeed the retiring Cardinal Kuharić as Archbishop of Zagreb. See *Globus* (Zagreb), 4 July 1997, pp. 4-6; and *AFP* (Paris), 5 July 1997, on *Nexis*.

81. See, for example, *Vjesnik*, 27 February 1980, p. 5.

82. Tomislav Šagi-Bunić, "Kršćanstvo i nacionalizam," in *Glas koncila*, 15 June 1969, pp. 4, 6. See also Tomislav J. Šagi-Bunić, *Katolička crkva i hrvatski narod* (Zagreb: Kršćanska sadašnjost, 1983).

83. *Oslobodjenje*, 12 January 1972, p. 5; *Washington Post*, 23 January 1972, p. A25.

84. *Washington Post*, 23 January 1972, p. A25.

85. *Borba*, 10 November 1986, p. 2; *Vjesnik*, 11 November 1986, p. 5.

86. *Vjesnik*, 14 April 1980, p. 5.

87. France M. Dolinar, "The Process of Normalization of the Relations Between the Church and the State in Yugoslavia," paper presented to the annual convention of the American Association for the Advancement of Slavic Studies, Washington, D.C., 25-29 October 1995.

88. Radio Vatican, 21 December 1984, trans. in *BBC Summary of World Broadcasts*, 9 January 1985; and Radio Vatican, 12 January 1985, trans. in *BBC Summary of World Broadcasts*, 16 January 1985.

89. Quoted in *New York Times*, 7 October 1984, p. 3.

90. *Delo*, 18 February 1989, summarized in *AKSA Bulletin*, compiled by Stella Alexander with Muriel Huppell, 20 May 1989, p. 7.

91. "Staat und Nationalität in Jugoslawien," *Wissenschaftlicher Dienst Südosteuropa* 19 (August 1970): 113-114.

92. Fuad Muhić, interview in *Start*, no. 283, 28 November-12 December 1979, pp. 13-14.

93. *Borba*, 10 May 1972, p. 5.

94. *Večernje novosti* (Belgrade), 2 July 1981.

95. "The Islamic Declaration," trans. in *South Slav Journal* 6 (Spring 1983): 68, 82.

96. *Archiv der Gegenwart*, 20 August 1983, p. 26903.

97. *Keston News Service*, no. 276 (28 May 1987): 12 and no. 278 (25 June 1987): 4-5; *Vjesnik*, 6 June 1987, p. 12. For an account of Yugoslavia's Muslims in the 1980s, see Abdullah Dedić, "The Muslim Predicament in Yugoslavia: An Impression," in *Journal Institute of Muslim Minority Affairs* 8, no. 1 (January 1987), pp. 121-131.

98. Kenneth Anderson, "Illiberal Tolerance: An Essay on the Fall of Yugoslavia and the Rise of Multiculturalism in the United States," *Virginia Journal of International Law* 33, (Winter 1993): 417, 427-428.

99. Details in Sabrina Petra Ramet, "The New Church-State Configuration in Eastern Europe," in Ramet (ed.), *Protestantism and Politics in Eastern Europe and Russia: The Communist and Postcommunist Era* (Durham, N.C.: Duke University Press, 1992), p. 319.

100. *Tanjug,* 28 March 1990, trans. in FBIS, *Daily Report* (Eastern Europe), 29 March 1990, p. 56.

101. Vladimir Dedijer, *Vatikan i Jasenovac* (Belgrade: Izdavačka radna organizacija 'Rad,' 1987), trans. as Dedijer, *The Yugoslav Auschwitz and the Vatican: The Croatian Massacre of the Serbs During World War II,* trans. from German translation by Harvey L. Kendall (Buffalo, N.Y.: Prometheus Books, 1992).

102. Such as *The Vatican's Tunnels,* published in Belgrade in 1994.

103. *Pravoslavlje,* 15 May 1991, p. 1.

104. "A Statement to the Public," given in the Patriarchate of Sremski Karlovci: 7 May 1991, trans. in *South Slav Journal* 13 (Spring–Summer 1990): 88–89.

105. *Pravoslavlje,* 15 July 1991, p. 8. For more details and examples of the Serbian Orthodox press's irredentist campaign in 1991–1992, see Ramet, "The Serbian Church and the Serbian Nation," pp. 313–314.

106. Details in Ramet, "The Serbian Church and the Serbian Nation," pp. 316–317.

107. Jure Kristo, "The Catholic Church in a Time of Crisis," in Sabrina Petra Ramet and Ljubiša S. Adamovich (eds.), *Beyond Yugoslavia: Politics, Economics, and Culture in a Shattered Community* (Boulder, Colo.: Westview Press, 1995), p. 432.

108. For details, see Sabrina P. Ramet, "The Croatian Catholic Church Since 1990," *Religion, State and Society: The Keston Journal* 24, no. 4 (December 1996). For further discussion, see Michael A. Sells, *The Bridge Betrayed: Religion and Genocide in Bosnia* (Berkeley: University of California Press, 1996).

109. Bill Yoder, "The Protestant Witness in War Zones of Former Yugoslavia," *Religion in Eastern Europe* 14 (June 1994): 28.

110. Archbishop Franjo Perko of Belgrade, interview with Predrag Popović, "Suživot je moguć," *NIN,* no. 2235 (29 October 1993): p. 30.

111. Milorad Pupovac, director of the Zagreb-based Serbian Democratic Forum, in interview with Bill Yoder, *Religion in Eastern Europe* 14 (June 1994): 30.

112. Quoted in *Danas* (Zagreb), 17 March 1992, p. 27.

113. Quoted here from an official Church translation of the memorandum of the Holy Synod of Bishops of the Serbian Orthodox Church, 28 May 1992.

114. Radio Belgrade Network (14 June 1992), trans. in FBIS, *Daily Report* (Eastern Europe), 16 June 1992, p. 42.

115. This paragraph is taken from Ramet, "The Serbian Church and the Serbian Nation," p. 318.

116. The statement was published in *Novi Vjesnik* (Zagreb), 26 September 1992, p. 9A; and *Politika—International Weekly* (Belgrade), 3–9 October 1992, p. 1.

117. *Politika,* 4 November 1992, p. 1; *Tanjug,* 26 November 1992, in FBIS, *Daily Report* (Eastern Europe), 30 November 1992, p. 41. See also *Srpska reč* (Belgrade), 28 September 1992, pp. 40–41.

118. This led *Christian Century* (27 September–4 October 1995, p. 881) to compare the Serbian Orthodox Church with pro-Hitler Christians in Nazi Germany.

119. Quoted in Paul Mojzes, "The Religiosity of Radovan Karadžić," *Religion in Eastern Europe* 15 (August 1995): p. 19.

120. *Süddeutsche Zeitung,* 29/30 October 1994, p. 4.

121. George L. Mosse, *Nationalism and Sexuality: Middle-Class Morality and Sexual Norms in Modern Europe* (Madison: University of Wisconsin Press, 1985).

122. *Religion and Human Rights* (New York: Project on Religion and Human Rights, 1994), p. 10. The overall project's general editors were John Kelsay and

Sumner B. Twiss. This passage is quoted from a chapter by David Little, Kelsay, John Mohawk, and Stanley Tambiah.

123. The skirmishes between the JNA and the Slovenian territorial militia occurred after months of escalating tensions and violence between Serbs and Croats in Croatia and between Serbs and non-Serbs in Bosnia, and they do not confute this interpretation.

124. For a balanced discussion of the media in this war, see Jasmina Kuzmanović, "Media: The Extension of Politics by Other Means," in Ramet and Adamovich (eds.), *Beyond Yugoslavia*, pp. 83–98. For an exceptionally balanced treatment of the war and its background, see Jasminka Udovički and James Ridgeway, eds., *Burn This House: The Making and Unmaking of Yugoslavia* (Durham, N.C.: Duke University Press, 1997).

125. *Tanjug*, 14 May 1992, trans. in *BBC Summary of World Broadcasts*, 19 May 1992.

126. *Christian Science Monitor*, 9 November 1993, p. 7.

127. *Tanjug*, 29 March 1994, trans. in *BBC Monitoring Service: Eastern Europe*, 4 April 1994.

128. *Oslobodjenje* (Sarajevo/Ljubljana), 12–19 January 1995, p. 24; and *Pobjeda* (Podgorica), 16 February 1995, p. 5.

129. *Večernji list*, 2 February 1995, p. 8.

130. This is so well documented that any citation of sources seems superfluous. But for those who wish more information on the destruction of Catholic churches by Serbian forces, see "The Croatian Catholic Church Since 1990," and on mosques, *Radio Bosnia-Herzegovina Network* (Sarajevo), 16 December 1993, trans. in FBIS, *Daily Report* (Eastern Europe), 16 December 1993, p. 37.

131. On the destruction of Serb Orthodox churches by Croatian forces, see *War Damage Sustained by Orthodox Churches in Serbian Areas of Croatia in 1991* (Belgrade: Ministry of Information of the Republic of Serbia, 1992); on the destruction of mosques, see, for example, *Globus*, 29 April 1994, p. 3, and *Tanjug*, 18 September 1994, in FBIS, *Daily Report* (Eastern Europe), 19 September 1994, p. 31.

132. On Croatian pressures on Serbian children to convert to Catholicism, see Ramet, "The Croatian Catholic Church since 1990"; on alleged Croatian pressures on Muslims to convert to Catholicism, see *Slobodna Dalmacija*, 15 December 1994, summarized in FBIS, *Daily Report* (Eastern Europe), 8 February 1995, p. 37. Evidence of pressures to convert to Islam are presented in the text.

133. Admitted by Bosnian sources. See *Radio Bosnia-Herzegovina Network*, 16 February 1995, trans. in FBIS, *Daily Report* (Eastern Europe), 17 February 1995, p. 38.

134. *Feral Tribune*, 22 August 1994, and *Globus*, 11 November 1994, both summarized in FBIS, *Daily Report* (Eastern Europe), 7 December 1994, p. 45.

135. Quoted in *NIN*, 16 September 1994, p. 9, trans. in FBIS, *Daily Report* (Eastern Europe), 18 October 1994, p. 59.

136. Ibid.

137. *Die Welt*, 11 May 1995, p. 4; "In War, Faith: An Interview with a Croatian Bishop," *America*, 31 August 1996, p. 22; *Süddeutsche Zeitung*, 27/28 May 1995, p. 2. See also *Radio Croatia Network*, 19 July 1995, trans. in FBIS, *Daily Report* (Eastern Europe), 19 July 1995, p. 20.

138. *National Catholic Reporter*, 2 June 1995, p. 15.

139. *Tanjug*, 1 June 1994, trans. in FBIS, *Daily Report* (Eastern Europe), 2 June 1994, p. 43.

140. *Reuter News Service,* 17 April 1996, on *Nexis.*

141. *Politika,* 18 October 1995, p. 13, and *New York Times,* 16 April 1995, p. 7.

142. *Politika,* 18 October 1995, p. 13.

143. HTV Television (Zagreb), 7 July 1994, trans. in FBIS, *Daily Report* (Eastern Europe), 8 July 1994, p. 39. The original FBIS translation refers to the "Jewish nation." The Croatian word *narod* can be translated as either "nation" or "people." I felt that the translation "Jewish people" probably comes closer to the meaning intended in the original Croatian and have therefore changed "nation" to "people" in two places in the translation.

144. See Jelena Lovrić, "Biskupska podvala," *Vreme* (Belgrade), 27 July 1996, p. 21.

145. Srdjan Vrcan, "The War in Former Yugoslavia and Religion," *Religion, State and Society: The Keston Journal* 22, no. 4 (1994): 374, 375.

146. It still bears that name today.

7. Romania's Orthodox Church

1. See Sabrina Petra Ramet, "Nationalism and the 'Idiocy' of the Countryside: The Case of Serbia," *Ethnic and Racial Studies* 19 (January 1996).

2. See Jay P. Dolan, *The American Catholic Experience: A History from Colonial Times to the Present* (Notre Dame, Ind.: University of Notre Dame Press, 1992).

3. L. S. Stavrianos, *The Balkans Since 1453* (New York: Holt, Rinehart and Winston, 1958), p. 596.

4. Quoted in Tom Gallagher, *Romania After Ceaușescu: The Politics of Intolerance* (Edinburgh: University of Edinburgh Press, 1995), p. 21.

5. Stavrianos, *The Balkans Since 1453,* p. 354.

6. Ibid., pp. 354, 597.

7. Gallagher, *Romania After Ceaușescu,* p. 23.

8. The number of Jews in 1939, cited in ibid., p. 47; the number of Lutherans in 1939, cited in Ernst Chr. Suttner, "Kirchen und Staat," in Klaus-Detlev Grothusen (ed.), *Rumänien* (Göttingen: Vandenhoeck and Ruprecht, 1977), p. 460; the number of Baptists in 1924, cited in George R. Ursul, "From Political Freedom to Religious Independence: The Romanian Orthodox Church, 1877-1925," in Stephen Fischer-Galați, Radu R. Florescu, and George R. Ursul (eds.), *Romania Between East and West: Historical Essays in Memory of Constantin C. Giurescu* (Boulder, Colo.: East European Monographs, 1982), p. 228. Numbers for all other faiths are as of 1930, as given in Sándor Bíró, *The Nationalities Problem in Transylvania 1867-1940,* trans. from Hungarian by Mario D. Fenyo (Boulder, Colo.: Social Science Monographs, 1992), p. 461. On Baptists, see also Earl A. Pope, "The Significance of the Evangelical Alliance in Contemporary Romanian Society," *East European Quarterly* 25 (January 1992).

9. Ursul, "From Political Independence," p. 217.

10. Ibid., p. 218.

11. Ibid., p. 230.

12. Quoted in R. W. Seton-Watson, *A History of the Roumanians: From Roman Times to the Completion of Unity* (Hamden, Conn.: Archon Books, 1963; reprint of 1934 orig.), p. 347.

13. Vlad Georgescu, *The Romanians: A History,* ed. Matei Calinescu, trans. Alexandra Bley-Vroman (Columbus: Ohio State University Press, 1991), p. 188.

14. Seton-Watson, *A History of the Roumanians,* p. 348; and Georgescu, *The Romanians,* p. 188.

15. Quoted in Seton-Watson, *A History of the Roumanians,* p. 349.

16. Quoted in ibid., p. 351.

17. Quoted in ibid., p. 352.

18. Ursul, "From Political Independence," pp. 236–237.

19. See Lloyd A. Cohen, "The Jewish Question During the Period of the Romanian National Renaissance and the Unification of the Two Principalities of Moldavia and Wallachia 1848-1866," in Fischer-Galați, Florescu, and Ursul (eds.), *Romania Between East and West,* pp. 195–216; also N. Jorga (Nicolae Iorga), *Geschichte des Rumänischen Volkes im Rahmen seiner Staatsbildungen* (Gotha: Friedrich Andreas Perthes Aktiengesellschaft, 1905), vol. 2, pp. 458–461.

20. See Keith Hitchins, *Orthodoxy and Nationality: Andreiu Saguna and the Rumanians of Transylvania, 1846–1873* (Cambridge, Mass.: Harvard University Press, 1977).

21. Keith Hitchins, *Rumania 1866–1947* (Oxford: Clarendon Press, 1994), p. 299.

22. On the irrationalist temper of the time, see Zeev Sternhell with Mario Sznajder and Maia Asheri, *The Birth of Fascist Ideology: From Cultural Rebellion to Political Revolution,* trans. from French by David Maisel (Princeton, N.J.: Princeton University Press, 1994). On the politics of Kantian rationalism, see Ronald Beiner and William James Booth (eds.), *Kant and Political Philosophy: The Contemporary Legacy* (New Haven, Conn.: Yale University Press, 1993).

23. Gallagher, *Romania After Ceaușescu,* p. 34.

24. Quoted in Irina Livezeanu, *Cultural Politics in Greater Romania: Regionalism, Nation Building, and Ethnic Struggle, 1918–1930* (Ithaca, N.Y.: Cornell University Press, 1995), p. 303.

25. Bíró, *Nationalities Problem,* p. 464.

26. Ibid., pp. 464–467.

27. Ibid., pp. 468–469.

28. Ibid., pp. 469–470.

29. Quoted in ibid., p. 471.

30. Ibid., p. 472.

31. Ibid.

32. Examples and documentation in ibid., pp. 474–475.

33. Ibid., pp. 479–482.

34. Ibid., pp. 485–486.

35. Alan Scarfe, "The Romanian Orthodox Church," in Pedro Ramet (ed.), *Eastern Christianity and Politics in the Twentieth Century* (Durham, N.C.: Duke University Press, 1988), p. 214.

36. Armin Heinen, *Die Legion 'Erzengel Michael' in Rumänien: Soziale Bewegung und politische Organisation* (Munich: R. Oldenbourg, 1986), p. 26.

37. Ibid., pp. 124–125.

38. Scarfe, "The Romanian Orthodox Church," pp. 215–216.

39. Ibid., pp. 217–218.

40. Heinen, *Die Legion 'Erzengel Michael,'* p. 319. For further discussion of the Iron Guard, see Stephen Fischer-Galati, "Fascism in Romania," in Peter F. Sugar (ed.), *Native Fascism in the Successor States, 1918–1945* (Santa Barbara, Calif.: ABC-Clio, 1971), pp. 112–121; Nicholas M. Nagy-Talavera, *The Green Shirts and the Others* (Stanford, Calif.: Hoover Institution Press, 1970).

41. Georgescu, *The Romanians,* p. 205. On Iorga, see Nicholas M. Nagy-Tala-

vera, *Nicolae Iorga: A Biography* (Iasi: Romanian Cultural Foundation, 1996), esp. pp. 354–357.

42. Georgescu, *The Romanians*, p. 207.

43. Ibid., p. 210. On this period in Romanian history, see also Dov B. Lungu, *Romania and the Great Powers, 1933–1940* (Durham, N.C.: Duke University Press, 1989).

44. For specifics, see Livezeanu, *Cultural Politics in Greater Romania*, p. 305.

45. Paul Mojzes, *Religious Liberty in Eastern Europe and the USSR: Before and After the Great Transformation* (Boulder, Colo.: East European Monographs, 1992), pp. 318–321.

46. Suttner, "Kirchen und Staat," pp. 461–462.

47. Ibid., p. 463; and Julian Hale, *Ceaușescu's Romania: A Political Commentary* (London: George G. Harrap, 1971), pp. 147–148. On early postwar Romanian politics, see Ghita Ionescu, *Communism in Rumania 1944–1962* (London: Oxford University Press, 1964).

48. Mojzes, *Religious Liberty*, p. 325.

49. Pedro Ramet, "The Interplay of Religious Policy and Nationalities Policy in the Soviet Union and Eastern Europe," in Ramet (ed.), *Religion and Nationalism in Soviet and East European Politics*, rev. and expanded ed. (Durham, N.C.: Duke University Press, 1989), p. 25.

50. Raoul Bossy, "Religious Persecutions in Captive Romania," *Journal of Central European Affairs* 15 (July 1955): 162; Emil Ciurea, "Religious Life," in Alexandre Cretzianu (ed.), *Captive Rumania* (London: Atlantic Press, 1956), p. 167.

51. Rumanian National Committee (Washington, D.C.), *Information Bulletin*, no. 46 (January 1953): 11; and Radio Vatican (6 January 1953), as cited in Ciurea, "Religious Life," p. 173.

52. Keith Hitchins, "The Romanian Orthodox Church and the State," in Bohdan R. Bociurkiw and John W. Strong (eds.), *Religion and Atheism in the USSR and Eastern Europe* (London: Macmillan, 1975), p. 316; Suttner, "Kirchen und Staat," pp. 458–459.

53. Scarfe, "The Romanian Orthodox Church," p. 222.

54. Hitchins, "The Romanian Orthodox Church," p. 319.

55. *The Times* (London), 2 January 1990, on *Nexis*.

56. Ramet, "Interplay of Religious Policy," p. 20.

57. Trond Gilberg, "Religion and Nationalism in Romania," in Ramet (ed.), *Religion and Nationalism*, p. 341.

58. Mark Almond, *The Rise and Fall of Nicolae and Elena Ceaușescu* (London: Chapmans, 1992), p. 145.

59. Quoted in Hale, *Ceaușescu's Romania*, p. 145.

60. *Agerpress* (Bucharest), 14 November 1986, in FBIS, *Daily Report* (Eastern Europe), 17 November 1986, p. H4.

61. Quoted in *Christian Science Monitor*, 17 January 1990, p. 19.

62. Recounted in *New York Times*, 10 February 1990, p. 11.

63. This was revealed by Metropolitan Antonie Plămădeală in an interview with the weekly magazine *22* in 1990, as reported in *Rompres* (Bucharest), 24 January 1990, in *BBC Summary of World Broadcasts*, 31 January 1990; and in *Reuter News Service*, 25 January 1990, on *Nexis*.

64. For details, see René de Flers, "Socialism in One Family," *Survey* 28 (Winter 1984): 165–174.

65. Almond, *Rise and Fall*, pp. 188–189.

66. Ibid., p. 228.

67. *Evening Standard* (London), 31 March 1994, p. 20.

68. Quoted in Robert Bacsvary, "National Minorities and the Roman Catholic Church in Rumania," in Norbert Greinacher and Virgil Elizondo (eds.), *Churches in Socialist Societies of Eastern Europe,* Concilium: Religion in the Eighties (New York: Seabury Press, 1982), p. 22.

69. Ibid.

70. *AZI* (Bucharest), 20 May 1994, p. 10, trans. in FBIS, *Daily Report* (Eastern Europe), 30 June 1994, p. 28.

71. *Rompres,* 27 March 1992, in *BBC Summary of World Broadcasts,* 30 March 1992.

72. *Reuter News Service,* 21 June 1992, on *Nexis.*

73. Quoted in ibid., 2 July 1992.

74. Letter dated 7 January 1992, published in *Új Magyarország* (Budapest), 9 January 1992, p. 4, trans. in FBIS, *Daily Report* (Eastern Europe), 14 January 1992, p. 31. The authorities took note of Tökés's letter and in due course published incriminating documents which appeared to indicate that Tökés had collaborated with the *Securitate* in Ceauşescu's time. On this point, see *Adevarul* (Bucharest), 29 December 1994, p. 2, trans. in FBIS, *Daily Report* (Eastern Europe), 3 January 1995, p. 24.

75. *Duna TV* (Budapest), 27 July 1995, trans. in FBIS, *Daily Report* (Eastern Europe), 28 July 1995, p. 19.

76. *Tineretul Liber* (Bucharest), 27 January 1990, trans. in FBIS, *Daily Report* (Eastern Europe), 9 March 1990, p. 85.

77. Serge Keleher, "The Romanian Greek-Catholic Church," *Religion, State and Society* 23, no. 1 (1995): 101. On the treatment of the Roman Catholic Church, see Emmerich Andras, "The New Organization of the Catholic Church in Romania," *Occasional Papers on Religion in Eastern Europe* 12 (March 1992): p. 27.

78. Gallagher, *Romania After Ceauşescu,* p. 107.

79. *Agence France Presse,* 2 July 1992, on *Nexis.*

80. *Reuter News Service,* 22 August 1995, on *Nexis.*

81. *Rompres,* 4 November 1991, in FBIS, *Daily Report* (Eastern Europe), 5 November 1991, p. 26.

82. The first quotation is from sociologist Mircea Kivu, the second from gynecologist Rodica Cojacaru, both in *Agence France Presse,* 28 June 1995, on *Nexis.* Both Kivu and Cojacaru are critics of the Orthodox Church's position on transsexualism.

83. As noted in *Daily Telegraph* (London), 27 December 1994, p. 11.

84. *San Francisco Chronicle,* 11 July 1994, p. A9.

85. Ibid.

86. *Rompres,* 25 May 1995, in *BBC Monitoring Service,* 27 May 1995.

87. UPI, 14 September 1995, on *Nexis.*

88. On the three-year penalty, see *Süddeutsche Zeitung* (Munich), 28/29 September 1996, p. 12. On the "control teams," see OMRI, "For the Record," compiled by Michael Shafir, 11 September 1996 (OMRI/Shafir).

89. OMRI/Shafir.

90. Ibid.

91. *Reuter News Service,* 19 April 1995, on *Nexis.*

92. *Agence France Presse,* 28 June 1995, on *Nexis.*

93. *Irish Times,* 7 March 1994, p. 9.

94. Quoted in the *Guardian,* 4 March 1994, p. 11.

95. *New York Times,* 21 November 1996, p. A3.

96. Ibid.

97. Almond, *Rise and Fall,* p. 249.

98. Ibid.

99. *Reuters,* 24 December 1989, on *Nexis.*

100. Quoted in *The Times* (London), 20 January 1990, on *Nexis.*

101. *Rompres,* 10 April 1990, on *Nexis;* and *Sunday Telegraph* (London), 22 April 1990, p. 14.

102. UPI, 5 April 1994, on *Nexis.*

103. Dan Ionescu, "Romanian Orthodox Leaders Play the Nationalist Card," *Transition* (Prague), 5 April 1996, p. 26.

104. *Reuters,* 14 September 1990, on *Nexis; AZI,* 23 November 1994, p. 2, trans. in FBIS, *Daily Report* (Eastern Europe), 13 December 1994, p. 20; *Rompres,* 19 May 1990, in *BBC Summary of World Broadcasts,* 25 May 1990; *Rompres,* 18 May 1990, in *BBC Summary of World Broadcasts,* 21 May 1990; and *Rompres,* 3 November 1993, in *BBC Summary of World Broadcasts,* 6 November 1993.

105. Ionescu, "Romanian Orthodox Leaders," p. 24.

106. Ibid., p. 25.

107. *Radio Bucharest,* 6 December 1991, quoted in Ionescu, "Romanian Orthodox Leaders," p. 26.

108. Ionescu, "Romanian Orthodox Leaders," p. 26.

8. Albania's Triple Heritage

An early draft of this chapter was published as "The Albanian Orthodox Church" in Pedro Ramet (ed.), *Eastern Christianity and Politics in the Twentieth Century* (Durham, N.C.: Duke University Press, 1988).

1. John Kolsti, "Albanianism: From the Humanists to Hoxha," in George Klein and Milan J. Reban (eds.), *The Politics of Ethnicity in Eastern Europe* (Boulder, Colo.: East European Monographs, 1981), p. 17.

2. Giuseppe Ferrari, "La Chiesa Ortodossa Albanese," *Oriente Cristiano* 18 (October–December 1978): 12, 14.

3. Šukri Rahimi, "Verska podeljnost i razvoj nacionalne svesti kod Albanaca u drugoj polovini XIX veka," *Jugoslovenski Istorijski časopis,* nos. 1–4 (1978): 299.

4. Ferrari, "La Chiesa Ortodossa," p. 16; J. Swire, *Albania: The Rise of a Kingdom* (London: Williams and Norgate, 1929), pp. 9, 39; and Peter Bartl, *Die Albanischen Muslime zur Zeit der Nationalen Unabhängigkeitsbewegung (1878–1912)* (Wiesbaden: Otto Harrassowitz, 1968), p. 25.

5. Ferrari, "La Chiesa Ortodossa," p. 16.

6. Rahimi, "Verska podeljnost," p. 300; and Bartl, *Die Albanischen Muslime,* p. 18.

7. Odile Daniel, "Nationality and Religion in Albania," *Albanian Catholic Bulletin* 11 (1990): 91.

8. Ibid., p. 92; Richard H. Siebert, "The Society of Jesus in Albania," *Albanian Catholic Bulletin* 14 (1993): 51.

9. Daniel, "Nationality and Religion," p. 52.

10. Stavro Skendi, "Religion in Albania During the Ottoman Rule," *Südost-Forschungen* (Munich) 15 (1956): 312, 316.

11. Stavro Skendi, *The Albanian National Awakening, 1878-1912* (Princeton, N.J.: Princeton University Press, 1967), pp. 17-18, 112.

12. Bartl, *Die Albanischen Muslime,* p. 24.

13. Ibid., p. 25.

14. Constantine A. Chekrezi, *Albanian Past and Present* (New York: Macmillan, 1919), p. 59; Charles and Barbara Jelavich, *The Establishment of the Balkan National States, 1804-1920* (Seattle: University of Washington Press, 1977), p. 226; Skendi, *The Albanian National Awakening,* pp. 133, 137-38; Edith Pierpont Stickney, *Southern Albania or Northern Epirus in European International Affairs, 1912-1923* (Stanford, Calif.: Stanford University Press, 1926), p. 95.

15. Skendi, *The Albanian National Awakening,* pp. 296, 299-300, 303.

16. Bernhard Tönnes, "Religionen in Albanien," *Osteuropa,* 24 (September 1974): 664.

17. Ferrari, "La Chiesa Ortodossa," p. 24.

18. For details, see Stefanaq Pollo and Asben Puro, *The History of Albania from Its Origins to the Present Day,* trans. Carol Wiseman and Ginnie Hole (London: Routledge and Kegan Paul, 1981), pp. 157-70.

19. L. S. Stavrianos, *The Balkans Since 1453* (New York: Holt, Rinehart and Winston, 1958), p. 717.

20. Teodoro Minisci, "Come si giunse all-Autocefalia della Chiesa Ortodossa Albanese—Note di cronaca," *Oriente Cristiano* 18 (October-December 1978): 72.

21. Bernd Jürgen Fischer, *King Zog and the Struggle for Stability in Albania* (Boulder, Colo.: East European Monographs, 1984), pp. 170-72.

22. Friedrich Heiler, *Die Ostkirchen* (Munich: Ernst Reinhardt, 1971), p. 85; Bernard Tönnes, "Religious Persecution in Albania," *Religion in Communist Lands* 10 (Winter 1982): 244, 246.

23. Minisci, "Come si giunse," p. 74.

24. Ibid., p. 76; and Fischer, *King Zog,* p. 172.

25. Italian text in "Tomos di Autocefalia," *Oriente Cristiano* 18 (October-December 1978): 83-86.

26. Skendi, "Religion in Albania," p. 311.

27. Ibid., pp. 312-313.

28. Ibid., pp. 313-314.

29. Bartl, *Die Albanischen Muslime,* p. 19.

30. Skendi, "Religion in Albania," pp. 316-317.

31. Bartl, *Die Albanischen Muslime,* p. 19.

32. Skendi, "Religion in Albania," p. 317.

33. Georg Stadtmüller, "Die Islamisierung bei den Albanern," *Jahrbücher fur Geschichte Osteuropas* 3, no. 4 (1955): 406.

34. See Bartl, *Die Albanischen Muslime,* pp. 117-124.

35. Ibid., p. 127.

36. Ibid., pp. 128, 149.

37. Ibid., pp. 147-148.

38. Barbara Jelavich, *History of the Balkans,* vol. 1: *Eighteenth and Nineteenth Centuries* (Cambridge: Cambridge University Press, 1983), p. 363.

39. Margaret Hasluck, "The Nonconformist Moslems of Albania," *Moslem World* 15 (October 1925): 391.

40. Bartl, *Die Albanischen Muslime*, pp. 171–172.

41. Ibid., pp. 176–177.

42. Bernd J. Fischer, "Albanian Nationalism in the Twentieth Century," in Peter F. Sugar (ed.), *Eastern European Nationalism in the Twentieth Century* (Washington, D.C.: American University Press, 1995), p. 37.

43. Ibid., p. 38.

44. Janice Broun, "The Catholic Church in Albania," in Pedro Ramet (ed.), *Catholicism and Politics in Communist Societies* (Durham, N.C.: Duke University Press, 1990), p. 238.

45. "The Jesuits in Albania," *Albanian Catholic Bulletin* 9 (1988): 55; Siebert, "Society of Jesus," p. 53.

46. Those mentioned were all Franciscans. See Vinçenc Malaj, "Apostolic and Educational Work of the Franciscan Order Among the Albanian People," *Albanian Catholic Bulletin* 11 (1990): 29.

47. Daniel, "Nationality and Religion," p. 90.

48. See Stephen Schwartz, "Some Notes on Albanian Jewry," *Albanian Catholic Bulletin* 12 (1991): 112.

49. Paul Mojzes, *Religious Liberty in Eastern Europe and the USSR: Before and After the Great Transformation* (Boulder, Colo.: East European Monographs, 1992), p. 119.

50. Anton Logoreci, *The Albanians* (London: Victor Gollancz, 1977), p. 73.

51. Palok Plaku, "Grave Violations of Religious Rights in Albania," *Albanian Catholic Bulletin* 6 (1985): 40.

52. Ibid., p. 41.

53. Gjon Sinishta, foreword to Giacomo Gardin, *Banishing God in Albania: The Prison Memoirs of Giacomo Gardin, S.J.*, trans. from Italian (San Francisco: Ignatius Press, 1988), p. 15.

54. Gardin, *Banishing God*, p. 56.

55. Ibid., p. 71.

56. On the Maliq marsh, ibid., p. 74; on the Vlorë prison, ibid., p. 115.

57. Zachary T. Irwin, "The Fate of Islam in the Balkans: A Comparison of Four State Policies," in Pedro Ramet (ed.), *Religion and Nationalism in Soviet and East European Politics*, rev. ed. (Durham, N.C.: Duke University Press, 1989), p. 385.

58. Frances Trix, "The Resurfacing of Islam in Albania," *East European Quarterly* 28 (January 1995): 534–535.

59. Bertold Spuler, *Gegenwartslage der Ostkirchen*, 2nd ed. (Frankfurt: Metopen, 1968), p. 140.

60. Quoted in Robert Tobias, *Communist-Christian Encounter in East Europe* (Indianapolis: School of Religion Press, 1956), p. 381.

61. Quoted in Peter J. Prifti, *Socialist Albania Since 1944: Domestic and Foreign Developments* (Cambridge, Mass.: MIT Press, 1978), p. 152.

62. Tönnes, "Religious Persecution," p. 248.

63. Quoted in ibid., p. 249.

64. Gjon Sinishta, *The Fulfilled Promise: A Documentary Account of Religious Persecution in Albania* (Santa Clara, Calif.: Author, 1976), p. 56.

65. Plaku, "Grave Violations," p. 41.

66. Ibid., p. 40.

67. Quoted in Prifti, *Socialist Albania*, p. 154.

68. Broun, "The Catholic Church in Albania," pp. 243–244.

69. *Zeri i popullit*, 27 June 1967, trans. in Foreign Broadcast Information Service (FBIS), *Daily Report* (USSR and East Europe), supp., 19 July 1967, p. 17. See also Louis Zanga, "Enver Hoxhas Krieg gegen die Religion," *Osteuropa* 30 (January 1980): 50–51.

70. Dilaver Sadikaj, "Revolutionary Movement Against Religion in the Sixties," *Studime Historike* (1981), no. 4, trans. in *Albanian Catholic Bulletin* 4, nos. 1 and 2 (1983): 23.

71. Trevor Beeson, *Discretion and Valour: Religious Conditions in Russia and Eastern Europe*, rev. ed. (Philadelphia: Fortress Press, 1982), p. 327. See also Bernhard Tönnes, "Religion und Kirche in Albanien," *Kirche in Not* 24 (1976): 101–109.

72. Quoted in Plaku, "Grave Violations," p. 42.

73. Sadikaj, "Revolutionary Movement," p. 25.

74. Logoreci, *The Albanians*, p. 157.

75. ATA (Tiranë), 16 September 1967, trans. in FBIS, *Daily Report* (USSR and East Europe), supp., 17 October 1967, p. 33. See also "Albanien: Götzen gegen Gott—'Die Religion des Albaniens ist der Albanismus,'" *Osteuropa* 24, no. 9 (September 1974).

76. Ramadan Marmullaku, *Albania and the Albanians*, trans. from Serbo-Croatian by Margot and Boško Milosavljević (London: Archon Books, 1975), p. 77.

77. Tönnes, "Religious Persecution," pp. 254–255; *Zeri i Rinise* (Tiranë), 25 March 1981, trans. in Joint Publications Research Service (JPRS), *East Europe Report*, no. 77958 (29 April 1981): 2.

78. Hulusi Hako, "Drejt krijimit te nje shoqerie plotesisht ateiste," trans. as "Toward the Creation of a Totally Atheistic Society," *Albanian Catholic Bulletin* 7–8 (1986–87): 24.

79. Ibid., p. 25.

80. "Religion Still Troubles Albanian Youth Leaders," *Albanian Catholic Bulletin* 9 (1988): 31.

81. Tommaso Ricci, "The Calvary of Nikollë Troshani," *Albanian Catholic Bulletin* 13 (1992): 25.

82. All information in this paragraph has been derived from the *Globe and Mail* (Toronto), 5 August 1995, p. D2.

83. *Christian Science Monitor*, 10 July 1995, p. 7.

84. IRNA, 25 July 1991, in *BBC Summary of World Broadcasts*, 27 July 1991; and *Večer* (Skopje), 26–27 December 1992, pp. 12–13, trans. in FBIS, *Daily Report* (Eastern Europe), 5 February 1993, p. 6.

85. *European Magazine* (London), 28 September–4 October 1995, p. 3; and *Moneyclips*, 14 February 1995, on *Nexis*.

86. *Moneyclips*, 14 February 1995, on *Nexis;* and *Neue Zürcher Zeitung*, 28/29 October 1995, p. 3.

87. *Moneyclips*, 8 December 1993, on *Nexis*.

88. Ibid., 3 October 1994.

89. Ibid., 19 February 1994.

90. *Jerusalem Post*, 14 June 1995, p. 7.

91. *Gazeta Shqiptare* (Tiranë), 24 August 1994, p. 1, trans. in FBIS, *Daily Report* (Eastern Europe), 1 September 1994, p. 2.

92. *Deutsche Presse-Agentur* (Hamburg), 12 June 1996, on *Nexis*.

93. Ibid., 5 September 1996.

94. *Prague Post,* 18 September 1996, and *Deutsche Presse-Agentur,* 21 September 1996, both on *Nexis.*

95. See, for example, *Tanjug* (Belgrade), 26 October 1996, in *BBC Monitoring Service: Eastern Europe,* 28 October 1996.

96. Quoted in "Albania's Supermarket of Souls," *Pozor* (Prague), October 1996, p. 41.

97. *The Times* (London), 17 April 1990, on *Nexis; Independent* (London), 21 July 1993, p. 10; *Guardian,* 7 November 1994, p. 8.

98. U.S. Department of State, *Albania Human Rights Practices, 1995,* on *Nexis* (March 1996).

99. *New Europe* (Athens), 25 February–2 March 1996, p. 39.

100. U.S. Department of State, *Albania Human Rights Practice, 1995,* on *Nexis* (March 1996).

101. *Independent* (London), 21 July 1993, p. 10; and *Reuters,* 4 July 1993, on *Nexis.*

102. *Inter Press Service,* 22 August 1994, on *Nexis.*

103. ATA (Tiranë), 6 August 1996, in *BBC Monitoring Service: Eastern Europe,* 8 August 1996.

104. Quoted in *Zeri i Popullit* (Tiranë), 23 October 1994, p. 4, trans. in FBIS, *Daily Report* (Eastern Europe), 21 November 1994, p. 2.

105. Ibid.

106. Albanian Radio (Tiranë), 8 November 1994, trans. in *BBC Summary of World Broadcasts,* 11 November 1994.

107. ATA, 4 May 1994, in *BBC Summary of World Broadcasts,* 6 May 1994.

108. Radio Tiranë, 19 October 1994, in FBIS, *Daily Report* (Eastern Europe), 20 October 1994, p. 1.

109. *Agence France Presse,* 6 November 1994, on *Nexis.*

110. *Koha Jonë,* 1 August 1996, p. 1, trans. in *BBC Monitoring Service: Eastern Europe,* 3 August 1996.

111. *Deutsche Presse-Agentur,* 7 August 1996, on *Nexis.*

112. Ibid.; and ATA, 1 August 1996, in *BBC Monitoring Service: Eastern Europe,* 3 August 1996.

113. Quoted in *Illyria* (New York), 8–10 August 1996, p. 5.

114. According to *Frankfurter Allgemeine,* 7 April 1993, p. 14. Reuters gives a lower figure of 250,000. See *Reuters,* 1 February 1993, on *Nexis.*

115. *Die Welt* (Bonn), 22 February 1991, p. 5.

116. *Frankfurter Allgemeine,* 7 April 1993, p. 14.

117. *Süddeutsche Zeitung,* 6/7 July 1991, p. 7; and *Neue Zürcher Zeitung,* 24 October 1991, p. 1.

118. "The Jesuits Return to Albania," *Albanian Catholic Bulletin* 12 (1991): 47–48.

119. ATA, 28 March 1993, in *BBC Summary of World Broadcasts,* 1 April 1993; and ATA, 30 September 1993, in *BBC Summary of World Broadcasts,* 6 October 1993.

120. ATA, 2 February 1993, in *BBC Summary of World Broadcasts,* 8 February 1993.

121. *Los Angeles Times,* 26 April 1993, p. 9; *Moscow News,* 23 December 1994, on *Nexis;* "Albanien—Der erste Kardinal," *Stimme der befreiten Kirche,* no. 1 (March 1995): 3–4.

122. *Chicago Tribune,* 11 April 1991, p. 12.

123. *Independent,* (London), 12 April 1991, p. 11.

124. *Jerusalem Post,* 12 April 1991, on *Nexis.*

125. Ibid., 21 April 1992.

126. Ibid., 11 April 1993.

127. U.S. Department of State, *Albania Human Rights Practices, 1995*, on *Nexis* (March 1996).

128. Quoted in *San Francisco Chronicle*, 12 December 1994, on *Nexis*.

129. Ibid.

130. Quoted in ibid. I have corrected the speaker's bad grammar.

131. Quoted in ibid.

132. As cited in *Die Welt*, 27 May 1992, p. 5.

133. *Liria* (Tiranë), 21 September 1994, p. 1, trans. in FBIS, *Daily Report* (Eastern Europe), 3 October 1994, p. 3.

9. The Russian Orthodox Church in Transition

I am deeply grateful to Nathaniel Davis for his most helpful feedback on an earlier draft of this chapter.

1. See Nathaniel Davis, *A Long Walk to Church: A Contemporary History of Russian Orthodoxy* (Boulder, Colo.: Westview Press, 1995), p. 17.

2. Philip Walters, "The Russian Orthodox Church," in Pedro Ramet (ed.), *Eastern Christianity and Politics in the Twentieth Century* (Durham, N.C.: Duke University Press, 1988), p. 71.

3. Quoted in ibid., p. 73.

4. *New York Times*, 18 February 1927, p. 2.

5. Quoted in Walters, "Russian Orthodox Church," in Ramet (ed.), *Eastern Christianity*, p. 73.

6. Daniel Peris, "Commissars in Red Cassocks: Former Priests in the League of Militant Godless," *Slavic Review* 54 (Summer 1995): 344–348; also Davis, *Long Walk*, p. 228, n. 18.

7. Dimitry Pospielovsky, *The Russian Church Under the Soviet Regime 1917–1982*, 2 vols. (Crestwood, N.Y.: St. Vladimir's Seminary Press, 1984), vol. 1, p. 178.

8. Quoted in *New York Times*, 19 February 1930, p. 20.

9. Ibid. Actually, one church in the Odessa region remained open. On this point, see Davis, *Long Walk*, p. 231, n. 63.

10. *New York Times*, 28 June 1930, p. 7. Metropolitan Evlogi refused to step down, however, and made preparations instead to transfer his parishes from Moscow's jurisdiction to that of the Ecumenical Patriarchate in Constantinople. See *New York Times*, 26 February 1931, p. 2.

11. Ibid., 1 May 1932, p. 1.

12. Ibid., 10 May 1932, p. 3.

13. Davis, *Long Walk*, pp. 12–13.

14. Charles Timberlake, *The Fate of Russian Orthodox Monasteries and Convents Since 1917*, Donald W. Treadgold Papers No. 3 (University of Washington, May 1995), pp. 18, 23, 26, 37. The swimming pool in question was the former Cathedral of Christ the Saviour. See Ryszard Kapuscinski, "The Temple and the Palace," *New Yorker*, 23 May 1994, pp. 72–76. Davis reported 1,025 in operation as of 1914. See Davis, *Long Walk*, p. 146 and p. 298, n. 18.

15. Oxana Antić, "The Russian Orthodox Church Abroad," in Ramet (ed.), *Eastern Christianity*, pp. 135–145.

16. William C. Fletcher, *The Russian Orthodox Church Underground, 1917–1970*

(London: Oxford University Press, 1971), pp. 153, 182, 196–201, 274–275, as cited in Davis, *Long Walk*, pp. 132, 139. See also A. V. Belov, *Sekty, sektantstvo, sektanty* (Moscow: Nauka, 1978), pp. 74–77; and Vladimir Moss, "The True Orthodox Church of Russia," *Religion in Communist Lands* 19 (Winter 1991).

17. Lev Regel'son, *Tragediia russkoi tserkvi 1917–1945* (Paris: YMCA Press, 1977), p. 188.

18. Philip Walters, "A Survey of Soviet Religious Policy," in Sabrina Petra Ramet (ed.), *Religious Policy in the Soviet Union* (Cambridge: Cambridge University Press, 1993), p. 17; Vladimir S. Rusak, *Istoriia russkoi tserkvi: So vremeni osnovaniia do nashikh dnei* (Jordanville, N.Y.: Author, 1993), pp. 477–479, 534; and Regel'son, *Tragediia russkoi tserkvi*, pp. 186–192.

19. For details, see Roman Solchanyk and Ivan Hvat, "The Catholic Church in the Soviet Union," in Pedro Ramet (ed.), *Catholicism and Politics in Communist Societies* (Durham, N.C.: Duke University Press, 1990), pp. 55–56. The closest that the Greek-Rite Catholic Church came to relegalization before Gorbachev was in 1953, shortly after Stalin's death, when KGB chief Lavrentii Beria, a contender for the succession, dispatched emissaries to initiate secret negotiations with Metropolitan Yosyf Slipyi, the Church's primate, who was then languishing in prison. The talks ended abruptly with Beria's arrest. See Amy Knight, *Beria: Stalin's First Lieutenant* (Princeton, N.J.: Princeton University Press, 1993), p. 189.

20. Davis, *Long Walk*, pp. 23–24. On this period, see also Dimitry Pospielovsky, "The 'Best Years' of Stalin's Church Policy (1942–1948) in the Light of Archival Documents," in *Religion, State and Society* 25, no. 2 (June 1997): 139–162.

21. Davis, *Long Walk*, p. 27.

22. Quoted in John Anderson, *Religion, State and Politics in the Soviet Union and Successor States* (Cambridge: Cambridge University Press, 1994), p. 7. The spelling in Anderson's translation has been Americanized.

23. Dimitry Pospielovsky, *The Russian Church Under the Soviet Regime, 1917–1982*, 2 vols. (Crestwood, N.Y.: St. Vladimir's Seminary Press, 1984), vol. 2, p. 327.

24. Anderson, *Religion, State and Politics*, p. 9.

25. Figures provided in Davis, *Long Walk*, pp. 147, 149–153. See also the figures in Gleb Rar, "Skol'ko v Rossii pravoslavnykh khramov?," *Posev* (Frankfurt), no. 1 (January 1974): 39–44. Different figures are given in Timberlake, *The Fate*, p. 37; and Walters, "A Survey," p. 21.

26. Quoted in Anderson, *Religion, State and Politics*, p. 19.

27. Quoted in ibid.

28. Davis, *Long Walk*, pp. 38–39.

29. Walters, "A Survey," p. 21.

30. Davis, *Long Walk*, p. 41.

31. Ibid., pp. 42–43.

32. Ibid., p. 112.

33. Anderson, *Religion, State and Politics*, p. 29; and Jane Ellis, *The Russian Orthodox Church: A Contemporary History* (Bloomington: Indiana University Press, 1986).

34. Anderson, *Religion, State and Politics*, p. 44.

35. Ibid., pp. 68, 72.

36. Davis, *Long Walk*, p. 112.

37. On the last point, see ibid., p. 52.

38. AFP (Paris), 28 November 1986, in Foreign Broadcast Information Service (FBIS), *Daily Report* (Soviet Union), 1 December 1986, p. R6.

39. Pedro Ramet, "Gorbachev's Reforms and Religion," in Eugene B. Shirley, Jr., and Michael Rowe (eds.), *Candle in the Wind: Religion in the Soviet Union* (Washington, D.C.: Ethics and Public Policy Center, 1989), pp. 279–286.

40. Jane Ellis, "Some Reflections About Religious Policy Under Kharchev," in Ramet (ed.), *Religious Policy*, p. 89.

41. Anderson, *Religion, State and Politics*, p. 174.

42. Ibid., p. 171. For more on the Russian Orthodox Church in the Gorbachev era, see D. V. Pospielovsky, "Church and State Under Gorbachev: What to Expect?," in Lawrence W. Lerner and Donald W. Treadgold (eds.), *Gorbachev and the Soviet Future* (Boulder, Colo.: Westview Press, 1988).

43. The first three paragraphs in this section are derived from my chapter "When Systems Collapse: Toward a Theory About the Relationship Between System Decay and Civil Strife," in Sabrina Petra Ramet (ed.), *Adaptation and Transformation in Communist and Post-Communist Systems* (Boulder, Colo.: Westview Press, 1992).

44. Ernst H. Kantorowicz, *The King's Two Bodies: A Study in Medieval Political Theology* (Princeton, N.J.: Princeton University Press, 1957). For a general treatment of religio-political interaction, see Sabrina Petra Ramet and Donald W. Treadgold (eds.), *Render Unto Caesar: The Religious Sphere in World Politics* (Washington, D.C.: American University Press, 1995).

45. Lilia Shevtsova, "Russia's Post-Communist Politics: Revolution or Continuity?," in Gail W. Lapidus (ed.), *The New Russia: Troubled Transformation* (Boulder, Colo.: Westview Press, 1995), p. 33.

46. Katherine Verdery suggests that analysts avoid use of the term "transition," which, she fears, does not sufficiently emphasize the *transformative* aspects of post-communist change. See Katherine Verdery, *What Was Socialism, and What Comes Next?* (Princeton, N.J.: Princeton University Press, 1996), pp. 15–16.

47. John Löwenhardt, *The Reincarnation of Russia: Struggling with the Legacy of Communism, 1990–1994* (Durham, N.C.: Duke University Press, 1995), p. 18.

48. See Samuel P. Huntington, *Political Order in Changing Societies* (New Haven, Conn.: Yale University Press, 1968).

49. See Nora Dudwick, "The Cultural Construction of Political Violence in Armenia and Azerbaijan," *Problems of Post-Communism* 42 (July–August 1995). On the fierce fighting in the summer of 1996, see *Neue Zürcher Zeitung*, 11 July 1996, p. 1; and *Süddeutsche Zeitung* (Munich), 3/4 August 1996, p. 6.

50. The figure was 70,000 according to *Christian Science Monitor*, 4 September 1996, p. 6; 80,000 according to *ITN World News* (London), 4 September 1996. See also *Neue Zürcher Zeitung*, 23 February 1995, p. 1; *Boston Sunday Globe*, 19 March 1995, p. 13; *Frankfurter Allgemeine*, 30 August 1996, p. 8; and *Christian Science Monitor*, 3 September 1996, pp. 1, 7. For analysis and discussion, see Martin Malek, "Zum Krieg in Tschetschenien," *Osteuropa* 46 (June 1996).

51. *Baltimore Sun*, 22 May 1994, p. 6A. See also Reinhard Eisener, "Zum Bürgerkrieg in Tadshikistan," *Osteuropa* 44 (August 1994); and Akbar Turajonzoda, "Tajikistan—Politics, Religion, and Peace," *Problems of Post-Communism* 42 (July–August 1995). See also *Neue Zürcher Zeitung*, 8 July 1996, p. 2, and 13 September 1996, p. 7.

52. See *Christian Science Monitor*, 19 September 1995, p. 6.

53. *Süddeutsche Zeitung*, 19 April 1995, p. 1.

54. *Krasnaya zvezda* (Moscow), 1 December 1992, p. 1, trans. in FBIS, *Daily Report* (Central Eurasia), 3 December 1992, p. 44.

55. *Daily Telegraph* (London), 13 April 1995, p. 13; see also *Itar-TASS World*

Service (Moscow), 12 April 1995, trans. in FBIS, *Daily Report* (Central Eurasia), 12 April 1995, p. 63.

56. *Ostankino Television First Channel and Orbita Networks* (Moscow), 19 October 1993, trans. in FBIS, *Daily Report* (Central Eurasia), 20 October 1993, p. 48.

57. *Süddeutsche Zeitung*, 1 March 1995, p. 7.

58. *Rossiyskiye vesti* (Moscow), 7 August 1993, p. 1, trans. in FBIS, *Daily Report* (Central Eurasia), 12 August 1993, p. 24.

59. On this episode, see Grigorii V. Golosov, *Modes of Communist Rule, Democratic Transition, and Party System Formation in Four East European Countries,* Donald W. Treadgold Papers No. 9 (University of Washington, August 1996).

60. On this item, see *Turkiye* (Istanbul), 10 August 1993, p. 13, trans. in FBIS, *Daily Report* (Central Eurasia), 12 August 1993, p. 58.

61. On the number of mobs, see *Boston Sunday Globe*, 11 June 1995, p. 86. On the Russian mafia's access to nuclear know-how, see *Boston Sunday Globe*, 12 June 1994, p. 8. For further discussion, see *Rossiyskiye vesti*, 21 November 1992, p. 5, trans. in FBIS, *Daily Report* (Central Eurasia), 8 December 1992, p. 22. On the activities of ethnic criminal gangs in Moscow, see *Kommersant-Daily* (Moscow), 17 March 1995, p. 14, trans. in FBIS, *Daily Report* (Central Eurasia), 30 March 1995, pp. 37–40.

62. *Neue Zürcher Zeitung*, 11 July 1995, p. 10; *Balkan News and East European Report* (Athens), 16–22 July 1995, p. 35, and 23–29 July 1995, p. 43; *Neue Zürcher Zeitung*, 12 October 1995, p. 11; and *New Europe* (Athens), 21–27 July 1996, pp. 8, 18. For more in-depth analyses, see Leonid Abalkin, "The Economic Situation in Russia," *Problems of Post-Communism* 42 (July–August 1995): 53–57; Anders Aslund, "The Political Economy of the Russian Transformation," *Brown Journal of World Affairs* 2 (Summer 1995): 91–96; Marshall I. Goldman, "The Consequences of Misguided Reform: Malignancies and Cancerous Growth," *Brown Journal of World Affairs* 2 (Summer 1995): 97–102; Avraham Shama, "Inside Russia's True Economy," *Foreign Policy*, no. 103 (Summer 1996): 111–127; and Peter Mieszkowski and Ronald Soligo, "Economic Change in Russia: 1985–95," *Problems of Post-Communism* 43 (May–June 1996): pp. 23–37.

63. *Balkan News and East European Report*, 16–22 July 1995, p. 37.

64. See, for example, Susan L. Clark and David R. Graham, "The Russian Federation's Fight for Survival," *Orbis* 39 (Summer 1995).

65. See *Christian Science Monitor*, 30 November 1995, p. 1. For that matter, Stalin was featured on a Russian stamp in 1995. See *Welt am Sonntag* (Hamburg), 7 May 1995, p. 27.

66. *Soveteskaia rossiia* (Moscow), 17 January 1995, p. 2, trans. in FBIS, *Daily Report* (Central Eurasia), 18 January 1995, p. 10.

67. This has been widely reported. See, for example, *The European* (London), 5–11 May 1995, p. 4.

68. *The European—élan* (London), 17–23 June 1994, p. 5.

69. *Frankfurter Allgemeine*, 6 April 1995, p. 38. Cultural appropriation is, of course, a two-way street, as illustrated by Italian wine producer Eros Rozza who in 1994 began marketing a red wine he called "Red Stalin," emblazoning the bottle with a prominent portrait of the Georgia-born despot. See *La Stampa* (Torino), 3 June 1994, p. 19.

70. Quoted in *New Europe*, 28 April–4 May 1996, p. 3.

71. *Itar-TASS World Service* (Moscow), 4 October 1993, trans. in FBIS, *Daily Report* (Central Eurasia), 5 October 1993, p. 26.

72. *The Times* (London), 17 May 1996, on *AmeriCast*.

73. *Zvyazda* (Minsk), 15 April 1995, p. 1, trans. in FBIS, *Daily Report* (Central Eurasia), 24 April 1995, p. 69.

74. *TVP Television First Program* (Warsaw), 4 September 1993, trans. in FBIS, *Daily Report* (Central Eurasia), 7 September 1993, p. 102.

75. *Segodnya* (Moscow), 14 September 1995, p. 8, trans. in FBIS, *Daily Report* (Central Eurasia), 26 September 1995, p. 101.

76. *Rossiyskaia gazeta* (Moscow), 2 June 1994, p. 6, trans. in FBIS, *Daily Report* (Central Eurasia), 7 June 1994, p. 63.

77. Yevgeny Polyakov, "The Activities of the Moscow Patriarchate During 1991," *Religion, State and Society* 22, no. 2 (1994): 148.

78. Quoted in ibid., p. 145.

79. Quoted in ibid.

80. Quoted in ibid., p. 146.

81. Dimitry V. Pospielovsky, "The Russian Orthodox Church in the Postcommunist CIS," in Michael Bourdeaux (ed.), *The Politics of Religion in Russia and the New States of Eurasia* (Armonk, N.Y.: M. E. Sharpe, 1995), p. 51. The report is published in German translation under the subtitle "Infiltration religioser Vereinigungen (1992)," in "Kirche und kommunistischer Staat: Dokumente einer noch ungeschriebenen Geschichte," *Osteuropa* 43 (November 1993): A602–A603.

82. Quoted in Polyakov, "Activities of the Moscow," p. 148.

83. Such as the possibility to publish a Russian translation of the Bible in CD-ROM. See *Süddeutsche Zeitung*, 22/23 April 1995, p. 12. See also William van den Bercken, "The Russian Orthodox Church, State and Society in 1991–1993: The Rest of the Story," *Religion, State and Society* 22, no. 2 (1994).

84. *Welt am Sonntag*, 8 January 1995, p. 7; and *The European* (London), 13–19 January 1995, p. 7.

85. *New York Times*, 16 July 1993, p. A9.

86. Quoted in *Segodnya*, 17 March 1995, p. 2, trans. in *Current Digest of the Post-Soviet Press*, 12 April 1995, p. 20.

87. Georg Seide, "Orthodoxie, Staatsmacht und Armee: Die neue Rolle der Russischen Orthodoxen Kirche," *Osteuropa* 46 (October 1996): 1015.

88. The communist-era figure comes from ibid., pp. 1008–1009. The contemporary figure comes from Keston Institute, *The Right to Believe* (October–December 1996), p. 1. Seide reports a markedly higher proportion of Orthodox among Russians, citing 75–85 percent, according to some polls.

89. Seide, "Orthodoxie," p. 1010.

90. *Moscow Times*, 18 May 1994, and *International Herald Tribune*, 20 May 1994, both on *Nexis*.

91. *The Times* (London), 16 October 1996, on *AmeriCast*.

92. Pospielovsky, "Russian Orthodox Church," p. 57.

93. Vsevolod Chaplin, "The Church and Politics in Contemporary Russia," in Bourdeaux (ed.), *Politics of Religion in Russia*, p. 98.

94. *New York Times*, 3 October 1994, on *Nexis*.

95. Quoted in Chaplin, "Church and Politics," p. 106.

96. *Russia TV Channel* (Moscow), 4 September 1995, trans. in *BBC Monitoring Service*, 7 September 1995.

97. *Rossiiskaia gazeta*, 16 October 1993, p. 2, trans. in FBIS, *Daily Report* (Central Eurasia), 19 October 1993, pp. 30–31.

98. On the Estonian Orthodox community, see Alexander F. C. Webster, "Split

Decision: The Orthodox Clash Over Estonia," *Christian Century*, 5–12 June 1996, pp. 614–623.

99. "Only a Pure Heart Can Transform Russia," Patriarch Aleksii II in interview with Pavel Popov, *Business in Russia* (Moscow), no. 67 (July 1996): 8.

100. D. E. Furman, "Religion and Politics in the Contemporary Mass Consciousness," from *Voprosy filosofii* (Moscow), 1992, no. 7, trans. in *Russian Social Science Review* 35 (September–October 1994): 7.

101. Ibid., p. 13.

102. Ibid., p. 14.

103. William C. Fletcher, "The Russian Orthodox Church and a Work Ethic," in Ramet and Treadgold (eds.), *Render Unto Caesar,* p. 295.

10. Ukraine's Fractious Churches

I am deeply grateful to Roman Solchanyk for sharing research materials with me and for generously giving of his time to answer questions of mine.

1. There were still *Pokutnyky* active as late as 1969. See John Anderson, *Religion, State and Politics in the Soviet Union and Successor States* (Cambridge: Cambridge University Press, 1994), p. 134.

2. See, in particular, Bohdan R. Bociurkiw, "Religion and Nationalism in the Contemporary Ukraine," in George W. Simmonds (ed.), *Nationalism in the USSR and Eastern Europe* (Detroit: University of Detroit Press, 1977); Vasyl Markus, "Religion and Nationality: The Uniates of the Ukraine," in Bohdan R. Bociurkiw and John W. Strong (eds.), *Religion and Atheism in the USSR and Eastern Europe* (London: Macmillan, 1975); Vasyl Markus, "Religion and Nationalism in Ukraine," in Pedro Ramet (ed.), *Religion and Nationalism in Soviet and East European Politics,* rev. and expanded ed. (Durham, N.C.: Duke University Press, 1989); Roman Solchanyk and Ivan Hvat, "The Catholic Church in the Soviet Union," in Pedro Ramet (ed.), *Catholicism and Politics in Communist Societies* (Durham, N.C.: Duke University Press, 1990).

3. Mikhail Dmitriev, "The Religious Programme of the Union of Brest in the Context of the Counter-Reformation in Eastern Europe," *Journal of Ukrainian Studies* 17 (Summer–Winter 1992): 30–31. This account is also confirmed in "Brest, Union of," in *The HarperCollins Encyclopedia of Catholicism,* ed. Richard P. McBrien (San Francisco: HarperCollins, 1995), p. 195.

4. Dmitriev, "The Religious Programme," p. 31.

5. Zenon E. Kohut, "The Problem of Ukrainian Orthodox Church Autonomy in the Hetmanate (1654–1780s)," *Harvard Ukrainian Studies* 14 (December 1990): 365.

6. Ibid., p. 367.

7. Paul Robert Magocsi, *A History of Ukraine* (Seattle: University of Washington Press, 1996), p. 545.

8. John S. Reshetar, "Ukrainian Nationalism and the Orthodox Church," *American Slavic and East European Review* 10 (February 1951): 42, 45.

9. Bohdan R. Bociurkiw, "The Ukrainian Autocephalous Orthodox Church," in Pedro Ramet (ed.), *Eastern Christianity and Politics in the Twentieth Century* (Durham, N.C.: Duke University Press, 1988), pp. 312, 313.

10. Ibid., pp. 313–314.

11. Roman Solchanyk and Ivan Hvat, "The Catholic Church in the Soviet Union," in Ramet (ed.), *Catholicism and Politics in Communist Societies,* p. 54.

12. Magocsi, *A History of Ukraine,* p. 629.

13. Paul Robert Magocsi (ed.), *Morality and Reality: The Life and Times of Andrei Sheptyts'kyi* (Edmonton, 1989), excerpted in Magocsi, *A History of Ukraine,* p. 632; confirmed in *Ukrainian Weekly* (Jersey City, N.J.), 20 November 1994, p. 7.

14. Quoted in Magocsi (ed.), *Morality and Reality,* excerpted in Magocsi, *A History of Ukraine,* p. 632.

15. As recounted in *Ukrainian Weekly,* 20 November 1994, p. 7.

16. The definitive treatment of the subject is Bohdan R. Bociurkiw, *The Ukrainian Greek Catholic Church and the Soviet State (1939–1950)* (Edmonton: Canadian Institute of Ukrainian Studies Press, 1996). See also Vasyl Markus, "The Suppressed Church: Ukrainian Catholics in the Soviet Union," in Richard T. De George and James P. Scanlan (eds.), *Marxism and Religion in Eastern Europe* (Dordrecht, Netherlands: D. Reidel, 1976), pp. 119–132.

17. Bociurkiw, *The Ukrainian Greek Catholic Church,* pp. 221–222; also *The European* (London), 14–20 April 1995, p. 4.

18. *Radyans'ka Ukrayina* (Kiev), 24 March 1981, p. 4, trans. in Joint Publications Research Service (JPRS), *USSR Report: Political and Sociological Affairs,* 19 August 1981, p. 34.

19. Ibid., p. 36.

20. *Radyans'ka Ukrayina,* 28 June 1981, p. 3, trans. in JPRS, *USSR Report: Political and Sociological Affairs,* 25 September 1981, p. 54.

21. Ibid., pp. 54, 55.

22. See Vasyl Markus, "Religion and Nationalism in Ukraine," in Ramet (ed.), *Religion and Nationalism in Soviet and East European Politics,* pp. 138–170.

23. On the revival of the Ukrainian Autocephalous Orthodox Church, see David Marples and Ostap Skrypnyk, "Patriarch Mstyslav and the Revival of the Ukrainian Autocephalous Orthodox Church," Radio Liberty, *Report on the USSR,* 11 January 1991; and Frank E. Sysyn, "The Third Rebirth of the Ukrainian Autocephalous Orthodox Church and the Religious Situation in Ukraine, 1989–1991," in Stephen K. Batalden (ed.), *Seeking God: The Recovery of Religious Identity in Orthodox Russia, Ukraine, and Georgia* (DeKalb: Northern Illinois University Press, 1993), pp. 191–219. On the revival of the Greek-Rite Catholic Church in Ukraine, see Bohdan R. Bociurkiw, "The Ukrainian Catholic Church in the USSR Under Gorbachev," *Problems of Communism* 39 (November–December 1990): 1–19.

24. *Svoboda* (Kiev), 5 March 1996, p. 1.

25. On the Muslims of Ukraine, see *Radio Ukraine World Service* (Kiev), 18 September 1994, trans. in Foreign Broadcast Information Service (FBIS), *Daily Report* (Central Eurasia), 19 September 1994, pp. 52–53; *Molod Ukrayiny* (Kiev), 27 September 1994, p. 1, trans. in FBIS, *Daily Report* (Central Eurasia), 29 September 1994, p. 48.

26. Andrii Krawchuck, "Religious Life in Ukraine: Continuity and Change," *Religion in Eastern Europe* 16 (June 1996): 18–19; Vasyl Markus, "Politics and Religion in Ukraine," in Michael Bourdeaux (ed.), *The Politics of Religion in Russia and the New States of Eurasia* (Armonk, N.Y.: M. E. Sharpe, 1995), pp. 172–173.

27. *Lyudyna i svit* no. 10 (1994): 10; *East-West Church and Ministry Report* 4 (Spring 1996): 14.

28. *Lyudyna i svit* no. 10 (1994): 10; *East-West Church and Ministry Report* 4 (Spring 1996): 14.

29. *Lyudyna i svit* no. 10 (1994): 10; *East-West Church and Ministry Report* 4 (Spring 1996): 14.

30. *Lyudyna i svit* no. 10 (1994): 10.

31. *Molod Ukrayiny,* 16 November 1995, p. 1, trans. in FBIS, *Daily Report* (Central Eurasia), 22 November 1995, p. 52.

32. Myroslaw Tataryn, "The Re-emergence of the Ukrainian (Greek) Catholic Church in the USSR," in Sabrina Petra Ramet (ed.), *Religious Policy in the Soviet Union* (Cambridge: Cambridge University Press, 1993), p. 303.

33. Ibid., p. 305.

34. Nathaniel Davis, "The Russian Orthodox Church: Opportunity and Trouble," paper presented at the annual convention of the American Association for the Advancement of Slavic Studies, Washington, D.C., October 1995, p. 10. On the death of Metropolitan Ioann in a car accident in western Ukraine, see *Ukrainian Weekly,* 20 November 1994, p. 2.

35. *Ukrainian Weekly,* 18 March 1990, p. 6.

36. Tataryn, "The Re-emergence," p. 304.

37. TASS (Moscow), 7 March 1990, in FBIS, *Daily Report* (Soviet Union), 6 April 1990, p. 100.

38. Radio Kiev, 13 March 1990, in FBIS, *Daily Report* (Soviet Union), 6 April 1990, pp. 100–101.

39. Statement of 12 April, quoted in TASS, 12 April 1990, in FBIS, *Daily Report* (Soviet Union), 17 April 1990, p. 116.

40. TASS, 12 April 1990, in FBIS, *Daily Report* (Soviet Union), 16 April 1990, p. 119.

41. Nathaniel Davis, *A Long Walk to Church: A Contemporary History of Russian Orthodoxy* (Boulder, Colo.: Westview Press, 1995), p. 81.

42. Miroslav Marinovic, "Le Chiese ucraine alla ricerca di un'identità," *La Nuova Europa* 4 (March–April 1995): 27.

43. Oleh W. Gerus, "Church Politics in Contemporary Ukraine," *Ukrainian Quarterly* 52 (Spring 1996): 37.

44. Davis, *Long Walk,* p. 97.

45. Ibid., p. 95.

46. Ibid.

47. Gerus, "Church Politics," p. 37; Davis, *Long Walk,* p. 98.

48. Gerus, "Church Politics," pp. 37–38; Davis, *Long Walk,* p. 99.

49. Gerus, "Church Politics," p. 38.

50. For a biography of Patriarch Volodymyr, see *The Times* (London), 26 July 1995, on *Nexis.* For another report, see *Ukrainian Weekly,* 31 October 1991, pp. 1, 10.

51. *Reuters,* 16 December 1992, on *Nexis.*

52. See, for example, *Moscow News,* 16 July 1992, on *Nexis.*

53. Ibid.

54. Gerus, "Church Politics," p. 39.

55. Davis, *Long Walk,* p. 101.

56. Davis, "Opportunity and Trouble," p. 12. For further discussion of UNA-UNSO, see Roman Solchanyk, "The Radical Right in Ukraine," in Sabrina Petra Ramet (ed.), *The Radical Right in Central and Eastern Europe* (University Park, Pa.: Pennsylvania State University Press, in press).

57. Roman Solchanyk, "Ukraine: The Politics of Reform," *Problems of Post-Communism* 42 (November–December 1995): 48.

58. Gerus, "Church Politics," pp. 43–44.

59. *Ukrainian Weekly,* 25 December 1994, p. 11.

60. Quoted in *Intelnews* (Kiev), 24 August 1995, in FBIS, *Daily Report* (Central Eurasia), 24 August 1995, p. 47.

61. *Intelnews,* 18 August 1995, in FBIS, *Daily Report* (Central Eurasia), 21 August 1995, p. 54.

62. *Intelnews,* 19 September 1995, in FBIS, *Daily Report* (Central Eurasia), 19 September 1995, p. 51.

63. *UNIAR News Agency* (Kiev), 21 July 1995, trans. in *BBC Summary of World Broadcasts,* 24 July 1995; *Deutsche Presse-Agentur* (Hamburg), 18 July 1995, on *Nexis.*

64. *Deutsche Presse-Agentur,* 18 July 1995, on *Nexis.*

65. Ibid.; *Reuters,* 19 July 1995, on *Nexis; Christian Science Monitor,* 21 July 1995, p. 6; *Der Spiegel* (Hamburg), 7 August 1995, p. 129.

66. Quoted in *Christian Science Monitor,* 21 July 1995, p. 6.

67. Quoted in *UNIAN News Agency,* 19 July 1995, trans. in *BBC Summary of World Broadcasts,* 21 July 1995.

68. Full text in *Radio Ukraine World Service* (Kiev), 22 July 1995, trans. in *BBC Summary of World Broadcasts,* 24 July 1995.

69. Full text in *Radio Ukraine World Service,* 26 July 1995, trans. in FBIS, *Daily Report* (Central Eurasia), 27 July 1995, pp. 69, 70.

70. Full text in *Vechirniy Kyyiv* (Kiev), 22 July 1995, p. 1, trans. in FBIS, *Daily Report* (Central Eurasia), 27 July 1995, p. 71.

71. Quoted in *Itar–TASS* (Moscow), 26 July 1995, in FBIS, *Daily Report* (Central Eurasia), 27 July 1995, p. 72.

72. *UNIAN News Agency,* 21 July 1995, trans. in *BBC Summary of World Broadcasts,* 24 July 1995.

73. *Interfax News Agency* (Moscow), 19 July 1995, in *BBC Summary of World Broadcasts,* 20 July 1995.

74. Quoted in *Los Angeles Times,* 7 August 1995, p. A6.

75. *UNIAN News Agency,* 23 August 1995, trans. in FBIS, *Daily Report* (Central Eurasia), 24 August 1995, p. 47.

76. *Ukrainian Weekly,* 23 June 1996, p. 1.

77. Ibid., 14 July 1996, p. 4, and 28 July 1996, p. 2.

78. Ibid., 19 November 1995, p. 16.

79. *UNIAN News Agency,* 26 October 1995, trans. in FBIS, *Daily Report* (Central Eurasia), 27 October 1995, p. 62.

80. *UNIAN News Agency,* 30 October 1995, trans. in *BBC Monitoring Service,* 31 October 1995.

81. Ibid.

82. Gerus, "Church Politics," p. 45.

83. *New Europe* (Athens), 24–30 March 1996, p. 5.

84. *Los Angeles Times,* 7 August 1995, p. A6.

85. Gerus, "Church Politics," p. 46.

11. The New Evangelism in Postcommunist Europe

1. Quoted in *Chicago Tribune,* 2 September 1992, p. 7.

2. Bellowed by evangelist Karen Podgorny through a bullhorn in front of Lenin's tomb in Moscow, as quoted in ibid.

3. UPI, 1 May 1992, on *Nexis*.

4. *Chicago Tribune*, 2 September 1992, p. 7.

5. *Washington Post*, 21 October 1991, p. A1.

6. *Independent* (London), 29 March 1993, p. 4.

7. BTA (Sofia), 12 July 1990, in *BBC Summary of World Broadcasts*, 16 July 1990.

8. *Warsaw Voice*, 2 October 1994, on *Nexis*.

9. *Financial Times*, 29 December 1990, p. 6.

10. *The Times* (London), 1 June 1991, on *Nexis*.

11. BTA, 7 November 1990, in *BBC Summary of World Broadcasts*, 9 November 1990.

12. *Christian Science Monitor*, 17 October 1995, p. 7.

13. *Observer* (London), 14 May 1995, on *Nexis*.

14. *East-West Church and Ministry Report* 1 (Fall 1993): 5. On the Czech Republic, see ČTK, 11 August 1991, on *Nexis*; on Macedonia, see *Sunday Telegraph* (London), 12 June 1994, p. 28.

15. On Moscow, see *Observer* (London), 14 May 1995, on *Nexis*.

16. *Sovetskaia Rossiia*, 29 August 1992, p. 2, trans. in *Current Digest of the Post-Soviet Press* 64 (7 October 1992): 2.

17. *Pravda*, 26 November 1992, pp. 6–7, trans. in *Current Digest of the Post-Soviet Press* 64, (23 December 1992): 24.

18. Quoted in UPI, 14 July 1993, on *Nexis*.

19. Quoted in *Balkan News and East European Report* (Athens), 30 July–5 August 1995, p. 8.

20. *Interfax News Agency* (Moscow), 22 July 1995, in *BBC Summary of World Broadcasts*, 24 July 1995.

21. Quoted in ibid. See also *Interfax*, 24 July 1995, in FBIS, *Daily Report* (Eastern Europe), 25 July 1995, pp. 64–65.

22. U.S. Department of State, *Belarus Human Rights Practices, 1994*, on *Nexis* (March 1995).

23. U.S. Department of State, *Moldova Human Rights Practices, 1994*, and *Armenia Human Rights Practices, 1994*, both on *Nexis* (March 1995).

24. *Moscow News*, 21 July 1995, on *Nexis*.

25. Ibid.

26. *Republic of Abkhazia Radio* (Sukhumi), 11 October 1995, trans. in FBIS, *Daily Report* (Central Eurasia), 12 October 1995, p. 73.

27. U.S. Department of State, *Lithuania Human Rights Report, 1994*, on *Nexis* (March 1995).

28. Patriarch Teoctist, head of the Romanian Orthodox Church, as quoted in UPI, 25 June 1996, on *Nexis*.

29. *Tanjug* (Belgrade), 4 April 1992, in *BBC Summary of World Broadcasts*, 8 April 1992.

30. Quoted in *Inter Press Service*, 21 April 1992, on *Nexis*.

31. "Bulgaria Human Rights Practices, 1993," in U.S. Department of State, *Department of State Dispatch*, 31 January 1994, on *Nexis*.

32. *New Europe* (Athens), 29 October–4 November 1995, p. 48.

33. *Prague Post*, 29 November 1995, on *Nexis*.

34. For some examples, see ibid.; *Slobodna Dalmacija* (Split), 21 May 1995, p. 11. See also Tomislav Branković, "Problemi definisanja suštine u karaktera sekti," *Marksističke teme* 11, nos. 3–4 (1987).

35. Quoted in *East-West Church and Ministry Report* 4 (Summer 1996): 5.

36. *Neue Zürcher Zeitung*, 29 November 1991, p. 4, and 11 December 1991, p. 4; *Süddeutsche Zeitung* (Munich), 14/15 December 1991, p. 7.

37. Quoted in *New York Times*, 7 September 1993, p. A9.

38. See UPI, 14 July 1993; *The Times* (London), 21 July 1993; *Süddeutsche Zeitung*, 27 July 1993, p. 6, and 4 August 1995, all on *Nexis*. A similar decree was actually adopted in Belarus in 1995. It regulated the order of invitation, length of stay, and activities of foreign clergy in Belarus, requiring, inter alia, that they coordinate their arrival with the department of religion. Archbishop Augustino Marcetto, papal nuncio to Belarus, met with Prime Minister Mihkail Chyhir on 2 August 1995 to express his concern about the decree. See *BELAPAN* (Minsk), 3 August 1995, in FBIS, *Daily Report* (Central Eurasia), 3 August 1995, p. 74.

39. See *Süddeutsche Zeitung*, 8 September 1993, p. 9.

40. *East-West Church and Ministry Report* 4 (Summer 1996): 1.

41. *Moscow News*, 28 October 1996, on *AmeriCast*.

42. *East-West Church and Ministry Report* 4 (Summer 1996): 1.

43. *Die Welt*, 19 July 1997, p. 7; *New York Times*, 23 July 1997, p. A1; *Christian Science Monitor*, 24 July 1997, p. 6; and *National Catholic Reporter*, 1 August 1997, p. 11.

44. *Warsaw Voice*, 2 October 1994, on *Nexis*.

45. *Independent* (London), 29 March 1993, p. 4.

46. *Christian Science Monitor*, 15 November 1995, p. 12. See also Bernice Martin, "New Mutations of the Protestant Ethic Among Latin American Pentecostals," and Paul Freston, "Pentecostalism in Brazil: A Brief History," both in *Religion* 25 (April 1995).

47. *Christian Science Monitor*, 3 June 1996, p. 7.

12. A Contrast of the Bulgarian Orthodox Church and the Polish Catholic Church

1. Quoted in Adam Michnik, *The Church and the Left*, trans. from Polish by David Ost (Chicago: University of Chicago Press, 1993), pp. 131-133. © 1993 by The University of Chicago. Reprinted by permission.

2. Regarding the *millet* system, see Charles and Barbara Jelavich, *The Establishment of the Balkan National States, 1804-1920* (Seattle: University of Washington Press, 1977), pp. 4-10, 100-105.

3. Lawrence Wolff, "Poland and the Vatican in the Age of Partitions: European Enlightenment, Roman Catholicism, and the Development of Polish Nationalism," Ph.D. diss., Stanford University, 1984.

4. Regarding Popiełuszko, see John Moody and Roger Boyes, *The Priest and the Policeman: The Courageous Life and Cruel Murder of Father Jerzy Popiełuszko* (New York: Summit Books, 1987).

5. For discussion, see James Cracraft, *The Church Reform of Peter the Great* (Stanford, Calif.: Stanford University Press, 1971).

6. Richard J. Crampton, *Bulgaria 1878-1918: A History* (Boulder, Colo.: East European Monographs, 1983), p. 11.

7. Ibid., p. 13.

8. Tatyana Nestorova, *American Missionaries Among the Bulgarians (1858-1912)* (Boulder, Colo.: East European Monographs, 1987), pp. 6, 9-10. See also Paul

Mojzes and N. Gerald Shenk, "Protestantism in Bulgaria and Yugoslavia Since 1945," in Sabrina Petra Ramet (ed.), *Protestantism and Politics in Eastern Europe and Russia: The Communist and Postcommunist Eras* (Durham, N.C.: Duke University Press, 1992), pp. 210–211.

9. Nestorova, *American Missionaries*, p. 47.

10. L. S. Stavrianos, *The Balkans Since 1453* (New York: Holt, Rinehart and Winston, 1958), p. 373.

11. Ibid., p. 374.

12. Crampton, *Bulgaria 1878–1918*, p. 34.

13. Spas T. Raikin, "The Bulgarian Orthodox Church," in Pedro Ramet (ed.), *Eastern Christianity and Politics in the Twentieth Century* (Durham, N.C.: Duke University Press, 1988), p. 162.

14. Ibid., p. 163.

15. Duncan M. Perry, *Stefan Stambolov and the Emergence of Modern Bulgaria, 1870–1895* (Durham, N.C.: Duke University Press, 1993), pp. 170, 202; Crampton, *Bulgaria 1878–1918*, pp. 133–134.

16. Perry, *Stefan Stambolov*, p. 148.

17. Raikin, "Bulgarian Orthodox Church," p. 170.

18. Janice Broun, *Conscience and Captivity: Religion in Eastern Europe* (Washington, D.C.: Ethics and Public Policy Center, 1988), p. 49; Raikin, "Bulgarian Orthodox Church," p. 171.

19. Raikin, "Bulgarian Orthodox Church," p. 171.

20. *Reuter News Service*, 19 July 1994, on *Nexis*.

21. Quoted in Djoko Slijepčević, *Die bulgarische orthodoxe Kirche 1944–1956* (Munich: R. Oldenbourg, 1957), p. 10.

22. Except from March 1954 until February 1957.

23. Wolf Oschlies, "Kirche und Religion in Bulgarien," in Paul Lendvai (ed.), *Religionsfreiheit und Menschenrechte* (Graz: Styria, 1983), pp. 189–190.

24. BTA (Sofia), 21 February 1992, in *BBC Summary of World Broadcasts*, 29 February 1992.

25. Pedro Ramet, *Cross and Commissar: The Politics of Religion in Eastern Europe and the USSR* (Bloomington: Indiana University Press, 1987), p. 119.

26. *Duhovna kultura* (1984), no. 9, trans. in *Keston News Service*, no. 219 (21 February 1985): 16.

27. Spas Raikin, "The Predicaments of the Bulgarian Orthodox Church Today," *Occasional Papers on Religion in Eastern Europe* 12 (February 1992): 21.

28. BTA (11 July 1991), in *BBC Summary of World Broadcasts* (17 July 1991).

29. Raikin, "Predicaments," p. 23.

30. BTA, 7 November 1990, in Foreign Broadcast Information Service (FBIS), *Daily Report* (Eastern Europe), 8 November 1990, p. 14; U.S. Department of State, *1991 Human Rights Report*, on *Nexis* (February 1992), and *1994 Human Rights Report*, on *Nexis* (March 1995).

31. BTA, 18 October 1990, in FBIS, *Daily Report* (Eastern Europe), 19 October 1990, p. 10.

32. *Tanjug* (Belgrade), 31 March 1989, in *BBC Summary of World Broadcasts*, 6 April 1989.

33. As noted and documented in Sabrina Petra Ramet, *Social Currents in Eastern Europe: The Sources and Consequences of the Great Transformation*, 2nd ed. (Durham, N.C.: Duke University Press, 1995), p. 282. See also BTA, 28 March 1989, in *BBC Summary of World Broadcasts*, 30 March 1989.

34. Janice Broun, "The Schism in the Bulgarian Orthodox Church," *Religion, State and Society: The Keston Journal* 21, no. 2 (1993): 209.

35. Quoted in *Los Angeles Times*, 19 November 1989, p. 1.

36. *Sofia Home Service*, 8 January 1990, trans. in *BBC Summary of World Broadcasts*, 11 January 1990.

37. Broun, "The Schism," p. 210.

38. Ibid., pp. 208, 211.

39. Quoted in *Inter Press Service*, 21 April 1992, on *Nexis*.

40. BTA, 21 February 1992, in *BBC Summary of World Broadcasts*, 29 February 1992; see also BTA, 1 June 1992, in *BBC Summary of World Broadcasts*, 5 June 1992.

41. BTA, 9 March 1992, in *BBC Summary of World Broadcasts*, 11 March 1992.

42. Janice Broun, "Bulgarian Orthodox Schism," *Religion in Eastern Europe* 13 (June 1993): 2–3.

43. Ibid., p. 3.

44. *Gazette* (Montreal), 17 July 1992, p. A1.

45. Broun, "The Schism," p. 213.

46. BTA, 1 June 1992, and 15 July 1992, in *BBC Summary of World Broadcasts*, 5 June 1992 and 23 July 1992, respectively.

47. BTA, 11 June 1992, in *BBC Summary of World Broadcasts*, 19 June 1992.

48. BTA, 5 November 1992, in *BBC Summary of World Broadcasts*, 9 November 1992. I have changed "intervene" to "interfere" for reasons of stylistic elegance.

49. Broun, "Bulgarian Church Schism," p. 4.

50. *Gazette* (Montreal), 17 July 1992, p. A1.

51. BTA, 24 August 1992, in *BBC Summary of World Broadcasts*, 27 August 1992.

52. BTA, 23 March 1993, in FBIS, *Daily Report* (Eastern Europe), 24 March 1993, p. 8.

53. BTA, 24 March 1993, in *BBC Summary of World Broadcasts*, 27 March 1993 (my emphasis).

54. *Reuters World Service*, 12 May 1994, on *Nexis*.

55. *New Europe* (Athens), 14–20 April 1996, p. 36.

56. Quoted in Antony Polonsky, *Politics in Independent Poland 1921–1939: The Crisis of Constitutional Government* (Oxford: Clarendon Press, 1972), p. 48.

57. Quoted in Neal Pease, "Nationalism and Catholicism in Interwar Poland," paper presented at the annual conference of the American Association for the Advancement of Slavic Studies, Washington, D.C., October 1995, p. 9.

58. Ibid., p. 6.

59. The complete authentic French text of the concordat is reprinted on pp. 117–125 as an appendix to Fritz Grübel, *Die Rechtslage der römisch-katholischen Kirche in Polen*, Leipziger rechtswissenschaftliche Studien, no. 59 (Leipzig: von Theodor Weicher, 1930).

60. Polonsky, *Politics in Independent Poland*, pp. 120–121.

61. Ibid., pp. 208–209.

62. Ibid., pp. 210–211.

63. From the complete text, reprinted as an appendix in Broun, *Conscience and Captivity*, pp. 330–332.

64. Andrzej Micewski, *Cardinal Wyszyński: A Biography*, trans. from Polish by William R. Brand and Katarzyna Mroczkowska-Brand (San Diego: Harcourt Brace Jovanovich, 1984), p. 69.

65. Ibid., pp. 79–80.

66. Tad Szulc, *Pope John Paul II: The Biography* (New York: Scribner, 1995), p. 173.

67. Barbara Strassberg, "Polish Catholicism in Transition," in Thomas M. Gannon, S.J. (ed.), *World Catholicism in Transition* (New York: Macmillan, 1988), p. 193.

68. Michnik, *The Church and the Left*, p. 69.

69. Ibid., p. 77.

70. Jan Kubik, *The Power of Symbols Against the Symbols of Power: The Rise of Solidarity and the Fall of State Socialism in Poland* (University Park: Pennsylvania State University Press, 1994), p. 111.

71. Ibid., p. 116.

72. The first national conferences of bishops were initiated in Europe after 1848 when Pope Pius IX fled Rome in disguise. The decision adopted at the Second Vatican Council in 1965 mandated the adoption of this structure throughout the Church. See "Episcopal conference," in *The HarperCollins Encyclopedia of Catholicism*, ed. Richard P. McBrien (San Francisco: HarperCollins, 1995), p. 473.

73. Quoted in Peter Hebblethwaite, *Paul VI: The First Modern Pope* (New York: Paulist Press, 1993), p. 446.

74. Ibid.

75. Quoted in ibid., p. 447.

76. Kubik, *The Power of Symbols*, p. 117.

77. Anna and Andrzej Anusz, *Samotnie Wśród Wiernych* (Warsaw: Wydawnictwo ALFA, 1994), p. 43.

78. Kubik, *The Power of Symbols*, p. 120.

79. Jane Leftwich Curry (trans. and ed.), *The Black Book of Polish Censorship* (New York: Vintage Books, 1984), p. 283.

80. Ibid., pp. 48-49.

81. Quoted in Kubik, *The Power of Symbols*, p. 173.

82. Krystyna Darczewska, *Katolicyzm we Współczesnym Społeczeństwie Polskim* (Wrocław: Zakład Narodowy im. Ossolińskich-Wydawnictwo Polskiej Akademii Nauk, 1989), p. 51.

83. Quoted in Stanisław Markiewicz, *Państwo i Kościoł w Polsce* (Warsaw: Krajowa Agencja Wydawnicza, 1984), pp. 108-109.

84. "Dialog, Pluralizm i Jedność," in *Spotkania*, no. 5 (October 1978): 41.

85. Szulc, *Pope John Paul II*, pp. 379-380.

86. Quoted in Carl Bernstein and Marco Politi, *His Holiness: John Paul II and the Hidden History of Our Time* (New York: Doubleday, 1996), p. 338.

87. See Jonathan Luxmoore, "The Polish Church Under Martial Law," *Religion in Communist Lands* 15 (Summer 1987): 134-135, 137-141, 143, 148; and Ramet, *Social Currents in Eastern Europe*, esp. pp. 185-190.

88. Another 24.6 percent claimed not to have an opinion on this question, while 8.6 percent gave other answers. See Darczewska, *Katolicyzm we Współczesnym*, p. 162.

89. Strassberg, "Polish Catholicism," p. 201. See also Barbara Strassberg, "Changes in Religious Culture in Post-World War II Poland," in *Sociological Analysis* 48 (Winter 1988): 347, 353-354.

90. Vincent C. Chrypiński, "The Catholic Church in Poland, 1944-1989," in Pedro Ramet (ed.), *Catholicism and Politics in Communist Societies* (Durham, N.C.: Duke University Press, 1990), p. 126.

91. See Ramet, *Cross and Commissar,* chap. 8 ("Religious Ferment, 1978–84") and chap. 9 ("Protestants and Catholics After Popiełuszko"); Ramet, *Social Currents in Eastern Europe,* chap. 7 ("Church and Dissent in Praetorian Poland").

92. Paul Hockenos, *Free to Hate: The Rise of the Right in Post-Communist Eastern Europe,* rev. ed. (New York: Routledge, 1944), p. 243.

93. *Frankfurter Allgemeine,* 6 May 1989, p. 12, and 18 May 1989, p. 6; *Tygodnik Powszechny,* 25 June 1989, pp. 1, 3.

94. Dobrosław Karol Pater, "Grandiose Visions: Changes in the Catholic Church After 1989," *Religion in Eastern Europe* 15 (August 1995): 3.

95. *Frankfurter Allgemeine,* 27 April 1991, p. 1; confirmed in *Süddeutsche Zeitung* (Munich), 27/28 April 1991, p. 9.

96. *National Catholic Reporter,* 31 May 1991, p. 7.

97. *New York Times,* 15 May 1991, p. A7.

98. *Süddeutsche Zeitung,* 30 September 1993, p. 8.

99. Hockenos, *Free to Hate,* p. 258. See also *Neue Zürcher Zeitung,* 13 July 1994, p. 2.

100. *Gazeta Wyborcza,* 9 August 1994, p. 1, trans. in *Polish News Bulletin,* 9 August 1994, on *Nexis.* On the other hand, a 1990 poll found that 75 percent of Polish adults *agreed* with the statement, "in sex everything is allowed." Reported in Irena Borowik, "Kóscielność i prywatność religijności w Polsce (1990–1994)," *Universitas,* no. 13/1 (1995): 73.

101. Hockenos, *Free to Hate,* p. 256.

102. Quoted in ibid., p. 247.

103. Ibid.

104. PAP (Warsaw), 20 August 1992, in FBIS, *Daily Report* (Eastern Europe), 21 August 1992, p. 15; *New York Times,* 22 April 1993, p. A7.

105. Renée Danziger, "Discrimination Against People with HIV and AIDS in Poland," *British Medical Journal* 308, no. 6937 (1994), on *Nexis* (30 April 1994).

106. *Rzeczpospolita,* 17 April 1996, p. 1, trans. in *Polish News Bulletin,* 17 April 1996, on *Nexis.*

107. Bogdan Tranda, "The Great Change and the Protestants," *Religion in Eastern Europe* 13 (April 1993): 32.

108. Quoted in *Reuter News Service,* 22 May 1995, on *Nexis.*

109. Quoted in *Warsaw Voice,* 16 July 1995, on *Nexis.*

110. Ibid., 11 September 1994, on *Nexis.*

111. *Guardian,* 12 July 1995, p. 12. Sources provide widely disparate figures for the number of abortions, ranging from 11,000 per year, to "tens of thousands," to 100,000. I know of no authoritative source for a precise figure.

112. Rebecca Pasini, "Piety Amid Politics: The Roman Catholic Church and Polish Abortion Policy," *Problems of Post-Communism* 43 (March–April 1996): 37.

113. Ibid., p. 39.

114. Ibid., p. 40.

115. Hockenos, *Free to Hate,* p. 248.

116. *Chicago Tribune,* 18 December 1992, p. 5.

117. PAP, 19 November 1992, in FBIS, *Daily Report* (Eastern Europe), 20 November 1992, p. 15.

118. Ibid.

119. PAP, 19 December 1992, in *BBC Summary of World Broadcasts,* 22 December 1992.

120. PAP, 30 January 1993, in FBIS, *Daily Report* (Eastern Europe), 1 February 1993, p. 35.

121. *Neue Zürcher Zeitung*, 19 February 1993, p. 4.

122. *Chicago Tribune*, 16 February 1993, p. 4.

123. *Reuter News Service*, 2 February 1993, on *Nexis*.

124. *San Francisco Chronicle*, 15 June 1994, p. D6.

125. *Guardian*, 12 July 1995, p. 12.

126. *Rzeczpospolita*, 18 June 1996, p. 2, trans. in *Polish News Bulletin*, 18 June 1996, on *Nexis*.

127. *Guardian*, 12 July 1995, p. 12.

128. *Rzeczpospolita*, 18 June 1996, p. 2, trans. in *Polish News Bulletin*, 18 June 1996, on *Nexis*.

129. *Warsaw Voice*, 30 April 1995, on *Nexis;* confirmed in *Scotsman*, 1 August 1995, p. 13.

130. *Warsaw Voice*, 4 June 1995, on *Nexis*.

131. Ibid.

132. Ibid., 29 May 1994, on *Nexis*.

133. *Reuter News Service*, 4 July 1994, on *Nexis*.

134. See *Süddeutsche Zeitung*, 16 June 1994, on *Nexis*.

135. Communiqué from the 270th plenary conference of the Polish Episcopate, published in full in *Gazeta Wyborcza*, 20 June 1994, p. 11, trans. in *Polish News Bulletin*, 20 June 1994, on *Nexis*.

136. *Reuter News Service*, 1 July 1994, on *Nexis*.

137. Ibid., 2 September 1994, on *Nexis*.

138. *Pismo Okolne* (press office of the Polish Episcopate), 19–25 October 1992, as quoted in Anna Sabbat-Swidlicka, "Church and State in Poland," *RFE/RL Research Report*, 2 April 1993, p. 48.

139. PAP, 30 December 1992, and *Süddeutsche Zeitung*, 10 May 1993, both on *Nexis*.

140. *Dziennik Ustaw* (Warsaw), 29 January 1993, pp. 62–72, trans. in U.S. Department of Commerce, *Central and Eastern Europe Legal Texts*, 29 January 1993, on *Nexis*.

141. *Wprost*, 18 April 1993, pp. 75–76, trans. in Joint Publications Research Service (JPRS), *East Europe Report*, 17 May 1993, pp. 10–11.

142. Ibid., p. 10.

143. *Warsaw Voice*, 4 December 1994, on *Nexis*.

144. *New Europa*, 10–16 September 1995, p. 20.

145. *Nowa Europa*, 14 July 1995, p. 1, trans. in *Polish News Bulletin*, 14 July 1995, on *Nexis*.

146. *Nowa Europa*, 6 December 1994, p. 2, trans. in *Polish News Bulletin*, 6 December 1994, on *Nexis; Radio Warszawa Network* (Warsaw), 5 December 1994, trans. in FBIS, *Daily Report* (Eastern Europe), 5 December 1994, p. 27; and PAP, 24 October 1994, trans. in FBIS, *Daily Report* (Eastern Europe), 25 October 1994, p. 21.

147. *Gazeta Wyborcza*, 29 December 1994, p. 3, trans. in *Polish News Bulletin*, 30 December 1994, on *Nexis*.

148. See also "Podkomisja do Spraw Dialogu Kosciola Rzymskokatolickiego i Kościoła Zrzeszonych w Polskiej Radzie Ekumenicznej," *Znak* 45 (June 1993): 83–84.

149. *TVP Television Second Program Network* (Warsaw), 23 February 1995, trans. in FBIS, *Daily Report* (Eastern Europe), 24 February 1995, p. 17.

150. *Reuter News Service,* 27 March 1995, on *Nexis.*

151. *Third Program Radio Network* (Warsaw), 22 March 1995, trans. in FBIS, *Daily Report* (Eastern Europe), 23 March 1995, p. 21; also *Reuter News Service,* 4 April 1995, on *Nexis.*

152. *Trybuna* (Warsaw), 2–3 May 1995, pp. 7–8, trans. in FBIS, *Daily Report* (Eastern Europe), 9 June 1995, p. 51.

153. Quoted in *Gazeta Wyborcza,* 19 June 1995, p. 3, trans. in FBIS, *Daily Report* (Eastern Europe), 20 June 1995, p. 29 (my emphasis).

154. Ibid.

155. "Konkordat Niezgody," in *Wprost,* 16 January 1994, p. 19; PAP, 28 December 1993, in FBIS, *Daily Report* (Eastern Europe), 30 December 1993, p. 19; and *Warsaw Voice,* 9 January 1994, on *Nexis.*

156. Andrzej Korboński, "A Concordat—But No Concord," in *Transition* 1 (9 June 1995): p. 15.

157. *Gazeta Wyborcza,* 28 January 1994, trans. in *Polish News Bulletin,* 3 February 1994, on *Nexis.*

158. PAP, 29 December 1993, trans. in FBIS, *Daily Report* (Eastern Europe), 30 December 1993, p. 20.

159. *Agence France Presse,* 1 July 1994, on *Nexis.*

160. Quoted in PAP, 5 July 1994, on *Nexis.*

161. Quoted in *Warsaw Voice,* 24 July 1994, on *Nexis.*

162. Quoted in ibid.

163. *Gazeta Wyborcza,* 9 August 1994, p. 1, quoted in *Polish News Bulletin,* 9 August 1994, on *Nexis.*

164. Quoted in *National Catholic Reporter,* 29 July 1994, p. 18.

165. Quoted in *Inter Press Service,* 6 August 1994, on *Nexis.* The statement about the "sick embryo" was Glemp's. See *Warsaw Voice,* 24 July 1994, on *Nexis.*

166. Twelve percent said they were "indifferent," while 32 percent expressed "no opinion." *Warsaw Voice,* 3 April 1994, on *Nexis.*

167. Quoted in ibid., 24 July 1994, on *Nexis.*

168. Quoted in ibid.

169. For example, Bishop Alojzy Orszulik of Lowicz in July 1995 and Bishop Józef Zycinski of Tarnow in September 1995. See *Polskie Radio First Program* (Warsaw), 26 July 1995, trans. in FBIS, *Daily Report* (Eastern Europe), 27 July 1995, p. 38; and *Polskie Radio First Program* (18 September 1995), trans. in FBIS, *Daily Report* (Eastern Europe), 19 September 1995, p. 53.

170. According to Prime Minister Józef Oleksy, as cited in *New Europe,* 24–30 September 1995, p. 20.

171. *Polskie Radio First Program Network,* 15 October 1995, trans. in FBIS, *Daily Report* (Eastern Europe), 16 October 1995, p. 60.

172. *PAP Business News,* 6 April 1995, on *Nexis.*

173. *Polskie Radio First Program Network,* 21 November 1995, trans. in FBIS, *Daily Report* (Eastern Europe), 21 November 1995, p. 61.

174. *Rzeczpospolita,* 26 October 1995, p. 1, trans. in FBIS, *Daily Report* (Eastern Europe), 27 October 1995, p. 32.

175. "Anti-religious" and "anti-God," Archbishop Tokarczuk, in PAP, 17 September 1995, trans. in FBIS, *Daily Report* (Eastern Europe), 18 September 1995,

p. 60; "neo-pagan," Cardinal Glemp, in *Reuter News Service,* 20 November 1995, on *Nexis.*

176. I have discussed the Polish presidential election of 1995 in more detail in my *Whose Democracy? Nationalism, Religion, and the Doctrine of Collective Rights in Post-1989 Eastern Europe* (Lanham, Md.: Rowman and Littlefield, 1997), chap. 4 ("Theocratic Impulses in Poland").

177. *Polish Radio 1* (Warsaw), 24 January 1996, trans. in *BBC Monitoring Service,* 25 January 1996. On Kwasniewski's olive branch, see, for example, PAP, 22 January 1996, on *Nexis.*

178. Quoted in *New Europe,* 24–30 September 1995, p. 21.

179. *Polish Radio 3,* 11 August 1996, trans. in *BBC Monitoring Service: Eastern Europe,* 13 August 1996.

180. *Süddeutsche Zeitung,* 4 July 1996, on *Nexis.*

181. *Rzeczpospolita,* 4 June 1996, p. 5, trans. in *Polish News Bulletin,* 12 June 1996, on *Nexis.*

182. Ibid.

183. *Reuter News Service,* 1 March 1996, on *Nexis.*

184. Ibid., 13 March 1996, on *Nexis.*

185. *Rzeczpospolita,* 7 June 1996, p. 2, trans. in *Polish News Bulletin,* 7 June 1996, on *Nexis.*

186. *Gazeta Wyborcza,* 9 August 1996, p. 3, trans. in *Polish News Bulletin,* 9 August 1996, on *Nexis.*

187. Ibid.

188. PAP, 10 June 1996, on *Nexis.*

189. *Rzeczpospolita,* 10 July 1996, p. 2, trans. in *Polish News Bulletin,* 10 July 1996, on *Nexis.*

190. PAP, 20 August 1996, on *Nexis.*

191. Ibid., 28 August 1996, on *Nexis.*

192. *Deutsche Presse-Agentur,* 30 August 1996, on *Nexis;* PAP, 30 August 1996, on *Nexis;* PAP, 30 August 1996, trans. in *BBC Summary of World Broadcasts,* 31 August 1996; and *Polish News Bulletin,* 3 September 1996, on *Nexis.*

193. Quoted in PAP, 1 September 1996, trans. in *BBC Summary of World Broadcasts,* 3 September 1996. See also *Deutsche Presse-Agentur,* 31 August 1996, on *Nexis.*

194. Quoted in *Independent* (London), 2 September 1996, p. 12.

195. Quoted in PAP, 2 September 1996, trans. in *BBC Summary of World Broadcasts,* 4 September 1996.

196. *Süddeutsche Zeitung,* 2 September 1996, p. 4.

197. *Neue Zürcher Zeitung,* 5/6 October 1996, p. 2.

198. *Chicago Tribune,* 25 October 1996, p. 3; *Neue Zürcher Zeitung,* 25 October 1996, p. 2; *The Times* (London), 25 October 1996, on *AmeriCast.*

199. *Polish News Bulletin,* 15 November 1996, on *Nexis.*

200. *PAP News Agency,* 20 November 1996, in *BBC Monitoring Service: Eastern Europe,* 22 November 1996; *PAP News Agency,* 25 October 1996, in *BBC Monitoring Service: Eastern Europe,* 28 October 1996. In May 1997 the Polish Constitutional Court found, by a vote of 9 to 3, that the liberalized law on abortion was inconsistent with the constitution. See *Süddeutsche Zeitung,* 30 May 1997, p. 9.

201. *PAP News Wire,* 20 April 1996, on *Nexis.*

202. Krzysztof Krzyzewski, "Does the Church Rule Poland?," *Nowa Europa,* 12–14 February 1993, trans. in *Polish News Bulletin,* 22 February 1993, on *Nexis.*

13. The Rise of Nontraditional Religions

1. For details, see Pedro Ramet, *Cross and Commissar: The Politics of Religion in Eastern Europe and the USSR* (Bloomington: Indiana University Press, 1987), pp. 167–169.

2. *East-West Church and Ministry Report* 1 (Fall 1993): 5.

3. Ibid. On the Church of Jesus Christ of Latter-Day Saints (Mormons) in the Czech Republic, see *Nedělní lidové noviny* (Prague), 21 August 1993, pp. 1, 3. On the presence of Children of God ("the Family") in Russia, see *Agence France Presse,* 22 April 1996, on *Nexis.* On the presence of Children of God in the Czech Republic, see Dušan Lužný, "Nová nabožemská hnutí," *Sociologický časopis* 30, no. 4 (1994): 502. On the teachings of cult founder David Berg, see *Daily Telegraph* (London), 25 November 1995, p. 4.

4. More details about the Theosophist Society can be found in Sabrina Petra Ramet, *Social Currents in Eastern Europe: The Sources and Consequences of the Great Transformation,* 2nd ed. (Durham, N.C.: Duke University Press, 1995), p. 173. On Scientology's plans to expand into Albania, see *Der Spiegel* (Hamburg), 7 March 1994, pp. 91–92.

5. For elaboration, see Angela A. Aidala, "Social Change, Gender Roles, and New Religious Movements," *Sociological Analysis* 46 (Fall 1985).

6. Quoted in *Inter Press Service,* 27 March 1995, on *Nexis.*

7. Rodney Stark and William Sims Bainbridge, *The Future of Religion: Secularization, Revival and Cult Formation* (Berkeley: University of California Press, 1985), p. 15.

8. Quoted in *Inter Press Service,* 27 March 1995, on *Nexis.*

9. For documentation on Poland, *Reuter News Service,* 21 November 1993; on Moldova, *Reuter Textline,* 16 November 1993; on Russia, Belarus, Moldova, the United States, Israel, Canada, and "Europe," AFP, 11 November 1993; on Ukraine, Moldova, Russia, Belarus, and Kazakhstan, *Warsaw Voice,* 28 November 1993. All documentation is on *Nexis.*

10. Pravoslavnaia Tserkov', *Sovremennye eresi i sekty v Rossii* (St. Petersburg: Izdatel'stvo Sankt-Peterburgskoi mitropolii "Pravoslavnaia Rus'," 1994), pp. 128–131.

11. *Moscow News,* 12 March 1993, and *New York Times,* 28 July 1993, both on *Nexis; Chicago Tribune,* 2 September 1992, p. 7; and Dimitry V. Pospielovsky, "The Russian Orthodox Church in the Postcommunist CIS," in Michael Bourdeaux (ed.), *The Politics of Religion in Russia and the New States of Eurasia* (Armonk, N.Y.: M. E. Sharpe, 1995), pp. 59–61.

12. *Observer* (London), 14 November 1993, p. 20, and *The Times* (London), 24 June 1995, both on *Nexis.*

13. Eliot Borenstein, "Articles of Faith: The Media Response to Maria Devi Khristos," in *Religion* 25 (July 1995): 252. See also Eliot Borenstein, "Maria Devi Khristos: A Post-Soviet Cult Without Personality," *Mind and Human Interaction* 5, no. 3 (1994).

14. *Warsaw Voice,* 28 November 1993, on *Nexis.*

15. Quoted in ibid.

16. *Moscow News,* 12 March 1993, on *Nexis.*

17. *Observer* (London), 14 November 1993, p. 20.

18. On Donetsk, see *The Times* (London), 24 June 1995, and on Lebork, see *Reuter Textline,* 23 November 1993, both on *Nexis.*

19. AFP, 10 November 1993, and *Reuter News Service,* 10 November 1993, both on *Nexis;* also see Borenstein, "Articles of Faith," p. 254.

20. Revelation 7:4, KJV.

21. Revelation 14: 1, 3, KJV.

22. Itar-TASS (Moscow), 12 November 1993, on *Nexis.*

23. See AFP, 13 November 1993, and *Reuter News Service,* 14 November 1993, both on *Nexis.*

24. Eliot Borenstein, "Maria Devi Khristos: A Post-Soviet Cult Without Personality," *Mind and Human Interaction* 5, no. 3 (1994): 114.

25. *Warsaw Voice,* 28 November 1993, on *Nexis.*

26. *Reuter News Service,* 14 November 1993, on *Nexis.*

27. *Financial Times,* 13 November 1993, p. xi.

28. *Observer* (London), 14 November 1993, p. 20.

29. *Press Association Newsfile,* 3 November 1993, and AFP, 11 November 1993, both on *Nexis.*

30. *Calgary Herald,* 14 November 1993, p. A5.

31. Ibid.; and *Sevodnya,* 13 November 1993, trans. in *Current Digest of the Post-Soviet Press* 45 (15 December 1993): 27.

32. UPI, 1 November 1993, and *Reuter News Service,* 1 November 1993, both on *Nexis.*

33. *Reuter News Service,* 10 November 1993, on *Nexis,* and AFP (Paris), 10 November 1993, in FBIS, *Daily Report* (Central Eurasia), 12 November 1993, p. 64.

34. Quoted in *Reuter News Service,* 24 November 1993, on *Nexis.*

35. Viktor Savchuk, a man in his forties, was skeptical but preferred to play it safe. He commented, "I've been coming to this square for days now. Of course, it's ridiculous—how can the world end here and not, for instance, in Moscow?" Quoted in *Reuter News Service,* 14 November 1993, on *Nexis.*

36. *Sevodnya,* 4 November 1993, p. 1, trans. in *Current Digest of the Post-Soviet Press* 45 (1 December 1993), on *Nexis.*

37. *Reuter News Service,* 24 November 1993, and *Warsaw Voice,* 28 November 1993, both on *Nexis.*

38. *Reuter News Service,* 24 November 1993, on *Nexis.*

39. *Interfax News Agency* (Moscow), 1 March 1995, in *BBC Summary of World Broadcasts,* 3 March 1995.

40. *Nezavisimaya gazeta,* 7 March 1995, p. 2, trans. in *Russian Press Digest,* on *Nexis.* See also *Ukrainian Weekly* (Jersey City, N.J.), 5 March 1995, pp. 1, 16.

41. Quoted in *The Times* (London), 24 June 1995, on *Nexis.*

42. *Moscow News,* 29 February 1996, on *Nexis.*

43. Ibid.

44. Ibid., 5 March 1996, on *Nexis.*

45. Penny Morvant, "Cults Arouse Concern in Russia," *Transition* (Prague), 5 April 1996, p. 21.

46. Thomas F. O'Dea, "Sects and Cults," quoted in Daniel A. Metraux, "Religious Terrorism in Japan: The Fatal Appeal of Aum Shinrikyo," *Asian Survey* 35 (December 1995): 1142.

47. Quoted in *New York Times,* 26 March 1995, p. 4.

48. *Inter Press Service* (Moscow), 27 March 1995, and *Reuter Textline,* 29 March 1995, both on *Nexis.* The Russian figure is confirmed in *Reuter News Service,* 18 April 1995, on *Nexis.*

49. AFP (Paris), 23 October 1995, in FBIS, *Daily Report* (Eastern Europe), 24 October 1995, pp. 5–6.

50. As cited in *New York Times,* 30 March 1995, p. A6.

51. *Inter Press Service,* 27 March 1995, on *Nexis.*

52. *Kyodo News Service,* 4 April 1995, and *Ukrainian TV* (Kiev), 20 June 1995, both on *Nexis.*

53. *Official Kremlin International News Broadcast,* 29 March 1995, on *Nexis.*

54. *New York Times,* 26 March 1995, p. 1.

55. *Inter Press Service,* 27 March 1995, on *Nexis.*

56. *New York Times,* 23 March 1995, p. A6.

57. *Die Welt* (Bonn), 19 April 1995, p. 10, and *Reuter News Service,* 18 April 1995, both on *Nexis.*

58. *New York Times,* 26 March 1995, p. 4.

59. *Welt am Sonntag* (Hamburg), 23 April 1995, p. 16.

60. Ibid., 16 July 1995, p. 14.

61. On Russian authorities, see *Interfax* (Moscow), 24 March 1995, in FBIS, *Daily Report* (Central Eurasia), 27 March 1995, p. 21; on Belarusian authorities, see Radio Minsk Network, 24 March 1995, trans. in FBIS, *Daily Report* (Central Eurasia), 27 March 1995, p. 63.

62. Itar-TASS, 4 April 1995, in FBIS, *Daily Report* (Central Eurasia), 5 April 1995, pp. 12–13; see also Itar-TASS, 12 April 1995, in FBIS, *Daily Report* (Central Eurasia), 12 April 1995, p. 12.

63. *Die Welt,* 16 May 1995, p. 12, and *Süddeutsche Zeitung* (Munich), 17 May 1995, p. 12.

64. *Die Welt,* 28 March 1996, p. 10.

65. *International Herald Tribune,* 14 February 1996, on *Nexis.* See also CTK, 11 September 1995, on *Nexis.*

66. *International Herald Tribune,* 14 February 1996, on *Nexis.*

67. Cited in *Slobodna Dalmacija* (Split), 21 May 1995, p. 10. For further discussions of reasons for conversion to cults and sects, see Stark and Bainbridge, *The Future of Religion,* pp. 15, 49, 56, 149, 151–153, 157, 172; Aidala, "Social Change, Gender Roles"; Dragomir Pantić, "Psihološki portreti pripadnika malih verskih zajednica," *Marksističke teme* 11, no. 3/4 (1987): 123–140; and Dragoljub Djordjević, "Zašto 'pravoslavci' prelaze u adventiste?," *Marksističke teme* 11, no. 3/4 (1987): pp. 141–149.

68. See Valerie Hansen, *Changing Gods in Medieval China, 1127–1276* (Princeton, N.J.: Princeton University Press, 1990).

69. *Harper's Encyclopedia of Mystical and Paranormal Experience,* by Rosemary Ellen Guiley (Edison, N.J.: Castle Books, 1991), p. 255.

70. Ibid., p. 258.

71. *Observer* (London), 14 May 1995, p. 20.

72. *The Times* (London), 9 April 1994, on *Nexis.*

73. Ibid., 28 December 1994, on *Nexis.*

74. On Poland, see *San Francisco Chronicle,* 24 May 1991, p. A14.

75. Quoted in *New York Times,* 28 July 1993, p. A1.

76. Quoted in *Observer* (London), 14 May 1995, p. 20.

77. Ibid.

78. *Reuter News Service,* 4 June 1995, on *Nexis.*

79. *The Times* (London), 9 April 1994, on *Nexis.*

80. *Newsweek,* 23 October 1989, p. 42.

81. *The Sunday Times* (London), 19 August 1990, on *Nexis.*

82. *The Times* (London), 14 August 1996, on *AmeriCast.* Vanga is also discussed in Pravoslavnaia Tserkov', *Sovremennye eresi,* pp. 180–181.

83. *Observer* (London), 14 May 1995, p. 20.

84. *Independent* (London), 14 November 1992, p. 1, on *Nexis.*

85. TASS, 13 November 1992, on *Nexis.*

86. *Independent* (London), 14 November 1992, p. 1, on *Nexis.*

87. *Financial Times,* 5 August 1989, p. 3.

88. *Harper's Encyclopedia,* p. 88.

89. *Slobodna Dalmacija* (Split), 21 May 1995, p. 11.

90. *The Sunday Times* (London), 5 March 1995, on *Nexis;* and *Marketing Week,* 10 March 1995, p. 98.

91. *Daily Telegraph* (London), 2 March 1995, p. 1.

92. Quoted in *Marketing Week,* 10 March 1995, p. 98.

93. Details in "UFOs—From Russia with Love," in *Unsolved UFO Sightings,* Summer 1995, pp. 65, 67–68.

94. See report in *Washington Post,* 13 October 1989, p. C1.

95. *Reuter News Service,* 8 August 1990, on *Nexis.*

96. *Süddeutsche Zeitung,* 22 April 1992, on *Nexis.*

97. Gallup poll of 1996, as cited in *Financial Times,* 25 June 1988, on *Nexis.*

98. *The UFO Encyclopedia,* compiled and ed. John Spencer (New York: Avon Books, 1991), p. 60.

99. UFO believers are sometimes inclined to interpret the "pillar of cloud and fire" recorded in Exodus as a UFO sighting and to associate the conversion of Saint Paul with an encounter with a space alien. For these and other UFO-linked reinterpretations of the Bible, see Barry H. Downing, "Did a UFO Part the Red Sea?," *UFO: A Forum on Extraordinary Theories and Phenomena* 5, no. 2 (1990): 16–21. Among the sources cited in this article is R. L. Dione's book, *God Drives a Flying Saucer.*

100. On the Czech Republic, see CTK National News Wire, 11 July 1995, and 21 July 1995, both on *Nexis.* On Slovakia, see CTK National News Wire, 10 August 1995, on *Nexis.* On Hungary, see *Reuter News Service,* 13 November 1989, MTI, 20 January 1991, *Reuter News Service,* 21 January 1991, *Reuter News Service,* 30 September 1991, and *Die Presse,* 8 November 1993, all on *Nexis.* On Croatia, see *Tanjug,* 21 September 1990, in *BBC Summary of World Broadcasts,* 25 September 1995; and Croatian TV satellite service (Zagreb), 10 August 1994, in *BBC Summary of World Broadcasts,* 12 August 1994. On Serbia, see Itar-TASS, 3 May 1992, on *Nexis.* On Romania, see AFP, 31 May 1991, on *Nexis.* On Albania, see *Reuter News Service,* 11 August 1995, on *Nexis.*

101. *Reuter News Service,* 27 July 1994, on *Nexis.*

102. Quoted in *The Times* (London), 16 August 1991, on *Nexis.*

103. On the societies, see MTI, 2 November 1992; and *The Times* (London), 28 December 1994, both on *Nexis.* On the UFO Congress, see MTI, 28 September 1994, on *Nexis.*

104. *Warsaw Voice,* 3 October 1993, on *Nexis.*

105. Ibid.

106. Ibid., 21 May 1995, on *Nexis.*

107. Quoted in ibid.

108. Ibid.; and PAP, 11 May 1995, on *Nexis*.

109. *Independent* (London), 17 August 1990, p. 8.

110. Ibid.

111. Lužný, "Nová náboženská hnutí," p. 505. Regarding religious cults centering on putative space aliens, see Robert W. Balch and David Taylor, "Seekers and Saucers: The Role of the Cultic Milieu in Joining a UFO Cult", *American Behavioral Scientist* 20, no. 6 (July/August 1977): 839–860.

112. *Newsweek*, 7 May 1979, p. 100.

113. *Independent* (London), 17 January 1991, p. 16; *Daily Telegraph* (London), 8 November 1993, on *Nexis;* and *The Times* (London), 17 October 1995, on *Nexis*.

114. Extract from the abstract for Mart Bax, "Ruža's Problems: Gender Relations, Popular Religion, and Violence Control in a Bosnian Village," in Sabrina P. Ramet (ed.), *Women, Society, and Politics in Yugoslavia and the Yugoslav Successor States* (University Park, Pa.: Pennsylvania State University Press, 1998).

115. *Warsaw Voice*, 24 February 1991, on *Nexis*.

116. Ibid.

117. Ibid.

118. Quoted in *Guardian*, 13 September 1993, p. 19.

119. *Nezavisimaya gazeta*, 30 July 1993, p. 5, trans. in *Current Digest of the Post-Soviet Press* 45 (25 August 1993), on *Nexis*.

120. *Danas*, no. 318 (22 March 1988): 67–70; *NIN*, 27 March 1988, p. 27; and *Danas*, no. 319 (29 March 1988): 76–77.

121. On the Czech Republic, see *ČTK National News Wire*, 3 December 1993, on *Nexis*. On Hungary, see *Budapest Home Service*, 20 November 1990, in *BBC Summary of World Broadcasts*, 27 November 1990. On Romania, see *Reuter News Service*, 1 June 1995, on *Nexis*.

122. For an account giving credence to the notion that Satanists may have been behind the explosions, see *MTI Econews*, 1 September 1994, on *Nexis*. For an account debunking the notion of a Satanist connection, see *Reuter News Service*, 1 September 1994, on *Nexis*. For a report concerning the spread of Satanism about German schoolchildren, especially ages 11 to 15, see *Welt am Sonntag* (Hamburg), 10 August 1997, p. 15.

123. Quoted in *Warsaw Voice*, 24 July 1994, on *Nexis*.

124. On this event, see *PAP News Wire*, 5 June 1994, on *Nexis*. On cemetery desecrations in Poland, see *PAP*, 4 February 1988, in *BBC Summary of World Broadcasts*, 8 February 1988; *PAP News Wire*, 16 October 1992, 28 January 1993, and 6 March 1995, and *Warsaw Voice*, 28 May 1995, all on *Nexis*. On cemetery desecrations in eastern Bohemia, see *CTK National News Wire*, 3 December 1994, on *Nexis*. On cemetery desecrations in Hungary, see AFP, 8 June 1993, and *MTI Econews*, 9 June 1993, both on *Nexis*.

125. Quoted in *San Francisco Chronicle*, 19 September 1994, p. A1.

126. *Encyclopedia of Psychic Science*, by Nandor Fodor (N.p.: University Books Reprint, 1966; originally pub. 1934), p. 267.

127. *Keston News Service*, no. 267 (22 January 1987): 16, and *Danas*, no. 263 (3 March 1987): 66.

128. On Poland, see *Warsaw Voice*, 6 November 1994, on *Nexis*. On Russia, see *Nedelya*, 12–18 February 1990, trans. in *Current Digest of the Post-Soviet Press* 42 (28 March 1990): 5.

129. On Besant and Theosophy, see *Harper's Encyclopedia of Mystical and Paranormal Experience*, pp. 611–615.

130. *San Francisco Chronicle*, 24 May 1991, p. A14; and A. S. Rogozhin (compiler), *Put' teosofii* (Petrozavodsk: Sviatoi Ostrov, 1992), p. 78.

131. *Slobodna Dalmacija*, 21 May 1995, p. 11.

132. *Novi list—Nedjelja* (Rijeka), 23 April 1995, p. 9.

133. TASS, 3 January 1994, on *Nexis*, and Pospielovsky, "The Russian Orthodox Church," p. 60.

134. *Moscow News*, 28 April 1995, on *Nexis*.

135. *Warsaw Voice*, 20 June 1993, on *Nexis*.

136. *The European* (London), 26 May-1 June 1995, p. 4. See also *Financial Times*, 25 May 1995, p. 3, and *Chicago Tribune*, 26 May 1995, p. 9.

137. *Warsaw Voice*, 9 January 1994, on *Nexis*.

138. *Observer* (London), 2 January 1994, p. 17.

139. TASS, 19 April 1993, on *Nexis*.

140. Małgorzata Ablamówicz, "Buddhist 'Protestantism' in Poland," *Religion in Eastern Europe* 13 (April 1993): 34–38. For further discussion, see Ramet, *Social Currents in Eastern Europe*, p. 171.

141. Pravoslavnaia Tserkov', *Sovremennye eresi*, p. 229.

142. *Keston News Service*, no. 296 (17 March 1988): 14, and *Vikend* (Belgrade), no. 1047 (17 June 1988): 12–13.

143. *Die Woche* (Hamburg), 8 July 1993, p. 16. For further discussion of this cult, see Oxana Antić, "The Spread of Modern Cults in the USSR," in Sabrina Petra Ramet (ed.), *Religious Policy in the Soviet Union* (Cambridge: Cambridge University Press, 1993), pp. 260–268.

144. On Albania, see *Radio Tiranë*, 29 June 1992, in *BBC Summary of World Broadcasts*, 1 July 1992. On Romania, see *The Times* (London), 23 February 1990, on *Nexis*. On Bulgaria, see AFP, 12 June 1992, on *Nexis*, and BTA, 20 May 1993, in *BBC Summary of World Broadcasts*, 24 May 1993. On Latvia, see *Irish Times*, 12 September 1994, p. 11. On Georgia, see TASS, 29 October 1993, on *Nexis*. On Abkhazia, see AFP, 1 August 1995, on *Nexis*. On Kazakstan, see *Kazakhstanskaya pravda* (Alma Ata), 21 July 1995, p. 1, trans. in *BBC Monitoring Service*, 25 July 1995.

145. On the centers in Moscow, Kiev, and Minsk, see Pravoslavnaia Tserkov', *Sovremennye eresi*, p. 139. On the number of Baha'i in Albania, see "Albania's Supermarket of Souls," in *Pozor* (Prague), October 1996, p. 38.

146. Lužný, "Nová náboženská hnutí," pp. 502–504, and *Novi list-Nedjelja*, 23 April 1995, p. 9. On the cult of Sai Baba, see *Večernji list* (Zagreb), 25 February 1996, p. 16.

147. Ananda Marga has followers in some 160 countries. See *Independent* (London), 18 December 1990, p. 24.

148. Quoted in Stark and Bainbridge, *The Future of Religion*, p. 23.

149. *Süddeutsche Zeitung*, 27/28 May 1995, p. 10.

150. *Moscow News*, 15 December 1995, on *AmeriCast*.

151. Ibid.

152. Morvant, "Cults Arouse," p. 21.

153. Pravoslavnaia Tserkov, *Sovremennye eresi i sekty v Rossii* (St. Peterburg: Izdatel'stvo Sankt-Peterburgskoi mitropolii "Pravoslavnaia Rus'," 1994), p. 90.

154. On Tantra, see *Inter Press Service*, 27 March 1995, on *Nexis*. On the Sri Radmish Mystical Cult, see *Nezavisimaya gazeta*, 30 July 1993, p. 5, trans. in *Current Digest of the Post-Soviet Press* 45 (25 August 1993): 19. On the Holic Group, see *Süddeutsche Zeitung*, 3/4/5 June 1995, p. 10. On the Santo-Daime cult, see *Der Spiegel*, 7 March 1994, pp. 110–111.

155. *Observer*, 4 October 1992, on *Nexis*.

156. Itar-TASS, 13 March 1992, on *Nexis*.

157. *Moscow Times*, 2 August 1994, on *Nexis*.

158. *Neue Zürcher Zeitung*, 8 August 1996, p. 2.

159. *Süddeutsche Zeitung*, 10/11 August 1996, p. 2.

160. *New York Times*, 30 October 1996, p. A6. For further discussion of the German government's dilemmas with Scientology, see Sabrina P. Ramet, "Religion and Politics in Germany since 1945: The Evangelical and Catholic Churches and New Religious Associations," in Brigitte Schulz (ed.), *Unified Germany: Domestic Problems and Global Challenges* (forthcoming).

161. *Novi list–Nedjelja*, 23 April 1995, p. 9.

162. In Russia, inspired by Viktor Bezverkhy, ed. the magazine *Volkhv* (Sorcerer). See *Moscow News*, 10 June 1995, on *Nexis*.

163. *Los Angeles Times*, 11 February 1993, on *Nexis*.

164. TASS, 18 April 1995, on *Nexis*. See also the reactions of the Catholic Church in Croatia and the Serbian Orthodox Church, as reported in *Arkzin* (Zagreb), 2 September 1994, p. 28.

165. Quoted in *Agence France Presse*, 12 November 1993, on *Nexis*.

166. *Izvestiia* (Moscow), 29 March 1995, p. 2, trans. in FBIS, *Daily Report* (Central Eurasia), 30 March 1995, p. 14.

167. For a Russian discussion of how counterculture, including religious innovation, relates to social stress, see I. G. Gromova and V. N. Leont'eva, "Kontrkul'tura kak adaptivnyi mekhanizm transliatsii sotsial'nogo opyta," *Sotsiologicheskie issledovaniia*, no. 10 (1991): 78–87.

168. Bryan Wilson, "American Religious Sects in Europe," in C. W. E. Bigsby (ed.), *Superculture: American Popular Culture and Europe* (Bowling Green, Ohio: Bowling Green University Popular Press, 1975), p. 108.

169. Quoted in *Der Spiegel*, 3 January 1994, p. 56. On the response, in Germany, to the Boston Church of Christ and other comparable organizations, see *Die Welt* (Bonn), 24 April 1997, p. 9.

170. R. I. Moore, *The Formation of a Persecuting Society* (Oxford: Basil Blackwell, 1987), pp. 91–94.

171. Theodor W. Adorno et al., *The Authoritarian Personality* (New York: Harper, 1950).

172. *Neue Zürcher Zeitung*, 11 December 1991, p. 4; *Süddeutsche Zeitung*, 14/15 December 1991, p. 7. See also *National Catholic Reporter*, 18 October 1991, p. 10.

173. See *Neue Zürcher Zeitung*, 23 November 1994, p. 2.

174. *Nowy Swiat* (Warsaw), 20 November 1992, p. 3, trans. in FBIS, *Daily Report*, 30 November 1992, p. 27.

14. The Nature of Religio-Political Interaction

1. Genesis 22: 2–3, 9 KJV.

2. Mark Juergensmeyer, *The New Cold War? Religious Nationalism Confronts the Secular State* (Berkeley: University of California Press, 1993), pp. 33–34. On this point, see also Russell Hardin, *Morality Within the Limits of Reason* (Chicago: University of Chicago Press, 1988), p. 13.

3. This list is adapted from Sabrina Petra Ramet, "Sacred Values and the Tapes-

try of Power: An Introduction," in Ramet and Donald W. Treadgold (eds.), *Render Unto Caesar: The Religious Sphere in World Politics* (Washington, D.C.: American University Press, 1995), pp. 12–19.

4. Sabrina Petra Ramet, "Spheres of Religio-Political Interaction: Social Order, Nationalism, and Gender Relations," in Ramet and Treadgold (eds.), *Render Unto Caesar*, pp. 51, 64.

5. See the discussion in Fritz Kern, *Kingship and Law in the Middle Ages*, trans. from German by S. B. Chrimes (Oxford: Basil Blackwell, 1948).

6. Cicero, *De Republica* 3.22, 33. On Cicero, see also Lloyd L. Weinreb, "The Moral Point of View," in Robert P. George (ed.), *Natural Law, Liberalism, and Morality* (Oxford: Clarendon Press, 1996), p. 200.

7. E. R. Dodds, *The Greeks and the Irrational* (Berkeley: University of California Press, 1951), pp. 31–32.

8. See Norberto Bobbio, *Thomas Hobbes and the Natural Law Tradition*, trans. from Italian by Daniela Gobetti (Chicago: University of Chicago Press, 1993).

9. I am taking an unabashedly Kantian position here. See Immanuel Kant, *Groundwork of the Metaphysic of Morals*, trans. and analyzed by H. J. Patton (New York: Harper and Row, 1964); and Immanuel Kant, *On the Old Saw: That May Be Right in Theory But It Won't Work in Practice*, trans. E. B. Ashton, intro. George Miller (Philadelphia: University of Pennsylvania Press, 1974).

10. Limited only by the harm principle, that is, by other dicta of Universal Reason. See Joseph Raz, "Autonomy, Toleration, and the Harm Principle," in Susan Mendus (ed.), *Justifying Toleration: Conceptual and Historical Perspectives* (Cambridge: Cambridge University Press, 1988).

11. I have attempted to demonstrate the existence of rationally derived absolute values in my essay "A Case for the Logical Derivation of Values" (under review). See also Immanuel Kant, *The Metaphysics of Morals*, trans. from German by Mary McGregor (Cambridge: Cambridge University Press, 1991); T. L. S. Sprigge, *The Rational Foundation of Ethics* (London: Routledge and Kegan Paul, 1988); and L. W. Sumner, *The Moral Foundation of Rights* (Oxford: Clarendon Press, 1987).

12. Quoted in Joseph M. Knippenberg, "The Politics of Kant's Philosophy," in Ronald Beiner and William James Booth (eds.), *Kant and Political Philosophy: The Contemporary Legacy* (New Haven, Conn.: Yale University Press, 1993), p. 165. For a loving treatment of Kant, see Karl Jaspers, *Kant*, trans. from German by Ralph Manheim, ed. Hannah Arendt (San Diego: Harcourt Brace, 1962), esp. pp. 64–70 and 150–154.

13. *Gazeta Wyborcza*, 10 June 1996, p. 2, trans. in *Polish News Bulletin*, 10 June 1996, on *Nexis*.

Index

Abortion, 338–339: in the German Democratic Republic, 86–87; in Poland, 296–299, 304–306; in Romania, 198–199, 201; in the Soviet Union, 22

Abraham (biblical), 335, 337, 338

Adorno, T. W., 334

Aetherius Society, 325

Agni Yoga "Living Ethic," 252

Albania, 7, 90–91, 202–226; Scientologists in, 309; UFOs sighted in, 323

Albanian Communist Party. See Albanian Party of Labor

Albanianism, 226

Albanian Orthodox Church, 203, 205–206, 207, 212, 213–219, 221, 222–224

Albanian Party of Labor, 216–219

Aleksandr, Archbishop of Kostroma and Galich, 332

Aleksii (Ridiger), Metropolitan, 254

Aleksii II, Patriarch, 240, 241, 242, 243, 270; as KGB agent, 255

Alexandria, Patriarchate of, 208

Alia, Ramiz, 218–219

Ali Pasha of Janina, 204

al-Mudaidab, Abdullah, 220

Ambrůz, A., 142

American Board of Commissioners for Foreign Missions, 277

Ananda Marga, 330

Anderson, John, 36

Anderson Community of God, 56

Andriy, Metropolitan of Halychyna, 261

Andropov, Yuri, 234

Andrs, J., 138

Anthroposophy, 4, 328

Anti-Catholic propaganda: distributed in Serbia, 172

Antichrist: Mariya Devi Khristos as, 314; Boris Yeltsin as, 314

Anti-Muslim graffiti: in Serbia, 171–172

Antioch, Patriarchate of, 208

Anti-Semitism: condemned by Croatian Catholic newspaper, 156; in Croatia, 178–179; in Romania, 185, 186, 189, 190; in Russia, 243

Antonescu, Marshal Ion, 4, 191

Antoniy (Masendych), Metropolitan, 256

Antrovis, Cult of, 324–325

Antunović, Ivan, 155

Apocalyptic associations, 311–319

Apostolic communities: in German Democratic Republic, 56, 59–61, 74, 83

Apponyi, Albert, 108

Aquinas, St. Thomas, 336, 337

Argjirokastriti, Bishop Grigor, 204

Armageddon, 269

Armenia, 4, 266, 271

Armenian Apostolic Church, 36, 271

Armenian Orthodox Church, 251

Arsenii, Bishop of Kostroma, 233

Arsenije III Čarnojević, Patriarch, 152

Asahara, Shoko, 316, 317–318

Assemblies of God: in Bulgaria, 282; in Cuba, 44; in East Central Europe, 267; in Russia, 273

Association for Contemporary Music, 21–22

"Astral ghost-warriors": expected in front of Lenin's mausoleum, 331

Atheism (Czechoslovak journal), 125

Aum Shinrikyo, 272, 311, 316–319, 332

Austria, 97–98, 151, 327

Austria-Hungary, 155, 156, 159–160

Avdić, Ibrahim, 170

Ayatollah Khomeini Association (Shkodër), 221

Azerbaijan, 239, 240

Babione, Bill, 225

Bachaists, 271
Bah'ai, 6, 309, 330; in Russia, 273
Bainbridge, William Sims, 310
Balaban, Metropolitan Dionysii, 247
Baláž, Bishop Rudolf, 142
Ballusek (criminal), 67
Baptists: in Albania, 225; in Armenia, 271; in Bulgaria, 277; in Cuba, 44; in German Democratic Republic, 55, 57, 71; in Romania, 4, 184, 185; in Russia, 274; in Ukraine, 252
Bartnik, Fr. Czesław S., 296
Bartolomeios, Patriarch, 272
Bassak, Gerhard, 76
Bavaria, 332
Bax, Mart, 326
Becker, Rev. Manfred, 81
Bekennende Kirche. See Confessing Church
Belak, Zoltán, 125
Belarus, 270; Aum Shinrikyo in, 317, 318; White Brotherhood in, 311
Belorussian Autocephalous Orthodox Church, 14, 23
Belorussian Orthodox Church, 4, 24, 35, 247
Benjamin, Hilde, 67
Beran, Archbishop Josef, 127-128, 131
Bereslavskii, Ioann, 311-312
Beresztóczy, Miklós, 109
Berisha, Sali, 222, 226
Berlin, Congress of (1878), 278
Besant, Annie, 328
Betto, Fr. Frei, 18
Bezbozhnik, 23
Bhagwan Rajneesh movement, 330
Bianu, Ioan, 187
Bible, study of, 58, 111, 225; translated into Albanian, 204; translated into Macedonian, 267; translated into Slovenian, 158
Bibles, 282; burning of, 31; importation of, 44, 219, 235; printing of, 38, 111, 137; shipped to Bulgaria, 267
Biblical Education by Extension, 267
Bierut, Bolesław, 32, 288
Bigamy, 15
Bilák, Vasil, 90, 132
Bíro, Imre, 110

Bíro, Sándor, 188
Bismarck, Otto, 96
Blavatsky, H. P., 328
Blessed Virgin Mary. See Virgin Mary
Blokhin, Andrei Ivanov, 4
Blüm, Norbert, 87
Bodin, Prince, 150
Bodnarchuk, Bishop Zhytomyr, 253
Bogomilism, 150-151
Bohemia, 322, 328. See also Czech Republic
Bolsheviks, 4, 35, 116, 229-230, 248. See also Russia; Soviet Union; Ukraine
Bonefačić, Bishop Kvirin Klement, 168
Borba, 168
Borets'kyi, Mykolai, 248
Boris III, King of Bulgaria, 279
Borisovna, Lyudmila, 315
Bosnia-Herzegovina, 148, 150-151, 153, 155, 167; Muslims of, 160, 169-171
Bosnian Church, 151
Bosnian Serbs, 173, 335
Bosnian War (1992-95). See Serbian Insurrectionary War
Brahma Kumaris, 309
Brest, Union of (1596), 95, 247, 339
Brezhnev, Leonid I., 36-37, 234, 321
Briedom, Msgr. Daniel, 128
Brikhnichev, Ivan, 230
Broun, Janice, 283
Budak, Mile, 178
Buddhism: in Bulgaria, 330; in China, 15, 26, 37, 38, 39; in Czechoslovakia, 330; in Estonia, 330; in Poland, 329-330; in Russia, 272, 274, 330; in Ukraine, 252
Bugaj, Ryszard, 303
Bukharin, Nikolai, 19
Bulgaria, 5, 6-7, 206, 308, 325; Aum Shinrikyo in, 317; evangelization in, 271-272; Orthodox Church in, 272. See also Bulgarian Orthodox Church
Bulgarianization, 205-206
Bulgarian nationalists: in Albanian regions, 205
Bulgarian Orthodox Church, 272, 276, 277-285, 306
Bulgarian Society of Psychotronics, 325

Buzálka, Bishop M., 116, 126

Calvary Chapel of Costa Mesa, 267
Campanella, Tommaso, 331
Campus Crusade for Christ, 267; in
    Albania, 225
Canada: White Brotherhood in, 311
Cance, Bishop Agathangjel, 214
Caritas: in Czechoslovakia, 127; in
    Poland, 100
Carol II, King of Romania, 190
Čarnojević, Patriarch Arsenije III. See
    Arsenije III Čarnojević, Patriarch
Čarský, Bishop, 128
Castrated, Sect of the, 3, 4
Castro, Fidel, 17, 30, 43, 44, 47
Catherine II, Empress of Russia, 94,
    247
Catholic Church. See Roman Catho-
    lic; Greek-Rite Catholic
Ceauşescu, Nicolae, 192–195, 197, 198,
    199, 201, 208
Censorship, 106; of Church press, 19;
    in Poland, 291
Central Asia, 21, 24
Čepička, Alexej, 127
Cerullo, Morris, 269
Channeling, 322–325
Charter 77, 132–133
Cheng, Rev. Marcus, 26
Chernenko, Konstantin, 234
Children of God, 272, 309
China, 14–15, 19, 20, 25–29, 34, 35,
    37–40, 46
Christ, 313, 333: Kondratii Selivanov
    as reincarnation of, 4; said to have
    been Serb, 152; those who follow,
    305; Maria Tsvigun as reincarnation
    of, 312–316; alleged to have come
    from Venus, 325
Christian Community: in the German
    Democratic Republic, 61
Christian evangelism, 265–274
Christian Peace Conference (Prague),
    281
Christian Science, 5, 320
Chrypiński, Vincent, 293
Chumak, Alan, 321
Churches: closed in Soviet Union,
    230; confiscated in Albania, 217;

destroyed by Stalin regime, 231;
    dynamited by Bosnian Serbs, 173;
    padlocked in Ukraine, 250; re-
    opened, 219; return of, 222, 282,
    294
"Church in Socialism," 69, 71, 79,
    82–83
Church of Christ, 267, 272, 333
Church of God: in Bulgaria, 282
Church of Jesus Christ of Latter-Day
    Saints. See Mormons
Church of John: in the German
    Democratic Republic, 5, 56, 62, 74,
    83, 88
Church of Satan. See Satan, Church of
Church Resources Ministries, 267
CIA, 288
Cicero, 336
Cieszkówski, August, 94
Clark, John, 319
Coba, Bishop Ernest, 217
Codreanu, Corneliu Zelea, 189, 190
Cojocara, Rodica, 198
College of St. Francis Xavier, 203
Committee for Religious Rights, Free-
    dom of Conscience, and Spiritual
    Values (Bulgaria), 282
Committee for the Salvation of Youth
    from Totalitarian Sects, 332
Communist Party of the Soviet Union
    (CPSU), 233
Concordat: in Albania, 212; in Aus-
    tria, 106; in Hungary, 106–107; in
    Poland, 19, 287, 294, 301–304; in
    Romania, 189, 190; in Yugoslavia,
    153, 156
Confessing Church, 64
Confucianism, 13
Congregational Church: in Bulgaria,
    5, 277
Congrua, 188
Conspiracies, 172, 242–243
Constantinism, 275–276
Contraceptives: in Poland, 297
Conversions: to Baptistry, in Ukraine,
    269; to Islam, in Albania, 203, 204–
    205, 209–210; to Orthodoxy, in
    Russia, 245
Counter-Reformation, 94, 104–105,
    113, 114, 119–120, 141, 143, 158

Craciun, Fr. Casian, 199
Crainic, Nichifor, 186, 189, 190
Croatia: Independent State of, 157; Satanism in, 326; spiritualism in, 328; UFOs sighted in, 323
Croatian Party of Right, 155
Crouch, Paul, 265
Crvenkovski, Krste, 164
Cserháti, Bishop József, 111
Cuba, 17–18, 19, 30–31, 34, 35, 42–44, 46–47
Cult of Antrovis. See Antrovis, Cult of
Cultural Revolution, 26–27, 37
Cvitković, Ivan, 121
Cyprus, Church of, 208
Cyrankiewicz, Józef, 33
Cywiński, Bohdan, 276, 292
Czarnecki, Ryszard, 302
Czech Brethren, 147, 237
Czechoslovak Communist Party, 121, 122; strategies of, 123–131
Czechoslovakia, 5, 6, 7, 90–91, 112–119, 120, 121–140, 308; Christian evangelism in, 268–269
Czech Republic, 7, 140–142, 144, 326; Jehovah's Witnesses in, 269; Messengers of the Holy Grail in, 311; UFO cultists in, 325; UFOs sighted in, 323

Dabčević-Kučar, Savka, 167
Dajani, Fr. Daniel, 214
Dalmatin, Jurij, 158
Damian, Archbishop, 217
Danube–Black Sea canal project, 191
Daoism. See Taoism
Davies, Norman, 94, 96
Davis, Nathaniel, 231, 234
Davitashvili, Dzhuna, 321
Dechet, Decan Jan, 128
Delo, 169
de Maiziere, Lothar, 61, 84
Demke, Bishop Christoph, 63
Democracy: and tolerance, 337–338; definitions of, 7; antipathy of Russian Orthodoxy toward, 244–245
Deng Xiaoping, 37, 38, 39
Dhanil, Mast, 204
Diakonia, Theology of. See Theology of Diakonia

Dias, Ivan, 224
Dibelius, Bishop Otto, 64–65, 66, 67, 68
Dimitrov, Filip, 285
Disneyland, 194
Divorce laws: in Poland, 294, 296
Dizdari, Nasuf, 225
Dmitriev, Mikhail, 247
Dmowski, Roman, 98
Dobrila, Bishop Juraj, 155
Doctor Zhivago, 47
Dodaj, Fr. Pal, 212
Doukhobors, 6
Dubček, Alexander, 82, 118, 130, 133
Dušan the Mighty, Tsar, 165
Dvorsky, Jan, 319
Dymtruk, Klym, 250

Eastern faiths, 329–330
Ecumenical Patriarchate, 206, 208, 223–224
Eggerath, Werner, 67
Endecja, 98, 287
Estonia, 266
Evangelical Church: in the German Democratic Republic, 5, 54–55, 56–57, 62–89. See also Hungarian Evangelical Church; Slovak Evangelical Church
Evangelical-Free Church Committees, Federation of: in the German Democratic Republic, 57–58
Evangelical Methodist Episcopal Church: in Bulgaria, 282
Evangelical Reformed Church: in Poland, 295
Evlogi, Metropolitan, 231
Extraterrestrial visitors, 322, 323–325

Fadilpašić, Fadil, 170
Faith Church, 310: in Hungary, 268; in Russia, 273
Faja, Baba, 213
Falcke, Heino, 72
Fausti, Fr. Gjon, 214
Fechner Decree, 66–67
Fejzo, Baba, 213
Felak, James, 116
Feranec, Bishop József, 125
Ferdinand I (Habsburg), Kaiser, 105

Ferdinand II (Habsburg), Kaiser, 113, 114
"50th Day" Church: in Armenia, 271
58th Testament, 331
Filaret (Denisenko), Metropolitan of Kiev, 241, 252, 254–262, 314
Filippovich, Danilo, 4
Fine, John, 151
Finzgar, Fr. Franc Saleški, 159
Flagellants. See Khlysty
Fletcher, William C., 245
Forck, Bishop Gottfried, 63, 84
Four-Square Gospel Church, 273
Franciscan Order, 127, 151, 154, 155, 158, 166, 167, 210, 214
Franić, Archbishop Frane, 166
Frank, Karl, 116
Frankel, Bishop Hans Joachim, 70, 76
Franz II (Habsburg), Kaiser, 106
Franz Josef (Habsburg), Kaiser, 106, 159
Fredro, Count Alexander, 97
Free Academy of Spiritual Culture, 4
Friedrich V (von der Pfalz), King, 113
Fromm, Erich, 333
Fuchs, Harmut, 75–76
Furman, D. E., 244
Fyock, Dave, 225

Gabris, Bishop Julius, 125
Gaj, Ljudevit, 154
Gallagher, Tom, 186
Gang of Four, 37
Gardin, Fr. Giacomo, 213, 214
Gari'c, Bishop Josip, 156
Gazeta Wyborcza, 302
Gender relations, 309
Genesis, book of, 335
Genischen, Peter, 75
Georgia, 266
German Democratic Republic, 5, 6, 54–89, 121
Germanization: in Slovenia, 166
Germany, Federal Republic of, 85–89, 331–332
Gerus, Oleh, 261, 262
Gestapo, 249
Gheorghiu-Dej, Gheorghiu, 191, 192

Ghibu, Onisifor, 186–187
Gienke, Bishop Horst, 63
Gierek, Edvard, 34, 44–45, 290, 291
Gilberg, Trond, 192
Gindirea, 189
Gjini, Bishop Fran, 214
Gjoka, Fr. Martin, 212
Glagolitic liturgy, 150–151, 154
Glaser, Msgr., 191
Glas koncila, 42, 166, 169
Glemp, Archbishop Józef, 102, 103, 104, 292, 296, 302
Głodz, Bishop Leszek Sławoj, 306
God, 338; alleged endorsement of Bosnian Serb conquests by, 174; alleged orders to Abraham to kill his son given by, 335, 337, 338; relationship to morality, 337, 338; Russians' belief in, 242, 321
Goeckel, Robert, 55, 85
Gomułka, Władysław, 18, 32, 33, 44, 45, 288, 289
Gorbachev, Mikhail, 43, 46, 47, 81, 134, 235, 240, 321; on UFOs, 324
Gordeev, Sergei, 321
Gorev, Mikhail, 230
Götting, Gerhard, 70
Gottwald, Klement, 131
Grachev, Pavel, 239
Great Novena, 100
Great Proletarian Cultural Revolution. See Cultural Revolution
Greco-Ottoman War (1897), 211
Greek government, 222, 223
Greek Orthodox Church, 208, 222, 332
Greek-Rite Catholic Church, 5, 94; among Albanians, 206, 214; in Bulgaria, 277–278; in Czechoslovakia, 117, 121; in Romania, 183, 185, 187–189, 191, 196; in Soviet Union, 35; in Ukraine, 232, 242, 248, 249–251, 252
Gregory VI, Pope, 278
Gronkiewicz-Waltz, Hanna, 303
Grósz, Archbishop József, 109
Grotewohl, Otto, 65, 66
Groza, Petru, 192
Grueber, Heinrich, 67
Guevara, Ernesto ("Che"), 30
Gurakuqi, Luigj, 211

Gysi, Klaus, 81

Hako, Hulusi, 218–219
Halík, Fr. Tomáš, 133
Hamel, Johannes, 69
Harapi, Fr. Anton, 212
Hare Krishna. *See* Krishna Society
Havel, Václav, 319
Healing, 319–322
Hebblethwaite, Peter, 289
Hegel, G. W. F., 45, 336
Hellenization: of Orthodox Church, 152; via Orthodox schools, 205, 222
Hempel, Bishop Johannes, 75
Henlein, Konrad, 116
Hildebrandt, Regine, 86
Himmler, Heinrich, 67, 249
Hitchins, Keith, 185
Hlinka, Fr. Andrej, 115–116, 119
Hobbes, Thomas, 237
Hockenos, Paul, 295
Holic Group, 331
Homophobia: in Poland, 294–295; in Romania and the United States, 339. *See also* Intolerance
Homosexuality, 197–198, 201, 333, 337
Honecker, Erich, 72–73, 75, 78, 83, 84, 88
Horthy, Admiral Miklós, 108
Hovhaness, Alan, 122
Hoxha, Ali, 221
Hoxha, Enver, 213, 216–217, 218, 220, 226
Hozjusz, Stanisław, 93
Hromádka, Josef, 131
Hua Guofeng, 37
Hubbard, L. Ron, 331
Huelsemann, Wolfram, 82
Hungarian Evangelical Church (Subotica), 147
Hungary, 6, 7, 90–91, 104–112, 120, 308, 309, 328; Christian evangelism in, 268; Satanism in, 326, 327; UFOs sighted in, 323–324; witchcraft in, 320
Huntington, Samuel P., 238
Hurko, Marshal Iosif, 96
Hus, Jan, 113, 121
Husák, Gustáv, 90, 118, 134
Hussites, 113, 115

Iannoulatos, Archbishop Anastasios, 222–223
Ierotheos, Bishop of Militopoli, 207
Iliescu, Ion, 196
Illyrianism, 152–153, 154
Illyrian Provinces, 158
India, 311
Inoue, Yoshihiro, 318
International Islamic Relief Organization, 220
Intolerance, 170, 172, 177–179, 333; in Albania, 221; defined, 181; vis-à-vis Jews in Romania, 184–190, 195–199, 337; in Poland, 294–295; relationship to degree of urbanization, 181–183; in Russia, 242–243. *See also* Anti-Catholic propaganda; Anti-Muslim graffiti; Anti-Semitism
Ioann, Metropolitan of St. Petersburg, 243, 269
Ionescu, Nae, 189, 190
Iorga, Nicolae, 182, 190
Irine, Bishop and Deputy-Metropolitan of Korçë and Gjirokastër, 214
Irine, Bishop of Appolonia, 214
Iriney, Archimandrite of Sofia, 279
Iron Guard, 189–190
Isaac (biblical), 335, 337
Islam: in Albania, 202–205, 209–211, 212, 213, 215–221; in Bosnia, 150, 159–161, 169–171; in Bulgaria, 282; in China, 15, 28–29, 38; in Russia, 272, 274; in Serbia, 177; in Soviet Union, 11, 24; in Ukraine, 251; in Yugoslavia, 30, 42, 179–180
"Islamic Declaration," 170–171
Ismail, Kemal Bey, 211
Iso Zen, 325
Israel, 225; White Brotherhood in, 311
Italo-Ottoman War (1911), 211
Italy, 212; Albanians in, 206, 209
Iuvenalii, Metropolitan, 241
Ivan the Terrible, Tsar, 247
Izetbegović, Alija, 170, 175

Jakeš, Miloš, 138
Jakob, Günter, 69
Jakova, Tuk, 216
Jakšić, Jovo, 161

Jan Kazimierz, King of Poland, 289
Janku, Vladimir, 138
Japan: Aum Shinrikyo in, 311, 317–318
Jarowinsky, Werner, 80
Jaruga-Nowacka, Izabela, 304
Jaruzelski, General Wojciech, 292
Jehlička, František, 116
Jehovah's Witnesses, 269, 272, 308, 309; in Abkhazia, 271; in Albania, 225; in Armenia, 271; in Bulgaria, 282; in Cuba, 44; in Czechoslovakia, 5, 121; in the German Democratic Republic, 56, 61; in Poland, 300; in Romania, 271, 273; in Soviet Union, 35; in Ukraine, 251
Jelinek, František, 136
Jeremiasz, Bishop, 295
Jesuits, 105, 114, 203, 212, 214
Jesus Christ. See Christ
Jesus Freaks, 272
Jews, 85, 142, 249; in Albania, 217, 224–225; in Bulgaria, 282; in Croatia, 178–179; in Romania, 184, 186, 189; in Russia, 274; in Serbia, 178; in Soviet Union, 35–36; in Ukraine, 251; in Yugoslavia, 177–178
Jiang Qing, 28, 37
Joachim, Ecumenical Patriarch, 278
John Paul II, Pope, 103, 123, 133, 134, 135, 141, 224, 253, 290, 293, 296, 305, 306, 319, 324, 334; alleged plagiarism from Tito, 177; visit to Vilnius, 273; visit to Zagreb, 177–178
Johnson, Benton, 330
Josef II (Habsburg), Kaiser, 105, 107, 123, 162
Journal of the Moscow Patriarchate, 233
Jovan, Metropolitan of Serbs in Croatia, 173
Jovan II, Patriarch, 151
Jowitt, Kenneth, 13, 34, 35
Joyu, Fumihiro, 317
Juergensmeyer, Mark, 335
Jugendweihe, 66, 68
Julianism, 186, 192, 193, 275–276
Justin (Moisescu), Patriarch, 193
Justinian, Byzantine Emperor, 202
Justinian (Marina), Patriarch, 191, 192–193

Kaczmarek, Bishop Csesław, 100, 288
Kádár, János, 91, 110, 111
Kakówski, Aleksander Cardinal, 286
Kalinik, Bishop of Vratsa, 284
Kállay, Benjamin von, 160
Kana, 42
Kann, Robert, 104
Kant, Immanuel, 185, 339
Kantian rationalism, repudiation of, 186
Kapetanović, Mehmedbeg, 160
Karadžić, Radovan, 173, 174, 177
Karadžić, Vuk, 152, 165
Karaites, 6
Kardelj, Edvard, 149, 167
Karimov, Islam, 240
Karpiński, Jakub, 8–9
Kashpirovsky, Anatoly, 321
Kastrioti, Gjergj. See Skenderbeg
Katolické noviny, 127, 308
Katolički list, 157; condemns Naziism, 156
Katyn massacre, 102
Kavalioti, Archpriest Theodore, 204
Kazakhstan: White Brotherhood in, 311
Kehnscherper, Rev., 65
Keleti, György, 324
KGB, 229, 234, 239, 241, 255
Khlysty, the, 3–4
Khmel'nyts'kyi, Bohdan, 247
Khomeini, Ayatollah, 221
Khristos, Maria Devi. See Tsvigun, Maria
Khrushchev, Nikita S., 25, 26, 36, 37, 233, 234, 249
Kiki (space alien in Plovdiv), 325
Kiril, Patriarch, 279
Kis, János, 110
Kissi, Bishop Kristofor of Synada, 207–208, 215
Klain, Manfred, 65
Klaus, Václav, 141
Kliment, Bishop of Tŭrnovo, 279
Klusak, Milan, 135
Knight, Judy, 322–323
Knowledge, absolute, 45
Kolakówski, Leszek, 122
Kolankiewicz, George, 34

Koliqi, Mikel Cardinal, 224
Kollonitsch, Count Leopold, 104
Komsomol, 23–24
Komsomol'skaia pravda, 123, 137, 235, 323
Kondulainen, Yelena, 239
KOR, 45, 101, 102
Koran: importation of, 219; instruction in, 176
Kordik, Fr. Josef, 132
Korec, Ján Cardinal, 140
Kosovo: Serbian Orthodox Church's politics in, 163, 165, 166
Kovalchuk, Vitaly, 312, 316
Kozkowska, Maria Felicja, 5
Kramer, Michael "Rogerius," 158
Krasiński, Adam, 95
Krasnaia zvezda, 323
Kraus, Ognjen, 179
Kravchuk, Leonid, 255, 256, 257, 260
Krenz, Egon, 84
Krishna Consciousness. *See* Krishna Society
Krishna Society, 5, 35, 252, 270, 271, 330; in Bulgaria, 282; in Poland, 309; in Russia, 273
Kristo, Jure, 173
Krivonogov, Yuri, 312–316
Križanić, Juraj, 154
Križkova, Marie Rut, 133
Krummacher, Bishop Friedrich-Wilhelm, 76
Krusche, Bishop Werner, 75
Krzyzewski, Krzysztof, 306
Kuchma, Leonid, 257, 258, 259, 260
Kuharić, Franjo Cardinal, 166, 168, 169, 172, 174
Kuhlman, Kathryn, 320
Kulturkampf, 96–97
Kuras, Ivan, 260
Kuratówska, Senator Zofia, 298
Kurila, Eulogio, 208
Kus, Bishop Kazimierz, 102
Kustić, Fr. Živko, 166, 168–169
Kuwait, 220
Kwan Um, 330
Kwaśniewski, Aleksander, 302, 303, 304, 305, 306

Laborem Exercens (1981), 103

Labuda, Barbara, 296, 303
Laco, Teodor, 221
Lamaist priests, 15
Lamentówicz, Wojciech, 295
Lange, Martin, 57
Lapshin, Mikhail, 239
Laskii, Jan, 93
László, Leslie, 112
Latvia, 266, 331
Lauer, Reinhard, 154
La Vey, Anton Sandor, 326
Lazar, Bishop (of Mother of God Center), 311
Lazar, Tsar, 166
Lazik, Bishop, 128
League for the Liberation of Ukraine, 248
League of Communists of Yugoslavia, 16, 148, 167, 168, 169, 171, 179–180; Eighth Party Congress, 40–41
League of Militant Atheists, 23, 24, 232
Lebed, General Aleksandr: opinions about nontraditional religious associations, 272
Lebeda, Bishop Ján, 125
Ledochówski, Archbishop Mieczysław, 96
Legitimacy, 236–237
Legitimation, 237, 336
Leich, Bishop Werner, 63, 80, 82, 83, 84
Lékai, Archbishop László, 110
Leo XIII, Pope, 98
LeoGrande, William, 31
Leopold I (Habsburg), Kaiser, 105
Leopold II (Habsburg), Kaiser, 105
Levaković, 154
Lew-Starówicz, Zbigniew, 295
Liebknecht, Karl, 80
Lin Biao, 27
Liška, Bishop Antonin, 125
Lithuania, 11, 95, 240, 253, 271, 273
Little Flock of Watchman Ni, 40
Lizna, Fr. František, 132
Lobov, Oleg, 317
Lopuszański, Jan, 334
Los von Rom, 117
Löwenhardt, John, 238

Lu Dingyi, 26
Lukashenko, Alyaksandr, 270
Luther, Martin, 73, 76–78
Lutheran Church, 6, 133; in Albania, 225; in Romania, 200; in Ukraine, 251. *See also* Evangelical Church; United Evangelical Church of Russia
Luxemburg, Rosa, 80
Lypkivs'kyi, Vasyl', 248

Macedonian Orthodox Church, 148, 149, 163–164
Mádr, Fr. Oto, 133
Magyarization: in Croatia, 162
Mahnić, Bishop Antun, 155
Maidonis, Fr. Chrysostomos, 222
Maiziere, Lothar de. *See* de Maiziere, Lothar
Maksim, Patriarch, 281, 283, 284, 285
Malachówski, Aleksander, 302
Malcolm, Noel, 150
Malý, Fr. Václav, 132
Mao Zedong, 13, 25, 26, 27, 28, 38
Marchuk, Yevhen, 258
Margjokaj, Fr. Paulin, 212
Maria Theresa (Habsburg), Kaiserin, 105
Mariavites, 5
Marlekaj, Fr. Luigj, 212
Marriage, "bourgeois," 14
Marxism: criticism of, 26; de-atheization of, 121; removed from school curriculum in Serbia, 165
Mary, Mother of God. *See* Virgin Mary
Masaryk, Tomáš, 114, 115
Maximilian II (Habsburg), Kaiser, 105
Mazowiecki, Tadeusz, 294
McKean, Kip, 272, 333
Mečiar, Vladimír, 142, 144
Medjugorje, 326
Medvedev, Roy, 25
Mehnert, Rev., 65
Mele, Vasil, 223
Meliev, A., 11
Mennonites, 4, 56, 59, 61
Merz, Ivan, 168
Meško, Fr. Franc Ksaver, 159

Messengers of the Holy Grail, 311
Meszaros, József, 320
Methodist Church: in Bulgaria, 277; in the German Democratic Republic, 55, 57, 71, 74; in Poland, 5
Metternich, Clemens von, 106
Meyer, Alfred G., 34
Michael, King of Romania, 190
Michael the Brave, 192
Michalik, Archbishop József, 301, 305
Michnik, Adam, 102, 208
Mielnik, Edward, 324
Miklós, Imre, 111
Millennial celebrations (1988) of the Christianization of Kievan Rus, 235
Millet system, 204, 278. *See also* Ottoman Empire
Milošević, Slobodan, 47, 48, 165, 166, 172, 174
Miłosz, Czesław, 102
Mindzenty, József Cardinal, 109, 110
Missionaries, Christian, 265–274
Mitrokhin, Lev, 274
Mitzenheim, Bishop Moritz, 60, 67, 68–69
Modern Buddhism, 15, 27
Modrzewski, Andrzej Frycz, 93
Moldova, 270; White Brotherhood in, 311
Monarchism: in Russia, 242–243
Monks: incarcerated in Czechoslovakia, 117; reduction in number in Romania, 191–192
Montenegrin Orthodox Church, 176
Moon, Rev. Sun Myung, 5, 331
Moonies. *See* Unification Church
Morality, 336–340
Morgenstern, Werner, 57
Mormons, 272, 309; in Albania, 225; in Bulgaria, 282; in the German Democratic Republic, 56, 61, 62, 74, 83; in Poland, 267–268, 274; in Russia, 273
Moroz, Oleksandr, 261
Moscow News, 256, 271, 316, 329
Moscow Patriarchate, 208, 214–215, 242, 247, 251, 252. *See also* Russian Orthodox Church
Mosse, George, 175

Mother of God Center, 311
Mstyslav (Skrypnyk), Patriarch, 253, 255, 256
Mukhortov, Pavel, 323
Müller, D. M., 70
Mulyun, Anna, 316
Müntzer, Thomas, 76–78
Music, 14, 21–22, 28, 32, 158
Muslims. *See* Bosnia-Herzegovina; Islam
Mussolini, Benito, 212

Nahum, Archimandrite of Russe, 279
Napoleon Bonaparte, Emperor, 158
Nastase, Adrian, 196, 198
Natanail, Bishop of Krupnik, 272
Nationalism: in Albania, 218; and anti-Ottoman rebellion, 152; co-optive, 104–112; disassociation from Catholicism, 112–120; among Croats, 154–156; and ethnogenesis in Bosnia, 150–151; oppositionist, 93–104; and religion in communist Yugoslavia, 162–171; and religious diversity, 183; in Romania, 185–190, 192, 195–196, 200; among Slovenes, 157–159; in Ukraine, 251; in Uzbekistan, 240
Native Ukrainian National Faith, 251
NATO, 16
Natural Law, 337
Navigators, 267
Navratil, Augustin, 138
Nazarenes, 5, 121, 308
Nedić, Milan, 153
Negovani, Popa Kristo, 206
Nenadović, Archpriest Matija, 152
Neofit, Bishop, 272
Neofit, Metropolitan of Vidin, 279
Neopaganism, 332; Kwaśniewski accused of, 303; in Ukraine, 251
Nestrova, Tatyana, 278
New Acropolis, 328
New Apostolic Church: in the German Democratic Republic, 56
Newsweek, 192
Nichifren Shoshu-Soka Gakkai, 330
Nicholas II, Tsar: canonized, 242
Nigris, Archbishop Leone G. B., 213

Nikodim, Metropolitan of Leningrad, 241
Nikolayev, Col.-Gen. Andrei, 242
Nikolayeva, Tamara, 320–321
NKVD, 249
Noah's Ark Society: in Croatia, 322
Noli, Bishop Fan, 206–208
Nontraditional Christian associations, 330–332
Nontraditional religious associations, 309–324
Novena: in Poland. *See* Great Novena
Nuns, 220; attacked by Bosnian Serbs, 177; incarceration of, 32, 117; resume activities, 137; reduction in number in Romania, 191–192
Nuschke, Otto, 67

Occult societies, 4, 328–329
Ochab, Edward, 32, 288
Oddi, Silvio Cardinal, 129
Ognjišče, 42
OGPU, 248
Old Believers, 4, 14, 35, 251
Old Catholic Church: in Croatia, 147, 162
Old Lutherans: in the German Democratic Republic, 56, 58
Oleksy, Jozef, 340
Omelchenko, Oleksander, 260
OMS International, 267
Oriental religious associations. *See* Eastern faiths
Ortega y Gasset, José, 337
Orthodoxy: among Albanians, 202–209. *See also* Albanian Orthodox Church; Belorussian Autocephalous Orthodox Church; Belorussian Orthodox Church; Bulgarian Orthodox Church; Greek Orthodox Church; Polish Orthodox Church; Romanian Orthodox Church; Russian Orthodox Church; Serbian Orthodox Church; Ukrainian Autocephalous Orthodox Church; Ukrainian Orthodox Church
Orwell, George: *1984*, 47
Oslobodjenje, 165
Ossoliński, Józef Maksimilian, 97

Ottoman Empire, 150, 151–152, 202–205, 209–211, 277, 306. *See also* Millet system
Ottoman-Venetian Wars, 210
Owen, David: recommends bestowal of award on Ceaușescu, 194

Pacem in Terris association, 124–125, 129, 137, 139
Paganism. *See* Neopaganism
Paisi, Metropolitan of Vratsa, 279
Paladi, Archimandrite of Vidin, 279
Palaj, Fr. Bernadin, 212
Panegyrics: in Romania, 192–194
Pankrati, Metropolitan of Stara Zagora, 284
Papmihaili, Papas Josif, 214
Parish bulletins, 6, 308
Parsifal Imanuel. *See* Dvorsky, Jan
Party of Love (Russia), 239
Pascu, Horia, 198
Pasternak, Boris, 47
Pasztor, Bishop Ján, 125
Patriarkhiia, 232
Paul VI, Pope, 132, 133, 139, 167, 289
Pavelić, Ante, 178
Pavle, Patriarch, 172, 174
Pavlišić, Archbishop Josip, 168
Pavlović, Teodor, 153
Pawelski, Jan, 98
PAX, 19, 33
Pázmány, Peter Cardinal, 104
Pazos, Felipe, 17
Peasant discontent: in Romania, 185
Pease, Neal, 286
Pecherska Lavra monastery, 257, 258, 259
Pejačević, F. K., 154
Pejkić, K., 154
Penitents movement. See *Pokutnyky*
Pentecostals, 320: in Bulgaria, 277; in Cuba, 44; in Romania, 4; in Soviet Union, 35
Perez, Faustino, 17
PERSIFANS, 14
Peter the Great, Emperor of Russia, 277
Petr, Metropolitan, 230
Petranović, Teofil, 153

Philaretos, Archbishop of Kastoria, 205
Piasecki, Bolesław, 19
Picha, Bishop, 128
Pieronek, Bishop Tadeusz, 302, 303, 304
Pijade, Moše, 161
Pilar, Ivo, 150
Pilate, Pontius, 315
Pilgrimages: in Czechoslovakia, 128; in Poland, 290
Piłsudski, Marshal Józef, 98–99, 276, 286, 287
Pimen, Metropolitan of Nevrokop, 283, 284, 285
Pimen, Patriarch, 240, 254
Pitirim, Metropolitan, 241
Pius VI, Pope, 162
Pius IX, Pope, 98
Plato, 337
Plesu, Andrei, 194
Plojhar, Josef, 117–118, 127
Pobozny, Bishop Robert, 128
Pohlin, Marko, 158
Pokutnyky, 246
Polák, Fr. Štefan, 134
Poland, 5, 6, 7, 11, 18–19, 20, 31–33, 34, 35, 44–45, 46, 47, 90, 93–104, 120, 237, 309, 320, 326, 328; constitutional debates in, 45, 291, 294, 300–301, 304; extraterrestrials in, 324–325; law on broadcasting, 299–300; Mormons in, 267–268, 274; Orthodox Church in, 295; parliamentary elections (1993), 301; White Brotherhood in, 311
Polansky, Ivan, 138
Poles: to be picked up on Mt. Sleza by space aliens, 324
Polgar, Steven, 109
Polish Catholic Lawyers' Association, 305
Polish Ecumenical Council, 295
Polish Federation of Pro-Life Movements, 305
Polish Orthodox Church, 208
Polish United Workers' Party, 18, 34, 288, 290, 291
Politika (Belgrade), 172

Pop, Valer, 187
Popescu, Emil, 198
Popiełuszko, Fr. Jerzy, 277
Poptodorov, Radko, 283
Popular Movement for the Reconstruction of Ukraine (*Rukh*), 253
Pospielovsky, Dimitry, 233, 241, 308
Possevino, Antonio, 247
Pravda (Bratislava), 137
Pravda (Moscow), 233-234, 270
Pravoslavlje, 42, 164, 165, 172-173
Pregun, István, 110
Prendushi, Archbishop Vinçenc, 212, 213
Pribojević, Vinko, 154
Priests: arrests of, 216; incarceration of, 32, 177, 213-214; labeled "enemies of the people," 214; shortage of, 124, 139-140, 224
Promiscuity, official encouragement of, 14
Proselytization: in Romania, 188-189
Protestant Churches, 35, 265-274, 309; in Albania, 219-220; in Bohemia, 105, 113-144; in Bulgaria, 277-278, 282; in China, 37, 39; in Cuba, 31; in the German Democratic Republic, 55-59; in Hungary, 107; in Poland, 93, 295-296; in Slovakia, 116. *See also* Baptist Church; Congregational Church; Evangelical Church; Lutheran Church; Methodist Church; Reformed Church
Punev, Blagovest, 284
Purivatra, Atif, 149

Quakers, 59, 71
Quidam episcopi (1982), 129

Rački, Friar Franjo, 154
Rajačić, Patriarch Josip, 152
Rajić, Jovan, 152
Ramtha (Egyptian warrior), 322-323
Ranković, Aleksandar, 41-42, 169
Ravel, Julie, 322
Raz, Joseph, 337-338
Red Guards, 27-28
Red paint, shortage of, 27-28
Reformation: in Germany, 76-78; in Poland, 93

Reformed Church, 6; in the German Democratic Republic, 55-56, 58, 71, 74; in Poland, 5; in Romania, 200
Religion: and absolution, 335; communist policy toward, 308; and cultural homogenization, 161-162; equated with crime, 272; and fascism, 189, 242; freedom of, 4-5; and legitimation of murder, 335; level of beliefs in Poland, 291; rights of (under Soviet law), 230; and violence, 173, 175; and war, 171-179
Religious innovation, 3, 310-325
Remes, Prokop, 319
Renovationist Church, 22-23, 35, 248
Repression, 210; in Albania, 213-218; in Czechoslovakia, 123-138; in Poland, 289; in Romania, 190-194; in Russia, 229-234
Revelation, book of, 269, 313, 314
Rey, Manuel, 17
Roberts, Oral, 320
Rocky (space alien in Sofia), 325
Rodionova, Yevgeniia, 256
Rodriguez, Carlos Rafael, 30
Roerich, Nikolai, 252
Rogge, Bishop Joachim, 63
Rogozin, General Georgi Georgievich, 239, 329
Roman Catholic Church, 147, 274; among Albanians, 202, 203, 205, 209-220, 224; and alleged collaboration with the *Ustaše*, 16; in Bulgaria, 282; in China, 15, 26, 37, 38, 39; in Croatia, 153-157, 166-169, 171-177, 179; in Cuba, 18, 31, 43, 44; in Czechoslovakia, 112-119; in the German Democratic Republic, 55, 61, 71, 83; in Hungary, 105-112; in Poland, 32-33, 44-45, 93-104, 247, 275-277, 285-307, 333, 336; in Romania, 187-189, 191; and Slovenes, 157-159, 166, 168; in Ukraine, 251; in Yugoslavia, 42
Romania, 4-6, 7, 121, 181-201, 206, 271, 308, 309; Satanists in, 327; UFOs sighted in, 323
Romanian Church News, 308
Romanian Orthodox Church, 183-201, 208, 337

Romzha, Archbishop Teodor, 250
Rozenblatt, Adam, 330
Rožman, Bishop Gregorij, 168
Rrota, Fr. Justin, 212
Rudé pravo, 129, 137, 138
Rudolf II (Habsburg), Kaiser, 113
Rukh. See Popular Movement for the
Reconstruction of Ukraine
Russell, Charles, 269
Russia, 4, 6, 229–245, 265–266, 270,
320–321, 322, 331; Aum Shin-
rikyo in, 317–319; spiritualism in,
328; UFOs sighted in, 323; White
Brotherhood in, 311. *See also* Soviet
Union
Russian agents, 204
Russian Association of Healers, 320
Russian Association of Proletarian
Musicians, 21–22
Russian Free Orthodox Church, 251
Russian Orthodox Church, 14, 36, 47,
48, 215, 229–245, 253, 272, 273, 274,
314, 329, 332; deaths of priests and
nuns, 24; in the German Demo-
cratic Republic, 55; number of
functioning churches, 24, 231, 232,
224; in Ukraine, 248, 253–254. *See
also* Moscow Patriarchate
"Russian Orthodox Church Abroad,"
230, 231, 242
Russification: of Ukraine, 248
Russo-Turkish Wars, 204
Ruthenian Orthodox Church, 251
Rutskoi, Aleksandr V., 317

Šagi-Bunić, Tomislav, 166, 167
Saint Catherine Convent, 303
St. Sava, 150; corpse burned, 151
St. Sophia Cathedral (Kiev), 258–259,
261, 315
Salečl, Renata, 166
Salvation, 310, 313, 324
Salvation Army, 267, 270
Sandžak, 176
Santo-Daime cult, 331
Santoyo, Rev. Orson Vila, 44
Šarčević, Boža, 155
Šarić, Archbishop Ivan, 156
Sarkander, Jan, 141

Satan, 314, 325–326, 331; tools of, 59
Satan, Church of (Poland), 325
Satan, First Church of (Czech Repub-
lic), 326–327
Satanism, 325–328; all religions other
than Orthodox Church character-
ized as, 243
Sathya Sai Baba, cult of, 330
Saudi Arabia, 220
Schmutzler, Siegfried, 67–68
Schönherr, Bishop Albrecht, 71, 75
Schröder, Richard, 83
Schumann, Erich, 65
Scientology, 309, 310, 331–332
Second Coming, 59
The Secret Doctrine, 328
Secularization, 3, 118–119
Securitate, 194, 197, 199
Seigewasser, Hans, 71
Self-mutilation, 4
Selimoški, Reis-ul-ulema Jakub, 174
Selivanov, Kondratii Ivanovich, 4
Selyunin, Vasiliy, 239
Serapion Brothers, 21
Serbia: spiritualists in, 328; UFOs
sighted in, 323
Serbian Insurrectionary War (1991–95),
172–179, 197, 236
Serbian Orthodox Church, 17, 42, 47,
48, 147, 208, 333, 335; and alleged
collaboration with Chetniks, 16, 153;
and nationalism, 149–153, 162–166,
171–176, 180
Serbs, Croats, and Slovenes, Kingdom
of, 153, 156–157
Sergii (Stragorodsky), Patriarch, 22,
36, 230–231
Seventh Day Adventists: in Albania,
225; in Armenia, 271; in Cuba, 44;
in the German Democratic Repub-
lic, 56, 61, 71, 74; in Poland, 5; in
Romania, 184, 185
Sex education, 295, 296, 305
Shakhnazarov, David, 271
Sheptyts'kyi, Metropolitan Andrei,
249
Shevtsova, Lilia, 237
Shllaku, Fr. Gjon, 212
Siberia, 322, 331

Sidorov, Vitaly, 312
Sima, Horia, 190
Skenderbeg, 209
Skoptsy. See Castrated, Sect of the
Skrabik, Bishop, 128
Skrypnyk, Mstyslav. *See* Mstyslav
  (Skrypnyk)
Slipyi, Metropolitan Iosyf, 249
Slomšek, Archbishop Anton Martin,
  159
Slovak Evangelical Church (Vojvo-
  dina), 147
Slovakia, 140, 141, 142, 144; Satanism
  in, 326; UFOs sighted in, 323
Slovenes: and Catholicism, 157–159,
  166, 168
Slovenia, 237
Slowo, 300
Socialist realism, 22
Socialist Unity Party (GDR), 65–66,
  69, 76–78
Sokol, Bishop Ján, 125
Solidarity, 294, 306
Soto Zen, 330
Southern Baptist Convention, 267
Soviet Union, 14, 16, 19, 20, 21–25, 34,
  36–37, 46, 229–241, 248–251, 309.
  See also Bolsheviks; Central Asia;
  Russia; Ukraine
Spanish Civil War (1936–39), 236
Spasov, Metodi, 283, 284, 285
Spiritualism, 322, 328
Spiroiu, Nicolae, 196
Spišak, Tibor, 125
Spulbeck, Bishop Otto, 55
Šrámek, Fr. Jan, 115
Sri Radmish Mystical Cult (Latvia),
  331
Stadler, Archbishop Josef, 160
Stakhanov, Aleksei, 22; and Stakha-
  novite movement, 22
Stalin, Josif V., 22, 25, 32, 36, 215, 230,
  231, 232, 241, 244, 250, 258; birthday
  of, 65; renewed popularity of, 239
Stambolov, Stefan, 279
Starčević, Ante, 155
Stark, Rodney, 310
Stasi, 76, 83, 86
Staszic, Fr. Stanisław, 94

Stefan Nemanja, Prince, 150
Stehlik, Antonin, 128
Stephen, King of Hungary, 111
Stephen the Great, 192, 195–196
Stepinac, Alojzije Cardinal, 16, 157,
  168, 171
Stier, Bishop Christoph, 63
Stojković, Bishop Dositej, 164
Stolojan, Theodor, 195
Stolpe, Manfred, 69, 75, 76, 86
Stoph, Willi, 82
Strassberg, Barbara, 293
Stravinsky, Igor, 32
Strossmayer, Bishop Josip Juraj, 154–
  155
Subev, Fr. Hristofor, 282, 283, 284, 285
Suchocka, Hanna, 294, 302
Sudoplatov, Pavel, 250
Sufi Brotherhoods, 35
Svetigora, 174
Svetokriški, Janez, 158
Svetosavsko zvonce, 42
Swedish evangelists: turned back at
  Sofia airport, 272
Synodal Church. *See* "Russian Ortho-
  dox Church Abroad"
Szafranek, Fr. Józef, 96
Szekelys: in Romania, 188–189
Szlávy, József, 159
Szwed, Robert, 326

Tantra, 331
Taoism, 15
Tashita, Seiji, 318
TASS, 314, 328
Tax, Church, 6
Tea-drinking rituals, 331
Templars, 332
Teoctist (Arapasu), Patriarch, 193,
  195–196, 197–198, 199
Teodor, Metropolitan of Skopje, 163
Teologičke texty, 139
Teološki pogledi, 42
Teresa, Mother, 219
Thaçi, Metropolitan-Archbishop
  Gasper, 213
Theocracy, 7, 295, 337, 338
Theological education, 183
Theological faculties, 54
Theology of Diakonia, 6

Theosophy, 4, 309
Theroux, Paul, 310
Third Testament, 311
Thirty Years War (1618-48), 113
Tiananmen Square, 39
Tikhon, Bishop (of Mother of God Center), 311
Tikhon, Patriarch, 229-230, 248
Tiso, Msgr. Jozef, 116, 119, 131
Tito, Josip Broz, 16, 17, 20, 40, 41, 157, 163, 164, 171
Tokarczuk, Archbishop Ignacy, 303
Tökés, László, 196, 199
Tolerance: and democracy, 337-338. *See also* Intolerance
Tomášek, František Cardinal, 124, 125, 129, 132-133, 135, 137, 138, 139, 143, 289
Tomb dwellers, 328
Tomislav, King of Croatia, 150
Torop, Sergei, 330-331
Townsend, Terry, 270
Tranda, Bogdan, 295
Transcendental Meditation, 194, 252, 331
Transsexuals, 300; in Romania, 197-198, 201
Trianon, Treaty of (1920), 108
Tripalo, Miko, 167
Trochta, Bishop, 128
Troshani, Bishop Nikolle, 217
Trubar, Primož, 157-158
True Orthodox Church, 4, 231
Tsankov, Dragan, 278
Tsvigun, Maria ("The Living God"), 312-316
Tucker, Robert C., 34
Tudjman, Franjo, 178, 179
Tukals'kyi, Metropolitan Iosyf, 247
Turkey, 182. *See also* Ottoman Empire
Turowicz, Jerzy, 288
Tygodnik Powszechny, 33, 288

UFO sightings, 323-324, 328
Ukraine, 7, 246-262, 270, 312-317, 333; Aum Shinrikyo in, 317; Baptists in, 269. *See also* White Brotherhood
Ukrainian Autocephalous Orthodox Church, 14, 23, 246, 248, 252, 253, 255-256, 261

Ukrainian Autonomous Orthodox Church, 253, 255
Ukrainian Exarchate of the Russian Orthodox Church, 254
Ukrainian Orthodox Church, 4, 24, 35, 247
Ukrainian Orthodox Church of the Kievan Patriarchate, 251, 252, 256-262, 314
Ukrainian Orthodox Church of the Moscow Patriarchate, 251, 252, 253, 254, 256, 258, 261
Ulbricht, Walter, 69, 73
UNA-UNSO, 257, 259, 260
UNESCO, 194
Unification Church of the Rev. Moon, 5, 309, 331; in Russia, 273
Union of Evangelical Congregational Churches, 269
Union of Evangelical Pentecostal Churches, 269; in Bulgaria, 282
Union of Orthodox Priests, 214
Union of Soviet Socialist Republics. *See* Soviet Union
United Arab Emirates, 220
United Evangelical Lutheran Church of Russia: statement regarding 1991 coup, 240-241
United States of America, 206, 218; White Brotherhood in, 311
Unity of Brethren (Herrnhut), 57, 71
Universal Reason, 337, 338
Universal White Brotherhood: in Bulgaria, 282
Urbanówicz, Juliusz, 313
Ustaše, 157

Valter, Jiří, 327
Values, 336
Vanek, František, 133
Vanga, 321
Vata, Fr. Gjergj, 213
Vechernyaya Moskva, 321
Vegetarianism, 331
Velimirović, Bishop Nikolaj, 165, 171
Venetian troops, 152. *See also* Ottoman-Venetian Wars
Verdery, Katherine, 238
Videnov, Zhan, 321

Vikentije, Patriarch, 17
Viktor, Bishop, 208
Violence: relationship to religion, 173, 175
Virgin Mary, 97–98, 289, 293, 305, 311–312, 319, 323, 324
Vissarion, Bishop. See Xhuvani, Bishop Vissarion
Vissarion Brotherhood, 330–331
Vitalii, Metropolitan, 242–243
Vjesnik, 168, 179
Vladimir (Sabodan), Metropolitan, 256, 257
Vlad Tepeš, 192
Vlahs: migrating to Bosnia, 150
Vlk, Archbishop Miloslav, 139
Vodnik, Fr. Valentine, 158
Vojtaššák, Bishop Jan, 116, 126
Vojvodina, 327
Volodymyr (Romanyuk), Metropolitan, 256, 258–260
von Kállay. See Kállay, Benjamin von
von Metternich. See Metternich, Clemens von
Voprosy filosofii, 244
Vovk, Bishop Anton, 168
Voznyak, S., 250–251
Vrana, Bishop Jozef, 125, 129
Vrcan, Srdjan, 179
Vymetal, Bishop František, 125
Vynnyts'kyi, Antonii: claimed title of metropolitan, 247

Wahrmann, Siegfried, 76
Wałęsa, Lech, 103, 296, 303; vetoes abortion bill, 299
War Pigs (Budapest), 327
Warriors of Christ, 271
We, 47
Weber, Max, 97
Wesselényi, Count Ferenc, 104
Wheaton College, 266, 309
White Brotherhood, 310, 311, 312–316
White Doves. See Castrated, Sect of
White-Haired Girl, The, 28

White Mountain, Battle of (1620), 105, 113, 114, 119
Wilcox, Bob, 320
Witchcraft, Church of, 320
Wojtyła, Karol Cardinal of Kraków. See John Paul II, Pope
World Assembly of Muslim Youth, 220–221
World Council of Churches, 193, 229
Wyszyński, Stefan Cardinal, 32, 33, 100–101, 277, 288, 289, 290

Xhuvani, Bishop Vissarion, 208, 209, 214

Yarema, Dmytriy, 256, 257, 261
Yaroslavsky, Emelyan, 23
Yeltsin, Boris, 239, 240, 241, 274, 317, 329; as the "Antichrist," 314
Yevtushenko, Yevgeni, 122–123, 235
Young Turks, 211
Yugoslavia, 7, 15–16, 19, 20, 29–30, 34, 35, 40–42, 46–47, 121, 147–180; Satanism in, 327; Theosophical Society in, 309
Yugoslav War (1991–95). See Serbian Insurrectionary War

Zahiragić, Munib, 170
Zakaryan, Ervand, 271
Zamiatin, Evgeni, 47
Zhao Ziyang, 39
Zhdanov, Andrei, 22
Zhelev, Zhelyu, 284, 321
Zhirinovsky, Vladimir, 321
Zhivkov, Todor, 282
Zichy, Count Nándor, 107
Zieliński, Tadeusz, 295
Znak, 33, 99
Znanie Society, 234
Zog, King, 207–209, 212, 226
Zogu, Ahmed. See Zog, King
Zorkaltsev, Viktor I., 273
Zrinyi, Count Miklós, 104
Zrinyi, Count Péter, 104
Zvěřina, Fr. Josef, 132, 133

Sabrina P. Ramet is a Professor of International Studies at the University of Washington. Born in London, England, she has lived for extended periods of time in England, Austria, Germany, Yugoslavia, and Japan, as well as in the United States. She is the author of six previous books, among them, *Social Currents in Eastern Europe: The Sources and Consequences of the Great Transformation,* 2nd ed. (Duke University Press, 1995), *Balkan Babel: The Disintegration of Yugoslavia from the Death of Tito to Ethnic War,* 2nd ed. (1996), and *Whose Democracy? Nationalism, Religion, and the Doctrine of Collective Rights in Post-1989 Eastern Europe* (1997), and editor or coeditor of eleven previous books. Her work has appeared in *Foreign Affairs, World Politics, Problems of Post-Communism, Orbis,* and other journals.

Library of Congress Cataloging-in-Publication Data

Ramet, Sabrina P.
Nihil obstat : religion, politics, and social change in East-Central Europe and Russia / Sabrina P. Ramet.
p.   cm.
Includes index.
ISBN 0-8223-2056-8 (alk. paper). — ISBN 0-8223-2070-3 (pbk. : alk. paper)
1. Religion and politics—Europe, Eastern—History—20th century.   2. Christianity and politics—Europe, Eastern—History—20th century.   3. Communism and religion —Europe, Eastern—History.   4. Communism and Christianity—Europe, Eastern— History.   5. Europe, Eastern—Religion—20th century.   6. Europe, Eastern—Church history—20th century.   I. Title.
BL65.P7R35   1998
322'.1'09470904—dc21   97-23350